Beyond State Crisis?

BEYOND STATE CRISIS?

Postcolonial Africa
and Post-Soviet Eurasia
in Comparative Perspective

Edited by

Mark R. Beissinger
and
Crawford Young

Published by Woodrow Wilson Center Press
Washington, D.C.

Distributed by The Johns Hopkins University Press
Baltimore and London

EDITORIAL OFFICES

Woodrow Wilson Center Press
One Woodrow Wilson Plaza
1300 Pennsylvania Avenue, N.W.
Washington, D.C. 20004-3027
Telephone 202-691-4010
www.wilsoncenter.org

Order from

The Johns Hopkins University Press
P.O. Box 50370
Baltimore, Maryland 21211
Telephone 1-800-537-5487
www.press.jhu.edu

2 4 6 8 9 7 5 3 1

Library of Congress Cataloging-in-Publication Data

Beyond state crisis? : postcolonial Africa and post-Soviet Eurasia in
comparative perspective / edited by Mark R. Beissinger and Crawford Young.
p. cm.
Includes bibliographical references and index.
ISBN 1-930365-07-1 (hardcover : alk. paper) — ISBN 1-930365-08-X
(pbk. : alk. paper)
1. Postcolonialism—Africa. 2. Postcolonialism—Eurasia. 3.
Postcolonialism—Former Soviet republics. 4. Africa—Politics and
government—1960– . 5. Eurasia—Politics and government. 6. Former
Soviet republics—Politics and government. I. Beissinger, Mark R. II.
Young, Crawford, 1931– .
DT30.5 B49 2002
947.086—dc21   2001006558

ABOUT THE CENTER

The Center is the living memorial of the United States of America to the nation's twenty-eighth president, Woodrow Wilson. Congress established the Woodrow Wilson Center in 1968 as an international institute for advanced study, "symbolizing and strengthening the fruitful relationship between the world of learning and the world of public affairs." The Center opened in 1970 under its own board of trustees.

In all its activities the Woodrow Wilson Center is a nonprofit, nonpartisan organization, supported financially by annual appropriations from the Congress, and by the contributions of foundations, corporations, and individuals. Conclusions or opinions expressed in Center publications and programs are those of the authors and speakers and do not necessarily reflect the views of the Center staff, fellows, trustees, advisory groups, or any individuals or organizations that provide financial support to the Center.

Contents

Part V: Beyond State Crisis?

List of Tables

Acknowledgments

In the long trail between conception and completion of this book, the editors have accumulated many debts. The very first is to Bogumil Jewsiewicki of Laval University in Canada, who in partnership with Prosser Gifford, who was then the deputy director of the Woodrow Wilson International Center for Scholars, conceived the idea of the comparison between former communist lands and Africa. In the Jewsiewicki version, the paired comparison was with eastern Europe rather than post-Soviet Eurasia, but his initiative broke new ground in perceiving a number of common themes defining the political process that were not at first evident to specialists on the two regions. A 1990 conference at Bellagio devoted to teasing out these parallels enlisted a substantial participation by scholars from the two regions, as well as those from western Europe and North America who specialized in one or the other of these regions. The dialogue, though stimulating, proved in some respects premature; eastern European scholars were not yet ready to perceive a genuine comparability between the states involuntarily enclosed within Soviet imperial space, whose point of reference was "normal" states in western Europe, and the states of Africa. The conference, however valuable, thus did not produce a sufficiently rich body of sustained comparison to justify a published volume, though some of the individual papers presented at the conference found their way into journals. But the idea was born; six years later, the intensification of state crisis in Africa, with a newly emergent category of "failed states," found even more evident parallels in the dysfunction of many of the successor states to the former Soviet Union. The editors were attracted to the possibility of reviving this comparative ambition but shifting part of its focus from eastern Europe to the former Soviet Union.

We initiated planning for the project in spring 1996, with the support and engagement of members of the Cultural Pluralism Research Circle (one of several interdisciplinary and cross-regional groups of faculty and graduate students operating within the framework of the University of Wisconsin's International Institute). The first step, we agreed, was to convene a scholarly conference built around an initial comparative agenda that we proposed. By the time that conference came to fruition in March 1999 in Madison, Wisconsin, an international team of prominent social scientists focused on both regions had been drawn into the project, including significant representation from both Africa and post-Soviet Eurasia. The enthusiastic reaction that the comparison elicited from this group fully confirmed our initial convictions. The conference proceedings themselves were structured thematically, with each panel representing a cross-regional dialogue on specific dimensions of state crisis and transition. After the conference, the editors selected what appeared to be the most promising papers for revision and publication. We are particularly grateful to those participants whose work is not directly represented here: Allen Buchanan, Cynthia Buckley, Kathryn Hendley, Bogumil Jewsiewicki, Michael Kennedy, Anatoly Khazanov, Charles King, David Laitin, Michael McFaul, Maria Nzomo, and Jennifer Widner. We are deeply indebted as well to the numerous commentators who participated in the conference and helped enhance its cross-regional interchange: David Abernethy, Leyla Alieva, Sergei Arutiunov, Michael Bratton, Valerie Bunce, Michael Chege, Timothy Colton, Georgii Derlugian, Peter Ekeh, Steven Fish, Oleksiy Haran, Jibrin Ibrahim, Robert Kaiser, Edmond Keller, René Lemarchand, Gaspar Munishi, Vladimir Popov, Peter Rutland, Michael Schatzberg, Masipula Sithole, Rotimi Suberu, William Zartman, and Olga Zdravomyslova. Their contributions find reflection in many of the essays selected for this volume.

Throughout this project, our aim has been to produce useful cross-regional comparisons that might shed light on individual cases, broader processes, and regional similarities and differences. Toward that end, after having benefited from the conference proceedings, authors were asked to revise their essays with the cross-regional comparison in mind if they had not already taken it into account. Moreover, in addition to the revisions encouraged by the editors, further comments aimed at enhancing cross-regional comparisons of each paper were solicited from two conference attendees, Valerie Bunce and René Lemarchand. Generally, our attempts to foster cross-regional comparison took the form of conscious efforts by authors or teams of authors to address similarities and differences across regions, either through direct comparison or through the pairing of regionally focused or case-focused comparisons addressing similar phenomena within each region.

In planning the first phase of this project, a major international conference, we recognized that substantial resources would need to be assembled to ensure its success. Like Jewsiewicki, we believed that substantial participation by scholars from Africa and post-Soviet Eurasia was indispensable to its success. We began by garnering a basic threshold of financial guarantees from within the University of Wisconsin at Madison. In this quest, we received constant encouragement and strong support from the International Institute and the dean of international studies, David Trubek. Also crucial was the backing of the Global Studies Program of the International Institute and its successive directors, Gay Seidman and Leigh Payne. Through the involvement of graduate students and faculty participating in the university's MacArthur Foundation–funded program with Stanford University and the University of Minnesota, we were able to draw some support from this consortium. Also contributing to local resources were some funds attached to the H. Edwin Young professorship of international studies, held by Crawford Young.

Supported by this degree of institutional backing, we were able to approach a number of external funding sources. Major backing was received from the United States Institute of Peace and the Kennan Institute of the Woodrow Wilson Center. Invaluable support to facilitate the participation of African and Eurasian scholars was received from the Rockefeller Foundation and the Lagos, Nairobi, and Moscow offices of the Ford Foundation. To these benefactors we extend our warmest thanks. We also wish to thank the Ford Foundation, the U.S. Institute of Peace, and the Rockefeller Foundation for helping to support publication of this volume, and Woodrow Wilson Center Press Director Joseph Brinley for his active cooperation toward this end.

The complexity of the organizational requirements for an event of this magnitude required the administrative assistance of many able hands. We are particularly grateful to the dedicated band of graduate students who worked closely with us at varying stages of the enterprise: Gwendolyn Bevis, Rick Tange, Stefanie Nanes, and James Shyne. Paul Beckett of the International Institute momentarily set aside his emeritus pursuits to bring his invaluable logistical expertise to the conference preparations. Carol Hansen of the Global Studies staff rendered tireless and selfless service to the project from beginning to end.

This project has engaged a good deal of the professional energy of both of us over the last five years. We elaborate on the intellectual rationale for the volume in the Introduction and thus will not repeat those points here. Suffice it to say that, for both of us, this venture has been very enriching; we have each learned a great deal from the comparison, about both our own region of specialization and the other's. We hope that the readers of this volume will feel equally rewarded.

Mark R. Beissinger
Crawford Young

Beyond State Crisis?

Part I

Overview and Retrospective

1

Introduction: Comparing State Crises across Two Continents

MARK R. BEISSINGER
AND CRAWFORD YOUNG

Africa and post-Soviet Eurasia today are united by many common travails. In both regions, the general euphoria that once accompanied the post-imperial moment has given way to a pessimism and sense of generalized crisis. The crises of these regions have multiple dimensions, but the most obvious undoubtedly has been the institutional incoherence of the state, visible in situations of manifest state weakness and, in some cases, state collapse.

This volume explores the state crises that have engulfed these two regions: their origins, their similarities and differences, the ways in which they interact with interstate relations and with the global processes of change (such as democratization and market reform) that have buffeted these regions in recent years, the effect of state crises on salient social divisions such as cultural difference and gender, and some of the pathways potentially leading out of crisis that are suggested by experience. Our ambition is to enrich understanding of the state crises widespread in both regions by systematic paired comparison of Africa and Eurasia, using each region as a mirror to illuminate the problems of the other. By turning the mirrors ordinarily used to view these societies so as to incorporate their joint reflections rather than viewing them in the separate contexts in which they normally have been placed or in juxtaposition to western Europe, North America, Asia, or Latin America, we seek to gain a new framework of comparison for issues that have traditionally been understood by scholars of both regions

3

as area-specific or have long been viewed with reference to other areas of the world.

Such a comparison is predicated on the assumption that this juxtaposition is not, in Giovanni Sartori's words, a "cat-dog" comparison (Sartori 1991): that is, however different the historical trajectories and cultural contours of the two regions, some powerful similarities exist in their contemporary situations that render this comparison meaningful and insightful. We believe this to be the case with respect to issues of state breakdown and crisis. Both regions entered the last decade of the twentieth century with severely dysfunctional and ultimately unsustainable political and economic institutions and practices. More significant, though they are far from identical, many of the ways in which state authority has disintegrated in the countries of both regions and the consequences of these cataclysms share enough similarities that meaningful insights into political processes can be generated when these situations are juxtaposed. Finally, the search for efficacious state authority hovers shadowlike over both regions and constitutes the predominant challenge confronting their societies in the first half of the twenty-first century.

By the end of the 1990s, both regions were suffering extreme consequences from unviable forms of political rule. Indeed, more than any other regions of the world, Africa and post-Soviet Eurasia symbolize the disarray of the high-modernist state that is characteristic of large portions of our planet. Criminalization of the state and the economy, the burgeoning of corruption, the disintegration of basic human services for populations, and heightened tensions between cultural groups have all been symptoms of the fundamental crises of the state that have enveloped these regions. Indeed, in the last decade of the twentieth century, Africa and post-Soviet Eurasia together constituted the chief source of new wars in the world, most of which had their roots in the combination of cultural diversity and dysfunctional state authority characteristic of both regions. In some instances, governments were captured by marauding criminal bands or organized criminal groups. At the end of the 1980s, both regions were profoundly affected by the Huntingtonian "third wave" of democratization (Huntington 1991). Yet, by the mid-1990s it was apparent that, in both Africa and post-Soviet Eurasia, transitions to democracy had become stalled and the democratic tide was, if anything, receding, leaving partially liberalized regimes in its wake. As experience in both regions demonstrates, predatory and incoherent political authority is fundamentally incompatible with democratic governance. But as the tremendous financial collapse of Russia in August 1998 also visibly demonstrates, so too is such authority incompatible with economic development. Already the sheer magnitude of the adaptations required to avert the downward spiral that has afflicted both regions has gone far beyond the challenges posed for any other areas of the world. Relatively stagnant economic growth or even decline, a high degree of external indebtedness, and marginalization within the world economy are both products and reinforcing causes of these crises of authority. By the end of 1998, Russia, the Sudan, Liberia, Congo-Kinshasa, Somalia, and Yugoslavia (in that order) were the six largest debtors on the books of the International Monetary Fund (*Economist* 1999).[1] For large numbers of Africans and residents of the former Soviet Union in the 1990s, real incomes declined, health prospects grew poorer, and physical and economic infrastructure significantly deteriorated. Official economies shriveled; barter, subsistence, and shadow economies took their place. Massive corruption, ineffectual regulation, and alternative systems of authority blossomed in the wake of the retreat and crisis of the state and remain the chief obstacles to achieving economic vitality in both regions.

Obviously, none of these problems is unique to these two regions; they can be found to varying degrees in parts of Asia and Latin America as well. Still, the Africa-Eurasia comparison that animates this volume places these issues in a new context, since the crises of the state in these two regions arguably were the most conspicuous in world politics in the 1990s and their consequences so glaringly destructive. The issues that grip Africa and post-Soviet Eurasia transcend region; they are global in scope. By juxtaposing analogous cases and processes in two regions that have normally been thought of in isolation from one another, we hope to draw attention to this fact.

We anticipate that for some readers the Africa-Eurasia juxtaposition that inspires this volume will seem odd given the enormous differences in the histories and cultures of the two regions. Although at first glance such a comparison may be jarring, through our own scholarly interaction we came to realize some of the strong elements of comparability in the crises that have overtaken states in both regions. In this respect we believe that in its fundamental approach this book pushes comparative analysis in new directions through its careful effort to foster crossregional (as opposed to case-specific) comparisons. The chapters in this book do not exclude case-

---

1. To distinguish between the two Congos, the chapters in this volume will refer to the Democratic Republic of the Congo (the former Zaire) as Congo-Kinshasa, and to the Republic of Congo as Congo-Brazzaville.

specific comparison, but they also attempt to add another component: comparison across sets of states from distinct regions of the world. Traditionally, comparative political analysis has tended to focus on similarities and differences in patterns of politics within individual states, across states within particular regions (the area studies approach), or across strategically selected states without regard to region (as in crossnational behavioral studies and, at times, historical sociology). Investigations that consciously attempt to compare across sets of states drawn from distinct regions that exhibit similarities in political processes and outcomes have been relatively rare. At one pole of inquiry, the area tradition within comparative politics has tended to treat the experiences of regions as unique and isolated from one another—formed largely through distinct historical processes that have fostered singular cultural areas. Despite the recent attacks on area studies within the social science community, there are powerful reasons why social scientists continue to practice their art within area-studies communities: knowledge of local languages, histories, and cultures remains critical to meaningful comparison, and analogous historical forces have often operated within geographically defined regions, producing social and cultural similarities that transcend contemporary state boundaries. For the most part, the social science community remains organized around area boundaries, and most social science theorizing has emerged out of the study of specific regions.

We do not seek to efface the very significant differences between the African and Eurasian political experiences. Rather, we take seriously the important kernels of truth: that postcommunist societies share their own set of problems emerging from their communist heritage (Bunce 1995) and that the African postcolonial state represents a "singular historical personality" (Young 1994). We readily acknowledge that the relatively more industrial and highly educated character of post-Soviet societies imparts a somewhat different dynamic to politics in that region than what obtains in African societies less advantaged in these respects. In spite of the extreme parastatalization of African economies and the rise of the would-be integral state on the African continent in the 1970s, the scope and effectiveness of state activity in the Soviet Union on the eve of its demise far exceeded that of most African states or their colonial predecessors. We fully expect that many of the economic, cultural, and political legacies of communism will remain distinct from those of the African colonial and postcolonial state.

Yet these discrepancies are all the more intriguing given some of the similarities in the dysfunctions of authority that we do perceive across the two regions. The combination of variable outcomes within and across regions of the world in comparable processes of state breakdown is precisely what gives rise to provocative questions of crossregional comparison. Why, for instance, has ethnic warfare often multiplied across state boundaries in Africa into severe regional conflagrations (as in the Great Lakes area), whereas in Eurasia ethnic warfare has more often been contained within state boundaries (as in Moldova, Georgia, or Chechnya)? Why have women suffered considerably from the dislocations of market transition in Eurasia, whereas disruptive market transitions in Africa have produced greater participation and opportunity for women? Why has the breakdown of the state's monopoly on violence in Africa largely taken the form of warlordism, whereas in Eurasia, although one can find isolated examples of warlordism, what Vadim Volkov calls in Chapter 4 "violent entrepreneurship" has more frequently assumed the form of organized crime? In short, not simply variation across states, but variation across regions needs to be explained, for such comparison can, when wisely posed, illuminate paradoxes and variations in outcomes that otherwise would remain invisible. These patterns become apparent only through the juxtaposition of sets of states experiencing analogous processes rather than through an area-studies approach only or by examining individual states in isolation from one another.

At the other pole of inquiry, the desire for generalization can at times lead to the assumption of like units when, in fact, dissimilar phenomena are being compared. This is the fundamental problem posed by Sartori. What has driven us (as well as the scholars represented in this volume) to be attracted to the Africa-Eurasia comparison are precisely issues of comparability—that is, the realization that in both of these regions many states lack many of the empirical qualities normally associated with the Weberian states of North America and western Europe. Indeed, in some instances state authority has failed completely. Thus, comparisons that take stateness for granted impose inappropriate assumptions on both of these regions. In both, the boundaries of states remain porous; their institutions lack coherence and cannot exercise effective control over their territories; some move in and out of various states of collapse.

Obviously, comparability is to a large extent a function of the perceptual frame imposed by the observer, and specifically, the observer's purposes and assumptions. The Africa-Eurasia comparison in this regard has been purposefully deployed in order to highlight particular issues that we observers see as critical in both contexts, but that we feel are often overlooked in theoretical assumptions flowing from the European and North American experiences—specifically, the fundamental issues of stateness. These are issues that, for a long time, were ignored within the Eurasian context and only in recent years have come to the foreground of analysis. Indeed, for many years specialists on the former Soviet Union and experts from the region itself resisted comparisons with Africa, believing that western Europe, North America, or Latin America was the proper referent for analysis. As the chapters in this book demonstrate, that the Africa-Eurasia comparison has now become thinkable among a significant number of experts on both regions reflects the shifting attentions of specialists on both areas to issues of stateness.

Thus we believe that there are serious intellectual reasons for pursuing crossregional comparison and that well-conceived crossregional analysis aids effective contextualized comparison in several ways. First, comparisons across regions allow one to ponder the role of broader global forces that might affect outcomes across multiple, disparate cases. This is particularly well illustrated by Chapter 11, written by Peter Stavrakis, on the similar ways in which international financial institutions have approached Africa and the former Soviet Union. But this purpose is evident as well in our own efforts in Chapter 2 to explain the emergence of state crises across Africa and Eurasia in part through the failure of the transformational state projects emerging out of high modernism and underlying pre-independence state experiences in both regions. Achille Mbembe's discussion in Chapter 3 of boundaries and sovereignty, Peter Lewis's observations in Chapter 12 on the contradictions and affinities between market reform and democratization (both induced and encouraged by external pressure), Lilia Shevtsova's and Richard Joseph's common concern with the "virtuality" of democracy in Russia and Africa (Chapters 9 and 10, respectively), and Donald Rothchild's attempts in Chapter 8 to generalize about the effects of weak states on interstate relations in the two regions all deal to varying degrees with the effects of global forces above the nation-state on political developments in both regions.

Second, crossregional comparison of analogous phenomena and patterns improves conceptual clarity and provides a better sense of the distinctive forces at work in shaping political processes within each region. We believe that a number of chapters in this book achieve this goal. William Reno's discussion in Chapter 5 of the differences between warlordism in Africa and organized crime in Russia, for instance, helps clarify the nature of violent entrepreneurship and its relationship to the state. Aili Tripp's discussion in Chapter 15 of the starkly different impacts of market transition and state crisis on women in Africa and Eurasia points to the significant ways in which prior political legacies within each context have shaped outcomes for specific societal groups. Chapter 7, by David Holloway and Stephen Stedman, probes the causes of different patterns of ethnic warfare across these two regions. A comparison of the Charles Fairbanks and Reno chapters (6 and 5, respectively) not only provides unique insights into the breakdown of military institutions and the emergence of private armies that have afflicted both Africa and post-Soviet Eurasia but also helps us to understand the reasons for the relative reticence (in comparison with their African counterparts) of militaries in the former Soviet states to assume the burdens of rule.

Third, pairing analogous outcomes and processes in different regions can enrich the search for possible pathways beyond state crisis by considering experiences not normally contemplated in area-specific research. Here the pairing of chapters by Ghia Nodia on Georgia (Chapter 16) and Crawford Young on Uganda (Chapter 17) provides insight into some of the factors that have allowed these states to move out of situations of state collapse to conditions of state weakness. They point in particular to the critical role played by the quality of leadership in altering the trajectory of state disintegration, though today neither Georgia nor Uganda could be understood as having transcended the challenges of stateness confronting their regions more generally. A similar pairing of Chapter 13, by Gail Lapidus, and Chapter 14, by Francis Deng, on the various ways in which African and Eurasian states have dealt with the challenges of cultural pluralism raises important questions about the applicability and transferability of ethno-federalism as an institutional means for containing conflict. And Volkov's chapter suggests an important role for the manipulation of economic interest and incentives in taming the challenges posed by organized crime for Russian state institutions. Thus in pursuing crossregional comparisons we have sought not to divert attention from the obviously significant variations in policies found within each region, but rather to use that variation to achieve new insights that would otherwise be obscured. Indeed, we believe that a knowledge of the variation in outcomes within regions is an essential precondition for effective crossregional comparison.

We believe that our contention that states in Africa and Eurasia have grown dysfunctional in some broadly comparable ways is supported by the increasingly frequent use of the same set of descriptors in political discourse on both continents: terms such as "lame," "quasi-," "patrimonial," "predatory," "criminal," "shadow," or "collapsed." These modifiers refer in fact to a number of different syndromes of politics that have spread widely in both regions and that are usually contrasted with the model of the Weberian state. As this volume will explore, in their specifics the crises of the states of these two regions may actually involve very different sets of actors and types of relationships, and lurking behind the common usage of these terms in some instances may be quite distinct phenomena. The criminalization of the state in Eurasia has been different from that of the African state, even though in both cases these behaviors may be situated outside the accepted norms that underlie our conceptions of modern authority. In this sense, the notion of state crisis used throughout this volume covers a multitude of sins. Its expansiveness allows for flexibility in comparison but also injects an unavoidable fuzziness into analysis. In some cases, the state crises with which we are dealing revolve around states whose actions are exceedingly predatory. In other cases, these crises revolve around states that are exceptionally weak and incapable of making their rules stick on society. In still other cases, state crises are actually instances of collapsed states, in which state authority exists in little more than juridical form. Moreover, in some circumstances these conditions are not mutually exclusive.

In this respect, what we mean by the term "state crisis" in this volume is not a singular outcome, but rather a set of outcomes connected with the massive failure of the state to live up to its own pretensions. In the Weberian conception that underlies so much of our thinking about the crises of the state in Africa and Eurasia, the modern state is defined as "a human community that [successfully] claims the *monopoly over the legitimate use of physical force* within a given territory" (Weber 1946, 78; emphasis in original). Others emphasize the relatively specialized and permanent institutions that allow states to exercise their claims to the exclusive right to rule within a bounded territory—i.e., the empirical qualities of statehood as opposed to its merely declarative existence (Migdal 1988, 19). Indeed, it is the contrast between the claim and the empirical reality that stands out so starkly and that prompts the sense of failure of the state project that is widespread in both regions (Jackson 1990). In both Africa and Eurasia, the state's ubiquitous and pervasive presence can be juxtaposed with its limited capacity for enforcing rules or generating legitimacy. Although the extractive and regulatory capacities of states in both regions remain low, the disaggregated extractive activity through rent-seeking behavior by the individuals who staff the state remains conspicuous. Activities not normally associated with the modern state (such as the use of state institutions to run private businesses) are widespread on both continents. At the same time, enforcement and regulatory functions normally associated with the modern state (such as policing, monetary emission, or tax collection) defy effective state control or are with considerable frequency carried out by private agents. At times, criminal organizations within society dominate the state, state actors function as a type of criminal organization, or paramilitary organizations function in place of the state. Little wonder that a generalized mistrust of state institutions as alien "other" reigns within populations of both regions.

As we observe in Chapter 2, state authority has not always been ineffective in Africa and Eurasia. Indeed, in certain respects both Stalinism and the African colonial state represented the peak of the development of the transformative state that materialized out of late-nineteenth- and early-twentieth-century Europe. In both Africa and Eurasia, state crises emerged in the aftermath of the failure of these grand transformational projects. Nor is it the case that all states in Eurasia and Africa have fared equally poorly. Yet even in cases judged as relative successes, such as in the Baltic states or Uganda, one observes a number of the same problems afflicting authority. In post-Soviet Latvia, for instance, 41 percent of citizens report that they feel comfortable offering bribes to officials (Deutsche Presse-Agentur 1998), smuggling and organized crime remain rampant (Handelman 1995), and international consultants estimate that in 1996 dishonest border officials stole more than $28 million (LETA News Agency 1997). In 1995 it was discovered that the Mercedes automobile used by Lithuania's top police official had been stolen from Germany and smuggled into the country via Poland—part of the vast smuggling enterprise that has overtaken Lithuania since independence (Filipov 1997). In Uganda, a 1999 National Integrity Survey revealed that 28 percent of respondents claimed to have been compelled to pay bribes to health services, 63 percent to police, 39 percent to local administration, and 40 percent to the Uganda Revenue Authority (*Monitor* 1999).

In short, we understand state crisis not as a category but rather as a set of syndromes that appears with considerable variation across the territories of contemporary Africa and Eurasia. The variation both within and across these regions is what provides the rationale for comparison. Viewing state crises in this way should defuse some of the anxiety that may accompany our lack of precision in defining the boundaries of these regions. Our tendency has been to use geographical descriptors to designate the collections of states that we are comparing: Eurasia and Africa. We are fully aware of the unsavory history and inherent fuzziness of the term "Eurasia" and expect some readers to object. The use of the term is meant to leave open rather than impart closure to our subject set, since the boundaries of regions are not simply geographic and cannot be established with precision. Is eastern Europe part of "Eurasia," and does it share some elements of the state crises described in the chapters in this book? The editors' use of the term "Eurasia" is primarily meant as a descriptor for the former Soviet Union. Yet, at the conference on which this book is based, Valerie Bunce argued strongly that the states of the Balkans fit many of the patterns of state crisis described in this volume and therefore deserve to be included in the analysis (though the same does not apply to the countries of east-central Europe, with their higher degree of stateness); Bogumil Jew-siewicki's paper at the conference compared communist Poland directly with colonial Africa (Jewsiewicki 1999; see also Jewsiewicki and Mudimbe 1995). Certainly, Africanists face many of the same issues of indistinct boundaries. Does North Africa belong in the same conversation as sub-Saharan Africa, and to what extent does South Africa exhibit the same problems of stateness as the rest of Africa? There are also issues of the time frame of comparison: Should contemporary Eurasia be compared with contemporary Africa, or is it more properly compared with Africa in the aftermath of independence?

We do not expect that these questions can or should be resolved. Indeed, we prefer to leave them open to creative interpretation and debate, in recognition that the utility of any comparison can be measured only by the degree to which it generates new and meaningful ideas. It is by this criterion as well that we invite our readers to judge the chapters that follow.

This volume is divided into five parts, structured by its vertebral thesis that protracted state crisis is the defining political attribute of Africa and Eurasia. We explore in turn its historical antecedents, its pathologies, the uneven and overall limited impact of efforts to repair state dysfunction through democratization and economic reform, and the interaction of protracted state crisis with the core societal cleavages of cultural plurality and gender, concluding with reflections on possible pathways beyond a dispiriting present. We begin with a chapter comparing imperial legacies, crucial to contextualizing the analysis. In Africa, the nature of the colonial state provided a procrustean bed that determined the character of its postcolonial successor to a far greater extent than expected by the independence generation of scholarly observers of Africa. The moral energies of anti-colonial nationalism swiftly dissipated in the face of the new imperatives of reproduction of sovereign statehood. The enduring force of the reproductive logic of state power imprinted on the postcolonial polity the bureaucratic authoritarian heritage of its predecessor, paradoxically reinforced by more expansive ambitions of state expansion as the presumed agency of transformative development. Legacy and overreach, combined with progressive patrimonialization, by the 1980s sowed the seeds of a sharp contraction of effective capacity. In the Eurasian case as well, the current state crisis is rooted in the historical character of the contiguous imperial domain constructed by the Russian tsars since the sixteenth century, then given new ideological form by the Soviet state. By the time of the 1917 revolution, a sharp sense of difference had taken form between the Russian imperial core and the non-Russian periphery, albeit in somewhat different forms in varying parts of the empire; the logic of state construction, as doctrines of modernity seeped into the empire, were fused with an awareness of the potential insecurity of the Russian hold on its subject periphery, a consciousness that became reinforced when the ideology of nationalism began to penetrate non-Russian zones in the later nineteenth century. The Soviet regime, to "solve" the nationality question, erected a system of ethnic federalism while retaining the inner logic of imperial control over the periphery. Ironically, the formal "internationalism" of the state socialist regime imported the sense of subject marginality into the Russian imperial core; the final blow to the Soviet Union came from the withdrawal of a now disaffected Russian center.

The second part of this book explores in various ways the pathologies of state crisis. The loss of Weberian stateness has multiple consequences. The attributes of external sovereignty partly dissolve—particularly, as Chapter 3 demonstrates, in the African instance. Boundaries, although etched on the maps and firmly implanted in the international normative system, become more permeable, and novel kinds of territorial reconfigurations are superimposed on the Westphalian geography of state-based territoriality. Networks of resource trafficking, armed militia, and criminal activity spring up in the interstices of a decaying state system. Transborder violence ultimately pits those possessing weapons against those with none. A prime characteristic of African civil wars, Chapter 8 shows, is their tendency to spill across borders, inviting the involvement of neighboring states. In the former Soviet Union, civil strife in the successor states has been an invitation to Russian army intervention, whether welcome or not (e.g., Moldova, Georgia, Tajikistan).

The shrinkage of effective internal sovereignty—the loss of a monopoly of coercion by states—opens space for diverse violent agents to emerge. Chapter 4 examines the emergence of what Volkov terms "violent entrepreneurship" in the Russian case. The inability of the state to provide a secure and legal environment for enterprises creates a market for diverse forms of protection rackets and private enforcement arrangements. These patterns of incivility, Chapter 5 demonstrates, contrast with the situations in Africa, where the violent entrepreneurs are warlords whose armed formations are much less interested in territorial occupation than in resource control. Skills in the illicit trade in high-value commodities such as diamonds, gold, or timber have developed since the 1980s, providing warlords with a capacity to acquire arms. Weakened states find great difficulty in combating such challenges to their domestic sovereignty, even though most of these marauding militias have virtually no popular support, and indeed do not really seek it. Chapter 6 examines the somewhat different pattern in the former Soviet Union: enfeebled states here as well create openings for private armies to take form. In Eurasia, however, such formations are of ethnic composition and primarily serve the security preoccupations of the communal groups from which they are drawn. They are frequently drawn from criminal or violent milieus, must support themselves through irregular activity, and frequently plunder.

Chapter 7 analyzes the relationship between civil wars, of which Africa and the former Soviet Union were the epicenter in the 1990s, and statebuilding. Historically, external warfare has been a crucial driving factor in the rise of the modern state (Young 1994, 33; Tilly 1992), making imperative the construction of an armed capacity and the revenue to support it. The state makes war, and war makes the state, runs the oft-cited Charles Tilly aphorism. In both Africa and Eurasia, however, interstate wars are improbable; the 1999–2000 war between Ethiopia and Eritrea is a striking exception. Internal wars are widespread in both areas, but civil war does not have the same state-enhancing effects; on the contrary, if protracted it corrodes stateness itself.

The relationship of state security forces to militias, warlords, ethnic armies, and the state itself is an important vector in relative state strength. Here there is a striking contrast between the regions under study. In the former Soviet Union, the official military has not sought power, reflecting a long-established pattern of military subservience to the state. However, desperately under-resourced, the successor military formations to the huge and elaborately armed Soviet army have frequently been driven to informal weapons sales, which in turn have fueled private armies. In the first three decades of post-independence Africa, more than eighty successful military coups occurred, and everywhere the army was a critical factor in the political equation. In the 1990s, the frequency of coups in Africa greatly diminished, and the Organization of African Unity now refuses admission to its annual summits to military rulers who seized power after 1998. Armies remain key players, however, and the ethnic composition of their command structures is a delicate issue in the era of partial democratization. As well, since 1979, in a number of instances (Uganda, Chad, Eritrea, Ethiopia, Somalia, Rwanda, and both Congos), armed insurgents swept to power from the periphery, resulting in the dissolution of existing armies and the disappearance of their personnel and weapons into hidden caches and private markets, a potent reservoir of arms and soldiers for violent movements.

The third part of this volume addresses the issues of political and economic liberalization in the two regions. In the political sphere, the dramatic collapse of state socialism in Eurasia and the sudden vulnerability to street action of long-standing African patrimonial autocracies in such countries as Algeria, Benin, Congo-Brazzaville, and Mali produced a seemingly irresistible tide of democratization. Economically, liberalization began earlier in Africa, but the external and internal imperative for dismantling command economies became equally intense in both regions by 1990.

Chapter 9, focused on the Russian Federation, makes clear how fragile and uncertain an "unconsolidated democracy" is in Russia. In place of a full constitutionalization of a liberal political order, the creation of a "superpresidency" under Boris Yeltsin (and its reinforcing by Vladimir Putin) evokes the profoundly rooted autocratic tradition of the Russian state. The enchantment of democracy, which swept Russia in the wake of the collapse of the Soviet Union, has long since given way to a deep disappointment with both political and economic liberalism. In Africa, Chapter 10 suggests, the formal external appearances of democracy too frequently conceal an inner reality redolent of the autocratic practices of yore. International presentability plays an excessive role in shaping liberalization. In addition, the dimensions of state weakening that have become apparent in the 1990s require a return of state-building to the agenda, conclusions that apply equally to Eurasia.

On the economic reform side, Chapters 11 and 12 take stock of the effects and consequences of adjustment programs in the context of parallel projects of political opening. Chapter 12 notes that in the moment of enthusiasm at the beginning of the 1990s, an optimistic reading of political economy emerged, postulating a "virtuous circle" linking political and economic liberalization. Economic reform fostered economic development, which in turn helps legitimate pluralist politics. Democratic regimes, in dispersing power, are also market-friendly. Thus political and economic liberalization, runs the argument, are mutually reinforcing.

This hopeful exegesis of modern history fares poorly set against African and Eurasian political economy in the 1990s. Though African economic performance in the 1990s was a modest improvement over the record of the 1980s, this improvement was far from sufficient to reinforce the legitimacy of a democratized political order. Although the patrimonial autocracy of the past clearly bore responsibility for the continental patterns of decline in the 1970s and 1980s, no strong evidence indicated a correlation between degree of democratization and quality of economic performance. In Eurasia, the command economy and the Leninist state provided a more extreme centralization and had greater historical depth than in its African counterparts. Outcomes showed more regional variation: at one pole were the Baltic states, with moderately effective political and economic reform; at the other were Central Asian countries, where the residue of the Soviet state was most pronounced. Overall, decline and stagnation were the most salient trends, punctuated by such acute crises as the Russian financial melt-down in 1998.

Chapter 11 traces the impact of externally imposed economic reform in both regions. Its evidence suggests negative consequences arising from insensitive and poorly informed diagnoses and remedies emanating from the international financial institutions and the donor community, whose voice drew strength from external indebtedness and the compelling need for external assistance in both regions. Unthinking imposition of radical reform measures, such as "shock therapy" in the Russian case, helped destroy state capacity, undermining both political and economic liberalization.

The fourth part of this book investigates the links between state crisis and social cleavage. The cultural pluralism so central to the politics of both regions is examined by Chapters 13 and 14. The dynamics of ethnic politics reflect the contrasting ethnic content of nation-state units in Eurasia and Africa. In their design of the Soviet state, Vladimir Lenin and Joseph Stalin created a formal federation based on "titular nationalities." This new territorialization of Russian imperial space then supplied the framework for its dissolution into fifteen units, all multiethnic polities with one nationality established as ascendant and others categorized as "national minorities." This model contrasts sharply with the African pattern, where the successor states to the colonial partition were with minor exceptions multiethnic, and the state as "nation" was a purely territorial notion. Rather than institutionalizing the dominance of a titular nationality, African states denied any ethnic content to the "nation."

Consequently, ethnic politics in these regions had a very different texture. In the former Soviet Union, the pivotal issues were the cultural and linguistic rights of "national minorities" and the degree of autonomy they might enjoy; in a number of cases, especially in the aftermath of Soviet collapse, secession demands were advanced. However, the successor states to the Soviet Union have, overall, stabilized themselves and their relationships with dissident minorities, though unsettled questions remain in such instances as Abkhazia, Nagorno-Karabakh, and Chechnya. The cultural balances in the successor states remain precarious in a number of instances, but they are more settled than they were a decade ago.

In Africa, as Chapter 14 demonstrates, cultural accommodation requires equitable access to the public realm and renunciation of any claim of a given community to dominance; the notion of a "titular nationality" is alien to the African state system. The violation of these precepts in the Sudan is responsible for a simmering civil war dating from independence in 1956; a decade of peace from 1973 to 1984 was followed by renewed and more intense warfare when the peace accords were subverted by a renewed assertion of Muslim and Arab hegemony. Sovereignty, this chapter argues, must be reinterpreted as comporting not the unlimited entitlement to the exercise of authority within a state, but rather an acceptance of responsibility for the equitable accommodation of diversity.

Chapter 15 offers a comparative overview of the gender dimension of state-society divisions. This chapter reveals a counterintuitive pattern, with sharply contrasting outcomes in terms of gender equity. In the former Soviet Union, women have lost ground, at least in terms of formal representation, and women's organizations have not been very visible. In Africa, democratization, however imperfect, has brought important benefits in opening space for articulation of a female voice. The removal of the prohibitions on autonomous organization characteristic of the single-party era has invited in many countries a proliferation of women's organizations that are frequently preoccupied less with national politics than with shared pursuit of common interests at the community level.

The concluding section returns to the core question that state crisis poses: How can an efficacious state be created in Africa and Eurasia that can carry the nearly six dozen polities of the two regions beyond endless impasse? We approach the issue in part by examining two cases in which indisputably failed states were carried part of the way back to political and economic health: Georgia and Uganda. Neither could be classified as possessing full stateness, yet both exhibited an intriguing resilience following catastrophic periods. Whether either or both can avoid relapse into incoherence and can continue on the path already trod from failed to weak state to become fully effective states remains uncertain; large questions arise in both instances. But they do point to possibilities for state restoration.

Our overall conclusions, drawing together the insights supplied by the many contributors to this project, stress the difficulty of the challenge, the dimensions of the obstacles, and the extended time frame required to achieve effective, democratic states and functioning market economies. Variability in outcomes is very likely, ranging from episodes of state failure and collapse to the moderately successful polities visible today in the Baltic states, Botswana, or Mauritius. Certainly, no instant erasure of deeply embedded historical impediments to "normal" statehood is possible.

References

Bunce, Valerie. 1995. "Should Transitologists Be Grounded? Transitions from Authoritarian to Democratic Rule in Eastern Europe." *Slavic Review* 54, no. 1: 111–27.
Deutsche Presse-Agentur. 1998. "Corruption in Latvia Takes Several Forms." 25 November.
Economist. 1999. "Money Can't Buy Me Love." 6 February: 23.
Filipov, David. 1997. "Lithuania Becoming Smugglers' Paradise." *Boston Globe*. 3 August: A1.
Handelman, Stephen. 1995. *Comrade Criminal: Russia's New Mafiya*. New Haven: Yale University Press.
Huntington, Samuel P. 1991. *The Third Wave: Democratization in the Late Twentieth Century*. Norman: University of Oklahoma Press.
Jackson, Robert H. 1990. *Quasi-States: Sovereignty, International Relations, and the Third World*. Cambridge: Cambridge University Press.
Jewsiewicki, Bogumil. 1999. "Post-Colonial and Soviet States: From the Disciplinary to the Predator State." Paper presented at the conference on "Beyond State Crisis? The Quest for the Efficacious State in Africa and Eurasia," University of Wisconsin at Madison, 11–14 March.
Jewsiewicki, Bogumil, and V. Y. Mudimbe. 1995. "Meeting the Challenge of Legitimacy: Post-Independence Black African and Post-Soviet European States." *Daedalus* 124, no. 3: 191–207.
LETA News Agency. 1997. 19 August.
Migdal, Joel. 1988. *Strong Societies and Weak States: State-Society Relations and State Capabilities in the Third World*. Princeton: Princeton University Press.
Monitor. 1999. (Kampala). 5 October.
Sartori, Giovanni. 1991. "Comparing and Miscomparing." *Journal of Theoretical Politics* 3, no. 3: 243–57.
Tilly, Charles. 1992. *Coercion, Capital, and European States, AD 900–1992*. Rev. ed. Cambridge, Mass.: Blackwell.
Weber, Max. 1946. "Politics as a Vocation." Pp. 77–128 in *From Max Weber: Essays in Sociology*, ed. H. H. Gerth and C. Wright Mills. New York: Oxford University Press.
Young, Crawford. 1994. *The African Colonial State in Comparative Perspective*. New Haven: Yale University Press.

2

Convergence to Crisis: Pre-Independence State Legacies and Post-Independence State Breakdown in Africa and Eurasia

MARK R. BEISSINGER
AND CRAWFORD YOUNG

The fathers have eaten a sour grape, and the children's teeth are set on edge.

—Jeremiah 31:29

The purpose of this volume is to explore similarities and differences in the state crises that have engulfed contemporary Africa and Eurasia, as well as various ways in which exits from these crises have been sought. But the obvious question raised by the core problematic of this project is why such a comparison has grown thinkable in the first place. Why, in such radically different contexts as Africa and post-Soviet Eurasia, should elements of comparability emerge? Why, in spite of their vast differences in history, culture, and experience, should these two regions have come to be subjected to what some observers believe are comparable sets of ailments?

One answer that we will pursue in this chapter lies in the shared legacy of imperial subordination. Nearly all of Africa and the non-Russian areas of the Russian empire and its Soviet successor were profoundly marked by the experience of subjugation to an imperial center. The respective imperial legacies introduce one important dimension of comparability, which we examine by identifying certain parallel features of these regions' distinct pre-independence state experiences[1] and the ways in which the structures, resources, assumptions, and practices emerging from these experiences were appropriated by self-interested actors in the transition to and from independence. These similarities revolve around the scope of pre-independence state power and the state's attempts at social engineering, the autocratic nature of that power, and the relatively recent timing of these experiences. We locate some important reasons for the analogous patterns of state breakdown that plague Africa and the former Soviet Union in the combination of autocratic state practice with the ideologies of high modernism that animated both Soviet communism and European colonial projects in Africa.

Indeed, many of the examples recounted by James Scott (1998) in his provocative study of the impact of high modernism on the behavior of states are drawn precisely from the African and Soviet experiences. We believe this to be no accident: both Soviet communism and European colonialism in Africa represented the high point of the tide of state power that swept the world in the early twentieth century, and both experiences involved attempts to impose a new social order through force. In contrast to western Europe, where the modern state evolved over centuries, and unlike Latin America, where the modern state emerged in the early nineteenth century after three hundred years of colonial experience, in both Africa and Eurasia the modern state emerged relatively late and largely at a time when belief in the transformative power of the state was at its height. Indeed, the critical periods of state formation in Africa and Eurasia materialized largely out of the coercive imposition of grand transformational state projects whose roots lay primarily in late-nineteenth- and early-twentieth-century European civilization. The unusual penetration of pre-independence state power; the state's extensive engineering of society for the dual purposes of modernization and control; its relatively recent imposition of bounded political order on complex multicultural populations; its absolutist, coercive character; and the widespread subversion that this power produced all proved critical to the subsequent deconstruction of the state in both regions. In both settings, pre-independence state practices established physical parameters and structures around which post-independence behavior flowed and created cultural understandings and expectations that structured the ways in which people behaved once independence emerged.

---

1. By "pre-independence state experiences," we are referring specifically to Soviet communism as well as the tsarist empire, and to European colonialism in Africa.

As we will see, the inertia of many pre-independence practices has proved irresistible on both continents. Nevertheless, broadly comparable features of state crises emerged only in the wake of the failure of these grand transformational projects and in the context of post-independence transitions, as pre-independence state experiences were appropriated by local social and political forces to produce "legacies." James Millar and Sharon Wolchik (1994, 1–2) have distinguished between what they refer to as the "legacies" of communism and the "aftermath" of communism, the former referring to "an enduring intergenerational transfer from the past to the present" and the latter to transient features emerging from a particular transitional context. "Legacies" understood in this sense are enduring social relationships, not temporary transitional phenomena. Yet "legacies" emerge as sustained and self-reproducing phenomena (i.e., they take on the characteristics of being legacies) only within particular transitional contexts. Our reading of the literature on both regions leads us to observe that Africanists have tended to place emphasis on legacies (in the sense of self-replicating social relationships) in explaining post-independence state crises, whereas scholars of postcommunist politics—especially in the first years after the collapse of communism—have tended to highlight the role of aftermaths (features emerging from the particular transitional context).

This difference in approach may in part be a reflection of the varying amounts of time that have passed since independence in the two regions; it is legacies, not aftermaths, that are so glaringly visible in Africa after forty years, while in the former Soviet Union only a decade after independence, it remains more difficult to distinguish aftermaths from legacies. Nevertheless, we are confronted with contrasting explanations of state crises: one focused on the continuity and reproduction of social relationships embedded by pre-independence political experiences, the other focused on the collapse of traditional instruments of social control exercised by pre-independence authority and the dysfunctional forms of authority that took their place. Our argument implies that these perspectives are not mutually exclusive and that neither on its own is sufficient to explain the unfolding crises of the state in Africa and Eurasia. In this sense, we think that both groups of scholars have something to learn from each other through this comparison. But we also suggest that these contrasting scholarly perspectives reflect to some extent the different transitional paths taken by Africa and Eurasia to and from independence and ultimately toward the state crises of the 1990s.

In conjuring in the title of this essay the terminology of convergence theory that was so prominent in scholarly thought about communism in the

1960s and 1970s, we do not mean to imply the kind of inevitable march toward a singular outcome that was frequently characteristic of this type of social scientific theorizing. On the contrary, we see considerable variation in
both regions in the degree to which state crises have become manifest.
Moreover, we speak not of a single crisis of the state in these regions, but
rather of a series of crises, some of which share comparable features. Multiple mechanisms in both contexts have produced a number of increasingly
parallel outcomes in different political circumstances. Among these, several
are conspicuous: a vacuum of purpose and agenda in the wake of the collapse of pre-independence transformational projects; the rapaciousness and
venality of elites, who have stolen the assets of formerly Weberian states; the
widespread evasion of authority within society; and the territorial grids that
have made the production of loyalty to a common state authority problematic. These causal mechanisms in turn emerged out of specific pre-
independence state experiences. Indeed, we would argue that, although the
global forces that have washed across both regions have magnified these
issues, the significant variation in the degree to which state crises are apparent across each of these regions has been more a function of the extent
to which these patterns hold than the influence of globalization per se.

In what follows, we review the distinctive features of pre-independence
experiences that in both contexts set these mechanisms in motion and that
in both contexts are critical to explaining post-independence state crises.
We then examine how these experiences shaped interests and understandings after independence and were themselves transformed into legacies of
dysfunctional state authority in the context of post-independence transitions. Obviously, the vast scale of the continental domains within our analytical lens necessitates a broad level of generalization, with many statements requiring nuance or attenuation that the constraints of space
unfortunately prohibit. We recognize this is the price paid for cross-
regional comparison but hope that this price is at least partially offset by
the utility of the insights generated.

Pre-Independence Experiences Compared

In both Africa and Eurasia pre-independence state experiences cast a long
shadow over the contemporary state and its travails. In the Eurasian case,
the rise of the tsarist empire can be traced back to a gradual expansion starting from the sixteenth century, as Muscovy conquered contiguous principalities and khanates in central Russia, the Middle Volga, and Siberia, sub-

sequently occupying parts of contemporary Ukraine and southern Russia in the seventeenth century, the Baltic region and Poland in the eighteenth century, and Bessarabia and the Caucasus in the first half of the nineteenth century. With the notable exception of Central Asia, whose conquest was nearly simultaneous with the sudden explosion of colonial expansion in Africa in the last quarter of the nineteenth century, in general the length of experience under Russian rule was far greater than that of Africans under European rule. Of course, as an overland (rather than overseas) empire, Russia could not so easily segment its nation-building and colonial policies as could the transoceanic empires of western Europe. Because of geography and the autocratic character of the tsarist state, Russia had a difficult time delineating who was a citizen and who was a subject. With a few exceptions in which the relationship remained more overtly colonial in character (particularly with regard to the mountain peoples of the Caucasus, the indigenous peoples of Siberia, and Central Asians), the tsarist state by the late nineteenth century treated its population as citizen-subjects, a status that applied equally to Russians and non-Russians. The idea of citizenship emerged in Russia from the late eighteenth to the mid-nineteenth centuries under heavy influence from the rise of nationalism in western Europe and analogous moves by European rulers toward incorporation of populations. In Russia, "the passage to citizenship in the borderlands was imagined as a kind of cultural revolution which would form a new social order and would turn rebellious natives into loyal citizens" (Yaroshevski 1997, 61). Yet the simultaneous reality of autocracy and the patrimonial character of the state universalized subject status as well. The Russian Revolution on the surface seemed to signal a break with the tsarist duality of state-building and empire-building, but in actuality the duality of authority came to be reinforced by Soviet modalities of rule. Ethno-federalism and a legitimating ideology of self-determination and internationalism were combined with hyper-centralized political control by Moscow and the widespread and intensified use of terror as an instrument of state policy, once again blurring the distinction between subject and citizen and between state and empire (Beissinger 1993, 1995). But communism layered a new element over empire: Marxist-Leninist ideology and its vision of modernist utopia. Tsarism was largely content to rule over traditional social structures and to leave them intact; Soviet power consciously sought to transform society and remake it in a new, industrialist image. Moreover, a distinct form of political organization was established to effect this transformation: the totalitarian party-state organized along monistic principles—one that, by Stalinist times, increasingly relied on the power of the secret police.

In contrast to Russia, in Africa the imperial moment was strikingly compressed, lasting in most areas less than a century (the exceptions being the French hold on northern regions of Algeria, the Portuguese settlements in Angola and Mozambique, a few coastal enclaves in West Africa originating in the slave trade, and the white colonies on the southern tip of the continent). In contrast to the tsarist/Soviet experience, colonial doctrine in Africa stipulated a clear distinction between the metropolitan domains and the African holdings, the territory and population of which held sharply demarcated subject status—only modestly blurred, in the French and Portuguese cases, by a patina of sporadically applied assimilationist ideology.[2] The African colonial state lacked the relentless enforcement of the monistic organization and ideology that were central in defining Soviet rule. Nor did Soviet political forms contain the overt notions of racial superiority that were intrinsic to the constitution of the subject within the African colonial experience. In reading the imperial experience with respect to the contemporary state crises, we should note that, in Africa, an implicit duality emerged more distinctly in the context of postcolonial transition, when the postcolonial African state silently incorporated its colonial origins (Young 1994). Although the era of formal colonial occupation in Africa came mostly to an end in the 1950s and 1960s, the habitus embedded by the colonial state remained and amalgamated dialectically with the state-building and power-reproduction imperatives of the postcolonial successor elite.

The distinct content of these histories is critical for explaining the contrasting scripts of contemporary politics in Africa and Eurasia. But some overarching parallels beckon our attention and provide a partial explanation for why both regions converged toward state crises in the wake of independence. First, the density and embeddedness of the impact of impe-

---

2. We note in passing that Ethiopia stands as an African exception more closely tracking the Eurasian dual-legacy model. Though a colony only during the abbreviated 1936–41 Italian occupation, Ethiopia assimilated imported doctrines of stateness in two stages. Beginning to some degree with Emperor Menelik II in the late nineteenth century, then more systematically with the consolidation of power by Emperor Haile Selassie about 1930, a traditional kingdom systematically reinvented itself and sought legitimation of its own subimperial expansion through wholesale importation of the European nation-state self-concept. With the destruction of the old Ethiopian order in 1974, the new military regime formally adopted Marxism-Leninism, fitfully applied Leninist nationality theory, and solicited comprehensive and intrusive Soviet security support and tutelage. The legacy of this sequence, when the Leninist experiment collapsed under the weight of armed uprisings around the periphery and vaporization of its external patron, was a post-imperial polity like those of Eurasia, compelled to acknowledge ethno-national segments as the basic constituent elements of a state struggling to neutralize the residues of its failed Marxist-Leninist moment.

rial/colonial experiences stand out in both instances—in large part because of the ways in which modernism was an integral part of imperial projects in both regions. The texture of contemporary stateness in both Africa and Eurasia today embodies the colonial/imperial cloth from which the successor states were tailored. Indeed, European colonialism in Africa and Russian imperialism in Eurasia (and that of its Soviet successor empire-state) were largely responsible for introducing the modern state to these regions. And perhaps more significant, because imperial domination in both cases lasted until the contemporary era, it fully reflected the apogee of expansion in the scope and reach of the modern state in the mid-twentieth century. As a result, the depth of state penetration stands out, well exceeding the reach of other imperial/colonial traditions, save perhaps only that of the Japanese (Young 1998, Myers and Peattie 1984). In both regions the expansion of state power in the pre-independence period was accompanied by massive social engineering by state authority. This fact is better known in the Soviet context than in the African. But as René Lemarchand observed, "the colonial state . . . must indeed be viewed as the single most powerful agent of societal transformation in the history of the [African] continent" (Lemarchand 1983, 45).

The expansion of the African colonial state was most starkly visible in the field of political economy. As Claude Ake noted,

The colonial state redistributed land and determined who should produce what and how. It attended to the supply of labor, sometimes resorting to forced labor; it churned out administrative instruments and legislated taxes to induce the breakup of traditional social relations of production, the atomization of society, and the process of proletarianization. . . . Indeed, it controlled every aspect of the colonial economy tightly to maintain its power and domination and to realize the economic objectives of colonization (Ake 1996, 2).

During World War II, a wide range of regulatory interventions appeared in response to emergency requirements: expansion of price controls and state monopolies on the marketing of key crops. Much of this extensive state intervention continued in the postwar years, acquiring through long usage an appearance of normalcy. In the final colonial era from World War II until independence, the revenue-generating capacity of the African colonial state expanded remarkably. The postwar years brought a sustained period of record prices for the major African agricultural and mineral exports; because the principal component of the fiscal domain was external trade, this translated directly into an extraordinary expansion in revenue. Also, for the first time on a significant scale, the major colonizers committed substantial funds to colonial development. These suddenly expanding resources permitted the rapid creation, from a tiny base, of a substantial social infrastructure of schools and health-care facilities. They also financed, alongside the traditional hierarchy of colonial command and control, a ramifying array of technical and social service agencies. As independence approached, the state acquired a formidable momentum of expansion. African society, especially in the rural areas, found access to valued social services that had been scarce or nonexistent in prewar years. The multiplication of primary schools across Africa in the late colonial period, the dramatic expansion of secondary schools, and the introduction of tertiary education, when combined with the long era of robust economic expansion, created an unparalleled moment of prosperity and, especially for the young, prospects for social ascension. Real wages rose for the only time during the colonial period. Urban employment was readily available. Secondary-school and university graduates had assured opportunities. Furthermore, as the discriminatory salary policies of high colonialism were swept away and elite African wages aligned with those enjoyed by Europeans, the emergent African middle class enjoyed an extraordinary rise in status and income. The historical memory of the colonial state among the older generation today is defined by a gilded recollection of an era of exceptional prosperity connected with the expansion of the colonial state and serves as a yardstick against which the harsh economic realities of the present are judged. For the middle class, often devastated by the prolonged economic crisis and incapacitation of the state, the gap between the rising hopes of the 1950s and their impoverished present condition is immense. Even where the colonial experience remained harsh and brutal until its final moments (as in Mozambique, for instance), field inquiry among peasants encounters surprising erasures in social memory of its repressive aspects. As one contemporary study suggests, "[p]art of the political legitimacy retrospectively conferred on the colonial state by peasants today [in northern Mozambique] . . . derives from a very negative evaluation of the postcolonial period" (Harrison 1998, 552). The parallels with the nostalgia today in many parts of the former Soviet Union for the years of Premier Leonid Brezhnev are striking.

A number of these same practices appeared in exaggerated form and at an earlier point of development in the Soviet case. Joseph Stalin's *velikii perelom* ("great break") of 1929 constituted one of the most important junctures worldwide in the enormous expansion of state power that occurred over the course of the twentieth century. Here, traditional society was subjected to violent frontal assault with the imposition of a uniform mold of economic and social institutions. Comprehensive imperative planning—treating all of society as a single economic complex whose productive capacities were to be harnessed and coordinated by bureaucratic fiat—was established as the dominant practice. Extensive networks of social and political control blanketed society. Class hierarchies were reconfigured, with mobility opportunities dependent on service to the state and privilege coalescing around one's place on the *nomenklatura* list. Though the peoples of the Russian empire at the turn of the century were extraordinarily diverse in terms of social structure, economies, and cultures, the Soviet state stamped a common institutional form and social structure on this diversity and enforced a common political discourse, creating in the process specifically Soviet cultural amalgams that loom large in the problems facing the region today.

To be sure, Soviet power crystallized in distinct ways across the expanse of the Soviet state, accounting in part for the continuing diversity of outcomes of state-building within the region. David Laitin (1998), for instance, has pointed to several models by which non-Russian territories were incorporated that defined the nature of state-society interactions: a "most-favored-lord" model pushing gradual assimilation, as in Ukraine; a colonial model, uprooting local society but establishing barriers to full assimilation, as in Kazakhstan; an integral model, in which local society was ruled over but retained a strong sense of autonomy and cohesion vis-à-vis metropolitan authority, as in the Baltic region. While these ideal types may not provide a perfect map, the basic point that Laitin makes holds true: the different ways by which central control was mediated by local elites at the point of contact left behind distinct variations in post-Soviet legacies. The penetration of Soviet state institutions undoubtedly exceeded substantially that of African colonial regimes, though the Soviet penetration was far from complete, and subversion was widespread. Nevertheless, the important commonality that subsequently contributed in both contexts to the crises of post-independence state authority was that, in both Africa and Eurasia, modes of domination effectively permeated and totally reordered their respective societal hierarchies in a modernist image, leaving behind embedded legacies touching multiple domains of everyday life within the modern sector of society: the structure of the economy, the nature of state institutions, systems of class stratification, and patterns of interface between state and society. Moreover, the very fact that colonial/imperial governments undertook and successfully enforced such wide-ranging societal transformations affected the habits, routines, and mentalities of governing and governed. In both contexts the state became not only the dominant focus for efforts at societal transformation, but the central vehicle for class mobility as well.

A second important commonality between the African and Eurasian pre-independence experiences was the critical role played by violence as a tool of social transformation and control, as well as the general trajectory of pre-independence state authority in the years leading up to independence—away from coercive state practice and toward more localized forms of bureaucratic authoritarianism. In both regions, autocracy and state-sponsored violence were defining attributes of pre-independence state projects and modes of modernization. These set a pattern of state-society interaction that proved tenacious. Stalinism, of course, was more than merely a personal despotism. As Barrington Moore (1954) observed, it was an institutionalized social and political system in which the authoritarian, arbitrary, and fundamentally violent exercise of state authority at the center was reproduced locally and in the workplace. Violence was wielded as a fundamental tool of social transformation by those who controlled the state. But these policies often played into particularistic interests at the local level, as land, living space, jobs, and amenities were redistributed on a vast scale through coercive practices.

Until the late 1980s the nature and legacies of Stalin's rule by terror could not be publicly aired. Yet within this continuing autocratic frame, authority evolved toward more diffuse and less capriciously violent forms. After Stalin's death, arbitrary terror halted and slave labor within the gulag was scaled back. Oligarchic modes of decision-making grew in importance, and efforts to introduce "socialist legality" tempered some of the worst abuses of the system. Some viewed this as a rationalization of autocracy, others as the incipient transition from totalitarianism. What is clear is that the end of terror was accompanied by a slow diffusion and localization of power. Centralization and personalization of authority, the arbitrary treatment of those opposing the regime, and rampant everyday abuses of power throughout the state hierarchy remained defining features of Soviet power into the late 1980s. The ingrained modes of behavior that this system implanted within the political class remain conspicuous today. As Boris Yeltsin (1990, 70) once reminisced about his power as Communist Party secretary of Sverdlovsk province during the later years of Brezhnev's rule, "[T]he power of a first secretary within his province is practically unlimited. And the sense of power is intoxicating. . . . In those days a provincial first secretary of the party was god, a czar—master of his province—and on virtually any issue the first secretary's opinion was final."

As those who worked closely with him in the post-Soviet period observed, Yeltsin's subsequent behavior as president of independent Russia demonstrated much of this same intoxication with power and a license in using it learned through years of climbing the Soviet hierarchy (Kostikov 1997, 338). The devolution of administration characteristic of the post-Stalin period was accompanied by the localization of patronage networks—developments that amounted to a greater penetration of local and unofficial social networks into party and governmental affairs. Clientelism and corruption blossomed, and much of the illicit politics that became so prominent in the post-Soviet period had their origins in state-society interactions of the late Brezhnev era. Although bureaucratic discipline was the basis of state authority in the Brezhnev years, the clearly authoritarian and hierarchical character of power was silently violated from within on a vast scale.

Within Africa, as well, autocracy remained the essence of the colonial state heritage. The highly competitive and swift nature of colonial conquest operated under a set of rules that necessitated rapid creation of an extractive hegemony. The requirement imposed by metropolitan treasuries on all participants in the African partition (save Italy)—that newly acquired African territories be financially self-sufficient—meant that African societies had to pay for their own conquest. Through the early colonial decades, state sustenance came in part from widespread use of forced or conscripted labor for portage, road and infrastructure construction, and military service. This in turn made imperative the identification and empowerment of a network of African intermediaries capable of recruiting labor levies, imposing direct taxation, or enforcing cultivation of taxable export crops on a subsistence-based rural populace. The result was a pattern of "decentralized despotism," to borrow the evocative Mahmood Mamdani (1996) concept, completed by a modest set of command institutions at the center, entirely alien in staffing and orientation and largely autonomous of subject society (excepting white settlers, where numerous) and the metropolitan center. Particularly in establishing the extractive practices that ensured the fiscal solvency of the colonial state, large quotients of brutal force were indispensable. Thus a singular form of state took shape, centralized and hierarchical at its center, operating in differentiated ways through its African intermediaries at the periphery—at its zenith a pure model of the bureaucratic authoritarian state.

Paternalism found its way deeply into the internal operative code of state action in both contexts. In the Soviet case, this amounted to more than simply the cradle-to-grave welfare system run by state and party-affiliated social institutions. As Peter Kenez (1985) pointed out, the propaganda state created by the Bolsheviks had its origins in the attempt to "enlighten" the population and played both a tutelary and prophylactic role. In Africa, of course, racism was deeply embedded in the paternalistic and expansionist premises of the African colonial state. The African as savage child required the stern discipline of the European agent or missionary. Here, too, the state, in loco parentis, presumed a didactic, tutelary role over the subject. When "developing the colonial estates" and "*mise en valeur*" entered state discourse in the 1920s, a corollary precept was the need to command the changes deemed necessary: introduction of a cash crop and cultivation practices, construction of a road, terracing of a hillside. Even though metropolitan states were sometimes, especially after World War II, under socialist governments, interventionist practices in the colonial territories owed little to progressive ideology in Europe and everything to a habit of paternalistic management of the subject.

A third critical similarity in the role played by pre-independence legacies in precipitating state breakdown lay in the territorial grids of authority imposed over these populations. These grids eventually became the basis for post-independence state systems, defined the conflictual character of cultural politics after independence, and persisted in spite of the extent to which juridical sovereignty outstripped empirical reality. The implications of these frames for state authority in both regions have been enormous. Turning to the African case, we may begin with the obvious: the geopolitical reconfiguration of the continent. Colonial occupation imposed a largely novel definition of territory. Partition reflected the accidents of European diplomacy and contingencies of military force; only rarely was an existing state incorporated within an imperial domain as a self-standing entity by negotiation (Lesotho, Swaziland) or force (Egypt, Morocco, Tunisia). Only Ethiopia, Egypt, and Morocco have an indigenous state tradition with substantial historical depth. Every political primer begins by noting the utterly arbitrary character of state borders within Africa. Once partition was in place, the colonial state breathed meaning into boundaries: more than mere lines on a map, the frontiers acquired visible demarcation, border posts, and restrictions (not always effective) that had never existed before on crossborder movements. Yet the territorial heritage of the colonial partition remains one of the most enduring elements of the current political landscape, coming under significant question only in the late

1990s. In its early stages, pan-African nationalism excoriated the "artificial frontiers drawn by the Imperialist Powers." But the long shadow of Westphalian doctrine soon silenced such radical demands. As soon as anticolonial nationalist leaders inherited the territorial entities fabricated by the colonial partition, their discourse changed. The first meeting of delegates of independent African states concluded that peace demanded "respect [for] the independence, sovereignty, and territorial integrity of one another." With the creation of the Organization of African Unity as a syndicate of independent states in 1963, African international normative doctrine went even further: acknowledgment of the extant territorial frame was not only unavoidable, but the frontiers were inviolable and states had a sacred obligation to uphold existing borders (Young 1991, 23). The ultimate consequence, increasingly apparent as deepening stress afflicted the state system in the 1990s, was to lock within a single territory communities that never would have chosen to share a common sovereign. The enduring force of the colonial territorial legacy finds eloquent proof in the persistence of the territorial state even in the face of its institutional collapse. Somalia continues as an imagined state in the absence of any functioning institutions since 1991. The exception that proves the rule is the reconstitution of state-like institutions in northern Somalia, itself a separate colonial fragment that was amalgamated with the former Italian colony at the time of independence in 1960; lacking formal recognition from the international system, Somaliland was a government without a state, while Somalia was a state without a government. Though Liberia and Sierra Leone lacked operating institutions that could exercise sovereignty over their territory for much of the 1990s, no one questioned their existence as states; sovereignty was merely in suspense, awaiting new agents for its exercise.

The discursive resources committed to a posthumous legitimation of the colonial partition have several explanations. Anticolonial struggle could be conducted only within the frame supplied by the colonial territory; in turn, the territoriality of the political mobilization rendered its agents tributary to its frame. Once in power and armed with formal independence, rulers required a normative script defining their domain. Colonial territories were no longer "mere geographical expressions," as Nigerian politician Obafemi Awolowo had once characterized Nigeria, but "nations" whose citizens were expected not only to obey but to love and cherish. The socializing instruments of school curricula and state media were marshaled to this higher purpose. The banal, everyday accouterments of nationality—stamps, coinage, flags, national soccer teams, and airlines—appeared to provide their quotidian imprint (Billig 1995). This naturalization of some degree of civic identification with the state undoubtedly had some success, in the relative absence of serious efforts to break up existing states (though a number of separatist movements have sprung up, with some degree of support). The only breakup to occur was the 1991 separation of Eritrea from Ethiopia, an independence claim grounded in the existence of Eritrea as a separate colonial state prior to its Ethiopian annexation. William Miles, in his captivating monograph detailing the myriad ways a boundary divides otherwise culturally identical, adjoining Hausa villages in Nigeria and Niger, ably chronicles the normalization of contrasting national identities, in spite of the daily flows and close social linkages across the line:

Incongruously, provocatively, [the border marker] towers on high: a fifteen-foot metal pole, springing out of the dirty brown Sahelian sand. No other human artifact is to be seen in this vast, barren, flat savanna. . . . One stares and wonders how, by beast and porter, such a huge totem could have been lugged there and erected in this desolate bush. But there it stands: a marker of an international boundary, a monument to the splitting of a people, a symbol of colonialism, an idol of "national sovereignty." . . . The poles would determine the identity, fate, and life possibilities of the people along and behind them (Miles 1994, 1).

One finds strangely similar descriptions of the boundary between parts of post-Soviet Ukraine and Russia, where, with the onset of independence, once-sleepy villages were turned almost overnight into lively border trading towns and springboards for smuggling across a barely marked border that, in Soviet times, no one seemed to know existed (Butuzova and Tuchnin 1998). Much like the colonial division of Africa, Soviet ethno-federalism formally divided and fixed political space for the first time in Eurasia. The invention of ethno-federalism was part of a larger strategy of divide and rule meant to advantage Soviet power in consolidating its control over non-Russian regions. Within the asymmetric federal system established by the Soviets, territorial units formed around ethnicities were not provided with equal status, but a complex hierarchy of units within units was established. Some populous groups were deprived of units altogether, and Russians functioned largely outside the ethno-federal hierarchy, as they were assumed to be its integrating core. Only by understanding ethno-federalism as a tool of cultural hegemony can one explain the significant anomalies in the way in which this vast and complex territory was carved up: Stalin's purposeful creation of multiethnic autonomous republics across the northern Caucasus that combined groups from different linguistic families; the division of the Muslims of the Middle Volga and the Muslims of Central Asia into numerous ethnic territorial units on a linguistic principle; the placement of the Abkhaz under Georgian rule or the division of Armenians and Ossetians into two federal units under separate lines of authority; or the use of the predominantly Slavic enclave of left-bank Pridnestr as a wedge for gaining control over Bessarabia by creating the Moldavian Autonomous Republic in the interwar period. But unlike the colonial division of Africa, Stalin's division of boundaries across Eurasia was guided by the assumption that every nationality officially recognized by the state deserved its own political-territorial unit. Of course, no drawing of boundaries would have produced full harmonization between cultural and political units in this complex, multicultural context; minorities would always be a fact of political life. Nevertheless, a significant number of the violent conflicts that engulfed the region after the fall of communism (e.g., the Armenian-Azerbaijani, Abkhaz-Georgian, Ossetian-Georgian, Ossetian-Ingush, and Moldovan-Pridnestr) trace their origin to Moscow's political misuse of boundary-making in the Soviet period.

Applying their own taxonomic logic of "state simplification" (Scott 1998) to complex, multicultural societies, both the African colonial and Stalinist states embarked on comprehensive cultural classification projects. Closely related to racism in the doctrine of the African colonial state was the constitution of the African subject as "native." To the extent that "native" was an undifferentiated subject category, a uniform body of law stipulated limited legal rights in such areas as property, movement, and political behavior, distinct in important respects from that applicable to citizens of the colonial power. But the subject, as Mamdani (1996) stresses, was more than a mere "native"; the African was also a member of a particular customary community. Here the impact of the colonial state was very large. The ethnic template that was superimposed on African society was in a number of respects transformative. Although ethnonyms were not simply "invented," they were subject to significant reinterpretation, extension of some categories, amalgamation of others, and obliteration of still others (Vail 1989). The revised ethnic mappings found local cultural entrepreneurs as well as customary authorities who acquired an interest in the colonial cultural classifications. Missionaries standardized languages with an eye to economy in evangelical investment. In emergent population centers, the novel social environment generated its own dynamic of category reduction. A fluid complexity of identity at the moment of colonial occupation, largely unencumbered by any ideological formulation of consciousness, became a more codified pattern of identity, awaiting mobilization by the political entrepreneur.

As in Africa, Soviet authority imbued new meaning in cultural difference through its ethno-federal categorization project, which in certain respects exceeded that of African colonial powers. As in Africa, groups were defined and classified, languages standardized, and all individuals coded with official categories of identity—in the Soviet case, through an internal passport system. But even more, literary idioms were established, histories written, and national intelligentsias created. One's place within the Soviet ethno-federal hierarchy established expectations around which behavior coalesced, determined flows of resources, and formed the contours of elites and bureaucracies (Suny 1993; Brubaker 1996). Moreover, unlike in Africa, where European colonialism consolidated ethnic/tribal identities as forces that stood in conflict with the state and left behind attempts to build civic nationalisms around postcolonial units, Soviet ethno-federalism accentuated and consolidated ethnic identities around political-territorial units, giving rise in the aftermath of independence to a plethora of nationalizing state projects based on claims to self-determination by eponymous cultural groups. The widespread perception in the post-Soviet period that politics in Uzbekistan should favor Uzbeks or that Ukraine should provide special privileges for the Ukrainian language is fundamental to eponymous ethnic groups of formerly Soviet ethno-federal units and contrasts sharply with the outwardly civic model characteristic of the African postcolonial state.

Asymmetric ethno-federalism also acted as a source of political ambitions in the post-Soviet period. A proliferation of claims to sovereignty emerged as the alter ego of Soviet hypercentralization. Since the Soviet collapse, Russians in Crimea, the Donetsk region, northern Estonia, northern Kazakhstan, and Pridnestr; Ukrainians in Transcarpathia; Poles in Lithuania; Gagauzy in Moldova; Lezgins in Azerbaijan; and Armenians in Georgia have all pushed at various times for autonomous territorial units as a solution to their claims of discrimination against them. Within post-Soviet Russia, where forty-five separate power-sharing arrangements (each different in content) were concluded between the central government and constituent units of the Russian Federation, asymmetric ethno-federalism led to a crippling paralysis of state authority, to the point that, depending on the region of Russia, effective power had drifted into the hands of local governmental satraps, paramilitary or criminal organizations, or local business enterprises—and often some combination of all three. Indeed, one of President Vladimir Putin's first acts as Yeltsin's successor was to try to reverse the extreme devolution of power that had taken place in the Yeltsin years. In both Africa and the former Soviet Union, the conflicts unleashed by the territorial grid imposed by pre-independence authorities have been dysfunctional for states, though in markedly different ways.

Yet the territorial boundaries imposed by Soviet authority, like those in postcolonial Africa, have had enormous staying power. In both contexts not only did pre-independence boundaries form the basis for the post-independence state systems; they became extremely difficult to challenge, due in large part to the role played by external forces in seeking to halt the dialectic of dismemberment that loomed over these regions. No state has recognized the claims of Pridnestr, Abkhazia, Karabakh, or Chechnya to the status of independent states (with the sole exception, in the latter case, of Taliban Afghanistan), even though these breakaway territories do attempt to function as states, organizing their own armed forces, courts, police, schools, flags, monuments, and, in some cases, even separate passports and currencies. Fragmented states such as Georgia, Moldova, Azerbaijan, and Tajikistan have continued to retain international recognition of their claimed boundaries, even though they do not control significant portions of their territories, mirroring many of the features of the African quasi-state model. Armenia's reluctance to annex Karabakh in spite of its ability to do so at any moment is strong testimony of the powerful international pressures operating against boundary change in the region.

A final critical vector of similarity revolves around the widespread practices of subversion of state power toward personal ends left behind by pre-independence state experiences in both Africa and Eurasia—forms of behavior and modes of alternative authority that, while differing in the two contexts, grew increasingly central to the political process in the wake of independence. For Africans and Eurasians, pre-independence state power constituted a distant and alien other to be simultaneously feared, milked, and deceived—a cause for distrust, self-protection, and booty. These widespread attitudes and forms of behavior naturally continued into the post-independence period. As one journalist has reported on public attitudes toward the state in contemporary Kazakhstan and Kyrgyzstan,

> There used to be a popular saying in Communist times . . . "If you don't steal from the State, then you're stealing from your own family." The higher up you were, the more you could, and usually did, steal. In this respect, little has changed in today's Kyrgyzstan and Kazakhstan. At the lower levels, petty corruption is a way of life, and the higher up you go, the bigger the theft gets. As in Soviet times, citizens

do not feel [that] they have a stake in the State. The State is not something to build up, something to feel proud of, or something that will protect you. There is no use contributing to the State, because the State is "Them" . . . [and "They"] care primarily about lining their own pockets and about pleasing their superiors (Bransten 1997).

The unusual scope of state authority in the former Soviet Union—particularly in the economic sphere—made subversion an economic necessity. As Merle Fainsod (1958, 85 and 209) observed, central controls that "looked so all-inclusive and deeply penetrating on paper" in fact "generate[d] their own peculiar techniques of defiance and evasion": the "family circle," embezzlement, bribery, false bookkeeping. In Soviet times a large portion of interenterprise transactions were conducted on the basis of informally arranged barter, enterprises hemorrhaged goods onto black and gray markets, and within the firm an alternative set of unofficial institutions emerged to support the underground economy (Berliner 1957). Shadow economy activity in the late Brezhnev era was estimated to involve up to 15 percent of the labor force at least part-time and to account for 30 percent of economic activity within the service sector (Hewett 1988, 180; Smith 1990, 266). Stephen Handelman (1995) deftly shows that the origins of organized crime in the former Soviet Union can be traced to the explosion of the second economy in the Brezhnev era and the roles played by both the criminal world and the *nomenklatura* itself in this activity.

A Nigerian scholar long ago drew the seminal distinction between the civic public realm, associated with the state, whose moral claims had no resonance, and the primordial public realm of operative communal values (Ekeh 1975). Parallel undercurrents of state subversion are clearly visible in Africa. Intrusive as the colonial state was in the exercise of its hegemonic ambitions, what Achille Mbembe (1988, 148–49) aptly termed "the historical capacity for indiscipline of the African subject" constantly reasserted itself. Goran Hyden (1980) two decades ago launched the influential if perhaps exaggerated thesis of the "uncaptured peasantry" as an explanatory touchstone of the African development crisis; in his analysis, neither colonial nor postcolonial state could deny the option of exit. Although direct confrontation of the colonial state was costly and difficult, innumerable escape routes were available through, for example, dissimulation, private ridicule, or concealment. Beneath the mask of formal deference often lay a project of subversion. Religion was a privileged field of disguised resistance: within the shelter of its sacred discourse, zones of autonomy could emerge. The proliferation of independent churches in both colonial and postcolonial Africa provides evidence of this fact (Fields 1985). Sufi Islam, although it often accepted accommodation with the colonial order, also retained a cultural space beyond the reach of the imperial order, as was true to some extent in the northern Caucasus as well. Within customary religious practice, the realm of the supernatural offered impenetrable domains for a subversive discourse with its own intellectual cadres (Geschiere 1995).

Inertia, Appropriation, and the Production of State Crises

Like pre-independence experiences themselves, the transitional contexts in which state crises emerged differed considerably in Africa and Eurasia. To be sure, both regions were buffeted by similar international pressures of change: global waves of democratization; international norms of self-determination; and pressures for economic restructuring. Yet the paths taken toward independence and to state crises were diverse. African independence for the most part did not come about as a result of mobilized challenge to the state or the breakdown of the colonial order; it was, for the most part, a result of a peaceful transfer of power. This transfer, once decided, in most cases occurred relatively rapidly, but state crises emerged in the wake of independence rather than as a precipitant of independence. By contrast, independence in the former Soviet Union came about as a result of the disintegration of communist authority amid its own efforts to reform itself, unleashing in some contexts considerable mobilization and conflict. The transition to independence in the Soviet Union was even more compressed than in Africa; even the possibility of republican independence did not enter the realm of the thinkable for the vast majority of inhabitants of the Soviet Union until 1990—a year before the country disintegrated—and for political leaderships in a number of republics (Belarus and Central Asia in particular), independence was not a desired outcome but rather a fact forced on them (as it was also for some elites in sub-Saharan francophone Africa). In Eurasia the collapse of the traditional social controls exercised by the Soviet state preceded and indeed very much precipitated independence.

Thus in certain respects one might argue that the transitional context played a more prominent role in the production of post-independence state crises in the post-Soviet cases than in the African, whereas continuity in mentalities and modes of governance were more significant in the African context than in the post-Soviet. Indeed, this divergence is largely reflected in the differing explanations one finds within the literatures on the two regions. Yet such a perspective would be misleading in certain respects. For one thing, in both contexts the newly independent states were not entirely new. Rather, they were fragments of pre-independence state authority, whose bureaucracies, resources, debts, informal relationships, and official privileges were handed over almost intact to new governing elites. Even those governing elites were not entirely new, as most had been schooled under the previous regime; in the former Soviet Union, many were even the previous regime's rulers. But the state crises that engulfed these regions were not mere continuations of pre-independence politics. They emerged in the process of transition to independence out of the combined effect of the inertia of past mentalities and modes of governance and the appropriation of these habits by well-positioned, self-interested actors toward their own personal ends. In short, for both regions an adequate explanation of state crises must focus on the interaction between pre-independence experiences and post-independence transitions.

Aside from instances in which independence occurred through armed insurrection alone (Algeria and the Portuguese territories), a progressive recognition in the 1950s by the colonial occupiers that African independence was ineluctable fundamentally altered the logic of rule for the withdrawing colonizers. The international presentability of the imperial achievement became a factor in the structures promulgated by the colonial powers; only a state modeled on the metropole was respectable. Thus in anticipation of independence the constitutional apparatus of representative democracy was grafted onto the robust trunk of colonial autocracy. Anticolonial nationalists clamored for democratic opening as well; political rights enabled swifter mobilization and offered international and local legitimacy for the successful competitors. In the wake of this moment of political opening, civil societies began to take form, and electoral battles were frequent fare. This transitional moment, in most instances, was very compressed, rarely occupying more than a few years when the arsenal of arbitrary and repressive legislation that armed the bureaucracy during high colonialism was dismantled or held in reserve. Yet the enduring legacy of the African colonial state was not the fragile flowering of democracy at its demise, but rather the patterns of autocracy that defined its operation until its final hours. The achievement of formal independence was at the time believed to open transformative possibilities, sweeping away the imperial past, suffusing an African personality throughout a colonial entity. The independent territory, in popular parlance, was a "new nation," a fulfillment of destiny. The text of nationalism was a comprehensive critique of colonialism, asserted all the more forcefully because responsibility for rule was withheld by the colonizers until the final moments. The alien super-structure of hegemony would, through its Africanization, become the authentic embodiment of the popular will. Paradigmatic of a vision projected by the leaders was the 1949 promise by Kwame Nkrumah, the first prime minister of Ghana, that with self-rule Africans would "transform the Gold Coast into a paradise in ten years" (Killick 1978, 34).

In innumerable ways, new rulers in Africa sought visible demarcation from the colonial past to establish the authenticity of African rule. State traditions do not simply dissolve, however, with the lowering of an imperial flag. A potent, invisible, inertial force emanates from long-established patterns of rule. The construction of the postcolonial state can be grasped as a dialectic process joining a continuing thrust for African demarcation with a self-reproducing disposition of the colonial state legacy. The project of demarcation proceeded on a number of fronts. The indigenization of the authority apparatus enjoyed high priority; visible command throughout the institutional fabric needed to be African. The instruments of socialization were also priority targets. The reform of school curricula, invariably prescribed by the state, began soon after independence—the goal being to "Africanize" educational content and enlist the school as an agent of "nation-building." Government-owned newspapers (often the only press permitted) and state radio had a similar mission. In the political realm, a ruling party, claiming to speak for the nation and to represent a popular will, was a novel element in the institutional complex. In a number of cases, the party apparatus became an important cog in the machinery of rule and, at the local level, a new competitor for social influence and an avenue of ascent for the ambitious. The state thus represented itself as a political rather than merely an alien bureaucratic agency. Its agents were keenly aware of the potential fragility of their domain, imperiled by the volatile ethnic and religious chemistry in many states, ultimately traceable to the artificiality of the state's borders and its vulnerability to the machinations of neocolonial conspiracy and great-power rivalry. Thus imperatives of security and legitimation drove the political concentration of power at the state center and an energetic campaign to establish the "nation" as the sole legitimate expression of identity in the public sphere, with religious and ethnic consciousness assigned to a private sphere.

The African demarcation project operated in the economic realm as well. Anticolonial nationalism painted a compelling portrait of the colonial state as politically oppressive and economically exploitative. Imperial capitalism was integral to the extractive scheme of the colonial occupant. Thus a public defense of a liberal market economy, even softened by Keynesian prem-

ises and the welfare state aura, contradicted core precepts of African nationalism. At the time of African independence, on the other hand, the
"camp of socialism" and its transformational project stood at the peak of
its prestige as a vehicle of rapid transformation. Even Western economists
in 1960 did not dispute the double-digit growth figures claimed by the
Soviet Union, and the contemporary Chinese "Great Leap Forward" had
not yet been exposed as an appalling economic catastrophe and the
hecatomb for thirty million. Although no African states formally embraced
Marxism-Leninism until 1969, many characterized their developmental
ideology as "socialist." The seductions of a command economy, central
planning, and expanded state ownership were potent. The state, thus empowered, appeared to acquire the weapons necessary for enforcing swift
economic growth and dismantling the colonial economy.

But the African colonial state legacy was not so easily exorcised, and indeed the irony of African attraction to the transformational ideologies of
socialism was, as we saw earlier, that it mirrored many of the high-modernist
assumptions about society embodied in the African colonial state. Moreover, an Africanized set of ruling institutions could not possibly govern with
a tabula rasa. The office bookshelves were filled with the collected laws, administrative manuals, and official gazettes of the colonial state, which could
be altered only slowly and incrementally. The files recorded the administrative history of particular policy spheres and pending questions; they fixed
the informational parameters of decision-making. The sartorial practices of
the colonial hierarchy were mostly maintained, at least initially. Agents of
authority characteristically made public appearances in uniform, redolent of
the largely military origins of the territorial administration. The everyday
deontology of administrative operation silently assimilated the habits, routines, mentalities, and hidden normative codes of the colonial state. As
scholar-activist Basil Davidson observed in his final work,

> Acceptance of the post-colonial nation-state meant acceptance of the
> legacy of the colonial partition, and of the moral and political prac-
> tices of colonial rule in its institutional dimensions. . . . Along with na-
> tion-state as necessary aim and achievement, the legacy of the parti-
> tion was transferred practically intact, partly because it seemed
> impossible to reject any significant part of that legacy, and partly, as
> one is bound to think in retrospect, because there was as yet no
> sufficient understanding of what the legacy implied (Davidson 1992,
> 162–63).

The ephemeral democratic moment of power transfer in Africa evaporated before the logic of the consolidation of power by the new rulers. The same undivided authority employed by the colonial state was needed for new purposes: to consolidate nationhood, to protect this still-fragile flowering from the attack of opposition forces suspected of playing the ethnic card, and to achieve a redoubled pace of economic expansion by insulating the state's planners and managers from attack and averting any dissipation of finite national developmental energies. The arsenal of repressive legislation stockpiled by the colonial state provided off-the-shelf resources for disciplining the unruly.

The colonial legacy became embedded in the African postcolonial state partly by inertial force; continuation of past practice and precedent is always the default option for the state agent. But the dialectic of African demarcation and the colonial legacy summoned agency of the new rulers as well. The first imperative of the ruler is the reproduction of power, and the search for a monopoly hold on the instruments of rule soon seemed indispensable for these purposes. In the 1960s and 1970s, this seemed to require the positioning of the dominant party as the sole occupant of political space and the subordination of the infrastructures of representation created by the terminal colonial state. The colonial state legacy of uncontestable authority, clothed in the radical language of anticolonial nationalism, had natural attractions.

The vision of modernity—not yet sullied by later disappointments or the voices of deconstruction—exercised a singular hold on the new African rulers. The silent corollary was the presumption that the elites' right to rule flowed from their schooled grasp of the secrets of development. As J. F. Ade Ajayi put it, "they staked their claims to leadership on their superior knowledge" of external models of modernity and "took for granted the masses' and the traditional elite's willingness to accept their leadership" (Ajayi 1982, 2). State agents thus operated as theologians of development. Although a discourse of participation accompanied the script of modernization, on a close listening distant echoes of the colonial legacy could be heard. Interior Minister Jean Colin of Senegal, speaking to a workshop of senior administrators a decade ago, contrasted the then-current state practice as an "administration of encadrement" rather then the command administration of colonial times (Young 1994, 284–85). But "encadrement," upon close inspection, reproduces previous notions of the state agent as bearer, interpreter, manager, and ultimately enforcer of modernity.

The ongoing dialectic between demarcation and legacy over time produced a formidable momentum of state expansion in Africa. In turn, the state became the prime, if not the sole, repository of resources. The drive for accumulation led ineluctably to the state. At the same time, the ruler found that the game of power could not be played by the same rules as those available to the colonial governors. Formal tables of organization and rules of hierarchy did not by themselves guarantee the discipline of the apparatus or the obedience of the subject. Clientele networks had to be built. "Big men" commanding regional followings were indispensable allies. Rewards and punishments became the currency of control; the source of incentives could only be the state. Thus was born the practice of prebendalism, given masterful exposition by Richard Joseph (1987). Initially practiced on a small scale, the patrimonial dynamic contained built-in escalator clauses that, by the 1970s, seriously compromised state action. The scale of resources diverted and the generalized perception of corruption that permeated the public by 1980 deeply subverted the legitimacy of the state.

In this dialectic there arose in many countries a moment of illusion, when the state appeared on the verge of achieving a comprehensive and perfected hegemony over society. In exaggerated form, this was apparent in Zaire under Mobutu Sese Seko in the mid-1970s (Young and Turner 1985). Reality, of course, fell far short of the pretensions, but the scope of the ambition stands out. Legacy and demarcation are both apparent in this vision. The colonial state imagined that it was, slowly and prudently, creating a "new African" who conformed to the norms of "civilization." The postcolonial vision was amended; the "new African" was now "modern." What was similar was the subliminal conviction that the African subject, even as citizen, was malleable clay in the hands of the enlightened ruler.

Social sites and practices undermining state hegemony became even more widespread after independence, as new domains of subversion opened. As would occur in the former Soviet Union, large-scale criminal activity emerged in Africa, often enjoying protection from or actual participation by state agents. Nigeria and several other African countries became major transit points for the narcotics trade (Bayart, Ellis, and Hibou, 1998). Informal economies exploded and, in countries such as Congo-Kinshasa, swallowed the formal economy. A *sauve qui peut* (fend for oneself) mentality was the key to survival for the everyday citizen in many lands; disorder, argue Patrick Chabal and Jean-Pascal Daloz (1998), became a veritable political instrument. With evil and sickness stalking the land, sorcery became a suspect cause as well as a site for contestation. Stephen Ellis and Gerrie ter Haar (1998, 183–84) cite the extraordinary text of a reborn Christian evangelist in Congo-Kinshasa who confessed his satanic past and revealed the existence of "diabolical underground conference centers," populated by all manner of sorcerers and magicians who flew in and out through an invisible international airport near Kinshasa. Sally Falk Moore, in her classic anthropological study of the Tanzanian Chagga, characterizes well the local realities that undermined the modernity project of the post-colonial state, expanding upon the developmental claims of its predecessor: "Now governments everywhere have large-scale designs to shape and control economies and polities. . . . The idea of control on the large scale is matched by a remarkable level of unpredictability or intractability on the ground" (Moore, 1986, 320).

An analogous atmosphere of optimism and demarcation characterized the immediate post-independence period within most post-Soviet states. In the heady days of 1990 and 1991, as Soviet power came undone, democratic transition was taken by many observers of the Eurasian scene to be accomplished fact, and attention shifted instead toward democracy's consolidation. The precipice separating central planning from the market was to be vaulted in a single, giant leap. Not a generation, but five hundred days would suffice. Naive assumptions underlay early understandings of the collapse of the Soviet Union. The Georgian dissident and nationalist leader Zviad Gamsakhurdia, himself a victim of persecution by the Soviet regime, is reported to have told his followers, "[W]e are being robbed by the Soviet occupiers; if we get rid of them, we will live well" (quoted in Sobchak 1993, 174). Yet, having attained power in Georgia in 1990, Gamsakhurdia quickly imitated his former tormentors, imposing a terror on his fellow Georgians that rivaled that of the Stalin years and unleashing a wave of interethnic violence in Ossetia and Abkhazia that soon turned Georgia into a mere shell of a state (Beissinger 1996). The habitus of power is not so simply dispelled.

The degree of continuity between old and new has varied across the post-Soviet states, but in some contexts its tangibility is overwhelming. One study of 320 members of the Kazakh political elite undertaken in 1997, for instance, indicated that 64 percent had been members of the old *nomenklatura* during the Brezhnev era and 41 percent had worked previously in the Soviet Communist Party apparatus (Tulegulov 1998). Little wonder, then, that the language of politics in Kazakhstan remains unmistakably Soviet (Schatz 1999). As another study of Kazakh politics concluded, "[A]lthough under other names, the basic elements of the command-administrative system [in Kazakhstan] have been preserved almost in their entirety" (Svoik and Lan'ko 1994, 17). A study in Russia in 1994 showed that a third of the political elite had been members of the *nomenklatura* in 1988, and that 70 percent of the economic elite in 1994 had been enterprise executives or ministerial employees in 1988, so that "a market economy was being created by those who managed the Soviet economy" (Ryvkina and Kosals 1997, 205–6). Even in the Baltic states, where the Soviet legacy has been less palpable, "chagrined reformers have had to admit that these so-called 'remnants' [of the Soviet period] have had a much greater staying power than the euphoria of the 'third national awakening' [i.e., independence from the Soviet Union] envisioned" (Plakans 1994, 4). The unbridled optimism of 1990–91 soon gave way to the realities of the "transition": collapsing economies, disintegrating state institutions, burgeoning corruption, and, at times, interethnic warfare.

As in postcolonial Africa, post-Soviet leaders also sought in many cases visible symbolic and substantive demarcation from the communist past. New national histories and symbols were quickly substituted for the old, and the postcommunist projects of transition (from plan to market, from communist autocracy to fledgling democracy, from colonial subject to nation) became central elements of the legitimating discourse of power in most former republics. But there remains a great deal more ambivalence toward demarcation in most post-Soviet states than was true in postcolonial Africa after the demise of colonial rule. This is hardly surprising within Russia, the former imperial metropole. But the ambiguity of state-building and empire-building in the Soviet era and the instability and disorder of the present have left significant pockets of nostalgia for the Soviet days in almost every post-Soviet state. Indeed, some regimes, such as Aleksandr Lukashenka's Belarus, openly glorify the Soviet past.

But even where demarcation has been less equivocal than in Belarus, Soviet ways of thinking and behaving, often unrecognized in those who practice them, remain conspicuous. Elements of transition ideology themselves resemble Soviet transformationalism: society is to be remade wholesale, this time in the equally utopian image of Western capitalism and democracy. It is one thing to carry out a social revolution such as shock therapy amid a significant national consensus about the need to "return the nation to Europe," as was true in the Baltic states, for instance. But elsewhere, the authoritarian implications of executing such a transition amid widespread resistance were not lost on many local observers. Dissent over the goals and methods of rapid economic transition essentially induced the breakdown of the first post-Soviet Russian republic in 1992–93 and brought about similar crises of authority in Moldova and Ukraine. In those cases, the crises generated by breakneck state-sponsored market transition intersected with the self-interested appropriations of power by *nomen-klatura*-tutored officials. This confluence took institutional form in the proliferation of presidential forms of government. With the exception of Latvia and Estonia, for instance, all of the post-Soviet countries have instituted presidential systems of power. The growth of voracious and powerful presidencies has been largely responsible for the stalled or receding tide of democratization and the growth of new authoritarianisms in the post-Soviet region. Ironically, presidential government arose for the first time in Eurasia only at the end of 1989 as a way for General Secretary Mikhail Gorbachev to make an end run around the Communist Party bureaucracy. It was duly imitated in the union republics and in most autonomous republics as they began to assert their sovereignty vis-à-vis the center—part of the larger hollowing-out of central control over localities that accompanied the collapse of communism. Although presidential government was an innovation at the time, it clearly upheld long-standing patterns of behavior and ways of relating to state authority. It has frequently been pointed out that the executive branch in post-Soviet states has come to play the coordinating role once played by Communist Party institutions; indeed, in many cases much of the staff of executive institutions was recruited directly from the former party apparatus, and in terms of size these bureaucracies often exceed their party predecessors. Although it is true that the Communist Party Business Office engaged in some significant economic operations during the Soviet period, since 1993 the amount of property owned by the Kremlin has increased tenfold; the Kremlin Business Office oversees the operations of 200 companies, including an airline, medical facilities, a network of hotels, and seventy-five factories (Ortung 1997). As Eugene Huskey (1999, 51–54) concluded in his study of the Russian presidency, in many ways the Kremlin Business Office has come to resemble more a business than a business office.

The collapse of communist authority in the 1988–91 period in itself was not sufficient to produce enduring state crises in Eurasia. Rather, state crisis became sustained and institutionalized precisely because the deconstruction of Soviet power and the transitions to the market produced opportunities for self-interested actors emerging out of the rubble to appropriate well-established resources, networks, and structures and to transform these elements into new forms of practice. On the surface, it appeared as if the Soviet order had been turned inside out. Black marketeers became business owners, and bureaucrats, factory managers, police, judges, and the KGB state security apparatus fused with the underground criminal world. In Moscow province the tax police themselves were engaged in marketing arms to criminals (Aleksandrov 1998). The Russian military had lost all coherence as an institution long before its invasion of Chechnya; in 1992–93, it had sold to the Chechens many of the weapons that were eventually used against it in 1994–95. State agents came to function as competitors and accomplices of organized crime: businesses seeking protection from criminal gangs were routinely required to make payoffs to the gangs or to state officials charged with protecting them from gangs; those who failed to obtain such protection from one force or the other were vulnerable to criminal attack (Shlapentokh 1996). The state had itself become the largest racketeer. Coteries of elites seized the state's assets, enriching themselves on a vast scale (Solnick 1998), while the economic infrastructure created by communism crumbled. Indeed, as Joel Hellman (1998) notes, the main threat to economic transition has come not from the losers, but from the winners of the reform process. The post-Soviet equivalent of Africa's "big men" were the new financial tycoons who made their fortunes primarily through their connections to the state and their ability to appropriate or control state assets (banks, oil and gas fields, diamond mines, television stations, etc.) by means of behind-the-scenes maneuvers. In some states, such as Heidar Aliev's Azerbaijan or Nursultan Nazarbaev's Kazakhstan, these assets came under the direct control of members of the president's extended family; in other cases, such as Yeltsin's Russia, the president's personal network (in an ironic twist, known informally in political circles as "the family") left other rival cliques in place, fostering a brisk competition among political and business groups for control over privatized state assets.

This wholesale merger of the dominant and the deviant sprang naturally out of the daily transactions of Soviet power and came to fill the void of authority left in communism's wake. Members of Brezhnev's family and his close confidants had been involved in similar schemes to bilk the Soviet state out of huge sums. And the various forms of subterfuge and noncompliance that were widespread in Eurasia before independence formed the basis for much of the hollowing of state authority in the aftermath of communism. But it is also clear that the scope of these behaviors exploded remarkably in the context of transition. The World Bank estimates that, among a sampling of countries belonging to the Commonwealth of Independent States (CIS), the underground economy grew from 12 percent of the given country's gross domestic product in 1989 to 37 percent by 1994 (Feige 1997, 29). By the late 1990s in most CIS countries, the shadow economy (which, by official definition, excludes smuggling and activities prohibited by law but includes lawful economic operations that are concealed or underrepresented by the individuals or businesses that conduct them, primarily for purposes of tax evasion) was officially estimated to account for from 45 to 50 percent of overall economic activity (Reuters 1998; Ziublio 1997).[3] The criminalization of politics and the economy, the personalization of the state, and the explosion of noncompliance have deep roots in communist rule. Nevertheless, they were not mere continuations of the past; they were appropriations and magnifications of the Soviet legacy—a massive inversion in which the implicit became the predominant practice.

Conclusion

In sum, state crises in Africa and Eurasia cannot be grasped outside of an understanding of the ways in which pre-independence state experience conditioned subsequent state breakdown. Subsequent chapters in this volume will explore the most salient faces of these crises and their consequences. But the search for pathways beyond the wreckage must necessarily begin with a clear diagnosis of the major causes of the present disorder in both regions.

As we have argued, the combination of high modernism with autocratic state practice proved fateful to subsequent state breakdown in both Africa and the former Soviet Union. The ultimate irony in both regions is that nowhere else were states built on the legacies of prior state formations that had such extravagant pretensions of a perfected, comprehensive hegemony. Yet the utter (and, at least in the short term, irremediable) deflation in state capacity that followed independence and that lies at the very heart of the crises of these regimes also has no match elsewhere. The establishment of effective state power is the sine qua non for fostering a political order in both regions that would be capable of rising above the devastation of the present. Undoubtedly, in such a quest one cannot expect complete erasure of the legacies that produced disorder in the first place—and indeed, in some contexts, any such attempt could end up reinforcing rather than eroding those legacies. Yet, as our diagnosis indicates, a better future cannot be found in the models of the past.

---

3. Official Russian sources contend that the "shadow" sector of the economy varies seasonally, expanding to 50 percent of the economy in summer and autumn and contracting considerably in winter (Interfax1999).

References

Ajayi, J. F. Ade. 1982. "Expectations of Independence." *Daedalus* 111 (spring): 1–10.

Ake, Claude. 1996. *Democracy and Development in Africa.* Washington: Brookings Institution Press.

Aleksandrov, German. 1998. "Sotrudniki nalogovoi politsii torgovali vzryvchatkoi." *Nezavisimaia gazeta.* 30 May: 2.

Bayart, Jean-François, Stephen Ellis, and Béatrice Hibou. 1998. *The Criminalization of the State in Africa.* London: James Currey.

Beissinger, Mark R. 1993. "Demise of an Empire-State: Identity, Legitimacy, and the Deconstruction of Soviet Politics." Pp. 93–115 in *The Rising Tide of Cultural Pluralism: The Nation-State at Bay,* ed. Crawford Young. Madison: University of Wisconsin Press.

———. 1995. "The Persisting Ambiguity of Empire." *Post-Soviet Affairs* 11, no. 2 (April–June): 149–84.

———. 1996. "State Building in the Shadow of an Empire-State: The Soviet Legacy in Post-Soviet Politics." Pp. 157–85 in *The End of Empire? The Disintegration of the USSR in Comparative Perspective,* ed. Karen Dawisha and Bruce Parrott. Armonk: M. E. Sharpe.

Berliner, Joseph. 1957. *Factory and Manager in the USSR.* Cambridge, Mass.: Harvard University Press.

Billig, Michael. 1995. *Banal Nationalism.* London: Sage Publications.

Bransten, Jeremy. 1997. "The More Things Change . . .: An Analysis." *RFE/RL Special Report: Central Asia in Transition.* 14 October.

Brubaker, Rogers. 1996. *Nationalism Reframed: Nationhood and the National Question in the New Europe.* Cambridge: Cambridge University Press.

Bunce, Valerie. 1995. "Can We Compare Democratization in the East versus the South?" *Journal of Democracy* 6 (July): 87–100.

Butuzova, Liudmilla, and Leonid Tuchnin. 1998. "Mify prigranichnoi polosy." *Moskovskie novosti* 23 (14–21 June): 6–7.

Chabal, Patrick, and Jean-Pascal Daloz. 1998. *Africa Works: Disorder as Political Instrument.* London: James Currey.

Davidson, Basil. 1992. *Black Man's Burden: The Curse of the Nation-State.* New York: Random House.

Ekeh, Peter. 1975. "Colonialism and the Two Publics in Africa: A Theoretical Statement." *Comparative Studies in Society and History* 17, no. 1: 91–112.

Ellis, Stephen, and Gerrie ter Haar. 1998. "Religion and Politics in Sub-Saharan Africa." *Journal of Modern African Studies* 36, no. 2: 173–202.

Fainsod, Merle. 1958. *Smolensk under Soviet Rule.* New York: Random House.

Feige, Edgar L. 1997. "Underground Activity and Institutional Change: Productive, Protective, and Predatory Behavior in Transition Economies." Pp. 21–34 in *Transforming Post-Communist Political Economies,* ed. Joan M. Nelson, Charles Tilly, and Lee Walker. Washington: National Academy Press.

Fields, Karen E. 1985. *Revival and Rebellion in Colonial Central Africa.* Princeton: Princeton University Press.

Geschiere, Peter. 1995. *Sorcellerie et politique en Afrique: La viande des autres.* Paris: Karthala.

Handelman, Stephen. 1995. *Comrade Criminal: Russia's New Mafiya.* New Haven: Yale University Press.

Harrison, Graham. 1998. "Marketing Legitimacy in Rural Mozambique." *Journal of Modern African Studies* 36, no. 4: 568–92.

Hellman, Joel S. 1998. "Winners Take All: The Politics of Partial Reform in Postcommunist Transitions." *World Politics* 50, no. 2 (January): 203–34.

Hewett, Ed A. 1988. *Reforming the Soviet Economy: Equality versus Efficiency.* Washington: Brookings Institution Press.

Huskey, Eugene. 1999. *Presidential Power in Russia*. Armonk: M. E. Sharpe.

Hyden, Goran. 1980. *Beyond Ujamaa in Tanzania: Underdevelopment and an Uncaptured Peasantry*. London: Heinemann.

Interfax. 1999. "Twenty Percent of Russian Economy in Shadow—Statistical Committee." 15 February.

Joseph, Richard. 1987. *Democracy and Prebendal Politics in Nigeria: The Rise and Fall of the Second Republic*. Cambridge: Cambridge University Press.

Kenez, Peter. 1985. *The Birth of the Propaganda State: Soviet Methods of Mass Mobilization, 1917–1929*. Cambridge: Cambridge University Press.

Killick, Tony. 1978. *Development Economics in Action*. London: Heinemann.

Kostikov, Viacheslav. 1997. *Roman s prezidentom. Zapiski press-sekretaria*. Moscow: Vagrius.

Laitin, David D. 1998. *Identity in Formation: The Russian-Speaking Populations in the Near Abroad*. Ithaca: Cornell University Press.

Lemarchand, René. 1983. "The State and Society in Africa: Ethnic Stratification and Re-stratification in Historical and Comparative Perspective." Pp. 44–66 in *State versus Ethnic Claims: African Policy Dilemmas*, ed. Donald Rothschild and Victor A. Olorunsola. Boulder: Westview.

Mamdani, Mahmood. 1996. *Citizen and Subject: Contemporary Africa and the Legacy of Colonialism*. Princeton: Princeton University Press.

Mbembe, Achille. 1988. *Afriques indociles: Christianisme, pouvoir et état en société postcoloniale*. Paris: Karthala.

Miles, William F. S. 1994. *Hausaland Divided: Colonialism and Independence in Nigeria and Niger*. Ithaca: Cornell University Press.

Millar, James R., and Sharon L. Wolchik. 1994. "Introduction: The Social Legacies and the Aftermath of Communism." Pp. 1–28 in *The Social Legacy of Communism*, ed. James R. Millar and Sharon L. Wolchik. Washington: Woodrow Wilson Center Press; Cambridge: Cambridge University Press.

Moore, Barrington. 1954. *Terror and Progress USSR: Some Sources of Change and Stability in the Soviet Dictatorship*. Cambridge, Mass.: Harvard University Press.

Moore, Sally Falk. 1986. *Social Facts and Fabrications: "Customary" Law in Kilimanjaro, 1880–1980*. Cambridge: Cambridge University Press.

Myers, Ramon H., and Mark R. Peattie, eds. 1984. *The Japanese Colonial Empire, 1895–1945*. Princeton: Princeton University Press.

Ortung, Robert. 1997. "Borodin Warns against Attempts to Remove Him." *Open Media Research Institute [OMRI] Daily Digest*. 12 March.

Plakans, Andrejs. 1994. "Latvia: 1991–1993." Paper presented at the annual convention of the American Association for the Advancement of Slavic Studies, Honolulu, November.

Reuters. 1998. "Georgian President Announces Anti-Graft Drive." 4 February.

Ryvkina, R. V., and L. Ya. Kosals. 1997. *Sotsial'nye posledstviia rynochnykh reform v Rossii*. Moscow: Institut sotsial'no-ekonomicheskikh problem narodonaseleniia.

Schatz, Edward. 1999. "The Politics of Familiar Symbols: Toward an Explanation of Non-Conflict in Multi-Ethnic Kazakhstan." University of Wisconsin. Photocopy.

Scott, James C. 1998. *Seeing Like a State: How Certain Schemes to Improve the Human Condition Have Failed*. New Haven: Yale University Press.

Shlapentokh, Vladimir. 1996. "Early Feudalism: The Best Parallel for Contemporary Russia." *Europe-Asia Studies* 48 (May): 393–411.

Smith, Hedrick. 1990. *The New Russians*. New York: Random House.

Sobchak, Anatolii. 1993. *Tbilisskii izlom, ili Krovavoe voskresen'e 1989 goda*. Moscow: Sretenie.

Solnick, Steven L. 1998. *Stealing the State: Control and Collapse in Soviet Institutions*. Cambridge, Mass.: Harvard University Press.

Suny, Ronald Grigor. 1993. *The Revenge of the Past: Nationalism, Revolution, and the Collapse of the Soviet Union*. Stanford: Stanford University Press.

Svoik, P., and E. Lan'ko. 1994. *Sud'ba Kazakhstana kak gosudarstva. Pervye shagi ot propasti.* Almaty: Evraziia.

Tulegulov, A. K. 1998. "Politicheskaia elita Kazakhstana: analiz biografii." *Saiasat* (January): 31–39.

Vail, Leroy, ed. 1989. *The Creation of Tribalism in Southern Africa.* Berkeley: University of California Press.

Yaroshevski, Don. 1997. "Empire and Citizenship." Pp. 58–79 in *Russia's Orient: Imperial Borderlands and Peoples, 1700–1917,* ed. Daniel R. Brower and Edward J. Lazzerini. Bloomington: Indiana University Press.

Yeltsin, Boris. 1990. *Against the Grain: An Autobiography.* New York: Summit.

Young, Crawford. 1991. "The Heritage of Colonialism." Pp. 19–38 in *Africa in World Politics,* ed. John W. Harbeson and Donald Rothchild. Boulder: Westview.

———. 1994. *The African Colonial State in Comparative Perspective.* New Haven: Yale University Press.

Young, Crawford, and Thomas Turner. 1985. *The Rise and Decline of the Zairian State.* Madison: University of Wisconsin Press.

Young, Louise. 1998. *Japan's Total Empire: Manchuria and the Culture of Wartime Imperialism.* Berkeley: University of California Press.

Ziublio, Aleksandr. 1997. "Anatolii Kulikov predstavil svoi nauchnye razrabotki po ekonomicheskoi bezopastnosti." *Izvestiya.* 3 July: 1.

Part II

Sovereignty, Violence, and War

3

At the Edge of the World: Boundaries, Territoriality, and Sovereignty in Africa

ACHILLE MBEMBE

From a philosophical point of view, globalization might be compared with what Martin Heidegger called "the gigantic" (*das Riesige*), for among the characteristics of the gigantic as he understood it were both the elimination of great distances and the representation—producible at any time—of daily life in unfamiliar and distant worlds. But the gigantic was for him, above all, that through which the quantitative became an essential quality. From this point of view, the time of the gigantic was that in which "the world posits itself in a space beyond representation, thus allocating to the incalculable its own determination and unique historical character" (Heidegger 1962, 124–25).

If at the center of the discussion on globalization we place the three problems of spatiality, calculability, and temporality in their relations with representation, we find ourselves brought back to two points usually ignored in contemporary discourses, even though Fernand Braudel had called attention to them. The first of these has to do with temporal pluralities, and also with the subjectivity that makes these temporalities possible and meaningful. Braudel drew a distinction between "temporalities of long and [of] very long duration, slowly evolving and less slowly evolving situations, rapid and virtually instantaneous deviations, the quickest being the easiest to detect" (Braudel 1984). He went on to emphasize—and this is the second point—the exceptional character of what he called "world time." For him, time experienced in the dimensions of the world had an exceptional character insofar as it governed, depending on the period and the location, certain spaces and certain realities. But other realities and other spaces escaped it and remained alien to it.[1]

This chapter, although it adopts the notion of long duration and relativizes the airtightness of the distinctions mentioned above, nonetheless differs in several respects from Braudel's theses. This chapter is based on a twofold hypothesis. First, it assumes that temporalities overlap and interlace. In fact, Braudel's postulate of the plurality of temporalities does not by itself account for contemporary changes. In the case of Africa, long-term developments, more or less rapid deviations, and long-term temporalities are not necessarily either separate or merely juxtaposed. Fitted within one another, they relay each other; sometimes they cancel each other out, and sometimes their effects are multiplied. Contrary to Braudel's conviction, it is not clear that there are any zones within which world history would have no repercussions. What really differ are the many modalities in which world time is domesticated. These modalities depend on histories and local cultures, on the interplay of interests whose determinants do not all lead in the same direction.

The central thesis of this chapter is that in several regions considered— wrongly—to be on the margins of the world, the domestication of world time henceforth takes place by dominating space and putting it to different uses. When resources are put into circulation, the consequence is a disconnection between people and things that is more marked than it was in the past (the value of things generally surpassing that of people). This disconnection and relative devaluation of people helps explain why the resulting forms of violence have as their chief goal the physical destruction of people (massacres of civilians, genocide, and other kinds of killing) and the primary exploitation of things. These forms of violence (of which war is only one aspect) contribute to the establishment of sovereignty outside the state and are based on a confusion between power and fact, between public affairs and private government (Mbembe 1999).

In this study, I am interested in a specific form of domestication and mobilization of space and resources: the form that consists of producing boundaries, whether by moving already existing ones, fragmenting them, or doing away with them. In dealing with these questions, I will draw a distinction between Africa as a place and Africa as a territory. In fact, a place is the order that determines how elements are distributed in relationships of coexistence. A place, as Michel de Certeau points out, is an instanta-

---

1. In his foreword, Braudel went so far as to assert that "there are always some areas world history does not reach, zones of silence and undisturbed ignorance" (Braudel 1984, 18).

neous configuration of positions (de Certeau 1984). It implies a stability. As for a territory, it is fundamentally an intersection of moving bodies. It is defined essentially by the set of movements that take place within it.[2] Seen in this way, it is a set of possibilities that historically situated actors constantly resist or realize (Lefebvre 1991).

Boundaries and Their Limits

Over the past two centuries the visible, material, and symbolic boundaries of Africa have constantly expanded and contracted. The structural character of this instability has helped change the territorial body of the continent. New forms of territoriality and unexpected forms of locality have appeared. Their limits do not necessarily intersect with the official limits, norms, or language of states. New internal and external actors, organized into networks and nuclei, claim rights over these territories, often by force. Other ways of imagining space and territory are developing. Paradoxically, the discourse that is supposed to account for these transformations has ended up obscuring them. Essentially, two theses ignore each other. One argues that the boundaries separating African states were created by colonialism, were arbitrarily drawn, and separated peoples, linguistic entities, and cultural and political communities that formed natural and homogeneous wholes before colonization. The colonial boundaries are also said to have opened the way to the Balkanization of the continent by cutting it up into a maze of microstates that were not economically viable and were linked more to Europe than to their regional environment. According to this view, by adopting these distortions in 1963, the Organization of African Unity adhered to the dogma of their intangibility and gave them a kind of legitimacy. Many of the current conflicts in Africa are said to have resulted from the imprecise nature of the boundaries inherited from colonialism. These boundaries could not be changed except in the framework of vigorous policies of regional integration that would complete the implementation of defense and collective security agreements.[3]

The other thesis claims that a kind of regional integration is already tak-

---

2. "Space occurs as the effect produced by the operations that orient it, situate it, temporalize it, and make it function in a polyvalent unity of conflictual programs or contractual proximities. . . . In contradistinction to the place, it has thus none of the univocity or stability of a 'proper.'" (de Certeau 1984, 117).

3. On this subject, consider views that are apparently divergent but are in fact ultimately based on the same misunderstandings: Nugent and Asiwaju 1996; Igué 1995; Herbst 1992; and the fantastic views of Herbst 1996—97.

ing place "from below." It seems to be occurring on the margins of official institutions, through socio-cultural solidarities and interstate commercial networks. This process is the basis for the emergence of alternative spaces that structure the informal economy, contraband, and migratory movements. Far from being merely regional, these interstate exchanges are connected with international markets and their dynamics. The commerce for which they provide the moving force is favored by a fundamental characteristic of African states, namely the relative lack of congruence between the territory of a state and areas of exchange.[4] Powerful religious and commercial networks with multiple ramifications have taken advantage of complementarities between areas of production, as well as legislation and monetary zones that differ from one country to another, in order to create markets that elude the states themselves (Grégoire 1997).

These two views are based on a simplistic notion of the role of boundaries in African history, as well as on a misunderstanding regarding the nature of colonial boundaries proper. There are two reasons for this misunderstanding. First, little effort has been made to understand the social imaginaries and autochthonous practices of space—which are themselves extremely varied—and the modalities through which a territory becomes the object of an appropriation or of the exercise of a power or a jurisdiction. Second, the history of boundaries in Africa is too often reduced, on the one hand, to the frontier as a device in international law and, on the other, to the specific spatial marker constituted by the boundary of a state.[5] In this context, the connection between a state and a territory is seen as purely instrumental, the territory making sense on the political level only as the privileged space of the exercise of sovereignty and of self-determination, and as the ideal framework of the imposition of authority (Kratochwil 1986; Clapham 1999). As a result, investigation is limited to the question of whether restructuring spaces of exchange does or does not contribute to the weakening of the state and to the erosion of its sovereignty (Evans 1997; Badie 1995).

In considering endogenous conceptions of space, it is important to keep in mind that before colonization, Africans' attachment to the territory and to the land was entirely relative. In some cases, political entities were delimited not by boundaries in the classical sense of the term, but rather by an imbrication of multiple spaces constantly joined, disjoined, and recom-

---

4. Cf. the contributions to *Autrepart* 1998.
5. Daniel Nordman (1998) shows not only that there are many different models of boundaries, the state boundary being in this respect only one variety in the immense range of limits, but that every boundary is first of all a paradox in space.

bined through wars, conquests, and the mobility of goods and persons (Kopytoff 1987). Very complex scales of measurement made it possible to establish productive correspondences between persons and things, the former and the latter being convertible into each other, as at the time of the slave trade (Miller 1988). It might be said that operating by thrusts, detachments, and scissions, precolonial territoriality was an itinerant territoriality. In other cases, mastery over spaces was based on controlling people or localities, and sometimes both together (Birmingham and Martin 1983; Jones 1963). Vast areas might lie between distinct polities, veritable buffer zones not subject to direct control, exclusive domination, or close supervision. A similar remark would apply to spaces of the former Russian empire—Central Asia, Siberia, and parts of the Caucasus and Arctic regions.

In still other cases, the spatial dynamics tending to make the boundary a genuine physical limit went hand in hand with the principle of dispersing and deterritorializing allegiances. In fact, foreigners, slaves, and subjects could be under the control of several sovereign powers at once. The multiplicity of allegiances and jurisdictions itself corresponded to the plurality of the forms of territoriality. The result was often an extraordinary superposition of rights and an interlacing of social ties that was not reducible to family relationships, religion, or castes alone. These rights and ties were combined with forms of locality, but at the same time they transcended them (Lovejoy and Richardson 1999). Various centers of power might have authority over a single place, which might itself fall under the control of another place that was nearby, distant, or even imaginary (Nair 1972). Whether the "boundary" was a state boundary or some other kind, it was meaningful only through the relationships it maintained with other forms of difference and of social, jurisdictional, and cultural discrimination, the forms of contact and interpenetration at work in a given space. It was a question not of boundaries in the legal sense of the term, but of the borders of countries and of interlaced spaces taken as a whole. These borders could shrink as a result of military defeats or be expanded through conquests or acquisitions. Thus it was very often a matter of boundaries capable of infinite extension and abrupt contraction. But this incompleteness did not in any way exclude the existence of specific forms of the bipolarization of space (Wilks 1975).

Multiple Geneses

It is clear that the boundaries inherited from colonization were not defined by Africans themselves. But contrary to a common assumption, this does not necessarily mean that they were arbitrary. To a large extent, every boundary depends on a convention. With the exception of flagrant cases of arbitrary division, some of the boundaries drawn by colonization are based on natural limits—oceans, rivers, or mountain ranges, for example. Others are the result of diplomatic negotiations or treaties of cession, annexation, or exchange among the imperial powers. Others take the old kingdoms into account. Still others are neither more nor less than imagined lines, as in the case of the boundaries separating the countries along the borders of the Sahara (Mali, Niger, Algeria) or the Kalahari Desert. All these boundaries marked geographical territories that were then associated with names, some of which were changed when independence was won. From 1960 on in Africa, they marked the limits of sovereignty among states. (The same became true in Eurasia following the 1991 dissolution of the Soviet Union.) As happens everywhere in the world, these limits of sovereignty have led, for example, to concrete arrangements with regard to tariffs, commercial policy, or immigration policy. In the same way, boundaries have been subjected to internal and external surveillance and contribute to the stabilization of relationships between states.

Thus to state that current African boundaries are merely a product of colonial arbitrariness is to ignore their multiple geneses. In fact, their establishment long antedated the Congress of Berlin, convened in 1884, whose objective was to distribute sovereignty among the different powers engaged in dividing up the continent. Their protogenesis goes back to the period of the trading-post economy, when Europeans set up agencies on the coasts and began to trade with the natives. The establishment of this economy explains, in part, some of the physical characteristics of African states: the distinction between the littoral areas and the hinterland that so deeply marks the geographical structure of various countries, or the enclosure of vast enclaves situated far from the oceans. Boundaries gradually crystallized during the period of "informal empire" (from the abolition of the slave trade up to the repression of the first resistance movements), thanks to the combined actions of traders and missionaries. The rise of boundaries took a military turn with the construction of forts, the penetration of the hinterland, and the repression of local revolts.

This complex dynamic compares and contrasts with the imperial dynamic of boundary definition in Eurasia. The still-precarious condition of the newly created socialist commonwealth in the early 1920s compelled its masters, Vladimir Lenin and Joseph Stalin, to redraw the administrative subdivisions inherited from the tsarist empire in ways incorporating the nationality principle, diluted by the calculus of state security. Thus was born the complex hierarchy of ethno-national territories, with the top rank of "titular nationalities" enjoying external borders that eventually defined the postimperial sovereign space. The inclusion of significant Russian or Russian-speaking minorities in various "union republics" and the division of others (Ossetians, Ingush, Armenians) across borders created in some ways the same phenomenon of imbricated peoples and purportedly "artificial" boundaries that many perceived in Africa.

Far from being simple products of colonialism, current African boundaries thus reflect commercial, religious, and military realities—the rivalries, power relationships, and alliances that prevailed among the various imperial powers, and between them and Africans through the centuries preceding colonization proper. From this point of view, their constitution depends on a relatively long-term social and cultural process (Lonsdale 1985). Before the conquest, they represented spaces of encounter, negotiation, and opportunity for Europeans and Africans (Adelman and Aron 1999). At the time of conquest, their main function was to mark the spatial limits that separated colonial possessions from one another, taking into account not ambitions but the actual occupation of the land. Later on, physical control over the territory led to the creation of devices of discipline and command, modeled on those of the customary chiefs where these did not exist. With the demarcation of districts, the levying of taxes, the spread of cash crops, a monetary economy, urbanization, and education, economic and political functionality were ultimately combined, the administrative power and the social power weaving a fabric that was henceforth to dominate the colonial state.

The decisive factor, however, was the internal boundaries the colonial enterprise defined within each country. In addition, it must be noted that colonialism structured economic spaces in several ways, which were themselves associated with specific territorial mythologies. This was notably the case in the settler colonies, where the erection of internal boundaries reached tragic proportions. In the case of South Africa, for example, the massive population shifts that took place throughout the nineteenth and twentieth centuries gradually led to the establishment, within a single country, of fourteen territorial entities of unequal status. Since membership in a race and an ethnic group served as the condition of access to land and resources, three types of territories emerged: the white provinces, where only Europeans enjoyed permanent rights (Orange Free State, Cape Province, Transvaal, Natal); the so-called Bantustans, or black homelands, composed of ethnic groups that were theoretically independent (Bophuthatswana, Venda, Transkei, Ciskei); and finally the "autonomous" Bantustans (KwaNdebele, KaNgwane, KwaZulu, Qwaqwa, Lebowa, and Gzankulu). Taking into account this legacy of fragmentation, the goal pursued by the current authorities is to encourage the emergence of new representations of identity and territory that transcend the racial, ethnic, and linguistic identities inherited from the old divisions (cf. *L'Espace géographique* 1999).

The same way of carving up space was used in the area of urban management. By defining urban spaces specifically reserved for nonwhites, the system of apartheid deprived the latter of any rights in the white zones. The result of this excision was to put on the black populations themselves the financial burden of reproducing themselves and to circumscribe the phenomenon of poverty within racially associated enclaves. Apartheid's stamp is also visible on the landscape and on the organization of rural space. The most characteristic marks of the latter are the differentiation of systems of property (individual property in commercial zones and mixed systems in communal zones), the racial appropriation and ethnic distribution of the natural resources most favorable to agriculture, and migrations resulting in a multilocalization of black families. Countries such as Kenya or Zimbabwe experienced the same process of dispossessing Africans of lands to the advantage of whites. Reservations were set up, while everywhere there prevailed legislation that sought to extend the mode of individual tenure and to limit the forms of tenant farming by blacks on white-owned properties. Thus reservoirs of labor were created (Elphick and Giliomee 1989).

This colonial structuring of economic spaces was not abolished by postcolonial regimes. The latter have often prolonged it; sometimes they have radicalized the logic of the creation of internal boundaries that was inherent in it, particularly in rural zones. To be sure, the modalities of state penetration have varied from one region to another, taking into account the influence of local elites, producers' cooperatives, or religious orders (Boone 1998). But as soon as independence was won, Africa began a vast enterprise of remodeling internal territorial entities even as it accepted the principle of the inviolability of boundaries among states. Almost everywhere, the redefinition of internal boundaries was carried out under cover of creating new administrative districts, provinces, and municipalities. These administrative divisions had both political and economic goals. But they also contributed to the crystallization of ethnic identities. In fact, whereas under colonization itself the attribution of space sometimes preceded the organization of states or went hand in hand with it, since the beginning of the 1980s the reverse has been happening.

However, a reclassification of localities into large and small areas is under way. These large and small areas are cut up on the basis of supposedly common cultures and languages. On these entities associated with family relationships, ethnicity, and religious and cultural proximities, the state confers the status of a federated state (as in Nigeria), a province, or an administrative district (Osaghae 1998). This bureaucratic work is preceded (or accompanied) by the invention of imaginary family ties. It is powerfully underpinned by the recent proliferation of ideologies promoting the values of autochthony. Everywhere, the distinction between autochthonous peoples and foreigners has been accentuated, the ethno-racial principle serving increasingly as the basis for citizenship and as the condition of access to land, resources, and elective positions of responsibility (Dozon 1997). As a result of the transition to a multiparty system, struggles over autochthony have taken a more conflictual turn, to the extent that they go along with the establishment of new electoral districts. The repertoires on which the protagonists in these struggles draw are not simply local, but also international. These processes closely match the dynamics of state reconfiguration in Eurasia.

Cultural and Symbolic Territorialities

One of the main legacies of colonization has been to set in motion a process of development that is unequal, depending on the regions and countries involved. This unequal development has contributed to a distribution of space around sites that are sometimes clearly differentiated, and to the emergence of cultural vectors whose influence on the reconfiguration of the map of the continent is generally underestimated. On the scale of the continent, a first differentiation thus contrasts regions where population is dense (on plateaus and around large lakes) to those that are almost unpopulated. From the 1930s to the end of the 1970s, two main factors contributed to the consolidation of the large population centers: the evolution of cash crops and the development of the great axes of communication (particularly the railway). The collapse of the production of certain cash crops and the transition to other forms of exploitation resulted in an accelerated—and sometimes region-wide—movement of populations toward the coasts or toward the great urban centers. Thus cities such as Abidjan, Cairo, Casablanca, Dakar, Douala, Johannesburg, Kinshasa, Lagos, and Nairobi became the destinations for regional migrations. They now constitute vast metropolises from which a new African urban civilization is emerging. This new urbanity, heterogeneous and cosmopolitan, is characterized by combination and mixture in clothing, music, and advertising as well as in practices of consumption in general (Simone 1997).

One of the most important factors regulating daily urban life is surely the multiplicity and heterogeneity of religious systems. With the proliferation of churches and mosques, a veritable territorial sphere has been constituted around places of worship. It is clearly distinguished from the territorial administration of the state, not only by the services that religious institutions offer, but also by the ethics they promote (Spruyt 1994). Alongside the religious foundations entrusted with running hospitals and schools, a religious individualism based on the idea of God's sovereignty is emerging. This sovereignty is exercised in all spheres of life, expressed in the form of grace and salvation. Grace and salvation are connected with the divine will and not with any human merit. The interiorization of grace is realized through strict moral codes, a taste for discipline and work, and concern for family life (marriage, sex) and the dead.

In Muslim countries, a territoriality based on networks provides the foundation for the jurisdictional power *marabouts* exercise over the faithful. Spread out within a national and often international setting, these networks tied to Sufi orders are connected with holy cities and figures to whom the faithful give allegiance.[6] The mosque, on the other hand, became in the 1980s one of the chief symbols of the reconquest of society and city by the religious. It has served sometimes as a refuge for those who were persecuted, and sometimes as a haven for those who could go no further. The ultimate resort for the desperate, it has become the primary referent for all those whose convictions have been shaken by the changes currently taking place. In North Africa, and even in some parts of Nigeria, the mosque has sometimes served as the point of emergence for a culture of protest, new figures of the imam coming to embody new practices of worship and preaching, and the Friday prayer becoming one of the main moments on the weekly calendar (cf. Dakhlia 1998).

In predominantly Christian countries, the proliferation of cults has given rise to a territorial logic of a capillary type. With the explosion of dogma, a plurality of meanings and institutional forms are assumed by preaching, the administration of the sacraments, the liturgy, and various rituals, including healing rituals. Wars, along with the volatility and hazards of everyday life, have led to reinterpretations of the narratives of the Passion and Calvary, as well as of the images of the Last Judgment, the Resurrection, and the Redemption (Werbner 1997). Sometimes this eschatological di-

---

6. See the case of the holy city of Touba (Senegal) studied in Ross 1995, 1996.

mension has found a ready-made outlet in armed movements character-ized by attendant ideologies of death and sacrifice (Grootaers 1998). Re-Islamization and re-Christianization have gone hand in hand, both processes confidently recombining disparate and even contradictory ele-ments of African paganism, of the ambient pietism, and of monotheistic patriarchalism.

The other territory on which the new frontiers of urban life are marked is that of sexuality. The dimension of individual behavior, the universe of norms, and the forms of morality that are supposed to govern private prac-tices have undergone deep transformations in Africa. The last twenty years have witnessed, in fact, a generalized loss of control over sexuality by fam-ilies, churches, and the state. A new moral economy of individual pleasures has developed in the shadow of economic decadence. Everywhere, the age of marriage has for the most part fallen. A general crisis of masculinity is occurring, while the number of female heads of families steadily increases. So-called illegitimate births have definitely ceased to be regarded as a seri-ous problem. Precocious and frequent sexual relations have become com-monplace. In spite of the resilience of traditional family models, many pro-hibitions have been lifted. Ideals of fecundity are in crisis, and contraceptive practices have increased, at least among the middle classes (Guillaume 1999). Homosexuality is becoming more common almost everywhere (see *Journal of Southern Africa Studies* 1998). Access to pornographic literature and films is more widespread. Concurrently, sexually transmitted diseases have extended their domain; acquired immunodeficiency syndrome (AIDS) now serves as the main regulator of demographic growth while at the same time it pushes to its ultimate limits the new cultural relationship between pleasure and death (Becker et al. 1999).

The other new form of polarization with regard to culture and identity is found in the refugee camps, under the combined impact of war, the col-lapse of state order, and the ensuing forced migrations. This phenomenon is structural to the extent that, first, the map of displaced populations, in addition to being drawn over a relatively long time, constantly extends to cover new centers while the number of these displaced populations con-stantly increases; second, the forced character of the migrations continu-ally assumes new forms; and finally, although we have witnessed sometimes spectacular cases in which refugees return to their homelands, the time refugees spend in the camps grows ever longer. As a result, the camp ceases to be a provisional place, a space of transit that is inhabited while awaiting a return home. From the legal as well as the factual point of view, what was supposed to be an exception becomes routine and the rule, within an or-

ganization of space that tends to become permanent. In these human concentrations with an extraterritorial status, veritable imaginary nations
henceforth live (Malkki 1995). Under the burden of constraint and pre-
cariousness, new forms of socialization are emerging (Nyers 1999; De
Smedt 1998). As bits of territory located outside the legal systems of the
host countries, the refugee camps represent places where the complete enjoyment of life and the rights implicit in it are suspended. A system based
on a functional relationship between territorial settlement and expropria-
tion leaves millions of people in a position in which the task of physical survival determines everything else.[7]

Still more important, the camp becomes a seedbed for the recruitment
of soldiers and mercenaries. Within the camps, new forms of authority are
also emerging. Nominally administered by international humanitarian organizations, they are secretly controlled by military leaders who are either
trying to retake power in their home countries or waging wars in the host
country for the benefit of local factions. These armies, composed of ado-
lescents and refugees, are financed in part through diasporic networks set
up in other countries. Children are used as supporting forces or as mercenaries in regional wars. Thus new social formations arise on the periphery
of the refugee camps. Veritable armies without a state, they often oppose
states without armies, which thus find themselves forced to recruit mercenaries as well, or else to solicit the aid of their neighbors in order to deal
with internal rebellions. This logic, which involves disconnecting the state
from war-making and using substitutes and mercenaries working for the
highest bidder, indicates that a complex social process is under way, and
that new political as well as spatial boundaries are being outlined beyond
those inherited from colonization.

The Territories of War

The examples cited above clearly demonstrate that most African wars do
not have their immediate point of origin in border disputes resulting from
colonial divisions. In fact, from 1963 to the present hardly a dozen conflicts
between states can be assigned to this category. From a normative point of
view, two major principles have guided the conduct of relations among
African states since independence: the first is based on the idea of nonin-

---

7. Compare this with what G. Agamben says about the concentration camps as the ultimate essence of modernity (Agamben 1997, 179–202).

terference in the internal affairs of other states; the second concerns the sacrosanct character of the boundaries inherited from colonization. Although it is evident that the principle of noninterference has been generally ignored, it is nonetheless true that the boundaries inherited from colonialism have remained essentially unchanged. Africans have accepted the territorial and state framework imposed by colonization. To be sure, there have been armed attempts to modify it, but in general they have not resulted in any redrawing of international boundaries such as those that followed the breakup of the Soviet Union or the former Yugoslavia. In these instances, the international system acknowledged only a derogation of recognized sovereignty to the previous component republics.

Until the mid-1970s, two types of war prevailed in Africa in which boundaries were directly at stake. First, there were the wars of secession. The two chief examples of this kind of war were the secession of Katanga from Congo-Kinshasa in 1960 and that of the self-proclaimed Republic of Biafra from Nigeria in 1967. Both the Congo and Nigeria put down these revolts and retained the integrity of their territories, whether by themselves or with the help of foreign forces. The only example of a successful secession is that of Eritrea from Ethiopia, which did not put an end to wars between these two neighbors, as the current conflict shows (Abbink 1998). Elsewhere, the secessionist or irredentist temptation has not disappeared. Efforts to escape the central power persist in Senegal (in Casamance), in Cameroon (in the English-speaking provinces), in Angola (in the province of Cabinda), in Namibia (in the Caprivi Strip), and in the Comoros (on the island of Anjouan).

The other form of conflict involving boundaries is constituted by wars of annexation, such as the Somali attempts to conquer Ogaden in Ethiopia in 1963 and 1978. These attempts ended in failure, but they led to important changes in alliances on the regional checkerboard, and ultimately to the partition of the Ethiopian state. The territorial conflict between Chad and Libya concerned Aozou, which Libya annexed in 1973. After several years of repeated wars punctuated by foreign military interventions (particularly on the part of France), the International Court of Justice ruled that the territory should be returned to Chad. This was also the case for Western Sahara, a former Spanish colony reclaimed and occupied by Morocco in 1956. The other boundary disputes represented dormant conflicts and had to do either with routes essential to the extraction of natural resources (oil, iron, diamonds) or with islands, notably in the dispute between Nigeria and Cameroon over the Bakassi Peninsula. These border wars have consisted more of skirmishes than of genuine, open conflicts.

Nonetheless, at the end of the twentieth century African countries continue to be involved in numerous border disputes, such as those between Nigeria and its neighbors on the Gulf of Guinea (Cameroon and Equatorial Guinea, in particular), in the Sahel area (Mali, Niger, Algeria), and between Namibia and Botswana. Most of these disputes have their origin not in the desire to make an ethno-cultural space coincide with the space of the state, but rather in the struggle to control resources considered to be vital, in particular water. The great hydrographic basins, involving both rivers (the Congo, the Zambezi, the Niger, the Nile, the Senegal) and lakes (Lake Chad, Lake Victoria), thus tend to become areas of conflict. Around these basins, not only economic activities but also serious contradictions have emerged. The noncoincidence of the borders of states with natural borders has opened the way to disputes over sovereignty. Since rivers and lakes generally combine distinct juridical elements (land and water), the question is how to reconcile the three requirements constituted by the freedom of use, the right of access for everyone, and sovereignty over the land through which the river flows.

In this regard, the example of the Nile speaks volumes. Ninety-five percent of the water that flows through Egypt comes from outside its boundaries (from Ethiopia and the Sudan, in particular). Demographic pressure in the region, the need to exploit increasingly less-productive lands, and the rapid growth rate of per capita consumption are leading most of the states in the region to consider constructing dams. Thus Ethiopia and Egypt are battling over the distribution of water resources in light of Ethiopia's plans for irrigation projects to improve farmlands in Ouollo and Tigray (Lebbos 1996). But the question of how the waters of the Nile should be distributed involves many other countries, such as Burundi, Kenya, Rwanda, Tanzania, Uganda, and Congo-Kinshasa.

Other river basins, such as those of the Zambezi, the Chobe, and the Okavango, reveal a different set of African boundaries that are a source of tensions among the main countries concerned: Angola, Botswana, Namibia, South Africa, Zambia, and Zimbabwe. An increase in the consumption of the waters of the Okavango in Namibia would automatically threaten the interior delta of this watercourse. Botswana's project to divert the river Chobe toward the river Vaal to supply South Africa immediately arouses tensions in the subregion. The same kinds of tensions are perceptible regarding the distribution of the fossil groundwaters in the Sahara, which concerns Chad, Niger, Libya, the Sudan, and, to the west, Senegal, Mali, and Mauritania. Libya has already begun a project to build an artificial Great River to exploit the Sahara's groundwaters, which extend under the soil of other countries. The boundaries of the continent are thus being re-drawn around the question of how to regulate the use of watercourses by the countries through which they flow, and these hydro-political conflicts exacerbate other disputes on which they are superimposed.

In the framework of the strategic ghetto that Africa has become in the aftermath of the cold war, another more basic spatial arrangement and an-other geopolitical situation are currently taking form. The processes they involve, separated in time but complementary in their effects, are situated within the major, ongoing movements of destroying and reconstituting the nineteenth-century state. Sometimes they occur in precisely the same spaces. Furthermore, dynamics that were introduced by colonization and essentially continued by the independent regimes are grafted onto these processes. Through the mediation of war and the collapse of projects of de-mocratization, this interlacing of dynamics and temporalities leads to the "exit from the state": it promotes the emergence of technologies of dom-ination that are based on forms of private indirect government and that have as their function the constitution of new systems of property and new bases of social stratification (Mbembe 1999).

The Three Fissures

Three major territorial configurations emerge from these interactive forces. The first two are the northern and southern extremities of the continent. Their respective positions with regard to the third, the heart of the conti-nent (the area G. W. F. Hegel called "true Africa"), are dissimilar.

Let us take the case of North Africa. All through the nineteenth century, North Africa was connected with the rest of the continent by three ancient corridors. In the western corridor, Moroccan influence made itself felt as far south as the countries in the bend of the Niger River. Conquests, raids, commerce, religious upsurges, and slavery made it possible to amass for-tunes and weave multiform networks of relationships (familial, commer-cial, religious, or military). Armed formations controlled the commercial routes and maintained clienteles (Webb 1995). Linkages between the Sahel and the desert were mediated by the Moors, the Tuaregs, and even the Dioula and the Bambara. On the religious level, a flexible and syncretic Sufism cemented the relationships between the two edges of the desert.

In the central corridor, religious, commercial, and political dynamics tra-versed the Sahara and, thanks to the Sanussi order of Sufis, connected Cyre-naica, the borders of Egypt, and Tripoli with Lake Chad, the Wadai district, and Borkou. The role played by the cities of Fez and Marrakech in the western corridor was played here by Ghadamis. In these two corridors, mixed and hybrid groups were to be found where the Arab-Berber world and the Negro African world met. Moving and fluid, these boundaries were characterized by a fragmentation into clans, families, and tribes, and by cycles of alliance and rupture.

A third corridor linked Egypt with the countries to the south. This latter linkage was based on the Nile River rather than the camel caravan. The third corridor reached as far as the borders of modern-day Uganda and included not only the lower Sudan but also part of northeastern Congo-Kinshasa.

In the context of the reorganization of the world, North Africa is today riven by parallel pressures. On a general level, part of North Africa is drawn toward the Mediterranean. Without necessarily espousing Europe's cultural values, it is trying to bind its economic future to that of western Europe. Its other side is turned toward the memorial sites of Islam in the Near East. The African nature of the Maghreb and the Mashriq is seen as problematic by other Africans as well as by the countries involved. In formulating North African autochthony solely in the register of Arabness, one ignores the role played by indigenous populations in this region, a role clearly reflected in all the local histories preceding the arrival of the Arabs and Islam. South of the Sahara, North African Muslim influence has increasingly been forced to compete with Saudi and Iranian activism. These two countries are involved in domains as various as the training of Islamic intellectuals, the socialization of preachers, the construction of mosques, the financing of charitable services, and the funding of foundations. Although it is receding, Moroccan influence still makes itself felt, particularly in Mali and Senegal in Muslim West Africa (El Farah et al. 1996). So also does that of Libya, in assistance rendered informally to impecunious West African states and in projects such as the short-lived Libya-Chad Union in 1980, or its energetically promoted African Union project, launched in 1999.

The channels linking the rest of the continent with the Middle East are controlled by a Lebanese diaspora that has long been established in the main centers of West Africa (Bierwirth 1998). But while North Africa is disconnecting itself from the rest of the continent, a process of deterritorialization is developing around the perimeter of the Sahara Desert. In a single movement, this process is eroding sovereignties in the northern part of the continent as well as in black Africa proper. A vast, moving frontier marks both sides of the desert. It reaches from the borders of Algeria to as far as Barkou, Ennedi, and Tibesti, at the western gates of the Sudan. In this vast space, segmentary logics are combined with the logics of clans and of exchange (Bennafla 1997). Here, indigenousness appears in the guise of itinerancy, an ancient mixture of races, and a mutual acculturation that combine several registers of identity. Those who move about in it include governmental and nongovernmental actors, nomads, merchants, and adventurers. Structured by a veritable chain of suzerainties, this space remains strongly marked by a culture of raiding and looting (Claudot-Hawad 1992). Here, more than elsewhere, the dominant form of territoriality is itinerant and nomadic.

The other extremity of the continent is constituted by South Africa, whose zone of influence extends from the Cape to Katanga. Internally, however, this diasporic and multiracial country is split into several worlds. On the one hand, thanks to active economic diplomacy, it succeeded, after the end of apartheid, in expanding its relations with Asia by means of a remarkable increase in exchange with China, Hong Kong, India, Japan, Malaysia, South Korea, and Taiwan. Asia's penetration of South African markets goes hand in hand with the strengthening of the latter's relations with the European Union and the United States. The consolidation of financial and commercial relations with the rest of Africa is carried out in different registers. South Africa is taking advantage of the institutional weakness of its neighbors by establishing asymmetrical relations with them—to the point that the flow of investments and regional networks of exchange have put Lesotho, Mozambique, and Swaziland well on the way to becoming South African provinces (Blanc 1997). Moreover, South Africa's policy of constructing transportation and maritime facilities (in the ports of Beira, Maputo, and Nacala) connected with the exportation of goods and services is transforming landlocked countries into captive markets (Arkwright et al. 1996). In the rest of Africa, the South African private sector invests in domains as varied as tourism, mining, transportation, electricity, banks, and breweries.

But South Africa's political, diplomatic, and cultural influence is far greater than economic power, which itself remains very relative. The country is, in fact, extremely vulnerable to international financial fluctuations. Moreover, the tension between its policy of social adjustment and macroeconomic choices intended to attract foreign capital is growing. The position of South Africa on the continent is still highly ambiguous, and the terms under which it can be reintegrated into the continent remain unclear. Its regional and commercial policies are strongly contested by the old front-line states (particularly Angola and Zimbabwe). Although South African diplomacy is still based on a minimal knowledge of the rest of the continent, businesses and particularly the mining companies are extending their tentacles as far as Mali, Ghana, and Guinea. This also holds true for security enterprises (Howe 1998). Trade in arms—both official and unofficial—is accelerating. The influx of legal and clandestine immigrants is leading to an extraordinary rise in xenophobia (Kadima 1999). In the hope of halting recent transregional migrations toward South Africa, expulsions have been systematized and police units charged with tracking down clandestine immigrants (particularly those of African origin) have been set up (Bouillon 1998).

Between these two continental extremities lies the "heart," the vast domain of Middle Africa, where the most dramatic territorial reconfigurations are in course. The area extending from the Horn of Africa in a southwestward arc through the Great Lakes and the two Congos to the Atlantic has become a vast interconnected war zone. In the nineteenth century, three processes structured this space. First was the establishment, around a triangle connecting Darfur, the Bahr el-Ghazal basin, and lower Egypt, of an extensive network for trade in ivory, weapons, and slaves, which was used by the Khartoumites, the Egyptians, the Syrians, and, later on, the Europeans. Constant wars and raiding allowed private fortunes to be made, but they also led to the destruction of social entities or their forced incorporation into larger configurations. Second, in the area around the Great Lakes (Buganda, Burundi, Ankole), small monarchies were established, based on armed force and characterized by a narrow conception of identity, on the one hand, and by intensive stock-raising, on the other. Finally, primarily in the center and in the south there emerged a patchwork of powers, including slave-trading principalities, caravan states, chiefdoms, brokering groups, and immense territories controlled by armed bands and warlords. Elephant-hunting, ivory-trafficking, and the slave trade supplied an interregional commerce whose outlets ran throughout the region, from the Atlantic to the Indian Ocean.

Over the past twenty years in Middle Africa, in the wake of nineteenth-century movements and behind the mask of authoritarian states inherited from colonization, a process of fragmentation has been proceeding. The relationships between the central state apparatus and the subjects it administers have grown steadily weaker. Similarly, military principalities have emerged in Rwanda, Uganda, and Burundi, and, to a lesser extent, in Ethiopia and Eritrea. One of the characteristics of these regimes is the recurrent use of force in implementing internal and external political strategies. Having taken power through violence and having been confronted with internal disorders, these regimes respond to their security obsessions in two ways: first, by creating "security zones" along their borders and, second, by extending their power into neighboring countries with the most fragile and unstable state structures, as happened to Congo-Kinshasa (Shearer 1999).

Incapable of colonizing a continental state whose structures are "unformalized" when they are not deliquescent, or even of simply conquering it, these military principalities ally themselves with their own long-established diaspora, even though the citizenship of those involved in this diaspora is contested in their home countries. The military principalities also acquire the services of "rebels," dissidents, and others available to the highest bidder, who provide a screen for the military regimes' intervention. Made up of "familiar" foreigners (whose assimilation within the autochthonous populations remains incomplete, as in the case of the Tutsi in Congo-Kinshasa) and of natives of the country (undisciplined and riven by constant factional battles), these armies of adolescent mercenaries are set up as para-governmental entities on the sites they control. This is the case in eastern Congo-Kinshasa, where, with the implosion of the country, the security problems created by the porosity of its borders has made it possible to structure rear-line bases from which armed groups opposed to the governments of Uganda, Rwanda, and Burundi undertake destabilizing missions (Lemarchand 1997; Barnes 1999).

Sometimes these wars result in the victory of a faction. Such victories are almost always temporary and result in a cycle of violence whose intensity constantly increases. In other cases, these struggles have led to the disappearance of states inherited from colonialism, as in the case of Somalia. In still other cases, the situation is such that none of the parties succeeds in decisively defeating the others. War is consequently prolonged, leading to the intervention of humanitarian organizations whose presence further obliterates the sources of sovereignty (Duffield 1997). Thus we witness the appearance of social formations in which war and preparation for war tend to become regular functions. Such wars set in motion a process of reproduction-destruction, made vivid by the cycles of massacres and human butchery as well as by the effects of pillage and looting on the model of nineteenth-century raiding (Behrend 1997; Doom and Vlassenroot 1999).

Yet another potent vector of reconfiguration emerges in the context of the internationalization of exchange and the development of new ways of exploiting natural resources. Three such resources may be distinguished: oil, forests, and diamonds. Oil, in particular, is the origin of an offshore economy whose center of gravity is now the Gulf of Guinea. In its extended definition, the gulf includes a long coastal area stretching from Nigeria to

Angola. Behind it lies a hinterland characterized by the exploitation of two types of spaces: the proximate interior forestlands and the peripheral continental zones (of which Lake Chad is the pillar). In the global geopolitics of hydrocarbons, the Lake Chad region has become one of the zones in which transnational and local factors are interlaced, leading to important recompositions of political and economic power and influence like that under way in the Caspian basin (Bolukbasi 1998).

Two factors have been fundamental to these African recompositions. First, during the 1980s governments of the countries around the Gulf of Guinea granted major concessions to various Western companies specializing in oil exploration. Whereas three companies (Shell, Agip, and Elf) dominated the region until the beginning of the 1980s, more than twenty firms now have permits (including Chevron, Texaco, Total, Fina, Norsk Hydro, Statoil, Perenco, and Amoco). Major investments such as the introduction of new technologies of extraction have made possible the discovery and then exploitation of new oil fields, some of them enormous (as in the case of Dalia, Girassol, Kuito, and Landana in Angola; Kitina, Moho, and Nkossa in Congo-Brazzaville; Zafiro in Equatorial Guinea; and Bonga in Nigeria), as well as the extension of earlier limits. This is particularly true of the deep offshore fields (zones at a depth of more than 200–300 meters). However, hydrocarbons are unequally distributed among the states of the Gulf of Guinea. The supremacy of Nigeria is increasingly being challenged by Angola, while countries such as Cameroon are about to be surpassed by Equatorial Guinea and Chad.

A comparable recomposition may be in process in Eurasia, with the jousting in process over exploitation of potentially vast oil and natural gas fields in the Caspian region and Central Asia. Issues of ownership and management of extraction and transport to zones of consumption jostle with questions of state consolidation and contestation. Hydrocarbon and pipeline politics permeate both interstate relations and internal dynamics from the Caucasus to the Chinese frontier.

The new oil frontier coincides, paradoxically, with one of the most clearly marked boundaries of state dissolution in Africa. In this respect, the situations of Nigeria, Angola, and Congo-Brazzaville are symptomatic. The deep movements of deterritorialization affecting Africa assume a vivid form in Nigeria. There, within a process of unifying a federal state, a set of embedded forms of control and regulation that were encouraged by colonial indirect rule are still dominant. Localities and internal divisions, some historical and others institutional or even cultural and territorial, are superimposed on the space of the state. Each locality is subject to several jurisdictions: state jurisdiction, traditional jurisdiction, religious jurisdiction. Different orders coexist within an interlacing of "homelands" and "communities." The coexistence of these different orders is disturbed by a multiplicity of local conflicts. Most of these conflicts are expressed in the form of an opposition between autochthonous populations and strangers. Citizenship is conceived in ethnic and territorial terms, and an individual's enjoyment of civil rights depends on his appurtenance to an ethnic group or locality.

The dissolution of the state is moving in two apparently opposed directions. On the one hand, several forms of territoriality intersect, confront, and substitute for one another, thereby producing an accumulation of mutually dissipating and neutralizing forces. On the other hand, the authoritarian imagination has taken multiple forms, notably that of a paranoid military institution. The regions at the epicenter of oil production are torn apart by repeated conflicts. Without taking the form of classical warfare, these conflicts set communities against each other within a single country, in regions known for their mineral wealth and for the intensity with which one or several natural resources are exploited by multinational companies. This is the case in the region of the Niger delta, a labyrinth of marshes, islands, and mangroves in which, against the background of an ecological catastrophe, the Ogoni, Ijaw, Itsekiri, and Urhobo are fighting among themselves and each group is involved in conflicts with the federal state and the oil companies (Osaghae 1995). Armed youths attack oil installations, sabotage pipelines, and block valves. Massacres regularly take place in the context of conflicts that are low in intensity but very costly in human lives (Manby 1999). Nonetheless, the fact that a major part of the exploitation of oil deposits takes place offshore means that disorder and profits, far from being antithetical, mutually complement and strengthen each other (Frynas 1998).

In the case of Angola, the dominant model is partition and dissidence. The boundaries of state sovereignty are blurred. Part of the territory is controlled by the government, while another part is under the control of armed dissidents. Each zone has its own rights and franchises and manages its own diplomatic, commercial, financial, and military affairs. In the model of partition, a first delimitation differentiates cities from rural regions. The Union Nacional paraa Independência Total de Angola (UNITA) dominates a major portion of the rural zones and, from time to time, some cities on the high plateaus of Andula and Bailundo, the valley of the Cuango River, and the area around the two Lunda provinces. One of the main tactics of the armed dissidents consists of causing the implosion of urban centers by sowing terror in the countryside, emptying the latter of "useless" populations and causing them to flee and amass in the cities, which are then surrounded and shelled.

The exploitation of diamonds is carried out by miners recruited both locally and in neighboring Congo-Kinshasa. In 1996, some 100,000 miners were working in the mineral deposits under UNITA's authority in the valley of the Cuango alone. UNITA's control extended to the Mavinga region and to certain parts of the province of South Kwanza. In the regions under the government's control, conscription has been introduced in the cities. But the draftees are called on to fight in rural areas. On the government side as well as on the rebel side, military service is performed in exchange for payments to the soldiers and to mercenaries. Salaries and compensations are often paid in cash that can be immediately circulated on the market, in particular among traffickers more or less specializing in supplying armies and dealing in the spoils of war. The war chest is composed of converted or convertible metals and of oil resources. The two parties to the conflict exploit gold and diamond mines or oil fields. The financial stratagems are complex. Almost all the oil fields are mortgaged.

Although it shares some characteristics with the Angolan case, the de facto partition of Congo-Kinshasa is of another order. Long ago, the Congolese state was transformed into an informal satrapy, conquered by henchmen armed by neighboring countries. In the context of a policy of reconstructing their own national states, the regimes of Burundi, Rwanda, and Uganda are attempting to change the regional balance in accord with a three-dimensional logic. Uganda's first goal is to weaken permanently the (phantom) state of Congo-Kinshasa by blurring its sovereignty over major parts of its territory. Next, it attempts to dismember the country into economically differentiated fiefs, each of which is endowed with specific resources (minerals, forests, plantations) that are exploited by way of monopolies and franchises of various kinds. Finally, it seeks to instrumentalize the collapse of the social order so as to establish informal domination over these economic fiefdoms. From then on, local and regional conflicts are interlaced, while constant wars set factions, ethnic groups, and lineages against one another within a framework that is thereafter regional in scope. Today, several African armies are facing off either directly or indirectly under the cover of pseudo-autochthonous rebellions sponsored by a group of neighboring states. Equateur (a province of Congo-Kinshasa) is under pressure from the Movement for the Liberation of the Congo; Kivu and some parts of Kasai are occupied by the Rwandans and the Ugandans; and a large part of the Lower Congo province is occupied by Angola. War and plunder go

hand in hand, and all these forces live off levies on minerals and other resources (timber, coffee) found in the territories they control.

In contrast to three other African countries of similar size (Nigeria,
South Africa, the Sudan), Congo-Kinshasa now appears to be a large, open
space that includes several boundaries, none of which corresponds to its
official place on the map. The territory is split between a multiplicity of
forces while the nominal central power struggles to survive. Part of the territory looks toward southern Africa, while the energies of the other part
are dissipated by the disorders in the Great Lakes region. Still another part
is sinking into the Sudan–Central African Republic orbit, while the Atlantic
corridor and the ancient lands of the Kongo are satellites of Angola. Against
a background of armed violence and a severe depreciation of currencies, alliances are constantly made and unmade. Ephemeral coalitions are formed
on the regional scale. But no force accumulates sufficient power to dominate all the others in an enduring way. Everywhere, lines emerge and vanish. Structural instability makes Congo-Kinshasa the perfect example of a
process of the delocalization of boundaries.

Congo-Brazzaville, on the other hand, is an example of extraterritorial-
ization. Here, the model is not that of partition proper, but rather of a vor-
tex. Violence is cyclical and its epicenter is the capital. Located in the hinterland, the capital itself has its center of gravity outside itself, in the relation
the state maintains with the oil companies operating offshore. The material bases of the state are essentially constituted by oil company advances
of future payments due. Outside this gelatinous structure, poorly controlled zones are dominant. Armed gangs and militias attempt to transform
themselves into genuine military units. They try to control bogus fiefs and
to capture what remains to be carried off (money, merchandise, small
household items), particularly when organized pillaging is involved (Dorier-
Apprill 1997; Bazenguissa-Ganga 1996).

Borders, Capitations, and Margins

In this nascent geography, composed of virtual, potential, and real limits,
three other configurations are emerging: the regions on the margins, the
coastal-savannah zone of contact and competition, and the sprawling
megacities and their hinterlands. Some whole regions suddenly find themselves on the margins of the major territorial mappings mentioned above.
This is the case of the countries in the Sudano-Sahelian region, which is
composed of small states that are often based on a differentiation between

forest lands and savannahs. Here, throughout the nineteenth century, the hawking of goods, the propagation of the Muslim faith, and ancient migrations led to a potent mixing of populations. During the colonial period, these population movements were reignited according to different logic, with the result that cleavages between coastal societies and those in the hinterland were accentuated. At the end of the twentieth century, the area is characterized by a contraction around the major urban areas situated along the Atlantic Ocean. These urban areas dominate a hinterland whose borders are often situated beyond the national state framework (as in the case of Abidjan and Dakar).

Today, the opposition between countries of the savannah and the countries on the coast is taking on new dimensions. A process of amalgamating ethnic groups under the banner of Islam has ensued. Organized into powerful networks, leaders of these communities have been able to amass fortunes on the margin of the state apparatus. Their spread in the subregion and their efforts to convert their mercantile power into political power within the framework of a multiparty system has accentuated debates concerning the relationship between citizenship and autochthony. On another level, we are witnessing the emergence of entrepôt cities or entrepôt states (as in the case of Touba in Senegal or of the Gambia), on the basis of which networks are woven and trafficking is organized, with both regional and international ramifications.

Finally, the region from Senegal to Liberia is full of apparently localized conflicts whose causes and consequences are connected with social structures and transregional histories. This is the case in Casamance, in Guinea-Bissau, in Liberia, and in Sierra Leone. These conflicts have repercussions in the Gambia, Guinea, the Ivory Coast, and Senegal. Social dynamics in the subregion are still marked by nineteenth-century developments. At that time, a migratory expansion of the Fulani from west to east, and then toward the south, touched off several *maraboutic* revolutions on a regional scale (Barry 1986). The river countries were at that time, as they are today, occupied by a conglomerate of peoples with fragmented power structures. The Fulani drive toward the south, the aim of which was to control the traffic in slaves, guns, livestock, and grains, was halted by colonization. Today, the structures of power that have crystallized in the course of this long century are once again being challenged.

As a result of international policies of conservation, whole territories are now outside state authority. This is not merely a matter of using the pretext of protecting rare species to impose Western imaginations of space (Neumann 1997). Managed on the concession model by international organizations seeking to protect the environment, these territories have a de facto ex-

AT THE EDGE OF THE WORLD

traterritorial status. Moreover, almost everywhere the development of tourism is leading to the establishment of tourist parks and hunting reserves.

Finally, there are the islands. Situated on the margins of the continent, they are all connected to a plurality of worlds from which they draw their basic resources. In this respect, they constitute a set of intersections. Thus Zanzibar, as a result of its history, lies at the intersection of "Africa proper" and the Arab world. Mauritius is situated at the confluence of several civilizations—African, Indian, and French. As major centers of slavery, the islands have generally constituted highly stratified societies. They are also connected to metropolitan centers on the coasts, such as Durban. Within these spaces structured by familial and diasporic networks, men, women, and merchandise circulate. There, a cosmopolitan, creole African culture is being born (Martinez 1998).

Three conclusions can be drawn from the observations made in this study. To conceptualize globalization adequately, one must make the classical distinction between spatiality and temporality more relative. Interpreted from what is wrongly considered to be the margins of the world, globalization sanctions the entry into an order where space and time, far from being opposed to one another, tend to form a single configuration. The domestication of global time proceeds by way of the material deconstruction of existing territorial frameworks, the excision of conventional boundaries, and the simultaneous creation of mobile spaces and spaces of enclosure intended to limit the mobility of populations judged to be superfluous.

In the regions of the world situated on the margins of major contemporary technological transformations, the material deconstruction of existing territorial frameworks goes hand in hand with the establishment of an economy of coercion whose objective is to destroy "superfluous" populations and to exploit raw materials. The profitability of this kind of exploitation requires the exit of the state, its emasculation, and its replacement by fragmented forms of sovereignty. The functioning and viability of such an economy are subordinated to the manner in which the law of the distribution of weapons functions in the societies involved. Under such conditions, war as a general economy no longer necessarily implies that those who have weapons oppose each other. It is more likely to imply a conflict between those who have weapons and those who have none.

References

Abbink, Jan. 1998. "Briefing: The Erythrean-Ethiopian Border Dispute." *African Affairs* 97, no. 389 (October): 551–65.

Adelman, J., and S. Aron. 1999. "From Borderlands to Borders: Empires, Nation-States, and the Peoples in between North American History." *American Historical Review* 104, no. 3 (June): 814–41.

Agamben, G. 1997. *Homo Sacer: Le pouvoir souverain et la vie nue*. Trans. M. Raiola. Paris: Le Seuil.

Arkwright, D., et al. 1996. "Spatial Development Initiatives (Development Corridors): Their Potential Contribution to Investment and Employment Creation." Working paper. Development Bank of Southern Africa, Midrand, South Africa.

Autrepart. 1998. "Exchanges transfrontaliers et intégration régionale en Afrique subsaharienne" (special issue). *Autrepart: Cahiers des sciences humaines* 6.

Badie, Bertrand. 1995. *La fin des territoires: Essai sur le désordre international et sur l'utilité sociale du respect*. Paris: Fayard.

Barnes, W. 1999. "Kivu: L'Enlisement dans la violence." *Politique africaine* 73 (March): 123–36.

Barry, B. 1986. *La Sénégambie*. Paris: L'Harmattan.

Bazenguissa Ganga, Remy. 1996. "Milices politiques et bandes armées à Brazzaville." *Les Cahiers du CERI 13*. Paris: Centre d'Etude des Relations Internationales.

Becker, C., et al., eds. 1999. *Vivre et penser le SIDA en Afrique: Experiencing and Understanding AIDS in Africa*. Paris: Karthala-CODESRIA.

Behrend, Heike. 1997. *La guerre des esprits en Ouganda, 1985–1986: Le mouvement du Saint-Esprit d'Alice Lakwena*. Paris: L'Harmattan.

Bennafla, K. 1997. "Entre Afrique noire et monde arabe: Nouvelles tendances des échanges 'informels' tchadiens." *Tiers-Monde* 38, no. 152 (October–December): 89–96.

Bierwirth, C. 1998. "The Lebanese Communities of Côte d'Ivoire." *African Affairs* 98, no. 390 (January): 79–100.

Birmingham, David, and P. M. Martin, eds. 1983. *History of Central Africa*. Vol. 1. London: Longman.

Blanc, M. O. 1997. "Le corridor de Maputo." *Afrique contemporaine* 184 (October–December): 133–40.

Bolukbasi, S. 1998. "The Controversy over the Caspian Sea Mineral Resources: Conflicting Perceptions, Clashing Interests." *Europe-Asia Studies* 50, no. 3 (May): 397–414.

Boone, Catherine. 1998. "State Building in the African Countryside: Structure and Politics at the Grassroots." *Journal of Development Studies* 34, no. 4 (April): 1–31.

Bouillon, A., ed. 1998. *Immigration africaine en Afrique du Sud: Les migrants francophones des années 90*. Paris: Karthala.

Braudel, Fernand. 1984. *Civilization and Capitalism, 15th to 18th Centuries*. Vol. 3, *The Perspective of the World*. Trans. Siân Reynolds. New York: Harper and Row. Original *Civilisation matérielle, économie et capitalisme (XVe–XVIIIe siècles)*. Vol. 3, *Le Temps du monde*. Paris: Librairie Armand Colin, 1979.

de Certeau, Michel. 1984. *The Practice of Everyday Life*. Trans. Steven Rendall. Berkeley: University of California Press. Original *L'Invention du quotidien: Arts de faire*. Paris: Union Générale des Éditions, 1980.

Clapham, Christopher. 1999. "Sovereignty and the Third World State." *Political Studies* 47, no. 3: 522–37.

Claudot-Hawad, H. 1992. "Bandits, rebelles et partisans: Vision plurielle des événements touaregs, 1970–1992." *Politique africaine* 46 (June): 143–49.

Dakhlia, J. 1998. *Urbanité arabe: Textes rassemblés par J. Dakhlia*. Paris: Actes Sud.

De Smedt, Johan. 1998. "Child Marriages in Rwandan Refugee Camps." *Africa* 68, no. 2: 211–37.

Doom, R., and K. Vlassenroot. 1999. "Kony's Message: A New Koine? The Lord's Resistance Army in Northern Uganda." *African Affairs* 98, no. 390 (January): 5–36.

Dorier-Apprill, Elisabeth. 1997. "Guerres des milices et fragmentation urbaine à Brazzaville." *Hérodote* 86–87: 182–221.

Dozon, Jean Pierre. 1997. "L'étranger et l'allochtone en Côte d'Ivoire." Pp. 779–98 in *Bataille les Entreprises Publiques en Côte-d'Ivoire: L'histoire d'un adjustement interne,* ed. Bernard Contamin and Harris Mernel-Fote. Paris: Karthala.

Duffield, Mark. 1997. "NGO Relief in War Zones: Towards an Analysis of the New Aid Paradigm." *Third World Quarterly* 18, no. 3: 527–42.

El Farah, Y. Abou, et al. 1996. *La présence marocaine en Afrique de l'Ouest: Cas du Sénégal, du Mali, et de la Côte d'Ivoire.* Rabat: Publications de l'Institut des études africaines, Université Mohammed V.

Elphick, Richard, and Hermann Giliomee, eds. 1989. *The Shaping of South African Society, 1652–1840.* Middletown, Conn.: Wesleyan University Press.

L'Espace géographique. 1999. "Afrique du Sud" (special issue). Vol. 2, no. 2.

Evans, Peter. 1997. "The Eclipse of the State? Reflections on Stateness in an Era of Globalization." *World Politics* 50, no. 1 (October): 62–87.

Frynas, Jedrzej George. 1998. "Political Instability and Business: Focus on Shell in Nigeria." *Third World Quarterly* 19, no. 3: 457–78.

Grégoire, Emmanuel. 1997. "Les grands courants d'échange sahéliens: Histoire et situations présentes." Pp. 121–41 in *Sahels: Diversité et dynamiques des relations société-nature,* ed. C. Raynault. Paris: Karthala.

Grootaers, J. L., ed. 1998. "Mort et maladie au Zaïre." *Cahiers Africains* 8, nos. 31–32.

Guillaume, A. 1999. "La régulation de la fécondité à Youpougon, Abidjan: Une analyse des biographies contraceptives." Documents de Recherche 7. Institut de Recherche pour le Développement.

Heidegger, Martin. 1962. *Chemins qui ne mènent nulle part.* Trans. W. Brokmeier. Paris: Gallimard.

Herbst, Jeffrey. 1992. "The Challenges to African Boundaries." *Journal of International Affairs* 46, no. 1 (summer): 17–31.

———. 1996–97. "Responding to State Failure in Africa." *International Security* 21, no. 3 (winter): 120–44.

Howe, Herbert M. 1998. "Private Security Forces and African Stability:" The Case of Executive Outcomes." *Journal of Modern African Studies* 36, no. 2 (March): 307–31.

Igué, J. O. 1995. *Le territoire de l'État en Afrique: Les dimensions spatiales du développement.* Paris: Karthala.

Jones, G. I. 1963. *The Trading States of the Oil Rivers.* London: Oxford University Press.

Journal of Southern Africa Studies. 1998."Masculinities in Southern Africa" (special issue). Vol. 24 , no. 4 (December).

Kadima, D. K. 1999. "Congolese Immigrants in South Africa." *CODESRIA Bulletin* 1–2: 14–23.

Kopytoff, Igor, ed. 1987. *The African Frontier: The Reproduction of Traditional African Societies.* Bloomington: Indiana University Press.

Kratochwil, Friedrich. 1986. "Of Systems, Boundaries, and Territory: An Inquiry into the Formation of the State System." *World Politics* 39, no. 1 (October): 27–52.

Lebbos, G. 1996. "La vallée du Nil." *Les Cahiers de l'Orient* 44.

Lefebvre, Henri. 1991. *The Production of Space.* Trans. D. Nicholson-Smith. Oxford: Blackwell.

Lemarchand, René. 1997. "Patterns of State Collapse and Reconstruction in Central Africa: Reflections on the Crisis in the Great Lakes Region." *Afrika Spectrum* 32, no. 2: 173–94.

Lonsdale, Jonathon. 1985. "The European Scramble and Conquest in African History." Pp. 680–766 in *The Cambridge History of Africa,* vol. 6, ed. Roland Oliver and G. N. Sanderson. Cambridge: Cambridge University Press.

Lovejoy, Paul E., and D. Richardson. 1999. "Trust, Pawnship, and Atlantic History: The Institutional Foundations of the Old Calabar Slave Trade." *American Historical Review* 104, no. 2 (April): 332–55.

Malkki, Lisa. 1995. *Purity and Exile.* Chicago: University of Chicago Press.

Manby, Bronwen. 1999. *The Price of Oil: Corporate Responsibility and Human Rights Violations in Nigeria's Oil-Producing Communities.* New York: Human Rights Watch.

Martinez, L. 1998. *La Guerre civile en Algérie.* Paris: Karthala.

Mbembe, Achille. 1999. *Du gouvernement privé indirect.* Dakar: CODESRIA.

Miller, Joseph C. 1988. *Way of Death.* Madison: University of Wisconsin Press.

Nair, K. K. 1972. *Politics and Society in South Eastern Nigeria, 1841–1906: A Study of Power, Diplomacy and Commerce in Old Calabar.* London: Frank Cass.

Neumann, R. P. 1997. "Primitive Ideas: Protected Area Buffer Zones and the Politics of Land in Africa." *Development and Change* 28, no. 3 (July): 559–82.

Nordman, Daniel. 1998. *Frontières de France: De l'espace au territoire, XVIe–XIXe siècle.* Paris: Gallimard.

Nugent, Paul, and A. J. Asiwaju, eds. 1996. *African Boundaries: Barriers, Conduits, and Opportunities.* London: Pinter.

Nyers, P. 1999. "Emergency or Emerging Identities? Refugees and Transformations in World Order." *Millennium* 28, no. 1: 1–26.

Osaghae, E. E. 1995. "The Ogoni Uprising: Oil Politics, Minority Nationalism, and the Future of the Nigerian State." *African Affairs* 94, no. 376 (July): 324–44.

———. 1998. "Managing Multiple Minority Problems in a Divided Society: The Nigerian Experience." *Journal of Modern African Studies* 36, no. 1 (March): 1–24.

Ross, E. 1995. "Touba: A Spiritual Metropolis in the Modern World." *Canadian Journal of African Studies* 29, no. 2: 222–59.

———. 1996. "Tûba: An African Eschatology in Islam." Ph.D. diss., McGill University.

Shearer, David. 1999. "The Conflict in Central Africa." *Survival* 41, no. 2 (summer): 89–106.

Simone, Abdumaliq. 1997. *Urban Processes and Change in Africa.* Dakar: CODESRIA.

Spruyt, Hendrik. 1994. *The Sovereign State and Its Competitors: An Analysis of Systems Change.* Princeton: Princeton University Press.

Webb, J. L. A. 1995. *Desert Frontier: Ecological and Economic Change along the Western Sahel, 1600–1850.* Madison: University of Wisconsin Press.

Werbner, Richard. 1997. "The Suffering Body: Passion and Ritual Allegory in Christian Encounters." *Journal of Southern African Studies* 23, no. 2 (June): 311–24.

Wilks, Ivor. 1975. *Asante in the Nineteenth Century.* Cambridge: Cambridge University Press.

4

Who Is Strong When the State Is Weak? Violent Entrepreneurship in Russia's Emerging Markets

VADIM VOLKOV

Economic historians and historical sociologists have studied the use of violence and the role of states in the development of capitalism. Despite these scholars' primary concern with events past, their findings are valuable for understanding the present dynamics of states in crisis. In the past, before markets had started to grow, territorial monopolies of force were established as a result of continuous warfare. Max Weber (1970, 77–78) claimed that the only plausible way to define the state sociologically was in terms of the specific means peculiar to it—namely, the use of physical force. His classic definition regards the state as the territorial monopoly of legitimate violence.

Norbert Elias (1993) substantiated this conception in his study of state formation in early modern western Europe. He also took a step further, showing that states came about as an unintended consequence of warfare rather than as the result of a conscious project of state-building by powerful princes. The rise of states was an effect of a dynamic relationship of forces engaged in continuous physical struggle—an "elimination contest," as Elias called it. Those who created states made various technical and tactical decisions only in order to increase the efficiency of violence, extract resources, win the war, and establish durable domination (Tilly 1985). The dialectic of violence was such that its increasing concentration in the hands of the state led to a decline in its actual application in day-to-day life (that is, to internal pacification), which proved crucial for the development of the peaceful economic activity of civil society. Combined with fiscal monopoly, the monopoly of force made possible the central function of the state: the enforcement of universal law and order and the exercise of justice.

Exploring the economic aspects of the use of organized violence, the economic historian Frederic Lane (1958) identified early modern governments as violence-using and violence-controlling enterprises that produced and sold a specific service: protection. His insights point to a specific political economy of force that assisted the accumulation of capital during the pre-industrial phase. The governments that commanded organized force received tribute for the protection that they sold to the subjects of economy and trade, but the latter could also gain from what otherwise appeared to be a mere protection racket. The customers (for example, Venetian merchants) earned protection rent, a kind of differential rent received because of the higher efficiency of their protector as compared with the protectors of their competitors. All merchants had to pay tribute to avoid harm, but those who paid less (due to more competitive prices) for protection of the firm in a dangerous business environment earned protection rent, reflecting their lower costs. Thus the institutionalized protection rackets that offered lower prices to clients grew at the expense of their rivals. Lane's major point is that "during the Middle Ages and early modern times protection rents were a major source of fortunes made in trade. They were a more important source of profits than superiority in industrial techniques or industrial organization" (Lane 1958, 410).

Private commercial relations between owners of capital and wielders of force, wherein both parties were players on the same entrepreneurial field, enabled the initial redistribution of resources and their concentrated accumulation but did not stimulate economic growth. Only when European states reached a high degree of centralization and functional differentiation in the late seventeenth century did the monopoly management of organized force become the source of a public good rather than of private profit. This chapter is not the place to describe all the intricate details of this transformation, but its long-term impact on economic activity should be mentioned. The creation of secure space, where access to organized force was no longer a matter of economic differentiation, enabled peaceful competition and thus allowed other factors (such as technical and economic organization) to determine economic performance. To be sure, the monopolization of protection and enforcement enabled the state to receive the monopoly profit. But because of economies of scale this monopoly also reduced the cost of protection and enforcement, thus freeing resources for other uses. In some cases these resources were unproductively consumed by political elites, which led to stagnation, but for the major European powers the monopoly surplus contributed to economic growth. As Charles Tilly (1990) showed in his study of coercion and capital accumulation in European history, the productive management of this surplus—whether the latter was controlled by owners of capital, by the state alone, or through negotiations between the two parties—constituted distinct patterns among the historical development of different European powers.

According to Douglass North and Robert Thomas (1974), states as organizations with a relative advantage in the use of violence protect property rights. Economic growth took place where states enforced property rights of a certain kind—namely, those that approximated public and private rates of return. It is therefore the capacity to enforce property rights and collect taxes in payment for the provision of such public goods (rather than the absolute might of coercive organs) that distinguishes the strong state. Where property rights are unclear or the state is incapable of enforcing them, private enforcers are likely to emerge and benefit from the state's weakness.

The economy of protection rackets and the monopoly management of organized force, so vital for the formation of European states, appear much more relevant to the distant past than to the immediate present. Theories of state formation hardly envisaged a reverse process, so powerful and stable did modern states, the Soviet Union included, appear. But today, when the post-Soviet states (like many of their African counterparts) are in deep functional crisis, the historical sociology of state formation can inform our vision of the processes unfolding in the present.

This chapter explores the use of organized violence in postcommunist Russia and its impact on economic markets and the state. "Violent entrepreneurship" can be defined as a set of organizational solutions and action strategies enabling the conversion of organized force (or organized violence) into money or other market resources on a permanent basis. If consumer goods, for instance, constitute the major resource for trade entrepreneurship, if money serves that purpose for financial entrepreneurship, if information and knowledge do the same for informational entrepreneurship, and so forth, violent entrepreneurship is constituted of socially organized violence, real or potential outside official state rule enforcement.

The main unit of violent entrepreneurship is the "violence-managing agency." In postcommunist Russia such agencies can be provisionally classified into three types: state illegal (units of the state police and security forces acting as private entrepreneurs), nonstate legal (private protection companies), and private illegal (the organized criminal or "bandit" groups). These three should be seen as ideal types; the boundaries between them are blurred in real life. Despite the differences in their legal status, violent entrepreneurial agencies perform similar functions and display similar patterns of action on the economic market. Their common practice derives from the specificity of their major resource: organized force.

The main function of violence-managing agencies within the emerging markets is "enforcement partnership" (*silovoe partnerstvo*)—a term used by one of my informants to describe the practice of his criminal group and that conveniently lends itself as an analytical category.[1] Enforcement partnership is the skillful, profit-motivated employment of actual or potential force, which enables the maintenance of certain institutional conditions necessary for business activities, such as security, contract enforcement, dispute settlement, and transaction insurance.

To reiterate, "violent entrepreneurship" is a conscious practice of violence-managing agencies; "enforcement partnership" is their function within the broader institutional context of emerging markets. The structural outcome of their activity is the covert fragmentation of the state's monopoly on violence, taxation, and rule enforcement. Thus the paradox of postcommunist Russia is that the state does not have unconditional dominance in those very areas that constitute it: protection, taxation, and enforcement. The major questions that drive this chapter, then, are how did this condition come about and what are the reasons for its persistence?

Enforcement Partnership

In Russia, enforcement partnership in the 1990s grew out of the regularized protection racket of the late 1980s, which in turn goes back to the practice of extortion in the Soviet-era shadow economy (black market). Nonetheless, the protection racket should be analytically distinguished from mere extortion: the latter lacks regularity, reference to a broader organization in the name of which the money is collected, and the claim to

---

1. In this study, I rely on data obtained from the following sources: recent journalistic publications and books; interviews with experts, businessmen, representatives of criminal groups, heads of private protection companies, and employees of the state police organs (nineteen in-depth interviews); and personal observations.

offer real or imaginary services in return. The surfacing of extortion and its conversion into regular observable patterns of protection occurred in 1987–88 as the cooperative movement, the first effect of the economic liberalization begun under Mikhail Gorbachev, gained momentum (Dmitriev and Kleimenov 1995, 115–21). Official statistics registered a 30 percent increase in racketeering offenses between 1987 and 1988. The scale of the phenomenon in question was no doubt much wider than its reflection in statistical accounts; according to expert estimates, only one victim in four appealed to police organs, the police reacted only in 80 percent of cases, criminal charges were pressed against every sixth racketeer only, and only in every eleventh case was a sentence served in prison. Moreover, the prison term for this kind of offense was a rather lenient maximum of three years (Diakov and Dolgova 1989, 98).

On the one hand, racketeer groups by their very methods created a dangerous business environment and proceeded to extract payments from economic subjects in exchange for reducing the danger they faced. As a matter of fact, any wielder of force can offer protection only insofar as it itself is capable of creating dangers. Any protection, therefore, inevitably contains at least some elements of racket. On the other hand, there was a range of factors that generated independent demand for a variety of enforcement services. Insufficient business experience and the propensity on the part of some business owners for dishonest conduct increased business risk and lowered the level of trust (Radaev 1998, 134–58). The resulting disputes and tensions could not be resolved by official institutions due to the poor definition of property rights, the inefficiency of state courts of justice (*gosarbitrazh*), and their incapacity to enforce decisions (Varese 1996, 97).

Having accumulated considerable force (physical as well as firepower) and perfected intimidation methods, multiple criminal groups, composed mainly of former athletes, arose to be the best private enforcers and mediators within disorganized and unpredictable markets, bringing at least some degree of order to them. Private protection and enforcement became the major engagement and source of regular revenue for criminal groups during the period of market reforms in Russia.

It would be misleading, however, to associate these groups with traditional forms of crime such as illicit trade (in drugs or arms, for instance) or theft, although these new *bandity* (bandits), as they were called, would readily provide protection to illicit dealers, just as they did for legal businesses. The new form of criminal business, protection, should therefore be distinguished from Soviet-era organized crime inasmuch as the market for private protection and enforcement can be distinguished from the market for stolen or illicit goods.[2] The old Soviet criminal underworld, formed in the severe conditions of the Soviet penal system and constrained by an elaborate set of mores, found itself challenged by a new generation of youth whose cohesion and mores were molded in gyms and sport clubs and who refused to recognize any authority apart from force. The old Soviet culture of *vory* (thieves) was a product of the strong repressive state (Chalidze 1977; Serio and Radzinkin 1995; Varese 1999). *Bandity,* on the other hand, appeared as an unexpected first fruit of liberalization and a symptom of state weakness. Since *vory* as well were compelled to adapt to the new economic conditions, they adopted new entrepreneurial values, so that the traditional criminal subculture disappeared (Volkov 1999, 744–45).

In the contemporary Russian business lexicon the functions of enforcement partnership are referred to by the modest phrase "to solve questions" (*reshat' voprosy*). What does this mean? The first racketeer groups were engaged mainly in physical protection from other such groups and in debt recovery. As private entrepreneurship developed and the number of transactions increased, the functions of enforcement partners diversified. They actively participated in business talks, giving informal guarantees of transactions and demanding the same from other enforcement partners involved in the deal. These tasks were performed either by organized criminal groups or by state police and security employees acting on an informal basis. Expert and interview sources indicate that even today in Russia the majority of high-value business agreements can be concluded only with the participation and mutual guarantees of enforcement partners. Apart from security, risk control, debt recovery, and dispute settlement, enforcement partners also came to mediate relations between private business and the state bureaucracy, helping to obtain permissions and licenses, registrations, and tax exemptions, as well as using state organs (police, fire inspection, sanitary control services, and the like) to close down their clients' competitors.

The evolution of patterns of enforcement partnership is described by my informants in three terms: "to get" (*poluchat'*), "to control" (*kontrolirovat'*), and "to hold a share" (*byt' v dole*). A brigade of racketeers "gets" (the tribute in cash) from a business in return for protection from other such brigades. A criminal group "controls" a business enterprise when, in addition to physical protection, it introduces into the enterprise its own bookkeeper or regular auditor who supplies information about

---

2. The argument for treating the market for private protection separately from the market for any other conventional or illicit goods was advanced in Gambetta (1996).

business transactions and their value, while the group supervises and secures major contracts and transactions for a fixed share of the profits. At this stage the group can be said to turn from racketeering to enforcement partnership. When a group of violent entrepreneurs that "solves questions" for a given business enterprise invests its own money into this enterprise and introduces its representative onto the board of directors, it becomes a "shareholder" and increases its share of the profits. Whereas at an earlier stage, enforcement partners preferred to achieve one-time big gains through active intimidation and violence, the increasing competition between them and their aspiration to control business produced incentives for creating a more favorable environment for sustained relations with clients in order to achieve longer-term gains.

The institution of enforcement partnership rests on the power of deterrence—the capacity to use force and cause physical damage to those who inflict financial or other losses on the business that the criminal group claims to protect. Thus the value of force is determined in proportion to the value of the potential damage—financial, material, or otherwise—that may be caused in the absence of protection. But later, if and when enforcement partners get involved in business transactions on a permanent basis and, consequently, turn from episodic damage and risk control to a broader set of tasks of securing and expanding the field of business activity of a given firm, it is the business skills involving, as it were, the nonviolent use of force that become the source of value rather than force as such. No fixed price list for enforcement partners' services has ever existed—the price has varied depending on the evaluation of risks, the income of the client firm, the duration and nature of its relations with the enforcement partner, and the latter's reputation. In retail trade and similar kinds of small business, simple protection was normally "offered" at the initial rate of $300 to $500 per month and then increased depending on the economic performance of the business. The average price of "question solving" or the full package of security and enforcement services, more relevant to larger-scale business activity, was established at a level of from 20 to 30 percent of the profit of the client enterprise. When the group holds a share, it claims up to 50 percent of the profit. The price of debt recovery stabilized at the level of 50 percent of the sum of the debt (Konstantinov 1997, 175).

Of course, violent entrepreneurs do not think in terms of the institutional functions that they perform, although generally they have a very positive image of themselves as people who exercise justice and help to maintain order as they understand these terms. These people think primarily in terms of material benefits. But in pursuit of these benefits they perform the function of enforcement partnership, reproducing the institutional structure that enables the development (although not necessarily the most efficient development) of certain segments of the private economy, which, in turn, feed the violent entrepreneurs.

The Organized Criminal Group

What is usually referred to by the Russian police as the "organized criminal group" (*organizovannaya prestupnaya gruppirovka*) can now be seen as an illegal violence-managing agency. How did these small groups initially form in Russia? Commonplace assertions about the territorial or ethnic base of such groups should be treated with caution. One should not infer that the criminal group is tied to the name-giving territory (e.g., *Solntsevskaya gruppirovka,* from Solntsevo, a Moscow suburb) or that it recruits its members on a strictly ethnic basis (e.g., from among the Chechens), although it is generally true that the name of the group refers to a territory or the type of ties that enabled initial trust between members and established their common identity. In St. Petersburg the first violence-managing agencies, called "brigades" (*brigady*), grew out of two types of institutional ties: nonresident students' communes (*zemliachestva*) and sports schools. The influential *Tambovskaya* group was formed in the late 1980s by several students from the town of Tambov who came to receive higher education in Leningrad institutes (including the Institute of Physical Culture). Many such nonresident communes from other cities (such as Murmansk, Vorkuta, Perm', and Kazan') became centers of gravity for other former athletes or violent young people willing to earn their living through the use of force. Thus emerged *Murmanskie, Vorkutinskie, Permskie, Kazanskie,* and similar such groups. Groups formed by Leningrad residents recruited local athletes (mainly boxers, weightlifters, wrestlers, and the like) whose primary cohesion and trust had formed over the course their joint sports careers. Unlike the migrant brigades that used topographical labels, the names of the local groups derived either from the kind of sport (e.g., *Bortsovskaya brigada,* the wrestlers' brigade) or from the name of the leader—as with the *Malyshevskaya* (from A. Malyshev), *Kudriashevskaya* (from P. Kudriashev), or *Komarovskaya* (from A. Komarov) groups.

Many groups gradually lost their original connection with some obscure suburb, sports club, ethnicity, or founding leader, however. The meaning of the criminal group's name thus came to lie in its practical usage. In the practice of violent entrepreneurship all such names are used as trademarks.

The license to use the trademark in practice means the right to introduce oneself as "working with" such-and-such criminal group. Such a license is supplied to a brigade or an individual member by the *avtoritet*, the leader of the group, normally after the candidates have been tested in action. For example, a certain Andrei F., for the murder of the managing director of St. Petersburg's northern airport, *Rzhevka*, received $500 cash and the right to introduce himself as *Murmanskii* (i.e., belonging to the *Murmanskaya* criminal group; *Operativnoe prikrytie* 1997, 10). The amount of cash he received may seem surprisingly low, but what really mattered in this particular case was the acquisition by the young bandit of the right to exploit the *Murmanskii* trademark.

The name of the group has a specific function in the practice of violent entrepreneurship: it guarantees the "quality" of protection and enforcement services and refers to the particular kind of reputation, built from the known precedents of successful application of violence and "question-solving." Because the functional demand for the institution of enforcement partners derives from high entrepreneurial risks, the media stories about "brutal" and "omnipotent" bandit groups only help to sustain high-risk expectations and support the reputations of such groups.

Before signing formal business contracts, companies acquire information about each other's enforcement partners ("With whom do you work?") and set a meeting (*strelka*) between enforcement partners. Besides that, each of the participating sides would check whether the others really belong to the group they claim to represent and seek additional information about the real power (reputation as well as actual firepower) of that group. The deal, with all its formal juridical and business attributes, will be signed only after the enforcement partners have recognized each other and given mutual guarantees. Likewise, a *strelka* will be set immediately if one of the sides fails or refuses to fulfill its obligations. The outcome may be either a peaceful solution as to how the damage will be repaired or a shootout (*razborka*). But in the long term, *razborka* may be a more costly and less efficient solution, especially if it leads to protracted warfare that causes severe damage—primarily to the business firms controlled by the warring opponents.

Elimination Contests

In the early 1990s, the number of criminal groups operating in Russia grew dramatically. According to official statistics, their number rose from 50 in

1988, to 952 in 1991, to 5,691 in 1993 (Gilinsky 1996, 77). Criminal
groups, many of whom were initially formed in and named after particular
territories (such as the Moscow suburbs Balashikha, Solntsevo, Podol'sk,
Koptevo, and Noginsk) or city districts (such as the *Tsentral'naya* and
Uralmashevskaya groups in Ekaterinburg), expanded rapidly to gain control of other territories, especially in large cities. Moscow suburban groups,
as well as groups from the Siberian industrial towns of Kurgan and No-
vokuznetsk, moved into Moscow to seize opportunities in Russia's largest
business area. The city of Kazan, notorious for its youth gang wars of the
late 1980s, also exported its criminal groups to Moscow and St. Petersburg. Some groups failed to establish permanent domains in large cities.
The *Kazanskie,* for instance, failed to find a niche in Moscow but succeeded in St. Petersburg. The *Permskie* (from the city of Perm in the Urals),
on the contrary, were unsuccessful in their persistent attempts to obtain a
share of the market in St. Petersburg. Apart from these new violent groups
of *bandity,* guided in their activities by sheer economic rationality, there
operated, especially in Moscow, the Urals, and the Far East, a large number of *vory v zakone* (thieves-in-law, or thieves professing the code) who
sought to use the authority of traditional criminal values and the power of
the old prison networks to secure their share and prevent the emergence
or expansion of new bandit groups. Ethnic criminal groups, especially
those from Azerbaijan, Chechnya, and Georgia, were also active in most
major cities. Their diasporas were traditionally strong in Moscow: Georgians had the highest ethnic representation in the ranks of *vory v zakone,*
whereas Chechens relied more on their own clan structures.

Thus, instead of a well-coordinated and uniform criminal system
wherein each subunit has its own clearly circumscribed territorial or business domain, Russia developed a rather heterogeneous, mosaic-like, and
diffuse realm where territories and businesses were divided in many different ways between criminal groups of different territorial, ethnic, institutional, and historical origin. Although groups often claimed control over
certain territories, the subjects of their divisions, rivalry, and cooperation
were opportunities rather than territories or sectors of the economy as
such. So there was no single feature common to all criminal groups except
for the means available to them—that is, organized force. Explanations of
the activity of criminal groups, therefore, should be sought not in the
groups themselves, their legal status, or the people that compose them, but
in their practice, determined by the opportunities opened by the emerging
market and the failing state.

The many groups that strove to seize new opportunities quickly got engaged in open as well as covert struggle with one another. However broad, the opportunities were limited, and those criminal groups that did not grow stronger became weaker and were gradually either eliminated or subsumed by more powerful rivals. The elimination contest of 1992–95 periodically erupted into massive shootouts, such as the one between The *Balashikhinskaya* and *Podol'skaya* groups in Moscow in May 1992 (Modestov 1996, 149–60). According to official statistics, 144 armed showdowns took place in Russia in 1991, and 305 were documented in 1992 (Diakov and Dolgova 1993, 25). But because strong leadership is the major factor in a criminal group's consolidation and success, carefully staged assassinations of leaders rather than gang wars became the routine method of violent competition. Of the original founders of criminal groups, only a few survived. These years were marked by numerous wars, such as between Slavic and Caucasian groups in Moscow, The *Uralmashevskaya* and *Tsentral'naya* groups in Ekaterinburg, and local and migrant groups in St. Petersburg and other cities. These contests were about opportunities, norms, and leadership. Whatever their causes and stakes, these violent conflicts steadily contributed to one general outcome: the emergence of a smaller number of larger groups, better organized and firmly integrated into the structures of the market economy.

In an interview with *Itogi,* a major weekly magazine, at the end of 1998, one Moscow-based criminal boss made the following claim: "Over the last two years we [criminal groups] have been the biggest investors in the Russian economy. One cannot imagine the country's economy without our investments" (Ryklin 1998, 16). Although exact figures for investments of this kind are unlikely ever to be established, such claims should not be discarded. As the wielders of force become owners of capital and especially in those cases where they take part in management, their ability to control their domains becomes conditioned on the logic and rules of economic action. To put this dialectic in a concise form, the more criminal groups strove to control the emerging markets, the more the markets controlled and transformed these groups. The acknowledgment by the wielders of force of the rules of economics—from the simple principle that violence, in the long term, is costly, to a more complex dependence on functionally divided management structures and the impersonal forces of the market—transforms the criminal group into a legal business enterprise. The *Tambovskaya* group, now strongest in St. Petersburg and other parts of northwestern Russia, clearly displays this transformation pattern. In 1992–95, the group went through a series of ruthless wars with the *Kazanskaya* and other groups in St. Petersburg, as well as through a bloody internal strug-

gle over leadership. It suffered heavy losses; its founder and leader, V. Ku-
marin, survived an attempt on his life but was severely wounded in June
1995. But in the end the group emerged stronger, concluded an informal
pact with the city authorities, and invested in the region's oil industry and
timber trade. The *Tambovskaya* now own the largest share of the Petersburg Fuel Company, one of the largest operators in the St. Petersburg and
northwestern oil and petrol market (*Obshchaya gazeta* 1998). Thus Ku-
marin, who has now adopted his mother's maiden surname, stated in a
recent interview, "In June 1998 I became vice-president of the biggest
holding—Petersburg Fuel Company. We have lots of problems to solve: we
have to draw up a budget and create a unified accounting office and consolidated holding management. Big changes have happened in my life"
(Konstantinov 1999, 390).

The Legalization of Private Protection

In 1992–95, rapid privatization and the rise of private financial institutions
brought new segments of the economy, including medium-sized and large
enterprises, into the sphere of free-market relations (Blasi et al., 1997). The
legal and institutional problems mentioned earlier were still far from being
resolved by the state powers, and the level of risk for businesses remained
very high. According to rough estimates, in the beginning of 1994 the
amount of unpaid business credits in Russia equaled 3.6 trillion rubles
($1.64 billion) and reached 8 trillion rubles ($1.75 billion) in 1995.[3]
Criminal groups, it seemed, were moving toward attaining full control over
the privatized economy. However, precisely at this stage, criminal syndicates encountered a powerful rival in the form of private protection and security agencies set up by former police and security employees.

A massive exodus of state security employees occurred in the wake of a
series of reforms of the KGB state security service in 1992–93. Several former KGB directorates were transformed into separate agencies under federal or direct presidential jurisdiction. Thus the formerly united organization was split into five separate agencies: the External Intelligence Service
(SVR), the Federal Agency for Government Communications and Information (FAPSI), the Federal Counterintelligence Service (FSK), the Chief
Guard Directorate (including the Presidential Security Service), and the

---

3. These figures were presented at a seminar of the chiefs of security services of Russian
banks in January 1995 and were reported in *Bdi* (1995).

Border Guard Service. In 1995, the FSK was renamed the Federal Security Service, or FSB (Korovin 1998, 80–86). Under a new federal law of August 1995, all of these agencies, plus the Interior Ministry (MVD), the Tax Police, and the Federal Customs Service, were authorized to carry out detective and operative work and to keep their own paramilitary units. In comparison with the Soviet period, the number of agencies entitled to maintain their own forces grew from three to seven. By mid-1995, Russia had fourteen state internal intelligence, security, and law enforcement agencies (Waller and Yasmann 1997, 198).

The restructuring of state security was accompanied by a reduction in its personnel. Negative public attitudes created moral pressure that devalued the status of this profession, while inflation and the shrinking of the state budget devalued wages. All these factors produced strong incentives on the part of security officers to look for alternative employment. More than twenty thousand officers left or were discharged from government service between September 1991 and June 1992. Attempts by the central government to use special antiterrorist security units as pawns in the internal political struggles of August 1991 and October 1993 caused frustration among the officers and led many to resign from service and find new employment. In 1992, President Boris Yeltsin ordered that the 137,000-strong central apparatus of the former KGB be reduced to 75,000 (a 46 percent reduction) in the process of restructuring. Although a substantial proportion of the former KGB staff was transferred in 1992–93 to newly established bodies (such as the SVR and FAPSI) and to regional FSB directorates, 11,000 officers had to leave state security employment for good (*Izvestiya* 1994a).

The federal law "On Private Detective and Protection Activity," adopted on March 22, 1992, provided an alternative employment solution for former state security employees. Previously, they had been engaged in the business of private protection on an informal basis. Now they were lawfully entitled to protect the legal rights and interests of their clients on a commercial basis. The law permitted private agencies to engage in a broad range of activities: to exercise physical protection for citizens and property, engage in security consulting, collect data for lawsuits, conduct market research, collect information about unreliable business partners, protect commercial secrets and trademarks, search for people who had disappeared, recover lost property, and conduct background investigations of potential employees of client companies. By 1998, private security agencies had absorbed nearly fifty thousand former officers of the state security and law enforcement organs (*Biznes i bezopasnost' v Rossii* 1999, 18–21).

Private Security Agencies

The 1992 law defined the licensing procedures for three types of security agencies and their personnel: private detective agencies (PDAs), private (company) security services (PSSs), and private protection companies (PPCs). PDAs normally execute narrow and specific tasks requested chiefly by private individuals with regard to their private matters. Consequently, autonomous detective agencies are few (there are just over a hundred for the whole country) and their services expensive. They will not concern us here.

All enterprises, irrespective of their size and form of ownership, were permitted to establish a special security subdivision, or PSS (in Russian, *chastnaya sluzhba bezopasnosti*). PSSs were set up in large numbers by private and state enterprises and financial institutions for physical and economic protection and for information-gathering and analysis. Security services of large banks and companies, especially those entrusted to deal with state financial assets or strategic resources, were organized and filled by former high-ranking state security officers. To give just a few examples, Vladimir Zaitsev, one of the former commanders of the special Alpha unit of the KGB, became the head of security at Stolichnyi Bank; Mikhail Gorbunov, who used to serve in the Chief Directorate of Intelligence Service (GRU) of the Soviet Army, continued as head of security at Inkombank; and the former deputy chief of the KGB, Filip Bobkov, headed the corporate security service of the Most financial group (Kryshtanovskaya 1995, 8). The thirteen-thousand-strong PSS of Gazprom, the natural-gas monopoly, is headed by the former KGB colonel Viktor Marushchenko and consists of forty-one subdivisions at the company's installations across the country ("Sluzhba bezopasnosti" 1997, 6). The majority of PSSs, however, are much smaller. Many were created to secure a one-time deal or simply to legalize armed bodyguards for the company's boss, and they exist today mainly on paper.

Originally, even before the adoption of the law on private protection, many future PPCs (in Russian, *chastnye okhrannye predpriyatiya*) started as private guards or informal security services for specific business projects. For example, a St. Petersburg PPC, Severnaya Pal'mira, headed by the former colonel of military counterintelligence E. Kostin, was initially set up as a security service for the city construction materials market, Muraveinik. Later, it became an independent supplier of security to a number of construction companies, such as Business Link Development and Com & Com, and to the official Peugeot dealer in Petersburg, Auto-France (Kostin

1998, 36). This case represents a typical pattern of evolution for a PPC, from being tied to particular clients to becoming an autonomous supplier of services on the market.

The corporate identity of employees of state security ministries has been sustained in the private security sphere. Many successful PPCs were founded by tightly knit communities of former officers of special-purpose units who sought to convert their skills and reputation into a marketable asset. Thus two former commanders of the KGB special antiterrorist unit Alpha, I. Orekhov and M. Golovatov, left the unit to set up a family of protection companies whose names openly point to the original affiliations of its staff: Alpha-A, Alpha-B, Alpha-7, and Alpha-Tverd' ("Vse problemy" 1998, 28).

Another KGB antiterrorist unit, Vympel, ceased to exist in 1993, as its duties were transferred to the jurisdiction of the MVD. Of the 350 Vympel officers employed at the time of its dissolution, only 5 decided to continue under MVD, 215 found new employment in the FSB and other state security organs, and 135 left to work in the sphere of private security (*Izvestiya* 1994b). Many of them were employed by the PPC Argus, set up by one of the former senior commanders of Vympel, Yu. Levitsky. Argus is now one of the largest security operators in the Moscow region. St. Petersburg's largest PPC, Zashchita, was set up by former employees of a special unit of the MVD and is known to actively recruit former officers of the Regional Anti-Organized Crime Directorate. A group of former Soviet Army paratroopers who shared combat experience in Afghanistan and in local conflicts were involved in setting up Aleks-Zapad, another large private security operator in northwestern Russia. In an interview with me, Boris Markarov, the chief of Aleks-Zapad, acknowledged his recruitment focus on former military officials, admitting that he personally trusts "the army caste much stronger than the militia or the KGB." Thus, most large PPCs rely on a preexisting corporate identity and resemble privatized segments of state defense and security ministries. The chiefs of PPCs also openly admit what they call "mutually beneficial cooperation" with state organs, meaning an exchange of operative information for money or equipment.

Soon after the adoption of the law on private security the new business sector began to expand at unprecedented rates, especially in Moscow and St. Petersburg. By the end of 1998, the number of private security agencies had reached 10,804, including 5,650 PPCs and 4,720 PSSs; the number of licensed security personnel had reached 165,600 (the total number of employees of such firms exceeds 850,000). The city of Moscow had a

total of 3,125 security agencies, and St. Petersburg 816, which amounted
to 29 and 7.6 percent of the total number of security firms in Russia, respectively. Between 1993 and 1996 the growth was especially dramatic: the
number of private security agencies almost doubled, reaching nearly 8,000.
After 1996 the growth continued, but the rate slowed as the possibilities
for extensive growth were exhausted (see Table 4.1 and Figure 4.1).

Legal versus Criminal Protection

The demand for private enforcers increasingly came from enterprise directors, who tended to avoid dealing with the official system of justice out of
fear that they would lose their personal influence if they relied on the impersonal legal institutions of the state (Hendley 1997, 228–51). Understandably, the large, established PPCs operate in those sectors that manage
to survive and are capable of generating profits, such as the oil and petrol
industries, banking, communications, high technology, and export-oriented
production, including the majority of foreign companies. Among the
clients of the PPC holding group Al'ternativa-M, for instance, are the large
chemical consortium Rosagrokhim and the Gromov aerospace research and
test center (*Mir bezopasnosti* 1997b, 10). In St. Petersburg, the PPC Staf,
headed by former KGB major M. Timofeev, started by collecting debts
from the clients of the telephone company Peterstar. Then it became the
security and enforcement partner of PTS, the major state-owned telephone
network, as well as of the main cellular phone operators in the northwestern region, Delta Telecom and GSM. As a result, Staf, which, as its chief
admitted, maintains close relations with the FSB, now supervises a vast
regional communications network (Timofeev 1998, 54–55).

With the entry of KGB and MVD cadres to the market as private agents,
the age of *krysha* (roofs) came into full being. *Krysha* is a key term in the
contemporary Russian business lexicon. It refers to an enforcement partner, criminal or legal, and signifies a complex of services provided by the
latter to its clients in order to protect them physically and minimize their
business risks. Unlike some other business terms that have gained currency
in recent years, *krysha* did not belong originally to criminal jargon but came
from the professional vocabulary of the intelligence service, where it
signified the official cover—diplomatic, journalistic, or other—of a spy.

Enforcement partnership (*krysha*) needs to be distinguished from mere
physical protection. The physical protection and security provided by
PPCs through their supplying of private guards and security equipment

Table 4.1
The Development of Private Security Businesses in Russia, 1992–98

	1992	1993	1994	1995	1996	1997	1998
Total number of agencies	0	4,540	6,605	7,987	9,863	10,487	10,804
Private protection companies	0	1,237	1,586	3,247	4,434	4,705	5,650
Private security agencies	0	2,356	2,931	4,591	5,247	4,973	4,720
Agencies closed down by authorities			73	640	622	978	1,364

Sources: *Mir bezopasnosti* 1997a, 49; *Biznes i bezopasnost' v Rossii* 1999.

on a contractual basis is not their primary mission. The actual practice of a successful PPC first of all includes the acquisition and analysis of information about the prospective business partners of its clients, the supervision of business transactions, and, most important, the ability to engage in informal negotiations with other enterprises and their enforcement

Figure 4.1
The Development of Private Security Businesses in Russia, 1992–98

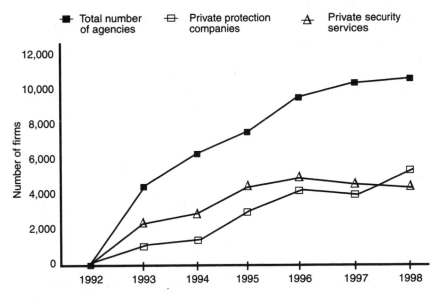

Source: Table 4.1.

partners in case of a breach of contract or failure to return debt. It is this informal practice of negotiation between enforcement partners, leading to the solution of the problem and thus allowing for the business to continue, that is most valued in business circles and that creates the reputation of the violence-managing agency, be it a PPC or a criminal group. Thus enforcement partnership is not just protection of individual clients but an activity and a function that relates to the institutional structure of the economy as a whole.

In conducting their business, private protection agencies have to steer between the increasingly tight legal regulations of the state authorities and the actual practice of private enforcement, which rests on informal dealings and the frequent use of semicriminal methods. This practice derives from the highly informal character of business relations in Russia and the heavy presence of criminal groups. Those criminal groups, too, strove to use the law on private protection to their advantage, creating their own PPCs in order to obtain licenses to carry concealed weapons and legalize their protection services. Thus in St. Petersburg, one of the oldest and most prominent protection companies, Scorpion, was set up and headed by A. Efimov (whose nickname is Efim), one of the leaders of the *Tambovskaya* criminal group, and used to actively draw on police officers to perform its *krysha* functions. Scorpion was closed down by the authorities at the end of 1996; its director managed to escape but was tracked down in Ukraine and arrested a year later (Leonov 1997, 8–9).

Yet on the whole, despite many cases in which PPCs have been involved in criminal affairs, the overall effect of their activity was more positive than negative. Although they are not manifestly anticriminal agencies, they nonetheless managed to weaken the economic basis of organized crime and limit its expansion. These effects were achieved by the higher quality and lower prices of services offered by PPCs and by their active interaction with state police organs.

By 1991, pursuing additional income to their devaluing salaries, informal groups of police and state security officers had begun offering private business an alternative solution to protection and enforcement and thus entered into direct competition with criminal groups. Those companies that managed to contract a police or KGB *krysha* no longer needed to fear visits by athletes-turned-gang-members offering their protection. The informal rule that "every businessman has to have a roof," well known to all entrepreneurs operating in the Russian market, was a peculiar way to acknowledge the thus of transaction costs, but it also presupposed multiple options and thus a competition between those who claimed these costs. Although it would require a separate study to assess the impact of private enforcers on economic growth and to establish which option is best for which type of business, it is possible to describe the basic noncriminal options, the logic of choice, and its consequences.

The cheapest solution is to have or make a friend among police officers, in particular in the special anti–organized crime unit. That gives the entrepreneur the opportunity to claim the police as a *krysha* and to ask the friend to help out in case of an attempt by a criminal gang to demand a protection fee. The owner of a small network of pharmacy shops in St. Petersburg whom I interviewed, for example, would be a typical client of such an informal "friendly" police *krysha*. His payment for protection may be occasional provision of free medicines for the police officer's parents (Vadim 1999). This solution pertains mainly to small businesses and gives advantages to those who happen to have the right kind of friends. Its reliability, however, is low, matching its low cost.

The hiring of an acting or retired FSB officer as a "manager" or "law consultant" is another widespread *krysha* arrangement that enables a company to avoid paying protection money to a criminal group. This "law consultant" acts as a kind of multipurpose fixer, shielding the company from criminal and bureaucratic extortion and mediating relations between the private business and state authorities. Interview sources indicate that the hiring (formally, as well as informally) of an FSB officer became a widespread practice in medium-sized companies, especially in Moscow. Such a "lawyer" would normally cost the company an equivalent of $1,000 or more per month. Thus a Moscow-based company producing silicon medical supplies was approached by a criminal group from Kazan, where the company's production site was located. Unwilling to submit to criminal protection, the director urgently had to find an alternative. First, he hired a retired KGB colonel and later an FSB acting officer as his company's *krysha*. Unfortunately, the officer was subsequently killed in Chechnya performing his state service duties. Then the company signed a contract with a PPC (Vladimir 1999).

Normally, a client company and a PPC sign a formal contract in which the range of services and the price are indicated. If the company requires armed guards, the price would be calculated on the basis of the standard $4–$6 dollars per guard per hour; the package could go up to $2,000 per month for an alarm system including a hot-line connection with a fast-reaction team normally kept by the PPC. To obtain regular information about another company costs $100–$300 per month (Kaledina and

Novikova 1999, 28). Another form of contract includes a monthly retainer fee of $250 or higher, depending on the size and nature of the business, paid to a PPC whose help is requested only in the event that a problem arises. If the problem is serious enough, such as the need to recover a debt or to resolve a dispute, especially if the adversary is a criminal group, the deal is likely to be negotiated on a noncontractual basis and the fee, normally quite high, would be adjusted to the value of the disputed property, the level of risk, and the amount of operative work. But not all PPCs provide such services. An alternative protection strategy, then, is to assist the client in engaging the state organs of justice to resolve the problem in a legal manner. In this case the role of the PPC is to ensure efficient treatment of its client by the state system of justice and to help enforce the state decision.

As my interview sources indicate, the contractual nature of the relationship, the higher degree of predictability of behavior, and the higher quality of services normally make the PPC a more competitive security solution than the criminal group. Unlike criminal groups, PPCs normally do not interfere in the business of their clients, but they also would not provide loans. Experts have estimated that clients of criminal groups are forced to relinquish up to 30 percent of their profits, and the cost of debt recovery is normally 50 percent of the debt's value (Konstantinov 1997, 175). The price of security and enforcement charged by noncriminal PPCs, on the other hand, is negotiable and varies depending on the size and the nature of the client's business. But it takes the form of a fixed regular payment rather than a tax on profits The charge for debt recovery typically varies between 15 and 40 percent of the sum of the debt (*Ekspert* 1996, 20).

Managers of large PPCs claim to provide better-quality services due to the professional experience of their personnel. While maintaining formidable firepower, large PPCs rely on the informational and analytic methods acquired by their management during their career(s) in state service. The major emphasis is said to lie not on direct physical protection or intimidation but on the preventive neutralization of potential conflicts and threats. The vice chairman of the security service of the Association of Russian Banks, A. Krylov, thus described the methods of legal enforcement partners: "To recover the debt one does not need recourse to violent means—it is sufficient just to demonstrate that you have information that compromises the debtor and the channels for its dissemination" (*Ekspert* 1996, 20). In an interview with me, the director of Aleks North-West claimed to have a database on all business enterprises in the region, which allowed the company to assess the reliability of its clients' potential partners before entering into business relationships.

Outcomes

Anyone looking back at the chaotic forces unleashed by the rapid collapse of the Soviet order and their violent struggle in the early 1990s, should not overlook the crucial structural outcome: the formation of a set of informal institutions shaping emerging markets. Organized force became a major market resource convertible into profits—irrespective of the origin and legal status of the group that managed this resource. Thus Russia witnessed the rapid proliferation of various types of armed formations, such as criminal groups, private guards, and paramilitary units attached to fragmented state security and police organs. Once the state failed to control the process of institution-building, it also lost the monopoly on force and the fiscal monopoly that were vital to its very existence.

Interesting contrasts as well as parallels may be noted in the African case. The weakening or even collapse of states in Africa has opened a market for private security services there. Some authors go so far as to identify the "criminalization of the state" as a central trend (Bayart, Ellis, and Hibou 1998; Chabal and Daloz 1998). What is at issue, however, is the complicity of ranking state officials in such illicit rackets as drug smuggling or the notorious Nigerian "419" schemes (so-called after Article 419 of the Nigerian criminal code, which proscribes the embezzlement of state funds), whereby gullible foreigners are invited to serve as partners in the export of purloined resources from the Nigerian National Petroleum Corporation. In South Africa, visitors are struck by the ubiquity in major cities, especially Johannesburg, of brightly colored cars advertising private security services assuring "instant armed response." However, in contrast to such firms in Russia, the services offered in South Africa are primarily protection of individual private property (vehicles, homes) in the face of the very high crime levels that are overwhelming the South African police force. As well, the existence of a large pool of personnel, specialized in various security functions and thrown into the private market by the demise of the apartheid order, provides the basis for private military services such as Executive Outcomes, available for rent by embattled regimes in Africa and elsewhere. (Such services are examined in Chapter 5 of this volume.) However, the greater sophistication of the Russian economy and the historic depth of its operations as a command system mean that the permeation of a newly privatized political economy with illicit enforcement and protection operations is far less comprehensive in Russia than in Africa.

In the beginning, Russian criminal groups did not aspire to participate in economic activity. They simply received a fixed amount of tribute, mainly from small and medium-sized companies in the wholesale and retail trade sector. Later they changed tactics, interfering in the management of enterprises under their protection or purchasing shares and introducing their own representatives onto the board of directors. But as some criminal groups managed to attain close control or ownership of economic enterprises, they became constrained by certain rules of economic action and began to adapt to the emerging business culture. In the late 1990s, many criminal groups and their leaders acquired economic assets of their own. This new responsibility compelled them to adopt more rational and risk-adjusted behaviors. Now they are undergoing an evolution toward becoming legal business enterprises playing by the formal rules and engaged in capital investment and charity.

Paradoxically, Russia's 1992 law on private protection can be seen as a successful example of legal development, whereby informal practices (in this case, of the private use of force and coercion) acquire legal status and become subject to state regulation. This was a rare instance in which the adoption of a law reflected an effort to acknowledge, codify, and regulate an already existing practice rather than to create something from above, although one may add that the state was simply incapable of the "from above" strategy. The growth rates of the new, now legal, business of private protection and enforcement testify to the success of this legal initiative and to the fact that it met a huge demand. It also enabled state authorities to achieve at least some degree of account of and control over the private use of force and coercion. The most controversial consequence of the privatization of state security and law enforcement and of the legalization of the business of private protection was its indirect, anticriminal effect, achieved by the growing competition in this domain.

One is only left to wonder at the dialectical nature of the legalization of private protection and enforcement in Russia. On the one hand, it can be seen as a juridical acknowledgment of the de facto fragmentation of the state monopoly on violence and justice. On the other hand, it may have been the first step toward the restoration of public control over the use of force and thus toward the reconstruction of the state.

References

Bayart, Jean-François, Stephen Ellis, and Béatrice Hibou. 1998. *The Criminalization of the State in Africa*. London: James Currey.

Bdi. 1995. No. 2.

Biznes i bezopasnost' v Rossii. 1999. No. 2.

Blasi, Joseph, et al., eds. 1997. *Kremlin Capitalism: Privatizing the Russian Economy.* Ithaca: Cornell University Press.

Chabal, Patrick, and Jean-Pascal Daloz. 1998. *Africa Works: Disorder as Political Instrument.* London: James Currey.

Chalidze, Vladimir. 1977. *Criminal Russia: Essays on Crime in the Soviet Union.* New York: Random House.

Diakov, Sergei, and Azaliya Dolgova, eds. 1989. *Organizovannaya prestupnost'.* Moscow: Yuridicheskaya literatura.

———. 1993. *Organizovannaya prestupnost'-2.* Moscow: Yuridicheskaya literatura.

Dmitriev, Oleg, and Mikhail Kleimenov. 1995. "Reket v Sibiri." *Sotsiologicheskie issledovaniya* 3: 115–21.

Ekspert. 1996. No.2.

Elias, Norbert. 1993. *The Civilizing Process.* Vols. 1–2, *The History of Manners and State Formation and Civilization.* Oxford: Blackwell.

Gambetta, Diego. 1996. *The Sicilian Mafia: The Business of Private Protection.* Cambridge, Mass.: Harvard University Press.

Gilinsky, Yakov. 1996. *Organizovannaya prestupnost' v Rossii: Teoriya i real'nost'.* St. Petersburg: SRAN.

Hendley, Kathryn. 1997. "Legal Development in Post-Soviet Russia." *Post-Soviet Affairs* 3, no. 13: 228–51.

*Izvestiya.*1994a. 2 March.

*Izvestiya.*1994b. 3 March.

Kaledina, Anna, and Tatiana Novikova. 1999. "Detektivnye rasskazy." *Den'gi* 24: 20–26.

Konstantinov, Andrei. 1997. *Banditskii Peterburg.* St. Petersburg: Folio-press.

———. 1999. *Banditskii Peterburg-98.* Moscow: Olma-Press.

Korovin, Vladimir. 1998. *Istoriya otechestvennykh organov bezopasnosti.* Moscow: Norma.

Kostin, Yevgenii. 1998. "Ya ne sebia v drugom Kachestve." *Lichnosti Peterburga. Bezopasnost'* 1: 36–37.

Kryshtanovskaya, Olga. 1995. "Nelegal'nye struktury v Rossii." *Sotsiologicheskie issledovaniya* 8: 92–101.

Lane, Frederic. 1958. "Economic Consequences of Organized Violence." *Journal of Economic History* 18, no. 4 (December): 401–17.

Leonov, Sergei. 1997. "Konets skorpiona—nachalo voiny?" *Operativnoe prikrytie* 1: 8–9.

Markarov, Boris. 1999. Interview with the author. 14 April.

Mir bezopasnosti. 1997a. No. 2.

Mir bezopasnosti. 1997b. No. 9.

Modestov, Nikolai. 1996. *Moskva banditskaya.* Moscow: Tsentrpoligraf.

North, Douglass, and Robert Thomas. 1973. *The Rise of the Western World.* Cambridge: Cambridge University Press.

Obshchaya gazeta. 1998. 20–26 August.

Operativnoe prikrytie. 1997. No. 2.

Radaev, Vadim. 1998. *Formirovanie novykh rossiiskikh rynkov. Transaktsionnye izderzhki, formy controlia i delovaia etika.* Mosocw: Tsentr politicheskikh tekhnologii.

Ryklin, Aleksandr. 1998. "Krysha." *Itogi.* 8 December: 16.

Serio, Joseph, and Viacheslav Radzinkin. 1995. "Thieves Professing the Code: The Traditional Role of *Vory v Zakone* in Russia's Criminal World and Adaptations to a New Social Reality." *Low Intensity Conflict and Law Enforcement* 4, no. 1 (summer): 72–88.

"Sluzhba bezopasnosti RAO 'Gazprom': Sostoyanie i perspektivy razvitiia." 1997. *Biznes i bezopasnost' v Rossii* 2: 6.

Tilly, Charles. 1985. "War Making and State Making as Organized Crime." Pp. 169–91 in *Bringing the State Back In,* ed. P. Evans et al. Cambridge: Cambridge University Press.

———. 1990. *Coercion, Capital, and European States, AD 990–1890.* Oxford: Basil Black-well.

Timofeev, Mikhail. 1998. "Menia raduet, chto staf vospital nostoiashchie kadry." *Lichnosti Peterburga. Bezopasnost'* 1: 54–55.

Vadim (last name withheld). 1999. Interview with the author. 16 January.

Varese, Federico. 1996. *The Emergence of the Russian Mafia: Dispute Settlement and Protection in a New Market Economy.* Ph.D. thesis, Faculty of Social Studies, Oxford University.

———. 1999. "The Society of the Vory-v-zakone, 1930s–1950s." *Cahiers du Monde Russe* 39, no. 4 (October–December): 515–38.

Vladimir (last name withheld). 1999. Interview with the author. 20 February. (Interviewee was the company's director.)

Volkov, Vadim. 1999. "Violent Entrepreneurship in Post-Communist Russia." *Europe-Asia Studies* 51, no. 5: 741–54.

"Vse problemy reshautsia mirno—s pomoshchiu Al'fy." 1998. *Biznes i bezopasnost' v Rossii* 9–10: 28–29.

Waller, Michael, and Victor Yasmann. 1997. "Russia's Great Criminal Revolution: The Role of the Security Services." Pp. 187–200 in *Understanding Organized Crime in Global Perspective: A Reader,* ed. Patrick Ryan and George Rush. London: Sage.

Weber, Max. 1970. "Politics as Vocation." Pp. 77–128 in *From Max Weber: Essays in Sociology,* ed. H. Gerth and C. Wright Mills. London: Routledge.

5

Mafiya Troubles, Warlord Crises

WILLIAM RENO

We have become a mafia state on a world scale. Everyone thinks that political issues could lead to an explosion but crime could as easily blow us asunder.

—Boris Yeltsin, quoted in Stephen Handelman,
Comrade Criminal: Russia's New Mafiya

Robert Kaplan writes of West Africa that the "increasing erosion of nation-states and international borders, and the empowerment of private armies, security firms, and international drug cartels are now most tellingly demonstrated" (Kaplan 1994, 45). Is this collapse of state institutions and their replacement by criminal networks—a "criminalization of the state" in parts of Africa (Bayart, Ellis, and Hibou 1997) and in the former Soviet Union—a sign of private, commercial networks superseding states?

This chapter compares the former Soviet Union and its informal (in the sense of nontaxed), nonregulated commercial organizations (or what Stephen Handelman calls "*mafiya*") to a category of organizations in Africa that makes serious, occasionally successful, bids to supersede state institutions to control people and resources directly—or what some call "warlords."[1] Crucial for this comparison is the observation that, although

---

1. States characterized by warlord politics are associated with weak formal institutions and armed groups that pursue military action without efforts to build local support or advance a particular political agenda and that devote significant portions of their organizational efforts to commerce. Such states in Africa include Angola, Burundi, Chad, Congo-Brazzaville, Congo-Kinshasa, Djibouti, Guinea-Bissau, Rwanda, Sierra Leone, the Sudan, and Uganda.

many of these groups in Africa collaborate with state officials, most demonstrate little interest in holding territory or administering populations. They operate as syndicates in the sense of pursuing the private interests of members and are not organized specifically to provide public goods from which individuals cannot be excluded. This appears to lead in the direction that Handelman sees in Russia: "The failure—often deliberate—of the state to impose its authority left mobsters free to sabotage what had been the most inspiring promise of the second Russian revolution: to create a new society based on the rule of law" (Handelman 1995, 25).

Some enterprising political and commercial actors in Russia and parts of the former Soviet Union do resemble their African counterparts. Like informal market syndicates in Africa, Russian *mafiya* undermine the capacity of state institutions to collect revenue and weaken state authority to regulate economic transactions. This chapter demonstrates, however, that specific aspects of state organization in Russia mitigate the influence of *mafiya* organizations in undermining Russia's economy and politics. A key difference lies in the relative capacity of Russian state agencies to predominate in the exercise of violence in comparison with their African counterparts in warlord-dominant states. In parts of Africa, the coercive capacities of nonstate groups exceed those of the state and impose a distinctive relationship among markets, power, and people. They use this superior capability to displace state agents and rules. Russia, on the other hand, possesses state institutions that, though marked by considerable arbitrary and ad hoc exercise of power by officials and often penetrated by criminal organizations, more closely approximate the condition wherein holding an office "is considered an acceptance of a specific duty of fealty to the purpose of the office" (Weber 1978, II, 959). In other words, Russia possesses to a greater degree than Africa institutions that adhere to Max Weber's definition: organizations that pursue an interest greater than the sum of the private interests of their staffs.

Overall, the relationship of Russian state power to *mafiya* organizations permits greater heterogeneity of outcomes compared with those that ensue in Africa. In some instances, local and regional administrators in Russia have found new ways to collect revenue and assert authority even while *mafiya* influence dominates other areas and economic sectors. Several regions of the former Soviet Union, and of Russia itself, however, more closely approximate African warlord conditions. As I discuss in this chapter, this difference is explained by a particular relationship of state power to violence and individuals' pursuits of private interests, a combination that creates a distinctive calculus of entrepreneurial opportunity.

To illustrate these different outcomes, I first provide a model for the relationship between formal state institutions and private syndicates. I use the term "shadow state" to describe relations between these two types of organizations in Africa—a notion that I have explored in greater detail elsewhere (Reno 1995). In setting out the model of the shadow state in Africa, I do not mean to imply that all African polities uniformly fit this concept. It certainly does not apply to South Africa or to the Arab tier of states to the north. It most closely describes West African states such as Liberia, Togo, Sierra Leone, and Nigeria (at least when it has been under military rule), and notoriously derelict countries such as the two Congos and the Central African Republic. States such as Senegal, Mali, Ghana, or Tanzania may exhibit some elements of the model without resembling it in all aspects of rule. My discussion of shadow states explains how private syndicates, especially those counting state officials among their members, promote the collapse of state institutions and state-sponsored order.

Next I ask whether Russia's *mafiya* are elements of a shadow state in this sense and thus agents of state collapse. I address this question by identifying similarities in the organizational logic of Russian *mafiya* and of the private syndicates that challenge state power in Africa. I also explore evidence that points to differences in the relationship between state and private power in Russia. I then deduce from this comparison why Russia and its *mafiya* only partially satisfy the conditions observed in shadow states and state collapse in Africa. In contrast to the situation in many African states, in Russia the *mafiya* are best understood as a manifestation of state weakness, not of state collapse.

Shadow States in Theory

The "shadow state" is a concept that was created to explain the relationship between corruption and politics in Africa. Shadow states are the products of personal rule, usually constructed behind the facade of formal state sovereignty. The governments of other countries recognize shadow states if it serves their interests. Robert Jackson (1990) observed that superpower support for the formal sovereignty of states that have very weak internal administrations relieves rulers of the need to strengthen institutions to protect productive members of society from whom those states could in turn extract income. Instead, rulers adopt a shorter strategic horizon, gathering critical resources either from superpower patrons or from capital holders willing to invest in relatively secure enclaves in zones of disorder.

These resources, acquired independently of the efforts of the country's population, give rulers the option of imposing heavy demands for resources on the people they control, even if these demands reduce overall societal productivity and wealth. In these circumstances, rulers have little prospect of attracting popular legitimacy or even compliance with their directives. Thus many rulers choose to conserve funds that might otherwise be spent on public services, instead paying key strongmen in return for loyalty and compliance. Such payouts include material ones, as in providing subsidies and preferred access to state assets, as well as discretionary ones, as in not prosecuting wrongdoing or otherwise exempting select individuals from regulations.

These private uses of state prerogatives and assets create a framework of rule outside formal state institutions—a "shadow" of formal structures of rule, based on these informal ties. As Weber observed, "The patrimonial office lacks above all the bureaucratic separation of the 'private' and the 'official' sphere. For the political administration, too, is treated as a purely personal affair of the ruler, and political power is considered part of his personal property which can be exploited by means of contributions and fees" (Weber 1978, II, 1028–29). Accordingly, Zaire's president, Mobutu Sese Seko, reportedly controlled $6 billion, a sum greater than the recorded economic output of his country in 1992 (Askin and Collins 1993). President Hastings Banda managed much of Malawi's business activities through family trusts, especially the notorious "Press Holdings" (Alexander 1991). President Samuel Doe of Liberia, after a decade in power, had accumulated a fortune equivalent to half of his country's gross domestic product (Kowenhoven 1989), and Sani Abacha of Nigeria was widely believed to have amassed more than $3 billion in less than five years of rule (*Africa Confidential* 2000, 1).

Another key element of the shadow state is the exclusion of free riders—individuals who benefit from the actions or resources of others by virtue of their presence and without having to contribute their own efforts or resources. A shadow state ruler may thus seek to make life less secure and more materially impoverished for subjects unless they demonstrate to the ruler that they contribute to his personal power. In other words, a ruler will minimize his production of public goods—benefits enjoyable by all, irrespective of their relationship to a ruler—to encourage all to seek his personal favor to acquire exemption from their otherwise insecure and impoverished conditions. The informal, nonbureaucratic connections that result constitute the networks of the shadow state.

Taken to the extreme, there are no shadow state–supplied public goods.

Nor can there be civil rights, as relations with authorities are entirely subordinate to the discretion of those authorities. Therefore, the ideal shadow state does not fulfill Robert Nozick's (1974) minimalist definition of a state as a monopoly over the control of force in a certain territory, protecting everyone, whether they like it or not—a basic public good. I have written that some shadow states enjoying global recognition as sovereign states are better understood as commercial syndicates—though I use the term "warlord politics" (Reno 1998). This definition makes the existence of a state a matter of degree rather than an all-or-nothing proposition, which allows one to speak of the growth or decay of a state. This definition of shadow states focuses on the conversion of organizational resources and outcomes as private benefits and leads us to two key propositions.

Proposition One: *A shadow state ruler who can no longer control free riding risks losing the loyalty of followers who do comply in return for payouts.*

A ruler's inability to control who gets benefits may leave open the possibility that groups will organize among themselves to force a ruler to heed their interests. In the context of the shadow state, however, this outcome is not likely. The growing inability of a ruler to control freelancing among members of informal syndicates is likely to lead to the collapse of order itself, since many freelancers in fact are agents of the shadow state. This would be especially true if a shadow state ruler had been successful in forcing as many people as possible to seek personal gain through the favor of the ruler and had repressed any signs of independent organization. To most observers, such a condition signals "state collapse," although I would argue that this particular phenomenon is the second part of a two-stage process, the first stage being the prior shadow state's dissolution of institutions and groups capable of asserting distinct interests apart from the private interests of their members. "State collapse" is the fragmentation of a shadow state whose key members had previously made deals with a ruler to receive protection for their pursuit of private interests.

Critical to this outcome of collapsing central authority is the fact that state officials and their allies, who together make up the informal shadow state, will have already abjured popular support through meeting the needs of the bulk of the population. Although shadow state rulers want key allies to be assured access to resources, they view differently the role of state agents such as teachers, health-care providers, and agricultural extension experts. These state agents undermine shadow state networks by giving would-be supplicants services and resources by right rather than in return for allegiance or contributions to a ruler. Furthermore, their costly efforts may drain scarce resources away from the tasks of managing associates.

Over time, rulers find growing incentives to protect those whom most people in society would view as criminals. To the extent that shadow state agents do business with other criminals, such as armed gangs or illicit international businesses, their enforcement of interests and agreements will be direct and violent rather than indirect and through legal institutions. As rulers become more reliant on shadow state networks to rule, the political costs of jettisoning their associates and diverting resources to build truly popular institutions grows. This progression leads to another observation regarding the character of shadow states.

Proposition Two: *Shadow state rulers have an incentive, in proportion to their reliance on shadow state networks, to destroy remaining formal institutions of the state.*

Rulers of shadow states logically ignore or abjure tasks and institutions commonly associated with states. This appears, for example, in the basic matter of postal services. U.S. post offices will refuse to accept mail being sent to some African countries because those countries do not possess postal services. The point is that not only do rulers save scarce political resources, they also ensure that other groups (including other shadow state agents) do not provide subjects with services, lest these activities overshadow the lesser attractions of accommodation with the shadow state. Even if society as a whole would be better off if some individuals organized a service for themselves, because all could enjoy it, from the ruler's perspective, officials or local organizers who appropriate resources and tasks nominally allocated to the state could easily curtail the ruler's authority if they were even modestly effective at providing a basic service. Thus rulers who do not offer postal services jealously guard the unfulfilled prerogatives of state sovereignty. Usually they obstruct the appearance of private services, preferring to incorporate entrepreneurs into their shadow state networks (or eliminate them from society altogether), and farm out postal duties to a politically neutral foreign firm such as DHL or UPS.

This view of shadow state power also motivates rulers to foster conflict within communities and among factions of the shadow state itself so as to encourage local strongmen to appeal to the personal favor of the ruler for the settlement of disputes and protection of followers. Mobutu personified this tendency, manipulating conflicts by siding with one faction, then another, in ways that forced all sides in conflicts to seek the president's favor to settle local scores (Schatzberg 1988).

The ruler's protection of some against others creates significant costs for most people, including those receiving protection. Nor will protection permit those so favored to develop independent means to provide for the needs of communities, for variation in the ruler's support demonstrates to followers that his favor can shift and must be sought continually and most strenuously. The benefits of a strongman's protection are not likely to become generalized in society as public order, since protection is sold as a private good and treated as such by buyers. Recipients of this protection have greater incentives to pursue purely private gain for themselves, even to the point of participating in what society as a whole considers exploitative or criminal behavior. They recognize that the ruler's favor both is unpredictable and punishes enterprise.

This strategy of rule through provoking insecurity and then providing private protection is likely to intentionally intensify ethnic frictions (Chabal and Daloz 1998). Lacking much in the way of formal military or civil institutions, Mobutu incited enmity in eastern Zaire against "newcomers" (albeit of two centuries' standing) in order to assert his authority. He incorporated local officials and armed bands into a coalition to loot the targeted population (Braeckman 1995, 387–94). Similar techniques appeared in Nigeria's Niger Delta under Abacha and Ibrahim Babangida. Quasi-official "task forces," often raised by a local faction or political figure, use political and commercial alliances with powerful national-level figures to settle political scores and share clandestine commercial gains with their patrons (Obi 1998). In Liberia, this strategy became a deliberate policy of President Doe, who protected ethnic-minority businessmen to extract commercial opportunities from them. Doe enhanced these individuals' need for protection by provoking popular ire at their privilege (Ellis 1995). In both places, state officials then lost control over ethnic and regionally based paramilitaries. A similar fragmentation of state control over violence appeared in Colombia: officials attempting to respond to a devastating earthquake in January 1999 found that local paramilitaries rebuffed central government efforts to reassert control. These paramilitaries, many involved in drug trafficking, were those that government officials had used as proxies earlier in a war against leftist rebels.

Robert Bates (1981) noted that rulers focused solely on private benefits prefer more rules and regulations, which they can manipulate to build constituencies and exclude free riders. Bates pointed out, however, that the use of formal administrative and legal regulations to provide and exploit private privilege detracts from predictable rule-based bureaucratic function, since institutions must remain flexible enough to serve needs based on constantly changing personal relationships and to discriminate on this basis (Krueger 1974).

A second reason that shadow state rulers prefer weak institutions (weak not only in terms of their adherence to rule-based principles, but also in terms of their ability to provide public goods) lies in the rulers' fears that enterprising rivals will use successful institutions to challenge the existing order. Administrators who provide popular services (such as security amid chaos) would inevitably gain popular support from beneficiaries of this public good (Migdal 1988). Fear of such an outcome reflects the dangers that coups and other violent actions on the part of subordinates pose to the physical security of rulers. John Wiseman (1993), for example, discovered that 60 percent of Africa's rulers from 1960 to 1992 left office for prison, exile, or an early grave. Security for African rulers has not improved during the 1990s: Nigeria boasts one civilian president removed by an incumbent military ruler (1993), an internal military coup (1993), and the suspicious nocturnal demise of a ruler (1998); Niger experienced two coups (1996 and 1999); Sierra Leone suffered not only a coup (1996) but also two rebellious military insurrections against a civilian president, causing him to flee (1997 and 1999); a rival politician's militia (with Angolan assistance) removed the president of Congo-Brazzaville (1997); and the Central African Republic's president survived three military uprisings over two years (1996–98) with help from French paratroopers and an international peacekeeping force.

This pattern reinforces the point that a ruler's failure to restrict or ration public goods (or from his private perspective, free riding) is likely to lead to his removal from power and, perhaps, his own death. Such a failure, however, is unlikely to evolve into state-building, at least not immediately, for the shadow state strategy of rule through informal networks destroys the institutional raw materials needed to organize groups for the provision of public goods, whether for the whole population or for a community within the country. Collapse of the shadow state is more likely to leave the field in the control of fragments of the shadow state: competing entrenched groups that seek to protect privilege on their own. As Mancur Olson observed, "The larger the group, the farther it will fall short of providing an optimal amount of a collective good" (Olson 1965, 35), because individuals will have incentives to forgo contributing to a common goal, especially if they can appropriate elements of a shadow state to provide themselves with private benefits. This prediction is especially accurate when a credible corpus of rules or recent positive experiences with state-level, rule-based behavior is not present for an elite challenger to easily exploit or for societal opposition to restore.

Is Russia's *Mafiya* a Sign of a Collapsing Shadow State?

How well does the shadow state model introduced in the preceding section apply to the appearance of *mafiya* organizations in Russia and other republics of the former Soviet Union? Comparison of these *mafiya* and elements of African shadow states reveals some similarities. Indeed, some responses of state officials to *mafiya* power in the former Soviet Union resemble relations between shadow state authorities and warlords in Africa.

First, informal syndicates organized around commerce have deep roots in many African states and in the former Soviet Union and were important in old-regime strategies of rule. Handelman (1995) observed continuity from a class of "fixers" from the socialist economy to contemporary criminal organizations (*vory v zakone;* see also Albini et al. 1997, 156–59). Others have observed that relatively autonomous societal organizations have survived in totalitarian regimes. Vivienne Shue points out that in Mao Zedong's China this survival was the result of "the collective capacity of small units and officials to evade, neglect, embellish, or distort central directives" and "their capacities to dissemble and to cheat their superiors where local interests were at stake" (Shue 1994, 70). She calls this a "cellularization" of society, a breaking apart of ties that bind groups together for a common struggle. In both Africa's shadow states and in Handelman's description of "fixers" and criminal groups, some pursue objectives through informal ties with (or in subversion of) regime officials in ways that blend business, crime, and government administration.

Writing of the Soviet period, Virginie Coulloudon observed that "the mafia and the state that ruled both politics and economics in an arbitrary manner became, we might say, one and the same" (Coulloudon 1997, 75). This convergence resembles the shadow state's melding of informal networks, where distinctions between public and private exercise of power are blurred. These intertwined, symbiotic relationships have far-reaching consequences if central power diminishes to the point that these structures predominate and no authority exists to provide a public good, whether to serve its own interests or those of society as a whole. Furthermore, previous state "cellularization" of society and collaborative links with nonstate groups, especially in commerce, undermine the autonomous efforts of any "civil society" groups that can articulate interests that threaten shadow state officials.

Post–cold war developments have weakened central power both in African shadow states and in the states of the former Soviet Union. As political bosses have lost control over "their" syndicates, their associates have set up new alliances and moved into new businesses, directly appropriating state assets. This process is manifest in the similarities between the "privatization" of state assets in Africa (van de Walle 1994) and that in the former Soviet bloc (Appel 1997). In Russia, state agents and their collaborators used their previous positions to take advantage of privatization (Kryshtanovskaia 1996). As Vadim Volkov discusses in Chapter 4 of this volume, private security firms in Russia often are rooted in the Soviet past. Olga Kryshtanovskaia reports that some members of state security services join private "coercive structures"—private armies—that collaborate with newly emergent *mafiya* figures. She estimates that twenty thousand people in the Moscow area work in these private security firms (Kryshtanovskaia 1996, 47–48). Once in business, these operators build new ties with friendly officials. To the extent that these officials exercise influence, "reform" is manipulated so that new bureaucratic measures protect the private interests of their commercial allies. This devotion to private interests enhances the tendency for remaining (and even new) bureaucracies to hinder efficiency (see Hellman 1998) such that all comers, even honest entrepreneurs, must make deals with *mafiya*-state syndicates to enjoy access to new opportunities.

Freelancing newcomers without special connections also take advantage of the proliferation of these networks to carve out their own areas of opportunity. In Liberia's civil war (1990–96), for instance, groups of armed young men engaged in looting, clandestine mining, logging, and exports of illicit substances through what some Liberians call a "Kalashnikov lifestyle." Led by individuals with colorful nicknames such as General Butt Naked, Colonel Blood, General Jesus, and Major Trouble (Ellis 1999; Huband 1998), these groups failed to exhibit clear internal hierarchies of command (titles notwithstanding) and usually moved quickly to eliminate any among them who became effective or popular on the battlefield. Some organized in order to exact revenge for previous indignities. In Sierra Leone, Commander Sam "Maskita" Bockarie promised to burn down much of Freetown to avenge the scorn he had endured from the educated elite.

The level of unstructured (in the sense of random and not easily avoidable) crime, however, is probably lower in Russia than in African shadow states. This difference suggests the presence of structures that either inhibit disorder or induce avoidance strategies of promoting conflict between groups. Something in society is attempting to provide a public good of relative security. A survey of Russians found that, for instance, crime ranked seventh in a list of popular complaints, below issues related to income distribution, economic management, and the decline of respect for institutions (*Current Digest of the Post Soviet Press* 1998). These popular concerns may reflect an awareness of collaborations between *mafiya* and the state, as well as the tendency of some *mafiya* activity to metamorphose into legal businesses, as demonstrated in Chapter 4. The ordering of these complaints also indicates that freelance crime poses relatively little threat to collaboration between officials and *mafiya* or to the resources and opportunities that they exploit. In other words, although corruption may be rampant, Russia's rulers do not substitute widespread disorder for an inability of state institutions to exercise power. Nor do their partners in corruption seek to control populations through imposing disorder. These factors point to a much higher level of existing (though compromised) state institutional structures throughout much of the former Soviet Union—a critical difference in circumstance that will be examined further in the next section.

In some of the post-Soviet republics, informal networks appear to blur distinctions between private and state authority, paralleling the warlord organizations of Africa. The Pridnestr Moldovan Republic within Moldova is close to this ideal type: it features freelancing military units that use direct control over people and economically useful territory to accumulate resources for the private benefit of the organization. In this case, according to the 1997 edition of *La dépêche internationale des drogues,* the activities of these groups include drug trafficking. It is also significant that former Soviet Army personnel from this area of Moldova have reputations in Africa as arms traffickers. Warlord-like collaborations between privatized military units and friendly state agents who appropriate state assets have occurred in Russia and other post-Soviet states. Dramatic varieties of these collaborations also surface at times in Africa. The Siberian diamond-mining firm Sakha Almazy Rossiya turned up in Angola's civil war, along with a privatized Soviet military "industrial security" force (*Intelligence Newsletter* 1997). Some Ukrainian and Russian military veterans appropriated military equipment on their own and then appeared in Sierra Leone to sell their services to a South African mercenary outfit (author's observations and Hooper 1997).

Tajikistan, Chechnya, Dagestan, and Georgia also saw varying degrees of a limited privatization of violence amid the collapse of central authority in the 1990s. In Chechnya, the collapse of state authority and its substitution by clan-based *mafiya* and militias bear a close resemblance to African warlord conditions, though this disorder in Chechnya is tempered by social norms concerning the use of violence (Lieven 1998). Within the rest of Russia, areas of weakest civilian control (such as in Kaliningrad and the northern Caucasus) are the same areas where security forces appear to exploit their autonomy to use military assets for economic gain (Galeotti 1999b). In Tajikistan, veteran politicians and newcomers such as Sungak Safarov headed their own militias, with weapons acquired from armed factions in neighboring states (Atkin 1997, 614–16). To the extent that these armed groups create and manage their own economic environments while pursuing political struggles, they begin to resemble warlord factions in Africa.

Areas containing valuable, portable natural resources or trading advantages (such as control over a frontier) also offer strongmen greater incentives and potential for privatizing their exercise of power. For example, the natural resource economies of Russia, Turkmenistan, Azerbaijan, and Kazakhstan offer rulers there the opportunity to appropriate rents from oil production for themselves and their associates, much in the fashion of African shadow states. If developments in these countries were in keeping with African experience, rulers should be expected to give up pretenses of serving a popular interest in fostering development or in using revenues for public purposes. Free from the need to tax populations, rulers could devote all their resources to personal enrichment—a tendency that Terry Karl (1998) observes in other oil-based economies. The nearly exclusive rent-seeking nature of the source of income lessens the cost of applying violence to commercial operations and to those who stand in the rulers' way, since repression or exclusion of the local population does not undermine this resource base. Defense against rivals already requires ruling groups to apply violence, which can be used to chase off those who are useless to the ruler and to exploit others with little fear of the consequences of overexploitation. This need can enhance the tendency among rulers to focus more on short-term gain and less on the productivity of "victims" who can be taxed.

Successive governments in Nigeria have shown "warlord" behavior of this sort, using control over oil to sustain a network of regime favorites, independent of obligations to provide services to a population in return for legitimacy or resources. By 1997, Nigeria's government depended on oil to provide 97 percent of the country's foreign exchange earnings (*Africa Confidential* 1998). This fact has rendered much of the country's population superfluous to the regime's pursuit of patronage resources, except insofar as individuals or groups contest the regime's control over oil. Any significant decentralization of power in such a context would be highly threatening to the shadow state regime, be it civilian or military, lest local demands of citizens cut off rulers from the political resources needed to entice compliance from strongmen.

In contrast, Peter J. Stavrakis et al. (1997) point out that Russian federalism has created a relatively decentralized political system, but not one of Moscow's intent. This situation enables local political actors to cut deals with *mafiya,* citizens, and outsiders and to localize rent-seeking economies, especially where state institutions are already weak. Regional politicians therefore have more room to innovate. Some regional rulers will nevertheless gear activities toward personal enrichment. Elsewhere, however, independent entrepreneurs or other societal groups may force local rulers to heed their demands. In shadow state federalism in Nigeria, by contrast, rulers use federalism as a tool to manipulate local factional battles. Local notables settle scores among themselves through appeals to the center, hoping for military and economic help to marginalize rivals—appeals that sit well with shadow state strategies that avoid the creation of effective institutions, whether as state bureaucracies or community self-help organs. Not surprisingly, federalism of the Nigerian sort leads to demands for ever-smaller divisions, as each enterprising politician or group seeks to cut its own deal with those in the capital (Oyediran 1997). Paradoxically, the weakness of the central state in Russia may have the beneficial (though unintended) consequence of permitting stronger (local) state institutions overall.

As we have seen, cases in some parts of the former Soviet Union show that *mafiya* can replace absent state authority, akin to the collapse of shadow states in Africa. But in most of Russia, *mafiya* organizations show evidence of remaining reliant on the continued autonomous exercise of state power and its dominance over the exercise of violence in ways that African warlords in the context of the shadow state collapse do not. Most *mafiya* activities—retail trade, wholesale marketing, and protection rackets—resemble more closely U.S. mafia activities than those of African warlords. The Russian and U.S. *mafiya* prefer to have weak local authorities but do not want to entirely subvert state provision of order. Thus, rather than sow disorder as a strategy for private gain, these mafia free ride on the state's provision of rules and order.

If that which *mafiya* "protect" operates in a taxable or at least a licit economy, their operation need not run counter to the revenue imperatives of building state institutions. Racketeering *mafiya* depend on an environment of prosperity and enterprise for profit. In contrast, a shadow state entrepreneur fears and needs to suppress enterprise and will tolerate the existence of prosperity among others. Comparison of tax receipts in Russia and several African states hints at the different incentives that influence the behavior of *mafiya* and warlords toward enterprise (see Table 5.1). States that are able to regulate economic transactions (measured in terms of their capacity to supply revenues through internal taxation) offer opportunities for criminal organizations to violate these strictures and to sell their help to others seeking exemption. But where internal economic regulatory capacity is very low, as in shadow states, informal networks cannot rely on state agencies to provide sufficient control to make exemption valuable and will be drawn toward more violent and exploitative commercial practices.

It is also likely that (as in Uganda and Ghana), where substantial wealth is derived from small producers and rent-seeking opportunities are comparatively limited, authorities will shy away from shadow state practices. States in such circumstances need to provide protection to farmers—at least enough for them to harvest—in order to tax them, even as the states' rulers may seek to enrich themselves and repress threatening signs of autonomous interests among groups less central to state finances.

Illustrating this dichotomous private relation to state power, Al Capone needed the state of Florida to provide enough order so that he could enjoy his sumptuous Miami mansion and the city's fabled sunshine. More important, Capone's racketeering activities depended on sufficient state provision of order to keep his victims in business. State capacity to declare certain activities illegal and to enforce those directives provided his business opportunities. Operators who then needed protection from state officials sought mafia services or were good targets for mafia solicitation. State regulations thus provide a "free good" to American-style mafia over

Table 5.1
Sources of Taxation, Russia and Africa, 1995

	Domestic tax as a percentage of GDP	Tax on trade as a percentage of GDP
Russia	27.4	4.1
Nigeria	7.0	16.0
Sierra Leone	6.4	2.6
Uganda	5.1	4.7
Ghana	10.3	4.5

Sources: Stotsky and Wolde 1997, 8; U.S. Bureau of the Census 1998, 1345.
Note: GDP = gross domestic product.

what mafia leaders may pay to state officials to gain protection for themselves and their clients against state enforcement of regulations.

The Limits of Applying the Shadow State
Model to the Former Soviet Union

Overall, there is little evidence among African warlords or their shadow state rulers of state-building of the kind that Douglass North and Robert Thomas (1973) saw in the growth of institutions that provide predictable protection for individuals' property and other rights vis-à-vis rulers. Indeed, most candidates for external recognition of sovereignty are themselves dominant commercial actors, thus eliminating (for them) the need for efficient institutions to negotiate and enforce bargains with other domestic groups. Among African warlords, societal wants have little to do with determining elite behavior. Thus, in contrast to Volkov's argument in Chapter 4 on Russia, shadow state rulers and warlords in Africa diverge from Charles Tilly's notion of states developing out of protection rackets (Tilly 1985, 170–72), since these private syndicates can profit without supplying a stable environment for most people, even though a syndicate may exercise a level of force theoretically capable of doing so. "The problem with many of the young fighters was that they had been addicted to blood and violence," reported an eyewitness to Liberia's civil war. "The material reward from war spoils was tempting enough to make some wish the war continued" (Ogunleye 1995, 137). Reinforcing this sense of private over public rights and interest, Wole Soyinka wrote of Nigeria's then-president, "Beyond the reality of a fiefdom that has dutifully nursed his insatiable greed and transformed him into a creature of enormous wealth, and now of power, Abacha has no *notion* of Nigeria" (Soyinka 1996, 15). These circumstances contrast with Tilly's observation that "state makers developed a durable interest in promoting the accumulation of capital" through fending off competitors and providing security to a population (Tilly 1985, 172).

In this sense, state agencies in post-Soviet Russia appear to exercise a considerably higher degree of autonomy in comparison with shadow states, at least in the eyes of the public. Public opinion surveys indicate that many Russians share the view that the state exercises some meaningful control over the use of force. On the one hand, a 1998 survey revealed that 80 percent of Russians polled believed that "criminal structures" exercise "significant influence" in Russia (*Obshchaya gazeta* 1998). The results of another poll showed that 51 percent affirmed the proposition that "real power in Russia belongs to criminal structures and the *mafiya*." Yet 46 percent believed that Russia's judicial system is fair "now and then." Sixty-eight percent reported that they would seek help from police, courts, and security service agents if their legal rights were violated. Only 7 percent reported that they would seek help from *mafiya* figures, and 10 percent would appeal to God (*Izvestia* 1998). In yet another survey, only 16 percent responded that their main complaint about government was that "its actions primarily benefit shadow-economy and *mafiya* capital"; more than twice as many people were concerned primarily about declining state provision of social services (*Moskovsky komsomolets* 1998).

Opinion polls are less common in Africa. Paul Beckett, however, reported a survey of Nigerian university students, who ranked stable government, followed by national unity, as their primary political concerns, ahead of democratic freedom and rapid economic development. In 1995, 81 percent of the students polled also believed that law and order was a more pressing concern than was economic development—in a country that has seen a 70 percent erosion of per capita formal economy incomes in the last fifteen years (Beckett 1998, 24–25). Many Sierra Leoneans refer to government soldiers as "sobels," or soldier-rebels, reflecting the predatory behavior of these armed men. A West African commentator has complained of "uniformed buzzards, soldiers [who are] . . . the scourge of the region . . . grossly ignorant of their own basic purpose in society" (Ayittey 1992, 139).

The fragmentation of the Soviet-era *nomenklatura* generally has not been accompanied by a complete fragmentation of the military organization along the same lines. Some *mafiya* organizations have or may become militarized, and some military units may be penetrated deeply by corruption and organized crime, but neither the *mafiya* nor corrupted military officers attempt to exercise the systematic and widespread control of violence that would enable them to marginalize the entire population in the process of exploiting natural resources (as has happened in Nigeria) or to become the sole authority in certain regions. The organizational coherence of the military, at least in terms of dominating the exercise of coercion, hinders *mafiya* attempts to apply violence against victims to create an exclusive private market for protection. In lieu of Tilly's or North and Thomas's "demand side" entrepreneurs who call for, then receive, protection for property, security in Russia is "supply side"; it follows from or subverts the interests of existing military or other coercive agents of the state that have distinct organizational identities, even if they are imperfect providers of security and order. Like African warlords, Russia's *mafiya* may not behave as state-builders, although some, as Volkov shows in Chapter 4, may transform into legal enterprises. Yet the existing state's relative control over coercion creates a structure that encourages Russia's *mafiya* to behave as free riders on the benefits the state provides, rather than destroying those benefits completely. Thus, unlike African warlords, Russia's *mafiya* do not seek to shape their own economic environment in the shadow state's noninstitutional image.

This relatively higher level of state control over coercion, at least when compared with Africa's shadow states, also reflects the character of the collapse of Soviet power. Soviet lobbies representing a particular industrial sector did not need to diversify their contacts to persuade Soviet officials to give them subsidies. But now, the terms of post-Soviet political competition mean that these groups (along with genuinely nouveaux riches) need to diversify their connections to further their own fortunes (Coulloudon 1999). Diversification occurs because supplicants are just that: they appeal to state officials or try to corrupt them. These circumstances promote economic inefficiency in situations where managers retain control over large labor forces and then claim to represent these groups in negotiations in a chaotic political marketplace, giving unproductive enterprises significant political value (Polishchuk 1997). Over the long term, notes Daniel Treisman (1998), entrepreneurs and officials alike desire more stable accommodations with each other so that the former can be assured that their bribes buy favorable action from the latter. The lack of organization among civilian administration and political parties, however, creates autonomy for each. Supplicants are forced to explore lucrative opportunities on their own. Politicians who serve supplicants "act as a screen between grass-roots protests and fundamental policy change" (Treisman 1998, 15).

Much of the difference in outcomes between African shadow states and Russian *mafiya* harks back to the contrasting relationship between coercion and enterprise. Security forces in the former Soviet Union survived their state's collapse with a greater sense of organizational mission and cohesion than that enjoyed by their African counterparts (that is, the Soviet forces were more institutional in a Weberian sense than most African militaries ever were). Supplicants in post-Soviet states are thus increasingly likely to exploit opportunities that the state's provision of order—a public good—makes possible. In doing so, their interests diverge from those of state agents. In these circumstances supplicants should reasonably seek to corrupt, but not to replace, the state authority that raises revenues from others to pay for security. It is easier to imagine in this setting clandestine enterprises organizing themselves as businesses (as Chapter 4 argues) rather than as warlords. This process also shows that corrupt officialdom is not the same thing as a shadow state.

Another possible factor explaining the different outcomes is that Russia's rulers appear to fear coups less than their African counterparts do. Evidence of political opinion among military officers indicates a general resistance to becoming involved in Russia's factional politics (Ball and Gerber 1996)—a conclusion that is reinforced by the difficulties that 1991 and 1993 coup plotters experienced in trying to draw military officers to the side of a political faction. The informal networks in Russia that concern Handelman focus more on filling in for deficiencies of the planned economy and less on replacing or paralleling suspect state security agencies, or hounding powerful local strongmen. This is not to say, for example, that Leonid Brezhnev's regime did not serve private interests, or that Soviet corruption was not widespread, as the epic scale of the Uzbek cotton scheme highlights (Handelman 1995, 94–95). Nor does it preclude recognition that officials and *mafiya* figures collaborate in ways that appear to lock in suboptimal outcomes (Hellman 1998). Nonetheless, a significant portion of these privatized gains rely on the state's provision of public order and the activities that this order, however weak and imperfect, permits.

Relations between Russia's formal state bureaucracy and its military provide evidence of the strength and autonomy of Russian state institutions relative to those of African shadow states. Officials in Moscow, for instance, appear capable of controlling military finances to the point of determining where and when they are withheld. This ability reflects in part institutional innovations that make up for weaknesses inherited from Soviet-era agencies. It may also reflect Russia's general economic crisis. Nonetheless, the Ministry of Finance demonstrates a capacity to control funding releases and to specify uses of resources (Galeotti 1999a, 8–10), to the extent that the ministry could withhold almost half of the military's funding during 1997, with no dramatic immediate consequence (Barany 1999, 58). This degree of budgetary control and the capacity to limit military resources has eluded Nigeria's rulers for decades; even modest calls for reining in Nigeria's military budgets (amid an economic crisis more serious than Russia's) have prompted direct military interference in politics (Peters 1997).

Russian state control over military resources reduces the chance that military units will disrupt public order or join with enterprising strongmen to do so, thereby providing at least some limited state-supplied security for private assets and investments. This security in turn limits the opportunities for local *mafiya* to engage in purely predatory strategies through militarizing commercial networks, providing further incentives for *mafiya* to exploit the state's provision of public order and to behave more like Capone-style racketeers. Although it still affords no paradise for economically stressed Russians, this state provision of (partial) order allows some experimentation with market reform among city and regional officials. Experimenting officials may eventually cater to autonomous groups who benefit from reform policies without posing a fundamental threat to the power of Russia's *mafiya*. The appearance of these local authorities in Africa would, however, present a fundamental challenge to the power of its shadow states and warlords, as demonstrated earlier in this chapter.

Global attention to Russia's economic problems enhances incentives for its rulers to create public goods. Russia has received since 1990 an estimated $200 billion from overseas creditors, including a $22.6 billion bailout from the International Monetary Fund in 1998. Critics of external support argue that Russian politicians frittered away this money, either through insider manipulation of economic policies or through support for politically motivated but economically inefficient policies. Even if this is true, external money and external pressure to balance budgets and to institute legal protections for property at least provide some incentive for greater state–society reciprocity. This external funding increases incentives for Russia's *mafiya* to behave as free riders on state-provided order rather than controlling their economic environment directly, as do shadow states. On the other hand, external sources of state revenues can encourage more exclusive rent-seeking behavior on the part of state officials. The effectiveness of external pressure should be measured by its success in promoting rule-based behavior among officials. Such a goal is more easily achieved in Russia compared with much of Africa, however, because significant pockets of rule-based behavior already exist in Russia and officials there have less fear of insubordination (and thus less incentive to buy off potential challengers or to fear efficient bureaucrats). Thus the external variable remains important despite criticism of Russian economic policies. Russia is too strategically important to all major industrial states for it to be abandoned, irrespective of the current low intensity of trade links, since disorder and state collapse in Russia could disrupt economic and social order in industrial states. Disorder in Africa, on the other hand, does not pose such a threat.

Conclusion

Overall, Russia's *mafiya* satisfy some of the key elements regarding the behavior of informal networks in shadow states and the decline of central control ("state collapse") outlined in Proposition One above. *Mafiya* often incorporate personnel associated with the ancien régime, who use official positions to advance the private interests of their syndicate partners. But we find in Russia much less tendency for *mafiya* to develop as syndicates that create overwhelming disorder for society as a whole in order to prevent outsiders from sharing in their rents. Where they do monopolize violence, and thus exercise a local form of control, Russia's *mafiya* resemble Africa's warlords mainly in areas that lack any central state control and therefore may be considered more a consequence of weak state control than a cause of it.

Nonetheless, Russia does not satisfy the assumptions of Proposition Two above that rulers logically fear rule-based formal state institutions and seek to weaken or destroy them. Thus Russia lacks a key element defining the African shadow state. This is particularly the case with regard to Russia's military. This condition has important implications for understanding *mafiya* in the post-Soviet states, because (1) it limits the degree and extent of militarization of commercial and factional conflicts, and (2) it provides for some level of public order and security. This selectively confirms Olson's observation that it takes resources and coordination by external authority to provide incentives to mobilize groups for collective action. Not surprisingly, it appears that where autonomous state institutions already exist or where incentives of self-interest to create them are high, *mafiya*-like organizations will adapt to these conditions. It is the existence of a state—however weak—that explains the behavior of Russia's *mafiya*. By contrast, the state's absence in parts of Africa explains the existence of warlords that are fundamentally hostile to public goods.

Of course, Russia's outcome is not a formula for democracy or reciprocity between broad interests in society as a whole and state authority. But a state need not be democratic, its officials morally upright, or its policies or behaviors very appealing in order to be considered a state. It may seem more like a state for some (such as oligarchs) and less for others (pensioners, perhaps). It must, however, force other groups to refrain from enforcing their own contracts, whether legal or clandestine, without having to absorb these groups into informal political networks or destroy them.

References

Africa Confidential. 1998. "Usman Optimism." 9 October: 8.
———. 2000. "High Street Havens." 27 October: 1–3.
Albini, Joseph, et al. 1997. "Russian Organized Crime: Its History, Structure and Function."

Pp. 153–73 in *Understanding Organized Crime in Global Perspective: A Reader,* ed. Patrick Ryan and George Rush. London: Sage.

Alexander, Caroline. 1991. "An Ideal State." *New Yorker.* 16 December: 53–88.

Appel, Hilary. 1997. "Voucher Privatisation in Russia: Structural Consequences and Mass Response in the Second Period of Reform." *Europe-Asia Studies* 49, no. 8 (December): 1433–49.

Askin, Steve, and Carole Collins. 1993. "External Collusion with Kleptocracy: Can Zaire Recapture Its Stolen Wealth?" *Review of African Political Economy* 57: 72–85.

Atkin, Muriel. 1997. "Tajikistan: Reform, Reaction, and Civil War." Pp. 603–34 in *New States, New Politics,* ed. Ian Bremmer and Ray Taras. Cambridge: Cambridge University Press.

Ayittey, George. 1992. *Africa Betrayed.* New York: St. Martin's.

Ball, Deborah, and Theodore Gerber. 1996. "The Political Views of Russian Field Grade Officers." *Post-Soviet Affairs* 12 (April): 155–80.

Barany, Zoltan. 1999. "Controlling the Military: A Partial Success." *Journal of Democracy* 10, no. 2 (April): 54–67.

Bates, Robert H. 1981. *Markets and States in Tropical Africa.* Berkeley: University of California Press.

Bayart, Jean-François, Stephen Ellis, and Béatrice Hibou, eds. 1997. *La Criminalisation de l'Etat en Afrique.* Brussels: Editions Complexe.

Beckett, Paul A. 1998. "Legitimizing Democracy: The Role of the Highly Educated Elite." Pp. 111–34 in *Dilemmas of Democracy in Nigeria,* ed. Paul A. Beckett and Crawford Young. Rochester: University of Rochester Press.

Braeckman, Colette. 1995. "Le Zaire de Mobutu, 'parrin' des Grands Lacs." Pp. 387–94 in *Les crises politiques au Burundi et au Rwanda (1993–1994),* ed. André Guichaoua. Paris: Karthala.

Chabal, Patrick, and Jean-Pascal Daloz. 1998. *Africa Works: Disorder as Political Instrument.* London : James Currey.

Coulloudon, Virginie. 1997. "The Criminalization of Russia's Elite." *East European Constitutional Review* 6, no. 4 (fall): 73–78.

———. 1999. "Corruption and Patronage in Russia (1979–1999)." Davis Center for Russian Studies, Harvard University. Photocopy.

Current Digest of the Post-Soviet Press. 1998. "Ratings as They Really Are." 15 April. Reporting a story in *Moskovsky komsomolets.*

La dépêche internationale des drogues. 1997. "Double jeu en Transnistrie." March: 8.

Ellis, Stephen. 1995. "Liberia 1989–1994: A Study of Ethnic and Spiritual Violence." *African Affairs* 94, no. 375 (April): 165–97.

———. 1999. *The Mask of Anarchy: The Roots of Liberia's War.* New York: New York University Press.

Galeotti, Mark. 1999a. "Decline and Fall—The Right Climate for Reform?" *Jane's Intelligence Review* 11, no. 1 (January): 8–11.

———. 1999b. "Russia's Criminal Army." *Jane's Intelligence Review* 11, no. 6 (June): 6–9.

Gregory, Paul. 1997. "Has Russia's Transition Really Been Such a Failure?" *Problems of Post-Communism* 44, no. 6 (December): 13–22.

Handelman, Stephen. 1995. *Comrade Criminal: Russia's New Mafiya.* New Haven: Yale University Press.

Hellman, Joel. 1998. "Winners Take All: The Politics of Partial Reform in the Post-Communist World." *World Politics* 50, no. 2 (January): 203–34.

Hooper, Jim. 1997. "Peace in Sierra Leone: A Temporary Outcome?" *Jane's Intelligence Review* 9, no. 2 (February): 91–93.

Huband, Mark. 1998. *The Liberian Civil War.* London: Frank Cass.

Intelligence Newsletter. 1997. "British-Russian Joint Venture." 30 January: 41.

Izvestia. 1998. 23 January.

Jackson, Robert. 1990. *Quasi-states: Sovereignty, International Relations and the Third World.* Cambridge: Cambridge University Press.

Kaplan, Robert. 1994. "The Coming Anarchy." *Atlantic Monthly.* February: 44–61.

Karl, Terry Lynn. 1998. *The Paradox of Plenty.* Berkeley: University of California Press.

Kowenhoven, Gus. 1989. Accountant's correspondence with his client, President Samuel Doe. 7 January.

Krueger, Anne. 1974. "The Political Economy of the Rent-Seeking Society." *American Economic Review* 64 (June): 291–303.

Kryshtanovskaia, Olga. 1996. "Illegal Structures in Russia." *Russian Social Science Review* (November/December): 44–64.

Lieven, Anatol. 1998. *Chechnya: Tombstone of Russian Power.* New Haven: Yale University Press.

Migdal, Joel. 1988. *Strong Societies and Weak States.* Princeton: Princeton University Press.

Moskovsky komsomolets. 1998. 11 March.

North, Douglass, and Robert Thomas. 1973. *The Rise of the Western World.* Cambridge: Cambridge University Press.

Nozick, Robert. 1974. *Anarchy, State, and Utopia.* Oxford: Blackwell.

Obi, Cyril. 1998. "Global, State and Local Intersections: A Study of Power, Authority and Conflict in the Niger Delta Oil Communities." Paper presented at Workshop on Local Governance and International Intervention in Africa, European University, Florence, March.

Obshchaya gazeta. 1998. 23 July.

Ogunleye, Bayo. 1995. *Behind Rebel Line: Anatomy of Charles Taylor's Hostage Camps.* Enugu: Delta.

Olson, Mancur. 1965. *The Logic of Collective Action.* Cambridge, Mass.: Harvard University Press.

Oyediran, Oyeleye. 1997. "The Reorganization of Local Government." Pp. 193–212 in *Transition without End: Nigerian Politics and Civil Society under Babangida,* ed. Larry Diamond, Anthony Kirk-Greene, and Oyeleye Oyediran. Boulder: Lynne Rienner.

Peters, Jimi. 1997. *The Nigerian Military and the State.* London: I. B. Tauris.

Polishchuk, Leonid. 1997. "Missed Markets: Implications for Economic Behavior and Institutional Change." Pp. 80–101 in *Transforming Post Communist Political Economies,* ed. Joan Nelson, Charles Tilly, and Lee Walker. Washington: National Academy Press.

Reno, William. 1995. *Corruption and State Politics in Sierra Leone.* Cambridge: Cambridge University Press.

———. 1998. *Warlord Politics and African States.* Boulder: Lynne Rienner.

Schatzberg, Michael. 1988. *The Dialectics of Oppression in Zaire.* Bloomington: Indiana University Press.

Shue, Vivienne. 1994. "State Power and Social Organization in China." Pp. 65–88 in *State Power and Social Forces: Domination and Transformation in the Third World,* ed. Joel Migdal, Atul Kohli, and Vivienne Shue. Cambridge: Cambridge University Press.

Soyinka, Wole. 1996. *The Open Sore of a Continent.* New York: Oxford University Press.

Stavrakis, Peter J., Joan DeBardeleben, and Larry Black, eds. 1997. *Beyond the Monolith: The Emergence of Regionalism in Post-Soviet Russia.* Baltimore: Johns Hopkins University Press.

Stotsky, Janet, and Mariam Asegedech Wolde. 1997. "Tax Effort in Sub-Saharan Africa." Working paper, International Monetary Fund, 97–107.

Tilly, Charles. 1985. "War Making and State Making as Organized Crime." Pp. 169–91 in *Bringing the State Back In,* ed. Peter B. Evans, Dietrich Rueschemeyer, and Theda Skocpol. Cambridge: Cambridge University Press.

Treisman, Daniel. 1998. "Dollars and Democratization: The Role and Power of Money in Russia's Transitional Elections." *Comparative Politics* 31, no. 1 (October): 1–21.

U.S. Bureau of the Census. 1998. *Statistical Abstract of the United States.* Washington: Bureau of the Census.

van de Walle, Nicolas. 1994. "Neopatrimonialism and Democracy in Africa, with an Illustration from Cameroon." Pp. 129–57 in *Economic Change and Political Liberalization in Sub-Saharan Africa,* ed. Jennifer A. Widner. Baltimore: Johns Hopkins University Press.

Weber, Max. 1978. *Economy and Society,* ed. Guenther Roth and Claus Wittich. 2 vols. Berkeley: University of California Press.

Wiseman, John. 1993. "Leadership and Personal Danger in African Politics." *Journal of Modern African Studies* 31, no. 4 (December): 657–60.

6

Weak States and Private Armies

CHARLES H. FAIRBANKS, JR.

The weakness of the postcommunist state is important to political scientists because it is the key transition development that we did not foresee. We were prepared for the success of democracy and the market in the states of the former Soviet Union, and even for the possibility of authoritarian rule. But few were prepared for the weak states that evolved out of the Soviet collapse. For this deficiency we had some excuse. There have been many failed democratic transitions, sometimes followed by brief periods of anarchy, but most such failures in the last two hundred years have ended within a few years in authoritarian rule. The outstanding exceptions, transitions that produced weak states, are Spain (1812–1975), Portugal (1820–1974), Latin America after independence, Greece (1828–ca.1950) and China after 1911; closer study of these transitions, we thought, might provide lessons about the transitions in the Soviet bloc.

Instead we saw something entirely different: the quick transformation of an overly strong state into a very weak state, which has occurred in a large number of former communist areas with widely differing histories and cultures. I can cite only the cases I know: in Chechnya there is essentially no state; in Albania, Republika Srpska (the Serb part of the Bosnian Federation), Bosnia, Trans-Dniestria, Abkhazia, South Ossetia, Georgia, eastern Tajikistan, and Cambodia the state seems, on balance, about as weak as it was in feudal Europe between 1100 and 1200; Russia, Belarus, Kyrgyzstan, and Azerbaijan are weak states, and Serbia, Ukraine, and Kazakhstan are stronger states that are getting weaker. Clearly, we need to ask now

129

whether there is something about the transition from communist rule that predisposes a state to become weak.

The question is even more relevant because it applies not only to the former communist realm but also to Africa. Until recently, African states were perceived as "overdeveloped" with reference to their societies, having inherited the autocratic nature of their colonial predecessors. Ambitious rulers aspired to construct leviathans, even if, when closely inspected, their creations were found to be "lame" (Callaghy 1984). But the African transition to a politically and economically liberalized polity has laid bare the gap between the aspiration for an "integral state" of perfected hegemony and the enfeebled condition of many African states today (Young 1994).

This chapter examines the relationship between state weakness and what I call "private armies." I have no space to discuss state armies, old or new. Much about their fragility will emerge in my analysis of private armies, because many units of new and even old state armies are more truly private— military forces that are formed by society from below, nonstate armies, what we often call "paramilitary forces" or "militias" (traditionally, *opolcheniya* in Russian, though they are most often called *gruppi boevikov* [groups of fighters] or *bandformirovaniya* [gang formations]). It is difficult to find a good term for these forces. I will argue that they are quite different from the guerrillas of the cold war period. "Paramilitary forces" is often used to describe states' militarized police and presidential guards. "Militia," the term I have employed in earlier works, once meant in the United Kingdom the national army reserves and in the United States was the earlier name of the National Guard. To avoid such confusion I will use the term "private armies," by which I do not mean organized military forces raised by private corporations and hired out to governments. William Reno (1997, 230) says that ninety such companies, which he calls "private armies," are active in Africa. Although mercenaries and foreign support are common in the former Soviet Union, I do not know of any such companies there. My primary examples of private armies are drawn from Chechnya and Dagestan, in the Northern Caucasus.[1]

---

1. Although I will make reference to the published literature, my most important sources are interviews with members of Western and Russian armies and intelligence services, members of private armies, involved state officials and citizens, and my own observation of some of these wars. Many of these interviews were conducted under conditions of confidentiality; I give no citations in such cases. Interested readers can supplement this essay with Fairbanks 1995, and the much longer and more documented unpublished study on which that piece was based. I describe there at length private armies in the former Yugoslavia and in Georgia.

Private Armies and the State

Chechnya, in the northeastern Caucasus, was inhabited before the recent wars by about a million people. The Chechens have lived in the area for thousands of years, without social classes or a Chechen state. Like some African peoples, modern Chechen identity is shaped by long struggles against colonial conquest (ca. 1763–1859) and by colonial rule. The struggle was led by a series of Muslim imams, culminating in the famous Imam Shamil. Over this long struggle, religion became fused with the ethnic identities of Chechens and many Dagestani nationalities, as also happened in Ireland, Spain, Poland, and Lithuania. But in the present time of rediscovery of Islam, bitter divisions have arisen about the correct interpretation of Islam.

It was the early Soviet regime that first established a Chechen administrative unit, which eventually became the Chechen-Ingush Autonomous Republic within the Russian Soviet Federative Socialist Republic. Chechens continued to rebel, however, and Joseph Stalin deported and scattered the entire people to Central Asia in 1944. In 1957, Chechens were allowed to return, but their close brush with genocide has marked Chechen relations with Russia ever since. In 1991, as the Soviet Union was breaking up, nationalist forces led by General Dzokhar Dudayev declared Chechnya's independence from the Russian Federation. In summer 1994, President Boris Yeltsin decided to subdue Chechnya, sparking an unequal war between tiny Chechnya and vast Russia, with its tens of thousands of nuclear warheads and millions of troops. By August 1996, however, the demoralized Russian troops had been routed and had withdrawn from Chechnya under an ambiguous, much-violated truce agreement. The war, like the Viking and Magyar invasions in western Europe centuries earlier, left strong private armies in Chechnya (see Table 6.1). After the end of the war, in January 1997, the Chechen commander-in-chief, the former Soviet artillery colonel Aslan Maskhadov, was elected president over a field of candidates that included warlord Shamil Basaev, the hero of the 1995 hostage-taking in Budyonnovsk. Maskhadov, who had spent his formative years in the Soviet army, clearly symbolized secularism and the normalization of Chechen life, including regular statehood and better relations with Russia. But relations with Russia remained tense. Nothing moved in the devastated economy. Crime, including kidnappings, only worsened when Maskhadov held office, losing him much of his active support.

This political opening was exploited by the private army commanders oriented, sincerely or tactically, toward political Islam. Originally, Maskha-

Table 6.1

Major Armed Forces and Private Armies in Chechnya,
Spring–Summer 1998

Name	Commander	Number of fighters (est.)	Notes
		Government forces	
National Guard	Khanbiev	3,000+	Intended as army, drawn from many warlords, possesses armor
Presidential Guard	Bakaev	350	Based in Grozny; also guards oil pipelines
Sharia Guard	Mezhidov	500	Enforces decisions of *sharia* (Muslim law) courts
Islamic Regiment	Baraev	Few	Loosely subordinated to Mezhidov, Alkhan-Kala, and Achkoy Martan
Antiterrorism Center	Israpilov, then Bargashev	500 (of which 300 make up the Special Group)	
National Security Service	Khultygov	450–500	Stationed in Grozny and Argun; Khultygov killed in car crash June 1998
Interior Ministry	Makhashev	5,500–6,500	Dispersed in small police forces
Department of Customs and Border Guards	Khatuev	400–2,000	Operates in border areas; subordinated to Khanbiev's National Guard
Internal Revenue Department	Ibragimov	100	3 units
Ecological Battalion	?	80	Possesses anti-aircraft equipment; scattered
Scorpio Unit	Basaev?	400?	Official part of Basaev's army; stationed in Grozny; existence denied by some

(continued)

Table 6.1 (*Continued*)

Name	Commander	Number of fighters (est.)	Notes
		Private forces	
—	Basaev	500–600?	Unofficial part of Basaev's army; number of fighters varies; stationed in Vedeno and elsewhere in in southeast; possesses armor
"Army of Dzokhar Dudayev"	Raduyev	40+	Unstable; operates in Grozny and Gudermes; strength and acts are often exaggerated
—	Gelayev	500	At one point to Ministry of Internal Affiars (MVD); stationed outside Grozny
—	Yamadayev bros.	150–250	Operates in Gudermes and eastern areas
—	Geliskhanov	30–100	Operates in Nozhai-Yurt and southeastern areas
—	Khalkhoroyev	150–300	Operates in Bamut and southwestern areas
—	Yelkhoyev	50	Operates in Znamenskoe and northwestern areas
—	Bugurayev?	100?	Operates in Ishcherskaya and northwestern areas
—	Khattab	200–300 at any one time	Operates religious and terrorist-training school; provides fighters to other forces; possesses armor

Sources: Information available from the most useful published sources—Kalinina 1998 and Blandy n.d.—then corrected with information obtained in author's interviews.

Note: Question marks by themselves indicate that information is unknown; question marks after a piece of information indicate that sources disagree substantially.

dov tried to form a consensus administration, making his rival Basaev interim prime minister and turning most other private army commanders into ministers or "army" unit commanders. Behind the "Islamic" warlords operated a rich civilian politician, Movladi Udugov, who was receiving major financing from the Arab world through Pakistan. In the summer of 1998, the tension between Maskhadov and the major warlords broke up the government. Maskhadov dismissed the warlord ministers, and they subsequently formed a *shura,* or council, that disputed Maskhadov's authority over the country. Prior to the second Russian-Chechen war in 1999, Chechnya, it seemed, was about to topple into full-scale civil war among various private armies. But it never did, nor did President Maskhadov use the large National Guard—the would-be Chechen army—against his domestic enemies.

Underlying the nominal Chechen state, it seems, was an ethnic group with a shared consciousness but no common institutions. Certain rules were enforced by consensus—such as not fighting other Chechens, or not interrupting the Baku-Novorossisk pipeline carrying Caspian oil, which was Chechnya's great economic hope. Thus Chechnya serves to introduce one of the reasons that the state is weak in many former Soviet republics: the noninstitutionalized ethnic community.

Those who watched the outstanding television coverage of the first Chechen war may have been struck by the fact that many private army fighters did not wear uniforms. These warriors had shifted abruptly away from the 1970s tendency in which leftist guerrillas or groups aped military practices. Then, tiny Italian leftist groups called themselves the "Red Brigades." In the United States, the "Symbionese Liberation Army" had its own flag. In Tajikistan, the "self-defense detachments" in Badakhshan and the Eleventh Brigade did not wear uniforms, nor did the Mkhedrioni private army in Georgia, most of the National Guard there, some of MVD (Ministry of Internal Affairs) colonel Iskandar Gamidov's fighters in Azerbaijan during 1992–93, and most of the Chechen fighters in both wars with Russia (Fairbanks 1995, 23; Goltz 1998, photos after 298, 361; Gall and de Waal 1998, 140–41, photos; Shihab 1999). Since the eighteenth century, uniforms have been a powerful symbol of unit loyalty and subordination to the state; the refusal to wear them in many postcommunist wars is quite significant. Private army fighters prefer macho symbols from Western pop culture: the words Mkhedrioni fighters scrawled on their Soviet armored personnel carriers were not Georgian but a kind of English—"Rainger" (Miller 1993).

These groups have characteristics very different from those of normal armies. People join and quit when they want (Fairbanks 1995, 23–24). Such units seem to be formed on two bases. The first is ethnic-nationalist enthusiasm, which produces volunteers against a ruling power or against an enemy ethnic group. Until the Soviet Union no longer formally existed, national armed forces could exist only in the form of private armies. Later they became a habit appealing to the deeply rooted antipolitical feelings of post-Soviet society. Many people from upper-middle-class backgrounds joined the various Georgian private armies and the Azerbaijani Popular Front in 1989–93 (Darchiashvili 1997, 39n107, 37n66; Tsintadze 1997; Alieva 1994). Thus these units were variegated in their social composition, as are the units of modern state armies.

Much more common is organization on the basis of families, clans, residential quarters, and patron-client networks. David Darchiashvili, the foremost civilian expert on the Georgian military, reports that military units were "party- or clan-based." "Tengiz Kitovani's armed units partly represent[ed] the . . . Union of Georgian Traditionalists and partly certain rural clans of central Georgia" (Darchiashvili 1997, 19). This "traditional" characteristic has been preserved in the present state army:

Despite the purges and the prohibition of illegal paramilitary units, the patriarchal mentality which displays itself in viewing these units as one's own fiefdom has largely been preserved. From the defense ministry to battalions, the enlistment of schoolmates, relatives, etc., is a universal practice. Despite the extra-territorial principle of enlistment, detachments are basically formed by the people with certain regional or other connections regardless of their professionalism (Darchiashvili 1997, 23).

The process of organizing political movements and their private armies has been studied by the Russian ethnologists V. E. Bushkov and D. V. Mikulskiy in Tajikistan. The "democratic" and Islamic detachments in Dushanbe, for instance, were formed on the basis of *avlodi*, or patrilineal clans. The Islamic bands that tried to take Khodzhent in 1992 had their family origins in (old) Matcha, a mountain region forced by the Soviet regime to resettle in the new Matcha *raion* north of Khodzhent. The bands were probably organized in much the same way that the "primary party organizations" of the Islamic Revival Party of Tajikistan (IRPT) were in the same areas—that is, along clan and quarter lines (Bushkov and Mikulskiy 1996, 136, 117, 119–20). The village of Pol'dork, whose people were also from Matcha, however, was largely opposed to the IRPT, a sign that postcommunist politico-military attachments were rooted in traditional tensions. Indeed, the patterns of support for the IRPT tended to follow patterns of participation and nonparticipation in the *Basmachi*, or anti-Soviet resistance, of 1918–31 (Bushkov and Mikulskiy 1996, 127; Medvedev 1992, 1993, 188, 191–94). In Khodzhent and some other cities, however, the Islamic organizations were composed of young people from various urban quarters, clans, and families (Bushkov and Mikulskiy 1996, 120–21). In accord with this pattern, many of the Islamic resistance's leaders, such as the organizer of the "National Guard," Said Kiemitdin Gozi, came from the families that traditionally provided *ishans*, or Sufi *shaykhs* (leaders—see Bushkov and Mikulskiy 1996, 127–28). A local branch of a Sufi order can be understood as a kind of patronage network, with the added element that the *murid*, or follower, is supposed to owe unconditional obedience to his Sufi master.

Soviet criminals were also organized in tightly structured patron-client networks, often rooted in the sports and martial arts subcultures. A number of leaders from this background, such as the ethnic Tajik and Kulyabi Sangak Safarov, the Lakai tribal and ethnic Uzbek Fayzali Saidov, and the Pamiri Rakhim Nurullobekov, became leaders of private armies in Tajikistan. In Georgia, warlords Tengiz Kitovani and Dzhaba Ioseliani had this background (oddly combined with art); in Chechnya so did Ruslan Labazanov and Beslan Gantemirov. The kind of loyalties that grew in these groups can be gathered from Safarov's comment about Rakhim: "He worked as a trainer, then went into a racket, he has his band" (Medvedev 1993, 200). Safarov himself was not only a criminal leader but a Kulyabi from the former *bekstvo* (autonomous fiefdom) of Baljuvon in the Emirate of Bukhara, a *sayyid* (descendent of the Prophet Muhammed), and the descendent of *ishans* who were *Basmachi* leaders. His ancestors had fought with Garmi *ishans*, whose descendents he fought in the Tajik civil war (Medvedev 1993, 188). These facts should give some sense of the overlapping group loyalties that probably work in the formation of most ex-Soviet private armies. Tajikistan was, with Dagestan, the most traditional society in the Soviet Union, but there are many signs of similar small-group loyalties in the postcommunist wars.

When private armies win, they often fall out among themselves. When they do, they tend to disintegrate along the lines of smaller groups. In Georgia, Gia Karkarashvili, a Soviet army captain, resigned and founded with army deserters the nationalist private unit White Eagle, which he confederated with similar units to form Ioseliani's Mkhedrioni. Subsequently Karkarashvili left the Mkhedrioni for Kitovani's National Guard, then left Kitovani to become, with his comrades, the nucleus of Georgian president

Eduard Shevardnadze's army (Darchiashvili 1997, 37n57). When Karkarashvili was dismissed as defense minister, many of his subordinates were dismissed with him. These dissensions and purges suggest important generalizations about post-Soviet private armies that may apply in other places: for one thing, the deepest motive for the formation of these private armies was not subethnic "patriotism" but the rewards of office.

But the private armies of common origin were often compelled to work together by the convention that they stood or fell together. Thus the Mkhedrioni split, then the National Guard; both split into smaller groups of narrower local origin. One gets the impression from such cases that most private armies are built up from small, face-to-face groups of fighters united by ancestry, place of origin, subethnicity, historical tradition, common experience during the nationalist-mobilizational phase, or several of these factors in combination.[2] Such smaller groups appear to have rather clear boundaries, with little opportunity to lose or add unrelated individuals.

Given the role of the salary in structuring modern states, its usual absence in private armies is crucial. As with sundry rebel forces in Africa today, the reward for fighting comes from plundering; from the income of plundered businesses or state bureaucracies; from selling equipment, food, ammunition, or weapons; and from the use of position and power to permit, for a fee, smuggling, particularly of drugs and arms. The border guards in Tajikistan, for example, both Russian and Tajik, are deeply involved in that trade. And some army units have seized resources or been given a source of income by the government. For instance, in Abkhazia, Russian and North Caucasian soldiers or adventurers who fought for Abkhazia were promised apartments, houses, land, passport registration, or dual citizenship in the Abkhaz vacationland (Chelnokov 1993; Nadareishvili 1997, 113, 131). And there are cases in the new armies (for instance, in Turkmenistan) where officers ordered soldiers to do construction work for private citizens (for instance, building dachas). The unit commanders received the pay for the completed dachas.

Just as with military power, in the case of Chechnya there are much greater financial resources outside the government than within it (see Table 6.2). Of course, this is also the case with modern capitalist democracies. The difference is that, in Chechnya, several individual warlords or leaders who are active contestants for political power, such as Basaev and Udugov,

---

2. Anthropologists should study the habits and symbols that draw these groups together, such as the "wolf ear" salute of the Azerbaijani Grey Wolves (Goltz 1998, 240) or the pseudomedieval neck medallion of the Mkhedrioni (Fairbanks 1995, 23).

Table 6.2

Sources of Income of Chechen Political Leaders and Warlords, 1998–99

	Number of personal fighters	Income sources
President Maskhadov	?	Primary sources: Transneft, Via Yunco Oil Company (transit fees); other Russian government sources: pipeline guarding fee, occasional pension payments; secondary sources: Islamists in Southeast Asia, business owners in Chechen diaspora, especially in Moscow and Turkey (e.g., Berkan Yasara); overall, has little money
Basaev	1,000?	Invested reserves from Abkhaz war and from Chechen business owners in Moscow; commissions on 1991–94 trade; protection services; gifts; possibly supporters in Saudi Arabia, the United Arab Emirates (UAE), possibly including Sait Ahmed Saidulayev; overall, a rich man
Udugov	None	Subsidies from Islamists in Saudi Arabia and the UAE, via Pakistan; earlier sources were personal donations by Fattakh, a wealthy Jordanian of Chechen origin who died in 1997; mobile phone monopoly; until recently, gifts from Russian oligarch Boris Berezovsky; overall, the richest person in Chechnya
Arsanov	?	Protection services, kidnapping rumored; possibly donations from the Russian intelligence service (FSB); overall, a wealthy man (pays bodyguards more than anyone else)
Raduyev	40	Industry and trade in eastern Chechnya; TV channel Marsho; illegal oil extraction, refining, and sale; gifts from Berezovsky; possibly contributions from supporters in Saudi Arabia, the UAE, and the FSB

(continued)

Table 6.2 (*Continued*)

	Number of personal fighters	Income sources
Israpilov	300	Well-off (his troops live in barracks)
Khattab	200–300	No reserves or business sources; continuous flow of donations from Saudi Arabia, the UAE, and Jordan, via Pakistan; possibly funds from Osama bin Laden; kidnapping rumored
Khultygov	450–500	Bribes to release people from jail
Barayev	Few	Kidnapping, other crimes; donations from Wahhabis; FSB sources (confirmed in 1999)
Gelayev	500	Little money; took Basaev's side for money
Kadyrov (Russian administrator of Chechnya in 2000; mufti of Chechnya; a Sufi)	none	Close to Yamadayevs (same *teip* [clan]); religious charity (with sources possibly from Southeast Asia); possibly FSB
Yamadayev bros.	200–250	Kidnapping; FSB likely
Khalkhoroyev	150–300	Kidnapping

Sources: Interviews; Gall and de Waal 1998.
Note: Question marks by themselves indicate that information is unknown; question marks after a piece of information indicate that sources disagree substantially.

have had more money at their disposal than the president can command for public purposes. This situation is reminiscent of feudal France, where after about 875 or 900 the king had less land (the equivalent of money in feudal society) in his family estates and was the feudal lord of an area (the Royal Domain) smaller than the similar territories held by several of his great vassals, such as the king of England/duke of Normandy, the duke of Aquitaine, and perhaps the count of Toulouse (Barraclough 1976, 84–97; Petit-Dutaillis 1964, 16). In fact, the kings faced a handicap in their struggle with the great vassals: because they were kings, they had more responsibilities, which they often could discharge only by giving someone part of the royal estates in return for his help. Similarly, the rulers of weak states have responsibilities such as representing the country abroad and the upkeep of the country's resources that their rivals do not have. Above all, they have to play the role of a national ruler; this frequently forces them to buy the support of powerful warlords by cutting into their country's resources or income. For instance, President Imomali Rakhmonov of Tajikistan bought the support, against other Kulyabi factions, of the criminals calling themselves the "Eleventh Brigade" by allowing them to take the revenues from the Central Market in Kurgan-Tyube.

A second problem that some rulers such as Maskhadov have faced is lack of a monetary reserve of the kind held by warlords such as Basaev and Udugov. Some other countries' rulers, such as Mobutu Sese Seko in Congo-Kinshasa, Slobodan Milosevic in Serbia, and Boris Yeltsin in Russia, accumulated substantial foreign reserves in banks and other investments. In a functioning modern constitutional system, the tax base serves as a broader functional equivalent of a reserve. In postcommunist weak states, however, people regard the Western style of taxation as strange and shocking; in the planned economy, most revenues were bookkeeping transactions within the government and formal taxes (and fees for services) tended to be low. Moreover, the postcommunist attitude toward the state comes into play: people simply do not want to pay.

For the first two reasons, weak state governments are often dependent on external revenue flows, making them fragile and easily controlled. Maskhadov's need for a continuous revenue flow rendered him to some extent dependent on Russia, his major peacetime financial backer. In Kosovo, the parallel Albanian government headed by Ibrahim Rugova was dependent on diaspora contributions, which suddenly dried up when the Kosovo Liberation Army was organized. In this respect the unrecognized "entities" are at a serious disadvantage: states such as Russia, Georgia, and Azerbaijan are able to draw on the International Monetary Fund (IMF) as a financial reserve. But Reno has pointed to cases where "freedom from creditors and . . . access to foreign firms" have given unrecognized entities greater capabilities than recognized states (Reno 1995, 179). This is an important insight; it would have been harder, for instance, for the finance minister of a recognized weak state to have put $4 million in bills in two used soap cartons and carry it back to Grozny on the shuttle-trader's flight (Gall and de Waal 1998, 134–36). Nevertheless, the advantage that Reno identified as accruing to unrecognized states did not prevail overall in any of the postcommunist cases. Because the "transition" in the former Soviet bloc has been seen as so important by Western states and by the IMF, recognized states have been granted considerable leeway. Africa in this sense is treated more harshly.

All these considerations pale before a fourth point: the internal resources of most weak states are simply miniscule in comparison with potential external resources. As Reno says, weak state rulers "are exposed much more than their strong-state colleagues" to the imperatives of the global market

(Reno 1998, 72). External resources, technological and financial, are available to private citizens as well as to rulers; in fact, they may not be equally available to rulers. The weakest of the weak states are the unrecognized "entities"—such as the late Srpska Krajina, Republika Bosna, Kosovo, Trans-Dniestria, Abkhazia, South Ossetia, Nagorno-Karabakh, Chechnya, the United Tajik Opposition–controlled parts of Tajikistan before the truce, and the former Ahmad Shah Massoud–controlled and present Taliban-controlled areas in Afghanistan. Such entities are often cut off from diplomatic relations, Western aid, human rights monitoring, travel, telephone, banking, and many other normal parts of the "global market." The forces to which they are exposed are a peculiar deformation of the global market. As a Russian reporter said of Trans-Dniestria, "This 'zero' land is a distinctive state that draws into itself romantics, adventurers, and soldiers of fortune . . . like some enormous funnel" (Chelnokov 1994).

The Organization of Private Armies

In the case of private armies, a unit designation, such as "regiment" or "company," depends for its meaning on the particular case. You cannot assume that the "First Brigade" or the "11th Battalion" is a unit of a certain size with a certain organization and equipment. In the Georgian National Guard, groups of 5–30 men, not the standard 400–800, were called "battalions" (Fairbanks 1995, 23). To fight in Tavildara during the Tajik civil war, a composite brigade was put together from troops belonging to the MVD, the Tajik KGB (state security service), and army ministries. But it was called the "Fifth Brigade" nevertheless. Normally, these private armies do not have a full set of ranks: they usually have an overall leader and other leaders at the normal platoon-size level.

Units tend to be headed by officers who were not trained as such (Darchiashvili 1997, 18–19). In the Chechen, Georgian, Azerbaijani, and Tajik cases, this tendency was initially necessitated by the small number of indigenous officers in the Soviet army (Darchiashvili 1997, 16–17, 37n52). For example, in 1992 only 4 percent of the officers of the Soviet army division that made up the Dushanbe garrison were Tajik (Ashurov 1992). The current Tajik Presidential Guard, the most competent military force under Tajik command, has three officers with professional military training. Its commander, General Ghafur Mirzoyev, comes from the *militsiya*, or ordinary police, a notoriously corrupt profession in the Soviet Union. He has, in fact, known criminal connections and comes from Baljuvon, the same Kulyabi village that is home to the president of the country. Clearly the favor given to this unit, which has its own military academy, its own budget, and the pick of the annual conscript pool, comes from the president's expectation that it will defend him out of regional or subethnic solidarity.[3] But the president does not rely solely on loyalty; he has given Mirzoyev the control of the Dushanbe Casino, a very lucrative source of income.

In post-Soviet parlance, such sources of income, which go to officials or bureaucratic units outside the state budget, are called "nonbudget funds" or, more rarely, "self-financing." They create a semifeudal situation. The dukes of Aquitaine were not always loyal to the French kings, their nominal superiors, above all because they were not on the royal payroll; they had their own sources of income and their own following. For this reason, it is not easy to draw a line between private armies created by society and armies raised, in the manner familiar to us, by the state. In a period when the Central Asian and Caucasian states are having great difficulty raising revenue, it is tempting, or necessary, to make army commanders raise part of their own budgets. If they do so, they become like the warlords controlling private armies, who raised and equipped their forces from the beginning.

Because these groups are not formed by government activity alone, they are not always controlled by governments. The relation of private armed forces to the state has never been better defined than by a Bosnian journalist, Tihomir Loza:

> Some of the gangs were created and are partly controlled by the government. But there is no absolute control and some of them have outgrown the government. Some gangs are loyal to one faction or another within the regime while some are independent and interested only in money. In fact, there are very narrow lines between the regular police, the military forces, and the private militia. Many gangs and militia steal and profit on the black market but fight bravely at the front (Loza 1993, 11).

As we have seen, many private army leaders emerged from the criminal world. At the end of the Soviet period the criminal culture began to penetrate the military. The military profession was not socially prestigious in the last years of the Soviet Union: it attracted either the children of serv-

---

3. This situation resembles the "ethnic security map" that characterizes the structuring of armies and their top command in Africa (Enloe 1980).

ing officers or people from parochial, disadvantaged parts of Soviet society, including the sports and martial arts subculture. The police, ordinary (*militsiya*) or political (KGB), were intimately involved through their work (as are American police) with the criminal world. But as the legitimacy of the Soviet regime waned, the wall separating public-spirited exploitation of criminal sources for law enforcement purposes from pure criminality crumbled as well. In the growing anarchy, as many civil conflicts broke out, access to weapons and criminal muscle became a valuable asset that could keep your family and friends prosperous in difficult times. In many non-Russian republics, where there were few local army officers, such ex-policemen supplied many new "army officers."

The disorder of private armies, their lack of discipline, and their frequent criminal connections assure numerous atrocities against civilians (for a discussion of this in the Abkhaz war alone, see Human Rights Watch Arms Project 1994; Argun 1994, 295, 433 ff.; Nodia 1998, 31). These traits do not go with military effectiveness. Generally, when private armies encounter an ordinary state army, they are routed. This was the outcome when Srpska Krajina and Republika Srpska encountered the American-trained Croatian army, when the Kosovo Liberation Army fought the Yugoslav army, when Zviad Gamsakhurdia's fighters in western Georgia met far smaller Russian units, and when the Armenian and Nagorno-Karabakh armies (the latter formed out of private armies) defeated the private armies calling themselves the "Azerbaijani Army." The great exception to this generalization is the Chechen victory over the Russian army in 1994–96.

There are also private armies that neither exist openly nor are clothed in the outward form of state armies—what might be called "latent private armies." In the Dagestan Republic of the Russian Federation, for example, there are many nationalities, with nine officially recognized languages. Each of those ethnic groups has a national movement. Both prominent politicians and the press have admitted in recent years that in these movements "groups of fighters exist, and are not hidden" (Abdulatipov interview 1997; Budberg 1996, 17; Kasaev 1996, 22).

Since the collapse of the Soviet Union there has been a shift from nationalism to Islam as a way of defining antiestablishment activity in Dagestan. The two are mixed in Nadir Khachilayev and his elder brother Magomed. Nadir is the bearded president of the Union of Muslims of Russia. He has hundreds of Dagestani followers, who hang around his house and the new mosque in Makhachkala, the capital. They revere him as their *shaykh,* the usual word for a Sufi leader, equivalent to an *ishan* in Tajikistan. Magomed is chairman of the Lak National Movement Gazi-Gumukh, which advocates a federalization of Dagestan. Because the Laks are few in numbers with little influence or respect, Nadir's Islamic orientation is as useful as it is pious. For some years Magomed headed Dagestan's offshore fishing and caviar monopoly, a fertile source of money.

The brothers are called a "mafia" by ordinary Dagestanis. They are playing many different cards, and used one of them in May 1998. After a murky incident in which their Humvee (a favorite warlord vehicle) was stopped and their house surrounded by police, the Khachilayevs and two or three hundred followers, now suddenly armed with pistols, Kalashnikovs, and rocket-propelled grenade launchers (and partly uniformed), occupied the local parliament building and seized the prime minister. Nadir told me later that the policemen simply fled, which reveals something about the state's weakness (Associated Press 1998; Khachilayev interview 1998). Their occupation of parliament ended in a peaceful, negotiated exit a few hours later. Neither Khachilayev nor his fighters suffered at this point from the authorities. This incident demonstrates another way in which private armies weaken the state. They not only can take power or get what they want by force, but can induce accommodations that make the state no longer look sovereign.

After several months of "investigation," however, the Russian government suddenly issued arrest warrants for the brothers. They nabbed Magomed, but his brother escaped, apparently to Chechnya. Although accounts differ, it appears that in August 1999 Nadir Khachilayev and several hundred of his followers joined cross-border attacks under the Chechens' Khattab (a nom de guerre) and Basaev to rescue Dagestani allies from the Russians. The Dagestani and Chechen private armies were eventually defeated, and in October Nadir was caught by the Russians in Dagestan (Sivertseva interview 1999), although he was released under an amnesty in spring 2000.

The sudden appearance, disappearance, and reappearance of Nadir Khachilayev's private armies make clear that such groups are not formed ad hoc in times of crisis, like American posses. In most cases, the arms and the social groups have a continuing existence. When private armies "appear," what is new is that the arms and the men appear together in public.

The attitude of the governments of Dagestan and of the Russian Federation toward the private army phenomenon is curious. On November 6, 1996, there were demonstrations in Dagestani areas along the Chechen border demanding the right to form self-defense detachments, which at first were prohibited by the Dagestani government but subsequently were allowed. An official newspaper, *Masliat,* gave this advice in late 1997: "In these conditions, *Masliat* calls on citizens through their national militias [*druzhini*], to include themselves in the defense of order in their cities and villages" ("Budni 'Masliat'" 1997, 1; cf. Beibutov 1997). During the Dagestani/Chechen invasion of 1999, the government once more handed weapons to citizens. In other words, the governments of Dagestan province and of Russia are legitimizing informal nongovernment armed units and the loss of state control over the means of coercion. Sometimes post-Soviet governments are forced into weakness, but sometimes they do not even wish to be strong.

Private Armies in the Former Soviet Union and in Sub-Saharan Africa: A Comparison

Any comparison of private armies in the area we have considered and in sub-Saharan Africa must be painted with a broad brush. The category "African" is a geographic artifact even more artificial than the assemblage of peoples in the Russian empire and in the Soviet Union.

The purposes of private armies in the ex-Soviet countries may be described as the acquisition of property and resources, ethnic defense and independence (often interpreted in terms of ethnic cleansing), attaining political power for the warlord, fighting feuds between warlords, and the amusement and self-assertion of the young men who compose them. All these purposes except ethnic assertion are shared by the African nonstate armed groups. On the role of ethnicity there is a major difference that I will consider below. There is a second important difference as well: the major African private armies have generally fought to bring the warlords who lead them to the position of leader of their country; in some cases, such as that of Charles Taylor in Liberia, they have succeeded. In no former Soviet republic or secessionist "entity," on the other hand, is the president a military officer brought to power by the use of force. In Chechnya, General Dzokhar Dudayev attained power in 1991 by seizing buildings; his accession was supported by a later plebiscite. His successors were, constitutionally, the poet Zelimkhan Yandarbiyev, succeeded after an internationally monitored free election by General Aslan Maskhadov, the victorious chief of staff of the Chechen army. Unlike the other leaders of private armies, Maskhadov apparently did not have his own group of fighters, and he was seen by the voters as a less "military" candidate.

As in the former Soviet space, acquisition can be closely linked with ethnicity: the assumption tends to be that resources will be dominated by one ethnic group or another. There are, however, marked differences in the role of ethnicity. Almost all of the private armies that flowered after the collapse of the Soviet Union and Yugoslavia were justified, and in many cases were really evoked, by ethnic self-defense. The extreme intensification of ethnic hatred in mixed, cosmopolitan societies with high rates of intermarriage, such as Bosnia or Abkhazia, has often been interpreted as artificially created by elites seeking to hold on to or seize power. This has been an important part of the reality. But we would not do justice to the real fears and dangers of postcommunist man if we did not admit that the Bosnian Muslims, Kosovar Albanians, Abkhaz, Tual (South Ossetian), Karabakh Armenians, and Udins have recently faced real dangers of annihilation as peoples. Such fears were reinforced by the historical memory of real or perceived attempts at genocide: the *Mukhazhirstvo* (in which Abkhaz, Chechens, and many other North Caucasian Muslim peoples were targeted) of 1864–66 and 1877–78, the Armenian massacres of 1915–21, Stalin's deportations of 1944 (which targeted Chechens, Ingush, and many other peoples), and the World War II massacres of Serbs and Croats.

But the immediate cause of danger was the collapse of state structures. The old definition of political order disappeared, leaving fear of the unknown. In the Soviet Union and in Yugoslavia, state institutions were much weaker in the federal units than in the national capitals because the economy, foreign policy, the military, the security police, ideology, and official appointments (the *nomenklatura* system) were controlled from the center. Thus from the moment of the federal republics' secession their state structures were decisively weaker than the earlier central state structure. The new states were also exposed to all the citizen aversion bred by decades of mobilizational pressure, while the rituals that had conferred a thin legitimacy were suddenly halted. The democratic mobilization and privatization promoted by the West weakened the institutions of the planned economy and existing authoritarian structures. In the absence of normal state institutions, a situation arose that was well described by the journalist Michael Ignatieff in *Blood and Belonging:* "If you can't trust your neighbors, drive them out. If you live among them, live only among your own. This alone appeared to offer people security. This alone gave respite from the fear that leaped like a brush fire from house to house" (Ignatieff 1993, 37, cf. 42–43). In the absence of an ideological justification for ruling over people, such as Marxism-Leninism, and of effective, politically neutral police and courts, communities fall back on the simplest, most instinctive definition of the political community: it is composed of people like us, neighbors who share our identity, ethnic or religious. What then is to be done about the others, who have an identity different from ours? Drive them out with ethnic private armies. In most cases (but not in Muslim Bosnia, Chechnya, Tajikistan, and Trans-Dniestria), ethnic self-defense was interpreted as ethnic cleansing, an extreme form of the demand for separation seen in autonomist and secessionist movements.

Reno's insistence on the importance of the distinction between collective and private interests (Reno 1998, 2–3) is very useful for examining post-Soviet politics, but it needs to be applied in a different way. Even nationalists, in my experience, understand that most private-army leaders, and other leaders, are crooks who are plundering collective resources for private ends. But they feel that, in weak-state conditions, these leaders must be supported to protect the ethnic group. There is a kind of implicit bargain: in this extremity, we will let you steal if you serve the overriding goal of ethnic survival. The bargain is helped by the fact that in these wars, the most visible and massive stealing is from the ethnic enemy. After the seizure and cleansing of Sukhumi by the Abkhaz and their Russian allies in September 1993, long lines of trucks could be seen taking the expelled Georgians' possessions to Russia. We see the opposite of this pattern in organized states, which become stronger and more authoritarian during wartime. In postcommunist weak states, disorder is at its maximum during wars of ethnic survival and ethnic cleansing. After wars were stabilized by truces or mutual exhaustion, publics in places such as Georgia, Azerbaijan, and Tajikistan supported national leaders in wiping out or co-opting the most prominent and rapacious private armies, creating a veneer of order and normal statehood over the continuing private appropriation carried out by the police and other officials.

Only in Rwanda and Burundi have African disorder and civil conflicts escalated to genocidal levels and led to ethnic cleansing. Yusuf Bangura has pointed out, "No armed group has made ethnic autonomy a major objective in Liberia" (Bangura 1996, 661). The same statement holds true of such private armies as the diverse insurgent groups in Congo-Brazzaville and the Allied Democratic Front in Uganda. Even where private armies are essentially ethnic in recruitment, such as the Cobra, Ninja, or Zulu armed factions in Congo-Brazzaville, or the Lord's Resistance Army in Uganda, their aim was control of the territorial state, not its dissolution. Although Africa has experienced secessionist movements, particularly striking is that those movements have almost without exception based their claim to sovereignty on a territorial entity of colonial derivation and not on ethnicity per se (e.g., eastern Nigeria, the southern Sudan, Katanga, Casamance, western Cameroon, Eritrea).

Indeed, African private armies often have little to do with ethnicity. In Sierra Leone, Congo-Kinshasa, and earlier Mozambique, private armies have been recruited from a wide range of ethnic elements. Ethnicity may well operate in patterns of participation, but the conflict does not congeal around a zero-sum struggle for ethnic survival.

The Somali private armies illustrate how ethnicity and armed conflict play a greater role in armed conflict there than elsewhere in Africa. Traditional Somalia was what anthropologists call a segmentary society: its population was almost entirely Somali, itself a strongly held consciousness. The Somalis were segmented further into smaller and smaller groups of clan-families, confederations, clans, and subclans, nominally structured by their genealogy (often fictitious) from the first ancestor. Members of all these kinship groups are supposed to unite against outside groups of similar size but fight each other when there are no larger external threats. Such nominal kinship groups are equivalent in the Somali context to subethnic groups such as the Mingrelians, Svans, Imeretians, and Kakhetians in Georgia or the Khujandis, Kulyabis, Pamiris, and Garmis in Tajikistan.

"In 1991/92," says the eminent Somali expert Ioan Lewis, "... the general tendency was for every major Somali clan to form its own militia movement" (Lewis 1994, 231). These kinship-based private armies fought the ongoing civil war. There have been some apparent exceptions. The Dulbahante and Warsangeli clans of the Majeerteen confederacy were united in the United Somali Party (Lewis 1994, 235), although other Majeerteen belong to the Somali Salvation Democratic Front. This sort of case does not conform to the nominal logic of segmentary society, in that the Dulbahante and Warsangeli were allied with the larger Isaaq clan-family against other Majeerteen. But the division of private armies repeats the nominal pattern of kinship, the Somali equivalent of subethnicity, in that all private armies seem to be made up of single clans or subclans, or coalitions of intact clans or subclans belonging to a larger confederation or clan-family, not of elements drawn from several clans or subclans and combined. On the other hand, Somali private armies are not coextensive with kinship groups; in "Puntland," the traditional Majeerteen sultanate, clans or groups of clans took actions to dissociate themselves from "their" kinship-based militias (Fox 1999, 6). Although Somali private armies have been organized along the lines of traditional kinship structures, they have not been otherwise traditional; Ahmed Samatar notes that they have dispensed with customary law, the authority of elders, and the veneration of Islamic *shaykhs* (Samatar 1994, 9). The automatic weapon, in the hands of young men, is a potent solvent of customary hierarchies and norms.

How does one explain the ethnic identity of postcommunist private armies, as contrasted with the more complex role of ethnicity in many African private armies? It seems to me that ethnicity played a similar covert role in the Soviet system and in much of postcolonial Africa, but different official discoveries of identity prevailed. "National in form, socialist in content" was the Soviet mantra. By contrast, "tribe" until recently was an illicit basis for formal political claims in Africa, viewed as an artifact of backwardness, relegated strictly to the private sphere.

Both communist and most postcolonial African political systems had ideologies and institutions that expressed poorly the real political forces; they needed organizing principles for common political action. In the Soviet case, this came from a state-sponsored and manipulated official "nationality" policy. Incessant campaigns were waged against "great power [i.e., Russian] chauvinism," "bourgeois nationalism" (that deviating from state-sponsored forms), and "Zionism," shifting frequently from one of these targets to another. These slogans served to legitimize one group within the elite as opposed to another. To take only the best-known example, the "Doctor Affair" and the "Mingrelian Affair" (accompanied by a bloody campaign against bourgeois nationalism) of 1951–53 served to signal and legitimize the ouster of Lavrenti Beria's Transcaucasian and Jewish followers and the Mingrelians in Georgia who were part of the political machine of his lieutenant, Mikhail Baramiya. Then, in 1953, the other Georgian groups that had replaced the Mingrelians were purged in turn. As the system became more corrupt, ethnicity gave one group, as opposed to another, access not only to office, with all its special privileges, but also to wealth. (Unlike in Africa, many Soviet ethnic groups enjoyed group rights such as entitlements to certain offices, privileges about publishing, and other aspects of national culture in "autonomous" republics, provinces, and districts inside union republics dominated by another ethnic group.)

In Africa before the democratic opening, although ethnicity was officially banished, in practice, through the mechanisms of patrimonial autocracy, an ongoing competition for disproportionate shares of the "national cake" took place. Favored access normally accrued to groups best represented at the political summit, although rulers did not normally entirely exclude significant ethnic groups. Rwanda and Burundi have been major exceptions: their post-independence regimes have operated highly exclusionary policies from the outset (with Tutsi ruling in Burundi except during a few months in 1993; Hutu running Rwanda from 1962 to 1994; and Tutsi ruling Rwanda since).

With the collapse of the communist order, a new and different pattern of ethnic conflict appeared in the countries of the Soviet bloc, but not in Africa. The Nagorno-Karabakh conflict flared in 1988 and was followed by ethnic cleansing in Azerbaijan proper and in Armenia, Croatia, Bosnia, South Ossetia, and Abkhazia in Georgia; North Ossetia and perhaps Chechnya in Russia; and Kosovo in Yugoslavia. The sudden weakening of the state is part of the explanation.

Elsewhere G. M. Tamas and I have developed an interpretation of the new ethnic cleansing, which I will only summarize briefly here (Tamas 1994; Fairbanks 1995, 27–28; 1997; 1999; forthcoming a; forthcoming b). When communism's deadening Truth, in which no one believed, crashed, it opened the former communist world to the impact of relativism. One side of relativism is a sudden absence of theories to justify the rule of one class, race, or religion over others. What today is called "multiculturalism" carries the refusal to judge other people into a refusal to assimilate the Other into a dominant culture or constitutional system. If we do not have the right to assimilate "inferior" cultures or lifestyles, having a culture or a lifestyle must be important. Having no right to judge what is good and bad, or which form of government is better or worse, we can only fall back on the only community that is given prior to any argument: the community of ethnicity and religion. Unfortunately, there is another side to relativism. If having a culture, community, identity, lifestyle, or "values" is really important, and there are people of fundamentally different identity within the community, what can be done? What is there to do but drive them out or kill them? The collapse of rationalism leaves no way of including them, the equality of values no excuse for ruling them. I have argued elsewhere that ethnic cleansing is not something atavistic or traditional, but "an appalling solution to a deeply felt quandary of modern man, who acknowledges no authority, who 'privileges' no discourse, worldview, or institution over others" (Fairbanks 1999, 23). If there is any truth to this argument, one would expect to find ethnic cleansing in more modern societies, and certainly much more in the former Soviet Union than in Africa, where the line of reasoning suggested is really not applicable. Such has been the case. In Tajikistan, the most traditional ex-Soviet society in which there were major ethnic wars, there was much brutality but little ethnic cleansing; the victorious Kulyabis turned the vanquished Garmis into something like serfs rather than expelling them.

In half a dozen African countries (Uganda, Chad, Ethiopia, Eritrea, Rwanda, and Congo-Kinshasa), the warlords of private armies installed themselves as presidents. The absence of a power seizure by armed insurgents from the periphery in the former Soviet space is a remarkable paradox. It is the more remarkable because, as we have seen, the goals of ethnic affirmation make ex-Soviet private armies more public-oriented than a number of their African analogues. Elsewhere I have speculated that "military leaders, themselves affected by the flight from the public world, want money and power more than glory and responsibility" (Fairbanks 1995, 29). The longer existence of the Soviet regime, and its greater control and intrusiveness, would be likely to produce a greater reaction against politics and the military, now so identified with politics. Maskhadov, the great Chechen general and a professional officer who led private armies to victory, recalls, "From childhood, from the school desk we were used to such commonplaces as 'the heroism of the masses,' 'people's war,' 'miracles of valor' and so on. With time all this rings with banality with every repetition" (Maskhadov n.d., 22).

All recruitment to private armies in the ex-Soviet space is voluntary. In every area where postcommunist wars have broken out, the fighters have been a small part of the population, by my calculations no more than from .05 to 5 percent. Many of the young men of Tbilisi, in a holiday mood, watched from the lofty vantage point of the Botanical Gardens, without interfering, as rival private armies destroyed the center of their historic capital (Dugashvili 1994). Even in Chechnya, where there are many part-time fighters, there are also many fierce nationalists who sat out the wars in Russian-occupied Grozny or abroad. This is not regarded with reproach; we are far from the guerrilla wars (and the vast world wars) of the recent epoch, where young men were shamed for not enlisting and guerrillas tried to mobilize entire populations, to involve them in their campaigns, and to provoke governments' retaliation that would drive them all into the resistance.

In Africa, by contrast, we find the remarkable practice of forced recruitment, which has been publicized through human rights organizations' protests against the forced recruitment of children (Amnesty International 1997, Cohn and Goodwin-Gill 1994, Human Rights Watch/Africa 1997, Human Rights Watch 1996). From these sources it is clear that private armies have recruited children by force in Liberia, Mozambique, Sierra Leone, the Sudan, and Uganda. This practice is also followed by private armies in some other "Third World" countries; it is the former Soviet space that is the exception. In some "Third World" cases, soldiers recruited by force seem to be in the majority, but there is always voluntary recruitment. The voluntary recruitment pool is mainly, as in the former Soviet republics, unemployed, largely lower-class young men eager for plunder.

No one has ever remarked on the military oddity of forced child recruitment, which seems likely to yield unenthusiastic, unreliable, and mutinous soldiers. So why do African abducted children fight, and why do their leaders trust them enough to use them? And why is the former Soviet space so different in providing no examples of child soldiers?

Child recruitment in Africa substitutes for all the military organization of modern armies the natural superiority of adults over children, and the possibilities of "training" them by a combination of brutality, fear, drugs, and armies' sense of rupture with their communities. In contrast, the exclusively voluntary recruitment of ex-Soviet private armies testifies eloquently to a fundamental resistance to coercion that has sprouted on that part of the earth. People associate coercion with the Soviet state. The Soviet state was so militarized that it seems to have created a dislike of the army and of military service; this partly explains the separateness of ex-Soviet private armies from the society, as well as their small size and partly criminal composition.

I am struck by how much the warlords in Liberia, Sierra Leone, and Uganda resemble nineteenth-century African leaders such as Samori, Tippu Tip, Zubeir Pasha, Rabih b. Fadlallah, Muhammad Al-Sanusi, and the Nguni leaders. Most of these leaders were men of modest birth who set up private armies or moving quasi-state structures by raiding less-well-armed and more poorly organized African peoples for slaves (as well as ivory and other plunder) that could be sold outside of Africa, turning other slaves into involuntary soldiers who continued the same process in more distant areas.[4] If so, one might conceive the forced recruitment of private armies in contemporary Africa to be a product of the contact between traditional African societies and more modern societies, as in the last century.

The military level of African armies recruited by force can be judged from the following interview with a child soldier in Uganda:

> The frontline was somewhere ahead of where I was, and the commander said, "Run, run to the front line!" It did not matter whether you had a gun or not. If you did not run they would beat you with sticks. . . . If you had a gun, you had to be firing all the time or you would be killed. And you were not allowed to take cover. The order from the Holy Spirit was not to take cover. You must have no fear, and stand up as you run into fire (Human Rights Watch/Africa 1997, 37).

---

4. The best description of this process of which I am aware is found in Cordell 1985 (79–135), which is based in part on interviews with surviving slave-soldiers.

Among the control mechanisms used to coerce children is the manipulation of supernatural beliefs; the child soldiers are persuaded that they are immunized against bullets by magical rites. Visible here is an element of magic or religion never found in ex-Soviet private armies.

If ex-Soviet private armies, other than the Chechen ones, have little combat capability, the African ones—given communications, tactics, and training such as the above—have even less. In both cases, it is the absence of competent state armies that enables them to exist and win. Here there is another contrast with the guerrilla armies of the previous era. Guerrilla warfare exploited the size and rigidity of the modern state and its armies, which offer so many targets. It exploited as well the media publicity and the civil liberties of democratic or quasi-democratic states to build its reputation and to operate more freely. Against an Attila, or a medieval king, guerrillas would have been helpless. Guerrilla warriors tried to trigger the massive repressive capability of modern states to build, by reaction, popular support. Thus guerrilla warfare and the modern state had a symbiotic relationship. Private armies, on the other hand, weaken existing weak states and create weaker states such as Abkhazia and Chechnya. Weak states, in turn, cannot inspire, discipline, or pay their soldiers, who desert to form private armies. This pair, too, nurse each other.

African and ex-Soviet private armies differ in the clarity of the borders distinguishing them from the rest of society and in their continuity. In Sierra Leone (and in Liberia), the "sobel" phenomenon—government soldiers who masquerade as rebels in order to loot—is well known (Jackson and Larsen 1998, 3-10, 5-1, 5-15). In Somalia there were "*mooryan*," or apolitical, heavily armed teenage gangs (Lyons and Samatar 1995, 22).

Similarly, there have been many internal splits in West African private armies. (Somali private armies have fissured and combined along the traditional lines of segmentary kinship, but rarely otherwise.) In 1994, there were eight identifiable private armies fighting in Liberia (Jackson and Larsen 1998, 5-9), some derived from internal splits within Charles Taylor's National Patriotic Front for Liberia (NPFL), others from various factions and ethnic groups that opposed him. The private army leader Roosevelt Johnson described the early history of the United Liberian Movement for Democracy (ULIMO) in this way: "We were open and the other tribes came in. The Mandingos also came in. We accepted them, not knowing that they had something up their sleeve" (Johnson 1997, 681). In subsequent "manipulations," as Johnson describes them, he quarreled with Alhaji Kromah, who split away many Mandingo fighters to form

ULIMO-K, and with one of his chiefs of staff, Armah Youlo, who joined Taylor's NPFL.

These shifting organizational permutations do not, generally speaking, characterize the former Soviet space. There were more similar cases in Georgia than in any other place. The Georgian National Guard that served Gamsakhurdia, the first president of independent Georgia, was already a composite of many armed groups; it was not surprising when a large part of it, under Kitovani, split away and attacked Gamsakhurdia. Subsequently, President Shevardnadze purged Kitovani with the help of Karkarashvili, one of Kitovani's lieutenants, and made him defense minister. After these changes, and the later ones, there were considerable purges of the departed leader's men, showing that we are dealing with relatively continuous organizational entities, not with a flux of betrayals and realignments. The ex-Soviet private armies seem to be composed of face-to-face groups of some 5–30 fighters, united in groups of 500–4,000 under a warlord of particular prestige (Fairbanks 1995, 23). To the extent that there are realignments, they are likely to be confined to the addition or subtraction of face-to-face groups, which themselves remain relatively solid. This situation is what might be predicted if the smaller building blocks of private armies are patron-client networks. In the old Soviet political system, there were strong informal rules against the betrayal of patrons, except at the very top level. Within Stalin's party apparatus, one could not expect advancement by shifting allegiance, unless at the very top (Fairbanks 1998, 369–72). The relative cohesion of Soviet clienteles probably reflects deeper forces in the nature of Soviet society, particularly the combination of universal education and opportunities to rise rapidly within an inefficient planned economy, with its resulting scarcity and the tremendous power of its administrative gatekeepers.

Ex-Soviet private armies tend to have rather definite borders, if one includes past members and potential members drawn from the same social group. Most of these organizations took form in response to ethnic warfare and totally excluded the members of the other contending ethnic group. (There have been relatively large numbers of foreign mercenaries, in the Abkhaz case possibly the majority of the fighters, who are valued for their skills but are not members in the same sense.) In two cases in Tajikistan, the Popular Front and its subsequent government handed out weapons in the Dushanbe stadium to anyone who would defend them, as did the Revolutionary United Front (RUF) in Sierra Leone.

A point of strong similarity between ex-Soviet and African private armies is the importance of foreign sponsorship. In the ex-Soviet insurgencies,

Russia, Armenia, Uzbekistan, Chechnya, Trans-Dniestria, and Taliban and Rabbani Afghanistan, together with international networks of Islamic radicals, have facilitated the operations of private armies. In West Africa, Liberia, Sierra Leone, "Taylorland," Libya, Burkina Faso, and the Ivory Coast have supported private armies in neighboring states. In both the former Soviet space and in West Africa, weak states have frequently been responsible for the formation of private armies on their own territory or others. (In calling them "private" I do not mean they are unrelated to the state.) The sense that the state ought to have a monopoly of the means of coercion has crumbled with surprising ease in both areas.

Private armies predictably are more likely to commit atrocities against their opponents and against civilians than are regular armies. Because ethnic antagonism was the very inspiration of many private armies during the disintegration of the Soviet Union, we might expect their violations to be graver than the offenses of African private armies. The harassment of civilians so as to evict them from the ancestral territory is the very purpose of many of these wars. Postcommunist wars of ethnic cleansing have indeed involved many rapes, massacres of civilians, mutilations of the dead—and sometimes of the living. But some African private armies have displayed a level of brutality far beyond anything in the former Soviet space. Insurgents in West Africa, especially the RUF in Sierra Leone, had a pattern of cutting off civilians' hands and feet, for no apparent reason beyond that of spreading fear. Child soldiers have often been "initiated" by being forced to commit brutal killings or rapes (Human Rights Watch/Africa 1997, 13, 26; Cohn and Goodwin-Gill 1994, 27; Amnesty International 1997, 14; Human Rights Watch 1996, 10–11). What explains the even greater inhumanity in some African private armies? Sometimes it has been hypothesized that the more picturesque cruelties are connected with secret societies or traditional religion (Jackson and Larsen 1998, 2–3). But since extreme, demonstrative brutality exists in many cultural areas, not just among the secret societies of the West African coast, a wider explanation is needed. Perhaps the atrocities are committed simply to inspire terror, in the absence of the excuse for plunder and domination provided by ethnic defense.

Reno has shown that African warlords support themselves by selling natural resources to international corporations, including some famous and state-owned ones. So can private armies be understood as an "attempt to deal with global capitalism" (Reno 1998, 39)? In Chechen private armies, a former political leader said, "It's all about money" (Usmanov 1998). But at the same time, something is obviously wrong with this view. International investment in the ex-Soviet countries that lack oil is low even by the standards of the "emerging markets." In Chechnya or Tajikistan or Abkhazia there is virtually no international investment. In Chechnya, one firm, Granger Telecom of the United Kingdom, was trying to install a cell phone system to compete with Udugov's system until its workers were beheaded. In my experience, major international corporations are extremely reluctant to become active in such places. Chechnya is a striking case, because the largest pipeline for Caspian oil to be put in operation runs through it. For the major corporations involved in the Azerbaijani consortia that will send oil through this pipeline, the stabilization of Chechnya would seem to be a high priority. Yet they have rigidly adhered to the position that they will pay Transneft, the Russian pipeline company, for transporting the oil, and that it is up to Transneft to deal with the problem of securing the Chechen route. Compare Angola: as civil war and the final battles of the cold war were being fought there, Western oil companies were pumping its oil, mostly from offshore platforms or secure coastal enclaves in Cabinda.

My impression is that the largest U.S. corporations prefer above all to simplify their business dealings in the former Soviet space. They have grown used to the strong state, with the protections and inconveniences it brings. They are ill-equipped to deal with a weak-state environment. On top of this, there is still the nervousness left over from the cold war, when both the Soviet and Western governments enforced business caution. Of course, some smaller firms specifically seek out difficult niches to exploit, and others come from different business cultures and have different expectations of the state (for example, the Japanese-owned Bridgestone-Firestone that operated in Liberia). On the supply side of economics, global capitalism has had little interest in post-Soviet weak states, especially unrecognized entities like Chechnya. If one wanted to show the real connection with global capitalism, I believe it would be better to consider the enormous demand in such places.

References

Abdulatipov, Ramazan. 1997. Interview. 29 April.

Alieva, Leila. 1994. Interviews. Spring.

Amnesty International. 1997. *Uganda: Breaking God's Commands, the Destruction of Childhood by the Lord's Resistance Army.* New York: Amnesty International.

Argun, Aleksey. 1994. *Abkhaziia: Ad v Raiu.* Sukhumi: Alashara.

Ashurov, Col. Mukhriddin. 1992. Interview. Interfax. 11 August.

Associated Press. 1998. "Daghestan Protestors Seize Prime Minister's Office." *Dispatch.* 21 May.

Bangura, Yusuf. 1996. "The Liberian Dilemma." *West Africa.* 29 April–5 May: 661–62.

Barraclough, Geoffrey. 1976. *The Crucible of Europe: The Ninth and Tenth Centuries in European History.* Berkeley: University of California Press.

Beibutov, Dekabr. 1997. "Home Guards Rather than Citizen's Militia Being Formed in Dagestan's Frontier Areas." Russian Information Agency-Novosti via Chechen List, Chechnya@plearn.edu.pl. 24 November.

Biebuyck, Daniel, and Mary Douglas. 1961. *Congo: Tribes and Parties.* R.A.I. Pamphlet no. 1. London: Royal Anthropological Institute.

Blandy, Charles W. N.d. "Chechnya: A Beleaguered President." Paper no. OB 61. Sandhurst: Conflict Studies Research Center.

Budberg, Aleksandr. 1996. "A Corollary of 'Strange War.'" *Moskovsky komsomolets.* 16 July. Trans. and reprinted in Foreign Broadcast Information Service, *FBIS-SOV,* 17 January.

"Budni 'Masliat." 1997. *Masliat.* October–November.

Bushkov, V. E., and D. V. Mikulskiy. 1996. *Anatomiia grazhdanskoi voiny v Tadzhikistane. Etno-sotsial'niye protsessy i politicheskaia borba.* Moscow: Institut etnologii i antropologii RAN.

Callaghy, Thomas M. 1984. *The State-Society Struggle: Zaire in Comparative Perspective.* New York: Columbia University Press.

Chelnokov, Aleksey. 1993. "Abkhazskii apokalipsis." *Izvestiia.* 6 October.

———. 1994. "Azartnie igri v strane 'zero.'" *Izvestiia.* 12 November.

Cohn, Ilene, and Guy Goodwin-Gill. 1994. *Child Soldiers: The Role of Children in Armed Conflict.* Oxford: Clarendon.

Cordell, Dennis D. 1985. *Dar al-Kuti and the Last Years of the Trans-Saharan Slave Trade.* Madison: University of Wisconsin Press.

Darchiashvili, David. 1997. "The Army-Building and Security Problems." NATO Fellowship Program. Photocopy.

Dugashvili, Tamaz. 1994. Interview. 27 July.

Enloe, Cynthia H. 1980. *Ethnic Soldiers: State Security in Divided Societies.* Athens: University of Georgia Press.

Fairbanks, Charles H., Jr. 1995. "The Postcommunist Wars." *Journal of Democracy* 6 (October): 18–34.

———. 1996. "Clientelism and the Roots of Post-Soviet Disorder." Pp. 341–74 in *Transcaucasia, Nationalism, and Social Change,* ed. Ronald Grigor Suny. Ann Arbor: University of Michigan Press.

———. 1997. "The Public Void: Antipolitics in the Former Soviet Union." Pp. 91–114 in *The End of Politics: Explorations into Modern Antipolitics,* ed. Andreas Schedler. New York: St. Martin's.

———. 1999. "The Wars of Hatred and the Hatred of War." *The National Standard.* (19 April):22–27.

———. Forthcoming a. "Party and Ideology in the Former USSR." In *Politics at the Turn of the Century,* ed. Richard Zinman, Jerry Weinberger, and Arthur Meltzer. Lanham: Rowman and Littlefield.

———. Forthcoming b. "The End of the Revolutionary Age?" In as yet untitled book, ed. Nathan Tarcov.

Fox, M. J. 1999. "Somalia Divided: The African Cerberus (Considerations on Political Culture)." *Civil Wars* 2, no. 1 (spring): 2–34.

Gall, Carlotta, and Thomas de Waal. 1998. *Chechnya: Calamity in the Caucasus.* New York: New York University Press.

Goltz, Thomas. 1998. *Azerbaijan Diary.* New York: I. B. Tauris.

Human Rights Watch. 1996. "Children in Combat." *Children's Rights Project* 8, no. 1 (January).

Human Rights Watch/Africa. 1997. *The Scars of Death: Children Abducted by the Lord's Resistance Army in Uganda.* New York: Human Rights Watch.

Human Rights Watch Arms Project and Human Rights Watch/Helsinki Reports. 1994. *Report on the War in Abkhazia* 7: 7.

Ignatieff, Michael. 1993. *Blood and Belonging: Journeys into the New Nationalism.* New York: Farrar, Straus and Giroux.

Jackson, Bruce, and Jeffrey A. Larsen.1998. "Analytical Study on Irregular Warfare in Sierra Leone and Liberia." SAIC-98/6039 & FSRC. Science Applications International Corporation, Foreign Systems Research Center.

Johnson, Roosevelt. 1997. "The 'Most Wanted Man.'" Interview with Ben Asante. *West Africa.* 28 April–5 May: 681–717.

Kalinina, Yuliia. 1998. "Chechnia. Bomba zamedlennogo deistviia na Kavkaze." *Moskovky komsomolets.* 21 April.

Kasaev, Alan. 1996. "Operation to Free Hostages Carried Out in Pervomaiskoye." *Nezavisimaia gazeta,* 16 January. Trans. and reprinted in *FBIS-SOV,* 16 January.

Khachilayev, Nadir. 1998. Interview. October.

Labazanov, Aslanbek. 1997. Interview. October 25.

Lewis, Ioan M. 1994. *Blood and Bone: The Call of Kinship in Somali Society.* Lawrenceville, N.J.: Red Sea.

Longrigg, Stephen H. 1945. *A Short History of Eritrea.* Oxford: Clarendon.

Loza, Tihomir. 1993. "A People with Tolerance, A City without Laws." *Balkan War Report* 21 (August–September): 11.

Lyons, Terrence, and Ahmed I. Samatar. 1995. "State Collapse, Multilateral Intervention, and Strategies for Political Reconstruction." Brookings Occasional Paper. Brookings Institution, Washington.

Maskhadov, Aslan. 1997. "Chest' dorozhe zhizni." Shtab podderzhki kandidata v prezidenty Ichkerii Aslana Alievich Maskhadova.

Medvedev, Vladimir. 1992. "Basmachi-obrechennoe voinstvo." *Druzhba narodov* 8 (August).

———. 1993. "Saga o bobo sangake, voine." *Druzhba narodov* 6 (June).

Miller, Krzystof. 1993. Photograph of Mkhedrioni fighters. Courtesy of Irena Lasota.

Murdock, George Peter. 1959. *Africa: Its Peoples and Their Cultures.* New York: McGraw Hill.

Nadareishvili, Tamaz. 1997. *Genocide in Abkhazia.* Tbilisi: Samshoblo.

Nodia, Ghia. 1993. Interview. October 4.

———. 1998. "Causes and Visions of the Conflict in Abkhazia." Working paper. Program in Soviet and Post-Soviet Studies, University of California at Berkley.

Ojukutu-Macaulay, Winston. 1998. "A Tale of Woe." *West Africa.* 9–22 November: 808–9.

Petit-Dutaillis, Charles. 1964. *The Feudal Monarchy in France and England from the Tenth to the Thirteenth Century.* Trans. E. D. Hunt. New York: Harper and Row.

Reno, William. 1995. *Corruption and State Politics in Sierra Leone.* Cambridge: Cambridge University Press.

———. 1997. "Privatizing War in Sierra Leone." *Current History* (May): 277–80.

———. 1998. *Warlord Politics and African States.* Boulder: Lynne Rienner.

Saffa, Harold. 1997. "Who Are the Kamajors?" *West Africa.* 28 July–3 August: 1214–15.

Samatar, Ahmed I. 1994. "Introduction and Overview." In *The Somali Challenge: From Catastrophe to Renewal?* ed. Ahmed I. Samatar. Boulder: Lynne Rienner.

Shihab, Sophie. 1999. "Tchetchenie: Les Islamistes quittent le bourg, les Russes bombardent." *Le Monde.* 20 September.

Sivertseva, Tamara. 1999. Interview. December 28.

Tamas, G. M. 1994. "Irony, Ambiguity, Duplicity: The Legacy of Dissent." *Uncaptive Minds* 7, no. 2 (26): 19–34.

Tsintadze, Lt.-Col. Archil. 1997. Interview. January 20.

Usmanov, Lyoma. 1998. Interview. November 10.

Vaughn, James H., Jr. 1970. "Caste Systems in the Western Sudan." Pp. 59–92 in *Social Stratification in Africa,* ed. Arthur Tuden and Leonard Plotnicov. New York: Free Press.

Young, Crawford. 1965. *Politics in the Congo.* Princeton: Princeton University Press.

———. 1994. *The African Colonial State in Comparative Perspective.* New Haven: Yale University Press.

7

Civil Wars and State-Building in Africa and Eurasia

DAVID HOLLOWAY
AND STEPHEN JOHN STEDMAN

John Lewis Gaddis has called the cold war the "Long Peace," on the grounds that it was an unusually long period without war between the major powers (Gaddis 1987). But numerous wars did take place during the cold war. By one count there were almost 130 wars between 1945 and 1989, with cumulative fatalities of more than twenty million people (Sivard 1989, 22). According to the same data set, there has been an increase in the number of wars in the 1990s, but as part of a post-1945 trend rather than as a discontinuous jump (Sivard 1996, 18–19). Another source identifies 184 wars between 1945 and 1992 and shows, after the late 1950s, a steady increase in the number of wars taking place in the world (Gantzel 1997). A third set of figures shows a decline in the number of wars in the world since 1990 (Sollenberg 1998). These data sets use different definitions of war, but they come independently to the conclusion that the number of wars has steadily increased since the 1950s, and that the end of the cold war did not mark a sharp break in that trend.

The data on war suggest a second conclusion: that there has been a shift in the balance between civil and interstate wars, and that this too is a post–World War II, not a post–cold war, phenomenon. Of the 160 or so

We would like to acknowledge the help provided by Kathleen Collins, Erin Jenne, Svetlana Tsalik, and Katarina Milicevic in the preparation of this chapter.

wars that took place from 1945 to 1995, only 25 or 26 can be counted un-
equivocally as interstate wars. The rest were internal wars in which nonstate groups—defined in ideological, religious, regional, ethnic, or other
terms—fought against each other or against established states (Sivard
1996; Tilly 1995; Gantzel 1997). According to one report, the preponderance of civil over interstate wars dates back to the 1950s, with the number of deaths in civil wars exceeding those in interstate wars by a wide margin over the last thirty years (Wallensteen and Sollenberg 1996, 356). The
growth in the number of wars taking place in the world in the last fifty years
can be accounted for largely by the increase in the number of civil wars and
by the longer duration of those wars compared with interstate wars. Although there has been a steady rise in the number of wars taking place in
any given year, the number of wars starting in a given year has not shown
a similar rise; therefore, wars are lasting longer (Gantzel 1997, 128).

Africa has been home to many of these wars, including some of the deadliest. The Nigerian civil war (1967–70) killed more than a million people
(Bercovitch and Jackson 1997). Civil war and state collapse led to more
than half a million deaths in Uganda in the early 1980s (Bercovitch and
Jackson 1997). In the Sudan, a war begun in 1984 rages on; it is estimated
that as many as 1.5 million people have died as a result (Bercovitch and
Jackson 1997). Between 1991 and 1993, 240,000 Somalis died from war-
induced famine (Sommer 1994). In a little more than two months in 1994,
nearly a million Rwandans fell victim to genocide. In October 1993, approximately 30,000–50,000 people lost their lives in Burundi during a
one-month eruption of ethnic violence; in the ensuing civil war an additional 100,000 people have died (Human Rights Watch 1997). When Angola's civil war resumed in late 1992, the death toll reached one thousand
people a day (Anstee 1996). Seven years of civil war in Liberia killed
150,000 people (Alao 1998). Sub-Saharan Africa now accounts for more
than half of the world's armed conflicts.

Although many analysts took notice of Africa's wars only in the 1990s,
political instability and violence have plagued the continent since most of
its countries became independent in the 1960s. As Table 7.1 shows, 11
civil wars erupted in Africa in the 1960s. In the 1970s the number of new
civil wars dipped to 5, but that rose to 11 in the 1980s. In the 1990s, 8
more civil wars broke out in Africa, fewer than in the 1960s or 1980s. But
because fighting continued in 9 wars that had begun prior to 1990, an observer of the continent in the 1990s might at a given time have seen as
many as 17 countries (about 30 percent of all the countries in sub-Saharan
Africa) at war.

Table 7.1
Civil Wars in Sub-Saharan Africa, 1960–99

	1960s	1970s	1980s	1990s
			Angola	
	Burundi I	Burundi II		
	Chad I	Chad II	Chad III	Chad V
			Chad IV	
				Congo-Brazzaville
			Ethiopia I	
				Ethiopia II
				Guinea-Bissau
				Liberia
			Mozambique	
			Namibia	
	Nigeria			
	Rwanda I			Rwanda II
			Senegal	
				Sierra Leone
			Somalia I	
			Somalia II	
			South Africa	
		Sudan	Sudan II	
		Uganda I	Uganda II	
			Uganda III	
	Zaire I	Zaire II		Zaire III
		Zimbabwe I	Zimbabwe II	
Wars begun	11	5	11	8
Wars underway at any given time	11	10	16	17

In the 1990s, the former Soviet Union, too, has been the site of a number of wars, each with various estimates of fatalities. The most careful and cautious suggest a total of about 100,000 deaths in all (Mukomel' 1997; Tishkov 1999). Of these conflicts the bloodiest have been the 1994–96 war in Chechnya, in which about 35,000 people were killed, and the civil war in Tajikistan, in which about 25,000 died (though some estimates put the number as high as 50,000–100,000). The war between Armenia and Azerbaijan over Nagorno-Karabakh has claimed more than 20,000 lives, and the war over Abkhazia several thousand. Other armed conflicts, such as those in South Ossetia and Moldova, appear to have resulted in about a thousand battle deaths each.

Thus the nature of war at the beginning of the twenty-first century is largely that of civil war (Van Creveld 1991; Kaldor 1999). The distinction between interstate and civil wars is not an absolute one, since outside states have often intervened in civil wars, and civil wars are sometimes an element in wider interstate wars. The shift from interstate to civil wars is nonetheless significant: it contradicts the prevailing assumption in political science that the international system is a sphere of anarchy, in contrast to the order that exists within the boundaries of the state.

In the dominant neorealist school of international relations theory, it is the anarchical nature of the international system—the lack of an authoritative institution above the sovereign state—that makes war possible. States have to rely on their own efforts to ensure their survival, and they may go to war if they see an opportunity to increase their power, or if they fear that another state is trying to become dominant. The state's attempt to provide for its own security may, regardless of its intentions, threaten others and lead to a spiral of arms competition, suspicion, and even, under certain conditions, a preemptive attack. International relations theory would predict that—other things being equal—the more states there are in the world, the more likely interstate war will be. But the growth in the number of states (from 61 in 1945 to 182 in 1999) has been accompanied by an increase in the number of civil wars, not by an increase in the number of wars between states.

Neorealism takes the state as the basic element of the international system and does not question the state's capacity to act as a coherent entity. But in civil wars it is precisely the state that is problematic. Some political scientists have argued that once a state begins to break down—i.e., once anarchy begins to emerge within the state—the mechanisms that lead to war between states come into play and may lead groups within states to go to war. Among the mechanisms analyzed in this way are the security dilemma, information failures, and problems of credible commitment (Posen 1993; Fearon 1994; Lake and Rothchild 1996). This has proved to be a fruitful approach in the study of internal wars, and it suggests interesting hypotheses about the consequences of state breakdown. But it is not clear that all civil wars take place in conditions of "emergent anarchy." More significantly, this approach focuses on the anarchy that follows the weakening of state authority; it does not explain what it is that weakens states in the first place. Consequently, it needs, at the very least, to be supplemented if it is to contribute to an understanding of the pattern of war since 1945.

This chapter looks at the processes of state formation in postcolonial Africa and the former Soviet Union and asks whether those processes make

African and Eurasian states especially vulnerable to civil war. In particular, we ask whether the experience of Africa's postcolonial states suggests a similar historical trajectory for the new states that emerged in Eurasia at the beginning of the 1990s. We argue that, despite important differences between the two historical experiences, conditions surrounding state formation in Africa and post-Soviet Eurasia have inhibited the formation of stable and legitimate states and have made war more likely.

The chapter begins by outlining three broad explanatory factors that scholars have used in trying to explain civil wars since 1945: ethnicity, nationalism, and globalization. We argue that these explanations neglect what Klaus Gantzel referred to as "the historicity of war," by which he means "the structural dynamics which condition the emergence and behaviour of actors" in any given period (Gantzel 1997, 139). We then suggest that a focus on state formation is helpful in providing the historical context for understanding civil wars. After surveying the experience of state-building in postcolonial Africa and in Eurasia, we conclude with comparisons and contrasts between the regions.

Approaches to Explanation

Perhaps the most common approach to recent civil wars has been to see them as manifestations of "ethnic conflict" (Brown 1993). Ethnic conflicts and civil wars are not the same, of course, but much attention has been devoted recently to studying how ethnicity can serve as an organizing principle for collective action (Hardin 1997). Some commentators assume that ethnic difference is itself a cause of conflict, but this is a mistaken view because most ethnic groups live together at peace. Others argue that the term "ethnic conflict" should be abandoned, precisely because it implies that ethnic difference per se is a cause of conflict. But this assertion goes too far, because the ethnic dimension has clearly been important in wars such as those in Bosnia, where "ethnic cleansing" took place, and in Rwanda, where a campaign of genocide was waged. The way in which the ethnic factor operates may vary from one war to another, but when the warring parties define each other in ethnic terms, that definition will help to determine the nature and dynamic of the conflict (Stavenhagen 1990, 74–84).

Various broad approaches can be used to understand ethnic identity (Young 1993). Constructivism stresses the way in which identity is shaped by the broader social context. Instrumentalism, on the other hand, the most common approach in political science, emphasizes the mobilization of ethnic sentiment by political leaders seeking to gain or retain power. Finally, primordialism, which sees identities as deeply rooted in human biology or the psyche, has fallen out of favor in academic circles but remains popular in the mass media.

These approaches are not always distinct in practice. David Turton has argued that, in order to understand the relationship between ethnicity and violent conflict, we need to explore not only "(a) the historical trends and conditions that shape and give salience to ethnic identities, without anyone's deliberate intent, and (b) the techniques of ethnic mobilization consciously employed by political and intellectual elites; but also (c) the special power of ethnicity to move human beings to collective action" (Turton 1997, 18). These three topics correspond to the questions raised by constructivists, instrumentalists, and primordialists. This suggests that the relationship between ethnicity and violence requires analyses of different kinds, that the ethnic character of a conflict is something that needs to be analyzed, not taken for granted. In some conflicts ethnicity may not be a factor at all; in others it may play a negligible role; in still others it may define the nature of the conflict.

A second and related approach to civil war is through the study of nationalism, understood as a political program linked to statehood, either that of an existing state or that of a state to which a group aspires. "Ethnic group" and "nation" are often treated as overlapping or interchangeable terms, as are "ethnicity" and "nationality." Yet it is important to distinguish between them. Ethnic consciousness is not always nationalist in the sense of implying a program of political action. And not all nationalism is ethnic, in the sense of defining membership of the nation in terms of ethnicity. Nationalism can also be civic, with membership of the nation defined in terms of citizenship—a legal status—rather than a particular ethnicity. Ernest Gellner (1983, 1) defined nationalism as a political principle that "holds that the political and the national unit should be congruent." It is, he writes, "a theory of political legitimacy, which requires that ethnic boundaries should not cut across political ones." (He elides here the distinction between ethnic and civic nationalism.) Many writers, following Gellner, accept that group conflict, including ethnic conflict, has always been found in history but regard nationalism as a product of modernity. Gellner related the growth of nationalism to the development of industrial society, which requires a high culture that is standardized and sustained by the state; hence the nationalist aim of making the political unit and the culture congruent.

According to Gellner's definition, the nationalist principle can be violated in several ways. The most obvious is when one nation rules another, as happens in empires. But other forms of violation are possible: if some members of the nation live outside the state, if foreigners live within the state, or if the nation lives in a number of different states. Nationalist movements have pursued independence, irredentism, secession, and unification in order to repair these violations of the nationalist principle. These four goals, which call into question either the legal status or the geographical location of existing borders, have been pursued in about half of the civil wars fought since 1945. A fifth goal related to nationalism is ethnic cleansing, which seeks to redefine, in ethnic terms, who has the right to live within particular borders. It is hardly possible to understand the wars of the twentieth century without taking the context of nationalism into account.

A third broad approach—in addition to ethnic conflict and nationalism—places civil wars in a global context. This approach can take many forms. For example, the "world polity," to use John Meyer's term, can be understood as the source of the categories in terms of which we think about political organization, and of the scripts that political leaders follow in building new states (Meyer 1987). Nationalism is therefore inscribed in global discourse and provides categories in terms of which claims—to independence, for example—can be made. This is another way of making Gellner's point that nations are the product of nationalism rather than vice versa.

Another version stresses the role of economic globalization. One report claims that "when the global economy pressures governments to engage in rapid political and economic reform, ethnic and sectarian entrepreneurs mobilize around ethnic or religious differences in an attempt to grab or restore positions of power and wealth" (Lipschutz and Crawford 1995, 1). According to this argument, ethnic or other groups mobilize, the weakened state is unable to repress these groups, and consequently civil war ensues. In other words, the root causes of internal conflict should be sought in those pressures—especially from the global economy—that disrupt the domestic political order and open up space for appeals to ethnic or religious solidarity as a response to those disruptions.

Stated in this way, the argument is too general to be useful. It is clearly inadequate on its own as an explanation for internal war, since the effect of global economic pressures on particular states will depend not only on the economies of those states, but also on the capacity of political institutions to adapt to change. The links between developments in the global economy and civil conflict need to be examined in a much more concrete way. And it needs to be asked whether the failure to enact reforms may not also precipitate internal conflict.

Nevertheless, the shift from a comparative perspective to one that emphasizes the relationship between the global and the local is interesting, because it provides another way of integrating individual cases into a broader picture. From this perspective, civil wars are not isolated events but part of a global context, and they have to be understood as such. It has been argued, for example, that globalization brings communities around the world into competition with one another. This "shrinkage of space" heightens ethnic consciousness, since ethnic identities can be seen as the product of contact rather than isolation. In this hypothesis, globalizing and localizing forces combine to weaken the state, which is now "too small to act as an autonomous and independent political and economic entity and too big to satisfy the aspirations and claims of its ethnic and other minorities" (Turton 1997, 27).

These three approaches suggest two broad perspectives for understanding the civil wars of the post–World War II period. The first perspective is that of a worldwide trend toward the politicized, though not necessarily violent or separatist, assertion of national and ethnic identities. Specific analysis is needed to determine which nationalist struggles or ethnic relationships become violent, and which remain nonviolent. The second, and related, perspective is to explain civil war as a consequence of the weakening of the state by intertwined globalizing and localizing pressures.

The state occupies a central position in both of these perspectives: civil war follows when the state's capacity to rule is undermined by ethnic rivalry, by nationalist claims, or by globalization. (The microanalytical approach in political science focuses on the mechanisms by which the weakening of the state leads to war.) What these perspectives lack is an explicit focus on the state and an analysis of the particular features of state formation and state-building that are conducive to civil war.

State Formation and Civil War

The number of wars in any given year since 1945 has grown along with the number of states in the world. Since most wars are civil wars, this suggests, as Holsti (1996) has argued, that new states may be especially liable to civil war. An examination of state formation in postcolonial Africa and the former Soviet Union, especially of those processes that might make African and Eurasian states vulnerable to civil war, can provide a broad historical context for the analysis of civil wars and enable us to study the pattern of war.

Charles Tilly noted that during the last five hundred years, three fundamental events have taken place in the political organization of the world:

"First, almost all of Europe has formed into national states with well-defined boundaries and mutual relations. Second, the European system has spread to virtually the entire world. Third, other states, acting in concert, have exerted a growing influence over the organization and territory of new states" (Tilly 1992, 181). These three developments have not occurred simultaneously. The formation of states took centuries in Europe. European states were not the product of conscious design; they emerged as a consequence of historical processes, and in particular of a complex interplay between capital and coercion, leading to different trajectories that resulted in military-bureaucratic Russia as well as trading states such as the Dutch Republic (Tilly 1992).

In contrast, the spread of the state model to the rest of the world has been a conscious undertaking on the part of conquerors and colonizers, and of indigenous reformers and revolutionaries, who saw in the state a model of political organization that they could copy. The founding of the League of Nations, and then of the United Nations, ratified and rationalized the organization of all the earth's peoples into a single state system. Most of the existing states in the world came into being in the twentieth century, largely in three waves. The first wave followed the breakup of multinational empires at the end of World War I. The second resulted from the collapse of the European overseas empires in the years after World War II. And the third wave of new states emerged from the collapse of communist rule in Eastern Europe and the Soviet Union.

Tilly's third point—that existing states have exerted a growing influence over the organization of new states—is important for understanding state formation in postcolonial Africa and the former Soviet Union. The first European states "took forms that mediated between the exigencies of external war and the claims of the subject population; to some degree, each state's organization adapted to local social and economic conditions" (Tilly 1992, 196). As the state system became established, the territorial dimensions and institutional structures of states were increasingly decided by other states, especially by victors in war. These external processes have become even more important as the state system has extended to cover the globe.

Tilly argued that the postcolonial states that entered the international system after World War II generally followed coercion-intensive paths to statehood. This was because they inherited little accumulated capital from the departing colonial powers but were left with military forces modeled on those that the colonial powers had used to maintain their rule. Furthermore, where they were able to draw revenues from commodity exports or military aid, the new rulers could set aside the need to bargain with their populations and were able to build large state apparatuses without popular consent. In Tilly's view, states that lack strong ties with the population become more vulnerable to forcible seizures of power and abrupt changes of government.

State formation is the process by which political entities acquire the attributes of statehood. Following Max Weber's work, we can define a state as an administrative and legal order that claims binding authority over the population of a given territory. This order is administered by an autonomous apparatus that is separate from other organizations on the same territory. Only if an organization of this kind exists in a given territory will the state be able to raise taxes and provide services, administer justice, and exercise its claim to the monopoly of the legitimate use of violence. State power also has an external face: to secure the state against threats from outside. This basic definition of the state is compatible with many different kinds of rule; states may differ, as well, in their degree of "stateness"—i.e., in the extent to which they can perform the functions of the state (Nettl 1968).

Much of the recent literature on Africa focuses on the weakness of post-colonial states and seeks to understand why many African states have failed to develop the attributes of effective statehood. Kalevi Holsti wrote that "the colonial state, an organism that left legacies primarily of arbitrary boundaries, bureaucracy, and the military, was taken over by leaders who believed they could go on to create *real* nations and master the new state" (Holsti 1996, 71). In Holsti's view it is the failure of state-building in Africa that has led to the rash of civil wars. In other words, the cause of African wars is to be found in the weakness of the postcolonial state, and that weakness is almost entirely attributable to the colonial legacy. Until recently, scholars paid much more attention to regime transition (e.g., from totalitarianism to democracy) in the post-Soviet world than to state formation. Now, however, the problems of state formation in the former Soviet Union are attracting more attention. An obvious question arises: How can the comparison with Africa help us to understand the trajectories of state formation in Eurasia?

Explaining civil wars in terms of state weakness is a bit dangerous. States with civil wars are by definition weak, because they are unable to exercise political authority over a given territory. Thus one risks lapsing into tautology in making the argument that weak states are vulnerable to civil conflict. To avoid that risk, it is necessary to find indicators of state weakness before a civil war begins. We will focus on several specific questions suggested by the discussion so far in this chapter. First, to what extent are the political and national units congruent in the state? Second, to what extent are the territorial dimensions and institutional structures of states defined by the international community rather than by political forces within the state? Third, has the state followed a coercion- or capital-intensive path of development? Fourth, have rulers been able to bypass their own populations by receiving support from abroad? And fifth, are the military organizations contained and constrained by civilian institutions?

Implicit in these questions is an argument about the conditions that may lead to war. The argument runs as follows. Arbitrary borders may lead to fragmented states that are liable to ethnic conflict. States formed predominantly by external influences may be unable to work out a stable relationship with their own societies, while states sustained from outside may lack the incentive to do so; such states may also be particularly vulnerable to shifts in the global economy or international politics. States in which the military is unconstrained will be liable to sudden changes of government. These are all factors that would inhibit the formation of stable and legitimate states. The argument is not that these conditions explain individual civil wars but that, if these conditions hold, war will be more likely. Other mechanisms may need to be invoked to explain why in one case there is war and in an analogous case conflict does not become violent. What the focus on state formation does provide is a context within which to explain the pattern of warfare, not individual wars.

Africa's Wars

Political instability and violence have plagued Africa since most of its countries became independent in the 1960s. Between 1960 and 1998, thirty-five civil wars took place on the continent. Almost one-third of the world's genocides between 1960 and 1988 (eleven of thirty-five) took place in Africa (Harff and Gurr 1988). Between 1963 and 1985, sixty-one coups d'état occurred in Africa—an average of almost three per year (Decalo 1990).

Three factors associated with state-building explain much of Africa's history of war. First, general aspects of state formation in Africa—artificial borders, quasi-states, low human capital, underdeveloped economies, a statist model of political and economic development—created a continent ripe for violence. Second, a more particular aspect of the African state formation process generated immediate violence, which continues to haunt the afflicted: the rapid, unplanned, turbulent transfer of power at independence, when little attempt was made to create the conditions for an orderly decolonization. This subgroup of African states—most, but not all, Belgian or Portuguese colonies—reads like a "Who's Who" of the worst atrocity-filled wars of recent memory: Angola, Zaire, Rwanda and Burundi, and the Sudan. Third, the historically late decolonization of southern Africa, a process not finished until the 1990s, produced three interlocking conflicts: wars for independence in Angola, Mozambique, Namibia, and Zimbabwe; the attempt by South Africa's National Party to maintain white supremacy; and South Africa's destabilization of its neighbors in the 1980s, a direct extension of its own civil war. From 1980 to 1988, between 1.2 and 1.9 million people were killed in war in Angola and Mozambique (Ohlson and Stedman 1994).

The roots of Africa's violence lie principally with the political and economic conditions that existed after independence and the policies pursued by elites to gain and consolidate power. Common patterns of state and class formation in Africa have led to endemic, intense internal conflict. Even in southern Africa violence was exacerbated by conditions inherited from colonialism and the policy choices of new elites.

Colonial powers established borders that corresponded little to African political, cultural, and economic life. Colonial governments were primarily policing and taxing organizations with few representative functions. Colonial economies exported primary products—agricultural goods and raw materials—to their respective metropoles and possessed little industrial capability. Colonial governments neglected the cultivation of Africa's human capital; when independence came, few Africans were trained to step in and operate large state bureaucracies. Strategists of colonial control manipulated ethnic division and exacerbated group conflicts over political and economic resources.

The first generation of African independence leaders accepted colonial borders and eschewed the arduous and politically volatile process of redrawing them. The charter of the Organization of African Unity places great emphasis on the permanence of existing borders and the principle of territorial integrity. Although many analysts attribute Africa's lack of interstate wars to this commitment, it guaranteed that internal instability would be rife throughout the continent (Foltz 1991; Herbst 1996–97). A few examples suffice to indicate the depth of the problem. Nigeria's territory included 3 major religions (Islam, Christianity, and animism) and 250 ethnic groups, the largest 3 (Hausa Falani, Yoruba, and Igbo) possessing "vastly different political values and institutions" (Sandbrook 1993). Zambia comprised 72 ethno-linguistic groups, and Tanzania, 120. Some states contained historical enemies: in the Sudan, Arabs in the north had enslaved Nuer and Dinka in the south; in Rwanda and Burundi, Hutu lived in near-feudal submission to Tutsi. The borders of Ethiopia, Kenya, and Somalia divided ethnic and clan groups, thus prompting periodic irredentist struggles.

If Africa's borders generated intense domestic conflicts over political identity, the lack of domestic economic capital ensured that states would become the object of intense distribution conflicts. As Larry Diamond has observed, the state structures established by the colonial powers "dwarfed in wealth and power both existing social institutions and various new fragments of modern organization." At independence, Africa's new elites sought to harness the power of their states to drive their economies. Regulatory and other state-sponsored bodies and widespread nationalization of foreign industries provided income opportunities for state officials. The state soon became the largest employer in these new countries: for example, 47.2 percent of Senegal's budget in 1964–65 was spent on administrative salaries, and 81 percent of that year's budget in the Central African Republic went to the civil service (Diamond 1987, 574).

As the state became the main source of employment and capital in the new countries of Africa, a pattern of patrimonial politics soon crystallized. Groups organized to ensure access to state largesse—the only way to accumulate wealth. Office-holders expropriated state resources to consolidate their power bases and reward their networks of clients. National interests were subordinated to the interests of politicians and their supporters, who viewed public office as private property (Callaghy 1984; Joseph 1987; Diamond 1987).

The rapidity of Africa's decolonization and the weakness of colonial efforts to prepare Africans for independence created an enduring paradox. As Africans rushed to take advantage of the resources and rewards that their new states could confer, and as African leaders expanded government offices to consolidate their patron-client networks, states became large, omnipresent bureaucracies. At the same time, a shortage of human capital robbed these bureaucracies of skilled civil servants and technocrats. The result, in Thomas Callaghy's (1987) memorable phrase, was the creation of "lame leviathans."

Colonial neglect of education posed nearly intractable problems for Africa's new states. There were, for example, no more than 1,200 university graduates in all of sub-Saharan Africa in 1960 (Sandbrook 1993). In Congo-Kinshasa, fewer than 20 persons held university diplomas at independence, although there were more than 300 priests with theological degrees. In Zambia, only 108 Africans had received a university education

(Chazan et al. 1988). In Tanzania, "there were only twelve African civil engineers, eight African telecommunications engineers, nine African veterinarians and five African chemists. No Africans had been trained as geologists or mechanical or electrical engineers" (Chazan et al. 1988, 228). When Mozambique became independent, the country claimed three African doctors and one African lawyer; 90 percent of the population was illiterate (Wastberg 1986).

Africa's new leaders consolidated their rule through access to state coffers. Some leaders, fearing potential ethnic conflicts, created inclusive coalitions that provided rewards for many societal groups (Rothchild 1997). In other cases, one ethnic group succeeded in capturing the state and shutting other groups out. In still other cases, political leaders chose to ignore ethnicity and insisted on establishment of a national identity as a unifying principle for the country.

Patrimonial politics eventually had devastating economic consequences. Most states were organized to redistribute wealth: existing resources were divided to buy and maintain political support. The production of wealth received short shrift. Domestic investment dried up, and foreign investment fled to more profitable regions of the world. The result was that most African countries suffered economic declines; in many, standards of living were worse in the 1980s than in the 1960s. To cope with the reduction in economic production and lack of investment capital, African states borrowed heavily from international financial institutions. African countries found themselves simultaneously marginalized from the international economy and dependent on international loans and assistance (Callaghy 1991). State formation became based on ties to international financial institutions or external patrons, either the superpowers or former colonial masters. Regime stability came to depend on the support of the few in society with access to state largesse and on the coercive force of the military and police. Those who held power perceived the costs of losing power to be devastating and therefore gutted constitutional provisions for turnover of office; alternative contenders for office were robbed of opportunities to contest succession, thereby creating a core of disgruntled elites. African militaries, lacking any institutional tradition of constitutionalism and playing the key role in providing for regime protection, soon became active competitors for state power. The state, in turn, became the biggest threat to individual security in Africa.

Two factors contributed to Africa's wave of political instability in the 1980s. At the end of the 1970s, an ideological revolution took place in international financial institutions: neoclassical theories of economic growth overtook models that emphasized state action. As international financial institutions grew impatient with the waste and corruption of African governments, they began to impose strict economic conditions on access to international aid. In order to maintain the flow of international loans and assistance, African leaders were forced to cut state employment, liberalize prices, sell off state-run businesses, and eliminate state regulation of markets. Economic conditionality cut at the heart of the patrimonial state. If African leaders followed the dictates of international financial institutions, they would divest themselves of the tools necessary to maintain the support of their clients. If leaders chose to defy these financial institutions, they would lose access to badly needed international capital. Either way, the patrimonial state was in jeopardy.

Some African states, however, could rely on superpower patronage and thereby sidestep the dilemma posed by economic conditionality. But the end of the cold war shut off this economic lifeline. Among the six largest recipients of American foreign aid from 1962 to 1988, only Kenya escaped war in the 1990s. The others—Liberia, the Sudan, Somalia, Ethiopia, and Congo-Kinshasa—would experience civil war in the 1980s and 1990s. The only regimes able to sustain shrinking internal patronage networks were those that oversaw economies that exported natural resources in world demand—for example, Gabon and Nigeria.

As Africa entered the 1990s, many regimes found themselves in a crisis of state legitimacy. African leaders responded in four ways. In the first category were countries such as Liberia and Somalia, where dictators refused to give up political power in the face of armed challenges. When no quick victory was forthcoming, the armed factions splintered into smaller camps. The result was state collapse and the proliferation of armed warlords who controlled small pieces of territory and who were sustained by plunder.

In the second category were countries such as Cameroon, Kenya, Nigeria, Togo, and Congo-Kinshasa, where despots initially conceded to demands for democratic participation but then manipulated the process to retain power through corruption, coercion, ethnic mobilization, and other divisive tactics. Given diminishing resources to buy internal support, leaders in these countries focused their patronage on smaller segments of society and politicized ethnicity as a means of maintaining their hold on power.

In the third category were countries such as Ghana and Uganda, where authoritarian leaders tried to build regime legitimacy from the top down. In both of these countries, for example, dictators invoked populist rhetoric, insisted on citizen participation in rebuilding the nation, implemented the structural reforms mandated by international financial institutions, and used coercion against internal dissidents. These regimes claimed that their countries were emerging from chaos and that political and economic discipline, not democracy, were needed—a claim largely accepted by donor nations and international financial institutions.

In the fourth category were countries such as Benin, Malawi, and Zambia, where authoritarian leaders ceded power to democratically elected forces. In these countries, civil society, emboldened by democratic successes in eastern Europe and elsewhere in Africa, asserted itself, producing multiparty elections and political freedoms. In these cases, former dictators did not have private sources of wealth that could be used to manipulate elections. Instead, they faced united opposition, which rendered the politics of ethnic hatred ineffective.

Only states in this last category have weathered the crisis, and they remain precariously balanced, attempting to establish multiparty political processes and implement tough economic reforms at the same time. Where dictators manipulated democratic processes to retain power, the potential for violence remains high. War finally engulfed Congo-Kinshasa in 1996 and led to its collapse. Cameroon, Kenya, and Nigeria have all experienced intermittent ethnic fighting. In countries that have pursued state-led reform, such as Ghana and Uganda, it remains to be seen whether leaders can avoid the fate of all of Africa's previous experiments in authoritarianism, where dictatorships became corrupt, fossilized, and ultimately brittle when confronted by strong populist challenges.

Wars in Eurasia

When the Soviet Union was dissolved in December 1991, the African experience was far from people's minds. Western Europe and the United States (and sometimes Japan), where "normal" states were to be found, provided the point of reference. Eight years later, interesting comparisons can be drawn with the African experience, especially in terms of state formation.

It was nationalism—the desire for independent statehood—that finally caused the Soviet breakup, but it was a more general crisis of the Soviet system that opened the way to nationalist mobilization. Soviet president Mikhail Gorbachev's reforms, a response to the systemic crisis, made it possible to voice nationalist claims and to organize nationalist movements (Suny 1993). In the last years of Soviet power, nationalist sentiments were very unevenly distributed: strong in some places, in particular the Baltic states and the Transcaucasus, and weak in others, especially Central Asia. Gorbachev responded, rather late, to these movements by seeking to negotiate a new Union Treaty. Work on the treaty began in June 1990, and in March 1991 a referendum was held on the preservation of the union. The overwhelming majority of voters supported maintaining a union of some kind. But the three Baltic republics refused to take part in the referendum, as did Moldova, Georgia, and Armenia; the latter two held votes on independence. The referendum showed that support for the union was strongest in Central Asia (Lapidus, Zaslavsky, and Goldman 1992).

Negotiations in May and June produced a new treaty, which was to be signed on August 20, 1991. But six union republics—the three Baltic republics and Georgia, Armenia, and Moldova—had not taken part in the negotiations and were unwilling to sign the treaty. After the failure of the August *putsch* (coup attempt), the Soviet Union crumbled, in spite of efforts by some republican leaders to negotiate a new form of union (Matlock 1995). The result was fifteen independent states instead of one. Some of these states had achieved independence; others had had independence thrust upon them.

Russian nationalism was an essential element in this story, for the popularly elected Russian leadership wanted to see the Soviet Union break up, even though it sought some form of association between the newly independent states. Thus Russia did not act like an imperial metropole resisting the movement of colonies to independence. On the contrary, in 1990 and 1991 the Russian leadership—as opposed to the Soviet leadership— supported the efforts of other union republics to acquire sovereignty and recognized them as states once they proclaimed their independence (Dunlop 1993). Boris Yeltsin, who had been elected president of the Russian Federation in June 1991, played a key role in defeating the August 1991 *putsch*, the main goal of which was to preserve the union.

As in the decolonization of Africa, the creation of fifteen new states on the territory of the former Soviet Union did not involve any redrawing of borders. The federal structure of the Soviet Union provided a salient solution to the problem of territorial organization, with independence granted to the republics that constituted the union and had the right of secession under the Soviet constitution. Fictional though it was in key respects, the federal structure of the Soviet state had been a concession to nationalist sentiment when the Soviet Union was formed in 1924, not something advocated by the Bolsheviks, who favored a unitary state (Pipes 1964). The union republics were ethno-territorial units, thus meeting—in theory at least—Gellner's definition of nationalism as a political principle: there was

supposed to be some correspondence between ethnic and political boundaries. In practice, however, the situation is far more complicated, since populations are intermingled in complex ways. Some of the post-Soviet states
include a large ethnic minority or multiple minorities (e.g., Latvia, Estonia, Ukraine, Kazakhstan, Georgia); in other cases a significant number of
the titular nation's co-nationals live outside the state (such as in Russia and
Armenia) (Laitin 1998).

Union republics were not the only ethno-national territories in the
Soviet Union. Autonomous republics, provinces, and districts, with their
own titular nationalities, existed in a number of the union republics. Under the Soviet constitution these entities did not have the right of secession, but in the last two years of the Soviet Union many of them began to
claim sovereignty. They were encouraged to do so by Gorbachev, who saw
them as a counterbalance to the union republics. Four of the six wars in
Eurasia have been about the status of autonomous entities of this kind. Armenia and Azerbaijan fought over the status of Nagorno-Karabakh, an autonomous province in Azerbaijan with a majority Armenian population.
Two wars were fought in Georgia over the issue of secession—in Abkhazia,
an autonomous republic, and in South Ossetia, an autonomous province.
The war in Chechnya, an autonomous republic within the Russian Federation, was fought over the attempt by Chechnya to secede from Russia.
Only a minority of the autonomous entities became the focus of violent
conflict, but political conflict surrounded many of the others, which have
claimed sovereignty on the basis of the principle of self-determination.

In Moldova, too, conflict has centered on the status of particular groups
within the state. The emergence of nationalist sentiment among the Ro-
manian-speaking majority in the late 1980s and the formation of the
Moldovan Popular Front stimulated a reaction among the primarily Russian and Ukrainian population on the left bank of the Dniestr River, where
the Dniestr republic was proclaimed in September 1990 with the avowed
intention of remaining part of the Soviet Union. In 1991 and 1992, fighting broke out between the Dniestrian community (with support from the
Russian 14th Army, stationed in Moldova) and Moldovan forces. The fighting ended with a cease-fire in 1992, leaving the Dniestrian community with
considerable autonomy on the left bank of the river (Kaufman 1996).

The war in Tajikistan had quite a different character. The traditional nationalist goals of independence, secession, irredentism, and unification
have not been involved in this conflict, nor are the participants defined
in ethnic terms. The war was precipitated by the collapse of Soviet rule,
with resulting rivalry among regional clans for control of the new state. In

Kyrgyzstan and Uzbekistan, where clans also play a key political role, clan leaders made pacts to secure stability during the transition. In Tajikistan, however, Soviet rule left an imbalance of power among the clans, making it more difficult to reach agreement on managing the shocks and strains of the end of the Soviet Union. Fighting broke out in May 1992 and continued until 1997, when a peace agreement was concluded, though fighting has persisted since then (Rubin 1998; Collins 1999).

The wars in Eurasia are sometimes referred to as the wars of the Soviet succession. In an important sense these wars were generated by the state system itself, which prescribed the political organization of the post-Soviet order (Lapidus 1998). The international community recognized the fifteen union republics as sovereign states but denied such recognition to other claimants to sovereignty. Thus the principle of self-determination was applied to peoples living on particular territories, not to individual nations or ethnic groups. This is also the way in which the principle of self-determination was applied in postcolonial Africa. Students of Africa have argued that one consequence of this has been to reduce the incidence of interstate war by making it very unlikely that the international community would recognize border changes brought about by force. But another consequence has been to sustain weak states, states that have juridical sovereignty but are unable to exercise effective rule over their territory (Jackson and Rosberg 1982). It is possible that the way in which the Soviet Union was dissolved will have the same consequences: low probability of interstate war, but persistence of weak states. But the international dimension has not disappeared entirely from post-Soviet conflicts. Armenia was deeply involved in the war over Nagorno-Karabakh, and Russia has played an important military and political role in the other wars.

Before its fundamental weaknesses were exposed in the 1980s, the Soviet Union was widely regarded as the epitome of the strong state. Gorbachev's opponents deplored the rapid weakening of the Soviet state to the point where it could no longer claim binding authority over the population on its own territory. For advocates of reform, however, the weakening of the state appeared to be desirable, for they wanted to reduce state regulation of the economy and society and to let the market and civil society develop. In other words, they believed that what was needed was a weaker state, with a restricted scope of authority. This view of the state was probably shared by most foreign analysts, who focused much less on issues of state capacity than on the kinds of regime—democracy, dictatorship, or variants of either—that would emerge from the post-Soviet transition.

In retrospect, however, the issue of state formation has turned out to be more complex than anticipated. The state has proved to be ineffective in many cases in performing its major tasks—maintaining order, collecting taxes, and providing services. Unlike the postcolonial states in Africa, the new post-Soviet states inherited extensive state bureaucracies, experienced and educated administrators, with many, if not most, of the administrative positions already occupied by members of the titular nationality. But the bureaucracies inherited from the Soviet Union were not always well suited to the new circumstances. Besides, the new states, with the exception of Russia, did not acquire institutions accustomed to formulating or implementing policy on a national level.

There is a third, and perhaps more profound, reason for the weakness of post-Soviet states, alongside the sometimes arbitrary territorial boundaries and ineffective bureaucracies. Most of the new states have fallen into a "transition trap," which seriously hampers the process of state-building. Only the three Baltic states have undertaken full-fledged economic and political reform. Belarus and Turkmenistan have introduced very few reforms, while Tajikistan is still torn by civil war. The other states, including Russia, occupy a halfway house on the road to reform in which a "symbiosis of property and illegal power" (Wolf 1999) undermines the state. The transitional period has seen a major reallocation of state property, with opportunities to "steal the state," in Steven Solnick's phrase (Solnick 1998). Some individuals and groups have used public office and political influence to gain access to licenses, to privatized state property, and to income streams and other privileges to enrich themselves and their friends. The result is a situation that deprives the state of resources, undermines the legitimacy of private property, and also discourages long-term investment and encourages capital flight. The legitimacy and effectiveness of the state both suffer, and full-scale reform is hindered by those who are benefiting from the conditions of partial reform (Hellman 1998).

When the Soviet Union collapsed, the Soviet system had been discredited in the eyes of most, though not all, of its citizens. In the circumstances, it was inevitable that governments, thrown precipitously into a turbulent process of transformation, should look abroad for help in carrying out reform. The international financial institutions, as well as foreign governments and nongovernmental organizations, became heavily involved in aiding post-Soviet governments to design new institutions and policies. The degree of external involvement has varied from case to case; nevertheless, the role of external institutions has been considerable. So, too, has the extent of financial aid, though it is hard to judge whether that level has been great enough to enable the new states to ignore their own populations and thus avoid negotiating a new relationship with their own societies. Most of the Eurasian states, however, have incurred high levels of indebtedness in the years since independence, leaving themselves open to pressure from international financial institutions and foreign governments. If the conditions imposed by foreign lenders and donors are needed to keep the post-Soviet governments on the road to reform, the leverage that foreign institutions enjoy may be a good thing. But it may also undermine the legitimacy of the new regimes, if their own people regard them as less responsive to the people's needs and wishes than to the instructions of foreign institutions. It is perhaps too early to make a final judgment on this, but the African experience cautions against assuming that outside intervention, even if undertaken with the best intentions, is always beneficial.

Although the Soviet Union was a highly militarized state, the military did not play a dominant political role because the Communist Party was firm in maintaining its own supremacy. After the collapse of the Soviet Union, Moscow initially hoped to treat the former Soviet Union as a unified strategic space but soon recognized that the new states wanted their own armies. The new states have been only partially successful in creating loyal armed forces out of the remnants of the Soviet military machine, however. The proliferation of military and paramilitary forces in Russia and some of the other states, examined in Chapter 6 of this book, reflects—and no doubt in turn reinforces—the fragmentation of power in those states and illustrates how far those states are from the Weberian ideal of statehood.

In spite of this fragmentation, however, the military has played a less significant political role in Eurasia than in postcolonial Africa. This may be because civilian institutions in Eurasia are stronger than those in postcolonial Africa. For Tilly it is a central paradox that although European states emerged as a by-product of war, it was preparation for war that led to the creation of civilian government. In order to raise armies, states created a civilian apparatus to extract resources, and in return for those resources granted social groups enforceable claims on the state. The military was contained and constrained by agencies established for the purpose of supporting and creating military power. Moreover, to extract resources from society, the state had to negotiate mutually advantageous relations between state and society—thus the central role of military power in the formation of civilian states (Tilly 1992). Although the Russian state was itself a product of the processes that Tilly analyzed, it is not clear that this logic will apply to the Eurasian states. If the argument about the low probability of interstate war is correct, states will have little incentive to engage in military preparations of the kind that would strengthen civilian institutions in the way that Tilly outlined.

Conclusion

We have reviewed the African and Eurasian experience in light of the questions posed at the end of the section on state formation and civil war. The answers to these questions point to some interesting comparisons. First, even though there are major violations of the nationalist principle (as defined by Gellner) in Eurasia, the political and national units are more congruent there than in postcolonial Africa. The borders of the union republics of the Soviet Union were drawn with at least some regard to the ethnic composition of the population. In Africa the borders are more arbitrary and the ethnic and linguistic diversity greater. Nevertheless, in neither region is the ethnically homogeneous state common. Given the way in which ethnic populations are intermixed, it is not clear that the situation could be very different. If borders were redrawn, political and national units might be more congruent, but states would still not be ethnically homogeneous. Africa and Eurasia are not unique in that regard, even though Africa is exceptionally heterogeneous. Very few states are ethnically homogeneous, and a world of such states—even if it were desirable—could be achieved only by massive movements of population and by the creation of numerous new states. One consequence of this condition is the "triadic configuration" discussed by Rogers Brubaker (1996), in which ethnic relations have to be understood not in terms of groups within the state, but rather in the context of interaction among a state, an ethnic minority within the state, and another state that is the national homeland of the ethnic minority.

Second, in both Africa and Eurasia the territorial dimensions of the new states were defined by the previous regimes. By mutual agreement these borders have remained in place, and the international community has not looked with favor on secessionist movements (such as those in Biafra and Chechnya, though Eritrea is an exception). In Africa this fact has reduced the likelihood of wars between states, according to some analysts, but also ensured the survivability of weak states (Herbst 1996–97). The same argument may apply to the former Soviet Union.

The situation is different in terms of institutional development. When African states became independent they had two paths of development to choose from—the Soviet and the Western models—and they could also devise a mixed strategy. What resulted in almost every case was state-led development. The shift to neoliberalism in Western thinking had, as we have argued, profound implications for African states dependent on foreign aid. When the post-Soviet states became independent, the neoliberal orthodoxy was still dominant and the Soviet model had, of course, collapsed. The International Monetary Fund and the World Bank, along with other aid agencies, played an important role in advising the nascent states on economic strategy and in developing economic institutions. The advice has not always been palatable to governments, but the international institutions have been a major force in post-Soviet transitions.

Third, in order to pursue a capital-intensive path of development, the new states of Africa and Eurasia need to create conditions favorable for investment by domestic and foreign capital. This has proved to be difficult, except in specific sectors such as oil and gas, which can to some degree be walled off from the rest of the economy. The main difficulty is that the patrimonial state or the partially reformed state does not provide conditions attractive to investors. This does not mean that coercion-intensive development is the only alternative. There is a third possibility: a low-level equilibrium in which an ineffective state is unable to pursue either a capital-intensive or a coercion-intensive strategy. This is what has happened to some African states, and some Eurasian states seem headed for the same fate.

Fourth, foreign aid and military assistance helped to sustain at least some African rulers in the 1970s and 1980s. This put those rulers in a difficult position when the international financial institutions changed their policies in the late 1970s and when the cold war led to a reduction in foreign aid. To that extent, it can be argued, some African rulers were able for a time to bypass their populations by receiving support from abroad. Post-Soviet governments have also received extensive loans and assistance from foreign governments and international institutions. This support was certainly intended to bolster reformers and assist the transition to the market and democracy, and the largest recipients of aid (Russia and Ukraine) have held parliamentary and presidential elections. To that extent, one might argue, foreign assistance has not removed from governments the need to seek the support of their own populations. The conditions on which aid has been given have often been unpopular, but foreign assistance has also given governments some advantages in generating popular support and the support of elites.

Fifth, there has been an important difference in the role played by the military in Africa and Eurasia. In postcolonial Africa, the military has been a key political actor, often ruling or determining who rules. In the post-

Soviet states, the military has not ruled, even though it has sometimes played an important political role. Tilly's analysis suggests that the explanation may lie in the differential development of civilian institutions in Africa and Eurasia. For all their failings, the civilian institutions of the post-Soviet states are much more developed than the equivalent institutions in most of the postcolonial African states. Imperial Russia and the Soviet Union were, after all, products of the European state-building analyzed by Tilly: in building up military power they created civilian bureaucracies that constrained the political role of the military. In postcolonial Africa, however, the state-building consequences of military preparations do not appear to have been the same as in Tilly's analysis of Europe, partly because military assistance from abroad has obviated the need to extract resources from society. Furthermore, if the argument about the low probability of interstate wars in Africa and Eurasia is correct, neither region will have the same incentive as Europe did to enhance the capacity and solidarity of the state. Whereas wars with other states can strengthen the state, wars within the state will inevitably weaken it, unless one side achieves a decisive victory and establishes its rule over the entire territory. War in Africa and Eurasia thus may not play the same role in state-building as it did in Europe.

One important issue that we have not discussed is the role of civil society. It is hardly possible to understand the modern European state without reference to civil society (Poggi 1978). Although it has not figured prominently in analyses of the postcolonial African state, civil society is an important issue in discussions of postcommunist transition. There are those who argue that the success of reform in central Europe can be explained, at least in part, by the relative strength of civil society in those countries, which were thus better prepared for transition than the post-Soviet states, where civil society was weaker. Yet civil society in the former Soviet Union may be stronger than in postcolonial African states, or at any rate may provide a stronger basis for state formation. As we have noted, there is in Africa a high correlation between the speed with which the colonial powers quit their colonies and the difficulties that new states have had in establishing their statehood. The same does not appear to apply to the post-Soviet states. This suggests that in the African cases what was important was not the speed of transition to independence but the degree to which certain conditions (education, administrative capacity, party formation, civil society, etc.) existed before independence.

Much of the political science literature on civil war focuses on processes that come into play when the state is weak and has begun to fall apart. We have tried in this chapter to look at some of the factors that account for the weakness of states in postcolonial Africa and in Eurasia. This provides some of the context in which the security dilemma, or commitment problems, or the triadic interactions among majorities, minorities, and neighboring states, play out. In focusing on state formation in Africa and Eurasia, we have not sought to idealize the European experience, which has been bloody enough. But comparison between Africa and Eurasia suggests some worrying parallels in the pattern of state formation.

References

Alao, Abiodun. 1998. *The Burden of Collective Goodwill: The International Involvement in the Liberian Civil War.* Aldershot: Ashgate.

Anstee, Margaret Joan. 1996. *Orphan of the Cold War.* New York: St. Martin's.

Bender, Gerald J. 1978. *Angola under the Portuguese: The Myth and the Reality.* Berkeley: University of California Press.

Bercovitch, Jacob, and Richard Jackson. 1997. *International Conflict: A Chronological Encyclopedia of Conflicts and Their Management.* Washington: CQ Press.

Brown, Michael E., ed. 1993. *Ethnic Conflict and International Security.* Princeton: Princeton University Press.

Brubaker, Rogers. 1996. *Nationalism Reframed: Nationhood and the National Question in the New Europe.* Cambridge: Cambridge University Press.

Callaghy, Thomas M. 1984. *The State-Society Struggle: Zaire in Comparative Perspective.* New York: Columbia University Press.

———. 1987. "The State as Lame Leviathan: The Patrimonial Administrative State in Africa." Pp. 87–116 in *The African State in Transition,* ed. Z. Ergas. London: Macmillan.

———. 1991. "Africa and the World Economy: Caught Between a Rock and Hard Place." Pp. 39–68 in *Africa in World Politics,* ed. John Harbeson and Donald Rothchild. Boulder: Westview.

Chazan, Naomi, et al. 1988. *Politics and Society in Contemporary Africa.* Boulder: Lynne Rienner.

Collins, Kathleen. 1999. "The Political Sociology of Regime Transition in Central Asia." Ph.D. diss., Department of Political Science, Stanford University.

Decalo, Samuel. 1990. *Coups and Army Rule in Africa: Studies in Military Style.* 2d ed. New Haven: Yale University Press.

Diamond, Larry. 1987. "Class Formation in the Swollen African State." *Journal of Modern African Studies* 25 (December): 567–96.

Dunlop, John B. 1993. *The Rise of Russia and the Fall of the Soviet Empire.* Princeton: Princeton University Press.

Fearon, James D. 1994. "Ethnic War as a Commitment Problem." Paper presented at the annual meeting of the American Political Science Association, 2–5 September, New York City.

Foltz, William. 1991. "The Organization of African Unity and the Resolution of Africa's Conflicts." Pp. 347–66 in *Conflict Resolution in Africa,* ed. F. Deng and I. W. Zartman. Washington: Brookings Institution Press.

Gaddis, John Lewis. 1987. *The Long Peace: Inquiries into the History of the Cold War.* New York: Oxford University Press.

Gantzel, Klaus Juergen. 1997. "War in the Post–World War II World: Some Empirical Trends and a Theoretical Approach." Pp. 123–44 in *War and Ethnicity: Global Connections and Local Violence,* ed. David Turton. Rochester: University of Rochester Press.

Gellner, Ernest. 1983. *Nations and Nationalism*. Ithaca: Cornell University Press.

Hardin, Russell. 1997. *One for All: The Logic of Group Conflict*. Princeton: Princeton University Press.

Harff, Barbara, and Ted Robert Gurr. 1988. "Toward an Empirical Theory of Genocides and Politicides: Identification and Measurement of Cases since 1945." *International Studies Quarterly* 32 (September): 359–71.

Hellman, Joel S. 1998. "Winners Take All: The Politics of Partial Reform in Postcommunist Transitions." *World Politics* 50, no. 2 (January): 203–34.

Herbst, Jeffrey. 1996–97. "Responding to State Failure in Africa." *International Security* 21, no. 3 (winter): 120–44.

Holsti, Kalevi J. 1996. *The State, War, and the State of War*. Cambridge: Cambridge University Press.

Human Rights Watch. 1997. *Stoking the Fires: Military Assistance and Arms Trafficking in Burundi*. New York: Human Rights Watch.

Jackson, Robert H., and Carl G. Rosberg. 1982. "Why Africa's Weak States Persist: The Empirical and the Juridical in Statehood." *World Politics* 35, no. 1 (fall): 1–24.

Joseph, Richard. 1987. *Democracy and Prebendal Politics in Nigeria: The Rise and Fall of the Second Republic*. Cambridge: Cambridge University Press.

Kaldor, Mary. 1999. *New and Old Wars: Organized Violence in a Global Era*. Stanford: Stanford University Press.

Kaufman, Stuart J. 1996. "Spiraling to Ethnic War: Elites, Masses, and Moscow in Moldova's Civil War." *International Security* 21, no. 2 (fall), 108–38.

Laitin, David D. 1998. *Identity in Formation: The Russian-Speaking Populations in the Near Abroad*. Ithaca: Cornell University Press.

Lake, David A., and Donald Rothchild. 1996. "Containing Fear: The Origins and Management of Ethnic Conflict." *International Security* 21, no. 2 (fall): 41–75.

Lapidus, Gail W. 1998. "Contested Sovereignty: The Tragedy of Chechnya." *International Security* 23, no. 1 (summer): 5–49.

Lapidus, Gail W., Victor Zaslavsky, and Philip Goldman, eds. 1992. *From Union to Commonwealth: Nationalism and Separatism in the Soviet Republics*. Cambridge: Cambridge University Press.

Lipschutz, Ronnie, and Beverly Crawford. 1995. "'Ethnic' Conflict Isn't." IGCC Policy Brief no. 2, Institute on Global Cooperation and Conflict, University of California, San Diego.

Matlock, Jack E. 1995. *Autopsy on an Empire: The American Ambassador's Account of the Collapse of the Soviet Union*. New York: Random House.

Meyer, John W. 1987. "The World Polity and the Authority of the Nation State." Pp. 41–70 in *Institutional Structure: Constituting State, Society and the Individual*, ed. George M. Thomas, John W. Meyer, Francisco O. Ramirez, and John Boli. Beverly Hills: Sage.

Mukomel', Vladimir. 1997. "Vooruzhennye mezhnatsional'nye i regional'nye konflikty. Liudskie poteri, ekonomicheskii ushcherb i sotsial'nye posledstviia." Pp. 298–324 in *Identichnost' i konflikt v postsovetskikh gosudarstvakh*, ed. Martha Olcott, Valery Tishkov, and Aleksei Malashenko. Moscow: Moscow Carnegie Center.

Nettl, J. P. 1968. "The State as a Conceptual Variable." *World Politics* 20, no. 4 (July): 559–92.

Ohlson, Thomas, and Stephen John Stedman. 1994. *The New Is Not Yet Born: Conflict Resolution in Southern Africa*. Washington: Brookings Institution Press.

Pipes, Richard. 1964. *The Formation of the Soviet Union: Communism and Nationalism*. Cambridge, Mass.: Harvard University Press.

Poggi, Gianfranco. 1978. *The Development of the Modern State*. Stanford: Stanford University Press.

Posen, Barry R. 1993. "The Security Dilemma and Ethnic Conflict." *Survival* 35 (spring): 27–47.

Rothchild, Donald. 1997. *Managing Ethnic Conflict in Africa: Pressures and Incentives for Cooperation*. Washington: Brookings Institution Press.

Rubin, Barnett R. 1998. "Russian Hegemony and State Breakdown in the Periphery: Causes and Consequences of the Civil War in Tajikistan." Pp. 128–61 in *Post-Soviet Political Order: Conflict and State Building*, ed. Barnett R. Rubin and Jack Snyder. New York: Routledge.

Sandbrook, Richard. 1993. *The Politics of Africa's Economic Recovery*. Cambridge: Cambridge University Press.

Sivard, Ruth Leger. 1989. *World Military and Social Expenditures (1989)*. Washington: World Priorities.

———. 1996. *World Military and Social Expenditures (1996)*. Washington: World Priorities.

Sollenberg, Margareta. 1998. *States in Armed Conflict 1997*. Uppsala: Department of Peace and Conflict Research, Uppsala University.

Solnick, Steven L. 1998. *Stealing the State: Control and Collapse in Soviet Institutions*. Cambridge, Mass.: Harvard University Press.

Sommer, John G. 1994. *Hope Restored? Humanitarian Aid in Somalia 1990–1994*. Washington: Refugee Policy Group.

Stavenhagen, Rodolfo. 1990. *The Ethnic Question*. Tokyo: United Nations University Press.

Suny, Ronald Grigor. 1993. *The Revenge of the Past: Nationalism, Revolution, and the Collapse of the Soviet Union*. Stanford: Stanford University Press.

Tilly, Charles. 1992. *Coercion, Capital, and European States, AD 900–1992*. Rev. ed. Oxford: Blackwell.

———. 1995. "State-Incited Violence (1900–1999)." *Political Power and Social Theory* 9: 161–79.

Tishkov, Valery. 1999. "Ethnic Conflicts in the Former USSR: The Use and Misuse of Typologies and Data." *Journal of Peace Research* 36, no. 5 (September): 571–91.

Turton, David. 1997. "Introduction: War and Ethnicity." Pp. 1–45 in *War and Ethnicity: Global Connections and Local Violence*, ed. David Turton. Rochester: University of Rochester Press.

Van Creveld, Martin. 1991. *The Transformation of War*. New York: Free Press.

Wallensteen, Peter, and Margareta Sollenberg. 1996. "The End of International War? Armed Conflict 1989–1995." *Journal of Peace Research* 33, no. 3 (August): 353–70.

Wastberg, Per. 1986. *Assignments in Africa: Reflections, Descriptions, Guesses*. New York: Farrar, Straus, and Giroux.

Wolf, Martin. 1999. "Caught in the Transition Trap." *Financial Times*. 30 June: 23.

Young, Crawford, ed. 1993. *The Rising Tide of Cultural Pluralism*. Madison: University of Wisconsin Press.

8

The Effects of State Crisis on African Interstate Relations (and Comparisons with Post-Soviet Eurasia)

DONALD ROTHCHILD

Although the great majority of Africa's states and borders remain intact, the African state system as designed by the continent's postcolonial leaders in the 1960s is beset with crisis, and external military interventions are increasingly evident. Africa's states, unable to provide security and economic well-being for their citizens, have become more and more aware of the risks they encounter from internal conflict and porous borders, as well as from the inability of regional organizations to enforce the rules of interstate relations. Parallels and differences can be found in the former Soviet Union; these will be examined below, though my focus will be primarily on Africa. In both regions weak states have generally lost their monopoly over the means of violence, and dangerous challenges, even civil wars, have at times erupted, undermining the state and, in Africa, state systems of conflict management (among others, see Ayoob 1995; Deng 1993; Goldgeier and McFaul 1992; Herbst 1989; Holsti 1996; Stedman 1996; Waltz 1979). Because of weak institutions, governments in both regions

An earlier version of this chapter was presented at Stanford University's Center for International Security and Cooperation. I wish to express my appreciation to my colleagues at CISAC (and especially to rapporteur Stephen John Stedman, as well as to Gail Lapidus and Kathleen Collins) for their helpful comments. In addition, I wish to thank the two reviewers, Valerie Bunce and René Lemarchand, for their thoughtful comments on this chapter.

are at times unable to control the activities of autonomous, private actors on their territories. Not surprisingly, such actors sometimes seize upon the lack of restraint resulting from state weakness to engage in economic and political practices antithetical to the well-being of both the state in which they reside and of neighboring states.

In such a context, states find themselves with little option but to take what measures they can to protect themselves. For example, South Africa defends its borders as best it can against Mozambican arms merchants, who accumulated enormous stockpiles of small arms and ammunition from de-mobilized soldiers following the negotiation of the 1992 peace agreement in their country (Honwana 1998). It also dispatched troops to Lesotho in 1998, in part to guard a reservoir that supplies critically needed water to South African consumers. Thus the weakening of international norms is threatening not only to weak states (which long looked to norms for pro-tection), but also to relatively better-functioning states (which are exposed to various perils from outside their borders).

Clearly, claims to state sovereignty can be undercut by such cross-bor-der predicaments. In Africa the complexities arising from these new inter-national encounters cause the accepted rules of interstate relations ham-mered out by the founders of the Organization of African Unity (OAU) at Addis Ababa in the 1960s to become increasingly blurred and ineffective. New types of local "externalities," or spillover effects, are emerging and threatening the security of political actors in the region (Lake 1997, 49; Keller 1997, 297). It therefore seems strangely incomplete when scholars of international relations concentrate attention on juridical norms of sov-ereignty or the balance of power between sovereign states, because such foci fail to reflect certain critical facets of the reality of internal and exter-nal relations currently occurring across Africa (and to some degree, across Eurasia as well). A more comprehensive, interactional outlook is neces-sary—one that takes account simultaneously of intra- and interstate rela-tions. Such an outlook must pay close heed to the way that weak states can create internal security threats capable of spreading across borders and ways in which other states respond collectively to these threats (David 1991).

In Africa, contemporary leaders have at times successfully overcome dis-trust and competing interests in attempting to cope with Africa's emerg-ing security predicaments. They have negotiated agreements on specific is-sue areas, organized international regimes, and established various multilateral organizations. Such regional and global security systems have facilitated cooperation in preventing and managing certain types of conflict. However, they have not given sufficient attention as yet to setting appropriate guidelines for dealing with challenges to security arising from the presence of dangerously incoherent states in their midst.

In examining this problem, I raise the following question: How can weakness in the structure and organization of a neighboring state create both incentives and disincentives for efforts by a state (or a constellation of states) to moderate the effects of local externalities? In an attempt to deal with this question, I will examine the conditions in Africa's weak states that give rise to the insecurity and instability of those states and thereby create the environment for possible external interventions. I will then analyze the negative external effects of state weakness on other countries in the region and in the wider African state system. After that, I will discuss the possible political, economic, and military/security alternatives open to state, regional, and continental actors for coping with negative externalities arising from the close proximity of a weak state (Lake 1997, 50). In my conclusion, I will consider the implications of weak states and declining international norms for the stability of the African state system in the twenty-first century. Along the way, I will draw some parallels and contrasts with the situation in Eurasia. The critical contrasts between the African and Eurasian contexts in this regard are the presence in the latter of a state that aspires to hegemony and the lower degree of formalized norms about intervention. These factors impart a distinctive character to the interstate consequences of weak states in the two regions.

Clearly, old legalistic norms of nonintervention and the integrity of sovereign states are losing some of their meaning in today's more fluid and sometimes more threatening African environment. Yet, despite this increased incoherence, African state borders have largely remained intact. Rather than explain this survival primarily in juridical terms, as some are inclined to do (see, for example, Jackson and Rosberg 1982), I view the durability of inherited borders and weak states largely in terms of the perceived domestic and international costs (relative to gains) faced by state leaders contemplating a decisive shift in their relations with weak state neighbors. Interventions in Africa are becoming increasingly common, as recent events in Liberia, Sierra Leone, Congo-Brazzaville, Congo-Kinshasa, and Lesotho make clear. Even so, most of Africa's fifty-three states remain weak and risk averse and consequently inclined to avoid the individual and collective actions necessary to resolve challenges to the norms of the contemporary African state system. As a result, the norms of the African state system continue to possess formal validity, but in practice they hang suspended in midair over regimes desperate for security in an increasingly anarchical continental order.

The Fragility of Connections in Weak States

The notion of a well-functioning state is a relative one covering a wide spectrum. It applies in a number of contexts where partially autonomous state elites can make use of institutions to allocate values and to implement domestic and international policies (Rothchild 1987, 119). The state is an arena with its own rules, relationships, and interests. It establishes both the parameters of choice and the explicit and implicit rules for making and implementing that choice. The state is not necessarily neutral, and it therefore may privilege certain groups more than others when providing resources and security. But the state cannot be dismissed as a mere tool of class interests, as some Marxist and other theorists would do, for it operates with a degree of autonomy from class and other interests in society.

What constitutes a relatively well-functioning state is contextual—dependent on the comparison set. Moreover, a state that functions relatively well in comparison with its neighbors in one period may become a weak state in another; the reverse, unfortunately, occurs less frequently. The weak state's capacity to regulate society and to implement public policies effectively throughout its territory remains uncertain. As I will refer to them in this essay, weak states include polities with collapsing economies and administrative structures and those ravaged by civil war or genocide. In some extreme cases (Somalia, Sierra Leone, Guinea-Bissau), the state has virtually disintegrated; in others (Chad, Burundi, the southern Sudan), chronic violence has become commonplace. At times, a weak state has the ability to take certain initiatives on its own, such as Tanzania's and Ethiopia's dramatic rural collectivization programs in the 1970s (Rothchild and Foley 1983, 313). But to the extent that the conflict-management system becomes merely a mask for elite repression and predatory actions (Halpern 1976), the postcolonial African state remains frail and incoherent. It is forced to rely on coercion to compensate for its lack of legitimacy. As Michael Schatzberg (1988, 135) notes regarding the dialectics of oppression in Zaire, not only was the citizenry caught up "in the grip of ever increasing insecurity" over the predatory designs of their rulers, but the ruling elite itself became insecure over its ability to survive in Mobutu Sese Seko's version of the state. Uncertainty is also a highly contextual phenomenon (Buzan 1991). At times, it emerges because the state is unable to protect its citizens from local predators (e.g., cattle thieves in Tanzania, local warlords in Liberia); at other times it reflects the state's inability to protect its citizens from cross-border raids and attacks (e.g., Sierra Leone, Rwanda, Congo-Kinshasa); and in different circumstances it appears because the state itself is the source of intimidation and violence (as in Somalia, the Sudan, and Uganda under Idi Amin). The looseness and contextual nature of the concept notwithstanding, insecurity of one type or another is prevalent across much of contemporary Africa, with weak states becoming the source of weakness in other states (whether relatively well functioning or weak themselves) in the region.

Noting the similarities between the postcolonial African states and the post-Soviet countries in this respect, Mark Beissinger and Crawford Young observe in this volume that both regions confront a common crisis of state "incoherence." As is the case for many of Africa's autonomous and "contested" regions within weak country structures, Eurasia's "quasi-states" include Chechnya, Nagorno-Karabakh, Abkhazia, South Ossetia, and Trans-Dniestria (Lapidus 1998, 6). Moreover, Tajikistan, a country plagued by civil war among regionally based factions, is a prominent example of state failure. Concerned that Tajikistan's internal instability might spill over into the wider region, Russia and the other members of the Commonwealth of Independent States (CIS) have stationed troops in the country in an effort to create stable internal power and to shore up the porous Tajik border with Afghanistan (Rubin 1998, 141). Paralleling Africa's experiences with external state intervention in the affairs of weak neighbors, Russian military forces have been involved in conflicts in other states in their region, such as in Abkhazia, Nagorno-Karabakh, and Trans-Dniestria. Although Russian leaders describe these interventions in disinterested terms, in fact their own security concerns have been evident. Thus the substantial Russian presence in Armenia has had the effect of deterring Azerbaijan from attempting to regain control of border areas (Furman and Asenius 1996, 147–48).

To understand the effect of state crisis on African (and, in a parallel manner, Eurasian) interstate relations, it will be necessary to start by probing some of the features of state softness that create security threats to other states and make military interventions possible. Taken together, the following main conditions of state softness give some insight into why a weak state environment often spills over dangerously into neighboring countries and invites retaliation.

A Low Level of Legitimacy

Weak legitimacy is characterized by the failure of the postcolonial state to secure public acceptance of an authoritative and effective political order. Where a public consensus exists over the valid exercise of public authority, it greatly strengthens state leaders in making difficult choices concerning state extractions and allocations. But such a consensus has often proved elusive. The assumption of authoritarian powers, often justified as a necessary means for spurring economic development, usually signals the arrival of a self-serving elite in power that is (or quickly becomes) alienated from its citizens. As this state elite disregards formal rules and procedures and acts to further its own private interests, the governing elite's legitimacy erodes and the public comes to perceive the state as an alien institution. Unable to maintain public support or to deliver on its promises, the governing elite turns to repression of opposition groups without dealing with the root causes of dissent. "The failure of the principle of governmental legitimacy," Christopher Clapham (1996, 13) observes, "dissolves the moral relationship that is assumed by the myth of statehood to exist between the population of the state and the people who run it." In these circumstances, the state itself becomes the source of exploitation and insecurity.

The indicators of weak state legitimacy vary. Military coups, the decline of confidence in the state's formal public institutions, disagreement over norms of conflict management, exclusion of minority interests, managed or irregular elections, the growth of informal economies, and the emergence of powerful militia leaders are all signs of a deteriorating citizen consensus for formal government norms and processes. When state and societal elites have diametrically opposed views on appropriate ways of organizing the state and its relations with civil society, the result can be unclear standards of behavior and a weakening of state purposes. For example, the call by some of Nigeria's Muslim fundamentalists to institutionalize a federal *sharia* (Islamic law) court competes with norms advocated by members of the state elite and others of a single court system for all. The potentially destructive nature of this issue became clear in 1991, when Mallam Yakubu Yahaya, the leader of the Shiite Muslim sect in the Nigerian state of Katsina, refused to recognize either federal or local government laws on the right to stage public demonstrations. At this time, Mallam Yakubu Yahaya declared, "If there is any grievance between Muslims and the government, we can only settle these grievances on the battle field and not on a round table" (*West Africa* 1991, 568). In this case, pursuit of one norm caused conflicts with another and contributed to state incoherence. This contradiction intensified in 2000, when the northern state of Zamfara unilaterally extended the application of *sharia* to criminal law, in apparent violation of the Nigerian constitution. Several northern states quickly followed suit, triggering lethal confrontations between Christians and Muslims in both north and south ("In God's Name" 2000).

As government fails to be sensitive to the stated or unstated preferences of the public, giving disproportionate resources to its own supporters and neglecting its adversaries, extensive corruption and unpredictability on the part of the ruling elite undermine the state's claims to legitimacy. In Congo-Kinshasa, note Crawford Young and Thomas Turner (1985, 183), "The progressive permeation of the patrimonial Mobutist state by venality to the point where corruption itself became the system . . . eroded its credibility, and in turn its legitimacy." Thus corruption, especially in its extreme form, leads to deep resentment over the misallocation of resources and abuse of power. In the face of such abuse, public reactions in Africa have ranged across a continuum from acquiescence (as when Ghana's president Jerry Rawlings spoke of a "culture of silence"), to disengagement from activities in the formal economy (by, for example, hoarding, exchanging currency on the black market, or smuggling), to open political opposition and armed resistance. Where a significant segment of the public becomes strongly disaffected, the weakened state may become vulnerable to opposition, even to possible alliances between regime opponents and external actors.

A Lack of Social Cohesion

Diverse interests in and of themselves do not make intense conflict inevitable. As long as perceptions remain pragmatic and demands reasonable, societal interests can feel secure and intergroup relations remain regular, moderate, and bounded (Rothchild 1997a). However, when perceptions become essentialist and demands inflexible, conflict among groups tends to grow increasingly adversarial and polarized. Especially where political leaders play an ethnic, religious, or ideological card, conflict seems prone to escalate and a paralyzing immobility marks social interactions. Thus the scapegoating tactics adopted by former president Mobutu Sese Seko in Zaire, harassing and stripping citizenship from the Banyamulenge people in Kivu, contributed to an ethnic view of the state as inherently biased. This view then led to an insurgent challenge and ultimately to state breakdown (Mafeje 1998, 10).

Because in Africa territorial boundaries were imposed by the outgoing colonial powers, the states of Africa tend to be artificial and to lack the sense of common identity that is so useful for integrating diverse peoples elsewhere in the world (David 1992–93, 132; Zartman 1998, 318). In this respect, post-Soviet Eurasian states seem to enjoy certain advantages that Africa never had, if only because in Eurasia the territorial frame of the state, also imposed by imperial power, is at least built on the principle of an eponymous nationality. In Africa, the political elite's material benefits, derived from maintaining the inherited state intact, give it an incentive to preserve the appearance of juridical sovereignty (Clapham 1996, 115; Jackson and Rosberg 1982). Because the state lacks the military capacity to achieve unity through coercion, political bargaining becomes essential for maintaining social cohesion. Thus the state negotiates out of necessity with powerful ethnic, religious, regional, and foreign interests (foreign corporations, security firms, crossborder trading partners) in order to maintain the territorial status quo (Hyden 1983). Inevitably, domestic interests display different levels of information, skill, and willingness to negotiate their differences over common problems. Unless these capabilities can be developed and the problems of commitment dealt with, social interactions may not become regularized and a security dilemma can emerge. Intergroup tensions in Rwanda over political power, representation in the military, and land ownership show how a process of conflict can escalate and deepen, bringing on the extremes of social polarization and genocidal fury.

Certainly the notion of the state as a unitary actor is a mythical one. Indeed, such a notion is at times quickly laid bare by politically powerful social and cultural identity groups that exhibit a high degree of autonomy and mobilize their members around common interests. The state elite's denial of multiethnic and multireligious interests is often highly destructive. Such a strategy tends to underestimate both the desire of identity-group members for inclusion in their group and their real or imagined fears of external aggression (Lake and Rothchild 1998). It also raises the critical question of who will be accepted as the enforcer of the implicit contract between the state and civil society (Lake and Rothchild 1998). The state elite's denial of group political legitimacy, then, gives rise to intense collective fears of the future (Ignatieff 1993, 24), and this denial ultimately acts to weaken the linkages that bind state and society together.

Such a lack of internal state cohesion can have significant international implications. In Africa, ethnic fractionalization and conflict in a weak Sudanese state opened the way to crossborder support for the southern-based Sudan People's Liberation Army (allegedly by Uganda, Eritrea, and Ethiopia) and, in retaliation, by the Sudanese government for the Lord's Resistance Army in Uganda. Such activities further weaken the already frail state system, creating uncertain connections outside as well as inside the state.

Ineffective Public Institutions

In many African countries, state institutions overexpanded relative to existing societal resources. African leaders, anxious to consolidate power and overcome the twin inheritances of colonial neglect and economic dependence, preferred to establish highly centralized states after decolonization. Yet such state centralization proved inefficient and costly, diverting scarce public resources away from rural producers (Bates 1981). This misallocation of resources led in turn to a loss of confidence in state leadership.

Because state structures tended to be overcentralized and overstaffed, they did not provide an adequate underpinning for effective administrative control. These overbureaucratized institutions themselves became major consumers of scarce resources and as such appeared to be relatively costly tools in the hands of the dominant political elite (a phenomenon with interesting parallels to Boris Yeltsin's Russia; see Stavrakis 1996). Basic public services existed formally in Mobutu's Zaire, but they were unable in practice to achieve the ambitious developmental plans of the hegemonic Mobutu state (Young 1994, 249, 263).

In addition, in some weak state environments (such as those in Liberia and Sierra Leone), informal patronage systems inside and outside the state have supplanted conventional bureaucratic institutions. Such patronage systems weaken the bureaucracy by denying it functions and resources (Reno 1998, 94). In Liberia, President Charles Taylor sold timber and minerals outside of bureaucratic control, leaving state structures unable to penetrate the rural hinterland or, for want of resources, to achieve the country's developmental objectives. As trade in diamonds and timber was diverted from formal to informal markets, the state in neighboring Sierra Leone was denied the resources it required for administrative and developmental purposes (Reno 1998, 116). The effect was to ensconce soft state institutions precisely when effective ones were so desperately needed. This situation resulted in the marginalization of the administrative, military, and police arms of the state and reliance instead on foreign security organizations such as Executive Outcomes to perform essential security tasks normally left to state institutions.

Limited Capacity for Economic Management and Resource Extraction

An overextended state, which is characterized in part by slow (even negative) growth in a country's gross domestic product, high levels of external debt, weak infrastructural support, and rapid population growth (at least in Africa, although not in most of the former Soviet Union), finds it difficult to manage economic development. Irresolute administration (i.e., tax collection) combined with weak economic performance leaves the state with inadequate revenue to create new choices for the unemployed and for despairing members of its society. The inability to generate taxable wealth creates difficult trade-offs. If state leaders seek to increase the price of foodstuffs in the face of mounting urban hardship (as proposed by the William Tolbert government in Liberia in 1979), they can spark violent demonstrations that can undermine the regime itself. And if the regime attempts to increase its resources for development by cutting back on military expenditures, it risks possible opposition from a key support group: military officers and their supporters. Weak states are trapped in an expenditure crunch that is in part of their own making, but one from which escape is extremely difficult. An important growth sector—the informal economy— emerges as more of a release valve than a source of taxable resources, largely because its evolution occurs outside of state control.

When self-generated resources are bounded, the leaders of weak states inevitably seek to compensate for shortfalls by looking outward for external support. But the world's potential donors are increasingly hesitant, even hostile, to the idea of extending aid to Africa's hard-pressed states. Recent data show that net capital flows to Africa declined from $16.8 billion in 1995 to $13.9 billion in 1996 (a decrease of some 17 percent). Moreover, net official aid flows to Africa in 1996 declined by 48 percent (to $3.2 billion), the lowest level in a decade; the International Monetary Fund's soft loan approvals to Africa through its enhanced structural adjustment facility also fell by 43 percent (Katsouris 1997, 1, 4). In this respect, Africa differs significantly from post-Soviet Eurasia, where major aid and loan programs have been in place (though a major flight of capital from Russia and other states has occurred). Declining levels of economic assistance, combined with increasing African debt payments, have complicated the problems of extracting resources for long-term investment. These constraints have further weakened the state's capacity to manage the economy and provide security. To be sure, there is no clear relationship between scarcity and legitimacy; nevertheless, there is evidence that those states that are ineffective in meeting legitimate public demands and expectations for an improving quality of life have often been the ones to falter in Africa. As seen with the Hilla Limann regime in Ghana, bare shelves in the present and inadequate planning for the future prove to be ominous indicators for survival.

Increasing Reluctance on the Part of External Enforcers

In the initial period after decolonization, the former colonial powers (particularly France) played a key role in shoring up the frail African state system, interceding diplomatically and militarily to support shaky state leaders against internal and external opponents. The OAU and the United Nations (UN) also were active in buttressing weak regimes, providing much-needed norms on recognition and nonintervention and backing vulnerable heads of state and governments with essential support against possible coup makers, insurgent forces, and external interveners. In the Nigeria-Biafra war, the OAU, protective of the African state system, gave meaningful support to the unity and integrity of the Nigerian state and shunned the role of a neutral mediator. Its visiting mission toured federal-controlled areas, but prudently avoided travel to Biafra (Rothchild 1997b). The effect of this international support for incumbent leaders and state integrity was to strengthen the state elite against its ethno-regional challengers (and their international allies).

Subsequently, as the cold war came to an end and the political costs of the American-led Somali intervention led to public opposition in the United States to multidimensional peacekeeping operations, the United States and other Western states largely disengaged militarily from Africa. The refusal of France to intervene to thwart the military overthrow of one of its key clients, Henri Bedie in the Ivory Coast in 1999, was a symbolic landmark in this respect. Despite evidence of repression and mass killings in Congo-Kinshasa, Rwanda, and the Sudan, the UN and the OAU have failed to play the role of peace enforcer, leaving weak-state leaders vulnerable to both internal and external threats. Some African leaders, shocked in the mid-1990s over the abuse of state power on the continent, have indeed made efforts to strengthen the OAU's role in preventing mass violence and managing disorder when it escalates dangerously. Even so, international norms have not proven sufficiently effective to prevent sovereign statehood from acting as a potential shelter for scoundrels, especially as there is no reliable regional or global authority willing and able to ensure that state rulers adhere to internationally accepted norms (Deng et al. 1996).

Russia, by contrast, is less reluctant to intervene in its so-called near abroad to guarantee its internal security, the security of ethnic Russians in other states, the security of its external borders, or its external ambitions to regional hegemony.[1] Unlike in Africa, which hosted multiple colonial powers, this single proximate hegemonic power has remained influential throughout Eurasia, where it has been actively involved in conflicts in Nagorno-Karabakh, Abkhazia, South Ossetia, Moldova, and Tajikistan,

---

1. Russia uses the term "near abroad" to refer to the now-independent states of the former Soviet Union.

among others. The contrasts between the regional organizations in the two regions are also relevant. Whereas the members of the OAU have agreed to formal norms of sovereignty, domestic jurisdiction, and external intervention, the CIS is not effective as a consistent body of formal, unified norms (Sheehy 1992). Although the governments of the Eurasian countries have not set down a prescribed normative system that is comparable to that existing in Africa, this is not to say that Russia, the hegemonic CIS member, does not conform to international standards of behavior. Russia's desire to be included in the new global system of relations and to attract international investment compels it to conform to some extent to widely accepted rules of international behavior (Rubin 1998, 171, 175). The European Union was in a position to press the Russians over the issue of Chechnya precisely because of Moscow's need for acceptability in Western circles (Lapidus 1998, 40).

State Weakness and External Threat

I have concentrated thus far on the internal dimension of state weakness, noting the potential threat it poses to individual and group well-being and to the security of other states. I turn now to the impact that the weak state has on its neighbors. Unlike the approach adopted at the turn of the twentieth century by realists, who were concerned over the presence of strong states on their borders, leaders of the relatively better-functioning African states now generally view the prospect of a weak state on their borders as being the greater danger. These relatively better-functioning states recognize that their security must take into account local and regional externalities, many of which arise because of the frail capacity of states in their region. Some of the possible threats arising from the presence of weak states abutting one's territory include the movement of arms, smuggling, currency manipulation, limits placed on the flow of water, the cutoff of oil exports, attacks on kinsmen across the border, a link between insurgent factions in neighboring countries and one's own opposition groups, hostile military coups, the export of violence and terrorism, belligerent radio and television broadcasts, and environmental degradation. The interdependence of regions creates insecurities at the same time that it provides new economic opportunities.

The externalization effect from weak or failed states has challenged the normative order on which African interstate relations rest. It appears menacing to the well-being of neighbors in part because the de jure sovereignty of these states complicates the possibility—once taken for granted in Europe—that weak states will be conquered and integrated into the domains of stronger states (Jackson 1990). Even if such a solution were still acceptable to the international community (which is not the case), Africa's relatively stronger countries generally lack the desire and capacity to intervene and absorb additional lands and peoples effectively (Ayoob 1995, 175). Consequently, the possible threat posed by a weak neighbor in today's political environment requires a carefully calibrated response.

Why leaders perceive what happens across their borders as a security threat is critical. Overlapping insecurities exist, but which threat is perceived as menacing and potentially costly is important in terms of its outcomes. An external threat from an adjoining state or private actor (to the economic well-being or physical safety of co-ethnics or co-religionists on the other side of borders, or to the borders themselves) may or may not be deemed sufficient reason to justify measures of self-help. Porous international frontiers may be regarded as comparatively harmless in some cases (as in Ghana's borders with Togo and the Ivory Coast), or they may be viewed as a threat to national security in others (as with Congo-Kinshasa's borders with Rwanda, Burundi, and Uganda to the east and Angola to the south). The presence of lethal weapons is not necessarily a good indicator of the perception of threat; however, if arms are used by a public or private actor in an adjacent state to launch attacks or to support attacks by others, then the external effects are usually perceived as negative indeed (for example, the Sudanese support for the Lord's Resistance Army along Uganda's border). State implosion or civil war becomes ominous for a neighboring state only when resulting incoherence becomes linked to negative externalization.

Clearly, it is important to guard psychologically against the tendency to overestimate the commitment of a rival to a threatening course of action (Jervis 1976, 350). Such an estimation can involve a number of calculations, including assessments about the nature of support that insurgent movements have among other states in the region, the extent that food and nonlethal aid will be provided by neighboring states and nongovernmental organizations to strengthen rebel guerrilla movements, and whether arms purchased on the black market or donated by supporters abroad will strengthen these movements decisively.

In some instances, the decline of a state's capacity to enforce peace in its own society has been perceived as threatening to the stability of the African state system. Rather than relying on effective rule and a monopoly of force, sovereignty in soft states involves the international community's recognition of a state elite's jurisdiction in a particular territory. In a rather passive way, the international community often finds it convenient to accept the credentials of weak state leaders, thereby preserving the fiction of a state system composed of fully sovereign entities. Only when the state is unable to ensure the security of its citizens does some kind of third-party enforcement mechanism legitimately come into play.

The weak state's lack of commitment to the stability of the state system takes various forms. When a ruling elite is unprepared to accept the internationally accepted norm on domestic jurisdiction, it has negative external effects. Other regional actors come to distrust the intentions of those refusing to bargain over intensely conflictive issues (Lake 1997, 51), causing the conflict to widen and possibly to escalate. The support of insurgencies by external states and private actors in contravention of OAU and UN norms (as occurred with Taylor's backing of the Revolutionary United Front forces in Sierra Leone and with Ethiopia's assistance to the opposition Sudan Alliance Forces; "Trumpeting the Horn" 1997, 5) is an obvious violation of a neighbor's internal jurisdiction. Such support further internationalizes an existing intrastate conflict.

Another internal factor threatening to the stability of the international state system involves a denial of civil and political rights to co-religionists and co-ethnics across a border. The treatment accorded to identity-group members in neighboring states can be a critical factor in interstate relations, because domestic publics can be expected to bring enormous pressure to bear on their leaders when they feel the rights of co-ethnics elsewhere are being violated. Thus Rwanda's vice president and defense minister, Paul Kagame, justified his country's assistance to rebel forces in eastern Congo-Kinshasa on the grounds that Congolese president Laurent Kabila was acting in a manner threatening to the stability of the region. Although his principal motivation for intervening was the threat that the *Interahamwe* (the extremist Hutu militia members) posed to the security of the Rwandan state, Kagame also stressed the threat to the Banyamulenge and other ethnic Tutsi peoples who earlier had migrated to Congo-Kinshasa and who have been denied full citizenship rights by recent Congolese governments. In Kagame's view, Rwanda's legitimate security concerns included stopping a possible genocide across the border (Pineau 1998a). With some similarities, a more powerful Russia also interceded in ethnic conflicts in the near abroad. In Moldova, for example, it intervened on the side of the Slavic-speaking secessionists of Trans-Dniestria. In the Abkhaz conflict, it used the occasion of ethnic conflict along its border to intervene, thereby pressuring Georgia to join the CIS. Thus a state like Russia that seeks to play the role of regional hegemon may view disorder on its borders as an opportunity to assert leverage on others.

The flow of migrants to and from a weak state can also cause conflicts between sending and receiving countries. The international migration of some three and a half million African refugees by the end of 1997 resulted from political instability and repression, famine, floods, civil wars, secessionist actions, and a lack of economic opportunities. In some cases, these conditions pushed large numbers of people to receiving countries that had a difficult time absorbing the influx (as when Mozambicans fled to Malawi, or Rwandan Tutsi streamed into Uganda). A similar refugee crisis exists in Eurasia. The presence of these migrants in Africa has had a destabilizing effect at times, allegedly causing increased crime, prostitution, smuggling, and conflicts over the distribution of scarce resources. Worse yet, the breakdown of international norms caused in part by state weakness has led to a situation of state irresponsibility, wherein the recipient state is too weak to police the refugees and in fact has an interest in embroiling them in internal wars or crossborder conflicts. There are reports, for example, that the Kabila regime has recruited Rwandan refugees to fight alongside government forces against rebel troops in Congo-Kinshasa (Schlein 1998). The presence of unwanted migrants can also be a conflict-producing factor between states, causing interventions by a state that is intent on preventing possible problems from arising (for example, the attacks by the Rwandese Patriotic Front government forces on refugee camps in Congo-Kinshasa and subsequent 1996 and 1998 invasions in support of Congolese insurgents).

Still another important source of strife resulting from the presence of a soft state in the neighborhood involves the spillover effects resulting from civil war and state collapse. Whether state leaders perceive these occurrences as sufficiently threatening to warrant an active response will differ from one country to the next (Weiner 1992–93, 104). What does seem clear is that events within a state (and particularly a weak state) are intertwined with the politics of its wider region. Recent findings regarding the diffusion of domestic African political conflict across state boundaries in the 1960s indicate the significance of internal-external interactions across a region. When past internal civil strife combined with discord in the region, an increased level of political conflict across state boundaries was predictable (Hill and Rothchild 1986, 726). The Tutsi minority in Burundi seized political power to ward off the threat of a Rwanda-type revolution that would give unrestrained power to the Hutu majority (Lemarchand 1994). Under these circumstances, states in the region, apprehensive over the spillover effects of state instability in their neighborhood, may decide to act (even to intervene) to protect their economic and political interests or "to prevent instability from spreading to them" (David 1992–93, 134).

External Responses to Threat

I now turn to the ways that relatively better-functioning states can respond to unfolding weakness in an adjacent state. In such a context, the notion of security applies broadly to internal and external threats to state borders, the effectiveness of state institutions, and societal integration (Ayoob 1995, 8–12). To be sure, most African states, with the exception of South Africa, Nigeria, and those in North Africa, have difficulties coping with external threats in their region. This is explained largely by their limited ability to deter or deal with challenges to their authority. Angolan government authorities, with a relatively strong military force at their command, have been able to alter the balance of forces in Congo-Brazzaville and to give substantial military assistance to President Kabila in Congo-Kinshasa, yet they have been unable to smash the insurgency by UNITA (the National Union for the Total Independence of Angola) in their own country. Moreover, the source of the problem can be critical—that is, a state can be crippled by a lack of capacity (as is Mozambique) or its leaders can be sustained by warlord practices and exhibit rapacious tendencies (as were Liberia's in the early 1990s). It is difficult at times for the rulers of better-functioning African states to negotiate with the leaders of disintegrating states, because the neighboring state's leadership often lacks effective countrywide regulatory capacity and is insulated from external pressures. Negotiations with predatory elites are gravely handicapped by problems of extreme ambition, irresponsibility, and reputations for deceit. Further complicating the difficulties of regularizing relations is the fact that some external actors— such as importers, smugglers, arms merchants, and private security firms— benefit handsomely from disarray.

Russian military influence in the post-Soviet region contrasts with this general picture of limited African force capacity, although the wars in Afghanistan and Chechnya indicate that its capacity must not be overestimated. In Eurasia, Russia nevertheless remains a hegemon and aspires to this role—that is, it wants to be a large power that can bring significant force to bear in its region when it deems such force to be necessary. Russian troops have been involved in four kinds of relationships in the near abroad: securing external borders (as in Tajikistan); guaranteeing Russia's own internal security (for example, in Chechnya); intervening to protect the interests of its co-ethnics (for instance, in Moldova); and taking actions to shore up its hegemonic position (as it did in Abkhazia and Nagorno-Karabakh). Because its influence remains significant, the countries in Russia's near abroad operate in the shadow of this previous colonizer and therefore exhibit varying degrees of discomfort over their unequal relationship. States such as Estonia, Latvia, Kazakhstan, and Ukraine, which include large ethnic Russian populations, are aware that there is pressure on the Russian government to reincorporate these countries in order to safeguard the interests of ethnic Russians. Although President Boris Yeltsin had defended ethnic Russians by means of diplomacy, the threat of force can never be entirely removed from these relationships (Kaplan 1998, 270).

Leaders of Africa's "quasi-sovereign" states (i.e., states whose survival is guaranteed by international norms but that lack the capacity to defend themselves; Jackson 1990, 24) may be internally protected outlaws: they are largely free from the responsibility of maintaining international norms but are in a position to use their acceptance as sovereign rulers to strengthen themselves. They can secure foreign aid, procure weapons, hire mercenaries, and enlist the support of other states at the OAU and the UN (Reno 1998, 8). The result is often a Hobbesian impasse, wherein the African state system is weakened and everyone's insecurity is heightened. Some of the strategic choices for stabilizing relations between better-functioning African states and their weak neighbors are relatively cost effective and long term in their consequences, whereas others are essentially short-term options that prove costly and difficult to implement.

One type of response to the external threat from weak states is to encourage them to adopt internal reforms or to engage in capacity-building initiatives. A decision by the state elite to retrain and encourage the professionalization of its police can be implemented on its own or, as in the case of the Mozambican peace agreements, with assistance from UN civilian police forces. Either way, the effect of such professionalization is to build long-term public confidence in the responsibility of the local police. As old memories of police high-handedness and abuse recede, an effective police force can gain public respect and strengthen citizen confidence in the legitimacy of the state and its institutions (Stanley and Call 1997). Confidence is also engendered by accommodative strategies or insurance incentives (Rothchild 1997a) that build minority trust in the good intentions of the leaders, thereby freeing up resources for developmental projects rather than security. Measures on proportionality in allocations and civil service recruitment, reserved seats, zoning for electoral purposes, inclusion in high-level government and party positions, and decentralization of power all represent concessions by the majority to the minority that have been adopted in various African states to mitigate conflict. Provided majority-backed governments are prepared to display the necessary goodwill toward their minority communities, such measures can be adopted at minimal financial cost and can reinforce trust in leaders and institutions. Moreover, such actions can encourage reciprocation, which can in turn lessen appeals to violent opposition.

Other alternatives, such as side payments to warlords and the use of private security services, can be more costly in their effects and do little to develop predictable state-society interactions. Because rulers such as Charles Taylor in Liberia and Valentine Strasser in Sierra Leone were insecure about their safety and because their militaries were underpaid and not committed to professional norms, they responded to internal or border violence by resorting to the use of irregular, private security forces. Their desire to work out collaborative relations with multinational firms may lead them to agree to the presence of mercenary forces, as was the case now and again in Sierra Leone in the 1990s. Such irregulars promote the security that enables private firms to operate effectively. These mercenaries also provide intelligence, train local forces, and furnish and service weapons (Shearer 1998a, 71). In addition, organizations such as Executive Outcomes and Sandline International have played a critical role in direct military engagements in such cases as Angola and Sierra Leone. Adaptable to local needs, quick to assemble, and easy to terminate, these mercenaries can be compensated out of a leader's personal extractions (Howe 1998; Reno 1998; Shearer 1998b). In today's disorderly environment in Africa, where powerful Western states have largely disengaged and international organizations are not always in a position to respond effectively to the turmoil caused by state weakness, the private security firm represents a seductive and expedient option for stabilizing relations with internal and external opponents. However, the use of such firms undercuts the norms of the African state system and does little to build durable institutions or relationships.

A second type of response can involve some form of intervention by the better-functioning state when lawlessness becomes evident in its region. To be sure, the disincentives on the part of leaders in the better-functioning states to eliminate threats from neighboring weak states are considerable, especially given these leaders' lack of an overwhelming capacity to crush the resistance of leaders and movements in weak states (Nigeria's troops, for example, were unable to triumph decisively over warlord militias in Sierra Leone in 1999). Accordingly, these leaders may be inclined to minimize some security threats to co-ethnics in border areas or to downplay

certain smuggling activities as not worth the costs of intervention. Moreover, with OAU norms proscribing external intervention, and with effective occupation complicated by the difficulty of absorbing new territories
and integrating hostile and scattered populations, the risks of protracted
military action seem high. Additional lands tend not to be valued in terms
of the financial outlays occasioned by occupation (Jackson and Zacher
1996, 23), especially when such seizures evoke the ire of publics at home
and in the wider region. Yet, with no external enforcer to rely on, the leaders in relatively better-functioning African states are increasingly viewing
some type of self-help as essential to reduce threats from violence on their
borders. These states often face a series of difficult trade-offs in their dealings with weak states in their neighborhood. Rather than overlook the disarray in crossborder areas, they can attempt to strengthen their own force
capacities and use them for interventionist purposes. Although often a potentially costly option, forcible state action remains a feature of self-help
with a long history in Africa. In such weak-state situations as Ethiopia's
Ogaden, Lesotho, Congo-Brazzaville, or Congo-Kinshasa, the threat of
intervention or its actual use in a weak-state situation depended in large
part on the militarily stronger state's capacity, domestic and international
support, and preparedness to intercede (Simon and Starr 1996). Intervention normally takes place to protect or advance perceived interests, such as
to protect investments, prevent smuggling, halt illegal arms transfers, stop
money laundering, gain access to water or minerals, and so forth. As Salih
Booker, a senior fellow at the Council on Foreign Relations, remarked,
"The Angolans didn't save Kabila because they're committed to his leadership or they think he's the solution, but because of their internal concerns" (Voice of America 1998).

Recent events in the Congo indicate both a decline in OAU norms on
nonintervention and a preparedness of African states to intervene militarily in support of vulnerable state leaders and insurgencies in neighboring
countries. Contending that the Mobutu regime failed to halt crossborder
raids by armed militias, Uganda and Rwanda argued that they had legitimate security concerns in eastern Congo-Kinshasa. These concerns, which
led the Ugandans and Rwandans to support the rebel Kabila in 1996, remained in evidence two years later. By 1998, alliance partners had shifted
and Kabila seemed unwilling or unable to restrain insurgent Rwandan and
Ugandan militias operating from Congolese territory. As Kabila acted aggressively toward Tutsi influences in his country, Uganda and Rwanda intervened to back those rebelling against his regime. Meanwhile, Angola,
Zimbabwe, Namibia, and Chad, seeking to buttress a fellow state leader

(which Kabila had by now become), sent military units to Congo-Kinshasa in an effort to overcome the rebellion. Clearly, a civil war had been internationalized, raising serious doubts about the future relevance of OAU norms on sovereignty and domestic jurisdiction in situations where ethnic and religious minorities have legitimate fears.

A third type of response to the international threat posed by weak states in the region involves initiatives undertaken by regional groups of states and international organizations. Weak states are magnets for external intervention not only for reasons of power and interest (as noted above regarding the Congo-Kinshasa interventions), but also because of human rights considerations. Increasingly, enlightened African analysts who hold that the international community has a right and a duty to intervene in domestic conflicts to prevent threats to international peace and security have advanced a new humanitarian intervention doctrine. Where scoundrels abuse sovereignty and minority interests are left exposed and unprotected, regional and global organizations cannot be expected to watch from the sidelines. Instead, as OAU secretary-general Salim Salim argued, they must intervene "to maintain a balance between national sovereignty and international responsibility" (Boutros-Ghali 1992; Deng et al. 1996; Gomes 1996, 41). Over time, such a reconceptualization of sovereignty represents the beginning of a new international order in Africa. In some respects, the intervention by ECOMOG (the Economic Community of West Africa Monitoring Group) in Liberia and Sierra Leone may be viewed as an early sign of such an emergent collective responsibility. Nevertheless, it should also be noted that this doctrine on responsible sovereignty has also prompted misgivings in weak states, where spokespersons express fears that it could represent blatant interference in an African country's internal affairs and could undermine OAU norms on state integrity and autonomy (thus, for example, Charles Taylor's criticism of ECOMOG's intervention in Liberia).

Collective state action to deal with the difficulties that weak states pose to the African state system is logically a means of enlarging choice, but because of competing preferences within regional and global organizations, it is more difficult to arrange (witness Burkina Faso's and the Ivory Coast's lack of support for ECOMOG in Liberia and the OAU's role in the Western Saharan and Rwandan conflicts). In practice, therefore, international coordination is plagued with uncertainties. Limited by budgetary considerations, agreement on a mandate, and the problems of enforcement, the UN and regional organizations are often unable or reluctant to launch new multidimensional peacekeeping efforts and frequently stand helplessly on the sidelines as the conflict runs its course.

Nevertheless, as was true with state-initiated self-help measures, some collective endeavors remain low-cost and offer high potential payoffs. Thus the gathering of early-warning information and other reliable data, so necessary for intelligence purposes, is best achieved as a collective undertaking. Similarly, collective diplomatic influence can prove a relatively low-cost and effective means for enlarging choice when it involves exerting regional and international pressure on warlords or rogue states who violate borders and give support to insurgent movements. Provided these interstate coalitions can overcome the costs of negotiating a common position among their members, they may be in a position to close off options for targeted private actors, insurgent movements, or states. They may also be able to expand the opportunities for alliance members, imposing sanctions and attempting to isolate targeted actors (as was the case in the initial period in Burundi, when seven regional governments imposed sanctions after Pierre Buyoya seized power in 1996).

Some creative but difficult possibilities available to alliance partners involve the reconfiguration of the state and the state system. Once one recognizes that the artificiality of some existing postcolonial states is the source of various identity and legitimacy problems, then measures aimed at "reconstruct[ing] sovereignty" may seem prudent (Hopkins 1995, 82). State and internally organized referenda on the partition of Ethiopia and Eritrea and the possibility of Western Saharan statehood display ways of rectifying borders or establishing new states. Various border adjustments and state reconfigurations have been proposed for coping with ethnic issues in central Africa; however, given the reluctance of African leaders to consider such changes in the past, and their inherent risks, efforts at state reconfiguration seem likely to encounter strong opposition from status quo–inclined regimes that will seek to uphold OAU norms on sovereignty and borders.

In addition, African leaders have proposed buffer zones as a confidence-building mechanism. Again, African state and international organization opposition to territorial alterations is likely to prove potent. Even so, Kagame has suggested the use of demilitarized areas as a security device in Congo-Kinshasa, arguing that buffer zones are a means of preventing border crossings by hostile forces and of addressing common security problems (Pineau 1998b). Significantly, under the 1993 Cotonou agreement, ECOMOG received authorization to create buffer zones between the borders of Liberia and those of Sierra Leone, Guinea, and the Ivory Coast in an effort to halt the spread of conflict (Adebajo 1998, 20). Intervention thus takes a variety of forms, and which form is relevant in a particular conflict situation is largely a matter of context and the capabilities of the political actors.

Conclusion

This paper adopts a bottom-up view of the current crisis in African inter-state relations, focusing on Africa's weak states as the source of destabilizing influences on the African state system and its normative order. Comparisons with experiences drawn from interstate relations in post-Soviet Eurasia are instructive, as they highlight the similarities and differences in these contexts. Because of the negative externalities resulting from interactions with weak states, the relatively better-functioning states of Africa are confronted with the prospect of an unpleasant choice between acting or failing to act in conformity with OAU norms on sovereignty and non-intervention while seeking to stabilize their region. In the former Soviet Union, by contrast, the CIS is a loosely structured economic and security organization that does not yet represent a consistent body of formal, unified norms. The challenge of designing effective strategies in both regions for coping with a wide range of illicit commercial activities, political and military assistance to co-ethnics in adjacent lands, and adventurist crossborder thrusts makes the regularization of relations between states challenging. In Eurasia, Russia's continuing aspirations to hegemony have tended to draw it into internal conflicts within neighboring weak states. By contrast, no state seeks to play this role in Africa; indeed, in Africa the reverse trend is visible: a withdrawal of influence by external great powers.

Weak states, which tend to favor private patronage networks and to place relatively little emphasis on institutions of diplomacy and bureaucratic management, differ from their better-functioning neighbors in terms of opportunities, costs, and benefits from formal interaction with neighboring states. In light of the prevailing incentive structure, it is difficult for weak-state rulers to forgo private patronage and the extension of private interest across their borders. The leaders of relatively better-functioning states in Africa generally have preferred a risk-averse strategy in the face of negative externalities, accepting the moderately painful status quo of life alongside weak neighbors to the possible gains that might be made from intervention, provided the threat to national security remains low to moderate (Levy 1994; Nincic 1997). Despite the presence of weak states in their neighborhood, they have been inclined to adhere to OAU norms on state sovereignty and to resist the temptations of seizing new territories or becoming involved in low-intensity wars that hold little promise of resolution. For the most part, their budgets are tight and resources scant, making it difficult for their political elites to pursue active interventionist policies over an extended time period. Thus, the risk-reward calculus more than likely inclines the leaders of most African countries to emphasize the avoidance of costs and to pursue cautious stances regarding interventions in the affairs of soft state neighbors. As a result, the challenge that the weak state presents to the African state system can be expected to take a continuing toll on stable inter-African relationships.

This calculus changes, however, when states feel that they have important economic or political interests in the affairs of neighboring countries or where the perceptions of external threat appear to require far-reaching decisions on self-help. Zimbabwe's support for Kabila is indicative of the former, while South Africa's willingness to send military forces into Lesotho, in part to protect its access to water reserves, and the willingness of Rwanda, Uganda, and Burundi to send troops into neighboring Congo-Kinshasa to help rebels and protect its security are suggestive of the latter. Either way, the risk-reward calculus in these circumstances overcame loss aversion and tilted rulers in favor of an interventionist course. In such cases, the leaders of these states accepted the perils of committing their forces, because they assessed the dangers of inaction to be unacceptable in terms of their interests, values, or externality costs. Their actions, however, have weakened the very norms of an interstate system that has protected all African countries directly or indirectly from loss of control of their borders and the instability and conflict that follow from such negative externalities.

References

Adebajo, Adekeye. 1998. "Liberia: A Banquet for the Warlords." Paper presented at the Center for International Security and Cooperation, Stanford University, 16 October.

Ayoob, Mohammed. 1995. *The Third World Security Predicament: State Making, Regional Conflict, and the International System*. Boulder: Lynne Rienner.

Bates, Robert H. 1981. *Markets and States in Tropical Africa*. Berkeley: University of California Press.

Boutros-Ghali, Boutros. 1992. *An Agenda for Peace*. New York: United Nations.

Buzan, Barry. 1991. *People, States, and Fear*. 2d ed. Boulder: Lynne Rienner.

Clapham, Christopher. 1996. *Africa and the International System: The Politics of Survival*. Cambridge: Cambridge University Press.

David, Steven R. 1991. "Explaining Third-World Alignment." *World Politics* 43, no. 2 (January): 233–56.

———. 1992–93. "Why the Third World Still Matters." *International Security* 17, no. 3 (winter): 127–59.

Deng, Francis M. 1993. "Africa and the New World Dis-Order: Rethinking Colonial Boundaries." *Brookings Review* 11, no. 2 (spring): 34.

Deng, Francis M., Sadikiel Kimaro, Terrence Lyons, Donald Rothchild, and I. William Zartman. 1996. *Sovereignty as Responsibility: Conflict Management in Africa.* Washington: Brookings Institution Press.

Furman, Dimitry, and Carl Johan Asenius. 1996. "The Case of Nagorno-Karabakh (Azerbaijan)." Pp. 139–53 in *Peacekeeping and the Role of Russia in Eurasia,* ed. Lena Jonson and Clive Archer. Boulder: Westview.

Goldgeier, James M., and Michael McFaul. 1992. "A Tale of Two Worlds: Core and Periphery in the Post–Cold War Era." *International Organization* 46, no. 2: 467–91.

Gomes, Solomon. 1996. "The OAU, State Sovereignty, and Regional Security." Pp. 37–51 in *Africa and the New International Order,* ed. Edmond J. Keller and Donald Rothchild. Boulder: Lynne Rienner.

Halpern, Manfred. 1976. "Changing Connections to Multiple Worlds," Pp. 9–44 in *Africa: From Mystery to Maze,* ed. Helen Kitchen. Lexington, Mass.: D. C. Heath.

Herbst, Jeffrey. 1989. "The Creation and Maintenance of National Boundaries in Africa." *International Organization* 43, no. 4: 673–92.

———. 1996–97. "Responding to State Failure in Africa." *International Security* 21, no. 3 (winter): 120–44.

Hill, Stuart, and Donald Rothchild. 1986. "The Contagion of Political Conflict in Africa and the World." *Journal of Conflict Resolution* 30, no. 4: 716–35.

Holsti, Kalevi J. 1996. *The State, War, and the State of War.* Cambridge: Cambridge University Press.

Honwana, Joao. 1998. "Implementing Peace Agreements in Civil Wars: The Case of Mozambique." Paper presented at the Center for International Security and Cooperation, Stanford University, 17 October.

Hopkins, Raymond F. 1995. "Anomie, System Reform, and Challenges to the UN System," Pp. 72–97 in *International Organizations and Ethnic Conflict,* ed. Milton J. Esman and Shibley Telhami. Ithaca: Cornell University Press.

Howe, Herbert M. 1998. "Private Security Forces and African Stability: The Case of Executive Outcomes." *Journal of Modern African Studies* 36, no. 2: 307–31.

Hyden, Goran. 1983. "Problems and Prospects of State Coherence." Pp. 67–84 in *State Versus Ethnic Claims: African Policy Dilemmas,* ed. Donald Rothchild and Victor A. Olorunsola. Boulder: Westview.

Ignatieff, Michael. 1993. *Blood and Belonging: Journeys into the New Nationalism.* New York: Farrar, Straus and Giroux.

"In God's Name." 2000. *Africa Confidential* 41 (3 March): 1–2.

Jackson, Robert H. 1990. *Quasi-States: Sovereignty, International Relations, and the Third World.* Cambridge: Cambridge University Press.

Jackson, Robert H., and Carl G. Rosberg. 1982. "Why Africa's Weak States Persist: The Empirical and the Juridical in Statehood." *World Politics* 35, no. 1 (fall): 1–24.

Jackson, Robert H., and Mark W. Zacher. 1996. "The Territorial Covenant: International Society and the Legitimation of Boundaries." Paper presented at the annual meeting of the American Political Science Association, San Francisco, 29 August–1 September.

Jervis, Robert. 1976. *Perception and Misperception in International Politics.* Princeton: Princeton University Press.

Kaplan, Cynthia S. 1998. "Ethnicity and Sovereignty: Insights from Russian Negotiations with Estonia and Tatarstan." Pp. 251–74 in *The International Spread of Ethnic Conflict:*

Fear, Diffusion, and Escalation, ed. David A. Lake and Donald Rothchild. Princeton: Princeton University Press.

Katsouris, Christina. 1997. "Sharp Fall in Resource Flows to Africa." *Africa Recovery* 11, no. 2: 1–4.

Keller, Edmond J. 1997. "Rethinking African Regional Security." Pp. 296–317 in *Regional Orders: Building Security in a New World,* ed. David A. Lake and Patrick M. Morgan. University Park: Pennsylvania State University Press.

Lake, David A. 1997. "Regional Security Complexes: A Systems Approach." Pp. 296–317 in *Regional Orders: Building Security in a New World,* ed. David A. Lake and Patrick M. Morgan. University Park: Pennsylvania State University Press.

Lake, David A., and Donald Rothchild. 1998. *The International Spread of Ethnic Conflict: Fear, Diffusion, and Escalation.* Princeton: Princeton University Press.

Lapidus, Gail W. 1998. "Contested Sovereignty: The Tragedy of Chechnya." *International Security* 23, no. 1 (summer): 5–49.

Lemarchand, René. 1994. *Burundi: Ethnic Conflict and Genocide.* Washington: Woodrow Wilson Center Press; Cambridge: Cambridge University Press.

Levy, Jack S. 1994. "An Introduction to Prospect Theory." Pp. 7–22 in *Avoiding Losses/Taking Risks: Prospect Theory and International Conflict,* ed. Barbara Farnham. Ann Arbor: University of Michigan Press.

Mafeje, Archie. 1998. "The Beast and the Icon: No End to Ali Mazrui's *Pax Africana* Muddles." *CODESRIA Bulletin* 2: 9–11.

Nincic, Miroslav. 1997. "Loss Aversion and the Domestic Context of Military Intervention." *Political Research Quarterly* 50, no. 1: 97–120.

Pineau, Carol. 1998a. "Kagame/International." On newswire of Voice of America, 16 September. Obtained at gopher.voa.gov/00/newswire/wed/KAGAME_-_INTERNATIONAL.

———. 1998b. "Kagame Security." On newswire of Voice of America, 18 September. Obtained at gopher.voa.gov/00/newswire/thu/KAGAME_SECURITY.

Reno, William. 1998. *Warlord Politics and African States.* Boulder: Lynne Rienner.

Rothchild, Donald. 1987. "Hegemony and State Softness: Some Variations in Elite Responses." Pp. 117–48 in *The African State in Transition,* ed. Zaki Ergas. New York: St. Martin's.

———. 1997a. *Managing Ethnic Conflict in Africa: Pressures and Incentives for Cooperation.* Washington: Brookings Institution Press.

———. 1997b. "Unofficial Mediation and the Nigeria-Biafra War." *Nationalism and Ethnic Politics* 3, no. 3: 37–65.

Rothchild, Donald, and Michael Foley. 1983. "The Implications of Scarcity for Governance in Africa." *International Political Science Review* 4, no. 3: 311–26.

Rubin, Barnett R. 1998. "Russian Hegemony and State Breakdown in the Periphery: Causes and Consequences of the Civil War in Tajikistan." Pp. 128–61 in *Post-Soviet Political Order: Conflict and State Building,* ed. Barnett R. Rubin and Jack Snyder. New York: Routledge.

Schatzberg, Michael G. 1988. *The Dialectics of Oppression in Zaire.* Bloomington: Indiana University Press.

Schlein, Lisa. 1998. "U-N Congo." On newswire of Voice of America, 25 September. Obtained at gopher.voa.gov/00/newswire/fri/U-N_CONGO.

Shearer, David. 1998a. "Outsourcing War." *Foreign Policy* 112 (fall): 68–81.

———. 1998b. *Private Armies and Military Intervention.* International Institute for Strategic Studies Adelphi paper 316. London: Oxford University Press.

Sheehy, Ann. 1992. *The CIS: A Progress Report.* Radio Free Europe/Radio Liberty Research Report 1, no. 38 (25 September): 1–6.

Simon, Marc V., and Harvey Starr. 1996. "Extraction, Allocation, and the Rise and Decline of States." *Journal of Conflict Resolution* 40, no. 2: 272–97.

Stanley, William, and Charles T. Call. 1997. "Building a New Civilian Police Force in El Salvador." Pp. 107–33 in *Rebuilding Societies after Civil War,* ed. Krishna Kumar. Boulder: Lynne Rienner.

Stavrakis, Peter J. 1996. "The Soft State and the Emergence of Russian Regional Politics." Pp. 185–205 in *Russia and Eastern Europe after Communism: The Search for New Political, Economic, and Security Systems,* ed. Michael Kraus and Ronald Liebowitz. Boulder: Westview.

Stedman, Stephen John. 1996. "Conflict and Conciliation in Sub-Saharan Africa." Pp. 235–65 in *The International Dimensions of Internal Conflict,* ed. Michael E. Brown. Cambridge, Mass.: MIT Press.

"Trumpeting the Horn." 1997. *Africa Confidential* 38 (9 May): 5–6.

Voice of America. 1998. "Crisis in the Congo." On newswire of Voice of America, 25 September. Obtained at gopher.voa.gov/00/newswire/fri/CRISIS_IN_THE_CONGO.

Waltz, Kenneth N. 1979. *Theory of International Politics.* Reading: Addison-Wesley.

Weiner, Myron. 1992–93. "Security, Stability, and International Migration." *International Security* 17, no. 3: 91–126.

West Africa. 1991. 15–21 April.

Williams, Pete. 1994. "Transnational Criminal Organisations and International Security." *Survival* 36, no. 1: 96–113.

Young, Crawford. 1994. "Zaire: The Shattered Illusion of the Integral State." *Journal of Modern African Studies* 32, no. 2: 247–63.

Young, Crawford, and Thomas Turner. 1985. *The Rise and Decline of the Zairian State.* Madison: University of Wisconsin Press.

Zartman, I. William. 1998. "Putting Humpty-Dumpty Together Again." Pp. 317–36 in *The International Spread of Ethnic Conflict: Fear, Diffusion, and Escalation,* ed. David A. Lake and Donald Rothchild. Princeton: Princeton University Press.

Part III

Democratization and Political Economy

9

Russia: Unconsolidated Democracy, Creeping Authoritarianism, or Unresolved Stagnation?

LILIA SHEVTSOVA

Russians are more and more skeptical about the results of postcommunist transformation. Few people in Russia any longer speak of a "triumph of liberal democracy." Harsher labels ("criminal oligarchic regime," "phony capitalism," "crony capitalism," "elected monarchy") are used to describe the political regime that has emerged in Russia since 1991 (Burtin and Vodolalazov 1998; Yavlinsky 1998, 67; Shevtsova and Klyamkin 1998). Over the course of the 1990s, Russia's continued progress toward democracy has stalled, dashing liberals' initial hopes that were raised by the collapse of communism. In this chapter I will assess Russia's democratization, focusing in particular on superpresidentialism and patrimonialism as the defining qualities of Russian democracy. As this chapter will show, these characteristics impart to Russia unique features in comparison with those of African regimes, but at the same time they raise certain parallels among the various countries in question.

Russia's Stalled Democratization

A preliminary assessment of the character and extent of Russia's democratization can be based on the following minimal criteria of democracy: accountability of government to the people, regular and fair elections, guarantees of citizens' rights to express their opinions freely and of freedom of the press, political pluralism, civilian control of the military, institutional checks in political life, and the rule of law (Schmitter and Karl 1991, 81). Another criterion might be the "democratic bargain"—i.e., the principle that whoever wins at the polls will not use that victory to suppress or persecute those who lost (Dahl 1970). On the surface, Russia meets nearly all these criteria to some extent, but it does so with a great ambiguity. This sense of a disappointingly incomplete democratization closely tracks many African cases.

Accountability to the People

Accountability still does not much concern Russian ruling groups; they have little fear of the consequences of their actions. Until recently, they did not even believe that mass protests were possible. In short, the ruling elite does not care about how it is viewed by the people. Its members have prepared their escape routes and extra parachutes in advance.

Elections

Many have been surprised at how eagerly the Russian political class has rushed to hold elections that have been characterized by voter turnouts so high that they put Western societies to shame. Electoral politics in Russia do not, however, testify to the democratic convictions of the establishment. Rather, they are an expression of the fact that the Russian ruling class is split and weak and cannot hold on to power through means other than abnormally frequent elections. It is true that elections provide society with the possibility of making choices. But Russians have had very limited, and not often reassuring, options. As Hortensio declared in Shakespeare's *The Taming of the Shrew,* "There's small choice in rotten apples." Although Russian citizens vote, most expect little, if anything, from those they elect. A large proportion of voters and politicians seems to be playing a game whose unspoken rules consist of preserving the status quo and leaving one another in peace. Such an electoral game gives rise to cynicism and discredits the concept of democracy in the eyes of the people.

Freedom of Expression

The state of freedom of expression and human rights in general in Russia appears to be satisfactory. Compared with the communist period, people are now freer than ever before. Boris Yeltsin did not encroach on individual rights and freedoms, as he could have done given the enormous powers he had acquired as president. On the other hand, he did little to expand or strengthen the guarantees of these freedoms. Freedom of expression loses much of its significance if public opinion matters little to those in power. Russia's press experienced a relatively short period of real freedom, but gradually the mass media have again become as partisan as ever, increasingly dependent on the state or on powerful financial groups that determine the views that the media are allowed to express. The Kremlin's attempts since 1999 to monopolize all resources of influence, including control over the media, have revealed how vulnerable to political pressure and machinations freedom of expression is in Russia. This issue has come to the fore under the Vladimir Putin administration as well; media tycoons critical of Putin have found themselves under attack by the state for tax evasion or embezzlement.

The basic civil rights established by the Russian constitution are constantly violated. Although significant repression is largely absent, Russian citizens are largely defenseless before the governing structures, especially in the provinces, where semi-authoritarian ruling groups have arisen. More alarmingly, the conflict in Chechnya demonstrated that the Russian government is not constrained from resorting to the barbaric destruction of its citizens if it so desires.

Political Pluralism

Russia has entered a phase of crisis in the arena of political pluralism. The Russian public is disappointed with the existing parties, and social and political interests remain unfocused. After the events of October 1993, when Yeltsin forcibly dissolved the Russian parliament, a new constitution placed limits on the parliament's independence, and since the parties do not influence the formation of the government, their role and impact are diminished. Decision-making has moved behind the scenes, a fact that increases the role of interest groups at the expense of the parties. The government does not care to reestablish mechanisms through which the will of the public could be expressed. Thus Russia's apparent political pluralism remains weak and fails to be constructive.

Civilian Control of the Military

The Soviet Union had a very strong tradition of civilian control of the military, and this mode appears to persist in today's Russia. The army, the troops of the Interior Ministry, and the special services are directly subordinate to the country's leader. Significantly, however, the command structure is based on personal rather than institutional loyalty. Embodied in this phenomenon is the potential danger of politicizing the power structures in the armed and police services, drawing them into conflicts between contenders for political and military leadership.

Checks and Balances

Russia lacks a system of institutional checks and balances, a condition that has led to an excessive focus on and the lodging of excessive power in individual personalities in Russian politics—an overpersonalization of politics. The political structure formed by Yeltsin after the dissolution of the parliament in 1993 was highly dependent on the physical condition, characteristics, and capabilities of the president. Such a situation has rendered institutions vulnerable, provoked a prolonged succession struggle, and left the country mired in uncertainty. With the accession of Putin and his dominance over the Duma (the lower house of the Russian parliament), that dependence on a single leader has only been reinforced.

The Rule of Law

The weakness of Russia's judicial system and the fragility of the rule of law are troubling. There are many indications that members of the elite have used public service as a vehicle for advancing their own private business interests. Although similar scandals have occurred in Western democracies, such affairs have been investigated by the courts, and the responsible people are usually prosecuted. Disturbingly, the Russian judiciary displays near-complete apathy about such legal violations; often it is used as a tool by one set of rivals against another.

The Democratic Bargain

Over time the possibilities for a "democratic bargain"—guarantees that new rulers provide to those leaving power—expanded in Russia, as irreconcilable political forces began to erase the differences among them. Certain groups came to understand the necessity of making a pact to preclude revenge-seeking after Yeltsin left his presidential post. However, the price of that bargain has been the entrenchment of the particular interests dominating the state—and specifically, the Yeltsin entourage itself.

In short, after a powerful push toward democracy in the late Soviet period, Russia today falls considerably short of a democratic polity. In this respect, it resembles a number of the African cases—particularly in the weak degree of accountability of rulers. As in Russia, elections have been frequent in Africa over the last decade, but many African intellectuals regard them as choiceless. The latitude of free expression enjoyed by the print media in Africa has greatly expanded, although the opposition press can be subject to diverse pressures. Although African judiciaries have shown some independence during the1990s, their institutional capacity to guarantee a "rule-of-law state" is limited.

In one important respect, however, the Russian and African experiences diverge: a secure tradition of civilian control of the military remains to be established in Africa. Although no seizures of power by the military have occurred in Eurasia since the Soviet collapse, such interventions—though far less frequent than previously—have occurred in Niger (twice), the Gambia, Guinea-Bissau, Nigeria, and the Ivory Coast.

Lost Chances

Why has Russian democracy fallen short of the democratic ideal? Nothing was preordained in Russia after the collapse of communism. In 1991, Russia had several options for its further development, including the possibility of following—for the first time in Russian history—the path of at least gradual democratization. At a minimum in 1991–92, broad segments of society supported democratic and liberal ideas, and Yeltsin and his group, at least rhetorically committed to democracy, had considerable influence. The pragmatists from the old ruling class who managed to retain power followed democratic rules, albeit reluctantly. Revanchist groups had been weakened, and the traditional "power structures" (the army, the Ministry of Internal Affairs, the former KGB intelligence service) were dispirited. Ordinary Russians were ready to make considerable sacrifices in the name of a more prosperous and democratic future. The international environment, too, was generally favorable for the implementation of both market and democratic reforms. At the time, many Russian observers believed that the Russian past and its legacy did not have to be an insurmountable impediment that would prevent the country from making a successful transition to liberal democracy.

Unfortunately, the opportunity for steady democratic development in Russia was not seized by the ruling group. A number of obstacles complicated Russian reforms. Russia's lack of democratic traditions did represent a hindrance. However, the most serious obstacle in the way of Russia's joining the Western political tradition of liberal individualism, of a search for equilibrium and stable rules of the game, and of an adherence to the system of checks and balances was a deeply ingrained rejection by the Russian ruling class of the division of power. The elites of influence have regarded power as an indivisible monolith—or, as some Russian analysts call it, a "monosubject."

The historical roots of postcommunist Russian developments are also evident in the personification of power, the succession struggle at the top, the greediness of so-called clans, court politics, nepotism and patrimonialism, and the all-absorbing thirst for power demonstrated by political leaders. The establishment of the "superpresidency" in Russia in 1993 preserved Russia's historic Byzantine model of governance: a leader (tsar, general secretary, president) becomes the concentrated focus of all power and the symbol of the nation, its arbiter, and its main guarantee of stability. In contrast to the Western political tradition, wherein power is based on rational ideas and institutions, the Byzantine tradition has always invested power in something sacred, irrational, and personal. The rulers are considered to be simultaneously the father of the nation and the omnipotent and unaccountable (personally and institutionally) ruler. Joseph Stalin was the full embodiment of the Byzantine tradition of irrationality, mystery, and contempt for society. Such patrimonialism in the late communist period acquired a collectivist ideological covering and the features of a kind of bureaucratic authoritarianism. As he tried to become a supreme arbiter in the Weberian sense, Yeltsin, with his sense of messianism and his aspiration to the role of father of the nation, seemed to have wanted to restore elements of this traditional patrimonialism. The past keeps Russia in its grip, and, as Yeltsin's behavior demonstrated, it is too early to reach final conclusions as to the ultimate interaction of continuity and change. Yeltsin's "Tsar Boris" behavior while society patiently waited for its leader to solve its problems echoed the past. In the crucial period of consolidation of the new political regime, in 1991–93, Russians exhibited no readiness, even on the part of democrats, to close the Byzantine chapter of Russian history.

At the same time, the emergence of the "presidential pyramid" was to a great degree determined by the logic of the political battle raging at the end of Mikhail Gorbachev's presidency and during the first years of the Russian transformation.[1] At the beginning of 1991, the nature of

---

1. Michael McFaul was right when he concluded that the Russian superpresidency not only is the result of Russian historical legacy, but "emerged directly from the transition process" (McFaul 1999, 11).

Yeltsin's—and Russia's—confrontation with the central Soviet authorities and with Gorbachev was transformed into a sharp public conflict within the old Russian republican parliament and into a split within its leadership. Subsequently, Yeltsin, whose legitimacy was to a large extent determined by the old Russian parliament, was forced to seek other ways of gaining public support and additional, broader legitimacy. Thus the post of the Russian presidency grew not merely out of Yeltsin's struggle with Gorbachev (who had created a Soviet presidency), but also out of Yeltsin's struggle with the newborn Russian political class to secure power through the creation of a directly elected presidency. The presidency was a new institution in Russia's political tradition, but by a circuitous route and through the twisted paths of the political struggle, it led directly back to the autocratic tradition (Klyamkin and Shevtsova 1999).

In short, the idea of the presidency was a new one, even a revolutionary one, as far as the means of constituting supreme power and the sources of its legitimacy were concerned; the old sources of legitimacy—hereditary monarchy and communist ideology—had exhausted their historical potential. But at the same time, this seemingly revolutionary invention was a step in a direction typical for Russia: toward a system in which power is completely personified and embodied in one individual. This marriage of the new with the traditional was reflected as a tension between democratic and autocratic strands in contemporary Russian politics, a tension that has not yet been resolved.

The presidential regime that came to life out of the political struggle in Russia and that was directly influenced by the nature of that struggle was at the same time a response to the legacy of the Communist Party of the Soviet Union (CPSU)—and in particular, to the impotence of the parliament-style soviets that were deprived of government support. Yet not only did the presidency fail to overcome the fundamental contradiction typical of the soviets, it actually resurrected it, albeit in modified form.

Formerly, the essence of this contradiction lay in the fact that the legal power of the soviets ran up against the claims of the CPSU to a monopoly on power. After the CPSU had exited the political stage, however, the line of conflict shifted to a different plane: the Supreme Soviet versus the president. Inevitably, the conflict took on an even more pointed character, since this time the struggle involved not a split between legitimate (the popularly elected soviets) and illegitimate (CPSU) power, but a battle between two government institutions both legitimized by popular elections (the parliament and the president).

Lasting close to two years, from 1991 to 1993, this confrontation of the president and the parliament exposed the lack of readiness of the Russian political class to reach an agreement on the division of power and on the observance of democratic norms. This political predicament differed significantly from the experience of other postcommunist countries, namely, those in eastern Europe. Fairly quickly, it became apparent that each side in the struggle intended to use democratic legitimation procedures to perpetuate the traditional monopoly of power. At the very least, the political actors hoped to erect a regime in which power would be shared among a hierarchy of institutions and in which one institution would dominate the others. The power configuration of 1991–93 both perpetuated centuries-old modes of Russian government and fueled a manipulation of democracy in the struggle for a monopoly on power.

Furthermore, in full accordance with state tradition, the parliamentary-style soviets tried at first to affirm their own omnipotence as a counterweight to the omnipotence of the CPSU. The union structure had been preserved in the Congress of People's Deputies—an unwieldy organ able to function only in a populist, mass-rally type of regime. Russia perpetuated the old model to a greater extent than did the other postcommunist republics. Granted almost unlimited powers, the congress was created in the last years of communist rule in order to allow the CPSU to gain hegemony in the democratization process. Although this goal was not attained, the very existence of this structure and its monopoly on power to a large extent predetermined Russia's political development vis-à-vis the other republics of the former Soviet Union. It is precisely because the Congress of People's Deputies was still legally the supreme organ of power in the Russian Federation that many liberal Russian deputies supported the introduction of the presidency.

In spite of its unlimited powers, the authority of the congress lacked one component absolutely essential within the context of Russia's political culture. The congress was not personified; it had no charismatic figure to compete with Yeltsin. Even its speaker, Ruslan Khasbulatov, who aspired to usurp Yeltsin's dominance over Russian politics, paled in comparison with Yeltsin's populist appeal. Moreover, the public viewed Yeltsin, the symbol of victory over communism in August 1991, as vested with supreme power. Thus a seemingly paradoxical situation developed: although defending the populace from the unpopular economic reforms that began in January 1992, the Congress of People's Deputies inspired even less trust among the Russian public than the president whose name was, to a significant extent, associated with these reforms.

Engulfed in a political struggle, Yeltsin could handle the Congress of

People's Deputies and the Supreme Soviet only through unconstitutional measures. These measures were based on the political capital he acquired through the April 1993 "referendum on trust in the president and support for his reform program." As shown by the events of September 21–October 4, 1993—beginning with Yeltsin's decree dissolving the Supreme Soviet and the Congress of People's Deputies through the armed storming of the building where the deputies were meeting—this capital proved more than sufficient.

Thus in 1993 a historical line was drawn, putting an end to the hybrid political regime of parliamentary-style soviets and the presidency. A continuation of the communist period, this regime provided a relatively painless way to overcome the omnipotence of the CPSU. But its inability to function and to survive made it necessary to add the institution of a popularly elected president. This institutional novelty resulted in a duality of power and in a concomitant degradation of the fledgling system of statehood. But even the new regime that arose after the violent eradication of this dyarchy could not free itself from the traces of the previous power arrangement. Although in an entirely different context and in more subtle ways, symptoms of dual power are still making themselves felt in the Russian political system.

Several other factors influenced the development of Russian postcommunist politics. The need to solve the problem of stateness and of the new national or multinational identity was critical and traumatic for Russia, significantly complicating both the democratization process and economic reforms. A coherent state with a clear set of rules and an effective governing apparatus is crucial for democratic consolidation. In the Russian case, the lack of such a state became one of the most difficult hurdles in the process of further democratization. Moreover, those who formed the first reform team around Yeltsin viewed the state as the major source of problems. Ironically, they believed that their major task was to weaken a state that had opened the way for "clannish," oligarchic dominance. The way in which the Soviet Union was dismantled—through a secret negotiation among the leaders of three of the Soviet republics and without democratic confirmation of this process—also had its impact on further developments, such as the strengthening of the role of leaders and the failure to generate institutional rules or legitimacy in postcommunist Russian politics.

The sequence of reforms also played a large role in degrading the Russian regime. The new Russian ruling class revealed absolute indifference to the issue of political rules and chose to privilege economic liberalization over democratic restructuring of the state. Juan Linz and Alfred Stepan correctly argue that this choice of agenda-setting "weakened the state, weakened democracy, and weakened the economy" (Linz and Stepan 1996, 392). However, not just Yeltsin but even the democrats in Russia were not concerned about defining new rules of the game or about generating a public consensus for the creation of new institutions. Comfortable with the idea of strong, charismatic personal leadership, they hoped to use the cult of personality as an instrument of furthering economic reform. Moreover, as Joseph Stiglitz (1999) pointed out, the "shock therapy" approach to reform was in a way based "on the Bolshevik approach to the transition from capitalism to communism" and used many "of the same principles for the reverse transition." As a result of this phenomenon, society was antagonized, and a political vacuum enveloped the regime. The legacies of the past were a heavy burden on the post-Soviet Russian state. The simultaneous needs to establish a new state, to create a new multinational identity, to carry out democratic and economic reforms, to overcome the legacy of seven decades of Soviet communism, and to find a new place in the world significantly complicated democratization in Russia. The absence of traditions of private property and of freedom of the individual slowed down the formation of civil society. Russia's position as the successor to the Soviet Union's superpower status, which bequeathed a powerful military-industrial complex, hegemonic ambitions, and a strand of messianic sentiment among both the elite and the masses, also put obstacles in the way of successful transformation.

As in many parts of Africa, elections in the new Russia became to some extent an expression of "electoralism." They were viewed by the elite as useful in order to create some surface manifestations of a democratic polity, such as parties, electoral laws, and contested campaigns. "Elections in themselves do not constitute democracy," writes Terry Karl; they can also impede democratization, as, for instance, when they simply "rectify existing power arrangements" (Karl 1986, 34).

One more obstacle to political and economic reform should be mentioned: Russia's vast mineral resources, especially gas and oil. A powerful gas and oil lobby, oriented toward moderate reform and cooperation with the outside world, emerged during Gorbachev's *perestroika* and the first stage of Yeltsin's rule. It helped to diminish the role of its rival, the military-industrial sector, and to begin the initial stage of marketization. But as early as 1993–94, the gas and oil sector, with its huge export-earning possibilities, began to block further reform. To a certain extent, the gas and oil sector helped those in power preserve stability. The assistance that the natural gas conglomerate Gazprom gave to the government in paying off pension and wage arrears serves as an example. More profoundly, however, stabilization of this sort simply postponed necessary restructuring.[2]

But the real blame for the failures of liberal-democratic reform in Russia deserves to be placed on the ruling elite: the bureaucrats at the top and, even more important, the intellectual elite, the democrats and liberals, among the politicians. They could have used the confusion in the ranks of the old elite to persuade Yeltsin to move more energetically in a democratic direction. Instead, they deliberately rejected the possibility of building strong institutions, adopting a new constitution, and creating a system of checks and balances. They preferred a model of authoritarian transformation through the presidential "pyramid" of power. By choosing "civilized authoritarianism," the liberals evidently aspired to influence Yeltsin and push him in the desired directions. They might have also hoped that through the president they could preserve their own power. Thus the reformers themselves were not ready to constrain the activities of the highest executive. Contrary to what happened in eastern and central Europe, in Russia the political elite neglected to build the new political system as a totality of institutions, mechanisms, and procedures that reproduce themselves automatically and dictate strict rules of the game that apply universally to any official. Instead, the ruling class preferred to put up with a personified regime. The old unreformed Communist Party emerged as one of the pillars of the newly constituted regime and was a crucial factor in the survival of the regime and its founders.

No less important was the fact that Russia's political elite failed to achieve consensus about the desired course of future development and its political structure. Time after time, compromises between the major political players reflected only their own temporary interests and failed to take a larger national interest into consideration. Moreover, the constitution of 1993 was the result of a victory of and domination by a single political force and could not be considered a social contract between government and society. The absence of any pact among the major political forces in Russia translated into an unwillingness of the members of Yeltsin's group to be constrained by the wishes of a plurality of interests. As events painfully demonstrated, the lack of compromise on the crucial issues of development in Russia turned out to be one of the major hindrances to reform.

---

2. "Exploitation of oil eventually encourages a type of oil-based contract among organized interests, but it does so at high cost. The advantages of this arrangement lie in the prolonged periods of regime stability that oil exploitation can foster . . . but this regime stability is based on a predatory relationship with the state and the perpetuation of oil dependency" (Karl 1998, 57–58). The same may be said of gas dependency.

A perception of the Russian public as totally undemocratic, however, is inadequate. The majority of the population has shown remarkable receptivity to liberal ideas and democratic processes. A 1996 survey by the Public Opinion Foundation showed that most individuals were "pro-private" rather than "pro-statist"; most were receptive to the idea of a market economy and desirous of a Western standard of living. Most Russians—between 67 percent and 98 percent of all social groups—agreed on the following fundamental principles: that the life of an individual is more important than any other consideration; that laws should apply to everyone, from the president to the ordinary citizen; that property is inviolable; that the main human rights are the right to life, to the defense of one's honor, and to freedom of the individual; and that freedom is as necessary to Russians as it is to people in the West. Communist or imperial ideology appealed to only about 15–20 percent of the population (Kutkoviets and Klyamkin 1997).

Thus one must ask why a consensus uniting a significant part of the population around liberal-democratic values has not emerged on the Russian political scene. The answer comes down to the fact that interpretations of these values vary, and there is still little agreement on their implementation. Moreover, even among people who support liberal-democratic values, one in five is ready to sacrifice one or another human right in the name of ensuring order and stability.

Some Russian observers believe that Russian society still is torn between two civilizations—that of the West and that of the traditional, patrimonial culture—and that it is simply trying to adapt to this division. The existence of this cleavage is partially due to the fact that these two value systems cannot merge; they have to keep competing with each other. Even more important, after a series of collapses of liberal-democratic steps, Russia experienced a temporary revival of traditional political mentalities (Achiezer 1997, 2–14).

The Paradox of Russia's Weak Patrimonialism and Superpresidential Regime

The constitution of 1993, confirmed by a popular referendum, legally consolidated Yeltsin's victory over the old parliament. It signified, in fact, the end of the Soviet period of Russian history and the beginning of a new, more democratic era in the country. But the process of organization of power in that era again reveals that the new system, brought about by a conflict of institutions aspiring to a monopoly on power (the presidency and the old parliament), overcame this very conflict not through compromise (a rejection of the very idea of monopoly) but by affirmation of the traditional principle of the indivisibility of supreme state power. Thus the baby was born with the same disease that its mother had. In the same manner that the sovereignty of the soviets had been reaffirmed as a reaction and in opposition to the sovereignty of the CPSU, the de facto presidential sovereignty consolidated in the 1993 constitution was a sharp rejection of the sovereignty of the soviets.

Formally, the Russian constitution establishes a separation of powers. However, the power of the president, as the head of state, both absorbs several of the most important functions of the other branches of government and allows for the neutralization of undesirable tendencies in the legislative, executive, and judicial branches. In this context, it is clear why the Russian president is more and more frequently referred to as a "tsar." This contextual framework also provides an easy and logical explanation for the seemingly perplexing phenomenon whereby Yeltsin's successor was chosen by Yeltsin himself. Had the constitution been strictly observed, Yeltsin may have had a preference but could not have "named" a successor. The actual context of presidential powers, however, unmasks the parallels between the Russian president and the tsar.

Although parallels with patrimonial regimes in Africa can be drawn, Russia's current political regime does not easily fit familiar categories.[3] It is a regime in which elements of many political systems—democracy, authoritarianism, post-totalitarianism, "delegative democracy," bureaucratic authoritarianism, oligarchic rule, sultanism, and even monarchy—are intertwined in sometimes peculiar ways. Moreover, the high degree of decentralization and asymmetry within the Russian Federation increases the patchwork character of Russia's political regime. The system uses democratic rhetoric but often resorts to statist and populist ideas. Its leadership is produced by elections, but the leader rules in a personalistic and arbitrary manner, without legal constraints. The ruling elite is drawn from family members, friends of the family, or groups that anticipate some reward. Citizen participation in the decision-making process is minimal. A description of post-totalitarian states offered by Linz and Stepan aptly depicts the state of affairs in Russia today: "Boredom, withdrawal and ultimately privatization of the population's values has become an accepted fact" (Linz and Stepan 1996, 44–45).

---

3. For an analysis of Yeltsin's regime, see Shevtsova 1999.

Russia's current regime also displays some of the elements that Guillermo O'Donnell identified in bureaucratic-authoritarian rule. As O'Donnell argued, this type of regime is committed to accomplishing two tasks: "the restoration of 'order' in society by means of the political deactivation of the popular sector, on the one hand, and the normalization of the economy, on the other" (O'Donnell 1979, 292).

Yet another Russia scholar, Michael McFaul, identifies the Russian political system as an "electoral democracy" and notes that "electoral democracies are not liberal democracies; elections are not the only component of a fully consolidated democracy" (McFaul 1997, 319). Fareed Zakaria contributes to the debate of incomplete democracies with the term "illiberal democracy" and applies it to cases where the political system is marked by elections but lacks constitutional liberalism (Zakaria 1997, 22–23). Russia's current political regime also bears some resemblance to the system that O'Donnell calls "delegative democracy." Such a polity, in his words,

rest[s] on the premises that whoever wins election to the presidency is thereby entitled to govern as he or she sees fit. . . . The president is taken to be [the] embodiment of the nation and the main custodian and definer of its interests. . . . Typically, winning presidential candidates present themselves as above both political parties and organized interests. . . . Other institutions—courts and legislatures—are [to the president] nuisances that come attached to the domestic and international advantages of being a democratically elected president. Accountability to such institutions appears as a mere impediment to the full authority that the president has been delegated to exercise. . . . Elections in [delegative democracies] are a very emotional and high-stakes event: candidates compete for a chance to rule virtually free of all constraints. . . . Presidents get elected by promising that they—being strong, courageous, above parties and interests, macho—will save their country. . . . [Theirs is] the government of saviors" (O'Donnell 1994, 59–62).

The model of "delegative democracy" parallels closely the Russian superpresidency, which in reality combines both omnipotence and impotence. But nepotism and Caesarism are also pronounced features of the Russian regime. In the Russian context, the probability remains small for a military coup along the lines of those experienced in many parts of Africa. The metaphor "virtual democracy" is also helpful in understanding the controversial interconnection among the institutional framework, official rhetoric, and the real political behavior and ambitions of Russian politicians. It is here as well that close parallels can be traced with Richard Joseph's description of the African experience. In both instances, the formal rules of the game produce unexpected, and not always desirable, effects.[4]

Outwardly, Russia's electorally determined presidency has a democratic cast, but in reality the presidency is totally independent of any political force and is endowed with immense powers. The presidency breaches its democratic mandate. The presidential post thus resembles a monarchy. The term "elected monarchy" sounds like political nonsense. This nonsense, however, reflects certain facets of the trap in which Russia finds itself and again underscores problems similar to those identified by Joseph. On the one hand, Russia seems unable to overcome the tradition of personalistic rule; on the other hand, the political regime is required to adopt some democratic procedures, because it has exhausted all other means of retaining power and requires external legitimation. But the incompatibility of the main features of such a regime makes it highly unstable and fragile; its structure is itself a source of major conflicts. Even more succinct in describing the regime are the terms "anti-systemic" or "quasi-systemic," which address one of the most important features of the Russian political mechanism: its formation not as a system of institutions with defined spheres of influence but as a personalistic regime that came at least partially to substitute for the system and even the state (Klyamkin and Shevtsova 1999).

A political regime built in the image of one man elected by the people cannot secure either a reliable transfer of power or the effective and stable functioning of the regime. Russia now has a regime with no institutional guarantees and with a strong potential for degeneration into conflict the moment the president becomes unable to govern. Such a system of government can be maintained by force, but the Russian federal government lacks (at least for now) the resources necessary for such an undertaking. Putin at least rhetorically seems inclined to gather these resources, but the outcome is far from certain.

Russia's regime of presidential power was shaped under the influence of Yeltsin's ambitions. His attempt to create a pure pyramid of power that needed no other institutions for its functioning was prevented by the fragmentation of society and the political class and by the devolution of power

---

4. This difference between rules and structures, on the one hand, and political behavior, on the other, exists in other countries as well (Putnam 1993, 17; Baylis 1996, 302).

from the center to the regions. In the end, the "presidential pyramid" transformed itself into a false front for a ramshackle regime built of ill-fitting parts. Although endowed with tremendous prerogatives, the president is in reality much weaker than the last of the communist leaders because he lacks the resources necessary to realize his prerogatives. Paradoxically, the Russian presidency was preserved only through a further devolution of power to the regions and to oligarchic groups in exchange for loyalty to the president. Thus the survival of such a regime would seem to rest on concessions to the regions and influential groups and on the degeneration of the state. Yet the aspiration to monolithic power pushes in the opposite direction. The superpresidential regime is therefore not stable; it can drift in any direction—changing its rhetoric, its goals, its balance of forces, and its major ideas. Fluidity, uncertainty, and ambiguity have become the regime's mode of survival.

References to the unconsolidated nature of Russia's government and to its fragmentation and divisiveness have become commonplace in Russian and Western analytical discourse. There is no lack of appeals for a consolidation of power. But can such a task be carried out while preserving the present superpresidential regime? Can it be accomplished in a system in which parliament, although it confirms a candidate for prime minister, escapes any responsibility for the latter's actions, or where the governors issue public ultimatums to the central government, blaming it for all their failures? The answers to these questions in today's Russia can only be negative. The president has no real interest in power consolidation, since it is only the weakness and fragility of the regime that allows him to play the role of arbiter. In this sense, Putin's attempts to gain greater control over provincial governors—in addition to generating resistance and subterfuge—will likely subordinate patrimonialism even more to presidential interests.

The concentration of power in individual hands in Russia does not contribute to the strengthening of presidential power but instead leads to its inevitable weakening. In other words, the delegitimation of presidential power is a corollary of Russia's failure to execute a functional division of powers. Without such a separation of powers a real democratic legitimation cannot take root. It is blocked, on the one hand, by the legally guaranteed monopoly of power on the federal level—i.e., the superpresidency "monosubject." This term is meant to imply not that there are no other political subjects on the Russian domestic political scene, but that one of the subjects, due to its immense range of powers, greatly surpasses the others. On the other hand, the goals of this superpresidency enshrined in the political system cannot be realized. As a result, the president is forced to maneuver among influential groups (financial-industrial, regional, bureau-cratic-official) pulling (or elevating) them closer to himself or pushing them further away, supporting them or depriving them of influence, try-ing to stifle conflicts between them or to unite them. In short, he must compensate for the weakness of his position through arbitration on the level of the political elite. But through this process the state inevitably loses the ability not only to realize its state interests, but even to define these in-terests and to articulate them coherently.

Until 1998, Yeltsin rather successfully manipulated his followers and adroitly kept some groups down and others up. Yeltsin himself called this mechanism a "spider web." He resolved conflicts among the main interest groups, maintaining a balance on the Russian political scene. By 1998, however, this mechanism was no longer effective for two reasons: first, the president had become physically unfit to continue as the balancer; and sec-ond, the complexity of the challenges facing Russia demanded a different way of responding. No arbiter can be effective without recognition by the main political actors and their readiness to comply with his decisions. Dur-ing the events of 1998–99, political actors began to show their fatigue with Yeltsin, thus bringing the functioning of the regime nearly to a halt. Cer-tain influential groups had already decided to push for a transition to a regime without an arbiter, preferring instead a weak, purely symbolic leader.

The growing role of oligarchic groups was evident. But Russian oligarchs are not the decisive political force that some assume them to be; they are dependent on the state and on their access to state resources. The presi-dent can still change the balance of forces, as Yeltsin did in 1998 when he delivered a blow to the oligarchic networks by toppling the government of Viktor Chernomyrdin, or in 1999 when he decided to side solely with one oligarchic group formed around his family. The financial crisis of the fall of 1998 degraded the previously powerful political and economic actors so much that they had to plead with the state and the West to help them sur-vive. In spring 1999, after investigations of corruption and money laun-dering charges began, the majority of Russian oligarchs left the country, thus demonstrating that the oligarchy failed to remain an influential polit-ical force. Putin likewise attacked oligarchs who refused to toe his political line, asserting his patrimonial dominance within the system. Forces within the bureaucracy and power structures also oppose oligarchic influence and are potential allies of presidential assertion over the oligarchs. When, in the president's struggle with the business elite or with the state apparatus, a significant danger arises, the president may address the nation and seek support from at least part of the population. The natural monopolies—Gazprom, the transportation system, the Unified Electric System—do have a lot of economic power, but they try to keep a low political profile.

Favorites other than the oligarchs might also play a crucial role in the regime, as they did in 1996 during the presidential campaign. They do not, however, dominate the political scene. The chief executive needs them in times of trouble, but he might just as readily diminish their role or reshuffle his favorites from time to time when he feels strong.

Russia's presidential regime, with its strong patrimonial features, in some ways functioned better during the revolutionary stage of the postcommunist transformation, helping to destroy the previous system, even if not always in the most effective way. However, it is not suited for the challenges of the postrevolutionary stage of development. Yeltsin attempted to survive by shuffling personnel, resorting to emergency methods, and creating tension. Although such "stabilizing by destabilizing" and by power-sharing with loyal interest groups in exchange for their support may have temporarily solved some tactical problems for Yeltsin, in the end it contributed to systemic decay of the whole construct.

Numerous centers of power, which are now the principal channel for harmonizing the interests of elite groups, became an important element of Yeltsin's regime. At different stages these included the presidential administration, the Security Council, the Defense Council, the "roundtable" with representatives of different political forces, and "the group of four" (the president, the prime minister, and the heads of the Duma and the Federation Council). In some respects, the system of power that evolved around Yeltsin resembled the Soviet system: the president played the role of the general secretary of the Communist Party; the presidential administration, the role of the Central Committee apparatus; the Federal Assembly, the role of the Politburo; and the government, the role of its Soviet counterpart, responsible only for managing the economy.

In contrast to African patrimonialism, in Russia fragmented state agencies and interests form a major element of the patrimonial bargain. Bureaucratic pluralism—a multiplicity of elite groups and their mutual patron-client relationships—is an important factor in the survival of the Russian system of government. Most interest groups were formed on the basis of previous sectoral, administrative, and regional divisions—such as, respectively, the fuel and energy lobby, the "power" structures, and regional groups (most notably that based in Moscow).

The regional elections of 1996–97 led to further decentralization of political and economic power. The inequality among the vast number of subjects of the Russian Federation enabled the federal center to manipulate them, especially when conflicts arose, such as those between rich, revenue-generating regions and poor, subsidy-receiving regions, agrarian regions and industrial regions, or ethnic republics and Russian provinces. The federal center, however, continued to decline in power. Its officials no longer had sufficient financial resources to buy the loyalty of all of the regions; nor did they have their former powers of coercion. Moscow's first invasion of Chechnya was a watershed event in the relations of the constituent parts of the Russian Federation with the center: the limits of the center's influence and capability became clear to all regional leaders.

The constitutional and political structure created during Yeltsin's rule—and designed to ensure domination by the leader and his close entourage—may not be capable of ensuring its own survival. Any lapse in the president's command automatically creates a vacuum of power. A super-presidential regime is incompatible with the loose federation that Russia has developed, and it prevents further state-building and the emergence of a viable party system. It is this conflict that has become central to the politics of post-Yeltsin Russia. It creates no incentives for the development of civil society, tries to freeze an unstable situation, and produces permanent conflicts that it cannot resolve. Thus the nominally democratic procedures used to preserve the status quo have only discredited democracy.

Can the Russian Political Regime Survive?

Several factors facilitate continuation of the current situation in Russian politics. The existence of a multiplicity of interest groups within the government plays a stabilizing role, both in the center and in the regions. The very diversity of these groups gives rise to constant tensions, but it also facilitates the leadership's ability to maneuver and balance among them. The same is true of the number of components of the federation: if, instead of eighty-nine, there were only fifteen or twenty powerful players, it would be far more difficult for the center to deal with them. The multiplicity of conflicts—at all levels, both in Moscow and in the provinces—prevents the emergence of a bipolar confrontation either within society or between the population and the regime. The system of under-the-counter deals also acts as a temporary force for stability because it facilitates the reconciliation of interests. In the provinces, for example, the ruling group is armed with both carrots and sticks and can also offer bribes to groups, such as miners, that might otherwise cause trouble for the authorities. In the long run, however, such an approach is highly destabilizing.

The present regime is a hybrid that exhibits some elements of durability. Its structures include representatives of nearly all political orientations: liberals, pragmatists, conservatives, left-wingers and right-wingers, advocates of Russia as a great power, and others. The "Russian accord" invented by the Yeltsin team drew opposition figures into the ruling structure on a personal basis rather than as representatives of defined political ideologies or forces. This device separated them from their obligations to their original constituencies or political parties. Putin has continued this practice. Thus diversity within the ranks of the ruling structure complicates the formation of any serious opposition to the regime.

Ironically, the new Communist Party, with its anti-Yeltsin rhetoric, also became an important factor in generating support for the regime. This rhetoric helped the Communist Party to preserve influence with a socialism-oriented audience, but a segment of the population, fearful of the return of the Communist Party to a position of power, reluctantly gave its support to the Kremlin. The Communist Party of the Russian Federation represents a certain disaffected segment of society, but it simultaneously bargains with the regime. The control of the Communist Party over this segment of the population and the party's willingness to engage with the regime makes this highly dissatisfied social group less of a threat to the authorities and also prevents the emergence of extremist groups. Even more surprising, perhaps, is the systemic role of the Liberal Democratic Party of ultra-nationalist Vladimir Zhirinovskii, who on all crucial occasions faithfully supported Yeltsin and his policies.

The current degree of stability in Russia is to a great extent the result of the overwhelming disillusionment and fatigue of a people who prefer not to risk losing what little they have. This type of stability is not grounded in economic growth or in trust of democratic institutions. The passive toleration of unsatisfactory governance only because apparent alternatives are worse leaves post-Soviet institutions with a large legitimacy deficit.

In the long term, tension in Russia could arise from several sources: the ineffectiveness of the system itself; the attempt to alter it; a further decline in the standard of living of a substantial part of the population; an increase in social differentiation; a broadening of the rift between the authorities and society; or the inability of the establishment to agree on basic questions of further development. The lack of a viable opposition could increase the possibility of spontaneous antigovernment actions, or it could push the frustrated masses to support a new, charismatic leader. The authorities' reliance on the military and police units may increase the danger of skirmishes between them and the regular military in the event of social upheaval. But the African path of military response to a seemingly democratic impasse, as was seen in the Ivory Coast in December 1999, is unlikely in Russia.

Official corruption and rampant crime have also become sources of constant public dissatisfaction in Russia. The criminalization of regional elites is even more dangerous; generally too weak to stand on their own, these elites at times find themselves dominated by criminal organizations. Such developments in several localities—particularly where natural gas and petroleum are produced—already provide evidence of the serious threat posed by criminal activities in the regions.

An enormous stratum of the population has lost out in the new Russia. Millions of Russians might choose to take decisive protest actions to force changes at the top, but this would require a confluence of several factors: a charismatic leader, consolidation of the socially active elements of society (notably the miners or workers in the transportation and energy sectors, with support from others in the industrial areas), support for the protest movement by elements within the government, and the neutrality or sympathy of the army and other power structures. To have an impact on all of Russia, such protest would require some triggering event and would have to be centered in Moscow or another big city. The possibility of mass protest and destabilization of the system cannot be completely ruled out, and the government cannot become complacent. Frustration persists in Russian society, creating grounds for constant tension, and no one can tell what spark might set off an explosion. So far, however, there are no signs that such an outcome is anywhere on the horizon.

Still, it would be naive to think that Russia's political regime can survive for an indefinite time in its current form. The only question is how it will change. The resources for self-transformation within the regime are extremely limited. It can acquire the supports it needs by strengthening either its authoritarian-monarchical component or its democratic one. Of course, the regime itself and Russian society as a whole can continue to stagnate as they have been doing for some time now, but sooner or later Russia will have to make a choice between authoritarianism and democracy, and the longer this decision is deferred, the greater the danger of the first option. The hope that stagnating stability can be preserved indefinitely is illusory.

During his brief presidency, Vladimir Putin has succeeded in achieving much more than Yeltsin did during his two presidential terms. Putin attempted a real regime revolution, changing not only the balance of powers but the style and structure of the regime he inherited from Yeltsin. Rejecting the previous principle of mutual tolerance and political decadence, he has tried to rely on the principles of compliance and subordination to create a greater sense of hierarchical power than Yeltsin was able to create. Putin has openly attempted to weaken the democratic and oligarchic elements of the political system in Russia, increasing the role of the bureaucracy and the power structures. But questions remain as to the extent to which these attempts to return to political uniformity and centralism are feasible in a pluralistic society with powerful group interests, and whether this type of regime can allow Putin to realize his major goal: to build a powerful and civilized Russia. In any case, Putin's revolution does not change the nature of the elected monarchy, leaving its major conflict—between democratic legitimation and authoritarian practice—unresolved.

Presidential power as personified in Yeltsin and Putin is unlikely to become authoritarian in the full sense, but it is not out of the question that other leaders in the future might turn to fully authoritarian means to consolidate the regime. Moreover, Yeltsin's policies toward the "power" structures—his introduction of the principle of personal loyalty to the leader in the selection of cadres and the inclusion of people with a military past in the highest echelons of the ruling elite—were bound to stimulate further politicization of those structures and their possible inclusion in the fight for the throne. It is true that Russia has no tradition of military involvement in politics, but as the experience of Africa demonstrates, the military can be pulled into a power struggle in the event of a fragmentation of the political class, stagnation, or a powerful longing within society for order and stability. Even if this authoritarian attempt fails, it would most likely destabilize the situation even further and could bring unpredictable shifts in Russian development.

On the basis of Russia's postcommunist experience, one might be tempted to conclude that Russia is clearly unable to handle democracy. But there is not a country on earth that could handle the kind of democracy that exists in Russia today. It is impossible to achieve accord among political forces (and the constituencies behind them) while completely blocking their influence on executive power. This difficulty leads to an even greater fragmentation of the political domain, since no effort has been made by ideologically compatible groups to form a coalition. The regime has also weakened the already fragile parties and other political unions. In this sense Putin's Unity Party exemplifies the patrimonial distortions of the party system, for it stands for little else than support for Putin. The chief (and most unfortunate) result has been that Russia's political regime cultivates irresponsibility in the majority of its political actors, who do not care about the country and act selfishly. Such a regime brings about the degeneration of parliamentary government and the party system. Ultimately, this trend paves the way for those opposed to the regime, even criminal elements, to obtain power.

A "democracy" that perpetuates political irresponsibility and the absence of agreement on the generally accepted rules of the game has no future. But responsibility and accord are unthinkable if numerous political actors have no access to real power. This situation means that, once again, Russia stands before a historic choice: either it must choose the path of democratic development, acknowledging that its corrupt partial reform cannot be preserved but will only go sour, or it must reconcile itself to the fact that the turn to authoritarianism described above is inevitable. In that case, society has no alternative but to wait patiently for a leader to appear in the Kremlin—Putin or someone else—who has the nerve and political will to turn to an "iron hand."

References

Achiezer, Aleksandr. 1997. "Dual Power in Russia." *Rubezhi* 8: 1–27.

Baylis, Thomas A. 1996. "Presidents versus Ministers: Shaping Executive Authority in Eastern Europe." *World Politics* 48, no. 3: 297–323.

Burtin, Yuri, and Grigory Vodolalazov. 1998. "Nomenklatura Democrats Are Set Up in Russia." *Izvestiya*. 1 August.

Dahl, Robert. 1970. *After the Revolution: Authority in a Good Society.* New Haven: Yale University Press.

Karl, Terry. 1986. "Imposing Consent? Electoralism vs. Democratization in El Salvador." Pp. 9–36 in *Elections and Democratization in Latin America, 1980–1985,* ed. Paul W. Drake and Eduardo Silva. San Diego: University of California Press.

———. 1998. *The Paradox of Plenty: Oil Booms and Petro-States.* Berkeley: University of California Press.

Klyamkin, Igor, and Lilia Shevtsova. 1999. *The Anti-Systemic Regime of Boris the Second: Some Pecularities of the Russian Post-Communist Development.* Moscow: Moscow Carnegie Center.

Kutkoviets, Tatyana, and Igor Klyamkin. 1997. "Russian Ideas." *Nezavisimaya gazeta,* 16 January.

Linz, Juan, and Alfred Stepan. 1996. *Problems of Democratic Transition: Southern America, Post-Communist Europe.* Baltimore: John Hopkins University Press.

McFaul, Michael. 1997. "Democracy Unfolds in Russia." *Current History* 96, no. 612 (October): 319–25.

———. 1999. "The Perils of a Protracted Transition." *Journal of Democracy* 10, no. 4: 4–18.

O'Donnell, Guillermo. 1979. "Tensions in the Bureaucratic-Authoritarian State." Pp. 285–318 in *The New Authoritarianism in Latin America,* ed. David Collier. Princeton: Princeton University Press.

———. 1994. "Delegative Democracy." *Journal of Democracy* 5, no. 1: 55–69.

Putnam, Robert. 1993. *Making Democracy Work: Civic Tradition in Modern Italy.* Princeton: Princeton University Press.

Schmitter, Philipp C., and Terry Lynn Karl. 1991. "What Democracy Is . . . and Is Not." *Journal of Democracy* 2, no. 3: 75–88.

Shevtsova, Lilia. 1999. *Yeltsin's Russia: Myths and Reality.* Washington: Carnegie Endowment for International Peace.

Shevtsova, Lilia, and Igor Klyamkin. 1998. "This Omnipotent Impotent Power." *Nezavisimaya gazeta.* 24–25 June.

Stiglitz, Joseph. 1999. "Whither Reform? Ten Years of the Transition." Paper delivered at the Annual World Bank Conference on Development Economies, Washington, 28–30 April.

Yavlinsky, Grigory. 1998. "Russia's Phony Capitalism." *Foreign Affairs* 77, no. 3: 67–79.

Zakaria, Fareed. 1997. "The Rise of Illiberal Democracy." *Foreign Affairs* 76, no. 6: 22–43.

10

War, State-Making, and Democracy in Africa

RICHARD JOSEPH

The 1990s were expected to be a decade of democratic renewal and resumed development in Africa and the former Soviet Union. The end of the cold war and the disintegration of the Soviet Union had exposed authoritarian African governments and the fragments of the Soviet state to domestic and international pressures for political reform and ushered the largest number of new states into independence since the termination of colonial rule in Africa in the 1960s. The building of liberal democracies and liberalized economies was expected to foster the emergence of stable developmental and constitutional polities in both regions. As the decade drew to a close, however, the situation in both Africa and post-Soviet Eurasia was more confused, complex, and uncertain than many analysts had anticipated.[1]

As in the former Soviet Union, in Africa the paradox of the state lies at the center of these dilemmas. Although the first leader of independent Ghana, Kwame Nkrumah, proclaimed the necessity of constructing the political kingdom, contemporary scholars as well as African citizens now confront the dire consequences of the failure to do so across much of the continent. It is poignant to read the opening sentence of an article by Crawford Young pub-

---

1. For overviews of democratization in Africa during the 1990s, see Widner (1994), Nwokedi (1995), Bratton and van de Walle (1997), and Young (1999). For an attempt to shift the focus to how regime power was reconfigured in response to pressures for political and economic liberalization, see Joseph (1999).

lished in 1988: "Few would dispute the proposition that the African state is beset with a profound crisis in the political, economic and social spheres." Of the three countries he then cited as illustrations, Mozambique has emerged from a brutal war and begun a long uphill process of reconstruction and development; the Sudan has sunk deeper into the mire of a horrific civil war; and Nigeria was further devastated by "the incorrigible venality of its ruling group" and "the corrosion of public institutions" during a subsequent decade of military dictatorship (Young 1988, 25).

Leading students of democratization, such as Guillermo O'Donnell, Adam Przeworski, and Juan Linz and Alfred Stepan, have recently argued the importance of viable statehood for democratic consolidation (O'Donnell 1993; Przeworski et al. 1995; Linz and Stepan 1996). In Africa, however, the insubstantial nature of many states has been exacerbated by endemic political violence, anarchic warfare, and predatory economic networks. Many scholars writing on statehood (or the lack thereof in Africa), including all those discussed in the next section, are critical and often dismissive of the prospects for democratization. Democratic transitions involving renewed electoral competition are often regarded as exercises in presentability to protect external sources of income and as reflecting the incomplete imposition by a triumphant West of its own political formulas (Joseph 1997, 1998). Significantly, one finds analogous opinions and concerns among many scholars of the former Soviet Union.

In Africa, statehood is often considered to be a fictive construct that deflects attention from the more salient nonstate entities that command power, resources, and allegiance. Scholars who find these analyses insufficient should, nevertheless, seek to distill the insights they contain. After conducting such an exercise, this chapter will argue the urgency of devising a framework of analysis that is not dismissive of incipient state renewal and political and economic reform in Africa (or, for that matter, in Eurasia). At this critical historical juncture at the beginning of the twenty-first century, we need to "take time," as Nigerians say, and critically examine the dilemmas confronted empirically by these societies and governments and those that we, as scholars, wrestle with in our attempts to understand their challenges.

African States and Nonstates: Alternative Visions

Many authors have tackled the paradox of statehood in late-twentieth-century Africa, including Jean-François Bayart, Stephen Ellis, and Béatrice

Hibou (1999), Patrick Chabal and Jean-Pascal Daloz (1999), William Reno (1997, 1998), Achille Mbembe (1999), Jeffrey Herbst (2000), and Christopher Clapham (1996). The contributions of scholars who venture onto this uncertain terrain, however, must be assessed as a prelude to devising a more satisfactory analytical framework.[2]

The well-known writings of Bayart on politics and the state in Africa, for example, have enriched our understanding of postcolonial Africa. Much of his earlier work—regarding the "politics of the belly" and the dualities of the "rhizome state," for example (Bayart 1993)—is consistent with the writings of other scholars on patrimonialism and prebendalism in Africa, such as Jean-François Médard (1982), Michael Bratton and Nicolas van de Walle (1994), and myself (Joseph 1984, 1987). In the more recent *Criminalization of the State in Africa*, Bayart, Ellis, and Hibou (1999) present an Africa that is increasingly consumed by the depredations of criminal networks, domestic and international. Resources provided by international agencies for economic and other reform programs are systematically diverted by state officials in league with criminal associates. Corruption, drug trafficking, money laundering, and the inventive financial scams perpetrated by Nigerian syndicates are backed by enhanced capacities to use violence. But while much of what these authors portray is undeniable, seldom indicate the relative importance of what is being presented. All states in the world experience criminality, and global criminal networks interweave with formal power in much of Latin America and post-Soviet Eurasia. By providing exhaustive details about criminal practices in any particular country, however, scholars are left uncertain how much weight to attach to these revelations.

William Reno has similarly probed the underside of African political and economic machinations—indeed, to such an extent that the area of his study has at times been facetiously dubbed "Renoland."[3] What remains unclear is whether Renoland represents the African condition more broadly or an extrapolation by the author based on his close examination of a particularly egregious example of a "failed state." Reno's impressive study of Sierra Leone (1995) focused on the emergence of financial networks involved in illicit mining and trading in diamonds and the ways in which they

---

2. For a mapping of this terrain on the eve of Africa's *abertura* (opening), see Bratton (1989). I argue in Joseph and Herbst (1997) that students of Africa do not engage sufficiently in critical but constructive assessments of one another's work, especially those that advance new frameworks of interpretation.

3. I first heard this term used by Christopher Clapham at the Conference on State, Markets, Law, and Democracy at Emory University in November 1998.

supplanted the formal state bureaucracy and economy. He subsequently expanded this model to war-torn Liberia and then to much of Africa. Although Reno writes about Africa's "weak states," he often implies that the dynamics he discusses are increasingly relevant to Africa's more conventional states as well. Most pertinently, he contends not only that bureaucracies, militaries, and other state structures have been undermined completely, but that new political units have emerged in Africa whose logics have a specific rationality that distinguish them from conventional notions regarding the construction of states and economies. Emerging in the continent, he argues, are "alternative rational forms of political organization" more suited to "Africa's marginal position in the changing global political economy" (1997, 493). An analogous argument is made by Reno in his chapter in this book comparing African warlords with Russian *mafiya* bosses (Chapter 5).

According to Reno, African rulers are increasingly inclined to disregard the building of formal bureaucratic state institutions and even to dispense with conventional notions of sovereignty and state boundaries. The "rational pursuit of power" induces them to tolerate and even foster the various forms of criminality and predation discussed by Bayart et al. (1999, 497). Although Reno's analysis are valuable, it is often difficult to assess how much his sweeping statements reflect reality. African rulers, even of weak states, tread a path between formal and informal structures, bureaucratic and nonbureaucratic forms, statism and statelessness. Moreover, as I will indicate later, such behavior is not unique to Africa. The nonstate political units that Reno postulates coexist with more bureaucratic and formal state entities. He underplays, for example, the extent to which African warlords, such as Charles Taylor, hanker after the legitimacy and authority of constituted states. Taylor would never have been content to govern a nonstate political unit from his regional redoubt in Gbarnga, Liberia, even if he could have procured all the resources he wanted. The same is true of Jonas Savimbi in Angola and Foday Sankoh in Sierra Leone.

The insights of the above-mentioned authors are carried to their culminating extreme by Patrick Chabal and Jean-Pascal Daloz (1999). Their book-length essay demonstrates the intellectual cul-de-sac of this particular line of argumentation. Unlike Reno, Chabal and Daloz purport to examine not the forces at work in Africa's weak states that are then projected onto others, but rather the African state *simpliciter*—in and of itself. This state is vacuous, noninstitutionalized, an empty shell. Not only is this entity inseparable from society and lacking the bureaucratic qualities of the Weberian (or Western) state; it is programmed to be that way. Politics is largely informalized. In agreement with Reno, Chabal and Daloz believe that there is a certain rationality to these forms and practices that escapes most analysts. There are strong disincentives, they further claim, for political elites to build institutionalized Weberian states because they profit so handsomely from not doing so. The most provocative argument made by Chabal and Daloz is that Africa is following a unique path of modernization that does not include development as this notion is currently understood in the West. Instead of regarding disorder in Africa as dysfunctional (a view, they argue, that results from looking at it through Western lenses), they contend that we should consider Africa's evolution from a non-normative, nonteleological standpoint. Viewed in this way, disorder will be seen as being put to positive use—i.e., instrumentalized—as Africa pursues its own path of modernization that involves elements of Westernization and traditionalism. So despite the absence of political institutionalization and economic development along Western and Weberian lines, Africa still "works" according to its unique set of rationalities and causalities.[4]

The problems with this type of argument are legion, but I will identify just a few that are relevant here—particularly for an understanding of democratization and state-building in Africa. The authors claim that their framework applies, in essence, to all of sub-Saharan Africa. But this is not shown empirically. Their generalizations about Africa are also matched by an idealization, or perhaps mythification, of the "West" that bears little resemblance to the countries we (Westerners) live in. Finally, their supposedly non-normative and nonteleological "analysis" can be shown to be both normative and teleological. What they are proposing, in effect, is the adoption of *their* conceptions of what is "useful," "rational," or "modern" in Africa, and that we regard Africa as "programmed" to be the way it is for the foreseeable future. In short, Africa's telos is predetermined by traditional and current practice. Any intellectual project concerned with the building of stable, constitutional, and democratic states in Africa is, from their standpoint, a delusional exercise. In the work of Chabal and Daloz, Afro-pessimism has been recast as Afro-realism, dysfunctionality as functionality, and economic decay as just a different, African kind of development.

Perhaps the most stimulating participant in this mode of discourse has been Achille Mbembe, in his chapter for this volume (Chapter 3) and in his other recent writing. His insights are often indispensable for an under-

---

4. For readers needing a solid exposition of what institutionalization involves, see Bratton and van de Walle (1997).

standing of the dynamics of state and society in contemporary Africa, and he avoids the inversions to which Reno and Chabal and Daloz readily succumb. For Mbembe, predation is predation, violence is violence, destruction is destruction. But Mbembe shares with the writers discussed above a particular vision of Africa: the formal state has been undermined by networks financed by profits from a shadow economy of drug and arms trafficking and sundry other criminal activities. Such networks have both domestic and external components. Mbembe echoes Reno and Chabal and Daloz when he refers to the likelihood in Africa of the "definitive defeat of the state," which lacks "the intrinsic qualities, attributes, and mode of operation" of classic states (Mbembe 1999, 3–4). Like these authors, he refers to the increasing irrelevance of official frontiers and the "reterritorializing" of Africa through organized violence. Private indirect government, which he presents as the dominant political mode in Africa today, is defined as "supposedly public functions and sovereign duties that are increasingly conducted as private operations for private ends" (Mbembe 1999, 25). Private indirect government, which combines the elements of prebendalism with what Reno called the "shadow state," is the organization of power based primarily on the use of violence to control financial resources within and across territories that are no longer properly functioning states. Although, like other authors, Mbembe does not examine the relative weight and internal dynamics of formal and informal state structures, unlike the authors discussed above he is more sensitive to the fact that European states went through a stage similar to the one he depicts. Like Charles Tilly and other historians, he sees the determining factor that enabled Europe to move beyond this stage as the shift from exaction to taxes and from privatized to legitimate uses of organized violence. Such a recognition already pushes us to consider the possibility of alternative modes of rule.

Similarly, Jeffrey Herbst (2000) makes a significant contribution to our understanding of the historical evolution of states and nonstates in Africa. He considers the central issue in Africa at the beginning of the twenty-first century to be the creation of viable states. Herbst recognizes certain continuities in the exercise of power and sovereignty within Africa and in the international regimes that influence and legitimate these processes. In precolonial Africa, power in statelike entities was more effectively exercised at the center and less so at the periphery. Borders were therefore weakly defined. The colonial authorities essentially replicated this system, Herbst argues, and, in most territories, seldom succeeded in establishing formal rule beyond the core areas. In practice the rules for legitimating imperial rule in Africa after the Berlin conference of 1884–85 enabled colonial powers to obtain recognition of territorial borders without effectively establishing control of the lands so demarcated. Following independence, this regime was adopted and given renewed sanction by the Organization of African Unity, which declared the inviolability of inherited colonial borders. From the precolonial through the colonial and postcolonial eras, according to Herbst, African states have been, to a significant degree, virtual states, existing more in the assertions of rulers than in their capacity to fully exercise and project power.[5]

But although Herbst recognizes the irrelevance of boundaries and the reality of trading networks and paramilitary forces that operate across them, he does not embark on a free-floating discourse about nonstate political entities and networks. Instead, he seeks to identify indices of relative stateness in Africa and undertakes pioneering comparative examinations of the impact of different degrees of road development and population distribution on state formation. In this sense Herbst has opened up a potentially fruitful area for empirical research. In trying to gain leverage on variations of stateness in Africa his book should inspire a new wave of comparative research based on the application of those and other indices of state-building.[6] Such research should begin by establishing an empirical basis for what we know impressionistically: that Africa is not exclusively Renoland, although Renoland is recognizably African; that Senegal, Ghana, and Botswana are empirical states comparable to those on any other continent; and that even where private indirect government prevails (for instance, in Cameroon, Kenya, Nigeria, or Zimbabwe), important elements of empirical statehood persist. A critical challenge confronting the scholarly community, then, is that of achieving a better understanding of the factors making for both viability and virtuality in statehood and acquiring the capacity to explain the relative balance and dynamic between them—in Africa, Eurasia, and elsewhere. At present, we lack such analytical tools and the understanding that such a capacity would generate.

Clapham has provided a realistic base for such an exercise. Following Robert Jackson (1990), he recognizes that although statehood has been more juridical than empirical in Africa, it provided local rulers the leverage to extort substantial resources from the international community. Clapham

---

5. "Virtual states" is my own terminology. I consider virtuality to be a critical feature of governance in Africa—an idea I intend to explore more fully elsewhere. The arguments in Herbst's book (2000) should be considered in relation to those presented by Crawford Young. Of particular importance is the schema developed by Young on the attributes and imperatives of statehood (Young 1994, 25–40).

6. In this connection, see Widner (1995).

delineates a complex terrain in Africa with regard to states and nonstates. While acknowledging "the evident disappearance of states from parts of the continent" and the appearance of authorities "whose entitlement to state-hood was contestable" (Clapham 1996, 9), his analysis is still grounded on the commanding importance of statism. The international community pro-vided powerful inducements to the maintenance of African states, however fictive and limited may have been the actual political control exercised by their leaders. Clapham makes a strong claim that a decisive shift in these dynamics occurred around 1975, and that a "second Cold War on Africa" delivered a devastating impact. At that time and subsequently, arms flows to Africa mounted precipitously, initially bolstering the military might of existing regimes but eventually provoking insurgencies, disorder, and state decay. A similar process occurred in the economic realm, with African regimes first losing control of economic policy to international financial in-stitutions, but then gradually recovering some leverage in their dealings with these institutions. Although structural adjustment programs under-cut the patronage basis of Africa's "monopoly states," in many instances these same programs helped bolster state power, as regimes obtained new inflows of financing while reducing their liabilities by scaling back the size of bureaucracies and slashing social benefits. The reforms also partially shifted economic policy toward wealth generation within the domestic economy, "rather than an economy which was manipulated by the patron-age available from the state" (Clapham 1996, 180). Clapham's book por-trays an Africa that is very recognizable to this author—i.e., involving con-tradictory processes: state erosion alongside state assertiveness; juridical sovereignty buttressed by elements of empirical sovereignty; external de-pendency contending with a residual autonomy; economic decay alongside economic renewal; and civil politics confronted by intermittent or persist-ent warfare. This recognition of variation and historical perspective are crit-ical for assessing democratization in the region and the prospects for con-structing effective states.

Warfare and the Struggle for Statehood

My own attempts to assess the somewhat disappointing outcome of the post-1989 wave of democratization in Africa forced me to return to ex-amining the paradox of the state and the impact of warfare on African pol-itics and society. The early 1990s, I wrote, spurred "democratic transitions as well as armed struggles. At first these seemed to be different kinds of phenomena. What is now evident . . . is the convergence and interpenetration of these two sets of dynamics" (Joseph 1998, 7). In addition to warfare that takes the form of more or less organized armed forces of states and insurgency movements, I argued, criminal networks and various forms of gangsterism also need to be considered. "Often there is no clear demarcation," I agreed with Mbembe, "between organized groups that pursue political objectives and those responsible for the criminalization of state and society through drug trafficking, mineral smuggling, embezzlement of public funds, money laundering, and other fraudulent practices" (Joseph 1998, 4–5).

But to move beyond such observations, we can benefit from another look at Tilly's trenchant essay on early-modern Europe, "War Making and State Making as Organized Crime." Tilly argues that organized violence was exercised by a variety of groups prior to the consolidation of the European state system: "the continuum ran from bandits to pirates to kings via tax holders, regional power holders, and professional soldiers" (Tilly 1985, 173). In fact, much of Europe as depicted by Tilly looks like Renoland today. It was not predetermined who would emerge as statebuilders in the extraction of resources from populations via organized violence. The eventual state-builders turned out to be those who succeeded in monopolizing the means of violence within a defined territory, in trouncing their rivals, and then getting this control acknowledged by other authorities. The eventual nature of the state apparatus in different countries reflected the pattern of alliances and structures used to secure political hegemony. Tilly often repeats what he regards as the basic formula: "war making, extraction, state making, and protection were interdependent" (Tilly 1985, 182).

In the case of contemporary Africa, colonialism followed by neocolonialism and cold war geopolitics provided a grid that upheld statehood throughout the continent. During the postcolonial era, virtually all African countries established some degree of empirical stateness: armies, physical and social infrastructures, and state and single-party bureaucracies. Beginning in the 1980s, as regimes came under increasing pressure to open their political systems to democratic contestation and to transform their patrimonial economies into market systems, their fragility and virtuality as states were simultaneously exposed. Instead of reflecting political and economic reconstruction, certain areas in eastern, western, and central Africa came to resemble a Tillyan landscape of "coercive and self-seeking entrepreneurs" possessing the capacity to organize violence, protect areas of extraction and tribute, and secure external acceptance of their partial or full hegemonies. Thus, contrary to the arguments of Reno and Chabal and Daloz, Africa is not pursuing some unique course of political organization. Rather, it seems to be replicating an earlier stage of the European experience. The laurel of state-making in Europe went to those who prevailed in the brutal conflicts and converted militias into armies, violence into legitimate constraint, and exaction into taxation. The crux of Africa's dilemma, however, is that it appears to be moving forward and backward across this continuum, and the relative pace and direction of that movement differ between countries and subregions.

From this perspective, there is no need to devise special theories of causality and rationality to explain the turmoil in contemporary Africa (or for that matter, in Eurasia). The intricacies of illicit capital accumulation discussed earlier would fall under Tilly's categories of banditry, piracy, and gangland rivalry (Tilly 1985, 170). What we currently lack, however, is a means of assessing how much formal state-building is occurring within this crucible of structuration and destruction, and determining what can be done to facilitate positive developments. In a published article based on the concluding chapter of his book, Herbst (1996–97) proposed, inter alia, that warfare should be permitted to take its course in the hope of generating more viable state units.[7] At the turn of the twentieth century, however, the international community cannot revert to an earlier era and allow warfare, plunder, anarchy, and the terrorizing of civilians to persist until sustainable states emerge from the carnage (Joseph and Herbst 1997). Crawford Young, for example, has pointed out that most of the "475 autonomous political entities that disappeared in Europe between 1500 and 1950" did so as a consequence of violence (Young 1994, 33). Yet he was not tempted by this observation to regard warfare as a way of reducing Africa's political entities into fewer and more viable units.

In Tilly's schema, all the key dimensions of state-making are premised on the successful organization and use of violence: the elimination of external rivals, the defeat or neutralizing of local ones, the subjecting of opposition clients to the victor's control, and the converting of extraction into bureaucratized taxation (Tilly 1985, 181). In the case of late-twentieth-century Africa, however, there is great uncertainty regarding which structures of power are likely to prevail. We can identify states, quasi-states, and nonstates; democracies, semidemocracies, and autocracies; civic polities, hybrid polities, and war-torn polities; and market economies, hybrid economies, and shadow economies. The new research agenda I would pro-

---

7. This position has recently been echoed by Marina Ottaway (1999).

pose would involve streamlining this typology, agreeing on how countries are best characterized, and then developing the analytical tools to disaggregate the relevant dynamics on a country and subregional level. Moreover, central to such a project would be devising ways to assess what is often ambiguous, in flux, or covert.[8] An analogous procedure may be relevant for understanding variation in state-making processes currently at work in Eurasia. In anticipation of these studies, I provide below an overview of statehood, civic order, and incipient democratization in three African countries that illustrate the ways in which progress is possible, even in the presence of disorder.

Order amid Disorder, Progress amid Distress

Developments in Ghana, South Africa, and Nigeria since 1989 demonstrate how state-making, civil institutionalization, economic reforms, and incipient democratization can co-exist with and sometimes prevail over disorder and proliferation of informal markets. I have chosen these three countries largely because of my personal experience, but other countries merit similar examination (for example, Benin, Botswana, the Ivory Coast, Mali, Mauritius, Mozambique, and Namibia). The governments of Ghana, South Africa, and Nigeria initially derived their authority from armed force, which was then legitimated via competitive elections.[9]

Ghana

The Provisional National Defense Council led by Jerry Rawlings (1981–92) in Ghana successfully established a monopoly of organized violence and withstood several coup attempts. Despite the transition to constitutional governance following the 1992 and 1996 elections won by Rawlings and

---

8. Although I believe that contemporary methods of statistical analysis should be applied more systematically to examining the issues discussed in this chapter, I am also conscious of how the fixed categories devised for such analyses often fail to capture the "multiple modes of existence" and other phenomena in Africa. For some relevant remarks, see Olukoshi (1999).

9. Although in Nigeria the federal government of Olusegun Obasanjo and governments at the state level assumed power following national elections in 1998–99, this transition was very much managed by an outgoing military regime that readily handed power over to a former military ruler. Not to be overlooked also is the role of retired military officers, now oligarchs, in financing the Obasanjo campaign. These factors do not contradict the determination of President Obasanjo to civilianize and constitutionalize the Nigerian political system, but they suggest some of the major challenges to be overcome.

his party, the National Democratic Congress, the government has maintained paramilitary structures alongside its highly professional armed forces. A constitutional state has not yet been fully consolidated, although considerable progress has been made in this direction (Gyimah-Boadi 1998). The level of extralegal violence resorted to by the regime has declined significantly during the course of the Fourth Republic, but the capacity and willingness to inflict it in highly demonstrative ways persist.

Ghana is an integrated polity that has successfully contained communal conflicts in its northern region and neutralized the greatest source of antigovernment resentment among the Ashanti in the south. After abandoning its socialist strategies in 1983, the regime has steadily fostered the expansion of a market economy and has used its hegemony to restructure public policy in keeping with adjustments advocated by international financial agencies. One longtime observer has nevertheless compared the patrimonialism of the post-1992 Rawlings government with that of the Nkrumah era (Sandbrook 1997), while another has criticized the self-serving fashion in which privatization reforms are being implemented (Gyimah-Boadi 1999a). Although civil society has regained much of its former vigor and autonomy, the Rawlings administration is itself an effective actor in civil society, fostering its own associational groups, rewarding perceived friends, and harassing presumed adversaries. Ghana is not yet a fully civic polity, but it is much closer to such status than many other West African states. Moreover, there are no other current examples in Africa to my knowledge of a military regime that has permitted, however reluctantly, a transition to a nearly constitutional system under the same political leadership of the preceding authoritarian era.[10]

Ghana's electoral system has moved from being highly manipulated and inadequate to becoming one of the most efficient and reputable in Africa today (Gyimah-Boadi 1999b). The Rawlings regime continued to make excessive use of the prerogatives of incumbency in the funding of party operations and in the conduct of government-owned media, but opposition groups won significant concessions to enhance the fairness of the electoral process and the autonomy of the private media. The importance of these changes was convincingly demonstrated by the defeat of the ruling party candidate by opposition New Patriotic Party (NPP) leader John Kufuor in the 2000 elections. Rawlings respected the constitutional prohibition on a third elected term and gracefully accepted his defeat. Critical in consoli-

---

10. For the sake of comparison, witness the continued reluctance of the regime of Yoweri Museveni in Uganda to permit such a transition.

dating the democratic process will be the vigilance of an independent press and civic organizations, improved organizational performance and strategies by political parties, and the alertness of the international community to attempts to derail further advances.[11] In short, a balanced appraisal of Ghana's evolution under a civilizing military regime would demonstrate that considerable progress has been made in moving a country that was a near "failed state" in the late 1970s toward becoming a stable, integrated, constitutional, and democratic polity (see Azarya and Chazan 1987; Chazan 1988; Herbst 1992).

South Africa

South Africa represents a peculiar conjoining of a state apparatus constructed under apartheid and the political and military structures of its former adversary, the African National Congress (ANC). To facilitate this reconfiguration, the South African state divested itself of its apartheid features and jettisoned its political leadership, while the ANC abandoned its independent military capacity and socialist ideology. The residual administrative, military, and police structures of the state then shifted their loyalties to the new political leadership after the 1994 elections, and the ANC neutralized its radical and antistate wings. Around this fundamental compromise, the rest of the South African polity has either sought accommodation or suffered marginalization. South Africa therefore represents a definite model of African progress toward consolidating state power, a civic socio-political order, liberal economic reforms, and democratization after 1989.

Nevertheless, all the features of informalization and criminalization discussed earlier are abundantly present in South Africa. Political corruption, now tied to a "culture of entitlement" among the new political elites, grows relentlessly. Organized crime flourishes alongside high levels of street violence. As prominent as these features have been, and despite the Hobbesian quality of life they bestow on certain parts of the country, they do not negate the positive elements of formal institutionalization in the postapartheid era. Many factors explain South Africa's relative good fortune, but two of them deserve mention: the high corporate level of development of the country's economy (and its transnational character) and the disciplined structures and leadership of the ANC. These factors con-

---

11. On the support bases and electoral strategies of the political parties, see Nugent (1999).

tributed significantly to the successful negotiation of the grand compromise.[12] White corporate elites acquiesced to the transitional endgame and the ANC's accession to power, while the latter accepted (with modest reforms to ensure greater black participation) the maintenance of the country's capitalist structures.

Success in consummating this transition during the 1990s does not guarantee its persistence as the country seeks to contain the explosion of demands in every conceivable sphere after decades of apartheid rule. Renewed strike action just months after the ANC won a resounding second election in April 1999 indicated that, although the black electorate may have accepted the political features of the negotiated transition, it is less patient with the accompanying gradualism in tackling the yawning social inequities. There is no certain outcome in the battle between the forces making for formalization or informalization, legality or crime, disarray or political order. The central grid of the judicial system, capped by the innovative Constitutional Court, has provided South Africa with an authoritative mediating instrument committed to entrenching the rule of law. Because of the government's commitment to maintaining its international reputation, great value is placed on the persistence of a vigorous civil society—including an independent media, respect for human rights, and considerable freedoms of political organization and electoral competition. South Africa can therefore be favorably compared with Mexico, Brazil, the Philippines, or Russia, which have also been involved in complex and contradictory transitions from authoritarian systems.

Nigeria

Throughout Africa, the struggle persists in varying ways to build viable states, promote a civic political culture, implement economic reforms, and advance democratization. In few countries, however, are the stakes and the obstacles as high as they are in Nigeria. Throughout its turbulent postcolonial history, and especially after its civil war ended and the oil boom commenced in 1970, criminality, informalization, violence, and authoritarianism have steadily undermined the positive norms and social values of the Nigerian polity (Joseph 1999). The dictatorial and Mobutuesque military regime of Sani Abacha (1993–98) brought Nigeria to the edge of a

---

12. For an explanation of the fundamental elements of the bargaining process in generic terms, see Bates (1999). The literature on the South African transition is now extensive. Helpful starting points are Friedman and Atkinson (1994) and Friedman (1995).

precipice from which Congo-Kinshasa had long since tumbled. By a still unclarified process, Abacha was eliminated in June 1998 through a conspiracy within the senior ranks of his regime. A transition then began in which concerted attempts were made to subdue the powerful forces that had eroded state authority, entrenched warfare in all its forms throughout the polity, criminalized economic activities, and promoted repression and autocracy.

Nigeria provides overwhelming evidence for all the assertions by Reno, Bayart et al., Chabal and Daloz, and Mbembe concerning the deformation of values, the expansion of structures of predation and violence, and the deceitful nature of the democratic transitions pursued by the Ibrahim Babangida and Abacha military regimes from 1985 to 1998. However, under the administration of President Olusegun Obasanjo after his inauguration in May 1999, Nigeria made a determined effort to extricate itself from this bog of repression and corruption, and it did so without illusions about the great obstacles to be overcome. The number of investigatory panels, policy changes, and institutional reforms instituted by the Obasanjo administration soon after its inception far surpassed what any analyst would have predicted. The government has been involved in a footrace, however, in which its opponents, overt and covert, are equally determined and prepared to use any tactics to protect their vast fortunes and areas of operational autonomy.[13]

The stakes in oil-rich Nigeria are enormous. Nigeria never developed the corporate structure that South Africa did—especially in the commanding oil sector, a business that has long been conducted on the basis of corrupt transactions between government officials and private speculators (see Turner 1978). Assassinations disguised as armed robbery attempts, proliferating communal conflicts over land and other resources, and semi-anarchy in the oil-producing delta region are just some of the challenges that confront the government at all levels and whose intensity is likely to increase in the near term. Workers who have watched their earnings and living standards plummet during the last two decades of kleptocratic government, both civilian and military, are now insisting on immediate redress. The privatization of violence and the deformation of social norms during Nigeria's prolonged descent are also reflected in the proliferation of covert

---

13. In addition to income from inflated government contracts, licenses to lift petroleum, drug trafficking, and other criminal activities during sixteen years of unaccountable military rule, the backwash from seven years of "peacekeeping" operations in Liberia has generated considerable resources for sub rosa networks.

and conspiratorial organizations, such as the secret cults that now pervade the educational system.

As the Nigerian people and their myriad traditional, civic, and religious organizations struggle to shift the balance of power away from the forces of criminality and predation to those promoting probity, accountability, and efficiency, a simultaneous challenge goes out to scholars to devise frameworks that capture these dynamics accurately and fairly. It would be an easy but irresponsible exercise to discuss post-Abacha Nigeria solely in terms of crime, violence, and disorder. During the twenty years that elapsed between the first and second Obasanjo administrations (1979–99), Nigeria also became endowed with a large and resourceful civil liberties and human rights community. One of its first actions during the Fourth Republic was that of forcing the resignation of the wealthy Speaker of the House of Representatives, Ibrahim Salisu Buhari, who had fraudulently misrepresented his age and educational credentials. That action sent a warning shot across the bow of a political class that had grown accustomed to acting corruptly and with impunity. Having come to power through the machinations of the very military establishment that imprisoned him from 1995 to 1999, President Obasanjo swiftly moved to establish control over that same body by forcibly retiring ninety-three senior officers who had held political appointments since 1985. His administration now proposes greatly reducing the size of the military corps and converting it into a professional and constitutional force. An anticorruption bill with an associated commission and ongoing probes of human rights abuses and fraudulent contracts are just some of the actions underway that attempt to shift Nigerian structures of government onto a path of greater honesty, lawfulness, and efficiency.[14] The Obasanjo government's abrupt cancellation of pending licenses to prospect for and lift oil and its removal of the barriers that had impeded the full functioning of the country's oil refineries have already demonstrated how fundamental aspects of Nigeria's distress are directly attributable to systematic obstructionism by corrupt public officials (see *Africa Confidential* 1999 and Onishi 1999).

Nigeria enters the beginning of the twenty-first century as Africa's foremost political and economic laboratory, with more than a hundred million citizens, divided by multiple attributes of region, ethnicity, language, religion, and wealth. If, in the face of these immense challenges, Nigeria is able

---

14. Commissions to probe corruption and unfulfilled government contracts are also being instituted at the state level, revealing the massive pillage of public funds in Nigeria's thirty-six states that mirrors what was occurring at the federal level.

to make progress toward building an efficacious state, creating a political order characterized by civil rather than violent competition and conflict, entrenching democratic procedures and the rule of law, and fostering a mixed economy in which the private sector becomes less dependent on the corrupt extraction of state resources, the country's government and people will have delivered the most decisive response to critics who postulate the "definitive defeat" of the African state or that African societies are "programmed" for disorder and predation. The forces of disorder are so extensive, entrenched, and ruthless in Nigeria, however, and their political mobilization assumes such insidious and virulent forms that they may still overwhelm the most determined efforts to promote salutary institutionalization. Nevertheless, there are no empirical or theoretical reasons that compel us to believe that success is axiomatic for one or the other side.[15]

The Imperatives of Statehood and Democracy

It is tempting to seek solutions to these dilemmas in the dissolution and transcendence of the state. Recently, Václav Havel suggested that "the evolution away from the dominance of the nation-state will not be as painful as the creation itself of those entities." There is "something of higher value," he contends, "than the state. That value is humanity" (Havel 1999, 4, 6). As laudable as this sounds, the evidence suggests that viable statehood, redolent of Hobbes, remains the most powerful deterrent to the horrors witnessed in African intrastate conflicts. Some close observers of these traumas, such as Timothy Longman in Rwanda, have expressed concern about the transformation of the state into a machine that devours its own people. Longman consequently regards the model of the Western state used by most scholars to be part of the problem rather than the solution (Longman 1999).

But where the state has been supplanted by nonstate entities (as it was for much of the 1990s in Liberia and Sierra Leone) or has been replaced

---

15. This account does not overlook the essence of Nigeria's "shadow" election of February 1999. Although conducted in the presence of several teams of international observers, the flaws in the process were numerous. In a less critical situation, they would have been fatal. That shortcoming has not, however, detracted from the high level of domestic and international legitimacy enjoyed by elected executives and legislators of the Fourth Republic. If the republic survives, the national elections of 2003 are likely to be even worse, because candidates will seek to avoid being outdone by their opponents in rigging and other fraudulent electoral behavior. Preventing such a disastrous situation will be one of the major challenges of the Obasanjo administration as soon as its more urgent reforms have been implemented.

by armed, clan-based structures (as it was in Somalia) life has certainly become poor, nasty, brutish, and short. The United Nations recently concluded that Somalia is now a "black hole" of anarchy in which criminal violence prevails (*New York Times,* August 19, 1999). Many of the normal functions performed by the state, it points out, are unmet, such as "providing social services, regulating the movement of goods and people, [and] controlling air space." The report concludes that the international community must seek ways "to help Somalia recover its sovereignty." Even President Daniel Arap Moi of Kenya, no stranger to the use of the state as an instrument of predation and political violence, expressed dismay at the anarchic situation in neighboring Somalia and the resulting cross-border banditry: "I have patiently waited for Somalia to form a government," he complained, "but in vain" (*New York Times,* August 25, 1999).

How can these dilemmas be resolved? Tilly warned not only that was state-making tied to war-making, but also that both were analogous to organized crime. He described the state as a protection racket that successfully acquires the advantage of legitimacy. In postcolonial Africa the state often did become a protection racket; that is the essence of the various neopatrimonial models. As it lost legitimacy through ineffectiveness and corruption, the citizenry disengaged from this instrument of predation that was sustained largely by its command of the means of coercion. Yet, in the early 1990s state reform was not generally regarded as an imperative alongside democratization and economic liberalization. Herbst recognized this oversight. The linkage between state-making and war-making, as mentioned above, led him to suggest that the international community should allow this process to take its course on the assumption that it would yield more viable states. To his credit, he was raising the most fundamental question: How can state viability be enhanced in Africa?

My experiences in a range of African states convince me of the continuing imperative in Africa of combining a state-building project involving the monopolization of the means of warfare with measures to constitutionalize and place checks on this capability within a democratic system.[16] State consolidation without democracy has allowed Ethiopia and Eritrea to heap destruction on each other over barren swaths of territory. A similar process in Burkina Faso has enabled the Blaise Campaoré regime to persist as a covert backer of warlordism in Liberia and Sierra Leone. The militarist po-

---

16. For a collection of case studies of various African countries in this regard, see Mengisteab and Daddieh (1999). Schedler, Diamond, and Plattner (1999) have appropriately conceptualized such a project as "the self-restraining state."

litical organizations of Yoweri Museveni in Uganda and Paul Kagame in Rwanda have gone from being regarded as dynamic regimes to being seen as feared self-aggrandizers in Congo-Kinshasa. Meanwhile, it is increasingly difficult to distinguish between statist and nonstatist forms of organized crime in war-torn countries such as Angola and Congo-Brazzaville, where control of mineral assets has become the prime resource (and often motivation) of competing armed groups. Entire populations are now held hostage to these machinations. As the executive director of the World Food Program declared with regard to Angola, the people there are now "living at a level of despair that exists virtually nowhere else in the world today" (New York Times, August 24, 1999).[17]

The most critically needed empirical and theoretical project, as many African countries limp into the twenty-first century, is one that seeks to identify how a virtuous cycle of state-building and institutional reforms can be facilitated over the competing dynamics of state decay, informalization, and crime. The fact that students of other regions of the world, such as post-Soviet Eurasia, are asking similar questions provides helpful comparisons as well as a counterbalance to the alarming tendency, signaled in this chapter, of Africanist scholars being enticed into speculative forms of theorizing based on notions of African exceptionalism. The ongoing work of such researchers as Béla Greskovits and Hector Schamis on how the paths of state-building and political and economic reform can connect or diverge, for example, serves as a model. Their examination of the ways in which differential degrees of stateness in eastern Europe and Latin America facilitate the implementation of political and economic reforms and how these, in turn, bolster state capacity could be replicated with regard to Africa (Greskovits and Schamis 1999). In directing attention to the most fundamental aspect of state capacity (i.e., that of monopolizing the legitimate means of coercion) as well as to more complex tasks of enforcing new rules of social and economic interaction, Greskovits and Schamis demonstrate the kind of responsible empirical and theoretical investigations that are now urgently needed in studies of Africa.

Three decades after Aristide Zolberg identified the precarious nature of the postcolonial order in Africa (Zolberg 1966), an effective state is perhaps the continent's most glaring deficiency. To be effective in the contemporary context, however, such a state must include institutions of popular participation and accountability. At the beginning of the 1990s, many

---

17. See also Jim Hoagland's searing editorial on "the turmoil, poverty and uncertainty that have descended across Africa" (Hoagland 1999).

students of Africa (including this author) believed that democratization, economic liberalization, and programs to enhance "good governance" would pull the continent into a virtuous cycle of renewed development (Joseph 1989a, 1989b, 1990). In retrospect, we put aside too quickly what we had learned from the mid-1970s about the factors and forces contributing to state erosion. That issue has now pushed its way to the forefront of our analyses. In taking up this challenge, however, while we endeavor to be as rigorously empirical as possible, we should not be unduly influenced by exhortations to avoid acting normatively and teleologically. Certain norms and social objectives have become imperative with the passage of time, no less for Africans than for any other people. They are peace and stability, development, social welfare, and democratic governance.

References

Africa Confidential. 1999. 40, no. 17 (August).

Azarya, Victor, and Naomi Chazan. 1987. "Disengagement from the State in Africa: Reflections on the Experiences of Ghana and Guinea." *Comparative Studies in Society and History* 29, no. 1: 105–31.

Bates, Robert H. 1999. "The Economic Bases of Democratization." Pp. 83–94 in *State, Conflict, and Democracy in Africa,* ed. Richard Joseph. Boulder: Lynne Rienner.

Bayart, Jean-François. 1993. *The State in Africa: The Politics of the Belly.* New York: Longman. Trans. Mary Harper, Christopher Harrison, and Elizabeth Harrison. Original *L'Etat en Afrique: La politique du ventre.* Paris: Fayard, 1989.

Bayart, Jean-François, Stephen Ellis, and Béatrice Hibou. 1999. *The Criminalization of the State in Africa.* Bloomington: Indiana University Press. Original *La Criminalisation de l'Etat en Afrique.* Brussels: Editions Complexe, 1997.

Bratton, Michael. 1989. "Beyond the State: Civil Society and Associational Life in Africa." *World Politics* 41, no. 3: 407–18.

Bratton, Michael, and Nicolas van de Walle. 1994. "Neopatrimonial Regimes and Political Transitions in Africa." *World Politics* 46, no. 4 (July): 453–89.

———. 1997. *Democratic Experiments in Africa: Regime Transitions in Comparative Perspective.* Cambridge: Cambridge University Press.

Chabal, Patrick, and Jean-Pascal Daloz. 1999. *Africa Works: Disorder as Political Instrument.* Bloomington: Indiana University Press.

Chazan, Naomi. 1988. "Patterns of State-Society Incorporation and Disengagement in Africa." Pp. 121–48 in *The Precarious Balance: State and Society in Africa,* ed. Donald Rothchild and Naomi Chazan. Boulder: Westview.

Clapham, Christopher. 1996. *Africa and the International System: The Politics of State Survival.* Cambridge: Cambridge University Press.

Diamond, Larry. 1996. "Is the Third Wave Over?" *Journal of Democracy* 7, no. 3: 20–37.

———. 1999. *Developing Democracy: Toward Consolidation.* Baltimore: Johns Hopkins University Press.

Friedman, Stephen. 1995. "South Africa: Divided in a Special Way." Pp. 531–81 in *Politics in Developing Countries: Comparing Experiments with Democracy,* 2d ed., ed. Larry Diamond et al. Boulder: Lynne Rienner.

Friedman, Stephen, and Doreen Atkinson. 1994. *The Small Miracle: South Africa's Negoti-ated Settlement.* Johannesburg: Raven.

Greskovits, Béla, and Hector E. Schamis. 1999. "Democratic Capitalism and the State in East-ern Europe and Latin America." Paper presented at the Annual Meeting of the American Political Science Association, Atlanta, 2–5 September.

Gyimah-Boadi, E. 1998. "The Rebirth of African Liberalism." *Journal of Democracy* 9, no. 2: 18–31.

———. 1999a. "Ghana: The Challenges of Consolidating Democracy." Pp. 409–27 in *State, Conflict and Democracy in Africa,* ed. Richard Joseph. Boulder: Lynne Rienner.

———. 1999b. "Institutionalizing Credible Elections in Ghana." Pp. 105–21 in *The Self-Restraining State: Power and Accountability in New Democracies,* ed. A. Schedler, L. Di-amond, and M. F. Plattner. Boulder: Lynne Rienner.

Havel, Václav. 1999. "Kosovo and the End of the Nation-State." *New York Review of Books* 46, no. 10: 4–6.

Herbst, Jeffrey. 1992. *The Politics of Reform in Ghana, 1982–1991.* Berkeley: University of California Press.

———. 1996–97. "Responding to State Failure in Africa." *International Security* 21, no. 3 (winter): 120–44.

———. 2000. *State and Power in Africa.* Princeton: Princeton University Press.

Hoagland, Jim. 1999. Editorial. *Washington Post National Weekly Edition.* 30 August: 5.

Jackson, Robert H. 1990. *Quasi-States: Sovereignty, International Relations, and the Third World.* Cambridge: Cambridge University Press.

Joseph, Richard. 1984. "Class, State and Prebendal Politics in Nigeria." Pp. 21–38 in *State and Class in Africa,* ed. Nelson Kasfir. London: Frank Cass.

———. 1987. *Democracy and Prebendal Politics in Nigeria: The Rise and Fall of the Second Republic.* Cambridge: Cambridge University Press.

———. 1989a. "Perestroika without Glasnost in Africa." Report on the inaugural seminar of the African Governance Program, Carter Center, Atlanta.

———, ed. 1989b. "Beyond Autocracy in Africa." Paper presented at the inaugural seminar of the African Governance Program, Carter Center, Atlanta.

———, ed. 1990. "African Governance in the 1990s: Objectives, Resources, and Con-straints." Paper presented at the 2nd annual seminar of the African Governance Program, Carter Center, Atlanta.

———. 1997. "Democratization in Africa since 1989: Comparative and Theoretical Per-spectives." *Comparative Politics* 29, no. 3: 363–82.

———. 1998. "Africa, 1990–1997: From *Abertura* to Closure." *Journal of Democracy* 9, no. 2: 3–17. Reprinted in Larry Diamond and Mark F. Plattner, *Democratization in Africa.* Baltimore: Johns Hopkins University Press, 1999.

———. 1999. "The Reconfiguration of Power in Late-Twentieth-Century Africa. Pp. 57–80 in *State, Conflict, and Democracy in Africa,* ed. Richard Joseph. Boulder: Lynne Rienner.

Joseph, Richard, and Jeffrey Herbst. 1997. "Correspondence: Responding to State Failure in Africa." *International Security* 22, no. 2: 175–84.

Joseph, Richard, Peter Lewis, Darren Kew, and Scott Taylor. 2000. "Nigeria." Pp. 545–606 in *Comparative Politics at the Crossroads,* 2d ed., ed. Mark Kesselman et al. Boston: Houghton Mifflin.

Linz, Juan J., and Alfred Stepan. 1996. *Problems of Democratic Transition and Consolidation: Southern America and Post-Communist Europe.* Baltimore: Johns Hopkins University Press.

Longman, Timothy. 1999. "State, Civil Society, and Genocide in Rwanda." Pp. 339–58 in *State, Conflict, and Democracy in Africa,* ed. Richard Joseph. Boulder: Lynne Rienner.

Mainwaring, Scott. 1999. "The Surprising Resilience of Elected Governments." *Journal of Democracy* 10, no. 3: 101–14.

Mbembe, Achille. 1999. *Du gouvernement indirect privé*. Dakar: CODESRIA.

Médard, Jean-François. 1982. "The Underdeveloped State in Tropical Africa: Political Clientelism or Neo-Patrimonialism?" Pp. 162–92 in *Private Patronage and Public Power: Political Clientelism in the Modern State*, ed. Christopher Clapham. London: Pinter.

Mengisteab, Kidane, and Cyril Daddieh. 1999. *State Building and Democratization in Africa*. Westport: Praeger.

Nugent, Paul. 1999. "Living in the Past: Urban, Rural and Ethnic Themes in the 1992 and 1996 Elections in Ghana." *Journal of Modern African Studies* 37, no. 2: 287–319.

Nwokedi, Emeka. 1995. *Politics of Democratization: Changing Authoritarian Regimes in Sub-Saharan Africa*. Münster: Lit Verlag.

O'Donnell, Guillermo. 1993. "On the State, Democratization and Some Conceptual Problems: A Latin American View with Glances at Some Postcommunist Countries." *World Development* 21, no. 8: 1355–70.

Olukoshi, Adebayo. 1999. "State, Conflict, and Democracy in Africa: The Complex Process of Renewal." Pp. 451–65 in *State, Conflict, and Democracy in Africa*, ed. Richard Joseph. Boulder: Lynne Rienner.

Onishi, Norimitsu. 1999. "Political Reforms Reach Nigeria's Gasoline Pumps." *New York Times*. 9 August: 1, 10.

Ottaway, Marina. 1999. "Keep Out of Africa." *Financial Times*. 25 February: 14.

Przeworski, Adam, et al. 1995. *Sustainable Democracy*. Cambridge: Cambridge University Press.

Reno, William. 1995. *Corruption and State Politics in Sierra Leone*. Cambridge: Cambridge University Press.

———. 1997. "War, Markets, and the Reconfiguration of Africa's Weak States." *Comparative Politics* 29, no. 4: 493–509.

———. 1998. *Warlord Politics and African States*. Boulder: Lynne Rienner.

Sandbrook, Richard. 1997. "Reforming Dysfunctional Institutions through Democratisation? Reflections on Ghana." *Journal of Modern African Studies* 35, no. 4: 603–46.

Schedler, Andreas, Larry Diamond, and Mark F. Plattner. 1999. *The Self-Restraining State: Power and Accountability in New Democracies*. Boulder: Lynne Rienner.

Tilly, Charles. 1985. "War Making and State Making as Organized Crime." Pp. 169–91 in *Bringing the State Back In*, ed. Peter B. Evans, Dietrich Rueschemeyer, and Theda Skocpol. Cambridge: Cambridge University Press.

Turner, Terisa. 1978. "Commercial Capitalism and the 1975 Coup." Pp. 166–97 in *Soldiers and Oil: The Political Transformation of Nigeria*, ed. Keith Panter-Brick. London: Frank Cass.

Widner, Jennifer A., ed. 1994. *Economic Change and Political Liberalization in Sub-Saharan Africa*. Baltimore: Johns Hopkins University Press.

———. 1995. "States and Statelessness in Late-Twentieth-Century Africa." *Daedalus* 124, no. 3: 129–54.

Young, Crawford. 1988. "The African Colonial State and Its Political Legacy." Pp. 25–66 in *The Precarious Balance: State and Society in Africa*, ed. Donald Rothchild and Naomi Chazan. Boulder: Westview.

———. 1994. *The African Colonial State in Comparative Perspective*. New Haven: Yale University Press.

———. 1999. "The Third Wave of Democratization in Africa: Ambiguities and Contradictions." Pp. 15–38 in *State, Conflict, and Democracy in Africa*, ed. Richard Joseph. Boulder: Lynne Rienner.

Zolberg, Aristide R. 1966. *Creating Political Order: The Party-States of West Africa*. Chicago: Rand McNally.

11

The East Goes South: International Aid and the Production of Convergence in Africa and Eurasia

PETER J. STAVRAKIS

It was not supposed to turn out this way. The collapse of the Soviet Union in 1991 was a cause for celebration and buoyant optimism that, at long last, a continent divided by cold war could enter the new millennium as a united community of liberal, free-market societies. Scholarly analysis reflected this optimism by connecting developments in eastern and central Europe to the democratic transitions sweeping through Latin America (Przeworski 1991). The former communist world was firmly linked to the progress of societies that held much promise for the future. Indeed, comparing Russia and its companion successor states to a region as troubled as Africa seemed positively mean-spirited at the beginning of the 1990s. Although Russia might have a rougher road to travel to enjoy the benefits of democratic governance and the wealth of the free market, Western policy-makers viewed this as associated more with the enormity of communist deconstruction than anything intrinsic to Russian culture or society. Once the institutional infrastructure of communism was dis-

I am indebted to Valerie Bunce, René Lemarchand, Peter Rutland, Nicolas van de Walle, Crawford Young, and William Zartman for providing me with comments and criticisms on earlier drafts of this chapter.

mantled, Russia's economy and society would quickly respond to the benefits of embracing the global liberal order.[1]

The dramatic collapse of Russian capitalism in August 1998 brought home to the West the reality of Russia's failed transition. Some commentators continued to stress the successes of democratic reform (McFaul 1999), but these arguments had to be made against the backdrop of a far more somber reality: eight consecutive years of economic contraction, decrepit and inefficient state institutions, pervasive criminalization of state and society, widespread public privation and ensuing withdrawal from society, and a physically enfeebled chief executive whose chief skill consisted of shuffling elites to preserve his own political stability. In sum, by the end of the 1990s most observers of post-Soviet states were persuaded by events that success had proven elusive and "transition" had produced a failing state, a spent society, and a self-serving political elite.

This chapter examines the international dimension of this seeming convergence between Africa and the former Soviet Union. Its central contention is that the assistance regime that lay at the core of the efforts of international financial institutions (IFIs) and Western governments to facilitate economic and political reform actually had the reverse effect—helping to undermine state capacity and stunt legitimate economic performance. The result was a failing state and an economy addicted to criminal and informal processes. Not surprisingly, then, some of the prevailing approaches in African studies constitute a useful comparative context for comprehending the modalities of the post-Soviet experience. Indeed, the concepts of the "presentability" of democracy and the "recomposition" of power recently articulated by Africanist scholars can also be powerful tools for explaining post-Soviet development.

Several potential criticisms that invariably accompany analyses of foreign assistance should be addressed at the outset. In particular, does not this effort overstate the influence and unity of the various aid actors? Moreover, does not a critical assessment of the efforts of the aid community fail to give sufficient credit to the West for addressing a complex and difficult process? It is undeniable that any global assessment of aid processes invariably sacrifices the richness and diversity present within the aid community. However, we ought not to begin a revisionist history of foreign assis-

---

1. An unspoken, yet important, factor that buoyed the hopes of Western policy-makers was the belief that Russia was a part of Europe and, as such, possessed the intellectual and cultural resources required to avoid the disastrous failures so prevalent on the African continent.

tance until we first come to terms with that aid's impact on the societies it was meant to affect. When the United States stepped forward with the ambitious aid agenda reflected in the 1992 Freedom Support Act—aimed at promoting democratic and market transitions in the postcommunist states—there was no question that the entire assistance community was suffused with the sense of a common set of objectives. And it was made abundantly clear that success could be achieved quickly. Western governments and international financial institutions began to think seriously about a realistic diversification of their approach only after the facile assumptions of an easy transition to free-market liberal democracy were shattered against the harsh terrain of post-Soviet realities.

Finally, it is important to acknowledge at the outset that in making the comparison with Africa, I draw on only those aspects of African states' reform experiences that resonate with the Russian case (with the potential extension to most other Soviet successor states). Many dimensions of the African experience remain fundamentally alien to Russian conditions, but the basic premise here is that even the persuasive presence of several strands of comparison provides some substantial progress in our knowledge of these societies.

Western Aid and the Shaping of the New Russia: The Economic Dimension

From the outset, the Western approach to the "transition" from communism rested heavily on neoliberal economics, with a secondary emphasis on building formal political institutions. International assistance institutions, however, presented no credible or persuasive argument as to how these two dimensions of the assistance program could be coherently reconciled. Russia thus embarked on its reforms plagued by the same inherent contradiction between neoliberal economic reform and democratic reform that characterized Western approaches toward assistance to the developing world. International financial institutions, led by the International Monetary Fund (IMF) and the World Bank, concentrated their energies on macroeconomic reform. Western countries, the United States in particular, directed their assistance efforts toward the creation of new political institutions and a nongovernmental sector that was deemed essential in catalyzing the transition.

Although the prospect of an inherent conflict between fundamental assistance objectives should have been cause for concern, changes in the global context—the U.S. victory in the cold war—permitted Western states to assume a casual attitude regarding the impact of assistance policies. Previously, international aid consisted of "modernist" as well as geopolitical components (Escobar 1995, 29–33); the former reflected a belief in uninterrupted progress from a traditional, authoritarian, and irrational society to the professional, stable, democratic Western state (Grant and Nijman 1998a). So long as the Soviet Union existed, however, the ineluctable march toward the modern risked being undermined by a competing social order, allowing geopolitical considerations to trump developmental ones. Once the great ideological contest ended in decisive victory for the West, international assistance gravitated toward a simple linear conception of development leading to liberal free-market democracy. As Richard Grant and Jan Nijman (1998a) point out, subsequent events in the post-Soviet world were to profoundly shake Western faith in this simplistic modernist approach. But as the cold war ended, it seemed possible to dichotomize the international system into those states that embraced Western society and those condemned to failure.

The modernist conception of societal development fostered an international aid policy toward Russia that rested heavily on faith in the power of market forces and trust in the essential decency of Russia's reformers. The bulk of assistance efforts concentrated on transforming the economic order and said little or nothing about the need to build the administrative capacity required for new institutions to function effectively. Indeed, Russia's first generation of reformers focused—with the explicit knowledge and consent of external institutions—on a simple formula for a speedy transition: destruction, stabilization, and construction. Soviet-era institutions of state power and economic management had first to be demolished to clear a path for realizing the ostensible benefits of market forces. Following this, the challenge of reform could be turned over to a new group of stabilizers who would focus on creating conditions for sustained economic growth. Finally, a new generation of builders (those skilled at wealth creation rather than destruction or stabilization) would be given the mantle of power, providing for the consolidation of a productive capitalist economy.

In 1992, when reforms first began, it was not unusual for Russia's "bold young reformers" to assume—with the hubris characteristic of those secure in their knowledge of economic science—that the entire process could be accomplished quickly. Their conviction was bolstered by the unabashed efforts of economist Jeffrey Sachs and his acolytes to accelerate the process of macroeconomic stabilization. Sachs excoriated the IMF in particular for being insufficiently aggressive in the application of "economic" shock ther-

apy in Russia. The faster shock therapy was implemented, the faster reformers would be able to deal a mortal blow to the sclerotic infrastructure
of the Soviet command economy and facilitate the consolidation of a capitalist economy. Russian reformers and their international supporters acknowledged that such an approach was bound to impose still more pain on
society. But this was considered to be a reasonable price to pay for a rapid
transformation. The reform of Russia's political institutions played a secondary role in this larger economic undertaking—yet it was no less important, in some respects, for the West had to demonstrate that no political alternative existed to the contemporary liberal state. Elections, a new
constitution for the Russian Federation, and the creation of effective legislative and judicial institutions were the initial principal foci of bilateral
Western assistance to Russia's political transition. The U.S. Agency for International Development (USAID) and the European Union's Technical
Assistance to the Commonwealth of Independent States (TACIS) initially
assumed that political reform could be smoothly integrated with economic
reform. But when tension subsequently emerged between the political and
the economic dimensions of international assistance, the West left little
doubt that it was committed first to defending the architecture of economic reform and only then to the institutionalization of democratic political institutions. In retrospect, it is hard to understand how the Western
assistance community could have expected a rapid transition to democracy
and capitalism when the historical record in Russia (as was also true on the
African continent) was bereft of apprenticeship in either. A key factor certainly had to be the false confidence bred from the collapse of communism,
which, as Peter Reddaway and Dmitri Glinski (1999) note, created an un-
obstructed path for an ideology of "market bolshevism."

But Russia and other successor states presented the West with a problem. Although the norms and institutions of the modern liberal state might
be the logical and desirable terminus for the transition process, there existed neither institutional infrastructure nor cultural legacy that would have
served as a base for achieving these ends. How then could a rational legal
order and a good state be built if the only implements and resources at the
West's disposal were rooted in past institutions and practices? The answer
appeared to be simple in concept: international assistance providers were
to place their trust in a select core of self-styled "reformers" whose macroeconomic credentials seemed beyond question. Hence, the fresh, young,
and appropriately Western faces of Yegor Gaidar, Anatoli Chubais, Peter
Aven, and others suddenly appeared extremely appealing. If such a group
were provided access to central power and given political cover by none

other than President Boris Yeltsin, they would be able to push through needed reforms rapidly. Chubais, for instance, repeatedly defended his resort to extralegal powers as necessary for implementing reform rapidly in the face of his possible removal from power. The West accepted this logic and thereby tolerated the reformers' abuse of the very principles that they sought to establish in Russia. Western institutions shunned other domestic groups and alternative reform programs and invested their financial, moral, and political support in a narrow clique of elites (Wedel 1998). Moreover, the linear logic of development that now prevailed internationally indicated that reformers had no alternative besides aspiring to the goals set for them by Western assistance institutions.

Yeltsin's reform team was described in the most favorable terms—"radical," "bold," "young," "pro-Western," "pro-capitalist"—whereas all who voiced doubts or opposition to the new course soon had a host of negative adjectives preceding their names in the Western press—"hard-line," "conservative," "nationalist," or "antireform." The West's need to find loyal cadres in Russia who promised rapid solutions along a predefined course had in one stroke reduced a remarkably complex array of social forces to a simple dichotomy: our (the West's) reformers and the rest.

The substance of Russian reform and Western assistance policy genuinely reflected a radical departure from the Russian past, but the political style of its implementation remained grounded in the more familiar terrain of personalistic and clientelistic elite groups and a highly authoritarian structure. Once the basic reforms were in place, Western policy-makers presumed that Russian reformers (who now stood to be the chief beneficiaries of a jury-rigged and deinstitutionalized system) would lead the way in supporting reforms that would undermine their own power. The West had not provided for the possibility that Russia's new elites would find the traditional mantle of power so appealing that they would refuse to take it off.

There were two justifications for delinking economic reform from public accountability, each of which was clearly recognizable to societies with similar reform experiences. First, the impact of macroeconomic stabilization policies would impose such hardship on the population and prove so politically unpopular that only an authoritarian leadership could secure the stable implementation of macroeconomic policy. Yeltsin's confrontation with the parliament in October 1993 confirmed to many within the aid establishment that a firm (read: nondemocratic) hand was justified. Anti–shock therapy elites in parliament, bitter at their effective disenfranchisement in the face of the government's economic policies, seized upon growing public discontent in an effort to pressure the Yeltsin government into making concessions on the new Russian constitution. Both sides in the constitutional debate—president and parliament—refused to budge, leading to political stalemate in late summer 1993. Yeltsin finally resolved the issue through the use of force, bombing parliament, arresting key leaders, and calling for new elections and a referendum on his version of the constitution. On December 12, 1993, the Russian electorate rendered a split decision on Yeltsin's actions by giving Vladimir Zhirinovskii's Liberal Democratic Party of Russia a stunning plurality of the public vote, yet approving the highly centralized Yeltsin constitution.[2]

Second, Western aid elites considered Yeltsin's authoritarian response to his opponents a necessary aspect of crisis management. At the beginning of Russia's reforms, the World Bank spoke approvingly of the need for a "crisis management" style of policy-making. The situation in Russia required urgent action, and state institutions either did not yet exist or were too fragile to respond adroitly. Hence, a tightly knit reform team would have to navigate through the institutional wreckage of the old regime to achieve the essential primary goals of macroeconomic stabilization. The urgency of the task also dictated that they be freed from legal and political constraints in implementing their policy. Once the critical phase had passed, the World Bank reasoned, it would be desirable to broaden the base of governance and link it firmly to formal institutions. Yet the bank provided no insight as to how this would be accomplished. Not surprisingly, as Russia lumbered from crisis to crisis, international aid providers found it easier to sustain the existing style of rule and postpone to the indefinite future the era of normal government.

But it was the privatization process—especially in its second stage—that dealt a mortal blow to the course of development of the Russian state. In a remarkable tour de force of political arrogance, Chubais (at the time a deputy prime minister) and Vladimir Potanin (the former head of Uneximbank) concocted a "loans for shares" arrangement in which a select group of seven "court" banks were provided controlling shares in the crown jewels of the Russian economy in exchange for loans that the Russian government badly needed to cover its budget deficits and continue its externally mandated course of reform. Theoretically, this arrangement per-

---

2. David White has noted that the chair of the Russian Central Electoral Commission during the vote admitted that the referendum, although it received a plurality of the popular vote, probably fell short of the absolute majority required by Russian law for adoption (White 1997). Confirmation of this admission is unlikely, as many of the ballots were destroyed in a fire shortly after the referendum.

mitted the government immediate access to finances, while preparing the ground for the sell-off of key industries that would generate still more revenue. The problem, however, was that the scheme was blatantly corrupt: the favored banks all had intimate links to the reform government, and they subsequently purchased Russia's richest assets for prices far below market value (Boldyrev 1996). This pillaging deprived the government of its anticipated revenue stream, leaving the attraction of foreign investors as the lone remaining option for generating revenue. Equally important, the financial oligarchy created as a consequence promptly engaged in the speculative sale of its new assets, undermining still further the chances for restoration of a productive economy.

Privatization policy also undermined the government's ability to develop a professional civil service. In an effort to assume direct control over the process, Chubais used foreign assistance funds to construct Russia's massive privatization program. Russian Privatization Centers (RPCs) were created to implement the program, yet the RPCs needed to recruit personnel. A ready pool of labor was found among government personnel loyal to Chubais, who were secretly paid for their consulting services. Chubais could count on finding many recruits, in large part because his government was responsible for the low wages paid to civil servants. Privatization thus triumphed in Russia only by compromising the possibility of a genuine civil service (Stavrakis 1998; Boldyrev 1996; Wedel 1998). In its place rapidly emerged tight networks of clientelistic ties that selectively allocated private enterprises to Kremlin intimates. The assistance policy designed to replace the patron-client networks that had formed the heart of the Soviet economy and politics instead paved the way for their resurrection.

The enervation of the state was paralleled by the emergence of speculation as a dominant form of economic activity. Lacking either legal protection or political support for their activities, enterprises rapidly saw that greater advantages accrued through asset-stripping (and subsequent sale on the black and/or international markets) rather than continued production of goods for which demand had collapsed and raw materials had grown scarce. Tax revenues accordingly shrank, and enterprise managers sought to avoid payment of taxes altogether. The Russian state, as Piroska Nagy recently argued (2000), had fallen victim to the zeal of its economic reform agenda.

The lone remaining option for salvation now lay in attracting foreign investors to the recently created Russian government bond (GKO) market. The GKO market initially proved successful, as the Russian government promised extremely attractive rates of return (as high as 150 percent in one year alone) on two-year ruble-denominated bonds, and it succeeded in obtaining emergency IMF funding to bolster its depleted coffers. Little more than a year later, the World Bank gave its stamp of approval to the GKO scheme by anointing Russia as the world's most attractive emerging market. But even this was not enough to reverse the downward course of the Russian economy. By 1998, in the wake of the Southeast Asian financial collapse, major Western investors began to cool their ardor for the Russian bond market, concerned that Moscow would be unable to honor its debt commitments. As foreign investment lagged, the financial crisis returned with renewed force, and Chubais was dispatched to Washington to negotiate an IMF bailout package designed to restore investor confidence. He persuaded the IMF (which pledged an additional $22.6 billion to prop up reform), but not Western investors, who failed to be swayed by the IMF endorsement.[3] Confidence in the Russian government's ability to avoid default and persevere in reform evaporated, and with it went bond prices and the stock market. Prime Minister Sergei Kirienko (another young reformer) initially attempted to stay the course, but he was forced to announce a debt moratorium and effective devaluation of the ruble. Shortly thereafter, Kirienko resigned, along with the entire complement of reformers in the government.

The appointment of Yevgennyi Primakov as prime minister two weeks later eased the political crisis, but Russia remained in deep economic trouble. Primakov's deliberate slowness in addressing the economic situation left Russia suspended at its lowest point since reforms began. For the international assistance community, however, the problem was even more profound, for it no longer had a single individual to whom it could point as the credible standard-bearer of reform. If Russia was to be rescued with renewed international assistance, a new accommodation had to be reached with the new elite that came to power in the Kremlin. This was in process in the spring of 1999, whereupon Yeltsin sacked Primakov and replaced him with Sergei Stepashin. The latter had only begun his own effort to accommodate Western demands when he, too, was replaced—by Vladimir Putin. Yeltsin clearly felt confident enough in Putin's ability to stay the course, since Yeltsin anointed him as his successor.

---

3. In a subsequent interview, Chubais claimed to have "conned" the IMF out of this money, implying that if the truth were known the IMF and Western investors would abandon Russia and reform. Chubais subsequently rescinded this claim, expressing regret that his words were interpreted in this manner. He did not, however, categorically deny the substance of the claim, or demand a retraction.

The Russian economic reform program endorsed by the West thus had a powerful corrosive effect on the state, neglecting or undermining the very institutional infrastructure responsible for managing the transition. Economic productivity, already reeling from the Soviet collapse, could not endure the plundering of a financial oligarchy created by a reformist clique that had employed economic crisis as a pretext for operating above the law. As the legal order was compromised, economic managers ventured into the darker corners of the speculative economy, compromising the much-desired breakthrough to a normal economy. But the reform government also learned the darker arts of global finance. The Russian Central Bank soon admitted that it had channeled perhaps as much as $50 billion of its reserves into FIMACO, an obscure offshore corporation on the Channel Island of Jersey, principally to prevent its recapture by Western creditors.[4] In its final moments, the Kirienko government had revealed that its commitment to transforming Russia had been secondary to the perquisites of power. As Kirienko and a stream of "bold young reformers" resigned en masse, they decried the collapse of reform in Russia, the political decrepitude of Yeltsin, and the crisis that now confronted Russia in the hands of the inept old guard. It was a remarkable performance, inasmuch as their actions were as much responsible for the collapse of reform as any one else's, and it was they who had massaged Yeltsin's ego and hidden behind his political shadow to cling to power.

Western Aid and the Shaping of the New Russia: Political Dynamics

Western assistance proved important in nurturing a political practice that exacerbated the impact of economic policy and degraded the prospects for the development of state institutions. On one level, the West—the United States in the lead—focused paramount attention on free and fair elections, political parties, and the separation of powers. Although the focus on political party formation fizzled early on, the United States aggressively

---

4. Sergei Aleksashenko, former deputy chairman of the Russian Central Bank, conceded that the sequestering of bank funds was done to protect them from Western creditors. FIMACO was a French corporation chartered in Jersey. Surprisingly, 78 percent of it was owned by the Russian government. The reform team had thus deftly exploited Western financial practices to securely channel money to themselves—beyond the reach of creditors. More on FIMACO and the Russian Central Bank (RCB) can be found in an audit of the RCB by PriceWaterhouseCoopers prepared for the IMF (PriceWaterhouseCoopers 1999).

sought to implement democratic parliamentary and presidential elections. Under the watchful eyes of hundreds of international observers Russians went to the polls in December 1993 and December 1995 and returned a parliament dominated by Communists and by forces largely hostile to the reform program. The centerpiece was the presidential election in June 1996, in which Yeltsin staged a remarkable comeback to defeat Gennadi Zyuganov, his Communist opponent. Americans congratulated Russians for freely electing their first president in history. Few seemed to be bothered by the fact that the choice was between a despot and a tsar.

In retrospect, the massive international effort succeeded in producing the appropriate election spectacle necessary for sanctifying Russia as "on track" toward democracy. Yet considerable evidence indicated that the elections were far from free and fair. The European Institute for the Media, pointing to the overwhelming monopoly of the airwaves by pro-Yeltsin forces, concluded in its final report that the elections were not free and fair. Moreover, Yeltsin's campaign manager, Chubais, did his best to rifle the government budget and foreign assistance funds to throw money at the Yeltsin campaign. The most glaring example of this was the "disappearance" of a $250 million tranche from the World Bank designated for relief of the mining sector, including payment of back wages. Not a nickel materialized there, and evidence now indicates that it wound up in the Yeltsin campaign coffers (Kramer 1997).[5] The Russian financial oligarchy created by earlier privatization policy made no secret of its massive assistance in support of Yeltsin's reelection bid. What they demanded in return was nothing less than a further crippling of the state's capacity in order to accommodate their personal interests. That the West did not protest these disturbing developments reflected the gradual emergence of the international community's real priorities for Russian political reform. If Russia embraced the rhetoric of reform and made marginal substantive steps—in short, if it provided the West with an image of presentability—Western agencies and governments would pronounce Russia to be a reform "success." The shift from substantive policy results to appropriate genuflection before the icons of free-market democracy proved remarkably easy for the Russian elite, and it was not long before virtually every political party and organization spoke the language of reform with accomplished fluency; only the Communists found this a challenge. International assistance agencies

---

5. The World Bank, for its part, proceeded in the issuance of the second $250 million tranche, after formally concluding there was no impropriety. The first allotment of money has never been found.

also found that this ritualistic embrace of transition goals provided them with the flexibility required to navigate difficult moments in the transition without having to claim that democratization had suffered serious reverses. Hence, Russia could now have a parliament, it could be populated with opposition forces, and it could even pass legislation that conflicted with the Yeltsin government's objectives. A strongly presidential constitution, however, empowered Yeltsin to circumvent or ignore such negative developments in virtually all cases, as Chapter 9 in this book shows.

The West's superficial investment in democratic institutions in Russia also meant that it would continue to tolerate endless conflict and political jostling between the informal "clan" networks that were the essence of Russian political life. Even when the patrimonial nature of Russian politics was publicly revealed to the West (Graham 1995), it caused only a momentary ripple in the tendency of Western governments and IFIs to cast Russian developments in the most favorable light. Hence, Russian political life acquired a two-tiered nature: the level of formal institutions that satisfied the rhetorical and ideological demands of Western policy, and the level of informal political struggle, where the serious political issues were resolved. Accountability of elites to the public was the principal casualty of this system, but Western aid officials attempted to deflect this by arguing that even imperfect elections were a major advance for Russia. This was the ultimate irony: the fabled Potemkin village, long the symbol of the Russian state's craven attempt to obscure its political backwardness, was now embraced by the West with relief. The traditional style of Russian politics had thus succeeded in a remarkable process of adapting to new conditions. The rhetoric and institutional framework had changed, and several new "clans" affiliated with the West had entered the political fray, but the hankering to live above the law and to resolve questions of power through semiclandestine struggles continued unabated.

The West's emphasis on economic reform and the presentability of political reform and its tolerance of unreconstructed clientelistic politics contributed to creating a "quasi-state" similar to that described by Robert Jackson: endowed with juridical statehood, yet lacking the political will, institutional capacity, and organized authority to protect human rights and provide socioeconomic welfare (Jackson 1990). Indeed, were one to consider Russia's accomplishments against the standard expected of modern states—provision for national defense, ensuring broad macroeconomic stability, maintaining social equity at politically manageable levels, and ensuring economic growth (M..andawire 1999)—the Russian state by 1998 had failed in all respects. The web of informal clan alliances among the Yeltsin political elite filled the void left by the breakdown of formal state capacity. Since the essence of clientelistic politics involves the amassing of power that transcends institutional boundaries, the triumph of traditional political behavior effaced the boundaries between state, society, and economy required for sustaining modern state institutions.

The primacy of informal "clan" politics allowed Yeltsin to develop a style of rule that prevented challenges to his authority even as it debilitated the pursuit of rational policy goals. This accounts for years of reshuffling his "reform team," which changed its political complexion on a regular basis. To balance the influence of Chubais and Boris Nemtsov, Yeltsin tolerated Prime Minister Viktor Chernomyrdin and his ally Boris Berezovskii. Then, as Chernomyrdin acquired too much presidential aura, he was sacked and replaced by political neophyte Kirienko. The latter's appointment, hailed externally as a triumph for "reform" by the West, was in reality designed to stabilize domestic politics and temporarily restrain personal ambitions. At the end of the 1990s, Yeltsin's erratic behavior increased. In spring 1999, he sacked Prime Minister Yevgennyi Primakov, evidently out of fear that the latter had also begun to compile a record of political success that might soon rival that of the president. Stepashin, Primakov's successor, lasted a mere eighty-four days, as Yeltsin again feared that the newest prime minister was exhibiting too much presidential ambition. The next prime minister, Putin, needed to avoid running afoul of the imperious Yeltsin until he could claim independent control over the presidency. In all of these exchanges, the Russian political elite bemoaned the subjugation of policy to despotic whim, yet none saw fit to challenge it directly. Instead, leaders were content to tolerate the situation so long as they remained at the center of the political game.

Understanding why Western aid and financial institutions tolerated this patrimonial style of rule allows us to achieve a closure between Western aid policy, Russian domestic politics, "presentability," and the rhetoric of reform.[6] Western states had resolved that only Yeltsin could push through the reform process; it therefore became imperative to permit him to secure his domestic political position. Yeltsin, however, had learned his political survival tactics in the old school; hence, if the president were to survive, he

---

6. Russian political elites tolerated this process, but for different reasons. The mutability of elite constellations under Yeltsin meant that, even if you were down, you were not yet out. Hence, it was better to find a sinecure in Moscow, bide your time, and hope to reinsert yourself into the process at a later date than to oppose the process altogether. The example of this par excellence was Chubais, who rotated in and out of government three times.

had to do so his way. This meant recourse to the comforting world of "clan" politics and clandestine intrigue rather than democratic processes. The West was forced to accept this reality and did so on the condition that the leading "clan" espouse the rhetoric of free-market democratic reform.

In the turbulent world of Russian domestic politics, however, no one could credibly guarantee the primacy of a single group of neoliberal reformers; moreover, such primacy would also risk depriving Yeltsin of the very flexibility in elite reshuffling that was required for ensuring his own predominance. The only way all of these contradictory imperatives could be reconciled was through the abandonment of the West's insistence on purely substantive reform and instead accepting a presentable image of Russia as a society in transition. Yeltsin, for his part, responded by developing what might be a textbook recipe for "presentable" transition: 1) seizing the rhetorical high ground and imposing on all Russian elites (except the Communists) the vocabulary of reform; 2) producing sufficient substantive change to permit the West to declare transition a success; and 3) exploiting the Communists' ineptitude to cast them as the perfect villains.

One area that was genuinely different from the Soviet era was in center-regional relations. At no point in Russian history had the likelihood of the disintegration of the Russian state appeared as great as during the 1990s. The period of greatest danger in this regard was 1992–93, when the central government had to confront the consequences of economic collapse outside Moscow yet lacked the institutional resources to do so. In a manner not unfamiliar to African states, Moscow adjusted to the "temporary" reality of its diminished power by sustaining regional relations through a web of ad hoc compromises and concessions to regional leaders (Rothchild 1987). As Russia achieved a modicum of stability in the middle of the decade, opinion was divided as to whether Russia would move in the direction of a federation or a recentralization of power.

By the late 1990s, it appeared that those optimistic about the emergence of a functioning federalism in Russia had been disappointed.[7] Despite the best efforts of a minority of regional leaders, the weakness of both Moscow and regional governments left a de facto structure tentatively in place—until one side or the other could impose another solution. Hence, personal relations between the president and regional leaders were preferred to legally binding federal practice, and regional governments were predominantly content to sequester substantial portions of their budgets to provide

---

7. This includes me; I earlier maintained that Russian regionalism was moving toward the institutionalization of federalism (Stavrakis 1996b).

for goods and services off the books. As this example illustrates, with rare exception the economic crisis in Russia brought about the system-wide failure of public institutions. Gogol's satirical depiction in his novel *The Inspector General* of the mutual mistrust and manipulation of both center and regional governments retained its currency.

The West largely missed this opportunity to assist in the decentralization of political power, which is partially attributable to an economic reform agenda that demanded all authority and attention be focused on Moscow. The logic of democratic reform suggests that decentralization of power and the creation of functioning federal structures were important objectives to the consolidation of democracy. Yet IFIs (followed somewhat less ardently by the United States) were openly hostile to any substantive decentralization. Their reasoning stemmed from the primacy, in their view, of economic reform: macroeconomic targets were best achieved only by strengthening central government institutions (Tanzi 1993), a paradox resembling the unraveling of Yugoslavia in the 1980s (Woodward 1995). The IMF and the World Bank obviously had in mind institutions such as the Ministry of Finance and the Russian Central Bank, but to the early neoliberal reformers this was political salvation, for they could use the guise of international aid to demolish the regional institutional bases of their political opponents. This also left some regional leaders in the awkward position of being on the front lines of democracy without enjoying the support of the central government, for local leaders stood first in line to bear the brunt of public disaffection with the consequences of shock therapy.

The United States eventually grasped the need to adjust its aid policy toward direct support for regional economies and governments. But this came late in the day. Moreover, the United States remained concerned lest direct assistance to regions offend the Kremlin. Hence, it proved difficult to keep foreign assistance money away from the black hole of Moscow. The most successful (and earliest) international initiative was the European Bank for Reconstruction and Development's Regional Lending Program. Generally, however, foreign investors seeking promising opportunities in the regions were often left to fend for themselves. Many of the regions, of course, were plagued with the same problems that afflicted central institutions: corruption and patronage. But some regions, such as Nizhnii Novgorod, succeeded admirably in forging ahead with reform and attracting foreign investors (at least until the August 1998 financial crisis) with relatively little help from Moscow. In sum, the emergence of regional politics in Russia proved a missed opportunity from the standpoint of international aid policy. Instead of being the centerpiece of a bold initiative in democratization, it lived in the shadow of macroeconomic imperatives and presidential politics. Consequently, the hoped-for transition from feudal to federal relations between center and periphery has yet to transpire.

The preceding sections indicate that Western assistance played an important role in fostering some of the same types of state pathologies in post-Soviet Russia commonly found in sub-Saharan Africa. Despite the formally distinct imperatives of "development" and "democratic transition," the striking parallels between the two regions in the areas of state failure and economic stagnation are attracting increasing attention. The tsarist empire and the African continent are products of widely differing patterns of historical development, but since 1991 the international aid regime has been a fixed constant in the efforts of these states to sustain political viability and economic growth. The common imprint of this regime can be discerned in several key areas, and it is to this that I now turn.

The Triumph of Neoliberal Economic Ideology

The West's triumph in the cold war explains a remarkable convergence in the economic dimension of international aid policy. Neoliberal economics, now unchallenged, stipulated that Western aid be directed less toward enhancing state capacity than toward aiding social forces deemed capable of satisfying the macroeconomic constraints established by government. Hence, African and post-Soviet states were viewed by international financial institutions as identical in the sense that, although the causes of the problems confronting African states and the post-Soviet states differed, the solutions prescribed were much the same.

A substantial deconstruction of the state was considered essential to developing a viable private sector in societies that did not possess one. De-emphasizing the state in the Russian case also initially served a dual political purpose: internationally, it undermined Soviet military structures that challenged American primacy; domestically, it demolished the basis of the command economy. Weak states were seen as indispensable for the development of civil society and private enterprise, and they conveniently minimized at the same time any military potential that might pose a threat to the West. Only later in the reform process did it become apparent that the state had been so critically impaired that it was unable to defend itself against the new social forces unleashed by reform (i.e., economic oligarchy, ethnic mobilization, and organized crime).

The demise of the African state as the agent of social transformation followed a different path from Russia's, only to arrive at the same result. Despite efforts to shore up weak administrative capacities, the African state's success in speeding the emergence of civil society proved disappointing. A growing number of scholars came to see the state as concerned primarily with producing and sustaining a new class of bureaucratic bourgeoisie (Shivji 1976), as aid intended for improving government capabilities was directed toward a new class that used the resources for its own benefit (Leys 1976). Strengthening an interventionist state in these circumstances amounted to supporting the efforts of an exploiting class to mold African society to its interest and appropriate for itself the benefits of state control.

In general, the solution seen by the donor community to the problems caused by the overdeveloped state lay in redirecting aid and technical assistance away from the state bureaucracy and toward nongovernmental organizations. This path blended conveniently with a new international emphasis on structural adjustment, economic liberalization, and privatization to support policies that explicitly bypassed the public sphere. The state "had been eclipsed in the eyes of donors by a veil of presumed obsolescence" (Doornbos 1990, 177–78). In its place, the new international community pursued the following objectives: 1) advocacy of privatization and increasing involvement of private enterprise in aid arrangements; 2) diversion of aid funds via nongovernmental organizations; 3) formation of donor-coordinating consortia, with corresponding counterpart "front" organizations, which assumed major policy roles; 4) preference for working with autonomous quasi-governmental organizations; and 5) introduction of highly advanced monitoring methods (for which national expertise was often insufficient) to constitute an effective counterpart in policy discussion and implementation. In Russia as in Africa, the result was a state chronically incapable of achieving basic societal objectives, let alone reform goals.[8] This ideologically mandated weakening of administrative capacity did have one perverse benefit for the strategy of shock therapy: it provided convincing evidence that state institutions were not up to the task of transition. The only alternative had to be devolving policy-making authority to a cohort of reformers.

---

8. A case with striking similarities to that of Russia is the Philippines. Paul Hutchcroft recently described the relationships there between a weak, patrimonial state and a powerful oligarchy of bankers (Hutchcroft 1998). The 1998 collapse of the Russian banking system indicates that, despite its weakened status, the Philippine state is still faring better than its Russian counterpart in reaching compromise with social forces.

The triumph of neoliberal economic ideology over reform also meant the victory of a severer vision of what had to be done and how it should be accomplished. Nothing less than a radical and painful restructuring (which in Russia had to be done wholesale) would suffice, and it had to be done with all deliberate speed. Advocates of more moderate, conservative approaches were denounced as defenders of the old regime. The tension between radical and piecemeal reform described by Albert Hirschman more than three decades earlier (1963) had been won decisively by the former. The harsh edge of reformist ideology also deprived post-Soviet states of some of their most important resources: economic managers. Neoliberal ideology depicted all Soviet-era managers as thoroughly incompetent and corrupt when, in fact, this was not entirely true.[9] A substantial number of managers were competent at their jobs and sincere in their desire to pursue reform—though they were unsure of how to proceed. But the very idea of economic management to many Western economists had unacceptable communist overtones. Transition policy, rather than making administrative competence the touchstone of acceptability, excluded everyone from the previous regime on the basis of their political coloration.

Ideological militancy in economic reform had the effect of replicating in Russia the same "choiceless" democracies described in the experience of many African states (Mkandawire 1999). The exigencies of economic transition, Thandika Mkandawire notes, required an undemocratic remolding of the traditional world and thus comfortably embraced authoritarian legacies. Especially important was the need to insulate institutions such as the Russian Central Bank and key ministries from the democratic process lest the transition be compromised. This explains the continuation of excessive secrecy, a lack of transparency, and the absence of accountability in freely elected governments. Key elements of the crisis management perspective were needlessly antidemocratic. In particular, a negative popular response was singled out as the greatest potential threat to neoliberal reform, as efforts to ameliorate economic and social hardships and shelter productive sectors of the economy threatened to compromise the basic premises of structural adjustment (Mkandawire 1999).[10] These considerations suggest

---

9. A similar example is the unsparing criticism Sachs had for the first RCB chairman, Viktor Gerashchenko, whom Sachs described as "the world's worst central banker." Gerashchenko was no prize-winner, but the revelations that his successor, Sergei Dubinin, profited by investing RCB reserves does little to distinguish high-minded reformers from their communist predecessors.

10. Ironically, postwar Germany and Japan were provided with minimal social and economic guarantees. The United States permitted the protection of some industries, reason-

that the crisis management style was less a temporary device than an alternative style of rule whose authoritarian character resonated favorably in both Africa and the former Soviet Union with traditional political culture.

The Recomposition of Power

The Russian case bears a close resemblance to the "reconfiguration" or "recomposition" of power in the African experience described in Chapter 3 of this book. Whereas international assistance focused on the objective of linear transitions to known societal destinations, traditional sources and forms of Russian power in fact proved remarkably adaptable, making political and social development an unpredictable, nonlinear process. Grant and Nijman refer to this as the "postmodern" perspective of development, where development signifies "a process of social change without a blueprint, a predictable path, or even a purpose, and largely beyond the control of governmental and non-governmental agencies" (Grant and Nijman 1998a, 190). Hence, Russia absorbed Western institutions and the vocabularies of macroeconomic theory yet remained unchanged in many of its traditional authoritarian proclivities for elite rule. The new Russia does not conform to the West's desired image of it, nor has it simply returned to the past. Regrettably, Western critics of Russia often fail to appreciate that, rather than slipping into the past, Russia is actually moving forward in a direction that Western institutions and norms cannot comprehend. This is not a happy outcome, for the contradictions embedded in such recompositions cannot be suppressed indefinitely; they create systems that are perennially unstable and prone to cycles alternating between spasms of development and collapse.

The most disturbing element of this process in Russia is the extent to which "normal" politics and economic behavior have been overtaken by pervasive corruption and organized crime. In the earliest days of Russian reform, foreign capital was to provide the backbone of the new economy and new practices. Bound as they were by the rule of law and norms of Western civil society, it seemed a reasonable bet that foreign business would insist on nothing less in its dealings in Russia. This assessment was, by and

---

ing—correctly—that rapid economic reconstruction was impossible without a vibrant core of economic activity. Of course, in the 1940s economic science had not yet graduated to the neoclassical stage. Moreover, in the 1990s there was no longer a competing power center in the international order that might make a better offer.

large, correct. The principal failing in this approach to reform, however, was that it subsequently deviated from the attraction of foreign investment and concentrated on the speculative redistribution of resources to the newly created domestic economic elite. Foreign investors thus had to sit out a critical window of opportunity and, when they returned to consider Russia, a financial oligarchy was already in place and accorded preferential legal status. Russia had taken, in keeping with Chapter 5, the "low" road of informal and illegal links to the international economy.

Presentability and "Virtual Democracy"

The toleration of a presentable external image of reform is where international aid to Russia reflects its most damaging similarity to recent African experience. IFIs and Western governments were too willing to tolerate the deformation of "reform," and the concept itself was converted into a hollow shell. The level of toleration in the case of Russia strains credulity: as evidence mounted of the pervasive corruption within government and its core privatization program, some Western officials retreated to a remarkable defense. The reform process might be unfair and corrupt at the start, but it nonetheless achieved the most important task of redistributing property. Now, provided the conditions were in place to guarantee the free and unfettered flow of information, property would eventually change hands until it reached the most efficient producers. The lack of democratic accountability was similarly easy to rationalize: Russia had made an excellent electoral start and, with several more iterations, would surely get it right.

It is difficult to comprehend policy-makers adopting such a view given the mounting evidence that Russia possessed a "virtual economy," consuming more value than it produced, and that the public continued in a still deeper withdrawal from civil society, only to have the void filled by organized crime. The answer to this seeming paradox is that Western institutions circled their wagons still more closely around their chosen ideology and instruments, settling for a presentable image of transition from the Yeltsin government. The West responded to the "reconfiguration" of power by reaffirming its faith in "transition." Descriptions of African presentability to the outside world evoke an eerie similarity to Russia: "hybrid regimes [in which] an outward democratic form is energized by an inner authoritarian capacity, especially in the realm of economic policy" (Mkandawire 1999). The "virtual economy" in Russia was thus paralleled by the construction of the "virtual democracy" described by Richard Joseph

(1997, 1999a), the elements of which were given formal basis in citizen rule but with key decision-making insulated from popular involvement: manipulation of democratic transitions by political incumbents, including the use of violence and election fraud; wider popular participation but narrow policy choices and outcomes; and external encouragement of multiparty elections on the premise that they would not threaten vested foreign and domestic economic interests. Two additional criteria could be added to flesh out fully the Russian case: the blurring of institutional boundaries and of any meaningful distinction between public and private spheres; and the shrinkage of public accountability to provide elites with a wide berth for circumventing legal, institutional, and political constraints.

Creating the Commercial Class

The international emphasis on mass privatization in Russia also helped create a form of state-economy relations with greater affinities with the African experience. Despite formal privatization, Russia never succeeded in enforcing a meaningful distinction between public and private spheres or monitoring the limit of state intrusion into social processes and institutions. This was due to the fact that Russian privatization, channeled through the hands of an unaccountable elite, created a corrupt fusion between the public and the commercial sectors. Olga Kryshtanovskaia observed that a process was at work in Russia not dissimilar from private sector development in some African societies: "reformist" elites played a crucial role in determining the specific content and character of financial and entrepreneurial strata (Kryshtanovskaia 1998; Reno 1995; Stavrakis 1998). Having created the private sector, government would be foolish not to rely on the private sector's resources in political struggles; new Russian capitalists likewise saw this as an opportunity to build their own political base in government. But this arrangement could function only if the rule of law were relaxed to permit a porous boundary between public and private.

An internationally acceptable image of distinct "state" and "private" sectors was created in Russia, but the reality of their interaction is still best captured by Jean-François Bayart: "In Africa, the state *is* the prime (though not the only) channel of accumulation. . . . Even the successful businessmen in the informal sector are highly dependent on the state because they need constantly to circumvent regulations and obtain official permits. It is, therefore, otiose to seek to establish a conceptual difference between the

private and public sectors" (Bayart 1986). Only in the two years following
the 1996 presidential elections did departure from this comparison
emerge, as Russian bankers (the "oligarchs") acquired sufficient strength
to become the dominant element in the state-economy relationship. But
the 1998 financial collapse provisionally returned the state to its more familiar position as master over a disintegrating economy.

The Personnel Factor: Domestic and International

The genuinely surprising aspect of international aid to the successor states
to the former Soviet Union has been almost exclusively neglected: the personnel responsible for shaping and administering bilateral international assistance policy were drawn predominantly from African, South Asian, and
(to a lesser extent) Latin American postings. USAID, for example, had no
area competence in the former Soviet Union. Early on, the agency scorn-
fully rejected the argument that existing personnel had to be retrained before being posted to the post-Soviet states or, alternatively, area specialists
had to be brought into the USAID bureaucracy. In effect, USAID staffed
its post-Soviet region missions with individuals ignorant of the cultural
and political context within which they operated. It was not surprising, for
example, to find key assistance personnel in Moscow, Kiev, Almaty, and
elsewhere whose previous postings had never allowed them to set foot outside of Africa or Asia. Consequently, the implementation of aid policy was
seen largely as a matter of bureaucratic routine developed in other areas
of the world. If post-Soviet Eurasia was indeed different, few in the bilateral assistance community were prepared to understand this reality and act
accordingly.

The ideology that animated the Bretton Woods institutions in the previous two or three decades was that of macroeconomic stabilization and
structural adjustment; regional specialization was irrelevant for the implementation of IMF and World Bank policies. Hence, as the IMF engaged
in a massive hiring binge to meet the expanded demands of assistance to
the post-Soviet world, it sought personnel whose knowledge reinforced
IMF values. The goal, after all, was to make these states adjust to a new
economic reality, and cultural variables counted for little in this regard. Finally, there was the key problem of finding a reform team that could be
trusted to administer the entry of Russia into the global economy and community of free-market societies. Again, the problem here was a familiar one
in the world of development assistance: the success of externally imposed

reform rested on its implementation by individuals who stood the most to gain from its success.

Explanations for Convergence

The uniform application of doctrinaire macroeconomic approaches through a common set of international institutions does much to explain the intertwining of Russian and African fates, yet several perplexing issues remain. It is unclear, in the first instance, why the West settled for the appearance of reform over lasting achievements. Several considerations in the present analysis provide at least some tentative explanations. Policy-makers, especially those responsible for foreign aid, found the modernist paradigm—with its assumptions of linear progress—far more reassuring than alternative understandings of the reconfiguration of power. The latter implied that we could not fully control the essence of development, nor could we be secure in the knowledge of what could be achieved within a given society. Moreover, it would have required a rare act of political courage for Western leaders to acknowledge that the result of their efforts in a place like Russia would fall far short of the free-market liberal state. What remained was an irresistible temptation to engage in wishful thinking by casting major systemic problems as minor glitches that could be overcome if only policy were applied more diligently.

The appearance of reform was also preferred because the West couched its efforts in the context of a false dichotomy: the traditional (read: authoritarian) world of the past and the democratic legal order that was promised. This view failed to appreciate the elasticity of traditional political culture, a feature that is at the heart of the recomposition of power. Western approaches have wrongly assumed that the systemic crises of Russian and African societies have reflected a rejection of traditional forms of domination. In reality, they are merely another turn in the cycle of perpetual instability that has characterized domestic politics.

This problem was compounded by the blatant hypocrisy with which the West sought to implement its reforms. Free-market democracy was the goal, yet it was to be achieved by sustaining in power an elite that could not survive a fair electoral contest without manipulation of the process. Similarly, mass privatization that provided unfair access to personal intimates of the ruling elite demonstrated not the hope for a different future, but merely a new set of opportunists. Domestic political elites were also quick to realize that the style of reform's implementation provided them with strong incentives to persevere in old patterns of behavior. If the choice was between a traditional political style and a world in which pious language masked the impulse to a familiar authoritarianism, there really was no choice at all.

The postcommunist experience of reform in eastern Europe provides the basis for a second, more serious, issue tied to this analysis. Some scholars (for example, Bunce 1999) have used the generally successful reform policies in eastern European societies to make the claim that there is no inherent contradiction between neoliberal economic reform and democratization. But such a conclusion seems premature, for although east-central Europe's successful transition adds complexity and comparative richness to the relationship between economic reform and democratization, it does not necessarily mean the absence of contradiction between the two. The eastern European case instead reveals that the presence of key social, political, and cultural assets during transition permits some societies to achieve macroeconomic stabilization while simultaneously blunting undue damage to their democratic evolution. In essence, higher levels of human capital and administrative capacity, combined with a less invasive and shorter communist history, provided some eastern European states with the resources to control the political damage that doctrinaire neoliberal economic reform would otherwise wreak. Russia's profoundly deeper and more destructive epoch of communist rule, by contrast, left it with no reservoir of administrative skill or institutional strength to check what amounted to a policy guided primarily by ideological zeal.

The focus of this chapter has been on the impact of foreign aid on transition in Russia (and Africa) rather than a thorough examination of the relationship between economic and political reform. In this regard, the evidence from the Russian case and its similarity to key syndromes manifest in African societies suggest that aid played an important role in bringing about negative results. Russia's transition era in particular reveals several major policy blunders committed by the assistance community that help explain why Russia succumbed to the destructive impact of neoliberal economic reform while some of its eastern European neighbors were spared the same fate. First, the Russian reform program concentrated on the intentional destruction of state capacity—a goal that ultimately undermined prospects for the emergence of the rule of law and civil society. Second, the Russian privatization program repeatedly appeared as a fundamentally destructive force. It was accorded such high political priority that it trumped any effort to develop sound economic policies and consolidate political reforms. It was, in fact, in the unregulated Russian privatization process that the central pathologies presently plaguing Russia were born. In short, not only did parts of eastern Europe amass a critical minimum of administrative capacity and possessed precommunist institutional memory to exercise a moderating influence on the macroeconomic reform processes, they also were spared the doctrinaire application of economic reform urged on Russia by the West. This suggests that had an alternative policy been pursued in Russia—one lacking the fixation on privatization at all costs—it might have been possible to reduce the negative political impact of neoliberal reform policy.

Were there credible alternatives to the specific aid policies pursued by Western states? Yes. Clearly, the urgency placed on rapid privatization was political, and not economic, in nature. Dismantling communism took precedence over the provision of a productive economy. A more balanced economic policy, entailing a gradual transfer of property to the private sector, would have been conducive to greater stability and reduced opportunities for a narrow clique to monopolize control over productive assets. On a more general level, Russia would have been better served by a policy designed to promote gradual transition to capitalism and democracy. The rapid destruction of state capacity, in retrospect, created the opportunity for a profound criminalization of Russian society while retarding economic reform that might have sustained a minimal level of productivity. Insufficient attention has been paid to the opportunities for the Russian economy and polity to reform in the absence of Western assistance. Similarly, a significant number of medium-sized entrepreneurs, relying largely on their own resources, emerged in the early part of the decade. Ironically, the subsequent introduction of massive World Bank assistance in certain respects impaired many of these new businesses (Stavrakis 1996a). This last point suggests that the West might have considered—in contrast to the calls for a new Marshall Plan—a far more modest program from which it would have derived far better and more consistent results. Ultimately, Western institutions would have been better served by finding a means to insert ideas and practices that incrementally modified the content and character of traditional political culture, rather than presenting reform as an alternative order. Such a transformation would have taken longer to accomplish and required Western institutions to comprehend how cultural and institutional variables could usefully constrain the debilitating impact of macroeconomic policy on democratic processes. Given the record of the international assistance community in helping to reduce two different regions in the international system to such low levels of promise and performance, there would seem to be little left to lose.

References

Bates, Robert H. 1999. "The Economic Bases of Democratization." Pp. 83–94 in *State, Conflict, and Democracy in Africa,* ed. Richard Joseph. Boulder: Lynne Rienner.

Bayart, Jean-François. 1986. "Civil Society in Africa." Pp. 110–25 in *Political Domination in Africa,* ed. Patrick Chabal. Cambridge: Cambridge University Press.

Bayart, Jean-François, Stephen Ellis, and Béatrice Hibou. 1997. *La criminialisation de l'Etat en Afrique.* Brussels: Editions Complexe.

Boldyrev, Yuri. 1996. "V strane sozdany ideal'nye usloviia dlia korruptsii." *Novaia yezhednevnaia gazeta.* 28 October: 1.

———. 1997. Interview with the author. Moscow. 15 January.

Bunce, Valerie. 1999. "The Political Economy of Postsocialism." *Slavic Review* 58, no. 4 (winter).

Clapham, Christopher. 1996. *Africa and the International System: The Politics of State Survival.* Cambridge: Cambridge University Press.

Cohen, Steven F. 1999a. "Russian Studies without Russia." *Post-Soviet Affairs* 15, no. 1: 37–55.

———. 1999b. "'Transition' Is a Notion Rooted in U.S. Ego." *New York Times.* 27 March.

Dietz, Ton, and John Houtkamp. 1998. "The Rise and Fall of Structural Development Aid." Pp. 89–102 in *The Global Crisis in Foreign Aid,* ed. Richard Grant and Jan Nijman. Syracuse: Syracuse University Press.

Doornbos, Martin. 1990. "The African State in Academic Debate: Retrospect and Prospect." *Journal of Modern African Studies* 28, no. 2.

Dornbusch, Rudiger, and S. Edwards. 1992. "Macroeconomics of Populism." Pp. 7–13 in *The Macroeconomics of Populism in Latin America,* ed. Rudiger Dornbusch and S. Edwards. Chicago: University of Chicago Press.

Ermath, Fritz W. 1999. "Seeing Russia Plain: The Russian Crisis and American Intelligence." *National Interest* (spring): 5–14.

Escobar, Arturo. 1995. *Encountering Development: The Making and Unmaking of the Third World.* Princeton: Princeton University Press.

Forrest, Joshua B. 1998. "State Inversion and Nonstate Politics." Pp. 45–56 in *The African State at a Critical Juncture: Between Disintegration and Reconfiguration,* ed. Leonardo A. Villalon and Phillip A. Huxtable. Boulder: Lynne Rienner.

Glaz'ev, Sergei. 1998. "Krakh 'stabilizatsionnoi programmy' i imperativ perekhoda k mobilizatsionnoi modeli." *Rossiiskii ekonomicheskii zhurnal* 9–10 (September–October).

Graham, Thomas. 1995. "Novyi rossiiskii rezhim." *Nezavismaia gazeta.* 23 November.

Grant, Richard, and Jan Nijman. 1998a. "The Emerging Transnational Liberal Order and the Crisis of Modernity." Pp. 183–95 in *The Global Crisis in Foreign Aid,* ed. Richard Grant and Jan Nijman. Syracuse: Syracuse University Press.

———, eds. 1998b. *The Global Crisis in Foreign Aid.* Syracuse: Syracuse University Press.

Gulhati, Ravi. 1990. "Who Makes Economic Policy in Africa and How?" *World Development* 18, no. 8: 1147–61.

Hirschman, Albert O. 1963. *Journeys toward Progress: Studies of Economic Policymaking in Latin America.* New York: Twentieth Century Fund.

Hutchcroft, Paul D. 1998. *Booty Capitalism: The Politics of Banking in the Philippines.* Ithaca: Cornell University Press.

Illarionov, Andrei. 1998. "Kak byl organizovan rossiiskii finansovyi krizis." Parts I and II. *Voprosy ekonomiki* 11–12 (November–December).

Israel, Arturo. 1990. "The Changing Role of the State: Institutional Dimensions." Working paper WPS 495, Public Sector Management and Private Sector Development, World Bank, August.

Jackson, Robert H. 1990. *Quasi-States: Sovereignty, International Relations, and the Third World.* Cambridge: Cambridge University Press.

Joseph, Richard. 1997. "Democratization in Africa after 1989: Comparative and Theoretical Perspectives." *Comparative Politics* 29, no. 3: 363–82.

———. 1999a. "The Reconfiguration of Power in Late-Twentieth-Century Africa." Pp. 57–80 in *State, Conflict, and Democracy in Africa,* ed. Richard Joseph. Boulder: Lynne Rienner.

———, ed. 1999b. *State, Conflict, and Democracy in Africa.* Boulder: Lynne Rienner.

Kosals, L. 1998. "Tenevaia ekonomika kak osobennost' rossiiskogo kapitalizma." *Voprosy ekonomiki* 10 (October).

Kramer, David J. 1997. "Missing Money in Russia." *Washington Times.* 7 March.

Kryshtanovskaia, Olga. 1998. "Smert' oligarkhii: Oligarkhiia soderzhala gosudarstvo v litse ego kliuchevykh chinovnikov." *Argumenty i fakty.* 11 November: 5.

Leys, Colin. 1976. "The 'Overdeveloped' Post-Colonial State: A Re-evaluation." *Review of African Political Economy* 5 (January–April).

Malia, Martin. 1999. "Communist Legacy Foreclosed Choices." *New York Times.* 27 March.

Mandeville, Bernard. 1997. *The Fable of the Bees and Other Writings.* Abridged and ed. E. J. Hundert. Indianapolis: Hackett.

Maravall, Jose Maria. 1994. "Myth of the Authoritarian Advantage." *Journal of Democracy* 5 (October): 17–31.

Mau, Vladimir. 1998. "Politicheskaia priroda i uroki finansovogo krizisa." *Voprosy ekonomiki* 11 (November).

McFaul, Michael. 1999. "The Demon Within." *Moscow Times.* 2 March.

Michalak, Wieslaw. 1998. "Assistance to Transitions." Pp. 113–29 in *The Global Crisis in Foreign Aid,* ed. Richard Grant and Jan Nijman. Syracuse: Syracuse University Press.

Mkandawire, Thandika. 1999. "Crisis Management and the Making of 'Choiceless' Democracies." Pp. 119–36 in *State, Conflict, and Democracy in Africa,* ed. Richard Joseph. Boulder: Lynne Rienner.

Nagy, Piroska Mahócsi. 2000. *The Meltdown of the Russian State: The Deformation and Collapse of the State in Russia.* Cheltenham: Edward Elgar.

PriceWaterhouseCoopers. 1999. "Report on the Relations between the Central Bank of Russia and the Financial Management Co., Ltd." 4 August. Obtained at www.legacyrus.com.

Przeworski, Adam. 1991. *Democracy and the Market: Political and Economic Reforms in Eastern Europe and Latin America.* Cambridge: Cambridge University Press.

Radaev, Vadim. 1998. "O roli nasilliia v rossiiskikh delovykh ontnosheniakh." *Voprosy ekonomiki* 10 (October).

Reddaway, Peter, and Dmitri Glinski. 1999. "The Ravages of 'Market Bolshevism.'" *Journal of Democracy* 10, no. 2.

Reno, William. 1995. *Corruption and State Politics in Sierra Leone.* Cambridge: Cambridge University Press.

———. 1998. "Sierra Leone: Weak States and the New Sovereignty Game." Pp. 93–108 in *The African State at a Critical Juncture: Between Disintegration and Reconfiguration,* ed. Leonardo A. Villalon and Phillip A. Huxtable. Boulder: Lynne Rienner.

Rothchild, Donald. 1987. "Hegemony and State Softness: Some Variations in Elite Responses." Pp. 117–48 in *The African State in Transition,* ed. Zaki Ergas. New York: St. Martin's.

Sachs, Jeffrey. 1998. "New Team, Old Answers, for Russia's Economy." *The Christian Science Monitor.* 14 September.

Schatzberg, Michael G. 1988. *The Dialectics of Oppression in Zaire.* Bloomington: Indiana University Press.

Shane, Scott. 1999. "Russia, Though Muddling, Will Recover Its Imperial Role." *Baltimore Sun.* 7 March.

Shivji, Issa. 1976. *Class Struggles in Tanzania.* New York: Monthly Review Press.

Simes, Dimitri K. 1999. *After the Collapse: Russia Seeks Its Place as a Great Power.* New York: Simon and Schuster.

Stavrakis, Peter J. 1993. "State Building in Post-Soviet Russia: The 'Chicago Boys' and the Decline of Administrative Capacity." Occasional Paper no. 254, Kennan Institute for Advanced Russian Studies, Woodrow Wilson International Center for Scholars, October.

———. 1996a. "Bull in a China Shop: USAID's Post-Soviet Mission." *Demokratizatsiya* 4, no. 2

———. 1996b. "The Soft State and the Emergence of Russian Regional Politics." Pp. 185–205 in *Russia and Eastern Europe after Communism: The Search for New Political, Economic, and Security Systems,* ed. Michael Kraus and Ronald Liebowitz. Boulder: Westview.

———. 1998. "Shadow Politics: The Russian State in the 21st Century." U.S. Army War College, Strategic Studies Institute, Carlisle, Penn, December.

Summers, Lawrence. 1994. "Foreword." In *Voting for Reform,* ed. Stephan Haggard and Sylvia Maxfield. New York: Oxford University Press.

Tanzi, Vito. 1993. *Transition to Market: Studies in Fiscal Reform.* Washington: International Monetary Fund.

van de Walle, Nicolas. 1998. "Globalization and African Democracy." Pp. 95–118 in *State, Conflict, and Democracy in Africa,* ed. Richard Joseph. Boulder: Lynne Rienner.

Villalon, Leonardo A., and Phillip A. Huxtable, eds. 1998. *The African State at a Critical Juncture: Between Disintegration and Reconfiguration.* Boulder: Lynne Rienner.

Wedel, Janine. 1998. *Collision and Collusion: The Strange Case of Assistance to Central and Eastern Europe.* New York: St. Martin's.

White, David. 1997. Lecture. Kennan Institute for Advanced Russian Studies, Woodrow Wilson International Center for Scholars, Washington, 1 April.

Woodward, Susan L. 1995. *Balkan Tragedy: Chaos and Dissolution after the Cold War.* Washington: Brookings Institution Press.

World Bank. 1982. *Russian Economic Reform: Crossing the Threshold of Structural Change.* Washington: World Bank.

12

Economic Reform and the Discourse of Democracy in Africa: Resolving the Contradictions

PETER M. LEWIS

In the 1990s, the currents of economic and political change converged in Africa. Throughout the preceding decade, the region had been beleaguered by a wide-ranging economic crisis. A host of countries had experienced a syndrome of declining economic growth, stagnant output, mounting external debt, general fiscal crisis, and widening domestic poverty. Facing severe budgetary constraints and balance-of-payments shortfalls, many governments had turned to the International Monetary Fund (IMF) and the World Bank for assistance in alleviating debt obligations and securing new resources. These multilateral institutions, along with bilateral donors, imposed conditions on the provision of aid to induce African governments to reform their economies. By the end of the decade, a majority of countries had embarked on donor-supported stabilization and structural adjustment programs. These policies were rarely pursued in a consistent or coherent fashion, and their effects differed significantly among states. Broadly speaking, however, African economies were substantially liberalized, and a number of countries showed hesitant signs of revival in growth and production.

The halting and uneven course of economic reform was accompanied in the early 1990s by widespread pressures for political renovation. As political transitions unfolded in eastern Europe, the former Soviet Union, and

South Africa, demands for democratization gained momentum throughout sub-Saharan Africa. Domestic forces and international influences prompted significant liberalization of African political systems. Here, too, there were diverse outcomes, encompassing democratic transitions, thwarted transitions, civil conflict, and even state collapse. Yet in a remarkably short span of time, many countries in the region shifted from relatively restrictive and noncompetitive systems to more open and plural politics. In 1989, nearly half the countries in Africa were ruled by military regimes, and most of the remaining states had long-standing single-party or dominant-party regimes. By 1994, only a handful of military regimes remained across the continent, and there were no longer any de jure single-party systems in the region (Bratton and van de Walle 1997). During this period more than thirty countries legalized multiparty politics, and at least sixteen made a transition to nominal democracy through elections that unseated incumbent regimes.

The problematic relationship between economic and political reform poses some of the leading questions in contemporary African development. Mainly by historical coincidence, numerous African countries are concurrently engaged in economic and political liberalization. As is the case in many of the former Leninist states of Eurasia, a number of African countries face basic problems of economic restructuring while they seek to consolidate democratic institutions and practices. Viewed comparatively, the origins, timing, and extent of reform have varied significantly in these regions. Economic reform programs were commonly initiated in Africa during the early 1980s, and the subsequent wave of political change merged with ongoing processes of economic adjustment. African countries rarely experienced the rapid simultaneous transitions witnessed in many of the former communist states. Moreover, political and economic reform in Africa have arguably created fewer abrupt departures from the institutions and symbols of the ancien régime than was the case in parts of the former Soviet Union and eastern Europe. The dynamics of dual transitions, however, raise some common questions. Can new democracies manage the demands of economic liberalization and restructuring? How does economic performance affect the consolidation of democracy? What patterns of reform are most likely to be successful and sustainable?

This chapter examines the reciprocal interaction of political and economic reform in Africa's new democracies. It concerns, first, the effects of political transition on economic performance and, second, the influence of economic outcomes on democratic consolidation. In the first instance, I focus on the crucial relationship between regime type and state capabilities. The second question is mainly concerned with the broad distributive effects of economic reform.

As observed elsewhere in this book, the problems of regime change and economic restructuring have been linked to a general crisis of the state in Africa. The debilities of African states have been a major source of poor economic performance in the region and, conversely, declining economies have undermined public institutions in many countries. Africa's weak states have largely been controlled (and shaped) by nondemocratic regimes. Given the close historical association among authoritarian rule, state decline, and economic malaise, we might reasonably infer that political liberalization would create possibilities for new directions in economic management and performance. In light of the variety of economic outcomes in new democracies, however, it is clear that regime change does not necessarily foster economic revival. Variations among democratic and nondemocratic regimes are more significant than regime type per se, and a discerning comparative framework is needed to account for differences in economic performance.

This analysis starts from the premise that economic recovery in the region relies on improved state capabilities. If the shift toward democratic governance is to yield economic advances, then new regimes must displace important features of the authoritarian legacy and enhance the developmental roles of states. Evidence from Africa's new democracies suggests that limited changes have been made in the political context of economic management, and regime change does not substantially affect economic performance in the near term. I analyze four factors influencing the relative effectiveness of state economic roles: the character of leadership, the configuration of supportive coalitions, the quality of peak institutions, and the international context of reform. In most democratizing African countries, these variables have reflected substantial continuity over the past decade. In particular, transitional regimes in Africa have not seen the emergence of strong coalitions for economic reform, and democratically elected leaders have often sustained clientelist politics. The range of policy choice for leaders has also been constrained by the requisites of international agencies and markets.

The character of economic reform in new democracies also affects the consolidation of transitional regimes and the constituency for future policy change. In this area, the distribution of gains from reform is decisive. If new governments foster consistent economic growth and allow for more broadly distributed gains, there is a greater likelihood for the coalescence of new constituencies for reform. Where traditional patronage structures endure, economic adjustment is usually compromised and elected regimes experience legitimacy problems. Although economic performance and distributive concerns may influence democratic consolidation, there is not a clear monotonic relationship among them; the persistence of poor economic performance does not necessarily invalidate democratic rule, and there is tentative evidence that citizens evaluate regimes on a range of qualities apart from the provision of economic goods.

The rest of this chapter proceeds as follows. The next section elaborates the linkages among state formation, political regimes, and economic performance in Africa. I then consider the challenges of parallel transitions in light of prevailing debates regarding the general relationships of democratization and economic development. In the succeeding section, I examine the specific problems of regime change and economic renovation in the African context, considering the attributes required in order for states to play a developmental role and the factors that influence the developmental capacities of regimes. The discussion addresses the key analytical features of leadership, constituencies, institutions, and international context as they are reflected in democratizing countries in the region. This is followed by an evaluation of economic policy and performance in countries undergoing political transition. I conclude with some observations about democratic sustainability and some comparative reflections.

States, Regimes, and Economic Performance in Africa

Africa's economic crisis prompted intense debate about the causes of continental decline. Alongside contending perspectives that focused on the effects of adverse global markets or domestic policy errors, a more explicitly political analysis emerged, linking the crisis of the region's economies with the infirmities of African states (Hyden 1983; Callaghy 1988; Sandbrook 1985). Africa's personalized, authoritarian regimes have manifestly failed to promote effective economic management or institutional development. This problem is directly related to the strategy of governance pursued by most leaders in the region. In this regard, the concept of neopatrimonial rule has provided insight into the region's political economies. Neopatrimonial systems reflect the trappings of Weberian bureaucratic states, although they are essentially structured and controlled along patrimonial lines (Clapham 1982, 1985; Bratton and van de Walle 1994, 1997; Lewis 1994, 1996). Beneath a veneer of formal administration and law inherited from the colonial regime, neopatrimonial states are organized by kinship, faction, and patron-client networks. Authority is highly concentrated, and the prerogatives wielded by personal rulers typically undermine the standing of laws and organizations. Governing largely through patronage politics, these regimes depend on a regular flow of resources to secure the loyalty of state agents and core constituencies.

Neopatrimonial rule has held sway in countries with a variety of ideological and policy orientations. Commonly, however, this pattern of state formation has yielded poor economic performance. Africa has certainly seen a range of outcomes, from the diffident growth policies of Kenya or the Ivory Coast to the predatory depths of Congo-Kinshasa under Mobutu Sese Seko, Ghana under I. K. Acheampong, or Liberia under Samuel Doe. Yet the secular trend in economic performance for the region's personalized, nondemocratic regimes was broadly downward, especially in the 1980s. Many factors influenced the continent-wide crisis, including exogenous price shocks, trends in global financial markets, the vagaries of weather, and widespread conflict, along with numerous policy distortions. There is also a clear link, however, between the character of political regimes and the region's economic travails. The effects of neopatrimonial rule can be seen in the domains of economic policy, fiscal management, and institutional change.

At the policy level, leaders who rely on patronage have a strong propensity to favor statist measures and relatively closed economies. Personal rulers extend their leverage through the political regulation of resources and markets, and interventionist regimes seek to expand their discretionary authority. Widespread administrative control over the economy fosters rent-seeking behavior, as private actors seek access to special gains in politically regulated markets. Although commonly rationalized in terms of economic development, statist policies have more often been driven by the requisites of clientelist politics, and impulsive interventions into African economies have undermined investment and production. Furthermore, measures to insulate African economies from global markets have impeded trade and capital inflows.

In the fiscal realm, the patrimonial character of these regimes is reflected in the lax distinction between public and private funds and the arbitrary use of state resources for personal aggrandizement or political advantage. Pervasive corruption, opaque budgeting, and the capricious use of finances give rise to chronic fiscal crisis. Public resources are commonly diverted to current consumption and lost through capital flight, rather than being channeled toward productive accumulation.

Over the long run, the institutional effects of neopatrimonial rule have been especially damaging. The interventionist goals of these regimes stand in sharp contrast to their limited capabilities. Autocratic control and mercurial administration have hindered the development of effective state institutions. In some respects the failure of institutions may be ascribed to scarce resources (often stemming from the fiscal crises noted above), but in many instances authoritarian rulers have systematically hobbled organizations that might offer countervailing power to their authority (Migdal 1988). African judiciaries, bureaucracies, central banks, and legislatures have commonly been politicized and manipulated by strong leaders. In addition, basic infrastructure and investments in human capital have been neglected. As a consequence, African states have been unable to provide the essential collective goods necessary for economic growth and transformation. Both state socialism and market-oriented approaches have foundered on the shoals of institutional weakness.

This political legacy has been inhospitable to the market-led strategies that have occupied most African countries since the late 1980s. Neopatrimonial regimes have great difficulty making credible policy commitments, given the hazards of reversal by impetuous leaders or bureaucratic fiat. In a context of weak formal institutions, states cannot establish stable property rights or reliably enforce contracts, two foundations of effective market systems. In addition, the traditional hostility of authoritarian governments toward civic organization has undermined the creation of private norms and enforcement mechanisms. Economic actors face high political risks in these circumstances, as their assets may be ruined by policy uncertainty or the arbitrary actions of officials. The common response is to avoid commitments to fixed capital, notably productive facilities, in favor of more liquid assets such as real estate, trade goods, or cash. Capital flight is a corollary of this strategy, as local capital-holders seek higher returns and greater security by investing abroad. The adverse political setting for investment and production in Africa has severely constrained economic growth, and market actors have provided a meager supply response to the incentives proffered by orthodox adjustment policies.

Neopatrimonial rule is also profoundly inequitable in its operations and effects. Although the distribution of patronage is evidently sufficient for the stabilization of many regimes, it reinforces skewed, rigid social divisions, whether defined along class or along ethnic lines. The pyramid of clientelist politics is narrow at the top, and these states have not provided mechanisms for the expansion of economic benefits or the redistribution of centrally controlled resources. They typically secure extravagant gains for the ruler and a small circle of retainers and cronies, while largely excluding popular groups from state largesse and protected markets. A few governments, such as those in Kenya or the Ivory Coast, have provided some benefits to broader elite and middle-class groups, whereas others, such as those in Guinea, Congo-Kinshasa, or Zambia, have pursued symbolic populist policies. Despite these variations in strategy and style, the inequitable effects of neopatrimonial rule are evident in weak entrepreneurship, the slow development of middle classes, high rates of poverty, and scant social provisions.

State decay and economic malaise proceeded in tandem in the 1970s and 1980s. Neopatrimonial regimes fostered stagnation in African economies through the cumulative effects of policy errors, fiscal dissipation, and institutional frailty. The resulting scarcity of output and revenues further eroded the resources of these states, instigating more rapid decline (Chazan and Rothchild 1993). This downward spiral, largely domestic in scope, was well advanced when the oil-price shocks of the late 1970s and the debt crisis of 1982 pushed African economies into rapid decline. Economic stagnation gripped most countries throughout the 1980s as governments were slow to respond to the initial crisis, and the subsequent adoption of stabilization or adjustment measures yielded only gradual results. Fiscal problems and dwindling foreign exchange dried up sources of patronage and rents through which leaders secured political allegiance. The need for debt relief accentuated the role of the multilateral financial institutions in promoting policy change, and the resulting orthodox reform programs further reduced patronage outlets and weakened government capabilities. Stricter budget constraints, more transparent public expenditures, a reduction in popular subsidies, and widespread privatization all served to loosen the control of neopatrimonial rulers over finances and markets. Orthodox reforms also prompted a contraction of state roles through spending cuts, retrenchments, and the shift of functions to private providers.

Ultimately, the decline of states and economies created conditions for the collapse of many neopatrimonial regimes. A number of scholars have attributed the wave of democratic pressures in Africa to the weakening of traditional elites and ruling coalitions in the region (Bratton 1994; Westebbe 1994; Herbst 1994). Severe reductions in the discretionary resources available to leaders prompted an unraveling of patronage networks and supportive constituencies for numerous authoritarian governments. With few sources of control apart from material inducement or coercion, many governments were vulnerable to opposition challenges from disaffected elites and popular groups.

The dramatic shifts in the international environment after 1989 served as a catalyst for regime change. With the rapid decline of cold war rivalries, governments and donors in the developed world signaled that they were no longer willing to subsidize neopatrimonial regimes simply for strategic gain, and African governments were subject to new pressures and conditions for reform. African states exhibit comparatively high levels of dependence on foreign aid, and the reduction of external support, including security assistance, weakened many authoritarian incumbents. The demonstration effects of democratic transitions in other regions and in neighboring states also served to embolden dissent and dishearten authoritarian leaders, quickening the process of change in many African countries.

It should be emphasized that these external forces did not determine the results of political reform in individual states. International factors can persuasively explain the timing of regime changes in Africa, but not the course of particular transitions. Government and opposition wielded different resources and pursued diverse strategies in different countries, and the range of reform outcomes should be traced to these domestic forces (Bratton and van de Walle 1992, 1997). Comparing Benin, Cameroon, and Liberia, for instance, we can identify the common influences of economic decline, state decay, and changing external relations in the decline of neopatrimonial rule. However, the distinctive actions of incumbents and the character of their opposition produced a democratic transition in the first instance, stymied reform in the second, and state collapse in the third.

Now that we have analyzed the political sources of Africa's economic decline and the factors contributing to regime change in the region after 1989, we will review the theoretical debates over the relationship between political and economic reform. This theory will frame the later discussion of states and developmental roles in Africa in a context of democratization.

Democracy and Economic Reform: Debates and Propositions

The "third wave" of global democratization coincided with an extensive process of economic adjustment in developing countries and a dramatic transformation of economies in the former communist states. These circumstances prompted a flurry of discussion about the relationship between democratization and economic reform. One view, derived from theories of modernization, regards economic and political liberalization as mutually reinforcing. More than four decades ago, the sociologist Seymour Martin Lipset emphasized the association between market economies and stable democracies, inferring that the process of economic modernization generated myriad effects that were beneficial for democratic politics (Lipset 1959).

The association observed by Lipset, although subject to some refinement, has largely been confirmed by subsequent research (Diamond 1992; Rueschemeyer, Stephens, and Stephens 1992). In recent years, the affinity between democracy and capitalism has been interpreted even more emphatically by some analysts who perceive a "virtuous circle" between market economies and pluralist politics. In their view, economic liberalization will tend to foster political liberalization, and political opening in turn will advance market reform. Successful market economies can enhance general welfare, disperse social power, and emancipate resources from the grasp of the state; these processes tend to undermine the control of centralized regimes while fostering social forces that challenge the arbitrary power of rulers. Economic well-being or positive assessments by the public of future prospects also encourage moderation and political stability. Conversely, democratization gives voice to such constituencies as private business and the professional middle classes, who have a stake in a liberal economy and a concern for responsible economic management. Political inclusion, especially of previously deprived groups, may also enhance equity. A number of observers, most notably the major international donors, have advanced these conclusions.

A divergent view holds that economic and political liberalization are more likely to be inimical. Democratic politics tend to encumber economic reform, and poor economic performance will undermine fledgling democracies. Rather than a virtuous circle, a vicious cycle is projected. In this view, economic reform gives rise to disruptive social tensions that erode political stability, and electoral regimes may be especially vulnerable to such pressures. Economic liberalization redistributes opportunities and resources, prompting a variety of interests to defend their entrenched positions (Przeworski 1991). Urban workers, government employees, middle-class wage-earners, and import-competing manufacturers are among the groups who mobilize against the loss of entitlements. Consequently, political leaders are faced with the alternatives of retreating from reform or pushing ahead through authoritarian means. In the postcommunist states, the particular inequities arising from rapid transition create additional tensions (Hellman 1998). In many states, the former party elites (*nomenklatura*) have cornered political power and the gains from privatization, and the rise of criminal syndicates is frequently associated with the emergence of a market economy, as Chapters 4, 6, and 11 in this book suggest.

One argument posits that authoritarian regimes evince some potential advantages in pursuing stabilization and economic growth. Cases as diverse as South Korea, Chile, and Ghana indicate that certain types of authoritarian regimes can assert relative autonomy from particularistic lobbying and successfully undertake politically risky economic restructuring. The stronger East Asian economies have also achieved relatively good levels of equity along with rapid growth, and they have initiated political liberalization after a burst of growth (Deyo 1987; Haggard 1990; Callaghy 1993).

These positions were delineated at the beginning of the democratic waves in Africa and Eurasia. During the ensuing decade, however, a more nuanced view emerged. The comparative experience of countries undergoing dual transitions has yielded few cases in which liberal democracy has developed *pari passu* with market capitalism. If the virtuous circle is not in evidence, neither is its strongest counterpoint. A number of new democracies appear capable of implementing basic reform policies and maintaining economic stability. Although there have been reversals or "recessions" of democracy in Africa and in post-Soviet Eurasia, it is often difficult to link these directly to the effects of economic malaise (although Chapter 11 presents a contrary view). This lack of direct evidence has led some analysts to propose that the implicit connection between economic and political reform may be more logical than real, and that these processes can be uncoupled, at least in the near term. This argument holds that democratization is a good in itself, and that democratic governments gain legitimacy from such attributes as elections, more open participation, improved human rights, and greater accountability (Diamond 1999). Although the delivery of economic growth and public services certainly influences legitimacy, they are not necessarily the main criteria affecting democratic consolidation. This conclusion is strengthened by evidence that citizens in new democracies attribute economic performance to particular leaders or parties rather than to whole political systems (Duch 1995; Haggard and Kaufman 1995). In short, some question remains as to whether popular approval for democracy is predicated mainly on instrumental concerns (Bratton and Mattes 1999). In addition, skilled leaders or political parties have considerable leeway to manipulate policies and public perceptions so as to evade the adverse effects of economic restructuring. Regimes are not necessarily doomed by economic failure, and adept politicians can use democratic institutions to manage reform.

The Challenges of Reform in Africa

The legacies of state weakness, shallow democratic endowments, and ineffectual adjustment create myriad challenges to political and economic transition in Africa. These legacies affect both the durability and the quality of democratization. Recent work in comparative democratization has suggested that, although transitions may occur at any level of development, democracies in poor countries have a greater likelihood of failure than those in higher-income settings (Przeworski and Limongi 1997). This inference seems to be borne out by the African experience. For instance, among the sixteen African countries that achieved democratic transitions between 1989 and 1994, six (the Central African Republic, Congo-Brazzaville, Guinea-Bissau, Lesotho, Niger, and Sao Tome and Principe) have experienced violent challenges to the new regime or the ouster of democratic governments. Another long-standing democratic government, that in the Gambia, was overthrown by the military. The historically high rate of democratic mortality in the region has persisted through the recent wave of change.

Apart from the question of regime survival, the character of democratic governance also forms a prominent concern. Democratic theorists have long distinguished between procedural forms of democracy, where a minimum set of democratic rules and rights are observed, and substantive democracy, in which citizens are broadly included in the political arena and the populace exercises an effective voice (Schumpeter 1942; Dahl 1971; Huntington 1991). A more contemporary formulation distinguishes electoral democracies, which simply allow for regular competitive elections, from liberal democracies, which fully develop government accountability, the rule of law, broad rights and liberties, and the inclusion of minorities and other traditionally marginal groups (Diamond 1999). These distinctions are relevant for evaluating the nature of regime change in both Africa and Eurasia, where there have been some transitions to liberal democracy but also many regime changes that have merely installed new institutions or leaders without significantly altering the substance of politics from the authoritarian era.

In the economic realm, we can identify structural and policy-related impediments to recovery. As noted earlier, Africa's economies embody weak foundations of human capital, infrastructure, and productive facilities. Essential institutions such as financial markets, legal codes, and regulatory mechanisms are often inadequate or lacking. Africa's position in the international economy poses fundamental problems: the issues of dependence and volatility in commodity-export economies have long been noted, and in recent decades the region has also experienced growing isolation from global trade and capital markets. This marginality has meant a declining market share for exports, reduced access to capital, and a tepid international response to policy reform (Callaghy and Ravenhill 1993). The adjustment measures adopted by African countries in the 1980s generally failed to elicit new investments, trade, financial resources, or debt relief.

It is also important to recognize the limited extent of economic reform in the region, whether of an orthodox variety or a heterodox "alternative." Regardless of how one views the merits of structural adjustment, it has not been extensively realized in Africa, notwithstanding the ostensible commitments of governments. Although the multilateral financial institutions successfully pressed for the adoption of orthodox stabilization and adjustment programs, the implementation of these policies has often been halting, uneven, and erratic (World Bank 1994; Gordon 1993; Lewis 1996). Many countries have achieved broad macroeconomic targets such as fiscal balance and lower inflation, and most have enacted nominal price reforms in such areas as exchange rates and agricultural producer prices. Other important policy and institutional changes, however, have been slower to emerge. Privatization has been hesitant and piecemeal, financial systems have not been revitalized, and regulatory regimes have not been augmented in most countries. Many governments have experienced "adjustment fatigue" when difficult austerity measures yield few evident returns, and a common response has been to relax or abandon reforms. Faced with inconsistent signals, investors and donors frequently question the credibility of reform, withholding needed investment and aid.

Analysts have observed the time-consistency problem in economic reform: groups that are adversely affected by adjustment measures are often quick to mobilize in defense of their interests, yet the potential beneficiaries of reform may be unsure of their potential gains or may face other collective action problems that inhibit participation (Fernandez and Rodrik 1991; Haggard and Webb 1994). Consequently, it is often difficult to gather coalitions in support of reform, and African governments typically push forward orthodox programs through executive fiat (Herbst 1992). These tensions are compounded by the imbalance of costs and benefits under structural adjustment. In most instances, neopatrimonial regimes have preserved returns for members of an elite inner circle, even if economic contraction reduces the web of patronage. Benefits are conferred through special access to privatization, new trade opportunities, financial speculation, or foreign currency transactions. These privileged gains are sharply contrasted with the general popular hardships under austerity.

In view of this historical inheritance and the ensuing constraints on development, Africa's political transitions elicit questions about the specific political requisites of economic advancement. What dimensions of democratic governance can enhance the course of economic development in the region? How will patterns of economic reform affect the legitimacy of democratic regimes and the credibility of liberalization? What is the record of performance in the region's new democracies?

Democracy and Development

At a minimum, democratic transitions introduce new political institutions, changes in the composition of leadership, and expanded opportunities for organization and participation. Whether these changes are sufficient to improve economic performance, however, depends on an array of subsidiary effects. A key question in African states is the degree to which new democracies serve to renovate the structures and coalitions associated with neopatrimonial regimes, or if traditional politics are instead resurrected in a different guise. Where earlier forms of authority, policy-making, and coalition-building persist under new governments, then regime change is unlikely to produce significant improvements in economic performance. Economic revival in the region requires an institutional evolution toward developmental states, and the relationship between regimes and developmental outcomes should be more carefully specified with regard to this challenge.

Politically, this trajectory of expansion and change has been associated with developmental states that can provide effective long-term economic management. The model of the developmental state has been derived from the experiences of the high-performing East Asian economies, although a number of analysts have abstracted features that may be relevant to other regions and historical settings (Deyo 1987; Haggard 1990; Leftwich 1995; Woo-Cumings 1999). Selected states in Southeast Asia and Latin America have also been described in this vein. Developmental states are especially capable in focusing public resources, policies, and institutions toward the goals of growth and productive transformation. These states have been relatively successful at sustaining macroeconomic stability while also pursuing selective interventions to promote entrepreneurship, investment, productivity, and trade.

Much of this success has been attributed to durable leadership with a vision of reform and substantial independence from particular interests or clients. Developmentalist leaders typically devolve policy authority to competent government technocrats and provide them with political insulation from particularistic lobbying. Technocrats in these states are often assisted by supportive bureaucracies. Indeed, merit-based Weberian administration is a core feature of successful developmental states. But the public service is only one element in the institutional capacity underlying these states. In general, they have been able to provide consistent and credible institutional support for market activities. The performance of legal and regulatory systems, information and reporting functions, and (sometimes) financial systems or capital markets all serve to reduce transaction costs and encourage private commitments to investment and production.

Developmental states reflect a distinctive political formation, including leadership committed to certain policy ideas; support coalitions of state officials and key producer groups; and a minimal set of capable, responsive institutions (Evans 1995). In the preceding discussion, I outlined a contrasting pattern of state and regime formation in Africa that has generally yielded poor economic outcomes. The syndrome of neopatrimonial rule comprises strong personal rulers, support coalitions constituted around the patronage and rents deployed by a narrow state elite, and weak formal institutions. Similar configurations can be found in post-Soviet Eurasian states as well. Consequently, we should refer to these structures and resources when assessing the process of change.

The Politics of Economic Change

Pursuing this line of analysis, we can identify three endogenous characteristics of democratic regimes that decisively influence the political context of economic change: the character of leadership, the composition of support coalitions, and the nature of peak institutions. In addition, the international environment frames policy choice and outcomes. But how did these variables affect the course of economic performance in Africa?

Democracy ostensibly provides the mechanism for a transfer of elites. Perhaps the most visible feature of Africa's transitions was the removal of long-serving authoritarian rulers in a series of transitional elections: Kenneth Kaunda in Zambia, Mathieu Kerekou in Benin, Didier Ratsiraka in Madagascar, Denis Sassou-Nguesso in Congo-Brazzaville, Moussa Traore in Mali, and Hastings Banda in Malawi were among the more prominent leaders who were ousted, and often humiliated, by electoral defeats (though Kerekou returned to power by electoral means and Sassou-Nguesso by armed seizure of authority). The rout of the executive was usually accompanied by a loss for the incumbent ruling party or military council and the implied rejection of elites associated with those institutions. In some instances as well, the new executive had a reform agenda: in Benin, Nicephore Soglo was a former official of the World Bank and in Zambia the prominent labor leader Frederick Chiluba replaced Kaunda.

Beneath these emblems of transition, however, there has often been considerable elite continuity in Africa's new democracies. Electoral rule was ushered in amid popular calls for a renovation of politics, yet political transitions were often supervised by incumbent leaders and set in motion by seasoned politicians (Bates 1994). The top-down character of liberalization created grounds for the continuation or renewal of patronage politics after the transitional elections. In a number of African countries the political opposition was populated by former cronies and political elites who decamped from the ruling circle, sometimes quite late in the transition process.

These factors have several implications for economic management. Generally, no definitive shift has been made in the modes of economic policy-making in democratizing countries. Many new executives embody policy ideas that vary minimally from those of preceding regimes. Although politicians have pragmatically adopted orthodox macroeconomic programs, they evince considerable suspicion toward engagement with the global economy as well as the role of domestic entrepreneurs and markets. Instead, their predominant mode of policy is a diffident embrace of donor-supported reform. Furthermore, many elected leaders draw on a sparse stratum of capable officials and advisers and have relied on a familiar roster of veteran ministers or counselors. The prevailing relationship between executives and technocratic elements can be seen in centralized "presidential" styles of policy formation, with few signs of delegation to insulated technocratic groups. In this respect, post-Soviet Eurasian states may well differ from the African experience in the more visible influence and presence of bureaucracy.

Finally, many leaders and governing parties in new democracies maintain support through the dispersal of patronage and by means of piecemeal negotiation with interest groups and clients. Governing parties in most new democracies face some degree of competition, along with a more restrictive economic environment, and few of these organizations can achieve the encompassing control of the "machine" politics associated with single-party rule (Bienen 1971). Although the scope of clientelist politics may be diminished, ruling groups evidently continue to cultivate support through discretionary spending and rentier outlets.

These relations between governing elites and societal groups echo the patterns of authoritarian policy-making, and democratic governments are scarcely more accountable for the delivery of collective benefits (such as the rule of law or improved administration) than were previous regimes. The Chiluba government in Zambia, for instance, has been assailed by public charges of official corruption and cronyism, while the Jerry Rawlings government in Ghana has directed benefits to allies among the business class, discriminating against those associated with opposition parties (Hart and Gyimah-Boadi 1997). Electoral regimes react to public sentiment in subsidies, tax policy, privatization, and other policy areas, but leaders are as likely to be disposed toward special preferences as toward nondivisible public goods.

This discussion directs our attention to another central dimension of transition: the nature of support coalitions. The constitution of interest groups under authoritarian rule created numerous impediments to economic reform. Ethnic alliances and patron-client networks have tended to dissipate strong class or ideological identities, and the region's political parties have not advanced forceful doctrines or policy ideas (Bienen and Herbst 1996). Neopatrimonial regimes have commonly relied on populist coalitions, including state employees, corporatist labor organizations, government-protected manufacturers, recipients of various subsidies, and clients of senior officials—all groups that evince a continued bias toward the status quo. Also, as noted earlier, time-consistency problems and other dilemmas of participation have blunted the efforts of social groups with a likely interest in economic liberalization, such as export-oriented farmers, middle-class professionals, or urban entrepreneurs. In consequence, few constituencies exist to impel governments in the direction of market reforms or improved management. The inequities in the application of orthodox reform have inspired further public antipathy toward economic adjustment.

In Africa's new democracies, we can discern varying and sometimes contradictory forms of interest group organization. Clearly, in many countries are emerging lobbies for better governance and economic reform. Local business groups, professionals, and journalists have been especially vocal in urging anticorruption measures, greater transparency in policy-making and budgeting, better delivery of public services, more equitable application of the law, and further engagement in global markets. These admonitions are often echoed by local representatives of the multilateral institutions and foreign businesses. On some issues (such as corruption and service delivery), social groupings such as women, students, or organized labor may also be active. Opposition parties find it easy to target government inefficiency and misconduct, offering additional pressure in these areas. In a number of cases, therefore, political liberalization has encouraged diverse popular pressures in the direction of improved economic management and policy reform.

The same political climate provides outlets for popular interests and traditional patronage networks that are largely antagonistic to economic liberalization. An array of groups with diverse motives and concerns are commonly opposed to orthodox reform measures. Government employees contest privatization and retrenchment; urban workers, students, and women are concerned about the loss of subsidies and social services; import-competing manufacturers call for continued protection; some academics and journalists decry the abandonment of economic nationalism and the opening to world markets; and particular ethnic or regional groups may fear entry into a more competitive economy. These pressures sometimes impel governments toward fiscal or monetary expansion and the preservation of populist measures.

In the neoclassical image of economic reform, a number of beneficiaries of liberalization will mobilize in support of policy change. In spite of the new political freedoms under democratic rule, however, the collective-action problems that hindered organization under previous regimes are still in evidence. Many interest groups with a potential stake in economic reform have remained politically marginal under democratic regimes. Rural constituencies, for instance, often have limited abilities to organize because of geographic dispersal, low educational levels, and fragmentation by ethnicity or activity (Bates 1981). Agricultural interest organizations have not had prominent roles in the region's new democracies, although rural voters have sometimes supported candidates backing reform. The inherited problems of civic associations in Africa, including scarce resources and thin institutional capacities, are reflected in weak participation by many popular groups (Lewis 1992). Some interests such as business associations display better organization and resources, but here, too, political influence may be diminished by sectoral or ethnic divisions. In addition, leaders have often co-opted business groups through patronage or shunned elements associated with the opposition. Where the organized private sector is divided or politically contained, it has not been an effective advocate of economic reform. In general, there is a limited basis for the types of producer coalitions that have fostered growth in successful developmental states.

The character of emerging party systems also influences the formation of support coalitions. Here, again, we find many points of continuity with the region's earlier politics. Political parties in Africa's new democracies have reflected traditional emphases on personalities, ethnicity, and region, with little differentiation on ideological or programmatic grounds. Parties have not generally forged strong alliances with elements of civil society such as labor or business. Most governing parties maintained their control in the second post-transition elections, and in the few instances where incumbents were overturned (as in Benin), the result could be explained in terms of expedient personal and geographic alliances (Magnusson 1999). Africa's "third wave" democracies have largely repeated the pattern of older democracies in the region (notably, Botswana and the Gambia), evincing little turnover. The importance for the present discussion is that most elected governments in Africa do not confront challenges from either reformist parties or strong populist organizations. In fact, a substantial consensus has emerged in most elections over the fundamentals of economic policy, largely in line with orthodox prescriptions.

The discussion of party systems raises the more general issue of institutional development. Nascent democracies confront the legacies of administrative weakness and societal alienation inherited from their autocratic predecessors, and most economies provide a tenuous basis for fortifying central institutions (Young 1994a; van de Walle and Gyimah-Boadi 1996). The reform of institutions can be conceived in two ways: as a problem of restraint or as one of capacity. A perspective derived from liberal theory and institutional economics stresses that democratic regimes must accept institutional constraints on their discretion and power (North and Weingast 1989; Weingast 1997). The introduction of "agencies of restraint" provides checks on the prerogatives of rulers and signals the adherence of governments to certain policies or practices (Collier 1991). Constraining institutions may include constitutions, independent central banks, autonomous regulatory bodies, or membership in regional or international organizations. Institutional "lock-in" allows governments to make credible commitments to the market actors and the general public about their programs and intentions.

Another view stresses the importance of institutional capabilities as a foundation for the government's effective management of the economy. The basic concern here is that governments require a range of organizations and resources to make and implement policy effectively (Brautigam 1996). Public authorities must be able to provide incentives to producers and investors, guarantees of property and contracts, and sanctions for non-performance or evasion. These abilities in turn entail a range of functions in planning, monitoring, regulation, allocation, and enforcement. As noted by several recent analyses, both dimensions of change are important for effective state tutelage (Evans 1995; Przeworski 1998).

Few signs indicate that democratization has served as catalyst for institutional reform in Africa, whether in the direction of restraint or in that of enhanced capacity. Liberalizing regimes have not generally encouraged central bank autonomy, arm's-length regulatory agencies, an assertive judiciary, or external watchdog organizations. Domestic scrutiny from elements of civil society and the political opposition may induce greater caution and a measure of accountability, but these are not effective institutional limitations on government. Executives and bureaucrats continue to wield high levels of discretion in economic management, continuing the dilemma of credible commitment to market actors.

The challenge of enhancing institutional capacity is hampered by limited resources, ambivalence on the part of governments, and external policy constraints. African economies performed slightly better in the mid-1990s than they had in the preceding five years, but still their average growth rate of 3.4 percent for selected democracies was hardly robust. This rate of growth offers inadequate surplus for the aggressive investments needed in human capital, key public infrastructure, and other basic state institutions, including the civil service, the judiciary, and the police. In addition, many governments are hesitant to strengthen institutions that might provide countervailing power to that of the executive branch. The external constraints on institutional change are equally noteworthy. The neoliberal goals of structural adjustment, stressing budgetary limits and the reduction of state roles, are not always compatible with a commitment to build state agencies' capabilities for effective management and intervention. External donors have underwritten steps toward "capacity-building" in select governmental organizations, yet these are pursued in the context of policies impelling a diminished state, a contradiction stressed in Chapter 11. Also, the prevalence of outside financing and technical assistance in these programs has paradoxically undermined the development of local capabilities (Brautigam 1996).

The role of donors and multilateral financial institutions brings us to a final issue, the international setting for reform. In this area, two factors deserve emphasis: conditionality and marginality. African governments face narrow policy options because of their heavy reliance on conditional aid and lending. At the same time, Africa's outlying position in global markets yields limited benefits from political and economic reform. Let us examine these factors in turn.

The movement toward orthodox economic policies in Africa was manifestly a product of external conditionality. African governments varied in their perception of the economic crisis of the early 1980s, and several leaders attempted "homegrown" austerity measures, which usually did little to arrest economic decline. Eventually, however, nearly all regimes were led to the IMF and the World Bank, which held the keys to debt restructuring and new financing. As discussed earlier, African leaders have been decidedly ambivalent toward orthodox prescriptions, while the mass public in most countries has been antagonistic toward structural adjustment. During nearly two decades of donor-sponsored reform, African policy-makers and elites have recognized that mainstream structural adjustment policies are a sine qua non for debt rescheduling, concessional financing, new commercial lending, or priority in bilateral development assistance. Many leaders and technocrats have also accepted the prudence of budgetary restraint, low inflation, fewer public enterprises, and more open trade policy. Regardless of the social stresses or political liabilities of orthodox policies, however, African governments have few alternatives to the general package sponsored by the multilateral institutions. Attempts by African regional organizations and analysts to define an alternative reform package have failed to produce a coherent program that can win assent in world markets.

Finally, it is important to note that the continued marginality of African economies in global markets has largely precluded any "democracy dividend" in aid, investment, or debt relief—in sharp contrast to the situation facing post-Soviet Eurasia. The legacy of political instability, adverse economic policies, and pervasive corruption has largely discouraged international investors from entering African markets. Although a few African countries have sought to join the club of emerging markets, portfolio investment in the region has been slim by international standards, totaling some $3.2 billion in 1996, a little more than half of which was directed to South Africa. Official development assistance, in real terms, doubled during the 1980s and then remained largely static, even declining slightly in the past several years. Democratizing countries have garnered few special considerations in negotiating debt relief. Debt retirement initiatives by the World Bank and bilateral lenders were introduced in the late 1990s, but these have been too complex and gradual to yield significant relief. In general, international markets have not spurred democratization in Africa, nor vice versa.

Economic Performance in Democratizing Africa

The discussion to this point has focused on the analysis of theoretical requisites for improved economic performance in Africa, and a general discussion of how those variables have been influenced by regime change. In the final sections, I offer some brief empirical observations on the comparative economic performance of new democracies and the influence of economic performance on democratic consolidation.

An assessment of regime change and economic outcomes should address two comparative questions: the relative performance of new democracies before and after transition and the relative performance of transitional and nontransitional regimes. Table 12.1 makes this comparison using representative subsamples of new democracies and countries that have not undergone regime change.

The most basic procedural definition of democratic transition is a regime change through competitive elections. This usually means alteration of the constitution, a transfer of governing parties, and a new executive. Drawing from a list of the seventeen nominally democratic governments in Africa in 1996, the subsample omits the cases of "postconflict" democratization (e.g., Namibia and Mozambique), for they likely garnered premiums from the end of war. It also sets aside some of the least populous countries (e.g., Sao Tome and Principe, though not Cape Verde) to avoid an overrepresentation of small markets and, of course, excludes the cases of democratic reversal (e.g., the Gambia, Niger, and Congo-Brazzaville). This yields a list of eight countries: Benin, Cape Verde, the Central African Republic, Ghana, Madagascar, Malawi, Mali, and Zambia. (Ghana is included because significant political opening had occurred by 1997, even though the change in executive took place after the time period covered by the table.) These transition cases are compared with an equal number of nontransition cases: Burkina Faso, Cameroon, Gabon, Guinea, the Ivory Coast, Kenya, Togo, and Uganda.

The periods of comparison are from 1985 to 1989—i.e., prior to democratic transition but generally well into the period of structural adjustment—and from 1992 to 1997, generally subsequent to democratic transition for most countries (excepting Malawi, whose transition was in 1994). Obviously, these figures indicate relatively inauspicious performance for most countries, but within this general setting there are some significant differences. As can be seen in the table, there appear to be few growth effects that can be attributed to regime change. Both transition and non-

Table 12.1

Economic Performance of Transition and Nontransition Countries in Africa

	Average GDP growth (%)		Average deficit as a percentage of GDP (%)		Average inflation (%)		Average growth of money supply (%)	
	1985–89	1992–97	1985–89	1992–97	1985–89	1992–97	1985–89	1992–97
Transition								
Benin	2.1	4.6	11.8	-1.8	n.a.	n.a.	-3.0	11.7
Cape Verde	5.1	3.9	-7.4	-13.6	5.8	6.7	8.0	9.8
Central African Republic	0.7	1.4	-4.5	-5.2	-0.8	7.5	2.0	14.8
Ghana	5.2	4.2	-2.7	-9.1	27.8	32.2	39.0	39.7
Madagascar	2.3	1.8	-3.6	-6.0	17.9	21.9	19.0	24.3
Malawi	1.9	5.2	-5.9	-12.0	20.4	40.5	24.0	29.8
Mali	3.9	4.2	-5.9	-3.1	n.a.	6.0	0.0	16.5
Zambia	2.3	1.7	-10.8	-4.1	57.0	90.7	45.0	26.0
Average	2.9	3.4	-3.6	-6.9	18.3	29.4	16.8	21.6
Nontransition								
Burkina Faso	4.4	3.3	-3.2	-2.5	n.a.	n.a.	10.0	16.8
Cameroon	-0.1	0.8	-5.2	-4.6	6.0	7.6	0.0	2.3
Gabon	-1.4	2.5	-7.1	-0.1	1.0	7.4	-1.0	9.5
Guinea	4.7	4.2	-5.5	-3.2	30.5	6.6	n.a.	7.5
Ivory Coast	2.2	3.6	-8.1	-6.3	5.3	8.9	-2.0	15.2
Kenya	5.9	2.1	-5.2	-3.7	10.0	20.6	11.0	20.0
Togo	3.4	2.8	-3.8	-7.5	0.7	10.4	-7.0	15.2
Uganda	3.4	7.4	-3.6	-3.5	158.9	16.4	84.0	28.0
Average	2.8	3.3	-5.2	-3.9	30.3	11.2	11.9	14.3

Source: World Bank 1999.

Notes: GDP = gross domestic product; n.a. = not available.

transition countries increased their growth rates between the late 1980s and the mid-1990s, in each case by about the same interval. Furthermore, half the countries in each sample accelerated growth in the 1990s, while the other half slowed. The general outcome suggests that many countries in the region, without regard to regime, benefited to some degree from policy reform and favorable trends in global markets during the 1990s. In this respect, many African states fared somewhat better than most of their post-Soviet Eurasian counterparts.

Other areas of economic performance reveal a clearer picture. On average, the new democratic governments displayed larger fiscal deficits, higher inflation rates, and faster monetary growth than their nondemocratic counterparts. One must be cautious about these numbers, as some trends are driven by a single case, and there may be alternative factors explaining performance in individual countries. Nonetheless, a preliminary reading of the data provides a distinctive impression. Among the transitional regimes, six of eight countries widened their budget deficits from −3.6 percent to −6.9 percent of gross domestic product, on average (an average interval of 3.3 percent), following transition, while seven of eight nontransition regimes narrowed their deficits from −5.2 percent to −3.9 percent, on average, a 1.3 percent reduction.

The record of inflation is particularly striking. The inflation rate in transitional countries rose from 18.3 percent on average to 29.4 percent (a 60 percent increase) after the change of regime, compared with a decline in the nontransition cases from 30.3 percent on average to 11.2 percent (a 63 percent reduction). Uganda's enormous drop in inflation is critical among the nontransition group, as is Zambia's increase in the transitions sample, but it is also noteworthy that all democratizing countries saw a rise in inflation. (These disparate results are not an artifact of the 1995 devaluation of the CFA franc [the currency used in most francophone states in western Africa], as CFA countries are represented in both samples.) Finally, there is a significant difference in monetary growth, as the transitional countries saw a rise of nearly 5 percent in the average rates of expansion in money supply, from 16.8 percent in the 1980s to 21.6 percent in the later period. In the nontransition countries there was also expansion from an average of 11.9 percent to 14.3 percent, though this rise, 2.4 percent, was smaller than that among transition countries. It should be noted that the nontransition group had lower overall monetary growth (though initially higher inflation) than the regimes undergoing transition.

This admittedly gross comparison raises some hypotheses and suggests avenues for further research. The proposition that macroeconomic discipline is diminished in new democracies has considerable plausibility. The converging increases in budget deficits, inflation, and monetary expansion in transitional regimes give substance to this premise. I raise the obvious conjecture that this reflects the combined pressures of popular constituencies and the inducements of electoral competition. At the same time there appears to be no growth liability for democratizing regimes, despite this weaker policy performance. The groups of transition and nontransition countries had almost identical growth rates in the late 1980s, and nearly equal, somewhat higher rates in the mid-1990s. This requires some qualification of the earlier statement that there is no "democracy dividend" in economic performance. If new democracies are able to preserve or improve growth despite worsening policy performance, then it is possible that donors or creditors have been more flexible toward countries pursuing political liberalization. In addition, transitions may reduce political risk in some countries, encouraging investors to enter these markets. These propositions merit additional inquiry.

Performance and Democratic Legitimacy

If, as I have argued, regime change has not significantly altered economic performance or elite politics in many African states, then it is important to ask whether these patterns influence the consolidation of democratic rule. Economic grievances were prominent in the ouster of the old regime, and this suggests that Africa's new democracies face substantial popular expectations for economic improvement. The continuing weak performance of the region's economies, the lopsided costs and benefits of reform efforts, and the evidence of persistent patronage politics in many electoral regimes could impair the legitimacy and longevity of democratic governments. A range of other factors, however, also potentially affect democratic consolidation, including civil-military relations, ethnic and regional interactions, the conduct of elected leaders, the efficacy of institutions such as parties and legislatures, and the evolution of new political values. The extralegal challenges to elected governments in recent years have generally borne the stamp of military factionalism or ethnic contention rather than economic discontent. Yet it is important to inquire how citizens evaluate democratic performance and how they weigh economic goods.

Here we turn to new data on citizens' attitudes in transitional regimes. Research by the Afrobarometer project in southern and western Africa offers some preliminary evidence on how Africans regard political and economic reform. The findings indicate that citizens in new democracies frequently distinguish between the system of democratic rule and the performance of particular governments. Moreover, there is a relatively firm commitment to democracy despite widespread disappointment over the results of economic liberalization. These results would seem to indicate that political and economic reform are separable to some degree and that citizens evaluate regimes on an array of material and political goods.

In a recent survey in Ghana, for instance, a large majority (76.5 percent) of respondents said they preferred democracy to all other forms of government, and most identified democracy with liberal qualities such as civil liberties or popular representation (Bratton, Lewis, and Gyimah-Boadi 1999). More than 80 percent of respondents offered high assessments of the state of basic rights, freedoms, and political choice under democratic rule, and a slight majority (54.4 percent) said they were satisfied with the workings of democracy in Ghana today. At the same time, two-thirds were dissatisfied with the state of the national economy, and less than half felt that democracy had produced economic improvements. A clear majority attributed economic performance to the current government, rather than to past military regimes or the multilateral institutions. Among those familiar with the government's structural adjustment policies, a little more than half were discontented with the results of the program, and a majority of respondents (57 percent) believed that reform policies had "hurt most people and only benefited a minority" who were closely allied to the government. Furthermore, more than three-fourths of those surveyed believed that "government officials are only out to enrich themselves."

These results suggest a clear distinction by the public between democratic institutions, economic policies, and particular governments. Ghanaians take a skeptical view toward orthodox adjustment policies, which are regarded as bringing few gains and widespread inequities. Many people believe the political elite to be corrupt and self-regarding. Much of the public is discontented with the economy and with the government's impact on economic performance. Yet there is substantial support for democracy as a form of government and satisfaction with the state of essential rights and liberties. These findings are reinforced by a comparative study of survey results in post-transition South Africa, Zambia, and Ghana (Bratton and Mattes 1999). The study finds, in all these cases, that general support for democracy as a system is higher than citizen satisfaction with democratic performance. The evaluation of democratic performance, moreover, extends well beyond economic provisions to encompass a range of political goods. The conclusion is that democratic consolidation in these countries is not predicated mainly on economic performance, and the public does not adopt an "instrumental" view of democratic governance. Africans value democracy as an ideal, though they also expect regimes to provide certain rights, liberties, and standards of governance. Moreover, high levels of inequality and corruption tend to reduce the legitimacy of democratic regimes.

Conclusion

In sub-Saharan Africa, as in post-Soviet Eurasia, the authoritarian legacy has shaped political and economic reform. Although the neopatrimonial inheritance in Africa is frequently different from the postcommunist heritage of Leninist parties and command economies, both regions face comparable problems of state capacity and institutional development. But the differences in degree deserve mention. The economic performance and reform of African economies, however tepid, were far less catastrophic in the 1990s than the trajectory of most of the former Soviet Union, with the notable exception of the Baltic states. Here we may note an important contrast—in the scope and nature of the adjustment. Colonial states in Africa practiced a paternalistic statism yet were ostensibly managing a particular form of capitalism, particularly for the sectors dominated by colonial corporations and European private interests. African states in the first three decades of independence expanded state sectors in pursuit of several things: "socialist orientation" for a number of them, mere economic nationalism for others, and neopatrimonial interest for all. But the economic command state was much less embedded in the everyday routines and practices of economic life than it was in the centrally planned economies of Eurasia. Time depth was an important factor as well: state socialism in the former Soviet Union continued for seventy years, whereas in Africa experiments in pervasive state seizure of the "commanding heights" subsisted for only a couple of decades.

Externally imposed economic reform in Africa began a decade earlier than in post-Soviet Eurasia and did not include anything remotely resembling the "shock therapy" in Russia. Nor has such privatization as has occurred in Africa given rise to plutocrats like Boris Berezovskii or Mikhail Khodorkovskii, with their political agendas and control of vast enterprises (Wolosky 2000). The sheer magnitude of Russia's resource base makes its colossal pilferage by a clique of tycoons eclipse even the performance of the late Nigerian dictator Sani Abacha, who, his successors have documented, embezzled $4 billion in less than five years of rule (1993–98). Diversion on this scale of essentially public resources in Africa can be carried out only by the rulers and their entourage, not by private actors.

Another major differences lies in the nature of the relationship with the international donor community. External leverage on African states is substantially greater than it is on Russia in particular. The Western stake in Eurasia, especially in Russia, is also substantially greater, and the aid sums involved, as Chapter 11 shows, are far greater than what is available to support economic reform in Africa.

This chapter emphasizes that regime change in Africa has been insufficient to revitalize and restructure regional economies because of substantial continuities lingering from the authoritarian era. Neopatrimonial systems, based on strong personal rulership and patronage politics, were incapable of providing the institutional foundations for effective market economies. If new electoral regimes are to foster improved economic performance, they must provide the political conditions for the emergence of developmental states. This entails shifts in leadership, support coalitions, and peak institutions, as well as the international environment. Although a number of African autocrats have been removed from office, the persistence of old elites, the inconclusive effects of participation and coalition formation, the continued deficiencies of key institutions, and the constraints of external policies and markets hinder a decisive transition in the region's economies. There is tentative evidence that democratization weakens basic macroeconomic management, though this does not seem to have a critical effect on growth outcomes. Perhaps more important for democratic legitimacy is the continued evidence of clientelist politics in democratizing regimes and the unequal distribution of burdens from economic reform. African citizens clearly include economic performance among other issues as a basis for assessing new democracies, but there is some evidence that the economy is not the litmus test for democratic legitimation. These findings suggest that economic and political reform in Africa are not integrally linked, in either a virtuous circle or a vicious cycle; rather, they are contingent processes with complex reciprocal effects. Different reform trajectories are likely in the region, depending on the variables enumerated in the preceding discussion. For Africa's weak economies and fragile democracies, the issue of state renovation provides the foundation of development.

References

Alesina, Alberto, Nouriel Roubini, and Gerald Cohen. 1997. *Political Cycles and the Macroeconomy.* Cambridge, Mass.: MIT Press.

Armijo, Leslie, Thomas Biersteker, and Abraham Lowenthal. 1995. "The Problems of Simultaneous Transitions." In *Economic Reform and Democracy,* ed. Larry Diamond and Marc F. Plattner. Baltimore: Johns Hopkins University Press.

Bates, Robert H. 1981. *Markets and States in Tropical Africa.* Berkeley: University of California Press.

———. 1994. "The Impulse to Reform in Africa." Pp. 13–28 in *Economic Change and Po-*

litical Liberalization in Sub-Saharan Africa, ed. Jennifer A. Widner. Baltimore: Johns Hopkins University Press.

———. 1999. "The Economic Bases of Democratization in Africa." Pp. 83–94 in *State, Conflict, and Democracy in Africa,* ed. Richard Joseph. Boulder: Lynne Rienner.

Bienen, Henry. 1971. "Political Parties and Political Machines in Africa." Pp. 195–214 in *The State of the Nations,* ed. Michael Lofchie. Berkeley: University of California Press.

Bienen, Henry, and Jeffrey Herbst. 1996. "The Relationship between Political and Economic Reform in Africa." *Comparative Politics* 29, no. 1 (October): 23–42.

Bratton, Michael. 1994. "Economic Crisis and Political Liberalization in Zambia." Pp. 101–28 in *Economic Change and Political Liberalization in Sub-Saharan Africa,* ed. Jennifer A. Widner. Baltimore: Johns Hopkins University Press.

———. 1997. *Democratic Experiments in Africa: Regime Transition in Comparative Perspective.* Cambridge: Cambridge University Press.

Bratton, Michael, and Robert Mattes. 1999. "Support for Democracy in Africa: Intrinsic or Instrumental?" Afrobarometer paper no. 1, MSU Working Papers on Political Reform in Africa, Dept. of Political Science, Michigan State University, October.

Bratton, Michael, and Nicolas van de Walle. 1992. "Popular Protest and Political Reform in Africa." *Comparative Politics* 24, no. 4: 419–42.

———. 1994. "Neopatrimonial Regimes and Political Transitions in Africa." *World Politics* 46, no. 4 (July): 453–89.

———. 1997. *Democratic Experiments in Africa.* Cambridge: Cambridge University Press.

Bratton, Michael, Peter M. Lewis, and E. Gyimah-Boadi. 1999. "Attitudes to Democracy and Markets in Ghana." Afrobarometer paper no. 2, MSU Working Papers on Political Reform in Africa, Dept. of Political Science, Michigan State University, October.

Brautigam, Deborah. 1996. "State Capacity and Effective Governance." Pp. 81–108 in *Agenda for Africa's Economic Renewal,* ed. Benno Ndulu and Nicolas van de Walle. Washington: Overseas Development Council.

Callaghy, Thomas M. 1988. "The State and the Development of Capitalism in Africa: Comparative and Theoretical Reflections." Pp. 67–99 in *The Precarious Balance: State and Society in Africa,* ed. Donald Rothchild and Naomi Chazan. Boulder: Westview.

———. 1993. "Political Passions and Economic Interests: Economic Reform and Political Structure in Africa." Pp. 463–519 in *Hemmed In: Responses to Africa's Economic Decline,* ed. Thomas M. Callaghy and John Ravenhill. New York: Columbia University Press.

Callaghy, Thomas M., and John Ravenhill, eds. 1993. *Hemmed In: Responses to Africa's Economic Decline.* New York: Columbia University Press.

Chazan, Naomi, and Donald Rothchild 1993. "The Political Repercussions of Economic Malaise." Pp. 180–214 in *Hemmed In: Responses to Africa's Economic Decline,* ed. Thomas M. Callaghy and John Ravenhill. New York: Columbia University Press.

Clapham, Christopher, ed. 1982. *Patronage and Public Power.* London: Frances Pinter.

———. 1985. *Third World Politics.* Madison: University of Wisconsin Press.

Collier, Paul. 1991. "Africa's External Economic Relations, 1960–1990." *African Affairs* 90, no. 358 (January): 111–17.

Dahl, Robert. 1971. *Polyarchy: Participation and Opposition.* New Haven: Yale University Press.

Deyo, Federick, ed. 1987. *The Political Economy of the New Asian Industrialism.* Ithaca: Cornell University Press.

Diamond, Larry. 1992. "Economic Development and Democracy Reconsidered." *American Behavioral Scientist* 35, nos. 4–5.

———. 1999. *Developing Democracy: Toward Consolidation.* Baltimore: Johns Hopkins University Press.

Diamond, Larry, and Marc F. Plattner, eds. 1995. *Economic Reform and Democracy.* Baltimore: Johns Hopkins University Press.

Diamond, Larry, Juan Linz, and Seymour Martin Lipset, eds. 1996. *Politics in Developing Countries*. 2d ed. Boulder: Lynne Rienner.

Drake, Paul, and Matthew McCubbins. 1998. *The Origins of Liberty: Political and Economic Liberalization in the Modern World*. Princeton: Princeton University Press.

Duch, Raymond. 1995. "Economic Chaos and the Fragility of Democratic Transition in Former Communist Regimes." *Journal of Politics* 57, no. 1: 121–58.

Encarnacion, Omar G. 1996. "The Politics of Dual Transitions." *Comparative Politics* 28, no. 4 (July): 477–92.

Evans, Peter. 1995. *Embedded Autonomy: States and Industrial Transformation*. Princeton: Princeton University Press.

Fernandez, Raquel, and Dani Rodrik. 1991. "Resistance to Reform: Status Quo Bias in the Presence of Individual-Specific Uncertainty." *American Economic Review* 81, no. 5: 1146–55.

Gordon, David F. 1993. "Debt, Conditionality, and Reform: The International Relations of Economic Policy Restructuring in Sub-Saharan Africa." Pp. 90–129 in *Hemmed In: Responses to Africa's Economic Decline*, ed. Thomas M. Callaghy and John Ravenhill. New York: Columbia University Press.

Haggard, Stephan. 1990. *Pathways from the Periphery*. Ithaca: Cornell University Press.

Haggard, Stephan, and Robert Kaufman. 1995. *The Political Economy of Democratic Transitions*. Princeton: Princeton University Press.

Haggard, Stephan, and Steven B. Webb. 1994. *Voting for Reform : Democracy, Political Liberalization, and Economic Adjustment*. New York: Oxford University Press.

Hart, Elizabeth, and E. Gyimah-Boadi. 1997. "Business Associations in Ghana's Economic and Political Transition." Paper presented at the Conference on Business and the State in Africa. American University, Washington, D.C., February.

Hellman, Joel S. 1998. "Winners Take All: The Politics of Partial Reform in Postcommunist Transitions." *World Politics* 50, no. 2 (January): 203–34.

Herbst, Jeffrey. 1992. *The Politics of Reform in Ghana, 1982–1991*. Berkeley: University of California Press.

———. 1994. "The Dilemmas of Explaining Political Upheaval: Ghana in Comparative Perspective." Pp. 182–98 in *Economic Change and Political Liberalization in Sub-Saharan Africa*, ed. Jennifer A. Widner. Baltimore: Johns Hopkins University Press.

Huntington, Samuel. 1991. *The Third Wave: Democratization in the Late 20th Century*. Norman: University of Oklahoma Press.

Hyden, Goran. 1983. *No Shortcuts to Progress*. Berkeley: University of California Press.

Joseph, Richard, ed. 1999. *State, Conflict, and Democracy in Africa*. Boulder: Lynne Rienner.

Leftwich, Adrian. 1995. "Bringing Politics Back In: Towards a Model of the Development State." *Journal of Development Studies* 31, no. 3: 400–427.

Lewis, Peter M. 1992. "Political Transition and the Dilemma of Civil Society in Africa." *Journal of International Affairs* 46, no. 1: 31–54.

———. 1994. "Economic Statism, Private Capital, and the Dilemmas of Accumulation in Nigeria." *World Development* 22, no. 3: 437–51.

———. 1996. "Economic Reform and Political Transition in Africa: The Quest for a Politics of Development." *World Politics* 49, no. 1 (October): 92–129.

Lipset, Seymour Martin. 1959. *Political Man*. Garden City: Doubleday.

Magnusson, Bruce. 1999. "Testing Democracy in Benin: Experiments in Institutional Reform." Pp. 217–37 in *State, Conflict, and Democracy in Africa,* ed. Richard Joseph. Boulder: Lynne Rienner.

Migdal, Joel. 1988. *Strong Societies and Weak States: State-Society Relations and State Capabilities in the Third World*. Princeton: Princeton University Press.

Ndulu, Benno, and Nicolas van de Walle, eds. 1996. *Agenda for Africa's Economic Renewal.* Washington: Overseas Development Council.

North, Douglass, and Barry Weingast. 1989. "Constitutions and Commitment: The Evolution of Institutions Governing Public Choice in Seventeenth Century England." *Journal of Economic History* 49, no. 4: 803–32.

Olson, Mancur. 1982. *The Rise and Decline of Nations.* New Haven: Yale University Press.

Przeworski, Adam. 1991. *Democracy and the Market.* Cambridge: Cambridge University Press.

———. 1998. "The State in a Market Economy." In *Transforming Post-Communist Political Economies,* ed. Joan Nelson, Charles Tilly, and Lee Walker. Washington: National Academy Press.

Przeworski, Adam, and Fernando Limongi. 1997. "Modernization: Theories and Facts." *World Politics* 49, no. 2: 155–83.

Remmer, Karen. 1991. "The Political Impact of Economic Crisis in Latin America in the 1980s." *American Political Science Review* 85, no. 3: 777–800.

Rueschemeyer, Dietrich, John Stephens, and Evelyn Huber Stephens. 1992. *Capitalist Development and Democracy.* Chicago: University of Chicago Press.

Sandbrook, Richard. 1985. *The Politics of Africa's Economic Stagnation.* Cambridge: Cambridge University Press.

Schumpeter, Joseph. 1942. *Capitalism, Socialism, and Democracy.* New York: Harper.

van de Walle, Nicolas, and E. Gyimah-Boadi. 1996. "The Politics of Economic Renewal in Africa." In *Agenda for Africa's Economic Renewal,* ed. Benno Ndulu and Nicolas van de Walle. Washington: Overseas Development Council.

Weingast, Barry. 1997. "The Political Foundations of Democracy and the Rule of Law." *American Political Science Review* 91, no. 2: 245–63.

Westebbe, Richard. 1994. "Structural Adjustment, Rent-Seeking and Liberalization in Benin." Pp. 80–100 in *Economic Change and Political Liberalization in Sub-Saharan Africa,* ed. Jennifer A. Widner. Baltimore: Johns Hopkins University Press.

Widner, Jennifer A., ed. 1994. *Economic Change and Political Liberalization in Sub-Saharan Africa.* Baltimore: Johns Hopkins University Press.

Wolosky, Lee. 2000. "Putin's Plutocrat Problem." *Foreign Affairs* 79, no. 2 (March–April): 18–31.

Woo-Cumings, Meredith, ed. 1999. *The Developmental State.* Ithaca: Cornell University Press.

World Bank. 1994. *Adjustment in Africa: Reforms, Results and the Road Ahead.* Washington: World Bank.

———. 1999. *African Development Indicators, 1998–99.* Washington: World Bank.

Young, Crawford. 1994a. "Democratization in Africa: The Contradictions of a Political Imperative." Pp. 230–50 in *Economic Change and Political Liberalization in Sub-Saharan Africa,* ed. Jennifer A. Widner. Baltimore: Johns Hopkins University Press.

———. 1994b. *The African Colonial State in Comparative Perspective.* New Haven: Yale University Press.

———. 1996. "Africa: An Interim Balance Sheet." *Journal of Democracy* 7, no. 3: 53–68.

Part IV

State and Society

13

Ethnicity and State-Building: Accommodating Ethnic Differences in Post-Soviet Eurasia

GAIL W. LAPIDUS

The unexpected and rapid dissolution of the Soviet Union in 1991 and the emergence of fifteen independent states on its former territory evoked apocalyptic predictions that imperial collapse would unleash an avalanche of ethno-political strife. Analysts and policy-makers alike feared that an unstable and indeed anarchic post-Soviet environment characterized by high levels of insecurity and unpredictability was likely to precipitate an uncontrollable escalation of ethno-political conflict and violence within and among the states of the region. The triumph of radical nationalism and the repression of minorities in the newly independent non-Russian states, juxtaposed with an increasingly assertive neoimperialism in Russia, was viewed as an explosive combination that threatened to destabilize the entire region.[1]

Their alarm was driven by a long list of potential dangers: the high level of ethno-national mobilization already manifest in the region, including unfulfilled aspirations for independence; large concentrations of "beached" Russians and Russian-speakers now stranded outside the Russian Federation who were facing potential discrimination and a profound transforma-

---

1. Indeed, President George H. W. Bush had given voice to these concerns even prior to the dissolution of the Soviet Union in a speech in Kiev in June 1991, in which he warned the Ukrainian leadership against pursuing what he labeled a "suicidal nationalism." For the argument that democratization encourages nationalist conflict, see Snyder (2000).

tion of their status in new and unstable states; minorities accustomed to relying on the imperial center for protection now vulnerable to pressures by newly independent nationalizing states; massive flows of refugees and "forced migrants" in search of more secure and hospitable environments; and rising nationalism and irredentism in Russia itself. All this occurred in a setting where weak states, lacking institutional capacity in general as well as real experience of democratic institutions and noncoercive ways of managing conflict, appeared highly vulnerable to internal unrest as well as to external interference. In short, the former Yugoslavia represented the nightmare scenario of what it was feared might transpire in the former Soviet space.

To date, these dire predictions have by and large not materialized.[2] In sharp contrast to Yugoslavia's recent history, the dissolution of the Soviet Union was a relatively peaceful process. Although the region has not been without its violent conflicts, including six regional wars involving regular armies and heavy arms, virtually all were precipitated by the combination of liberalization and state breakdown associated with Soviet president Mikhail Gorbachev's reforms, and their onset was concentrated in the period from 1988 to 1992 (Gurr 1993; Rubin and Snyder 1998). With the exception of the civil war in Tajikistan, they involved wars of secession by ethnic groups that enjoyed an institutional base in the form of autonomous republics and that received support from external actors, most commonly Russia.[3] With the exception of Chechnya, these conflicts are now essentially frozen. Despite the efforts of several of the governments involved as well as of a variety of regional and international actors to find a path to ac-

---

2. It should be noted that a number of Russian analysts have painted a far more negative picture of current trends in the non-Russian states. The term "ethnic cleansing" has been widely and indiscriminately used, and some analysts have argued that former Yugoslav president Slobodan Milosevic's behavior in Kosovo hardly differs from widespread practices in the newly independent states. In attacking Western intervention in Kosovo, for example, Sergei Rogov, the prominent director of Russia's Institute for the Study of the USA and Canada, recently asserted, "Look at the leaders of almost all the newly independent states. Like Milosevic, they used to be leaders of the Communist Party before the collapse of Communism. And if you look at how they treat the ethnic minorities in the newly independent states, you'll see that Milosevic fits the pattern. He's not perceived [by Russians] as something outstanding." Quoted in Wines (1999).

3. The involvement of Russian military forces in Trans-Dniestria and Abkhazia and the participation of Armenia in the Nagorno-Karabakh conflict contributed decisively to the outcomes. The war in Chechnya, by contrast, was largely confined to the two parties to the conflict (Chechnya and Russia). Despite the involvement on the Chechen side of a small number of individual volunteers from other countries, Chechnya received no significant military support from any other state.

commodation, they have resisted resolution. But what is particularly significant and indeed striking is the fact that no new violent ethno-political conflicts have erupted in the post-Soviet region in the past few years.[4] Although the process of state-building and the formation of new identities is proceeding slowly and amid enormous challenges, a stabilization—however precarious—appears to be taking place.

A number of factors help explain this tendency. First and foremost are the shift in priorities from the struggle for national liberation to the effort to consolidate statehood and the ethno-political demobilization across the region that has accompanied that shift. Stability is increasingly recognized to depend on the successful integration of ethnic minorities, which has in turn encouraged more inclusionary and accommodationist strategies by titular elites as well as national minorities than those pursued during and immediately after the struggle for independence.[5] Moreover, by depriving national movements of their central raison d'être, the demise of the Soviet system brought economic, social, and regional cleavages to the fore (Dawson 1997; Alexseev 1999; Lapidus 1999). It remains to be seen whether Russia becomes an exception to this trend, but even here the process of federalization, as well as the ongoing economic and political crises, has altered the constellation of identities and interests in ways that increase the political salience of regionalism rather than ethnicity.

A second stabilizing element was the fact that the achievement of independent statehood was the result of a process of "pacting" among the leaders of the former union republics rather than of a revolutionary struggle against the imperial center. The peaceful dissolution of the union and the mutual recognition of borders and territories entailed in the December 1991 Belovezhskoe Forest and Almaty agreements transformed the internal boundaries of the republics into international borders. This arrangement was swiftly legitimated and endorsed by international recognition of

---

4. The recent violence in Dagestan involved radical Islamic groups supported by militants from Chechnya, rather than an ethno-political conflict.

5. The Georgian case provides a particularly dramatic illustration of this broader trend toward diminishing the use of the "ethnic card" in electoral competition. The accession to power of Zviad Gamsakhurdia in 1990 represented the victory of an extreme and counterproductive form of Georgian nationalism that alienated the republic's non-Georgian populations and triggered the attempts at secession by Abkhazia and South Ossetia. His replacement by Eduard Shevardnadze brought a dramatic shift in policy aimed at promoting conciliation among Georgians themselves and in their relations with other ethnic minorities. Constitutional provisions as well as public discourse have sought to define a civic conception of the political community and envision the formation of a new federation in which a peacefully reintegrated Abkhazia and South Ossetia would enjoy substantial autonomy.

the fifteen successor states.[6] As in the case of Africa, where the Organization of African Unity's early decision to affirm the sovereignty of the newly independent states and recognize existing borders helped to contain conflict in the aftermath of decolonization, early endorsement by the international community had a stabilizing effect on interstate relations across the region, precluding protracted struggles over borders and territories among the new states and the mobilization of domestic forces around borders, a result that might have accompanied a lengthy negotiating process. International affirmation also constituted a significant barrier to irredentist movements and to imperial revival.

Third, a relatively benign international environment and the rapid integration of the new states into a virtual alphabet soup of international institutions injected new norms of human and minority rights and ethnic conciliation into political discourse. In addition, it provided incentives to moderation and deterrents to extremism and conflict. Not only were the new states subjected to close scrutiny and even intrusive interventions in their domestic affairs, particularly by the Organization for Security and Cooperation in Europe (OSCE) and its high commissioner for national minorities, but key organizations such as the Council of Europe also conditioned future membership on adherence to certain standards concerning human rights and the treatment of ethnic minorities (Hurlbutt 1999; Hopmann 1999; Chayes and Chayes 1996). These different forms of international involvement in the region have contributed significantly to increasing security and defusing tensions, particularly in the case of those states—the Baltics, for example—that attached a high priority to integration into Europe. In many instances, the desire to improve bilateral relations with neighboring states served as an additional incentive. Although this has clearly been an important factor in the treatment of Russian-speaking communities, Lithuania's treatment of its Polish minority, too, was favorably influenced by its desire for Poland's support in joining European institutions and the North Atlantic Treaty Organization. Moreover, a great variety of international and local nongovernmental organizations (NGOs) have been actively promoting and monitoring respect for human rights and the rule of law and have launched training programs on conflict resolution and mediation, offering additional outlets for the expression of grievances by individuals and groups and providing new channels for redress.

---

6. This contrasts sharply with the case of Yugoslavia, where no such consensual agreement among its constituent republics was possible and where Western governments were sharply divided over how to deal with the situation, and indeed whether to define it as secession or dissolution.

Finally, populations as well as states in the region have been tenuously adapting themselves to the new realities, notwithstanding the lingering nostalgia for a time when travel across the entire region was unencumbered by borders, visas, or new currencies. Especially significant have been the changes in the consciousness of Russians themselves. In contrast with the non-Russian populations of the republics, who even in the Soviet period overwhelmingly tended to consider their republics to be their homelands (*rodina*), Russians typically identified the Soviet Union as their homeland. Since 1991, however, growing numbers of Russians as well as non-Russians appear to identify themselves with the states in which they reside (Arutiunian 1994, 1996). The trend is particularly striking in the Russian Federation, which was long conflated with the Soviet Union itself and lacked a distinct identity as well as key institutions of its own. Over the past decade, however, a growing share of the federation's population identifies itself as citizens of Russia (Levada 1999). Even in Latvia and Estonia, which granted automatic citizenship only to those who had been citizens prior to World War II and their descendants and established criteria for naturalization for other residents, growing numbers of Russian-speakers are actively seeking to qualify for citizenship.[7]

State-Building and Nation-Building: The Challenge of Multiethnicity

With the dissolution of the Soviet Union, the challenge of state-building became the central priority across the region, coupled in varying degrees with a general commitment to political democratization and economic transformation. Conceptions of statehood remained powerfully shaped by the Soviet legacy. Whether under the leadership of communists-turned-nationalists or under leaders who had emerged from the nationalist opposition movements, state-building was conceived as inseparable from nation-building and drew on the discourse of national revival.

The national idea had served to mobilize populations against Soviet rule; it now also served as the basis of legitimacy, an instrument of political consolidation, and a form of compensation for populations experiencing the economic and psychological hardships of the transition. But these efforts at nation-building confronted the fact that—with the exception of Arme-

---

7. A January 1997 opinion poll of Russian residents of Estonia aged 18–29 found that two out of three desired Estonian citizenship, and 75 percent considered Estonia their home (Markus 1997).

nia, which was already relatively ethnically homogeneous and which would shortly lose its remaining Azerbaijani population—the new states were multinational societies embracing substantial ethnic and religious minorities whose loyalty was critical to the state's internal stability and international legitimacy. As Table 13.1 indicates, the share of nontitular groups in the populations of the new states ranged at the time of independence from a low of 10 percent in Azerbaijan and 18 percent in Russia to a high of 54 percent in Kazakhstan. The major challenge of managing these cultural differences presented itself from the start.

That the new non-Russian states would seek to privilege the cultural and political role of their titular nationalities was the unsurprising legacy of Soviet rule. The Soviet leadership had conceived of ethnicity in primordial terms and had made it a critical attribute of individual and group identity. By the late 1930s, nationality had become an official criterion for classifying Soviet citizens (Hirsch 1997). It was established as a census category, it was inscribed on internal passports and on numerous other official documents, and it was embedded in a variety of educational, occupational, and political quota systems. Group identities were in turn territorialized in an ostensibly federal system. The Soviet Union was a hierarchy of ethno-territorial units, in effect a system of "tactical nation-states"(Massell 1974) viewed as national homelands "owned" by their titular nationalities. At the same time, Soviet ideology as well as practice viewed national identities and loyalties as atavistic, if not subversive, and sought to weaken and undermine their hold in constructing a supranational socialist community. The principle of republican sovereignty was in fact thwarted in practice; the republics were subjected to a highly centralized and coercive system of controls, with key political and economic decisions made in Moscow.[8]

The political liberalization introduced by Gorbachev invited efforts to give real substance to these claims and encouraged the formation of new political movements in which demands for reform of the Soviet system were increasingly joined to calls for national revival and republic sovereignty (Lapidus 1992). Although in some cases these movements were led

---

8. Two features of Soviet policy exemplified the constraining role of central policies: 1) rapid industrial development accompanied by organized population movements that radically altered the demographic composition of a number of republics and threatened to transform the titular population into a minority; and 2) language policies that amounted to an asymmetrical bilingualism, in which Russian became the universal official language throughout the Soviet Union, while Russians outside the Russian Soviet Federal Socialist Republic were under no pressure to learn the languages of the republics in which they lived and worked (Lapidus 1992, 83).

Table 13.1
Ethnic Composition of Post-Soviet Eurasian States

Country and total population	Percentage of total population that is:			
	of titular nationality	Russian	of other major group(s)	of all other (nonmajor) groups
Armenia 3,421,775	93	2	3 (Azeri)	2
Azerbaijan 7,855,576	90	3	3 (Dagestani) 2 (Armenian)	2
Russia 146,861,022	82	82	4 (Tatar) 3 (Ukranian)	12
Lithuania 3,600,158	81	9	7 (Polish) 2 (Belarusian)	2
Uzbekistan 23,784,321	80	6	5 (Tajik) 3 (Kazakh)	7
Belarus 10,409,050	78	13	4.1 (Polish) 3 (Ukrainian)	2
Turkmenistan 4,297,629	77	7	9 (Uzbek) 2 (Kazakh)	5
Ukraine 50,125,108	73	22	1 (Jewish)	4
Georgia 5,108,527	70	6	8 (Armenian) 6 (Azeri)	10
Tajikistan 6,020,095	65	4	25 (Uzbek)	7
Moldova 4,457,729	65	13	14 (Ukrainian) 4 (Gagauz)	5
Estonia 1,421,335	64	29	3 (Ukrainian) 2 (Belarusian)	3
Latvia 2,385,396	57	30	4 (Belarusian) 3 (Ukrainian)	6
Kyrgyzstan 4,522,281	52	18	13 (Uzbek) 3 (Ukrainian)	14
Kazakhstan 16,846,808	46	35	5 (Ukrainian) 3 (German)	11

Source: CIA 1998.

Note: figures are estimated as of July 1998, except those for Armenia (1989), Azerbaijan (1995), Uzbekistan (1996), and Turkmenistan (1996). Almost all Armenians live in the separatist Nagorno-Karabakh region. For Georgia, the population of all other (nonmajor) groups includes 3 percent Ossetian and 2 percent Abkhaz. In Tajikstan, the Russian population is currently declining.

by former dissidents and human rights activists challenging the Communist Party establishment, in most cases elements of the party leaderships themselves became advocates of republic sovereignty and self-rule. Not unlike the pattern that prevailed in postcolonial Africa, the territorial arrangements created by the Soviet system and the assumptions and expectations that went with them shaped and indeed determined the state units that emerged from the Soviet Union's demise.

The very process of imperial collapse itself also shaped the forms of state- and nation-building that emerged in its wake. By contrast with cases of imperial attrition, wherein core institutions survive and continue but the territory under their control gradually shrinks or decays, the collapse of the Soviet Union was sudden and largely unanticipated and was in large measure the result of defection by its core political unit, the Russian Soviet Federal Socialist Republic (Lapidus forthcoming; Dunlop 1993). On the one hand, Russia's defection contributed to a peaceful dissolution of the union based on the consensus or acquiescence of the elites of the key union republics. On the other hand, it resulted in the emergence of new states that had little preparation for independent existence and that—with the exception of Russia itself—largely lacked effective political, economic, or foreign policy institutions and expertise. Again in contrast with the states of Africa, which were former colonies of distant overseas empires, the post-Soviet states were doomed by geography to live in the shadow of their powerful Russian neighbor—which itself faced the unexpected challenges of adjusting to a traumatic loss of territories and populations and defining a radically unprecedented nonimperial identity within historically novel borders. And unlike the situation in post-independence Africa, both geography and geopolitics endowed the Russian Federation with a considerable stake in developments in the region as well as considerable leverage over its neighbors, while at the same time generating continuing suspicion over Russian motives and intentions.

Moreover, the process of dissolution also left unfulfilled the aspirations of other, subordinate units in the former Soviet ethno-territorial hierarchy—suddenly deprived of the accustomed protection of the Soviet "center," their aspirations to sovereignty or autonomy unfulfilled, and their past entitlements threatened by newly empowered independent republic governments. The political struggle between Gorbachev and Boris Yeltsin and their competition for support from Russian elites had considerably enhanced these elites' political influence; it had also served to increase the inherent tensions among different levels of the ethno-territorial hierarchy— tensions that became even sharper in the process of dissolution.

The effort at state- and nation-building in the new "nationalizing states," to use the apt term of Rogers Brubaker (1995), brought to the forefront a key challenge: how to privilege the cultural and political leadership of the titular group without alienating key minorities or jeopardizing the stability and integrity of new states. Three issues were key to this challenge: defining state identity, elaborating language policies, and establishing the criteria for membership in the political community. Policy-making in these three areas was simultaneously complex and contentious, in view of the broad range of contending views among domestic constituencies as well as the need to simultaneously address a variety of attentive external audiences—from neighboring states to international organizations to NGOs. Moreover, to the extent that language, culture, and religion are significant building blocks in all state-building efforts, as well as in projects of national revival, the effort in the non-Russian republics to replace the previous hegemony of Russian culture and of Russian elites with that of the titular group was not in itself sufficient warrant for labeling these states "ethnocratic," as many Russian critics alleged. Notwithstanding important similarities across the region, both the specific challenges posed by cultural differences and the outcomes of policy varied considerably from one country to another. Although it is impossible to address them adequately in a single chapter, a wide range of practices emerged across the region, involving differing degrees of inclusiveness toward other groups and cultures.[9]

State- and Nation-Building: The Borderlands

A major source of variation in state policies and practices across the region stemmed from structural differences in the composition or organization of ethnic minorities in the new states. Briefly, each of these groups fell into one of four broad categories. The first consisted of ethnic minorities that had enjoyed the status of autonomous republics in the Soviet period and therefore not only possessed political institutions—and, consequently, organizational capacities—of their own but enjoyed certain political and cultural rights associated with that status. The ethno-national mobilization that swept many of the union republics during the late Gorbachev period and the growing demands for sovereignty also extended downward to the autonomous republics, exemplifying Donald Horowitz's argument that, as

---

9. For a more extensive treatment, see Rubin and Snyder (1998); Smith et al. (1998); Laitin (1998); Arbatov et al. (1997); Bremmer and Taras (1997).

the importance of a given political unit increases, so does the importance of the highest available level of identification below it (Horowitz 1975).[10] In most cases, particularly in the Russian Federation, the former autonomies sought to maximize their power within the framework of existing state structures. In several instances, however, particularly where they could rely on external homelands or other supportive actors for political and military support, they opted for secession.

A second category comprised the Russians and Russian-speaking populations "stranded" outside the Russian Federation at the moment of dissolution and facing as a consequence a radical change in their status and power, particularly acute problems of identity. Both the sudden change of position—from a hegemonic Soviet-centered elite to a national minority—and the presence of a powerful and neighboring "homeland" created the triangular relationship among these national minorities, the nationalizing states in which they now found themselves, and Russia, setting the stage for a distinctive dynamic superbly depicted in the work of Brubaker (1995, 1996).

A third category consisted of minority groups—whether compact or dispersed—that were indigenous to a particular republic and lacking an external homeland. By contrast with the previous groups, their demands tended to center on issues of economic and cultural rights, political recognition, and, in some instances, cultural survival. On the whole, the demands of this category were least threatening to the new states and could most readily be accommodated, but by the same token these groups lacked significant political protection against discrimination.

Finally, the category of "punished peoples" posed unique and difficult challenges. Deported from their homelands during the Joseph Stalin era and only partially rehabilitated under Nikita Khrushchev, their efforts to return to their previous homelands, restore their statehood, and regain lost land and homes clashed with the interests and expectations of current inhabitants and, in a number of instances, resulted in outbreaks of serious violence. The Ossetian-Ingush conflict over the Prigorodnyi *raion* in 1992, the first case of large-scale violent conflict on the territory of the Russian Federation, remains unresolved to this day. In the Crimean region of Ukraine, the return of the Crimean Tatars has also been a source of tension, albeit one that has not actually taken significant violent form.

---

10. The political importance of the autonomous republics was further enhanced by the conflict between Gorbachev and Yeltsin, each of whom sought their support in the struggles over a new Union Treaty. Indeed, in an effort to dilute the power of the union republics, Gorbachev sought to allow the autonomous republics to sign the treaty as separate subjects of the Soviet federation.

To this list should also be added two additional categories: "foreign" minorities, including Germans and Koreans, whose putative homelands lay outside the borders of the former Soviet Union and whose status was strongly affected by Soviet relations with their respective states, and religious/confessional minorities, many of whom had been persecuted during the Soviet era and now sought guarantees of their rights of association as well as, in many cases, restitution of religious properties. These important topics, however, lie outside the scope of this chapter.

Consolidating Statehood, Defining Identity

Whether or not they had actively sought sovereignty or independence in 1991, the new states of the region were compelled by the dissolution of the Soviet Union to define the identity on which their new statehood would be based. Although these states recognized to varying degrees that they were multinational states and defined their identity in civic rather than ethnic terms, for all of them (with the exception, as we shall see, of Russia) it was the European nation-state, however incompletely understood, that served as a model for their state-building projects.

In a variety of formulas, the new constitutions and discourses of the region sought to affirm the idea that power flowed from all the peoples of the country. In conformity with Western practice and new norms, most also eliminated the designation of ethnicity or nationality from passports and other official documents, accepting the principle that individuals have the right to freely choose, or to refuse, such identities. At the same time the continuing assumption that the new states were the national homelands of the titular group gave rise to other provisions that privileged the political and cultural role of the titular nation as the core of its identity. How the two discourses were balanced against each other in practice varied from country to country, as well as with the speaker and the audience. Clearly, consociationalism had scarcely entered the vocabulary of the region, and although cultural autonomy was generally viewed in positive terms, political autonomy and federalism (particularly when claimed by groups with external homelands) were viewed with suspicion, except in the Russian Federation.

Also of importance was the general refusal to acquiesce to pressure from the Russian government to introduce dual citizenship. Fearing that such agreements would provide a legal basis for Russian interference in their domestic affairs, all the states of the region with the exception of Turkmenistan and Tajikistan rejected these proposals. (As we shall see, however, this refusal has not deterred the Russian government from allowing its consulates in these states to grant Russian citizenship to residents without informing their local hosts.)

Although all the new states sought to define their identity in civic rather than ethnic terms, the approaches to state- and nation-building in the Baltic states diverged from the broader pattern and were based on a distinctive restorationist discourse. Briefly, this discourse was premised on the view that the independent statehood of these countries had been interrupted by the Soviet occupation of 1940 and that the events of 1991 had not created new states but had restored their prior statehood. This position had a variety of juridical consequences, but its most significant effect in the cases of Latvia and Estonia bore on the question of membership in the political community. In all the other post-Soviet states, citizenship was automatically extended to all those residing on their territories at the time of the union's dissolution—in effect, the "zero option." The governments of Estonia and Latvia, however, took the position that the demographic changes resulting from large-scale in-migration to these republics during the Soviet period constituted a form of illegal occupation in violation of the Geneva Convention and other international norms. Therefore, only those who had been citizens of the interwar republic and their descendants, irrespective of nationality, were entitled to automatic citizenship; all other residents would be obliged to apply for naturalization. Moreover, specific conditions were attached to naturalization, including a prescribed level of competence in the Estonian or Latvian language, knowledge of the respective country's constitution, and a defined period of residency. By compelling the substantial and largely Russian "settler communities" to treat citizenship not as an automatic entitlement but as a privilege requiring conscious choice and commitment, this approach induced high levels of anxiety even as it promoted a psychological adaptation. It also served to exclude these populations from significantly influencing the political process during the period when the basic rules of the game concerning political and economic reform were being established. Nonetheless, the tensions over this issue appear to be diminishing, a process of accommodation and integration is well under way, and there has been no significant wave of emigration of noncitizens from these states. Although the Baltic states' higher living standards and growing ties to Europe are an incentive to accommodation, the low propensity to emigrate also reflects the sense of security afforded to national minorities by these countries' relatively democratic political institutions, civil rights and legal protections, and the availability of a variety of official and nongovernmental channels through which to express grievances and adjudicate conflicts.[11]

Identity and Language Policy

Even before the dissolution of the Soviet Union, language policy had become a major focus of the new national movements. Soviet policy had promoted a pattern of asymmetrical bilingualism, with Russian enshrined as the dominant and officially compulsory language throughout the country, while national languages played a limited and varying role in the non-Russian republics and were largely ignored by the Russian population.[12] This situation was dramatically challenged in 1989 as new laws were passed in one republic after another making the titular language the state language and seeking to expand its use in official settings, in higher education, and in the media.

Although these laws were initially intended to revive national languages and protect them against further erosion or extinction, the effort to oust Russian as the dominant language and to enshrine the titular language as the official one subsequently became the core of nation-building projects and served as a catalyst for mobilizational efforts. In several cases the new language policies also included efforts to change the script in which national languages were written—from Cyrillic to Latin in the cases of Moldova and the Turkic Central Asian states, or to Arabic in the case of Tajikistan. Because of the close connection between language and access to education and employment, the issue had important instrumental as well as symbolic significance. However, these laws would remain largely symbolic unless followed up by serious efforts at implementation, and there was wide variation among the new states in both the level of commitment to this goal and the resources devoted to its fulfillment.

Broadly speaking, the language policies pursued by the new states tended to fall into five broad patterns. In Georgia, Armenia, and Azerbaijan, the knowledge and use of national languages had remained strong in the Soviet

---

11. A recent account in the *Los Angeles Times* of the sharp contrast in living conditions between the relatively prosperous city of Narva in northeastern Estonia, once a hotbed of Russian irredentism, and the decaying Russian city of Ivangorod just over the border captures a key feature of current trends (Paddock 1999, 1).

12. Soviet linguists claimed that this did not reflect the unequal status of national languages but rather was an indication of the universal respect and love for the Russian people and their language (Kreindler 1997).

period, and all three already treated their national languages as virtually official languages. The new, post-independence language laws basically strengthened and supported the existing trends, in which the use of Russian began to diminish but retained its function as a language of interstate and interethnic communication within the region (Kreindler 1997). Even this function has begun to be threatened by the rapid spread of English, not only in the southern Caucasus but throughout the entire region, particularly among aspiring and upwardly mobile economic and political actors and among the younger generation.

A second pattern involves the deliberate and extensive promotion of national languages as a substitute for Russian; Estonia and Latvia exemplify this pattern. From the earliest days of the popular fronts, there was a clear commitment to a national revival in which language and culture were defined as central and in which Russian was associated with foreign occupation and repression. With independence, policies were adopted that created major incentives and pressures designed to encourage Russian-speakers to learn and use the titular languages in public settings. These measures, including the citizenship laws discussed above, introduced language competence as a requirement for citizenship (as well as for certain categories of employment in the state and service sectors and some of the professions) and eliminated any lingering doubts about the seriousness of purpose that underlay them.[13] The fulfillment of these requirements was hampered by the limited availability of language-training programs, particularly outside the capital cities, as well as by a mixture of resistance and hesitation. But even though these policies were initially a source of considerable anxiety, the relative clarity and unambiguity of intention, as well as the tendency to reward good-faith efforts, accelerated the process of adaptation. As the work of David Laitin and others has suggested, the general trend of the past few years is toward serious efforts to master these languages and, among younger generations, to achieve real fluency (Laitin 1998).

---

13. Although this effort was under continuous assault from Moscow, which insisted that these policies constituted a fundamental violation of human rights and sought to use a variety of international forums as well as direct pressure to alter them, the Council of Europe maintained that neither the European Convention on Human Rights nor any other international human rights convention recognized the right to a certain citizenship as a human right, and it affirmed that any state had the right to determine the conditions for acquiring its citizenship (Parliamentary Assembly 1992, 239). More recently, the European Union's enlargement commissioner, Guenter Verheugen, praised the passage of amendments to the Estonian language law on June 14, 2000, affirming that the language law is now in total compliance with all OSCE and European Union norms (M. H. 2000).

A third pattern, particularly characteristic of Ukraine, Uzbekistan, Kazakhstan, and Moldova, shared this general commitment to language revival but considerably softened its actual implementation. Lacking the resources, capacity, and indeed the political will to energetically promote a transformation of language use, particularly in a situation where Russian-speaking political and cultural elites themselves resisted change, these states have tended to define the desired language shift as a gradual one and to envision a longer time frame for accomplishing it. In the case of Ukraine, where the closeness of the Ukrainian and Russian languages eases the process, the use of Ukrainian is gradually expanding and is becoming the norm for official purposes at the national level. At the local level, Ukrainization has made few inroads in the predominantly Russian eastern regions and in the Crimea, but flexibility has served to mitigate conflict. In the spring of 2000 the Ukrainian government proposed new measures to broaden and accelerate the use of Ukrainian, particularly among government officials and civil servants, but the proposals elicited sharp criticism from Moscow and precipitated a strident debate between Russian and Ukrainian officials.[14] In Kazakhstan the widespread Russification of Kazakh elites, their own resistance to learning Kazakh, and the lack of resources to teach the language on any large scale have together tended to subvert the nationalist program and to sustain the belief that learning Kazakh is not really necessary (Laitin 1998). In Uzbekistan, where Uzbek was already widely used, especially in rural areas, the shift to Uzbek has been faster and fuller than in the rest of Central Asia, despite some relaxation of the initial timetable.

A fourth set of cases, represented by Kyrgyzstan, Turkmenistan, and Tajikistan, involves efforts to forestall the departure or alienation of much-needed Russian specialists by preserving a substantial role for the Russian language and giving it equal or special status. In Kyrgyzstan and Turkmenistan, Russian was made a second official or state language, and both Tajikistan and Kyrgyzstan went further still in creating Slavonic universities intended to reassure their Russian communities that they could enjoy a rich cultural and educational environment in Russian in independent Kyrgyz and Tajik states. The civil war in Tajikistan, however, precipitated

---

14. Iakuda (2000). Russia's human rights commissioner, Oleg Mironov, asserted that restrictions on the official and business use of Russian violated "norms of civilized relations among peoples" and the basic rights and freedoms of citizens, and he asked the Council of Europe and the OSCE to monitor the situation (J.A.C. 2000a, 2000b). Meanwhile, Ukrainian officials have accused their Russian counterparts of distorting the real situation and of intervening in Ukraine's domestic affairs.

a massive exodus of Russians, which even exceptionally accommodating cultural policies could not have reversed.

A final and unique case is presented by Belarus. Under the leadership of its authoritarian and erratic president, Aleksandr Lukashenko, and despite an opposition that has attacked him for sacrificing Belarusian sovereignty to the pursuit of a Russia-Belarus union, the primacy of Russian has now been restored. The teaching and use of Belarusian in schools and the media is once again being circumscribed (Maksymiuk 1999).

Although Russian continues to serve as the lingua franca throughout the region, particularly among elites and the older generation, the erosion of Russian linguistic and cultural preeminence has been a cause of some alarm within Russia itself. Indeed, the Russian government has attempted in a variety of ways to defend and preserve the role of Russian across the region, even submitting a draft law on languages to the Commonwealth of Independent States (CIS), which ultimately proved unacceptable to CIS members. Interestingly, Russian writers on the issue have often cited Africa as a desirable model for the region, referring approvingly to the continuing role of English as a lingua franca in its now-independent states.

Cultural Pluralism

These approaches to state- and nation-building were not necessarily incompatible with support for considerable cultural pluralism. Indeed, in reaction to the Soviet legacy of national and religious repression the national movements had adopted a discourse that gave explicit emphasis to the development of civil societies and to freedom of cultural expression for different national groups. Following independence, there was considerable openness to expanding the rights enjoyed by many groups, particularly the right to establish cultural organizations and other institutions designed to protect and develop national heritages. Different forms of national and particularly cultural autonomy that had been circumscribed or eliminated in the Soviet period were revived. Islam, of course, experienced a significant renaissance, not only throughout Central Asia but in the Caucasus and in parts of Russia as well; Jewish communities enjoyed greater freedom, including the opportunity to establish new educational institutions; the Hungarian minority in Transcarpathian Ukraine was granted rights more extensive than it enjoyed anywhere else in Europe; and the Latvian state began to restore a diverse cultural infrastructure that included state financing for schooling in Polish, Ukrainian, Hebrew, and Lithuanian. A wide variety of new initiatives intended to promote interethnic communication and conciliation were also launched, including both governmental and unofficial nationality forums and roundtables from Estonia to Kazakhstan.

These years also saw a considerable expansion of opportunities to restore and develop ties with compatriots and co-religionists abroad—ties that had been severed or constrained during the Soviet period. Indeed, for Tatars, Koreans, and Jews, to mention just a few, such ties were transformed from liabilities to assets, offering access to new economic and political resources from abroad in support of local efforts at cultural and religious revival. Access to such resources became a critical determinant of the success or failure of such efforts, as local sources of funding virtually dried up.

Notwithstanding this greater openness to cultural pluralism, the ability to make use of these new opportunities was sharply constrained by the economic crisis that enveloped the region. State funding dwindled or ended, and the promotion of these activities depended almost exclusively on the energies and resources that could be mobilized internally or externally by local activists. By the same token, these external ties and support—especially in the case of religious groups perceived to threaten established religious institutions—also provoked suspicion and repression.[15]

Responsible judgments about the extent to which independent statehood has affected the political and economic opportunities available to different ethnic groups—a much broader definition of citizenship than the narrower juridical one—require a more substantial base of data than is currently available. Existing evidence suggests that the main beneficiaries of the political transformations of the last decade have been the political elites of the titular nationalities. Their predominance is most evident at the level of national politics, where they are increasingly displacing Russian officials in key executive positions and in legislative bodies. In some cases, personnel changes also carry with them great symbolic importance: the replacement of several prominent figures in the government of Kazakhstan, for example, or in the Georgian Ministry of Defense is widely interpreted as an affirmation of control by the titular group and an assertion of independence from Moscow; the recent appointment of a number of Russian officials to key positions by President Lukashenka is taken as a further indicator of the erosion of Belarus's sovereignty under his leadership (J. M. 2000).

---

15. Hostility to "incursions" and proselytizing by nonindigenous evangelical Christian groups and restrictions on their registration and activities have been widespread across the region and have provoked considerable Western criticism, as well as OSCE human rights monitoring (see also Lord 1997).

The impact of economic marketization, however, is more ambiguous; as Amy Chua has argued, marketization is likely to benefit a market-dominant minority even as electoral democracy increases the power of the relatively impoverished majority (Chua 1998). To the extent that Russians tended to be concentrated in major urban centers, to dominate the managerial and administrative as well as military-industrial sectors of the economies, and to be underrepresented in agriculture and in rural areas, they enjoyed relatively favorable opportunities in many instances to convert political advantage into control over important economic assets during the early stages of the transformation. They also benefit from their role as intermediaries in still-significant economic relationships with Russia. In countries where language requirements have significantly affected access to employment in the state sector and services, however, as in Estonia and Latvia, growing income inequality may disadvantage the Russian-speaking population because of its lower levels of representation in these sectors (Titma, Tuma and Silver 1998).

Over the longer term, the uneven distribution of political power and economic resources among different regions and groups and the perception of discrimination and injustice could well precipitate new forms of ethnic mobilization and interethnic tension. The absence of effective power-sharing arrangements that give all major groups both a voice and a stake in governance, combined with the weakness of central and especially local government institutions, could seriously threaten the stability and governability of many of the states in the region and exacerbate the separatist tendencies that have already compromised the statehood of several.

Statehood Compromised

Leaving aside the civil war in Tajikistan, the most serious threat to the political and territorial consolidation of several of the new states—specifically, Georgia, Moldova, and Azerbaijan—was the violent ethno-political conflicts and secessionist wars that erupted in the earliest stages of independence. These conflicts threatened their security and indeed viability as states, diverted energy and resources from political and economic consolidation, eroded the legitimacy of their political leaders, and threatened them with near-disintegration. They also proved to be exceptionally resistant to all efforts at accommodation.

These ethno-territorial, secessionist conflicts tended to share several common features. First, they involved ethnic groups that had enjoyed under Soviet rule an institutional base in the form of territorial autonomy. (Trans-Dniestria, which was not an autonomous republic in the 1977 Soviet constitution, declared itself one during *perestroika*. Moreover, in the interwar period, the Trans-Dniestria region had constituted a separate administrative unit within Ukraine—the Moldavian Autonomous Soviet Socialist Republic.) Second, the warring ethnic groups based their claims on the principle of national self-determination as well as on notions of historical justice, insisting that their borders or status had been unjustly imposed, that their status and entitlements were threatened by the republics of which they were a part, and that as peoples they enjoyed the right to determine their own fate, up to and including independence. The rights of other peoples inhabiting the same territories were largely ignored. Third, when the conflicts escalated into violence, they culminated in military victories by the secessionists, notwithstanding their smaller numbers; these outcomes resulted from the secessionists' high levels of preparation and motivation but also from overt or covert support from an external actor: Armenia in the case of Nagorno-Karabakh and Russia in the case of Trans-Dniestria, Abkhazia, and South Ossetia.

Fourth, all of the conflicts resulted in large flows of refugees and in the "ethnic cleansing" of the territories involved; these demographic changes were in turn an instrument for consolidating political control. Fifth, and in contrast with most ethno-territorial conflicts in Africa, which have tended to end in decisive military victory by one side or the other, these conflicts in Eurasia remained essentially frozen, without any political resolution and with the potential to erupt in the future. They have resulted in the creation of several quasi-states with de facto control of their own territories but are unlikely to be recognized by the international community. And sixth, these conflicts have been used by the Russian Federation to preserve its political and military influence in the region, including to compel membership in the CIS, to secure and extend basing rights for Russian military units, to maintain control over the external borders of other CIS states, and to preserve elements of the Soviet unified air defense system.

In seeking to restore their territorial integrity and to find mutually acceptable political compromises with the secessionist leaderships, the states involved have turned to regional and international organizations—initially to Russia and the CIS, but later to the OSCE, the United Nations, and friendly Western governments—for assistance in managing or mediating the negotiating process, in dealing with the humanitarian needs of large numbers of refugees, and in pressing the Russian government to play a more constructive role. They have sought to accommodate demands for a significant degree of self-rule by proposing or acquiescing in a variety of new federal arrangements, often drawn from broader international experience, as well as security and confidence-building arrangements that would alleviate fears of retribution. While the offer of a high degree of autonomy has been a useful strategy for conflict prevention, serving to forestall serious conflict in a number of other instances, from Crimea to Gagauz to Ajaria to Tatarstan, it has been less successful as an instrument of post-conflict resolution. In the aftermath of these secessionist wars the victors have held out for full independence or for loose confederal arrangements that have often been viewed by the governments involved as an unacceptable violation of their sovereignty and territorial integrity.

A Contested Identity: The Case of Russia

The dissolution of the Soviet Union created a distinctive set of challenges for state- and nation-building in the Russian Federation. Stripped of a significant part of the territory that had once formed the Soviet state and of much of its non-Russian population, the post-Soviet Russian state was a far more homogeneous entity than the Soviet Union had been, with Russians constituting some 82 percent of its population. But it also emerged from this process stripped of its superpower status and of both the imperial and Soviet identities that had long defined it. The effort to virtually invent a new Russian state and a novel national identity in these radically new conditions—including defining the new state's borders, its interests in relation to populations and states now outside them, and its internal ethno-political and constitutional structure—proved far more problematic and contentious than was the case in the other fourteen successor states and became the source of major political cleavages and contestation.

The sudden and traumatic dissolution of the Soviet state, indistinguishable for many from the end of the Russian empire, provoked exaggerated if not obsessive fears of the possible disintegration of Russia itself and contributed over time to a shift within the political elite from a liberal-democratic orientation to an increasingly statist and nationalist one. The growing controversy over Russia's federal structure, fueled by changes in the composition and policy orientation of the political elite, made issues of center-republic relations particularly contentious. As the new Russian state struggled to create constitutional and federal arrangements in an environment of state breakdown and high levels of uncertainty, efforts to halt the centrifugal tendencies that had been unleashed during *perestroika* became a key priority in Moscow and a major source of conflict in center-periphery relations—a conflict that would take its most extreme and intractable form in the relations between Moscow and Chechnya.

Reinventing Russia

A broad framework for constructing a new Russian state and national identity had begun to take shape even prior to the dissolution of the Soviet Union. As the personal and political conflict between Gorbachev and Yeltsin came to focus on the nature and future of the Soviet Union, Yeltsin and his advisers—drawn at that time largely from radical democratic circles associated with the Democratic Russia movement—began to articulate a conception of Russian statehood that sought to distance Russia from its imperial past and to create the institutional foundations of a liberal and democratic political order (Szporluk 1994; Dunlop 1993; Lapidus 1992, 1994; Breslauer and Dale 1997). In his 1990 campaign for election to the Russian presidency, Yeltsin had embraced the notion of Russia's revival based on a liberal and anti-imperial national identity, inclusive and civic rather than ethnic in its conception, appealing for the support of all citizens of Russia (*rossiyane*) rather than to ethnic Russians (*russkie*) alone (Tishkov 1995). He painted a picture of Russia as a multinational and democratic state based on individualism and human rights, a "normal European country" in which the interests of all its peoples would be represented and in which their distinct ethnic and cultural traditions would be protected and advanced. This essentially civic conception of Russia remained central to his presidency (even though it underwent modification over time) and would contrast sharply with the views of various opposition figures who advocated scenarios based on Russian ethnic nationalism and imperial restoration.

The territory to be embraced by this new Russian state was to become a particularly contentious issue. Although his approach would be challenged by an increasingly outspoken and assertive opposition, Yeltsin's Russia was a state defined by the Russian Federation's borders of 1991. The Belovezhskoe Forest agreement and the subsequent Almaty agreement were predicated on the mutual recognition of existing borders by the signatories and were in turn endorsed and legitimated by the international community. This approach was consistent with Yeltsin's earlier support for the aspirations of national and independence movements in the Baltics and other republics and for the creation of a commonwealth of sovereign states.[16] This stance was tempered in practice in response to growing political pressures on Moscow and on the Yeltsin leadership to defend the interests of the large Russian or Russian-speaking communities "beached" outside Russia's borders after the dissolution of the union and by pressures to support separatist movements that looked to Moscow for assistance. Nonetheless, the Yeltsin government on the whole refrained from efforts to mobilize separatist movements in the Russian diaspora, especially after the government's expressions of concern for the fate of compatriots in the Baltic republics—joined to veiled threats of military action—provoked pointed Western commentaries about historic parallels with the claims of the Third Reich (Zevelev 1996; Smith et al. 1998).[17]

The absence of a clear and compelling conception of Russia's national identity among reformers and democrats made them especially vulnerable to attacks by a variety of opposition groups espousing statist and nationalist ideas. Already in the Gorbachev era, a rapprochement had begun to take place between communist and nationalist extremists, a "red-brown" coalition opposed to Gorbachev's reforms that sought to unite all "patriotic forces" in defense of the Soviet fatherland and to prevent the destruction of the Soviet state by what it described as a clique of domestic and Western enemies. Opposing Gorbachev's attempt to criticize and ultimately to delegitimize key features of the Soviet system, members of this coalition denounced the Belovezhskoe Forest agreement as treason and viewed the dissolution of the Soviet Union as a national catastrophe.

This opposition was far from homogeneous. It embraced different conceptions of Russian identity and statehood and different views about the role of Russians and non-Russians in a future Russian state (Tolz 1998). The dominant strain, however, was "restorationist:" to re-create as much of the former Soviet Union as possible, whether in the form of a new union or through the restoration of a Russia-centered empire. Although today some advocates of this position would shrink from any resort to violence to achieve these goals (assuming the necessary instruments were at their disposal), others—both nostalgic communists and "Eurasianists"—have a more ambitious, indeed aggressive, agenda. This restorationist impulse,

---

16. Among the several explicit attacks on this position, see Andronik Migranian's diatribe treating Russia's recognition of Baltic independence as a serious mistake and the result of the "naiveté and dilettantism of the Russian leadership" (Migranian 1994).

17. Notwithstanding some sympathy and even support for several separatist movements, the Russian government strongly endorsed the principle of territorial integrity with a view to deterring external support for separatist challenges to the Russian Federation itself.

however, no longer draws on the internationalist ideology of Soviet Bolshevism but rather evokes Russian imperial ambitions. It also envisions a political community that unmistakably bestows on ethnic Russians a privileged place above the other national groups of both the Russian Federation and the successor states. In contrast with civic and inclusive notions of Russian identity, it argues that Russia should be viewed as the national state of ethnic Russians.[18]

A second orientation focuses on Slavic rather than Russian identity. It views post-Soviet Russia as a "divided nation" and advocates pursuing the reunification of the Slavic heartland—essentially Russia, Ukraine, and Belarus, with the addition (as proposed by novelist and political activist Aleksandr Solzhenitsyn) of the largely Russian-settled territories of northern Kazakhstan. Heartened by the recent Russia-Belarus union, supporters of this vision see the union as merely the first step in the larger process of Slavic consolidation. Some advocates of this approach are prepared to contemplate the loss of the northern Caucasus and possibly other Muslim regions of the Russian Federation and attach little importance to Central Asia or other non-Russian regions. Others appear to contemplate a broader union that would extend beyond ethnic Slavs to embrace a broader community of Christian peoples of the region, from Armenia to Serbia.

At times this view is linked to the argument (as expressed by the radical nationalist politician Sergei Baburin) that "there has been, and still is, a genocide taking place against the Russian people, directly and indirectly . . . and [we should] condemn those who are guilty"(Simonsen 1996, 19). Russian neofascists such as Aleksandr Barkashov go even further in defining Russian identity in racial terms and maintaining (as his communist allies would not) that the Soviet regime pursued a "racial program . . . so that the Russians would to the largest possible extent lose their national appearance and traits of their national-racial Indo-European (Aryan) genotype." His program includes "the [Russian] Nation as the highest value" (Simonsen 1996, 35) and assigns responsibility for the humiliation of Russians to Jews.

These views are increasingly echoed among a wider public. Recent public opinion surveys show increasing support for the view that Russians have been deceived, exploited, and victimized by the developments of the past years and that foreigners—whether Caucasians, Jews, or Westerners—are

---

18. Valery Tishkov (1995) has argued for an inclusionary strategy, and indeed for renaming the country "Rossia"; by contrast, the writings of Migranian (1994) exemplify the exclusionary perspective.

to blame for the tribulations that have befallen Russia (Payin 1999). Correspondingly, there is a growing feeling that Russians deserve to enjoy special rights and privileges. Data gathered by the highly respected All-Russia Center for the Study of Public Opinion in December 1988 found that 43 percent of respondents supported the idea that "Russia is for ethnic Russians"; 30 percent rejected the statement as tantamount to fascism.[19] Should such tendencies grow stronger and become more widespread in the months and years ahead they could be seriously destabilizing both within the Russian Federation and in the region as a whole, weakening support for pluralism and accommodation domestically and encouraging more assertive and aggressive policies toward neighboring states.

Accommodating Ethnic Differences in Russia

In the first years of independent statehood, the Russian government adopted a number of measures that sought to accommodate some of the political and cultural interests of ethnic minorities and to reduce interethnic tensions. In keeping with the inclusive conception of Russian state and national identity, the citizenship law adopted by the Russian Federation extended the right of citizenship to anyone who had been a citizen of the Soviet Union, whether or not he or she was already a citizen of another state. This stance had both an accommodationist and a threatening aspect to it. On the one hand, it relieved the anxieties of large numbers of refugees who flooded into Russia from neighboring states, while also reassuring those outside the borders of the Russian Federation that, should the environment in these states prove less than hospitable, emigration to Russia was, in principle, an option. However, it also became a way of introducing dual citizenship by stealth. As mentioned earlier, even though most of the new post-Soviet states refused to accede to Russian pressures to allow dual citizenship, Russia instructed its consulates to issue citizenship documents to citizens of other states without the knowledge of host governments.[20]

Other constitutional provisions and legislative acts also testified to the

---

19. *Kommersant* 1999, pp. 1, 3. A June 1999 survey found that 38 percent of respondents felt that Russia should accept only ethnic Russian refugees; 35 percent agreed with the statement that a candidate's ethnicity should be a factor in elections and appointments; and 20 percent upheld the view that ethnic Russians should enjoy special rights and privileges (Kakovkin 1999, 5).

20. For example, in 1997 the Russian embassy in Estonia reported that some 120,000 persons had obtained Russian citizenship, but it declined to provide the Estonian government with a list (U.S. Department of State 1999).

liberal inclinations of the new Russian state: guarantees of extensive individual rights, including equality before the law regardless of race, nationality, or language; guarantees of group rights, including the right to use and develop native languages; a law on cultural autonomy that sought to define the rights of cultural institutions; and a legislative provision that made it a crime to incite ethnic hatred. However important these were as statements of principle, most of these provisions remain little more than pieces of paper.[21] Their implementation has been the victim of state breakdown, a lack of financial resources, and outright bureaucratic sabotage, while evidence continues to multiply of serious discrimination and hostility—toward Jews, Caucasians, Roma, and more recently Chinese and others viewed as "outsiders"—further intensified by economic crisis and deteriorating living conditions.

Arguably the most significant and successful of the Yeltsin government's efforts to avert ethnic conflict and accommodate many of the demands of important ethnic communities and elites was the development of a form of asymmetrical federalism—a set of bilateral, treaty-based relationships negotiated with each of the federation's republics as well as with other subjects of the federation.

The Russian Federation had inherited from the Soviet Union a particularly complex ethno-territorial structure, which included five distinct types of administrative territorial units. These were consolidated into two types of units between 1991 and 1993: 20 (later 21) ethnically defined republics and 66 territorially defined regions, with the former enjoying significantly greater rights (Lapidus and Walker 1994). Faced in 1991 with some of the same centrifugal forces as those that had undermined the Soviet Union, the Russian government leadership rejected proposals to eliminate the existing ethnic units as potentially destabilizing and concluded in 1992 a new Federation Treaty (signed by all republics except Tatarstan and Chechnya) that granted the constituent units broad but vague economic and political rights and described them as "sovereign." Yeltsin had further promised that the treaty would be incorporated into the new constitution then being

---

21. A recent illustration of the problem involves the law against incitement of ethnic hatred. This law has not in fact been used to prosecute offenders, including self-proclaimed adherents of neo-Nazi organizations. In one highly publicized case brought against a neofascist publication for inciting anti-Semitism, scholarly testimony was presented to the court on behalf of the defense that argued that the terminology involved had no pejorative connotations. More recently, an episode involving an anti-Semitic speech by a parliamentary deputy, General Albert Makashov, brought neither a rebuke from the Communist Party parliamentary faction of which he was a member nor any immediate response from the government.

drafted. In the course of subsequent political struggles, elements of these agreements were whittled away: the Federation Treaty was not ultimately incorporated into the constitution, the language describing the republics as "sovereign states" was removed, and the largely Russian regions were granted many of the privileges previously enjoyed by the republics alone.

Nonetheless, the outcome did not represent a full victory for the advocates of a strong centralized government or a purely territorial federation. Significant powers were to be exercised jointly by the central and republic (and regional) governments, including the protection of human rights and the rights of ethnic minorities, ownership of land and mineral resources, and environmental protection within the republics' territory. In addition, the republics (and regions) were awarded limited powers of independent legislation and taxation and the right to establish state languages (to mention just two of the most important provisions). But the adoption of the constitution could not and did not provide a definitive and final resolution of a whole range of key issues, all of which remained subject to continuous renegotiation and to behind-the-scenes bargaining between central and local authorities.

Of crucial importance during these years was the fact that the conflict with Tatarstan was eventually resolved peacefully. Following difficult and protracted negotiations a treaty was finally signed in February 1994 that granted Tatarstan considerably broader competencies and rights than had been granted to other subjects of the federation, including significant economic concessions and the right to its own international and economic relations with foreign states. This agreement was criticized—from opposite positions—both in the republic and in Moscow, but the process of mutual accommodation through negotiations served to defuse separatist sentiments, enhance the loyalty of republic elites, and avoid the deadly use of force. And it set a useful precedent for subsequent efforts to resolve jointly such contentious issues as republic citizenship.

The agreement with Tatarstan was the first of a long series of bilateral treaties that were negotiated between Moscow and the republics and regions in subsequent years, with differing terms corresponding to the distinctive features of each case. This process was not without its serious problems: the proliferation of bilateral treaties conferring different rights on different constituent units arguably weakens the development of a single and uniform legal order and economic space for the federation as a whole (Lysenko 1998). Yet on balance this asymmetrical federalism in Russia represented a constructive and flexible response in a period of great fluidity to a Soviet legacy that created aspirations, expectations, and institutional arrangements that could not be dismantled without risking destabilization. It tailored center-periphery relations to the varying needs and demands of different subjects of the federation, allowing for a useful degree of diversity and experimentation in a country as large and variegated as the Russian Federation. It also created a framework for satisfying the aspirations of major ethnic groups for recognition, security, and meaningful political participation and has provided opportunities for the preservation or enhancement of ethno-linguistic and cultural diversity, thereby defusing the potentially separatist connotations of republican sovereignty and transforming it into a legitimate form of regionalism (Drobizheva 1998a). It located decision-making on some key issues closer to the ground and facilitated cooperation between moderates and pragmatists in Moscow and their counterparts in the regions and republics. At the same time, it has helped to marginalize or isolate extremists on both sides. Proposals to abolish the ethnic republics and replace them with purely territorial administrative units along the lines of the tsarist *guberniya*—an approach endorsed in part by former prime minister Yevgennyi Primakov—were widely perceived, by the general population as well as by republic elites, as both unrealistic and needlessly provocative.

The most profound weakness of Russia's evolving federal structure was not its asymmetrical character; asymmetry is a feature of most multinational federations. Rather, it was the absence in Russia of institutionally embedded mechanisms and credible guarantees to ensure that a division of powers and competencies between the national government and local units is in fact observed. As Alfred Stepan has argued, only a constitutional democracy can provide both the relatively autonomous constitutional, legislative, and judicial systems a genuine federal system requires and the credible guarantees that the prerogatives of subunits are in fact respected. The Russian Federation lacked both (Stepan 2000; Mendras 1999).

Vladimir Putin's ascendancy to the presidency of Russia and his commitment to restoring the authority and power of the Russian state radically challenged these prevailing arrangements. While refraining from a direct challenge to the existing ethno-territorial structure, Putin moved aggressively to strengthen the vertical structure of power and to curtail the political and economic power of republic and regional leaders. Equating "order" with centralization and federalism with fragmentation and separatism, he superimposed on the existing structure seven super-regions—corresponding to Russia's military districts—whose appointed heads, typically drawn from the military and security services, report directly to the president. He also initiated a radical change in the composition of the Fed-

eration Council (the upper chamber of parliament) by replacing oblast governors and republic presidents with less-influential representatives. At the
same time his government launched an aggressive campaign to annul
regional laws that contradicted federal legislation, to reduce the share of
revenues controlled by regional governments, and to arrogate the right to
dismiss errant elected officials. It also threatened unilaterally to review, alter, and possibly even annul the bilateral republican treaties, including the
1994 treaty between Tatarstan and the Russian Federation that was mentioned above.

This aggressive campaign was tempered by more conciliatory gestures,
including the creation, by presidential decree, of a new consultative body:
the State Council of the Russian Federation, which includes Russia's
regional and republic leaders in its membership and Tatarstan's influential
president in its presidium. Nonetheless, the continuing yearning for a more
centralized, unitary, and cohesive state and the misperceptions and controversy surrounding the very notion of federalism demonstrate the complexity and the fragility of current arrangements.

From Accommodation to Force: War in Chechnya

If the treaty between Russia and Tatarstan represents a model of successful peaceful accommodation of ethnic and regional interests, the resort to
military force in Chechnya is the most potent symbol of failure. The
conflict had its origins in a fundamental misperception by Moscow of the
nature of the challenge posed by Chechnya and its tendency to view the
situation not as a unique case but as the first of a series of potential "domi-
noes" that would result in the destruction of Russian statehood. Its escalation into full-scale war in 1994–96 was also the product of institutional
breakdown in both Moscow and Grozny, which resulted in a highly personalized and subjective style of decision-making in both capitals in which
hard-line figures hostile to accommodation gained the upper hand
(Lapidus 1998, 1999; Payin and Popov 1996). In Moscow it was mani-
fested in a poorly institutionalized policy-making process, exacerbated by
bitter intra-elite struggles and institutional rivalries and the divergent and
conflicting interests of a variety of ministers and presidential advisers (as
well as of the shadowy business interests with which they were associated).
Lacking more subtle instruments to influence the conflict and seeking a
clear demonstration of state power, President Yeltsin and his Security
Council made a deliberate decision to resort to military force.

These weaknesses on the Russian side were compounded and exacerbated by state breakdown and intra-elite conflict in Chechnya. Unlike in Tatarstan, where the state institutions inherited from the Soviet era were largely adapted by the Mintimer Shaimiev leadership to a nation-building project, Chechnya experienced a revolutionary transformation that undermined Soviet institutions but brought virtual anarchy in its wake. Weak institutions, the lack of experienced leadership, and the diversion of economic resources from public to private ends undermined the ability of Chechnya to function as a state, while regional cleavages and competition among rival clans drove elite politics. Weak political and economic capacity in turn created additional incentives and opportunities for a variety of illegal activities, including trade in drugs and weapons, whose availability had been increased by the disorganized withdrawal of Soviet military units from the Caucasus. These problems were compounded by Chechen president Dzokhar Dudayev's own political inexperience, mercurial temperament, provocative behavior, and poor judgment. His use of anti-Russian discourses to delegitimize his opponents, consolidate his own political support, and compensate for the absence of other bases of legitimacy in turn played into the hands of hard-line political and military figures in Moscow, who favored "settling" such problems by force.

Russian military defeats combined with widespread public hostility to the war created a propitious opportunity for terminating the war. The Khasavyurt agreements of 1997 pledged both sides to renounce the use of force "forever" in mutual relations, deferred the issues of Chechnya's status for five years, and facilitated new presidential elections in Chechnya under OSCE supervision—elections that brought to power Aslan Maskhadov, a moderate figure seeking cooperation with Russia. But the opportunity afforded by peace was squandered. The Russian government failed to commit resources to rebuilding the infrastructure of the region and alleviating the economic and social desperation that bred for radicalism and banditry. Lacking a coherent policy toward the region, it vacillated between isolating the republic and vilifying it.

The Russian government's renewed resort to massive military force in August 1999 was an undiscriminating and disproportionate response to two crises: two incursions from Chechen territory into Dagestan by armed militants (many of them Dagestani) in support of Islamist insurgents there, incursions that were neither supported nor approved by the Maskhadov government or by the Chechen population more broadly; and three bombings of apartment buildings in Moscow and Volgodonsk that were immediately blamed on Chechen terrorists without any convincing evidence. Playing on the fears of the Russian population, and following up on military assaults on Wahhabi villages in Dagestan, the government seized on the opportunity to launch a full-scale military attack on Chechnya, repudiating the Khasavyurt agreements, denouncing the Maskhadov government as a criminal regime (much as it had earlier denounced the Dudayev government), and refusing to engage in any negotiations.

The Putin government sought to portray its actions in Chechnya as a limited and carefully targeted counterterrorist operation aimed at eliminating the threat to Russia posed by "international terrorism." Although the presentation was novel and sought to exploit Western concerns over international terrorism, the actions in fact amounted to a resumption of the 1994–96 war, now pursued with even greater determination by the Russian military and political leadership, with even greater disregard for civilian casualties and refugees, and with a more sophisticated military and public relations strategy designed to minimize military casualties and sustain widespread popular support.

The military assault was initially portrayed as a targeted attack on armed terrorist formations, but its scope progressively broadened. Whether by design from the start or as a product of "mission creep," the objectives progressively escalated: from the creation of a cordon sanitaire, to military occupation of northern Chechnya up to the Terek River, to a massive military campaign across the entire territory of Chechnya without any clear political endgame. It involved artillery and air bombardment of civilian settlements and populations, the destruction of the city of Grozny as well as of most of the republic's infrastructure, and the flight of more than two hundred thousand refugees to Ingushetia.[22] It has been accompanied by tight control over the media and an effort to downplay casualties so as to capitalize on public support, minimize protest, and promote Putin's political popularity. Allegations that Russian behavior in Chechnya is tantamount to "ethnic cleansing" feed on dramatic statements, such as that of former Russian vice president Aleksandr Rutskoi advocating that Chechnya "should be turned into a Gobi Desert" (Rudakova 2000)—a statement endorsed by 34 percent of respondents in a subsequent opinion poll (Radzikhovskii 2000).

One year later, no clear victory was in sight. Refusing all negotiations with Maskhadov, the Russian leadership attempted to install its own pro-Moscow leadership in Chechnya. The appointment of Mufti Kadyrov was,

---

22. The war was conducted with such flagrant disregard for international norms that respected human rights organizations charged the Russian authorities with massive war crimes against civilian populations (Human Rights Watch 2000).

in effect, an effort to create a fig leaf of authenticity around what was de facto an occupation regime. Decisions to station a permanent, major military contingent in the northern Caucasus were a clear indication that Russian interior forces would be unable to control the situation unaided. It remains unclear how they will win the loyalty of an increasingly embittered population. Thus Russian actions have further undermined the possibility of drawing the majority of the Chechen population into support for and cooperation with Russia and of making the Russian Federation a country of which they want to be part.

Quite apart from the destabilizing consequences of the war itself, it has exacerbated the stereotyping, dehumanizing, and demonizing of Caucasians generally, of Islam and Muslims within the Russian Federation (especially after the Soviet experience in Afghanistan), and of Chechens in particular. In cities such as Moscow, popular suspicion and hostility have been given official sanction in campaigns to expel from the city persons "of Caucasian appearance," fueling widespread suspicion and discrimination, arbitrary seizures and shakedowns of suspects, and growing alienation of the targeted groups. Overall, the devastating consequences of this brutal and tragic war have proven infinitely more costly to the process of state- and nation-building in Russia than the concessions made to Tatarstan.

Conclusion: Stability and Potential Conflict

With the exception of the new war in Chechnya, the late 1990s were marked by a considerable degree of stabilization across the ethno-political landscape of the Soviet successor states. It may well herald an accommodation, however reluctant and imperfect, among potentially conflicting parties. But stability remains precarious, and the potential for future conflict remains high.

There is among the fifteen successor states a considerable and indeed growing differentiation in political orientations and prospects, from democratizing to authoritarian (Fish 1998; Bunce 1998). Yet everywhere we observe a striking failure to create strong and efficacious states where the rule of law and the protection of minorities are not only enshrined in institutions and law but also assimilated in the dominant political culture and patterns of behavior. And although the latter process is bound to take time, there is little evidence that most of the governments of the region have either the intense commitment or the institutional and economic resources to make power-sharing and fostering multiethnic tolerance serious priorities.

Moreover, in a number of the region's states the present stability and accommodationist discourse have been closely identified with the personality of a particular leader. Before very long the succession of the present incumbents will create new uncertainties, and the political struggles apt to accompany the succession process may well undermine the stability sketched above. In those states where competitive elections shape political outcomes there are substantial incentives for candidates to engage in competitive ethnic outbidding. In more authoritarian and repressive political environments, as in parts of Central Asia, discontent may find outlets in Islamist or separatist insurgencies.

Perhaps the most salient development in many of the post-Soviet states (with the partial exception of the Baltic states) has been the ongoing economic crises and growing socio-economic disparities. Although these problems have thus far resulted in large measure in focusing popular preoccupations on sheer survival, the dynamics of deprivation could readily spill over into ethnic conflicts. Both in Russia and in the new states rising aggressiveness, scapegoating, and interethnic tension could easily assume even uglier forms.

The evolution of political conditions in the Russian Federation will be critical to stability and to interethnic concord in all the states of the region. Stability in Russia has thus far been supported by state weakness, the preoccupation with severe domestic problems, and the relatively moderate dispositions of the Yeltsin leadership in Moscow, which acted with greater restraint in relations with neighbors than it was widely expected to. But the activities of extreme nationalist and neofascist movements that blame Jews, Caucasians, and other ethnic and religious minorities for Russia's problems are a continuing danger. The growing assertiveness and militarization of groups such as the Cossacks in the northern Caucasus and Central Asia, indications of rising political mobilization among the Russian population in northern Kazakhstan, and the possibility of harnessing the frustration and bitterness of refugees and "forced migrants" in Russia to a larger political movement all provide a potential base of support for a Russian leader seeking to restore order, status, and power. These trends have converged in support of President Putin and have focused on the military campaign in Chechnya. As Major-General Vladimir Shamanov, then commander of Russian forces in western Chechnya, summarized it, "[T]his war is above all to restore the trampled-upon honor of my motherland" (York 1999).

All of these elements could have seriously destabilizing consequences for the other states of the region and invite turmoil in a variety of areas—from the Crimea to the Caucasus to Kazakhstan, and perhaps the Baltic republics—as well as in Russia itself. In comparing post-Soviet politics of cultural pluralism with those of Africa, one finds both striking parallels and sharp contrasts. The most important similarity is the relative absence of direct interstate violence. The sanctity of colonial partition boundaries proclaimed by the Organization of African Unity at its creation in 1963 has been generally respected. Although there has been some skirmishing arising out of disputes as to where these boundaries lie (e.g., Algeria-Morocco, Mali–Burkina Faso, Nigeria-Cameroon, Libya-Chad), by and large interstate warfare has been remarkable for its absence. A sharp difference is that the African state system is not based on "titular nationalities"; the only exceptions are Botswana, Lesotho, Swaziland, and Somalia. The first three have substantial number of co-ethnics in neighboring South Africa, but these would never be considered as "beached" and are not a source of controversy. Only Somalia at an earlier phase harbored irredentist ambitions, a mantra of state ideology from independence in 1960 until its crushing defeat by Soviet- and Cuban-reinforced Ethiopians in 1977. However, in the 1990s, the growing pattern of crossborder spillover and interpenetration of internal civil conflict has characterized the region, with some distant echoes of post-Soviet patterns.

As Mark Beissinger reminds us, surges in nationalist violence in Eurasia are closely connected with shifts in state authority: "[S]tate authority plays a key role in encouraging, condoning, aiding, and in some cases directly perpetrating acts of nationalist violence" (Beissinger 1998). The successions and elections that lie ahead could well result in the political victory of groups of more assertive nationalist orientations, groups whose geopolitical agendas are also far less oriented toward integration with the West than has been the case thus far. Under these circumstances there is a real danger that resort to ethnic and nationalist outbidding as an instrument of political competition could provoke escalation of the kinds of conflicts in the region that have long been feared but thus far have largely been avoided.

References

Alexseev, Mikhail A., ed. 1999. *Center-Periphery Conflict in Post-Soviet Russia: A Federation Imperiled*. New York: St. Martin's.

Arbatov, Alexei, et al., eds. 1997. *Managing Conflict in the Former Soviet Union: Russian and American Perspectives*. Cambridge, Mass.: MIT Press.

Arutiunian, Ju. V. 1994. *Russians: Inhabitants of the Capital*. Ethnosociology in Figures series. Moscow: Russian Academy of Sciences.

———. 1996. *Uzbekistan: Inhabitants of the Capital.* Ethnosociology in Figures series. Moscow: Russian Academy of Sciences.

Beissinger, Mark R. 1998. "Nationalist Violence and the State: Political Authority and Contentious Repertoires in the Former USSR." *Comparative Politics* 30, no. 4 (July): 401–22.

Bremmer, Ian, and Ray Taras, eds. 1997. *New States, New Politics: Building the Post-Soviet Nations.* New York: Cambridge University Press.

Breslauer, George W., and Catherine Dale. 1997. "Boris Yeltsin and the Invention of a Russian Nation-State." *Post-Soviet Affairs* 13, no. 4: 303.

Brubaker, Rogers. 1995. "National Minorities, Nationalizing States, and External National Homelands in the New Europe." *Daedalus* 124, no. 2: 107–32.

———. 1996. *Nationalism Reframed: Nationhood and the National Question in the New Europe.* Cambridge: Cambridge University Press.

Bunce, Valerie. 1998. "Regional Differences in Democratization: The East versus the South." *Post Soviet Affairs* 11, no. 3: 187.

Chayes, Abram, and Antonia Handler Chayes, eds. 1996. *Preventing Conflict in the Post-Communist World: Mobilizing International and Regional Organizations.* Washington: Brookings Institution Press.

Chua, Amy. 1998. "Markets, Democracy and Ethnicity: Toward a New Paradigm for Law and Development." *Yale Law Journal* 108, no. 1 (October).

Dawson, Jane. 1997. "Ethnicity, Ideology and Geopolitics in Crimea." *Communist and Post-Communist Studies* 30, no. 4: 427.

Drobizheva, Leokadia M., ed. 1998a. *Asimmetrichnaia federatsiia. Vzgliad iz tsentra, respublik i oblastei.* Moscow: Izdatelstvo Instituta Sotsiologii RAN.

———, ed. 1998b. *Sotsialnaia i kulturnaia distantsii. Opyt mnogonatsionalnoi Rossii.* Moscow: Izdatel'stvo Instituta Sotsiologii RAN.

Dunlop, John B. 1993. *The Rise of Russia and the Fall of the Soviet Empire.* Princeton: Princeton University Press

Fish, M. Steven. 1995. *Democracy from Scratch: Opposition and Regime in the New Russian Revolution.* Princeton: Princeton University Press.

———. 1998. "Democratization's Requisites: The Postcommunist Experience." *Post-Soviet Affairs* 14, no. 3: 212–47.

Gurr, Ted Robert. 1993. *Minorities at Risk: A Global View of Ethnopolitical Conflicts.* Washington: U.S. Institute of Peace Press.

Hirsch, Francine. 1997. "The Soviet Union as a Work-in-Progress: Ethnographers and the Category 'Nationality' in the 1926, 1937, and 1939 Censuses." *Slavic Review* 56, no. 2: 251–78.

Hopmann, Terrence P. 1999. *Building Security in Post–Cold War Eurasia: The OSCE and U.S. Foreign Policy.* Washington: U.S. Institute of Peace Press.

Horowitz, Donald L. 1975. "Ethnic Identity." Pp. 111–40 in *Ethnicity: Theory and Experience,* ed. Nathan Glazer and Daniel P. Moynihan. Cambridge, Mass.: Harvard University Press.

———. 1985. *Ethnic Groups in Conflict.* Berkeley: University of California Press.

Human Rights Watch. 2000. *"No Happiness Remains": Civilian Killings, Pillage and Rape in Alkhan-Yurt, Chechnya.* Russia/Chechnya 12, no. 5 (D). New York: Human Rights Watch.

Hurlbutt, Heather F. 1999. "Preventive Diplomacy: Success in the Baltics." Pp. 91–107 in *Opportunities Missed, Opportunities Seized: Preventive Diplomacy in the Post–Cold War,* ed. Bruce W. Jentleson. Carnegie Commission on Preventing Deadly Conflict Series. Lanham, Md.: Rowman and Littlefield.

Iakuda, Viktor. 2000. "Na Ukraine gotoviatsia zapretit' russkii iazik." *Segodnia.* 3 February.

J. A. C. (pseudonym). 2000a. "More Russian Officials Criticize Ukraine's Language Policy." *Radio Free Europe/Radio Liberty [RFE/RL] Newsline.* 11 February.

————. 2000b. "Russia Tells Ukraine 'Nyet' to Curbs on Language." *RFE/RL Newsline*. 20 July.

J. M. (pseudonym). 2000. "Popular Front Says Russians in 'Practically All' Key Posts in Belarus." *RFE/RL Newsline*. 21 February.

Kakovkin, Grigorii. 1999. "V nashi vagony, na nashi puti nashi gruzit drova." *Izvestiya*. 26 June.

Kommersant. 1999. 2 February.

Kreindler, Isabelle. 1997. "Multilingualism in the Successor States of the Soviet Union." *Annual Review of Applied Linguistics* 17: 91–112.

Laitin, David D. 1998. *Identity in Formation: The Russian-Speaking Populations in the Near Abroad*. Ithaca: Cornell University Press.

Lapidus, Gail W., ed. 1992. *The Nationalities Problem in the Soviet Union*. New York: Garland.

————, ed. 1994. *The New Russia: Troubled Transformation*. Boulder: Westview.

————. 1998. "Contested Sovereignty: The Tragedy of Chechnya." *International Security* 23, no. 1 (summer): 5–49.

————. 1999. "Asymmetrical Federalism and State Breakdown in Russia." *Post-Soviet Affairs* 15, no. 1: 74.

————. Forthcoming. "Transforming the 'National Question'": New Approaches to Nationalism, Federalism, and Sovereignty under Gorbachev." In *The Erosion of Marxism-Leninism under Perestroika*, ed. Archie Brown. London: Macmillan.

Lapidus, Gail W., and Edward W. Walker. 1994. "Nationalism, Regionalism, and Federalism: Dilemmas of State-Building in Post-Communist Russia." Pp. 79–114 in *The New Russia: Troubled Transformation*, ed. Gail W. Lapidus. Boulder: Westview.

Lapidus, Gail W., Victor Zaslavsky, and Philip Goldman, eds. 1992. *From Union to Commonwealth: Nationalism and Separatism in the Soviet Republics*. Cambridge: Cambridge University Press.

Levada, Yuri. 1999. "People and Their Values: Hopes Associated with Perestroika Have Given Way to Nostalgia for the Past and Efforts to Adapt to New Realities." All-Russian Center of Public Opinion Studies, Moscow, March.

LeVine, Steve. 1999. "Lesson in Caucasus: War Has Rules." *New York Times*. 14 February: 15.

Lord, Karen S. 1997. "Religious Liberty in the OSCE: The Caucasus." *CSCE Digest* 20, no. 10 (October): 112.

Lysenko, Vladimir I. 1995. *Razvitie federativnykh otnoshenii v sovremennoi Rossii*. Moscow: Izdanie Instituta Sovremennoi Politiki.

————. 1998. "Distribution of Power: The Experience of the Russian Federation." Pp. 97–115 in *Preventing Deadly Conflict: Strategies and Institutions*, ed. Gail W. Lapidus and Svetlana Tsalik. Proceedings of a conference in Moscow, Russian Federation, April. New York: Carnegie Commission on Preventing Deadly Conflict.

Maksymiuk, Jan. 1999. "Belarusians Pray for Mother Tongue." *RFE/RL Newsline*. (28 June).

Markus, Ustina. 1997. "Citizenship Poll in Estonia." *OMRI* [Open Media Research Institute] *Daily Digest*. 6 January.

Massell, Gregory J. 1974. *The Surrogate Proletariat: Moslem Women and Revolutionary Strategies in Soviet Central Asia, 1919–1929*. Princeton: Princeton University Press.

Mendras, Marie. 1999. "How Regional Elites Preserve Their Power." *Post-Soviet Affairs* 15, no. 4 (October–December): 295–311.

M. H. (pseudonym). 2000. "EU Praises Changes to Estonian Language Law." *RFE/RL Newsline*. 15 June.

Migranian, Andronik. 1994. "Rossiia i blizhnee zarubezh'e: vse prostranstvo byvshego SSSR iavliaetsia sferoi zhiznennykh interesov Rossii." *Nezavisimaia gazeta*. 18 January.

Paddock, Richard C. 1999. "Ex-Soviet State Dares to Dream." *Los Angeles Times*. 24 August: 1

Parliamentary Assembly of the Council of Europe. 1992. "Human Rights in the Republic of Estonia." *Human Rights Law Journal* 13, nos. 5–6.

Payin, Emil. 1999. "The Russian Question: From Internationalism to Nomenklatura Nationalism: Article II." *Literaturnaia gazeta*. 27 January.

Payin, Emil, and Arkady Popov. 1996. "Chechnya." Pp. 9–30 in *U.S. and Russian Policy-making with Respect to the Use of Force,* ed. Jeremy Azrael and Emil Payin. Santa Monica: Rand Corporation.

Radzikhovskii, Leonid. 2000. "Ostanovit' nel'zia prodolzhat." *Segodnia*. 18 January: 3. As reported in *Current Digest of the Post-Soviet Press* 52, no. 3 (16 February): 9.

Rubin, Barnett R., and Jack Snyder, eds. 1998. *Post-Soviet Political Order: Conflict and State Building*. New York: Routledge.

Rudakova, Diana. 2000. "Governor: Putin Not to Cede to Pressure on Chechnya." ITAR-TASS newswire (in English). 17 January.

Silver, Brian D., and Barbara A. Anderson, eds. 1997. *Estonia's Transition from State Socialism: Nationalities and Society on the Eve of Independence*. Armonk: M. E. Sharpe.

Simonsen, Sven Gunnar. 1996. *Politics and Personalities: Key Actors in the Russian Opposition*. Oslo: International Peace Research Institute.

Smith, Graham, et al., eds. 1998. *Nation-Building in the Post-Soviet Borderlands*. Cambridge: Cambridge University Press.

Snyder, Jack. 2000. *From Voting to Violence: Democratization and Nationalist Conflict*. New York: Norton.

Stepan, Alfred. 2000. "Russian Federalism in Comparative Perspective." *Post-Soviet Affairs* 16, no. 2 (April–June): 133–76.

Suny, Ronald G. 1993. *The Revenge of the Past: Nationalism, Revolution, and the Collapse of the Soviet Union*. Stanford: Stanford University Press.

———. 1998. *The Soviet Experiment: Russia, the USSR, and the Successor States*. New York: Oxford University Press.

Szporluk, Roman, ed. 1994. *National Identity and Ethnicity in Russia and the New States of Eurasia*. Armonk: M. E. Sharpe.

Tishkov, V. A. 1995. "Chto est' Rossiia?" *Voprosy filosofii* 11.

Titma, Mikk, Nancy Brandon Tuma, and Brian D. Silver. 1998. "Winners and Losers in the Postcommunist Transition: New Evidence from Estonia." *Post-Soviet Affairs* 14, no. 2: 114.

Tolz, Vera. 1998. "Conflicting 'Homeland Myths' and Nation-State Building in Postcommunist Russia." *Slavic Review* 57, no. 2: 267.

U.S. Central Intelligence Agency (CIA). 1998. *World Factbook*. Washington: CIA.

U.S. Department of State. 1999. *Estonia Country Report on Human Rights Practices for 1998*. Washington: U.S. Department of State, 26 February.

Wines, Michael. 1999. "Double Vision: Two Views of Inhumanity Split the World, Even in Victory." *New York Times*. 13 June.

York, Geoffrey. 1999. Report of TV interview. *Globe and Mail* (Toronto), 8 November. As posted by Johnson's Russia List, no. 3613 (9 November). Available at www.cdi.org/russia/johnson/3613.html##4.

Zevelev, Igor. 1996. "Russian and the Russian Diasporas." *Post-Soviet Affairs* 12, no. 3: 265–87.

14

Beyond Cultural Domination: Institutionalizing Equity in the African State

FRANCIS M. DENG

Cultural domination is a characteristic of inequity in a multiethnic state. In Africa, the cultural inequities associated with the state take two principal forms. One entails the domination of some cultural, ethnic, or religious groups by other groups; the other is the marginalization of African indigenous cultures by the colonial and postcolonial state. The first of these forms is a function of cultural pluralism that poses a challenge to governance—which can be, and often is, a source of conflict. The other effects a cultural disconnect between the state system and its alien origins and institutions, on the one hand, and the African cultural heritage, on the other. This divide denies cultural legitimacy to the state and may weaken the effectiveness of the state as an embodiment of national identity, values, and institutional capacity.

Cultural domination is particularly ominous because it also implies the existence of stratifications that determine who gets what in the political, economic, social, and cultural life of the country. Cultural domination is essentially a conflict of identities rooted not merely in differences, but rather in the discriminating implications of those differences. Indeed, it is the reaction to the injustices of such discrimination that engenders violent conflicts. Conflicts in Africa are provoked by gross injustices, real or perceived.

The situation is rendered even more complex by the parodoxical approaches taken to African cultures and indigenous institutions. African "tribal" or "ethnic" groups and their indigenous values and institutions have been the primary victims of statecraft and nation-building in Africa. By the nature of its ideology, institutions, and operations, the colonial state overshadowed indigenous ethnic groups and values. But colonialism also recognized and in some instances invented tribes and tribal authorities. On balance, however, indigenous cultures and institutions were subordinated and even marginalized in the process of state formation.

The marginalization of indigenous cultures in the political, economic, social, and cultural development of African countries in most cases set the state apart from the cultural context of its people. This result was, of course, to be expected in the colonial state. But independent African states have tended to be even more oblivious to indigenous cultures than were the colonial masters. Nevertheless, the fact that colonial administrations gave traditional values and institutions a measure of recognition and reinforcement, not to mention the inherent entrenchment of those traditions, makes them resilient and assertive against the suppressive measures of the postcolonial state.

With the contest over state power, resources, and institutions often a conflict between identity groups, each of which seeks to capture the state, break away, or pursue its own autonomous development, the state ceases to be the embodiment of the collective national consciousness. This situation creates a crisis of national identity, which can result in vacuums of responsibility for the security and general welfare of the citizens who fall outside the dominant identity framework of the state. The victims of the humanitarian tragedies that often result from violent conflicts, especially if those victims are not members of the dominant group, become dispossessed by their own governments, unprotected, and unassisted. In their desperation, they can only turn outside the state framework to seek and receive humanitarian assistance and sometimes human rights protection from the more compassionate international community. But even here, the outside world and the needy victim community are often confronted by a negative assertion of state sovereignty as a barricade against foreign scrutiny and intervention.

The state system implies an international order in which the state is the centerpiece. The inequities of the African state must therefore be seen in the context of the prevailing international climate. Two major trends characterize developments in international relations since the end of the cold war. On the one hand, internal and regional conflicts are now seen in their proper context instead of distorted as episodes in the global confrontation between the superpowers. This new outlook is undoubtedly a positive development. But the withdrawal of the major powers after the end of the global strategic rivalry of the cold war has also led to the marginalization and even neglect of certain regions, foremost among them Africa. This is, of course, a negative development. The international community remains engaged primarily on humanitarian grounds and to a lesser extent to ensure the protection of human rights universally. But this involvement usually provides only reluctant, often belated, "Band-Aid" responses to crises of grave magnitude.

Two implications arise from these two trends. First, difficult situations must be analyzed contextually to identify critical problem areas, probe their root causes, and explore appropriate solutions. And second, responsibility for addressing the problems has been reapportioned, with primary responsibility now placed on the states concerned; responsibility and accountability are now shared among the subregional, the regional, and, residually, the international levels. The international community remains the ultimate guarantor of universal human rights and humanitarian standards.

In this emerging policy framework, national sovereignty acquires a new meaning. Instead of being perceived as a means of insulating the state against external scrutiny or involvement, it is increasingly postulated as a normative concept of responsibility, requiring a system of governance based on democratic citizen participation, constructive management of diversities, respect for fundamental rights, and equitable distribution of national wealth and opportunities for development. For a government or a state to claim sovereignty, it must establish legitimacy by meeting minimal standards of good governance or responsibility for the security and general welfare of its citizens and all those under its jurisdiction.

This concept of sovereignty as responsibility is essentially the outcome of an evolutionary process that began with the Westphalian perception of sovereignty as the prerogative of a monarchy with absolute control over territory and population to ensure order and stability, considered essential to international trade and interstate relations. Beginning with the American and French revolutions, this idea then shifted to a more assertive demand of the people for effective democratic representation and participation, or popular sovereignty. Since the end of World War II, a more rigorous involvement by the international community in the internal affairs of states has sought to ensure humanitarian and human rights protections for the victims of internal misrule. The end of the cold war removed the ideological barriers that once shielded allies or dependents of the superpowers from international scrutiny, opening windows on internal political problem areas and enhancing accountability to domestic and international constituencies.

This chapter tries to address issues connected with these overarching themes of cultural domination, the inequities of state institutions in Africa, and the emerging demand for a normative framework of sovereignty, responsibility, and accountability. First, it outlines the African policy context: the major problem areas confronting the continent, their root causes, and the measures required to address them. There then follows a brief account of the evolution of trends since the inception of the state system through colonial intervention and the way diversities have since been managed. This is followed by a discussion of culture as a factor in indigenous political and economic development. The chapter concludes with a policy perspective that underscores the need to balance globalization with localization through a process that builds on African indigenous values and institutions but links all levels of human interaction, from local to global, with national sovereignty perceived as a concept of responsibility. Along the way, I will note some of the interesting parallels and divergences between the African experience and that of the post-Soviet world.

The African Policy Context

An appropriate normative framework for Africa must place the challenge in its proper context by addressing multifaceted policy questions: What are the critical problem areas that call for analysis and policy formulation? What are the root causes of these problems, what can be done about them, and where does the responsibility for addressing them lie? Africa's list of problem areas must place internal conflicts highest in the order of priorities, followed by human rights violations, dictatorial or authoritarian systems of government, and flawed economic policies—all of which are closely interconnected in a chain of cause and effect. The corresponding solution list would include conflict resolution, human rights protection, democracy, and sustainable development.

The case is often made that Africa's problems are primarily due to underdevelopment and abject poverty, which would place development highest on the list of priorities (Ake 1996). In creating preconditions for development, African leaders saw human rights and democracy as luxuries to be sacrificed or postponed until African economies were sufficiently advanced. Development was articulated in terms of the war against the "real enemies"—poverty, ignorance, and disease.[1]

Despite the priority given to development, it is one of the areas in which Africa's performance has been dismal. Although the failure to live up to expectations can be attributed to a myriad of reasons, bad governance in general and internal conflicts in particular constitute the most significant factors. Economic growth is impossible in a country where war, insurgency, and terrorism destroy lives and property at random, prevent agricultural production, create multitudes of refugees and displaced persons, and divert precious resources into massive arms purchases and military buildups.[2] Whatever their order of priority, these problem areas, put together, paint a picture of a continent in crisis, desperately in need of rescue operations— a continent that some have gone so far as to say is not worth saving (Kaplan 1994).

The plight of the continent in large measure lies in the disconnect between Africa's indigenous values and institutions in the process of development and nation-building and the implications and consequences of an increasingly globalizing context in which Africans are disadvantaged, impoverished, incapacitated, and marginalized. Without the resilience and resourcefulness that would come from Africa building on its own roots to generate a dynamic process that transforms tradition while deriving motivation and legitimacy from it, African development and nation-building concepts will always appear alien and ungrounded. An effective policy reform agenda must reverse this helpless, foreign-driven sense of Africa's destiny.

The irony is that the principal modern agent of Africa's political and economic development, and therefore the legitimate actor in the international arena, is the state—itself a creature of foreign intervention. Although Africans have, for the most part, accepted the state with its colonially defined borders, the African state lacks the indigenous cultural and moral values and integrity that should be the sine qua non of internal legitimacy. Even worse, it is often not representative of or responsive to the demands and expectations of its domestic constituencies. It is important in this con-

---

1. These have been described as "'the unholy trinity' against which the nationalist swords were drawn" (Mkandawire 1997, 10).

2. Ultimately, the question arises as to whether development has actually received genuine priority or has been used as a pretext for other self-serving political objectives. As Claude Ake notes, "[T]he ideology of development was exploited as a means for reproducing political hegemony; it got limited attention and served hardly any purposes as a framework for economic transformation" (Ake 1996, 8—9).

text to distinguish between recognizing the unity and territorial integrity of the state and questioning its normative framework. The latter might be attributable to a regime or might be more structural, evoking calls for a fundamental restructuring of the state—normatively, institutionally, and operationally. Reconceptualizing the state to build on indigenous values and institutions would undoubtedly enhance its normative legitimacy.

The description of this disconnect with tradition should be nuanced, however, because apart from the fact that a degree of continuity is nearly always inevitable, colonial administrations built in part on indigenous values and institutions through their policies of indirect rule. These indigenous factors are thus a reality that cannot be disregarded with impunity. In this respect, comparisons with the situation in the countries of the former Soviet Union (as described in Chapter 13) are intriguing. The Soviet Union recognized nationalities, even according them the rights of self-determination, and yet repressed them through a paradoxically centralized federation. The dissolution of the Soviet Union brought these nationalistic identities to the fore, with institutions that were relatively well developed and intact despite their prior marginalization. It is perhaps the extent to which these ethnically based nationalities had been developed that distinguishes the case of the Soviet Union from that of African ethnic groups.

Although colonial states in Africa, especially those under British rule, sometimes relied on an ethnic principle in constituting administrative subdivisions, Africa's independent states, which have frequently redrawn provincial and local boundaries, have generally aimed to avert the identification of large ethnic blocs with defined territorial subunits of the state. The major exception is Ethiopia, whose internal reconfiguration was inspired by Leninist nationality theory during its Marxist-Leninist period (1976–91). Once established, Ethiopia's titular nationality principle could not be overturned after the demise of the Afro-Marxist regime. But for the rest of Africa, without titular nationalities, the increasingly resonant international normative discourses regarding "national minorities" or "indigenous peoples," important for the former Soviet Union, have not permeated debates about accommodation of diversity.

Another distinguishing factor may be the greater degree of ethnic diversity in African countries compared with that in the states of the former Soviet Union, where majorities and minorities are more discernable. Indeed, the realities on the ground leave Africa precariously pulled in the opposite directions of unity and localization. Cultural groups demand both local control and effective national participation. Although the centerpiece is the state (a relic of European intervention), the internal challenge of localization requires a more effective use of indigenous cultural values and institutions for nation-building and self-reliant development. Externally, state linkages to regional and international contexts raise questions about the objectives and scope of sovereignty, which stipulates the basis of relations with the outside world but should be predicated on domestic legitimacy. Inherently, these processes pose serious dilemmas for Africa, whose borders, though artificially drawn and still porous, have become sacrosanct, but whose normative legitimacy is at best contested.

By both local and global standards, Africa is now facing a call for democracy, which is posing a formidable challenge for pluralistic states that are acutely divided on ethnic or religious grounds. Because democracy has become closely associated with elections, in which Africans tend to vote on the basis of politicized ethnic or religious identities, democracy risks becoming a dictatorship of numbers, with the majority imposing its will on the minority. For this reason, the suitability of democracy for Africa is being questioned, both within and beyond the continent (Zakaria 1997, Kaplan 1997).

But Africans cannot accept dictatorship as the alternative. The increasing assault on democracy is based on a narrow definition that places overwhelming emphasis on the procedural aspect (elections), then uses the negative consequence of this narrow definition to question democracy as a normative concept. A balanced perspective should draw a distinction between the principles of democracy and the institutional practices of its implementation. Given the tendency of Africans to vote according to their ethnic identities, democracy will have to mean more than electoral votes. In the context of ethnic diversity, true democracy would require some forms of devolution of power through decentralization to the local level combined with some method of ensuring the representation of those who would otherwise be excluded by the weight of electoral votes. In any case, democracy, however defined or practiced, implies accommodation of differences and a special responsibility for the protection of minorities.

In the African context, this definition of democracy is complicated by the fact that in many countries the multiplicity of ethnic groups makes it difficult, if not impossible, to speak of "majority" and "minority." Some countries, of course, have clearly discernable majorities and minorities. Such was true for Zanzibar under the Jamshid dynasty and is today the case in Burundi and Rwanda—precisely why the situations in these countries have been more acutely polarized. Where diversities and cleavages are more complicated by multiplicity, the nature of the state becomes even more complex—but that fact in itself offers more opportunities for alignments across ethnic cleavages. Still, groups that find themselves threatened with marginal status may resist incorporation into a national framework that excludes them. This resistance poses a serious challenge to the legitimacy of the regime, if not the state itself, as it may lead to a call for either secession or a major restructuring of the polity.

Thus, although democracy broadly defined in terms of normative ideals or principles is universally valued, it needs to be contextualized by taking into account African realities and making effective use of indigenous values, institutions, and social mores to make it homegrown and sustainable. However, this contextualization must not be allowed to degenerate into a pretext for relativistic authoritarianism that is inimical to traditional African political theory and practice. In much of traditional Africa, rulers governed with the consent of the people, who participated broadly in their own self-administration, were free to express their will, and held their leaders to high standards of transparency and accountability. To suggest how positive aspects of the African political heritage can serve in the creation of a sustainably democratic and culturally accommodative political order, it is therefore necessary to trace the historical process by which the African policy agenda has evolved and the challenges that it presents for reform.

Connecting to the African Heritage

There is a logic to developments on the continent and a reason that things are the way they are. The starting point for understanding modern Africa is colonial intervention, which disrupted evolutionary processes from within and set the continent on its contemporary course. Since the decolonization process swept across Africa in the late 1950s, starting with the landmark independence of the Sudan, Morocco, and Tunisia in 1956 and Ghana in 1957, the continent has been driven by lofty slogans that have produced contradictions and countercurrents. Foremost among the principles that have shaped developments has been the 1963 decision by the founders of the Organization of African Unity (OAU) to preserve the colonial borders. Although this decision has maintained peace and stability among states, it has provided a breeding ground for internal conflicts among racial, ethnic, cultural, and religious groups. Given the fact that ethnic diversity is a pervasive reality in virtually all African countries, including the supposedly homogeneous Somalia, and considering that ethnic groups generally demand a place in the political and economic life of their countries, managing diversity constitutes a principal challenge to nation-building in Africa. The paradox of colonial borders is that they are artificial yet sacrosanct.

The oppressive implications of forcing on diverse groups a unitary system of government within the confines of those borders are now challenging their inviolability. Of course, state borders are a reality that cannot be wished away, but they also remain figments of foreign imagination, often defied by realities on the ground.[3] Some, including David Holloway and Stephen Stedman in Chapter 7, suggest that retention of colonial partition boundaries reduced the likelihood of interstate wars. But as one observer asks rhetorically, "[D]id not the same policy lead, 40 years down the road, to collapsed states, ethnic conflicts, . . . predatory rule and a general political alienation of grass roots Africans?"(Englebert 1997). The challenge is not necessarily to question borders but to create conditions for managing diversity more equitably and constructively within those borders. On the other hand, where the state fails to create conditions for peace, and where ethnic or religious groups are victims of genocide, indiscriminate killing, or intolerable indignities, then people feel impelled to challenge the status quo and may even threaten to dismantle the very foundation and structure of the state. Unity within these artificial borders was never, or should never have been, intended as an end in itself; it should be a means to achieve higher goals. The overriding objective must be to ensure people's sense of dignity and belonging as citizens and to promote their participation on equal terms with all others, majorities and minorities alike.

Perhaps the most outstanding characteristics of traditional African society are the autonomy of component elements of the political and social order and the devolution of power and decision-making processes down to local units—territorial subdivisions, lineages, and extended families. Colonial rulers recognized these characteristics to a degree but exploited them; postcolonial states have disregarded and even discredited them, much to their own peril. The process of sharing power at all levels of the social struc-

---

3. John Ravenhill notes, "In recent years we have witnessed the growth of intra-African territorial aggrandizement, which has changed the *de facto* boundaries of African states. Elsewhere similar *de facto* changes have resulted from the success of anti-government forces, including secessionist movements. Whether *de facto* changes in boundaries and international jurisdictions will be translated into *de jure* changes is more problematic. Recent trends away from respecting the sovereignty of African states, however, can be expected to continue and intensify" (Ravenhill 1988, 284–85). Ravenhill is even more assertive in his prediction: "There have been significant changes in a number of these dimensions in recent years, greatly increasing the prospects that there will be a *de facto* redrawing of the map of Africa" (286).

ture is particularly pronounced in stateless or acephalous societies in which the autonomy of various components of the segmentary lineage system is emphasized down to the level of the family and even the individual. As John Middleton and David Tait explain in their introduction to *Tribes without Rulers* (1958), relations of local groups to one another are seen as a balance of power, maintained by competition between them in the political and social hierarchy. Although relations may be competitive at one level, in another situation the formerly competitive groups may come together in a mutual alliance against an outside group. Each group at a given level has competitive relations with other groups, aimed at maintaining its identity and rights as a corporate entity. Units that are separate in one context merge into larger aggregates in other contexts. This wider aggregate may in turn be in external competition with other, similar segments. An entire series of such segments may exist in a state of complementary opposition (Middleton and Tait 1958, 6–7).

The heritage of the segmentary lineage system may sit uneasily with centralizing projects of the state and may also divide members of its own camp. Such a situation prevails among the Nilotic peoples of the southern Sudan, notably the Dinka and the Nuer, who constitute the bulk of the forces of the Sudan People's Liberation Movement and its army (SPLM/SPLA). Although this movement has been fighting on behalf of the non-Arab, non-Muslim south against domination by the Arabized Muslim north, it has also suffered severely from internal factionalization between and within its major constituents, the Dinka and the Nuer. This factionalization within an otherwise common cause emanates from the individualized yet collective quest for permanent identity and influence through the lineage system. Values engendered in the system are deeply individualistic, rooted in the egocentric yearning of everyone to have a respected place in the family and in the agnatic chain of descent. As Godfrey Lienhardt explains about the Dinka,

> [They] positively value the unity of their tribes, and of their descent groups, while also valuing that autonomy of their component segments which can lead to fragmentations. The basis of this occasional contradiction of values lies in each Dinka ambition. . . . A man . . . wishes to belong to a large descent group, because the greater the numbers of his agnatic [paternal] kin who have still not formally segmented with separate agnatic groups, the wider the range of people from whom he can hope for help . . . in quarrels either within the tribe or outside it. On the other hand, each man wants to found his own

descent group, a formal segment of the sub-clan which will for long
be remembered by his name, and wants to withdraw from his more
distant agnatic kin in order not to be required to help. . . . These values of personal autonomy and of cooperation, of the inclusiveness and
unity of any wider political or genealogical segments and the exclu-
siveness and autonomy of its several subsegments are from time to
time in conflict (Lienhardt 1970, 117–18).

E. E. Evans-Pritchard, describing the system among the Nuer, notes,

There is . . . always a contradiction in the definition of a political
group, for it is a group only in relation to other groups. . . . [T]he political system is an equilibrium between opposed tendencies towards
fission and fusion, between the tendency of all groups to segment, and
the tendency of all groups to combine with segments of the same order . . . an equilibrium between . . . contradictory, yet complementary,
tendencies (Evans-Pritchard 1940, 147–48).

As was the case in Somalia, where Muhammad Siad Barre manipulated
the clan system based on a segmentary lineage principle to divide and rule,
the Sudanese central government in Khartoum has exploited, with relative
success, the contradictions of the similar Nilotic system in order to weaken
the southern liberation movement, causing devastatingly violent confrontations between increasingly fragmentary factions (Young 1991, 339).
For the purposes of designing culturally oriented policies, it is important
to bear in mind these characteristics of independence and autonomy at the
various levels of political and social structures and processes.

Ironically, despite Nilotic egalitarianism and sense of independence,
leadership is of critical importance to the Nilotic value system. Chiefs of
the Sacred Spears (their symbol of authority) among the Dinka or Chiefs
of the Leopard Skin (their regalia) among the Nuer are indispensable to
the maintenance of peace and public order. However, a chief among them
is not a ruler in the Western sense but a spiritual leader whose power rests
on divine enlightenment and wisdom. In order to reconcile his people, the
chief should be a model of virtue and righteousness—"a man with a cool
heart"—who must depend on persuasion and consensus-building rather
than on coercion and dictation. Lienhardt writes,

I suppose anyone would agree that one of the most decisive marks of
a society we should call in a spiritual sense "civilized" is a highly de-

veloped sense of practice of justice, and here, the Nilotics, with their intense respect for the personal independence and dignity of themselves and of others, may be superior to societies more civilized in the material sense. . . . The Dinka and Nuer are a warlike people, and have never been slow to assert their rights as they see them by physical force. Yet, if one sees Dinka trying to resolve a dispute, according to their own customary law, there is often a reasonableness and a gentleness in their demeanor, a courtesy and a quietness in the speech of those elder men superior in status and wisdom, an attempt to get at the whole truth of the situation before them (Cited in Deng 1995, 194–95).

Similarly, Evans-Pritchard observes of the Nuer settlement of disputes,

The five important elements in a settlement of this kind by direct negotiation through a chief seem to be (1) the desire of the disputants to settle their dispute, (2) the sanctity of the chief's person and his traditional role of mediator, (3) full and free discussion leading to a high measure of agreement between all present, (4) the feeling that a man can give way to the chief and elders without loss of dignity where he would not have given way to his opponent, and (5) recognition by the losing party of the justice of the other side's case (Evans-Pritchard 1940, 164; see also Deng 1995, 195).

These accounts should not be interpreted as painting a "Merrie Africa" mythical glorification of tradition, against which many observers have correctly warned. To emphasize the peacemaking role of the chiefs and elders in Nilotic societies is not to imply that these societies were nonviolent. Quite the contrary: the Nilotics were warlike and prone to violence. It can indeed be argued that the emphasis placed on the ideals of peace, unity, mediation, and persuasion emanates from the pervasiveness of violence in Nilotic life. Internal violence can in turn be attributed to a generational distribution of roles and functions and to the exaggerated sense of dignity young members of the warrior age-sets acquired from their identity and status as warriors. They were defenders of the society from aggression, a function they overzealously displayed, resorting to violence at the slightest provocation. By the same token, leaders, even when young, were required to disavow violence and be men of peace. One chief, reacting to the assertion that in Dinka society force was the deterrent underlying the social order, articulated the delicate balance between the violence of youth and the peacemaking role of leaders in these words:

[I]t is true, there was force. People killed one another and those who could defeat people in battle were avoided with respect. But people lived by the way God had given them. There were the Chiefs of the Sacred Spear. If anything went wrong, they would come to stop the . . . fighting . . . and settle the matter without blood. . . . Men [chiefs] of the [sacred] spear were against bloodshed (Deng 1980, 58).

In the words of another chief, "There was the power of words. It was a way of life with its great leaders . . . not a way of life of the power of the arm" (Deng 1980, 42). It is particularly noteworthy that despite the lack of police or military forces, civil order was maintained with very low levels of crime other than those associated with honorable fighting.[4] It was what Evans-Pritchard describes with detectable admiration as "ordered anarchy."[5]

Colonialism undermined the indigenous African political, social, and economic systems fundamentally by its imposition of the state in the image of the European model, modified to suit the needs of conquest, oppression, and domination. The autonomous character of the old order was replaced by the control mechanisms of the state and its monopoly on power, which ultimately rested on military force. Once the initial phase of military pacification was accomplished, this crude force was softened by the system of indirect rule, which made use of traditional leaders as the extended arm of state control over tribes or local communities. This gave the imposed system a semblance of legitimacy for the masses, but paradoxically it also endangered the legitimacy of the institution as measured by traditional yardsticks. Adding to this appearance of legitimacy was the introduction of a welfare system by which the state provided social services and development opportunities. Because of the scarcity of resources, this system benefited only certain regions and privileged sectors of society, thereby introducing or aggravating cleavages among ethnic groups, regions, and even within families.

---

4. Sir Gawain Bell, who served as district commissioner among the Ngok Dinka and the Missirya Arabs under the British colonial regime, observed, "I can't remember that we ever had any serious crime in that part of the District. Among the Baggara of Missiriya . . . there was a good deal of serious crime: murders and so forth; and the same applied to the Hamar in the North. . . . The Ngok Dinka were a particularly law-abiding people" (cited in Deng 1995, 282).

5. The introduction of the police, who often harassed alleged wrongdoers, and the prison system was seen as a source of great indignity and humiliation of what the Dinka called *adheng*, best translated as "gentlemen." It was often a subject of songs of lamentation and protest (Evans-Pritchard 1940, 168; see also Deng 1974).

With eyes now focused on the state, which controlled national resources and development opportunities, competition for access to central power inevitably intensified along newly politicized ethnic lines. But ironically, while the colonial rulers exploited ethnic rivalries in their policies of divide and rule, they also played the role of third-party moderators of ethnic coexistence by imposing a superstructure of law and order that maintained relative peace and stability among various groups.

The independence movement was a collective struggle for self-determination that reinforced the notion of unity within the framework of the newly established state. Indeed, independence came as a national achievement that did not initially disaggregate who was to get what from the bequeathed power and wealth. Once the control of these centralized institutions and resources passed on to nationals, the struggle for control ensued; the outcome was conflict over power, wealth, and opportunities for development. This made the quest for unity and the preservation of inherited borders a more pressing priority to which the conflictual demands of diverse groups had to be subordinated, if not totally suppressed.

Managing Diversity

African elites were eager to disavow what was generally termed "tribalism" as divisive. Unity was pursued after independence in a way that assumed a mythical homogeneity or manipulated diversity. Kwame Nkrumah of Ghana outlawed parties organized on tribal or ethnic bases. Félix Houphouet-Boigny of the Ivory Coast co-opted ethnic groups through a shrewd distribution of ministerial posts, civil service jobs, social services, and development projects. Julius Nyerere, himself a scion of tribal chieftaincy, stamped out tribalism by fostering nationalistic pride in Tanganyika and, later, after the union with Zanzibar, Tanzania. Jomo Kenyatta of Kenya forged a delicate alliance of ethnic groups behind the dominance of his Kenyan African National Union party. In South Africa, apartheid stratified race and ethnicity to a degree that was not sustainable. Postapartheid South Africa, however, remains poised between a racially, ethnically, and tribally blind democratic system and a proud ethnic self-assertiveness, the prototype of which is represented and exploited by Zulu nationalism.

The Sudan offers an extreme example of an identity crisis resulting from mismanaged diversity. The dominant north is a hybrid of Arab and African racial, cultural, and religious elements, who are trying to resolve their region's racial and cultural anomalies by being more Arab and Islamic than their Middle Eastern prototypes. Worse still, this distorted self-perception, heightened by the agendas of political elites, is projected as the framework for unifying the country through assimilation of non-Arabs and non-Muslims, generating a devastating zero-sum conflict between the Arab-Muslim north and the indigenously African south, whose modern leadership is predominantly Christian. The rebellion of the SPLM/SPLA is essentially a resistance to Arab-Islamic domination and the threat of assimilation.

The decision of the founders of the OAU to respect the colonial borders has been unsuccessfully challenged in several cases (for example, Katanga and Biafra). Even in the case of the one successful revision of these borders, the breakaway of Eritrea from Ethiopia in 1991, Eritrean liberation fighters could never secure OAU sympathy during their thirty-year struggle, until the 1991 dissolution of the Ethiopian regime made independence a fait accompli. Paradoxically, Eritrean independence can be seen as consistent with OAU doctrine, since the country had been an Italian colony. Likewise, the de facto breakaway of northern Somalia, though recognized neither by the OAU nor by the international community, can be seen as a restoration of colonial borders, since the territory was once British Somaliland. Even in the Sudan, often said to be a good candidate for partition, any proposed division could be rationalized as an extension of the British colonial policy that governed the country as two separate entities.

In most African countries, the determination to preserve national unity after independence provided the motivation behind one-party rule, excessive centralization of power, oppressive authoritarian regimes, and systematic violations of human rights and fundamental liberties. The participatory process of decision-making in traditional African society was later exploited by nationalist leaders to justify the one-party system, the rationale being that since Africans traditionally sat and debated until they all agreed, the multiparty system was antithetic to African culture. The delicate balance between the interest of the individual and that of the community was also misconstrued to give undue emphasis to communalism at the expense of individualism and was used to justify the imported concept of socialism, euphemistically dubbed "African socialism."

Managing ethnic diversity is one of the challenges that postcolonial African governments were reluctant to face or treated negatively. As one African observer put it, "The new governments mistook any manifestation of ethnic identities or articulation of ethnic claims as divisive and consequently treasonable . . . Authoritarian rule saw itself as the guardian of the nation against the divisive demons of tribalism . . . a major blind spot . . .

that was to make even manageable conflicts so devastating" (Mkandawire 1997, 4–5).

Given its centrality and pervasiveness, ethnicity is a reality no country can afford to completely ignore. But no strategic formula for its constructive use has been developed (Rothchild 1997, 20–21), despite the fact that an overwhelming majority of Africans, however urbanized or modernized, identify with their ethnic origins and remain in one way or another connected to their groups, often in flexible or adaptable ways. Ethnic identities in themselves are not conflictual, just as individuals are not inherently in conflict merely because of their different identities and characteristics. Rather, it is unmanaged or mismanaged competition for power, wealth, or status broadly defined that provides the basis for conflict. Today, virtually every African conflict has some ethno-regional dimension to it (Cohen and Deng 1998). Even conflicts that may appear to be free of ethnic concerns involve factions and alliances built around ethnic loyalties. Analysts tend to hold one of two views on the role of ethnicity in these conflicts: some see ethnicity as a source of conflict; others see it as a tool used by political entrepreneurs to promote their ambitions.[6] In reality, it is both. Ethnicity, especially when combined with territorial identity, is a reality that exists independently of political maneuvers. To argue that ethnic groups are unwitting tools of political manipulation is to underestimate a fundamental social reality. On the other hand, ethnicity is clearly a resource for political manipulation and entrepreneurship, which African states are loath to manage constructively. Ethiopia, after Eritrea's breakaway, can claim credit for being the only African country that is trying to confront the problem head-on by recognizing territorially based ethnic groups, granting them not only a large measure of autonomy, but also the constitutional right of self-determination, even to the extent of

---

6. According to one source, ethnicity is important in African politics because it serves as an "organizing principle of sound action," which makes it "basically a political . . . phenomenon" (Chazan 1988, 110, 120). U.N. Secretary-General Kofi Annan, in a paper presented to an international conference on "The Therapeutics of Conflict" when he was still undersecretary-general for peacekeeping operations, observed,

Many of [the civil wars] have also been perceived as showing strong symptoms of ethnic conflict. Ethnic conflict as a symptom is, at best, extremely difficult to assess. . . . Ethnic differences are not in and of themselves either symptoms or causes of conflict; in societies where they are accepted and respected, people of vastly different backgrounds live peacefully and productively together. Ethnic differences become charged—conflictual—when they are used for political ends, when ethnic groups are intentionally placed in opposition to each other (Annan 1996, 176).

secession.[7] Ethiopia's leaders assert emphatically that they are committed to the right of self-determination, wherever it leads. Giving the people the right to determine their destiny, one can argue, leads them to believe that their interests will be safeguarded, which should give them a reason to opt for unity.

Self-determination does not necessarily mean secession. After all, one of the options of self-determination is to remain within the state. But perhaps even more significant is the reconceptualization of self-determination as a principle that allows a people to choose their own administrative status and machinery within the country.[8] It has been noted that internal self-administration "might be more effectively used in a way that would help avoid suffering of the kind that so regrettably became commonplace when communities feel that their only option is to 'fight for independence'" (Danspeckgruber and Watts 1997, 1).

In that sense, self-determination becomes closely associated with democracy and the protection of human rights and fundamental freedoms, rather than being synonymous with independence. As Sir Arthur Watts, one of the principal proponents of internal self-determination, has observed, independence is a complicated process that can be traumatic. For many communities, it is not necessarily the best option. Often, no advantage is gained by insisting on independence, excluding other kinds of arrangements, especially if they would grant a community all it wants without the additional burdens of a wholly independent existence (Watts 1997, 23).

Ultimately, the only sustainable unity is that based on mutual understanding and agreement. Unfortunately, the normative framework for national unity in modern Africa is not the result of consensus. Except in postapartheid South Africa, Africans won their independence without negotiating an internal social contract that would forge and sustain national consensus. Of course, the leaders of various factions, ethnic or political, negotiated frameworks that gave them the legitimacy to speak for their coun-

---

7. The constitution of the Federal Democratic Republic of Ethiopia (enacted December 8, 1994) provides in Art. 39, sec. 1, that "[e]very nation, nationality and people in Ethiopia has an unconditional right to self-determination, including the right to secession." In Art. 39, sec. 3, it states that "[e]very nation, nationality and people in Ethiopia has the right to a full measure of self-government which includes the right to establish institutions of government in the territory that it inhabits and to equitable representation in regional and national governments."

8. This is the essence of the proposal that Liechtenstein presented to the General Assembly of the United Nations in 1991 and that aimed at establishing a new international legal framework in which self-determination, defined primarily as self-administration, might be pursued within the existing state framework. See Danspeckgruber and Watts (1997).

tries in their demands for independence. Political elites certainly negotiated a common ground for independence in Zimbabwe, Namibia, and, with less satisfactory results, Angola. Independent leaders debated over federalism in Nigeria and ethnic representation in Kenya, Uganda, and the Ivory Coast. Indeed, in virtually every African country, independence was preceded by intense dialogue and negotiation among various groups, parallel to negotiations with the colonial powers. But these were tactical agreements to rid the countries of the colonial yoke and were in any case elitist negotiations that did not involve people at the grassroots level, as the South African negotiations did through a broad-based network of political organizations and elements of civil society.

Typically, the constitutions that African countries adopted at independence were drafted for them by colonial masters and, contrary to the authoritarian modes of government adopted by the colonial powers, were laden with idealistic principles of liberal democracy with which Africa had no experience. The regimes built on these constitutions were in essence grafted foreign conceptualizations with no indigenous roots, and they therefore lacked legitimacy. In most cases, they were soon overthrown with no remorse or regrets from the public. But these upheavals involved only a rotation of like-minded elites or, worse, military dictators, intent on occupying the seat of power vacated by colonial masters. They soon became the images of those colonial masters. In the overwhelming majority of countries, the quest for unity underscored the intensity of disunity, sometimes resulting in violent conflicts. Many of these conflicts have intensified in the post–cold war era, as evidenced in Burundi, Congo-Brazzaville, Liberia, Sierra Leone, Somalia, Rwanda, and Congo-Kinshasa, to mention only a few. It can be argued that the gist of these conflicts is that the ethnic pieces that were welded and kept together by the colonial glue and reinforced by the cold war began to pull apart and reassert their autonomy or demand the total restructuring of the state to be more representative. African states must respond to the demands of justice, equity, and dignity or risk disintegration and collapse.

Comparing and contrasting the experience of the former Soviet republics in this respect reveals significant similarities and differences. As noted in Chapter 13, the sudden dissolution of the Soviet Union led many to predict chaos and generalized instability, accompanied by an uncontrollable rise in ethnic political conflict and violence within and among the successor states. The ensuing six regional wars involving regular armies and heavy arms were, with the exception of that in Tajikistan, secessionist wars by ethnic groups that had been well established as autonomous republics or provinces during Soviet times and that received support from external sources. These conflicts have now been frozen, and no new conflicts have erupted. According to Chapter 13, although the process of state-building and the formation of new identities is progressing rather slowly and is confronting enormous challenges, the situation appears to be stabilizing, however precariously.

Although a number of regional and international factors are responsible for these developments, the manner in which the legacy of Soviet policy on national identities has been a factor in both generating secessionist conflicts and consolidating post-Soviet states is crucial. These states are based on dominant ethno-national identities but must also accommodate minority rights to be effective and legitimate regionally and internationally. The fact that Russia remains keenly interested in the welfare of ethnic Russians in the countries of the former Soviet Union provides both the carrot and the stick for this balanced approach.

The similarities and contrasts with the African experience are striking. Colonial administrations in Africa recognized "tribes" or ethnic groups and granted them indirect rule that was basically tactical. This recognition did not rise to the level granted the "titular nationalities" of the Soviet Union, but it was significant enough to pose a threat to poor colonial administrations. Precisely because it was confined to local or rural administration, the concession to African ethnic groups did not provide a sound basis for structuring new entities after independence and, with rare exceptions (for example, Buganda), could not provide a basis for independence movements.

The critical issues in the experience of the countries of the former Soviet Union crystallized in a definition of the new national identity, the elaboration of language policies, and the formation of citizenship criteria. Language, culture, and religion are building blocks in constructing a new sense of national identity. But beyond making use of these elements of nation-building, the liberalization process generated by the dissolution of the Soviet system unleashed a process of cultural and religious revivalism not dissimilar to the current African experience. In particular, the resurgence of Islam in North African countries and in the Sudan has significant parallels with the renaissance experienced by Islam not only throughout Central Asia, but also in the Caucasus and in parts of the Russian Federation.

Four policy options are available for managing pluralistic identities. One is to create a national framework with which all can identify without any distinction based on race, ethnicity, or religion. Although this prescription is perhaps the ideal, it is also problematic, as it implies homogenization and therefore assimilation of minority cultures. At a time when groups are asserting their separate identities, such an approach would in fact be resisted.

The second option is to create a pluralistic framework to accommodate diversity in nations that are racially, ethnically, culturally, or religiously divided. Under this option, probably a federal arrangement, groups would accommodate each other's differences with a uniting commitment to the common purpose of national identification and nondiscrimination. This might involve recognizing various shades of decentralization, federation, and confederalism. However, such an approach implies that minorities are identifiable with specific territorial borders. Where they are dispersed, the issue of how to manage diversity becomes more complex.

For more seriously divided countries, the third option may be some form of power-sharing combined with decentralization that expands federalism into confederalism. In many ways, the solution adopted by South Africa, which gives special recognition to racial and ethnic pluralism, is an example of this approach, as is the approach to the autonomous territories in the former Soviet Union. Where even this degree of accommodation is not workable, and where territorial configurations permit, the fourth option, partition, ought to be accepted.

The Cultural Dimension in Development

The dilemma of ethnicity in nation-building also raises questions about the related issue of the role of cultural values and institutions in the political and economic development of a country. Botswana stands out with its remarkable stability and economic success; its development was based on a dynamic reinterpretation and transformation of tradition as a foundation and a resource for promoting a progressive process of transitional integration that is self-reliant and self-sustaining. Replicating this approach to state-building would make development not something from outside the culture, but a process of self-enhancement from within.

Culture is "a set of shared and enduring meanings, values, and beliefs that characterize national ethnic or other groups and orient their behavior" (Faure and Rubin 1993, 3). It connotes a defined group with a set of value-objectives, organizational structures, and patterns of behavior in pursuit of those objectives, with certain outcomes and effects, all of which constitute a system. According to the definition propagated by the United Nations Educational, Scientific, and Cultural Organization, "[C]ulture . . . is . . . the whole complex of distinctive spiritual, material, intellectual and emotional features that characterize a society or social group. It includes not only arts and letters, but also modes of life, the fundamental rights of the human being, value systems, traditions and beliefs" (Deng 1994, 466).

Paradoxically, despite their disregard of "tribal" or "ethnic" identities and corresponding values and institutions, postcolonial African leaders sought to justify their policies with reference to indigenous cultural values. Such concepts as African socialism and the one-party system were often explained in those terms. Nkrumah wrote of "consciencism" as founded in the African values of social consciousness and communal solidarity. Nyerere founded his socialism on the concept of *ujamaa* (familyhood), which also focused on communal cooperation. Léopold Senghor in Senegal wrote of *négritude* and the African personality as cultural bases for the pan-Africanist movement. Mobutu Sese Seko in Congo-Kinshasa advocated *authenticité* as a principle of indigenization. And Kenneth Kaunda in Zambia sought his ideology of governance in what he called "Humanism." In reality, except for Nyerere, who gave his African socialism a degree of intellectual depth and cultural authenticity, much of the philosophy espoused by socialist leaders was rhetorical justification for Marxist ideologies imported from the Soviet bloc. Others tried to legitimize their own innovations to entrench themselves in power. Ironically, Nyerere's philosophy of building on indigenous African cultural values to promote a self-reliant concept of development became so appealing to donors, especially the Scandinavian countries, that they chose Tanzania as a country of concentration for their economic aid. This eventually undermined the very ideology they were supporting, as Tanzania became particularly dependent on foreign aid.

Some scholars have argued that patronage government in modern Africa has its roots in African tradition (Hyden 1998). This, in my opinion, is a misconception. Patronage government is more a response to the objective realities of the socio-economic conditions of Africa today than it is a well-formulated method of building a modern system on indigenous values and institutions. It is widely recognized that there is always high pressure exerted on elected politicians to become benefactors to their kin group or ethnic constituencies, whether financially or in terms of social services and development projects. The abuse of power for the acquisition and private disbursement of wealth under those conditions, rather than the result of some indigenous propensity toward corruption, may well be the outcome of a felt need caused by the demands of new standards of living and raised expectations, contrasted with scarcity of resources and gross inequities in the modern patterns of income generation and distribution. Power and control of wealth became concentrated in the central government, in contrast to the broad-based autonomous and self-reliant means of production and distribution in traditional society. Combined with this concentration is the very limited access to power at the center, achievable only through the few members of the community who occupy elected or civil service positions.

In the sense that traditional communities have been deprived of their autonomy and self-reliance and rendered dependent on government-controlled resources, corruption can indeed be attributed to modern rather than indigenous factors. It can even be argued that a more constructive use of traditional institutions in the political process could invoke and mobilize traditional values and practices that would constrain the unscrupulous exploitation of public trust for material gains. Under those conditions, the community can be an effective watchdog on its leaders in accordance with the indigenous norms of leadership. It has indeed been noted that the numerous instances of state failure and the massive evidence of societal exit derive from the very exogeneity of the state, its lack of embeddedness, its divorce from underlying norms and network of social organization. Patterns of predation, neopatrimonialism, rent-seeking, urban bias, and administrative decay can be thought of as deriving from the legitimacy deficit of the African state.

History cannot be remade, of course; the colonial state has become an African reality that cannot be wished away. At the same time, the issue of the role of indigenous values and institutions in the development of Africa remains a matter of grave concern. Instead of being perceived as a self-reliant process of building on what existed in traditional society and the enhancement of the quality of life from within, past policies saw development as an imported commodity. But tradition has continued to assert itself. As Ake explains, "African culture has fiercely resisted and threatened every project that fails to come to terms with it, even as it is acted upon and changed" (Ake 1996, 15). The reaction to this resistance, however, has been an attempt to eradicate tradition in favor of modernization. Instead of seeing traditional culture as an asset that the development paradigm should build on positively, many look upon it with disdain. The more Africans resist, the more they are faced with hostility against tradition as an obstacle to development. Agents of development "castigated peasants for being bound to tradition, for being conservative and emotional in their attitudes. The impression was given that Africans, particularly the rural people, are, by virtue of being themselves, enemies of progress" (Ake 1996, 15).

A mounting call is being made for a change of policy in this regard. As Ben Kwame Fred-Mensah has observed, "[T]here is a growing consensus among some African and Africanist writers, development experts, and the donor community that indigenous institutions, values, and practices are the motors of grassroots participatory development strategies. Consequently, there is a growing demand not only for the utilization of indigenous institutions, but also for their rationalization and formalization" (Fred-Mensah 1992, 7; see also Deng 1984, Serageldin and Tabaroff 1994, Dia 1995, Cole and Huntington 1997).

Development should be perceived as a process of self-enhancement from within by improving on what the people have in fact done for tens, hundreds, and perhaps thousands of years. People have always cultivated food; they could always do better by increasing the quality and quantity of their produce to yield a surplus that can be marketed to acquire cash for other necessities or values. People have always tried to increase the size of their herds, improve their quality, and protect them from disease; they could always do more with feeding, breeding, and disease-control programs. People have always built dwellings appropriate to their environment; they could always improve the quality of their houses to provide for more space, lighting, ventilation, insulation, and protection against the elements. People have always endeavored to ensure their health and general well-being through various preventive and curative methods; they could always do better to prevent disease by improving the quality of their hygiene, their nutrition, their potable water, their sanitation, and, of course, their curative methods. People have always traveled and transported their goods on land and water; they could always facilitate their movement by constructing country roads and using animals, bicycles, carts, or more mechanized vehicles. And there are those whose exceptional drives have always extended their horizons far and wide—traders, innovators, and adventurers who, more than others, explore, adopt, and adapt new ways to improve their conditions. Within this range and more, much can be done by building on the old, acquiring what is new, and cross-fertilizing to enhance the quality of life.

Conclusion

Africa's turbulent transformation, initiated by the colonial scramble for the continent in the nineteenth century, constrained by external domination for much of the first half of the twentieth century, reactivated by the independence movement at the second half of the century, and subdued by the cold war bipolar control mechanism, is now gaining a renewed momentum of self-liberation from within. The context in which this is taking place is poised delicately between globalization and isolation, bordering on the marginalization of Africa. Paradoxically, ideological withdrawal by the major powers is being counterbalanced by pressures for humanitarian intervention. This calls for a more cost-effective sharing of responsibility, with Africans assuming the primary role and their international partners lending a distant but affirmative helping hand.

The policy framework that apportions responsibilities in accordance with this emerging scale places the first tier of responsibility on the state. At the next level up the international ladder, regional actors are increasingly being challenged and motivated by the realization that their own national security is closely connected with the security of their neighbors. This has propelled a range of initiatives in which neighbors offer their good offices for third-party mediation in internal conflicts, but if their counsel is not heeded, they intervene unilaterally or collectively to achieve their objectives.

A number of African leaders have embraced programs of political and economic reforms that would enhance regional security and stability. Some of their peers remain doggedly committed to authoritarian methods of governance. The international community, weary of shouldering responsibility for Africa's problems, is striving to win over the leaders intent on reform, give them the support they need to carry out their programs, and thereby provide them with the incentive to do so in earnest. This implies the stipulation of national sovereignty as responsibility with regional and international accountability.

An important dimension of this reconceptualization of sovereignty is to reform state structures, institutions, and processes to be more equitable in their management of diversities. This will require reversing Africa's international dependency to enhance the autonomy of internal actors, ethnic groups, and members of civil society to mobilize and engage in self-reliant processes of governance and sustainable development. The state has been the intermediary and often the bottleneck in the chain of Africa's dependent relationship with the outside world. The required reform must broaden the scope of decision-making through extensive and genuine decentralization. It must make more constructive use of indigenous structures, values, and institutions for self-governance and sustainable development from within. The values of this system reflect both the competitiveness of individuals and groups and communal solidarity based on kinship and other corporate associations. A government genuinely committed to reform should have no difficulty in supporting this approach; those governments that would insist on centralization of authority wittingly or unwittingly expose their authoritarian disposition and risk regional and international scrutiny or admonition, and maybe condemnation and reprisals.

As a polarity emerges between African governments committed to participatory democracy, respect for human rights, and responsible international partnership and those bent on repression and resistance to reform, the international community should adopt a dual strategy that effectively supports reform with positive incentives and discourages resistance with punitive action. Although the international community has made some progress in responding to humanitarian tragedies, much more needs to be done to ensure that governments adhere to the responsibilities of sovereignty by ensuring the security, fundamental rights, civil liberties, and general welfare of their citizens and all those under their domestic jurisdiction.

References

Ake, Claude. 1996. *Democracy and Development in Africa*. Washington: Brookings Institution Press.

Annan, Kofi. 1996. "The Peacekeeping Prescription." Pp. 174–90 in *Preventive Diplomacy,* ed. Kevin M. Cahill. New York: Basic Books.

Chazan, Naomi, et al. 1988. *Politics and Society in Contemporary Africa*. Boulder: Lynne Rienner.

Chege, Michael. 1992. "Remembering Africa." *Foreign Affairs* 71, no. 1: 146–63.

Cohen, Roberta, and Francis Deng, eds. 1998. *The Forsaken People: Case Studies of the Internally Displaced*. Washington: Brookings Institution Press.

Cole, David, and Richard Huntington. 1997. *Between a Swamp and a Hard Place: Developmental Challenges in Remote Rural Africa*. Cambridge, Mass.: Harvard Institute for International Development.

Danspeckgruber, Wolfgang, and Arthur Watts. 1997. "Introduction." Pp. 1–20 in *Self-Determination and Self-Administration: A Sourcebook,* ed. Wolfgang Danspeckgruber and Arthur Watts. Boulder: Lynne Rienner.

Deng, Francis M. 1974. *The Dinka and Their Songs*. Oxford: Oxford University Press.

———. 1980. *Dinka Cosmology*. London: Ithaca Press.

———. 1984. "Crisis in African Development: A Social and Cultural Perspective." Pp. 7–18 in *Rockefeller Brothers Fund Annual Report*. New York: Rockefeller Brothers Fund.

———. 1994. "Cultural Dimensions of Conflict Management and Developments: Some Lessons from the Sudan." Pp. 465–510 in *Culture and Development in Africa,* ed. Ismail Serageldin and June Tabaroff. Technical paper no. 225. Washington: World Bank.

———. 1995. *War of Visions: Conflict of Identities in the Sudan*. Washington: Brookings Institution Press.

Dia, Mamadou. 1995. *Africa's Management in the 1990s and Beyond: Relocating Indigenous and Transplanted Institutions*. Washington: World Bank.

Englebert, Pierre. 1997. "The Contemporary African State: Neither African nor State." *Third World Quarterly* 18, no. 4 (September): 767–75.

Evans-Pritchard, E. E. 1940. *The Nuer*. Oxford: Oxford University Press.

Faure, Guy Olivier, and Jeffrey Z. Rubin. 1993. "Culture and Negotiation: An Introduction." Pp. 1–13 in *Culture and Negotiation: The Resolution of Water Disputes,* ed. Guy Olivier Faure and Jeffrey Z. Rubin. Newbury Park: Sage.

Fred-Mensah, Ben Kwame. 1992. "The Dilemma of Much-Needed Institutional Change in Africa." *Social Change and Development News* 4, no. 1: 7.

Hyden, Goran. 1998. "Sovereignty, Responsibility and Accountability: Challenges at the National Level in Africa." Pp. 37–66 in *African Reckoning,* ed. Francis M. Deng and Terrence Lyons. Washington: Brookings Institution Press.

Kaplan, Robert. 1994. "The Coming Anarchy." *Atlantic Monthly.* February: 44–76.

———. 1997. "Was Democracy Just a Moment?" *Atlantic Monthly.* December: 55–80.

Lienhardt, Godfrey. 1970. "The Western Dinka." Pp. 97–135 in *Tribes without Rulers: Studies in African Segmentary Systems,* ed. John Middleton and David Tait. New York: Humanities.

Middleton, John, and David Tait. 1958. "Introduction." Pp. 1–32 in *Tribes without Rulers: Studies in African Segmentary Systems,* ed. John Middleton and David Tait. London: Routledge and Kegan Paul.

Mkandawire, Thandika. 1997. "Shifting Commitments and National Cohesion in African Countries." Center for Development Research, Copenhagen. Photocopy.

Ravenhill, John. 1988. "Redrawing the Map of Africa." Pp. 282–306 in *The Precarious Balance: State and Society in Africa,* ed. Donald Rothchild and Naomi Chazan. Boulder: Westview.

Rothchild, Donald. 1997. *Managing Ethnic Conflict in Africa: Pressures and Incentives for Cooperation.* Washington: Brookings Institution Press.

Serageldin, Ismail, and June Tabaroff, eds. 1994. *Culture and Development in Africa.* Technical paper no. 225. Washington: World Bank.

Watts, Arthur. 1997. "The Liechtenstein Draft Convention on Self-Determination through Self-Administration." Pp. 21–45 in *Self-Determination and Self-Administration: A Source Book,* ed. Wolfgang Danspeckgruber and Arthur Watts. Boulder: Lynne Rienner.

Young, Crawford. 1991. "Self-Determination and the African State System." Pp. 320–46 in *Conflict Resolution in Africa,* ed. Francis M. Deng and I. William Zartman. New York: Brookings Institution Press.

Zakaria, Fareed. 1997. "The Rise of Illiberal Democracy." *Foreign Affairs* 76, no. 6 (November–December): 22–43.

15

Women and Political Change in Post-Soviet Eurasia and Postcolonial Africa

AILI MARI TRIPP

In both Africa and Eurasia women lived through somewhat analogous processes of political opening and economic liberalization in the 1990s. Yet the outcomes of the processes in these two regions were in some ways remarkably different. In Africa, democratization and economic reform have on the whole generated greater opportunities for mobilization of and representation by women than in the past. In the former Soviet Union, on the other hand, it is generally accepted that these same processes have led to a marked deterioration in the position of women.

This chapter seeks to explain this divergence. It does so by focusing on the quite distinct historical legacies and political economies of women's situations in Africa and the former Soviet Union. In the former Soviet Union the paternalistic legacy of enforced modes of equality without genuine voice led in the 1990s to the swift dismantlement under marketization of welfare provisions supporting families and of social protection for women and to a sharp deterioration under liberalization in women's representation within the political sphere. By contrast, in Africa in the 1990s the relative autonomy and mobilizational capacity of women's organizations helped to fuel a concerted move by women into the political sphere. In both regions women have suffered from state crisis. However, in some senses, given their starting points, women in Eurasia had more to lose than

African women did. Although women on both continents bore the brunt of the burden of structural adjustment and political disorder, the extensive experience of African women in seeking survival strategies outside the state provided them with significantly greater resources and capacity for responding to changed circumstances.

The Changing Status of Women in the 1990s

Economic and political changes left women in the former Soviet republics without the net of social security provisions, low-cost child care, job security, and relatively high levels of political representation that they had enjoyed under communism. Economic decline and state retreat similarly wrought new hardships on women in Africa. The opening of political spaces propelled women in both regions to form independent organizations addressing a host of new issues, ranging from human rights to the environment, welfare concerns, reproductive rights, and female political representation. For women in Africa in the 1990s the agenda gradually shifted from one of focusing almost exclusively on income generation and economic development to a new interest in strategies to advance women's political representation. For Eurasian women, the focus was on reclaiming what had been lost, but within a new context in which the role of the state had shifted dramatically.

Women in both regions experienced deterioration in their status and welfare under the impact of economic change. In Africa, their conditions had been declining since the late 1970s and 1980s, whereas in Eurasia the most dramatic changes took place in the 1990s. This is not to say there were no serious problems for women in the Soviet period, when the state addressed political and economic equality without attending to inequalities in the household. Nevertheless, in the Soviet Union in 1991, women earned about 75 percent of what men could earn. Yet by the end of the decade Russia had one of the largest gender gaps in wages in the world, with women making about 40 percent of men's wages. In Ukraine women made only one-third the amount that men earned. Similar percentages could be found in the other Eurasian states. Prior to the 1990s, Soviet women had one of the highest rates of labor-force participation in the world (Rimashevskaia 1992, 5). By the end of the 1990s all the former Soviet republics were experiencing growing rates of female unemployment. In Russia, Ukraine, and many of the other republics women made up over 70 percent of those unemployed. Women also suffered disproportionate discrimination in the labor market, holding poorly paid jobs with low job security. One of the many new consequences of women's unemployment and lack of job security was the growing problem of sex trafficking, in which criminal groups lured young women with the promise of working as waitresses and barmaids overseas and then confiscated their passports, sometimes raping and beating them into submission and forcing them to work as prostitutes. The numbers of women trafficked from Ukraine, Russia, and other former Soviet republics were among the highest in the world, matching or even surpassing the numbers drawn from Asia and Latin America (Blagov 1999).

After the collapse of the Soviet Union, family benefits and child care services declined precipitously, adding to women workload (Tserkonivnitska 1997). Women were particularly burdened by declines in health services, especially in the areas of childbirth, abortion, and contraception (Slater 1994, 32). Moreover, women were often left saddled with finding ways of coping with soaring consumer prices.

Changes in women's political status were also stark. This problem is evident from the sharp drop in the number of women deputies in all-union, republican, and local legislatures (see Tables 15.1 and 15.2). A quota system had basically guaranteed women 33 percent of the seats in the Soviet Union's Congress of People's Deputies. But when the quota system was dropped in Russia in the 1990 republican elections, women occupied only 5 percent of the seats in the republic's Congress of People's Deputies. Female representation rose to 13.5 percent of the Russian Duma with the 1993 election, largely from the efforts of the Women of Russia electoral bloc, but dropped to 9.8 percent in the 1995 elections and to 7.3 percent in 1999. Moreover, in the legislature women were virtually excluded from the centers of decision-making, including the factions and deputies' groups, the leadership of legislative committees, and the Council of the State Duma (Shvedova 1999). In Azerbaijan, to take another case, the same pattern was repeated: at the beginning of 1991, women representatives made up 40 percent of the Supreme Soviet of the Azerbaijan Republic; by 1992, however, women comprised only 6 percent of the deputies in the legislature, although this number increased slightly to 12 percent in the 1995 elections.

Of course, because power was not always concentrated in the legislature, such representation had its limitations. Even though women claimed 16 percent parliamentary representation in a country like Turkmenistan, they clearly remained isolated from the reins of power. A council of elders who advised the president served as the main power brokers in the country, yet

Table 15.1

Percentage of Seats Held by Women in Eurasian Legislatures, 1959–2001

	Supreme Soviets of union republics			Local councils of peoples' deputies			Legislative bodies
	1959	1967	1985[2]	1959	1967	1985[2]	2001
Turkmenistan	34	35	36	37	41	50	26
Estonia	33	35	36	39	47	50	18
Latvia	31	33	35	37	46	50	17
Tajikistan	33	33	36	33	44	50	13
Lithuania	28	32	36	35	43	50	11
Kazakhstan	32	34	36	33	38	50	10
Azerbaijan	30	32	40	40	41	48	10
Kyrgyzstan	33	35	36	38	41	50	10
Belarus	37	36	37	37	43	50	10
Moldova	37	38	36	45	48	50	19
Russia[1]	33	34	35	40	44	51	8
Ukraine	34	34	36	36	41	50	8
Georgia	30	31	36	44	43	51	7
Uzbekistan	29	31	36	34	44	49	7
Armenia	32	33	36	41	41	50	3
Average	32	34	36	38	43	50	11

Sources: Inter-Parliamentary Union web site (www.ipu.org/wmn-e/world.htm); Central Statistical Bureau 1985.

[1] 1959–85 figures are for the Russian Soviet Federated Socialist Republic; 1999 figures are for the Russian Federation.

[2] For all 1985 figures, elections were held in 1984.

none of its members were women, and there did not appear to be any effort to include women in such institutions.

The changes for women in the post-Soviet legislatures were perhaps more symbolic than real, in the sense that in spite of the decreases in representation, women in the Soviet period were almost completely excluded

Table 15.2

Percentage of Seats Held by Women in the Supreme Soviets of the Republican and Autonomous Republican Governments of the Soviet Union, 1958–89

	1958	1967	1975	1985	1989
Supreme Soviet of the Soviet Union	27	28	31	33	19
Supreme Soviets of union republics	26	35	39	31	16
Supreme Soviets of autonomous republics	27	35	39	35	21

Sources: Lapidus 1978; Central Statistical Bureau 1985; Buckley 1992b.

from key policy-making institutions such as the Communist Party Central Committee and the Council of Ministers (Moses 1977, 334; Lapidus 1978, 206). This was also the case at the local and regional levels, where political recruitment for central institutions started (Moses 1977, 336). Moreover, those women who in the past filled the reserved seats got there because of their loyalty to the Communist Party. These women in particular were not about to challenge the status quo or adopt positions on women's issues that were independent of the party. Thus women's impressively high levels of representation in the Soviet era were somewhat illusory in that they did not reflect women's genuine political involvement. Still, developments in the post-Soviet period indicate no signs of female political empowerment and, in comparative terms, a relatively low degree of representation (see Table 15.3).

Women in most African countries never enjoyed such high levels of female representation in political institutions (real or symbolic) as their counterparts did in the Soviet Union, nor did they experience such high levels of employment, education, and social benefits. Protracted state and political crisis left African women considerably worse off. They suffered from economic decay and later from International Monetary Fund and World Bank structural adjustment programs that introduced austerity measures. They had to contend with plummeting real wages, declining employment, food shortages, and declines in public and social services. With structural adjustment, user fees were introduced in medical facilities and food subsidies were dropped, hurting women in particular as the primary providers of food and health care in the family.

Thus women in both regions in the 1990s were preoccupied with dealing with a collapsed state-sponsored safety net and with economic decline. But there were some crucial differences. Eurasian women perhaps had more to lose but at the same time were more dependent on the state, whereas women in many African contexts had long sought strategies of survival outside the state and had more experience and resources (not necessarily monetary resources) to use in responding to such changing circumstances. In both regions, the division of labor within the household placed much of the burden of the survival of families on women. Women sought income-generating projects in the informal economy and private sector businesses, in addition to a variety of collective solutions to their economic difficulties in the form of voluntary associations. It is of enormous significance that for the first time in recent history, women in the former Soviet republics were after 1990 able to organize independently around issues of their own choosing and in ways they themselves determined (Buck-

Table 15.3

Percentage of Senior Government Positions in Post-Soviet Governments Held by Women, 1996

	Ministerial	Subministerial	Total
Latvia	11.1	19.0	17.6
Estonia	0.0	16.8	14.3
Kyrgyzstan	10.5	12.0	11.4
Lithuania	0.0	6.8	7.3
Azerbaijan	7.7	6.9	7.1
Belarus	5.3	7.0	6.6
Moldova	0.0	7.0	4.3
Tajikistan	3.7	3.9	3.8
Georgia	0.0	4.7	3.4
Russia	2.4	2.6	2.6
Turkmenistan	3.1	0.0	2.2
Armenia	0.0	2.9	2.1
Kazakhstan	2.6	1.7	2.1
Ukraine	0.0	2.2	1.7
Uzbekistan	2.6	0.0	1.3
By region			
Baltic states (Latvia, Lithuania, Estonia)	3.7	14.2	13.1
Caucasus (Armenia, Azerbaijan, Georgia)	2.6	4.8	4.2
Central Asia (Kazakhstan, Kyrgyzstan, Tajikistan, Turkmenistan, Uzbekistan)	4.5	3.5	4.2
Western CIS (Belarus, Moldova, Russia, Ukraine)	1.9	4.7	0.8
Non-Nordic OECD member states	13.5	12.8	13.0
Nordic OECD member states	33.1	19.0	22.3

Sources: UNICEF 1999; Inter-Parliamentary Union web site (www.ipu.org/wmn-e/world.htm).
Note: CIS = Commonwealth of Independent States; OECD = Organization for Economic Cooperation and Development.

ley 1992a, 54). Mary Buckley underscores the variety of groups and orientations and the general political fragmentation of women in the former Soviet Union. Some supported democracy and economic reform, whereas others opposed a market economy; some identified themselves as feminists, whereas others promoted the return to traditional conceptions of women's role in society; some promoted religion, or political, social, or cultural interests; mothers in some republics mobilized against their sons being sent as soldiers to suppress nationalist unrest, whereas mothers in the Baltic countries, by contrast, encouraged their sons to enlist in the army.

Many women's organizations in both regions focused on entrepreneurship, self-employment, and income generation. They also concentrated on helping women who had suffered disproportionately from the cutbacks; in post-Soviet Eurasia, these victims were predominantly unemployed women, single mothers, and pensioners (Racioppi and See 1995a, 194). Some women's groups also increasingly sought greater influence in the legislature to shape laws affecting women and the welfare of their families.

Women and the State

In Eurasia and Africa in the 1990s, women leaders and women's organizations sought to negotiate a new relationship with the state, but for different historic reasons. In the post-Soviet period some women were eager to abandon the public arena and seek refuge in domesticity because of what the public arena had meant to them under communism. Interviews with Russian women activists by Linda Racioppi and Katherine O'Sullivan See reveal in particular how women were reluctant to be spoken for, rescued by someone else, or forced into a false solidarity. "Am I an object of the state? Am I being manipulated by the state?" asked Elivira Novikova, founder of the Women and Creativity Association in Moscow, which explores issues of women's consciousness (Racioppi and See 1995b, 193). Novikova's statements reflect the widespread suspicion of state-sponsored equality that characterized women's responses in the former Soviet Union. Thus, although women activists have some interest in influencing the state, they also are keenly aware of the importance of keeping women outside of state control so that women's emancipation does not come to be defined solely by the state (Racioppi and See 1995b, 842–43, 845).

By contrast, in Africa one finds much the same resistance to the way the state had shaped women's lives and mobilization in the past, but considerably less interest in retreating from the public sphere—in part because the reach of the state there was never as extensive and all-encompassing as that of the Soviet state. Much of the post-Soviet Eurasian concern is a reaction to forced emancipation under Soviet rule, which pushed women into the workforce but left them also doing most of the time-consuming and back-breaking housework and child care. Moreover, with liberalization the family became the refuge against a state that always knew what was best for people—hence the retreat into domesticity.

Thus, whereas in Africa the movement for equal rights gained momentum throughout the 1990s, in Eurasia there was greater ambivalence in this regard, especially with the breakup of the Soviet Union. Some women in the postcommunist states at least initially appeared reluctant to embrace claims to equal rights that all too often were associated with the communist state's interpretation of gender equality, because of the burdens it had placed on women in the past. Moreover, because women's emancipation had in the past been defined in ways that served only the needs of the state, women in Eurasia had to struggle to reconceptualize it in a way that corresponded more directly with their own interests.

After the 1917 Bolshevik Revolution, the regime introduced reforms to improve women's status: marriage, abortion, and property laws were changed. But it was not long until the aspirations of Bolshevik feminists took a back seat to other goals of establishing the socialist state. These feminists drew on the Marxist rationalization that women's emancipation lay with their participation in social production. The family was a bastion of tradition and backwardness that needed to be undermined so that people's energies could be redirected to the public domain and toward building up the economy to create a socialist state. Economically independent women were critical to this shift, but in order to create such women the functions of the household needed to be shifted to the public domain (Lapidus 1993, 138).

By the time Joseph Stalin came to power, only the Soviet state and the Communist Party were to define women's interests, set priorities, and implement policies that "served the causes of national consolidation, economic construction, and, later, the war effort" (Racioppi and See 1995b, 820). Industrialization required rising birthrates. These were to be generated by banning abortion, making divorces more difficult, and promoting traditional family values. In the post-Stalin period, state policy shifted again, as abortion was legalized and divorce restrictions lifted. Day-care centers, summer camps, and subsidies for mothers reduced some of the burden of juggling domestic and employment responsibilities. With the disintegration of the centrally planned economy in the late 1980s and early 1990s, economic crisis resulted in a massive loss of jobs by women, creating yet a new set of state legacies vis-à-vis women. Under President Mikhail Gorbachev, the earlier image of woman as worker-mother began to be replaced by a stay-at-home-mother image to allow women to "rest from production work" (Posadskaya 1993, 162)—again, another form of withdrawal from the public sphere. The renewed emphasis on devotion to the responsibilities of caring for the family paralleled women's changing employment opportunities, as even well-educated women were among the first to lose their jobs (Racioppi and See 1995b, 820–24).

The breakup of the Soviet Union brought additional negative consequences upon women. In many former Soviet republics, state subsidies of social benefits were cut dramatically. In Russia, President Boris Yeltsin promoted the view that women should leave their jobs and return to caring for the family as a solution both to the problems of alcoholism and crime and to the precipitously declining birthrate. The revival of religious beliefs and practices in Islamic parts of the former Soviet Union also at times resulted in setbacks in women's status. In southern Kyrgyzstan, to take one example, one finds both increased incidences of bigamy and prohibitions on girls attending secondary school (Galieva 1999).

Some observers were surprised by the lack of protest in much of the former Soviet Union when the numbers of women legislators dropped sharply with the lifting of the quota system and with the other setbacks experienced by women in the economic sphere. The lack of resistance was at times explained as a consequence of the psychology of dependence and passivity and the widespread sentiment that a paternalistic government would take care of issues of equality. Others saw the initial quiescence as a manifestation of the lack of political influence women had had in the Soviet Union and their lack of experience with autonomous mobilization (Konstantinova 1992, 207).

As it became clear that women were losing out on many fronts with dire consequences for the welfare of their families, women began to mobilize. In countries such as Kyrgyzstan, women's groups have been involved in promoting female parliamentary candidates and in trying to bring about changes in family law as it pertains to women and children. Indeed, there are more than five hundred nongovernmental organizations (NGOs) in Kyrgyzstan, of which the strongest are women's groups. Many of these associations have worked with divorced women, widows, and other women who have suffered most from the weakening of the social security net. Others have sought policy changes and to influence public opinion regarding unemployed women, single mothers, and pensioners (Galieva 1999).

But the ideological underpinnings of these new women's organizations are unclear. While rejecting state-sponsored gender equality, many female activists in the former Soviet republics do not necessarily embrace feminism either. Nor is there any reason to expect that they will. Much as in African women's movements, Eurasian women's activism suggests the emergence of what Racioppi and See call a "pragmatic feminism," one that is not extensively theorized but that focuses on the building of coalitions and agendas by hundreds of organizations—particularly in the areas of small business, the environment, mothers of soldiers, soup kitchens, and political and religious concerns (Racioppi and See 1995b, 830). Few groups actively identify themselves with feminism. Most that do comprise academics, artists, journalists, or professional women. Indeed, interviews reveal a suspicion of Western feminist ideas and influences among some Russian women's activists. Many make appeals to Western feminists to allow them the necessary space to sort out their own direction and talk about the need to be listened to by feminists from around the world rather than to be told how to analyze their own circumstances (Racioppi and See 1995a, 194). For others, feminism is yet another ideology, and given their experiences under Soviet rule, they feel that ideology is to be avoided at all costs. Others have been influenced by the popular media and its associations of feminism with deviance and with negative foreign influences. Still others have associated feminism with the Soviet exploitation of women in the labor force by relegating them to low-paying jobs with a second shift of domestic duties at home (Lipovskaia 1992, 72). Attitudes toward feminism have been changing in countries where links with international women's organizations are being strengthened. Organizations in the Baltic states, in particular, have been less reluctant to draw on international influences in building their movements, more readily establishing ties with Nordic women's organizations and feminists throughout the world.

Undoubtedly there have been African women activists who have similarly been hesitant to embrace the term "feminism," primarily because of its Western connotations and its association with a kind of selfish individualism that negates the family and community. But these perceptions have changed rather rapidly in recent years as African women activists have appropriated the term and defined feminism for their own purposes and in their own ways, thus diminishing its association with the West. Moreover, women's movements in Africa have been in extensive dialogue with international women's organizations and networks for some time. They have fought and at times won battles over questions of global economic inequalities, poverty, and other concerns that African women want placed higher on international agendas. African women have also struggled with

Western women to bring a new awareness of the cultural context of female genital cutting and other such controversial issues. Thus there has not been the same ambivalence toward feminism and international women's movements in Africa as has been evident in parts of Eurasia.

Changing Agendas in Women's Movements

In many African countries, women activists saw the opening of political space as a chance to assert themselves in new arenas and challenge the worst characteristics of neopatrimonialism, clientelism, personal politics, and the politicization of ethnicity and religion. Because of past gender-based exclusions from formal political and economic life, women often had less at stake in maintaining the status quo and subsequently had the potential for greater openness to change and for adapting more easily to new incentive structures. It is no accident that women such as Zimbabwean parliamentarian Margaret Dongo, Kenyan parliamentarian and former presidential candidate Charity Ngilu, Kenyan environmental activist Wangari Maathai, and Ugandan parliamentarian Winnie Byanyima have emerged among the fiercest and most visible opponents of corruption and patronage politics in their respective countries. Many women's organizations and leaders have little to gain from allying themselves with state-related corruption and therefore have less to lose materially and politically by opposing it (although Maathai and Dongo live in fear for their lives because of their outspokenness). The Russian counterpart to these women was Galina Starovoitova, one of the country's best-known female politicians, who was assassinated mafia-style in 1998, most believe, because of her outspoken advocacy of democracy and human rights. Other populist women politicians in post-Soviet politics, such as Natalia Vitrenko in Ukraine, stand for an ideology entirely polar to Starovoitova's—calling for a restoration of Soviet values.

Women today see formal politics as a way to challenge the worst tendencies in many African states. But this has not always been the case. A shift has taken place in African women's movements over the past decade. In the past, wives of the leaders of the country ran mass women's organizations that were tied to the ruling party and regime through patronage. In the last decade, however, we have witnessed the proliferation of new independent organizations replacing the dominance of these mass organizations. Under one-party rule, organizations such as Umoja wa Wanawake wa Tanzania (the Tanzanian Women's Union), Organização da Mulher

Moçambicana (the Organization of Mozambican Women), the 31st December Women's Movement in Ghana, the Women's League in Zambia, and Kenya's Maendeleo ya Wanawake (Development of Women) dominated the landscape when it came to women's mobilization. Ruling parties kept these organizations depoliticized. They acted in the service of the party as vote-getting mechanisms and in solidifying women's support of the regime. They were generally unable to set their own agendas or select their own leaders. Women's wings of parties and mass women's party organizations often served in celebratory functions, cooking food, dancing, and hosting guests of the party. Moreover, when one spoke of women's mobilization in Africa prior to the 1990s, it was almost always a reference to "development"-related activities—income-generating projects and handicrafts.

Although many of these characteristics of female mobilization are still evident in Africa, today there are also significant numbers of new, autonomous women's associations on the scene taking advantage of the new political spaces that have opened up as a result of state retreat. Through these organizations women are trying to gain better political representation. This is a relatively new phenomenon. Some countries, such as South Africa, have 30 percent female representation in parliament; the Seychelles have 25 percent, Mozambique 30 percent, and Namibia 25 percent. By 2001 women held on average 12 percent of parliamentary seats in Africa, which is more than in the former Soviet Union, where the average is 11 percent (see Tables 15.1 and 15.4).

Until the 1990s it was almost unheard of in Africa for women to run in presidential races. Indeed, prior to the 1990s the only African country to have had a female prime minister was the Central African Republic in 1975–76. But during the 1990s, a number of women rose to the forefront of politics in Africa. Liberia had a woman chairing its six-member collective presidency council in 1996–97. Women sought party nominations to run in presidential races in Nigeria, Tanzania, Angola, the Central African Republic, Guinea-Bissau, Kenya, Sao Tome and Principe, Liberia, and Burkina Faso. Undoubtedly, women will run in greater numbers in future presidential races in these and other countries. Uganda has had a woman vice president since 1994. Rwanda and Burundi both had women prime ministers in the early 1990s. The only comparable examples from Eurasia are from the Baltic states: Kazimiera Prunskiene, who became prime minister of Lithuania briefly in 1990–91, and Vaira Vike-Freiberga, the president of Latvia, who spent almost all of her adult life in exile in Canada. Women's organizations have been active in lobbying for and bringing

Table 15.4
Women's Legislative Representation in Africa, 2001

	Election year	Total number of seats in lower or single house	Number of seats held by women	Percentage of seats held by women
Mozambique	1999	250	75	30.0
South Africa[1]	1999	399	119	29.8
Rwanda	1994	74	19	25.7
Namibia	1999	72	18	25.0
Seychelles	1998	34	8	23.5
Tanzania	2000	274	61	22.3
Uganda	1996	281	50	17.8
Botswana	1999	47	8	17.0
Senegal	2001	120	20	16.7
Angola	1992	220	34	15.5
Eritrea	1994	150	22	14.7
Burundi	1993	118	17	14.4
Mali	1997	147	18	12.2
Congo-Brazzaville	1998	75	9	12.0
Cape Verde	2001	72	8	11.1
Zambia	1996	158	16	10.1
Zimbabwe	2000	150	15	10.0
Sudan	2000	360	35	9.7
Malawi	1999	193	18	9.3
Gabon	1996	120	11	9.2
Sao Tome and Principe	1998	55	5	9.1
Ghana	2000	200	18	9.0
Guinea	1995	114	10	8.8
Sierra Leone	1996	80	7	8.8
Ivory Coast	2000	223	19	8.5
Burkina Faso	1997	111	9	8.1
Madagascar	1998	150	12	8.0
Guinea-Bissau	1999	102	8	7.8
Liberia	1997	64	5	7.8
Ethiopia	2000	547	42	7.7
Central African Republic	1998	109	8	7.3
Benin	1999	83	5	6.0
Mauritius	2000	70	4	5.7
Cameroon	1997	180	10	5.6
Equatorial Guinea	1999	80	4	5.0
Togo	1999	81	4	4.9
Kenya	1997	224	8	3.6

(continued)

Table 15.4 *(Continued)*

	Election year	Total number of seats in lower or single house	Number of seats held by women	Percentage of seats held by women
Nigeria	1999	351	12	3.4
Swaziland	1998	65	2	3.1
Chad	1997	125	3	2.4
Gambia	1997	49	1	2.0
Niger	1999	83	1	1.2
Djibouti	1997	65	0	0.0

Source: Inter-Parliamentary Union web site (www.ipu.org/wmn-e/classif.htm).
[1]Figures on the distribution of seats do not include the thirty-six special rotating delegates appointed on an ad hoc basis, and the percentages given are therefore calculated on the basis of the fifty-four permanent seats.

about constitutional and legislative changes in countries such as Kenya, Malawi, Zambia, Uganda, South Africa, and Tanzania.

Today women's organizations in Africa are no longer simply focusing on "developmental" (i.e., economic empowerment) issues. They are also trying to improve women's leadership skills, promote civic education, assist women running for office, and pressure political parties to endorse more women candidates. Women's movements are addressing issues that never would have been touched by the old single-party-sponsored women's organizations—issues ranging from women's political representation to those of domestic violence, rape, sexual harassment, reproductive rights, disparaging portrayals of women in the media, and other concerns. They are involved in issues that affect the broader population, such as land rights in Tanzania and Uganda. The critical difference between those women's movements that have shifted to this more political and expanded agenda and those that remain developmental is the extent to which they have been able to assert their autonomy from the state. This autonomy is crucial to their success, although it is often tempered by the inability or unwillingness of the state to respond to women's demands and by state hostility to independent mobilization.

What, then, accounts for women's increased visibility in the political arena in Africa? A combination of reasons must be considered in explaining women's new interest in politics. First, the move away from single-party to multiparty systems reduced the importance of party-sponsored mass women's organizations funded and directed by the ruling party. As these mass organizations diminished in importance, new independent women's organizations proliferated in the 1990s to fill in the opening political spaces, to advance women's economic status, and to address their social welfare needs. Of course much the same dynamic was visible in the former Soviet republics, where the large Communist Party–sponsored women's unions were dissolved or reconstituted as independent organizations and women joined the new women's groups that were proliferating.

Second, as more African women became educated, especially at the tertiary level, this gave added impetus to the formation of these new organizations. Third, women often had longer experiences with mobilization than did men. Until the late 1980s in Africa, women's autonomous mobilization was curtailed in most one-party states and military regimes. However, even then women had considerable experience with their own market associations, trading associations, dual-sex women's councils, small informal credit associations, and farming, marketing, and other informal groups. Even in countries where mobilization at the national level was sharply curtailed, women still had YWCAs (Young Women's Christian Associations), religious associations, family planning associations, and some international professional associations. Thus, in contrast to the situation in the former Soviet Union, women had these traditions of independent associational life to build on and as a result were in some ways better situated than men were to take advantage of the new political spaces of the 1990s. This is why today most registered NGOs in Africa tend to be women's organizations. In Tanzania, for example, 80 percent of the registered NGOs are women's organizations (Meena 1997). In short, African women had more experience with autonomous mobilization than did post-Soviet Eurasian women, making it easier for them to respond to the changes that came with political liberalization.

Fourth, the new availability of donor funds through international and local NGOs, religious bodies, international foundations, and bilateral and multilateral donors also spurred women's mobilization in Africa—especially the new interest in funding democratic political action. These trends were also evident in the former Soviet republics—although there, as in Africa, most organizations, especially smaller ones, remain self-financed, contrary to common public perceptions. There is, however, a greater amount of government financing of women's organizations in the former Soviet republics than in African countries—in part a legacy of the previous regime.

Fifth, in some African countries leaders found it expedient to introduce party quotas and reserve parliamentary seats for women. Indeed, such measures account in part for the high levels of female representation that one finds in Uganda, Tanzania, Mozambique, South Africa, and elsewhere. Uganda set an important precedent for Africa by providing for one-third female representation in local councils, as well. Pressures to introduce such affirmative action measures have been mounting in other African countries. By contrast, in post-Soviet Eurasia similar quotas were removed in the 1990s. In this regard, the trends for the two regions were remarkably divergent.

Sixth, the international women's movement has given added impetus to women in Africa in addressing questions of political representation. These issues were raised, for example, as central concerns for women at the 1995 United Nations Conference on Women, held in Beijing. International influences were also evident in the former Soviet Union, although to a lesser degree than in Africa, in part because, until recently, Communist Party control of the women's network there isolated Soviet women's groups from their international counterparts. Women in Eurasia also seem to be more hesitant to embrace the feminist thinking prevalent in international women's organizations.

Finally, much of formal politics in Africa and Eurasia is controlled by informal patronage. Women tend to operate on the margins of such networks. But where clientelistic ties have broken down as a result of state crisis and economic decline in Africa, women have been able to make some political inroads, drawing on their own independently acquired wealth. This is especially true in local politics in Africa, but the same has not yet occurred in post-Soviet Eurasia.

Women's organizations in Eurasia have tried in a variety of ways to respond to the new challenges posed by liberalization and state contraction, and many of their motivations parallel the African cases. *Perestroika* and *glasnost* opened the door to a new kind of activism around women's issues, one not promoted by the party or state but initiated by women themselves (Racioppi and See 1995b, 827). The tight political control exercised by communist regimes until the late 1980s meant that relatively few women had experience with autonomous political activity or mobilization—even fewer than among African women, as explained above. This legacy posed difficult challenges for post-independence mobilization.

The landscape of Eurasian women's organizations parallels the African landscape in some ways. Independent women's organizations in Uzbekistan, for example, carry out many of the same functions as their counterparts do in many African countries, and these organizations have been growing exponentially since 1991. The Association of Businesswomen of Uzbekistan, formed in 1992, is the largest independent such organization, with 13 branches throughout the country. It educates women about business skills and acts as an advocate for business women's rights. Other organizations promote women's reproductive health and rights; women's health and an ecologically healthy environment; employment and social protection; rural women's concerns and education; women's legal, social, economic, and political status; and women's leadership skills, among other things. Women's organizations are particularly concerned with social issues that have traditionally fallen under women's purview, such as child and family health, education, care for the disabled, and other areas where state support has decreased.

Thus women in Uzbekistan appear to be more involved in nongovernmental organizations than men are (Sheridan n.d.), in part because the cutbacks in these areas have impinged more directly on women as a result of the division of labor in the household, and therefore women have had to find solutions to directly respond to these changes. Moreover, women have also at times found that political avenues for dealing with certain issues have been closed to them, forcing them to address these issues through alternative strategies. Women are also realizing that they need to find ways to stop the deterioration of women's rights, and NGOs are one of the few mechanisms for doing this.

In many African countries as well, women are more likely to be involved in NGOs than are men. In Uganda, as in other African countries, women's organizations have taken up issues similar to the Uzbek example. They have fought for greater female representation in parliament and governmental bodies and have addressed issues of domestic violence, rape, reproductive rights, sex education in the school curriculum, sexual harassment, women's rights as human rights, the representation of women in the media, and other such concerns. Some groups have focused on women's economic empowerment, others on women's legal rights, and others on the rights of particular groups of women—e.g., widows, the disabled, domestic servants, or second wives. The numbers of organizations have proliferated to the point where women are networking to an unprecedented degree with regional, national, continental, and international organizations.

Obstacles to and Strategies for Political Participation

Women in both regions face many of the same obstacles to increased participation in politics. In Africa, women generally lack the resources, political experience, education, and political connections to run for office. Moreover, they often do not have the necessary clientelistic ties that are so critical for success in the formal political arena.

In many African contexts, popular views would have women remain in the home rather than make forays into the political arena, where they are apt to be subject to vicious gossip and be labeled prostitutes, loose women, or poor mothers and wives (Ferguson with Katundu 1994, 18; Andersen 1992, 260–63). Jealous husbands may place restrictions on them or undermine their activities. Women who are elected to office often find they are not listened to or taken seriously. They may even be subject to sexual harassment by other members of parliament or local councils, as Sylvia Tamale revealed in her study of Ugandan parliamentarian women (Tamale 1997, 131–34). In Uganda, married women politicians often find it difficult to find a constituency in which to run: if they run in the constituency where they were born, they are told to go to the constituency where they are married; when they run in their husband's constituency, they are told, "You came here to marry not to rule" (Tripp 2000a).

Some obstacles have particular cultural manifestations, but many are fairly universal. Thus it comes as no surprise that Eurasian women face restrictions in the political arena that generally parallel those of African women. A 1997 survey of Belarusian women politicians representing various political parties suggested that women faced considerable sexual stereotyping, were excluded from cliques of male politicians, received little financial organizational support from their political parties, and found a low level of awareness among fellow politicians and the public when it came to women's participation in politics, which is still generally considered a male arena.

A 1995 survey in Kazakhstan found gender stereotypes to be salient among the population. University students were given copies of a speech by President Boris Yeltsin; half were told that it was written by a man, while the other half were told it was written by a woman. Those who thought it was written by a woman were consistently more skeptical of the competence of the politician than were those who thought it was written by a man and were less sympathetic to the politician's views on all topics, ranging from foreign policy to social concerns (Herrick and Sapieva 1997).

It is these kinds of attitudes among the population, politicians, and party leaders that have often forced women to resort to women-only parties or to run as independent candidates in the hope that their interests can be better represented through such alternative strategies. Women politicians in the former Soviet republics, for example, found it hard to gain political leverage through positions in the *nomenklatura* or patronage networks to which they did not have access until recently. What political visibility many gained was a result of their own involvement in public events and meetings and through campaigning.

On the one hand, such political independence allows politicians to challenge the status quo and make important critiques that party discipline might not permit. On the other hand, the lack of resources and support from a party tends to marginalize women—or push them right out of the picture. Zimbabwe's Margaret Dongo is one leader who has made the most of her independent status. She was one of only three opposition candidates in parliament until the opposition party Movement for Democratic Change gained seats in the 2000 parliamentary election. Until then, Dongo was one of the only members of parliament to speak out against abuses of power, corruption on the part of the president's family, and state control of the media. Even the parliamentarians of the ruling party ask her to publicly condemn bills they are afraid to attack openly (McNeil 1996).

Women have at times actively sought to organize their own separate women's parties in Lithuania, Russia (where several were formed in the early 1990s), Armenia, and Belarus. Inonge Mbikusita-Lewanika started the National Party in Zambia in 1991, and in Lesotho Limakatso Ntakatsane formed the party Kopanang Basotho. But these were parties initiated by women, not women's parties. The idea of forming a women's party has been floated in several African countries for the same reasons some Eurasian women have opted for this strategy (exclusion from male-dominated hierarchies), but so far such parties have not materialized.

In post-Soviet Eurasia, this strategy has provided some degree of women's representation. Of the 34 parties that emerged in Belarus after 1991, most women leaned toward the socialist and social-democratic parties, including a women's party, Nadzeya, which was formed in 1994 under the rubric of the Federation of Trade Unions. With the exception of Nadzeya, none of the parties made any effort to promote female candidates or set quotas. A small, independent women's movement emerged, much of it aimed at getting women into political positions. The most important organizations pushing for women's political advancement were the Women's Christian-Democrat Movement and Nadzeya, which also drew support because of its focus on social issues. Of course, the imposition of the dictatorship of Aleksandr Lukashenka has limited the opportunities for any form of representative influence—including that of women.

With the exception of Women of Russia in the 1993 elections, most women's parties in Eurasia have had limited success. In 1995 the Lithuanian Women's Party won one seat in a parliament in which twenty-four seats

(17 percent of the total) were won by women. The women's party Shamiram won eight of the twelve seats held by women (6 percent of the total seats) in the National Assembly in Armenia in 1995, doing better than Women of Russia in that same year. But representation of women's parties has been unstable and, in general, relatively small.

Women of Russia has been the most publicized of these women's parties, but its future is very much up in the air. The Women of Russia electoral group was made up of an alliance of three groups, including the Association of Businesswomen of Russia, the Union of Women in the Navy, and the Union of Women of Russia. The Union of Women of Russia drew on women's groups that had constituted one of its precursor organizations, the Committee of Soviet Women, which had well-established networks throughout the country. Part of the success of the Women of Russia as an electoral bloc, therefore, could be attributed to the fact that it was able to take advantage of the networks and connections formed by its predecessor (Racioppi and See 1995b, 845). In Russia, the 1993 parliamentary election saw an unprecedented 170 percent increase in female representation over the previous (1990) election, largely due to the efforts of Women of Russia. Women won 15 percent of the Duma seats, which included 13 women in addition to the 21 seats won by Women of Russia; 26 women were elected from single-member districts. (Half of the Duma is elected via a party list/proportional representation system, the other half by a system of single-member districts.) Women of Russia won their votes largely as a result of the resistance of women to the political and economic changes taking place in the country. Their main platform had to do with creating a lawful, socially responsible state that observed human rights. They also focused on questions of social protection of the family and quality-of-life issues, to be addressed by tax, wage, and price policies. In particular, they were concerned with child care, women's health (including childbirth, abortion, and contraception), and the high costs of essential goods (Rule and Shvedova 1996, 45; Slater 1994, 32).

However, Women of Russia's gains were not sustained, largely because the bloc was unable to gain the required 5 percent of the party list vote necessary for gaining any of the seats elected through proportional representation. One factor in its decline was a switch in the strategies of left and center parties, which placed women higher up on their party lists, suggesting to the electorate that it was unnecessary to vote for a women's party to advance women's status and promote women as leaders (Rule and Shvedova 1996, 56). Women of Russia also faced an unprecedented and harsh smear campaign. Political opponents launched public misogynist attacks on women as politicians for which the bloc leaders, by their own admission, were not prepared. The media played up opponents' claims that the bloc had taken contradictory positions on budget issues and the Chechnya conflict. Women of Russia had also failed to broaden its voter base and to build necessary coalitions at a time when the electorate was expanding (Buckley 1997, 176–77, 180–81). Thus the number of Women of Russia deputies dropped from a high of 23 in 1994 to 3 after the 1995 election. Following the 1995 elections a separate Women's Movement of Russia was formed by Yekaterina Lakhova, former co-leader of Women in Russia, suggesting serious internal conflict and dissension within the coalition. In the December 1999 parliamentary elections, Women of Russia received only 2 percent of the vote.

The Importance of Autonomy

One of the issues women's organizations on both continents wrestle with is the issue of autonomy. The process of shifting from the dominance of state- and party-sponsored women's organizations to a preponderance of autonomous associations in both regions has not been smooth. Examples of attempts by the government to curtail the autonomy of associations, including women's associations, are numerous in Africa. Some of the most autonomous organizations have faced suppression, intimidation, and outright efforts to ban them. In Zimbabwe, the independent Association of Women's Clubs was suspended in 1995. The matter was taken to court, and in 1997 the courts struck down a key part of the Private Voluntary Organisations Act on the grounds that it violated Zimbabwe's constitution. The court order also allowed the organization to resume its activities.

In Tanzania, the independent Tanzanian Women's Council (BAWATA) faced similar government repression. In 1996 it was suspended under pressure from the Tanzanian ruling party's women's organization, Umoja wa Wanawake (UWT), and from the Ministry of Community Development, Women's Affairs, and Children. BAWATA had been formed by the UWT to be a semi-independent organization. When the BAWATA leadership unexpectedly steered it toward complete independence, began to carry out civic education, and started lobbying for legislative change, the ruling party and the UWT turned against the organization and suspended it. BAWATA took the matter to the High Court and challenged the country's Societies

Ordinance on the grounds that the government action was unconstitutional and in violation of international human rights conventions to which Tanzania is a signatory. Although BAWATA eventually won its case against the government, in the process the organization was destroyed, and the intimidation of its leadership left local chapters in disarray (Tripp 2000b).

Deep-seated distrust of the state in Eurasia persists and is extended to all organizations that have touted state programs in the past. For this and other reasons, some organizations have disbanded or tried to become independent or semi-independent. Some organizations changed their names but kept the same leadership and continued to maintain their funding through state companies and other state sources. Few of these groups have a genuine interest in changing the status of women, according to Olga Lipovskaia (1992, 73).

Nevertheless, the prior association with the Communist Party and the state often lingers on with organizations that have sought autonomy. Organizations such as the Union of Women of Russia have had to wrestle with this stigma. The Union of Women of Russia's predecessor, the Soviet Women's Committee, broke with the state in 1990 and reconstituted itself as a voluntary union of women's councils. Yet the Union's association with the state was difficult if not impossible to shake. During the Soviet period, its precursor had focused on peace as a women's issue and on showing how the party had solved the "woman question." After 1990 it focused on unemployed women by helping women find employment and providing them with retraining and strategies to survive unemployment (Racioppi and See 1995b, 832). However, its former incarnation as the Soviet Women's Committee and therefore as a front organization for the Communist Party of the Soviet Union made groups like the Center for Gender Studies, its sister umbrella group the Independent Women's Forum, and the Independent Women's Democratic Initiative NEZhDI (Do Not Wait) suspicious of the organization. Some feminists, for example, criticized the Union of Women of Russia for voting too closely with the Liberal Democrats and the Communist Party (Buckley 1997, 169). The Independent Women's Forum, however, did collaborate with the Union of the Women of Russia to support various female candidates at the local level. The forum explicitly promoted links between independent women's groups and women of all political persuasions (Slater 1994, 28). What makes the issue of autonomy especially complicated is that even many independent organizations receive state sponsorship, making it difficult to distinguish between those that are autonomous and those that are autonomous in name only.

Conclusions

Both post-Soviet Eurasian and post-colonial African countries saw the expansion of women's organizations and mobilization in the 1990s in response to state retreat and economic decline. Women took advantage of some of the new spaces that emerged with the breakup of the Soviet Union and with political reform in Africa to form organizations independent of the state and the ruling party, a break from the single-party dominance of women's organizations on both continents. As difficult as these crises have been for women in both regions, Eurasian women had more to lose and had fewer coping mechanisms at their disposal. African women suffered enormously from the economic downturn of the 1980s as well as the subsequent economic reform measures that were introduced. Nevertheless, they never had the high levels of employment, job security, literacy, social benefits, and political representation (however questionable) that Soviet women "enjoyed." When these gains, however problematic, began to dissipate, women in the former Soviet republics did not have the same experience that African women had with autonomous mobilization, nor had they had the same latitude in devising alternate economic survival strategies.

The hardships that Soviet women had faced in dealing with forced emancipation, which had pushed them into the labor force without addressing inequalities on the domestic front, left women overburdened with work and domestic responsibilities. Given this legacy, the issue of defining gender equality was a far greater challenge in the Eurasian context than in the African one and left women with enormous dilemmas as they confronted ideas of feminism associated with the international women's movement, not to mention temptations of retreating into domesticity as a reaction to the Soviet state's solutions to the woman question. Many women sought to respond to their deteriorating political and economic situation by mobilizing. In the process, questions of autonomy became salient as organizations sought to disentangle themselves from the legacies of close association with the state in the past. The relationship of these groups to the state has yet to be worked out, as some of the largest women's organizations that have relied on the state for funding confront the implications of that dependence.

In the African context, one of the biggest changes in the 1990s for women was the shift from a focus on economic empowerment through various income-generating strategies to a new interest in gaining access to political power. For the first time, women became presidents, vice presidents, and prime ministers, and greater numbers sought representation in parliament. Women's organizations began to take an interest in civic education, leadership training skills, advocacy, and the promotion of women running for office. As in Eurasia, this new interest in political activity was a consequence of the opening of new political spaces as a result of liberalization. But in Africa, additional factors provided impetus to these new trends: women had previous experiences in local-level mobilization from which to draw, they expanded their contacts with international women's organizations, donors took a new interest in promoting women's groups and democratization, greater numbers of educated women were available to lead organizations, and some governments chose to introduce party quotas and reserved parliamentary seats for women to promote female leadership. These developments mean that the organizational terrain in Africa shifted from domination by a single-party or state-sponsored mass women's organization to a proliferation of new, independent organizations that had complete autonomy in selecting their own leaders and in setting more expansive agendas. This new interest in political representation and influence stood out as a most dramatic departure from earlier forms of female mobilization.

References

Andersen, Margrethe Holm. 1992. "Women in Politics: A Case Study of Gender Relations and Women's Political Participation in Sukumaland, Tanzania." Ph.D. diss, Aalborg University, Denmark.

Blagov, Sergei. 1999. "Rights Russia: Equal Opportunities for Women a Long Way Off." *IPS* (Moscow). 7 March.

Buckley, Mary. 1992a. "Political Reform." Pp. 54–71 in *Perestroika and Soviet Women,* ed. Mary Buckley. Cambridge: Cambridge University Press.

———, ed. 1992b. *Perestroika and Soviet Women.* Cambridge: Cambridge University Press.

———. 1997. "Victims and Agents: Gender in Post-Soviet States." Pp. 3–16 in *Post-Soviet Women: From the Baltic to Central Asia,* ed. Mary Buckley. Cambridge: Cambridge University Press.

Central Statistical Bureau. 1985. *Tsentral'noe Statisticheskoe Upravlenie SSSR, Zhenshchiny i deti SSSR: Statisticheskii sbornik, Moskva: Finansy i statistika, 1959, 1967, 1985.* (Central Statistical Bureau of USSR, Women and Children of the USSR: Statistical Handbook, Moscow, Finances and Statistics, 1959, 1967, 1985). Moscow.

Ferguson, Anne E., with Beatrice Liatto Katundu. 1994. "Women in Politics in Zambia: What Difference Has Democracy Made?" *African Rural and Urban Studies* 1, no. 2: 11–30.

Galieva, Zairash. 1999. "Civil Society in the Kyrgyz Republic in Transition." *Central Asian Monitor.* Obtained at www.undp.uz/gid/eng/KYRGYZSTAN/index.html.

Herrick, Rebekah, and Almira Sapieva. 1997. "Perceptions of Women Politicians of Kazakhstan." *Women & Politics* 18, no. 4: 27–40.

Konstantinova, Valentina. 1992. "The Women's Movement in the USSR: A Myth or a Real Challenge." Pp. 200–217 in *Women in the Face of Change: The Soviet Union, Eastern Europe and China,* ed. A. Phizacklea, Hilary Pilkington, and Shirin Rai. New York: Routledge.

Lapidus, Gail W. 1978. *Women in Soviet Society.* Berkeley: University of California Press.

————. 1993. "Gender and Restructuring: The Impact of Perestroika and Its Aftermath on Soviet Women." Pp. 137–61 in *Democratic Reform and the Position of Women in Transitional Economies,* ed. V. M. Moghadam. Oxford: Clarendon.

Lipovskaia, Olga. 1992. "New Women's Organisations." Pp. 72–81 in *Perestroika and Soviet Women,* ed. Mary Buckley. Cambridge: Cambridge University Press.

————. 1997. "Women's Groups in Russia." Pp. 186–99 in *Post-Soviet Women: From the Baltic to Central Asia,* ed. Mary Buckley. Cambridge: Cambridge University Press.

McNeil, Donald, Jr. 1996. "Zimbabwe Opposition: Ex-Guerrilla Is a One-Woman Tempest." *New York Times.* 13 May: A4.

Meena, Ruth. 1997. "Changes in Gender and Civil Society." U.S. Agency for International Development, Dar es Salaam, Tanzania. Photocopy.

Moses, Joel. 1977. "Women in Political Roles." Pp. 333–73 in *Women in Russia,* ed. D. Atkinson, Alexander Dallin, and Gail W. Lapidus. Stanford: Stanford University Press.

Posadskaya, Anastasia. 1993. "Changes in Gender Discourses and Policies in the Former Soviet Union." Pp. 162–79 in *Democratic Reform and the Position of Women in Transitional Economies,* ed. V. M. Moghadam. Oxford: Clarendon.

Racioppi, Linda, and Katherine O'Sullivan See. 1995a. "The 'Woman Question' and National Identity: Soviet and Post-Soviet Russia." Pp. 173–202 in *The Women and International Development Annual* 4, ed. R. S. Gallin, A. Ferguson, and J. Harper. Boulder: Westview.

————. 1995b. "Organizing Women Before and After the Fall: Women's Politics in the Soviet Union and Post-Soviet Russia." *Signs* 20, no. 4: 818–49.

Rimashevskaia, Natalia. 1992. "Perestroika and the Status of Women in the Soviet Union." Pp. 11–19 in *Women in the Face of Change: The Soviet Union, Eastern Europe, and China,* ed. A. Phizacklea, Hilary Pilkington, and Shirin Rai. New York: Routledge.

Rule, Wilma, and Nadezhda Shvedova. 1996. "Women in Russia's First Multiparty Election." Pp. 40–59 in *Russian Women in Politics and Society,* ed. W. Rule and N. C. Noonan. Westport: Greenwood.

Sheridan, Blair. N.d. "Women and the NGO Movement in Uzbekistan." United Nations Development Programme. Photocopy.

Shvedova, Nadezhda. 1999. "The Challenge of Transition: Women in Parliament in Russia. Report." In *Women in Parliament: Beyond Numbers.* Stockholm: International Idea. Obtained at www.int-idea.se/women/parl/studies2a.htm.

Slater, Wendy. 1994. "Female Representation in Russian Politics." *RFE/RL Research Report* 3, no. 22: 27–33.

Tamale, Sylvia. 1999. *When Hens Begin to Crow: Gender and Parliamentary Politics in Uganda.* Boulder: Westview.

Tripp, Aili Mari. 2000a. *Women and Politics in Uganda.* Madison: University of Wisconsin Press; Oxford: James Currey; Kampala: Fountain.

————. 2000b. "Political Reform in Tanzania: The Struggle for Associational Autonomy." *Comparative Politics* 32, no. 2: 191–214.

Tserkonivnitska, Marina. 1997. "Where Have All the Women Gone? Increasing Women's Representation in Parliamentary Bodies in the Former Soviet Union: The Case of Ukraine." Paper presented at Gender and Global Change Colloquium, Cornell University, Ithaca, 27 March.

United Nations Children's Fund (UNICEF). 1999. "Women in Transition: The Monee Project." CEE/CIS/Baltics Regional Monitoring Report no. 6. Florence, Italy: UNICEF.
United Nations Development Programme. 1999. *General Trends of Women's Participation in the Public Life*. Obtained at www.undp.uz/gid/eng/TURKMENISTAN/index.html.

Part V

Beyond State Crisis?

16

Putting the State Back Together in Post-Soviet Georgia

GHIA NODIA

The disintegration of the state went further in Georgia than anywhere else in the former Soviet Union with the sole exception of Tajikistan. Georgia went through two ethno-territorial wars for secession (in the regions of Abkhazia and South Ossetia), a military coup followed by episodes of civil war, a period of near anarchy and warlordism, and a spectacular collapse of the economy. During 1989–95, the country's gross domestic product (GDP), according to the official statistics, dropped some four to five times (United Nations Development Programme 1996, 156).[1] Against that backdrop, however, Georgia has enjoyed a dramatic turnaround since 1995: though still not an accomplished, stable, or, if one can use the term, "normal" state, it is nevertheless no longer a particular failure in comparison with other post-Soviet countries, and at least a basic level of order and stability does not seem to be challenged anymore.

How can the collapse or regeneration of the state be measured? The literature on the collapse of the state in the developing world (which pre-

---

1. I make the reservation "according to the official statistics" because they are not necessarily reliable. First, the system of statistics collapsed together with the state. Second, whereas in Soviet times both producers and the state had an incentive to exaggerate production figures in order to report high achievements, after communism the opposite incentive prevailed: producers did not report their activities in order to avoid taxes, and the leadership welcomed low GDP figures in order to be eligible for international assistance.

dominantly uses examples from Africa) proposes an opposition between "strong" ("normal" or "effective") states modeled on the modern Western state and "weak," "failed," or "quasi-" states that are internationally recognized but whose capacity to deliver on traditional state obligations domestically is dramatically challenged (Jackson 1990; Zartman 1995; Migdal 1988). This framework seems to be fully applicable to the recent Georgian experience. But its rigid duality may also be a handicap: there are considerable differences among states that are not as effective as the advanced Western model implies. The binary model does not make clear exactly how weak the state should be to be counted among "failed" or "quasi" ones. For instance, this is how Robert H. Jackson characterizes the "quasi-state" in his frequently quoted book:

> [Quasi-states] disclose limited empirical statehood: their populations do not enjoy many of the advantages traditionally associated with independent statehood. Their governments are often deficient in the political will, institutional authority, and organized power to protect human rights or provide socio-economic welfare. The concrete benefits which have historically justified the undeniable burden of sovereign statehood are often limited to fairly narrow elites and not yet extended to the citizenry at large (Jackson 1990, 21).

Here, failure to "protect human rights" and "provide social-economic welfare" are the two most specific issues in which the weakness of quasi-states expresses itself. But these functions have been associated with the idea of statehood only since the late nineteenth or early twentieth centuries, whereas the history of modern statehood is approximately four centuries long. Is the modern state the same as the modern liberal-democratic state—that is, preoccupied with the protection of human rights? Was Adolf Hitler's Germany "weak" or a "quasi-state"? Is a despotic state also a "quasi-state" by definition? Many developed Asian states provide much less of a social security net than do European states. Does this in itself make them "weak" or "quasi"? I do not think many states in the world outside the West would pass these tests.

A workable checklist of basic and necessary functions of statehood should be shorter. The classical Weberian criterion of monopoly on the legitimate use of force within a given territory should be taken as a starting point. One could expand on this by saying that a "minimal" state should not have competitors in its basic role as arbiter of law and order (at least not overt competitors, other than those that the state itself accepts). It should be the only agent that raises taxes for the public good and should have reasonable control over its own officers. These criteria do not preclude corruption: a high level of corruption marks a serious deficiency of the state but may not necessarily challenge the manageability of the bureaucratic hierarchy. Beyond this, a state (or, more widely, a polity) should define for itself the functions that it undertakes.

With that in mind, I propose a three- rather than two-level classification of state efficacy. I will call "strong," "effective," or "normal" those states that are capable of carrying out functions that they themselves claim and that they are reasonably expected by their populations to carry out. This means that an effective state is not by definition supposed to be liberal or welfare-oriented, but a state cannot be effective if it does not enjoy some critical level of legitimacy with its own population. On the other pole one would place "failed" or "quasi-states" that cannot meet the minimal criteria of statehood as defined above. If a state is seriously challenged in carrying out these minimal tasks, then its very reality may be legitimately questioned. In the grey area between these two poles one would find what I call a "weak" state: one that meets the minimalist functions of a state throughout or in most of its territory but is seriously challenged in its capacity to implement some major state functions and policies that have been reasonably defined by political actors and are expected from it by its own population. This usually means that a weak state's authority is openly or tacitly challenged on some parts of its territory (though maintained on most parts), that its ability to tax its population is dramatically lower than its own legislation and policies require, that the smooth operation of basic institutions of power cannot be taken for granted, and that the general failure of institutions is a real possibility that is systematically taken into account by major political actors. Although a weak state may be deficient in many ways, it provides to its citizens an important level of basic security and economic opportunity, in contrast to a "quasi-state," where people are obliged to look for alternative sources of security or economic opportunity that explicitly challenge the state order.

The intermediary position of a weak state implies the twofold concern of its population and ruling elites: on the one hand, its domestic constituency cannot be satisfied with the current condition and wants the state to deliver on obligations that the population expects it to fulfill—that is, to become a "normal" state. On the other hand, it faces the danger of collapse and is preoccupied with efforts to preclude this. The problem here is that these two concerns may clash: measures taken to pursue objectives of long-term development and short-term survival are different and may contradict one other. Although this kind of contradiction is also widespread in "normal" democracies, where short-term interests of the electoral cycle may clash with long-term national goals, in weak states it is the fate of the whole political system rather than a certain party that is at stake.

Based on this classification, in the course of the last ten years Georgia made a transition from being part of a strong (or at least ostensibly strong[2]) Soviet state to a failed state and then later partly recovered, so that it can now be placed in the category of weak states. The goal of this chapter is to understand the causal factors underlying such a crooked odyssey. I will start with a brief general outline of the dynamics of state development in Georgia and then will examine those factors that directly led to the collapse and partial reconstruction of statehood. In the end I will propose some general interpretations of the reasons for the particular fragility of the Georgian state in comparison with others in the post-Soviet region.

From a "Failed" State to a "Weak" State

From 1992 to 1994, following the military ouster of Zviad Gamsakhurdia (the first democratically elected president of Georgia) and as a result of the two-week-long "Tbilisi war" from December 1991 to January 1992 (also sometimes known as the "Christmas coup"), Georgia represented a classic case of a failed state. It conspicuously failed to meet the Weberian criterion of exercising a monopoly over the legitimate use of force. The army (more often referred to as the National Guard) formally existed, but it actually represented a loose federation of "battalions," each of which was controlled by the personality of its commander (if controlled by anyone at all). The most efficient and organized armed force, the Mkhedrioni (meaning "riders" or "warriors") militia, was headed by the charismatic Jaba Ioseliani, a formerly prominent criminal and then popular playwright and professor of arts. The Mkhedrioni was not even part of the National Guard and operated outside any state control. The police retained some traits of institutional structure (anonymous hierarchy and subordination and general acceptance of control by political authority) but were blatantly humiliated by the National Guard and the Mkhedrioni. However, the warlords did not

---

2. I call the Soviet state "ostensibly strong" because, at least in its last stages in the 1970s and 1980s, it lacked an important (though often overlooked) component of strong statehood: legitimacy. I believe that this deficiency primarily explains its unexpected but fast implosion. But from the position of an ordinary citizen, it seemed strong until the bluff of its strength was called.

claim full political power either; they were aware that an open military (or, rather, paramilitary) dictatorship would have a slim chance of gaining internal legitimacy and international recognition (and they were probably just reluctant to take on full government responsibilities). Instead, they invited Eduard Shevardnadze, the world-famous and well-connected former communist leader of Georgia and Soviet foreign minister under President Mikhail Gorbachev, to act as the formal political authority, without any real intention of transferring adequate power to him. They wanted instead to exploit his image and international connections.[3] In March 1992, Shevardnadze became the chair of the State Council, a quasi-parliamentary body created by the military victory in the Tbilisi war. After the elections of October 1992, Shevardnadze was elected chair of parliament and was endowed with the authority of the head of the executive branch of power. But elections did not change much; the actual tools of power at his disposal were very scarce.

In lieu of effective central authority the country disintegrated territorially as well, with different regions exhibiting various degrees of defiance of a largely symbolic political center. Abkhazia and South Ossetia opted for open and militarily asserted separatism (in both cases, separatist forces successfully repelled the military effort of the center to bring the breakaway regions under control). Parts of western Georgia were controlled by militias supporting the ousted president (the "Zviadists"), who theoretically recognized the unity of Georgia but not the acting government. The Ajarian Autonomous Republic, in the person of local strongman Aslan Abashidze, professed a version of soft separatism, recognizing both Georgian unity and the acting government in principle but defying the government's authority in practice. Some other regions (and sometimes towns and villages) did not challenge the center politically but in practice were controlled by local power "clans," petty warlords, or simply criminal gangs. Roadblocks and local "customs" checkpoints were erected in different parts of Georgian territory, so that moving around the country was extremely unsafe, and there was no single power able to enforce control over transportation routes.[4]

---

3. Tengiz Kitovani alluded to this during his press conference on April 26, 1993, when the breach with Shevardnadze had already developed. He openly expressed his resentment at the latter's attempt to meddle in his business (*Georgian Chronicle,* April 1993).

4. Compare this with the African context of state failure: "A sign of declining institutional capacity in [the Ivory Coast] at the end of the 1980s was the proliferation of roadblocks manned variously by custom officials, the police, the gendarmerie, the army, and the forest police" (Widner 1995, 133).

The state was unable to carry out economic functions as well. Though a provisional national currency, the Georgian coupon, was introduced in August 1992, it soon became worthless and was never used in actual transactions; the Russian ruble and the U.S. dollar shared the functions of a national currency. One could hardly speak of the implementation of any economic policy. Hyperinflation made salaries paid in national currency worthless (the minimal salary dropped to the equivalent of $1 per month), which meant that state employees were in practice not paid by the state (and in a state that had just emerged from communism, the majority of the workforce consisted of state employees). The social security system was purely symbolic.

The only state function that remained under the firm control of Shevardnadze and was carried out in a more or less "normal" way without direct challenge from the warlords was foreign policy.[5] Arguably, however, against the backdrop of the general failure of statehood, this latter function made less and less sense, since Georgia came very close to losing its international sovereignty altogether. After losing the war in Abkhazia in October 1993 (a loss attributable, according to common Georgian estimation, to Russian military support of the separatists) and facing the Zviadist insurrection, which he was not able to suppress, Shevardnadze decided to make a deal with Russia, which meant becoming its strategic satellite in exchange for Russian support for the restoration of stability in Georgia. Protégés of the Russian government were appointed to head the Security Service[6] and the Ministry of Defense. The presence of Russian military bases, Russian border guards on the Georgian-Turkish border, and Russian troops as peacekeepers in Abkhazia was legitimized.[7] It was assumed in political circles and the media in late 1993 and early 1994 that in a matter of a few months Georgia would give up its provisional currency and join the "ruble zone." At that time, this author was often asked by Western diplomats and journalists whether Georgia could be considered a truly independent country.[8]

---

5. Even in this area a kind of challenge existed. Shevardnadze did not trust his foreign minister, Alexander Chikvaidze, an appointee of his rivals, and so implemented his foreign policy not through the Foreign Ministry, as one would expect, but through the office of his national security adviser.

6. Afterwards, in August 1995, this Russia-backed minister of security, Igor Giorgadze, allegedly masterminded an attempt on Shevardnadze's life.

7. The presence of Russian military bases was not fully legitimized. Although Shevardnadze, as head of state, signed an agreement to do so, it was never ratified by the Georgian parliament.

8. The point that Georgia could be considered only a *formally* independent country was made by David E. Mark (1996).

This dramatic moment, however, proved to be a turning point. The new alliance with Russia brought positive results swiftly: the Zviadist insurrection was suppressed with restricted but decisive Russian help, and a reasonable level of state control was established in formerly rebellious provinces. Shevardnadze used the ensuing momentum to build on these successes. By skillfully maneuvering between different political forces and taking advantage of considerable good luck (which included narrowly surviving two assassination attempts), he gradually managed to broaden his power base and to neutralize major warlords (the leaders of the National Guard and the Mkhedrioni both ended up in jail), so that after the October 1995 elections he was clearly in charge of the institutions of state power. Criminality was also reduced; it reached a level where it was threatening to particular citizens but not to the overall political order. This success was not reached at the expense of instituting a dictatorial rule. Although Georgia is an imperfect democracy in many ways, political pluralism is not hindered, parliament is a working institution genuinely balancing presidential political power (with a variety of political parties, many of them strongly opposed to the government, competing for power), and the media are quite free to express a diversity of opinion.

With regard to territorial disintegration, Shevardnadze's success was mixed. Control over the separatist regions of South Ossetia and Abkhazia was lost, and protracted negotiations over their status led nowhere, though the independence of these self-proclaimed states was not recognized by anyone, and formally they continued to remain part of Georgia. Ajaria continued its policy of defiance of central authorities, and tensions between the center and the region persisted. The uncertain status of these territories was the main reason why the parliament, in adopting a new Georgian constitution in August 1995, decided not to include any provisions on the territorial arrangements of states until the existing conflicts (especially that with Abkhazia) were resolved. However, on the rest of the territory some basic homogeneity of political order was achieved. Most important, after their defeat in the fall of 1993, supporters of the former president had no territorial power base and could not pose a serious challenge to the existing government (small, dispersed armed groups still created a problem of terrorism, however). Roadblocks and local "customs" ceased to exist. National (rather than regional or ethnic) parties competed in all levels of elections. The Union for Democratic Revival, Abashidze's party based in Ajaria, was the only notable exception, but even it tried to redefine itself as a national party and became the core of the major opposition coalition for the 1999 parliamentary elections.

The state gained a capacity to implement economic policy (again, how these policies are evaluated is another question). A new national currency, the lari, was introduced in 1995 and proved to be a success. It maintained its stability until late 1998 and ousted the Russian ruble from the market (save for in a few border areas). Strict economic policy following International Monetary Fund (IMF) guidelines brought inflation considerably down. Privatization of small and medium-sized enterprises was carried out, and that of large enterprises was begun. In 1996–97, the country enjoyed an annual growth of GDP in the range of 10–11 percent. Of course, these figures were made possible only against the backdrop of a very low starting point.

Still, the state continues to be seriously challenged in carrying out its obligations. At least two major deficiencies place Georgia into the "weak state" category. First is the dramatic inability of the state to raise tax revenues. Despite all the efforts of the government, the rate of tax collections stands at about 9 percent of GDP (Ramishvili et al. 1999) compared with at least 30 percent in most liberal Western economies. Nevertheless, the state maintains a massive apparatus and theoretically has not given up its general commitments in the social sphere (the constitution defines the economic structure of Georgia as a "social market economy"). As a result, the state cannot provide a living wage to the vast majority of its employees, and salaries are often delayed for several months. In practice, this means that the state cannot afford honest and competent employees, which translates into structural corruption reflected in a form of "crony capitalism." It is widely recognized that formal taxation is systematically replaced by paying shares to political "roofs" in exchange for "protection," so that pursuing serious business without political connections is extremely difficult.

A second fundamental challenge, as already mentioned, pertains to the territorial distribution of power. The presence of the breakaway territories of Abkhazia and South Ossetia is the most obvious problem. I would argue, however, that this is not the most serious problem in this area. People living in the breakaway territories in fact constitute separate political communities; these territories have different dynamics of development, and whatever happens there has only an indirect impact in Georgia proper—or, at least, the potential impact is less than, for instance, that which would result from a change of government in Russia or a redefinition of priorities by the IMF. Of course, the importance of the problem should not be downplayed too much: Georgia has not given up the intention of regaining those territories, and the presence of a considerable refugee community (numbering more than 200,000) is a constant reminder that the problem is not solved and represents a looming destabilizing factor. The six-day war in May 1998, which resulted in thirty to forty thousand Georgians being driven out of their homes for the second time in five years, had disastrous consequences for Georgia (among other things, it launched a serious fiscal crisis; see *Black Sea Press,* 1993, 1998a). The Georgian guerrilla movement in the Gali district, a buffer region between Abkhazia and Georgia proper, may become a basis for re-creating uncontrolled militias along the 1992–93 model. However, though the lack of a final settlement in Abkhazia and South Ossetia constitutes a considerable problem, the overall experience since 1993 shows that the country may achieve sizeable progress even without having solved those two problems. One could reasonably summarize this by saying that, for the time being, the Abkhazian and South Ossetian problems have been bracketed out of domestic Georgian politics, something that may be considered the "second best" option after a final settlement of these problems.

The problem of Ajaria may represent a more immediate challenge to state development precisely because this region does not strive to separate itself from Georgia but at the same time consistently defies the constitutional order. For instance, attempts by the Georgian state to improve the efficiency of its customs office with the help of the British company Intertek Testing Service met fierce opposition from Ajarian authorities. Abashidze described the state's efforts as an attempt of the center to institute an "economic blockade" against Ajaria (*Black Sea Press* 1999b). Since customs constitute an especially lucrative source of illegal income, solving this problem has proven difficult and has caused greater polarization in society. Moreover, Ajaria represents a different model of political evolution and a different political culture. Whereas Georgia in general is an imperfect but pluralistic democracy, Ajaria is a one-man dictatorship with no independent media or functioning opposition. The rift was exemplified by the November 1998 local elections: the voter turnout in Ajaria was well over 90 percent, with 97–98 percent voting for representatives of Abashidze's party, while in all of Georgia the average turnout was about 40 percent, and in many regions opposition coalitions prevailed over the ruling party (*Adgilobrivi tsarmomadgenlobiti organoebis* 1999).

Regions with dense minority populations (such as the south, with its Armenian population, and the southeast, populated by Azerbaijanis) have not posed any serious challenges to central authority so far, but the lack of integration of these minorities into Georgian society is the basis for legitimate concerns that these regions may attempt to form separate political societies in the future.

Factors of Disintegration

Though the theme of this chapter is the reconstruction of the Georgian state, it is important to ask why the state failed in Georgia in the first place. Certainly the 1991–92 Christmas coup was an obvious breaking point, but focusing on it would hardly be sufficient. Military coups can represent attempts to either prevent the disintegration of or restore state power, and this may create the basis for some degree of legitimacy for them. In this case, however, the coup was a stage in the further disintegration of the state. It would be incorrect to define the "Tbilisi war" as a military coup because there was no real military (no armed forces united by a sense of discipline, institutional hierarchy, and anonymous loyalty to the state) in the country, and this was probably the main problem. The adversaries of the president were represented by unstable militias that depended on individual enthusiasm and their leaders' charisma, and the defenders of "legitimate power" were not much different.

What factors led to this condition? Three obvious ones come to mind: the abrupt breakdown of state legitimacy in the face of mass political mobilization (which may be just another way of describing a revolutionary change of political regime); rival claims to political sovereignty from ethnic minority communities that disrupted the majority drive to establish a unitary nation-state; and the incompetence of the first postcommunist leadership, which led to conflict within the new ruling elite.

None of these factors has sufficient explanatory power on its own. The recent history of breakdown of communism in the former Soviet Union and its European satellites provides a whole array of models of regime *ruptura:* gradual and orderly takeovers of power through a political process recognized by preexisting authority (Poland and the Baltic states); nonviolent "velvet" revolutions (Czechoslovakia); violent revolution (Romania); and a mixture of these (Russia). In none of these cases, however, did the breakdown of the state ensue (though one can speak about different degrees of state weakness). New elites took hold of existing state institutions, rapidly consolidated their power, and in some cases proceeded to a fairly orderly process of political and economic reform. The specificity of the Georgian case was that the process of change of the political regime happened to be both revolutionary in character and protracted in time. There was an intermediate period of divided rule (April 1989–October 1990), and it was in this period that the first signs of the breakdown of state authority appeared.

Although the "Tbilisi war" was the clear landmark in the final demise of the state, one can also define the exact date when the state started to disintegrate in Georgia: April 9, 1989. On that morning, the Soviet army crushed pro-independence demonstrators in Tbilisi who had been rallying round the clock for several days in front of the parliament building. Twenty people, mostly young women, were killed as a result of the army action. A state of emergency was declared, tanks came to patrol the streets of the capital, and organizers of the rally were put in jail.

Initially this looked like the Soviet state reasserting its power by brutal but efficient methods—something it was expected to do in the face of mass disturbances. Prior to *glasnost,* the Soviet totalitarian regime was as a rule successful enough to prevent such trouble altogether, but on rare occasions when people took to the streets, it was never shy in using harsh and decisive methods to restore order. In Georgia, older people well remembered the March 9, 1956, episode in Tbilisi, when a huge rally protesting the new de-Stalinization policy of the Communist Party was met with machine-gun fire. Order was swiftly restored, and people did not dare protest further.

In the wake of the April 9, 1989, massacre, however, both the public and the government behaved in a radically different way. The events in Tbilisi strongly contradicted the image of liberal reformer sought by Mikhail Gorbachev, while the same established Georgian intellectuals who had been considered the ideological stronghold of the regime publicly denounced the actions of the army. The regime backed off, the local Communist Party chief resigned, the state of emergency was soon lifted, imprisoned leaders were released, and the attitude toward the media and independent political activities drastically liberalized. The result was that, although formally the Communist Party retained power, it lost all remaining traits of legitimacy (even the official media started openly denouncing communism), as well as any nerve to govern further.

Had Georgia been an independent country already, the opposition would probably have taken power promptly under these circumstances. But fear of Russian power was still strong enough to prevent that, and what ensued was a period of de facto divided rule. The government was allowed to carry out most of its routine functions, but the mobilized national independence movement was successful in paralyzing the government's capacity to make political decisions and in resisting any action that the government decided to take. The condition of responsibility without power led to further discrediting of state authority, while the condition of power without responsibility encouraged the nationalist movement to develop in a radical and anarchic direction. The idea of taking control of the existing state institutions through elections, an idea that guided almost all liberation movements in the late communist period, was the least popular in

Georgia. The political scene was dominated by "irreconcilable" groups that believed in a "clean" new start through staging unofficial elections not recognized by the existing state. In practice, however, this meant that the opposition to the Communist regime developed into disruption of the state as such. Since the political regime was considered an "illegitimate" foreign occupation (one of the buzzwords of the day), it was "legitimate" to ignore the state and take extralegal actions. Whereas prior to April 9 the nationalist movement had developed in a peaceful way, after that date various militias, resentful of any concept of state control but based on some vague understanding of "national interests," started to develop.

Here the topic of ethno-territorial conflict comes into play. It is in no way peculiar to Georgia that newly independent states (or states trying to assert themselves as independent) are challenged by ethnic separatist movements. Indeed such challenges can in some cases become a factor of regime consolidation around nationalist slogans. Croatia serves as a good example: a direct challenge to national integrity was used there for consolidation of a not fully democratic but reasonably stable regime. Turkey may be widely criticized for the way in which it handled the Kurdish issue, but the Kurdish challenge did not destroy Turkish state institutions; rather, the challenge was instrumentalized for state consolidation. During the late communist stage of developing statehood in Georgia, however, the test of ethnic separatism proved disastrous. The authorities' inability to meet the challenge became an important legitimizing factor for the creation of independent militias. If the government cannot protect national interests, the thinking went, someone should. The conflicts in Abkhazia and South Ossetia became testing grounds for these new militias as early as 1989 (see, for instance, Zverev 1996, 13–71; Nodia 1998b). Most of them were formally or informally linked to newly emerging political parties. The Mkhedrioni, which claimed a peacekeeping role in South Ossetia, emerged as the brightest star among those groups. This was also the period when the first conflicts between different paramilitary groups began.

The period after parliamentary elections in October 1990 (which were swept by Gamsakhurdia's "Round Table" coalition) may be considered the first attempt to overcome anarchy and to reconstruct state power. His broad popularity and mass enthusiasm about the "peaceful revolution" (which was how his election victory was officially defined) seemed to provide a good basis for meeting that challenge. Despite his anticommunist and anti-Russian (and therefore, pro-independence) rhetoric, it was Ioseliani's Mkhedrioni and other rival radical nationalist groups rather than Moscow that Gamsakhurdia considered (correctly) to be the major threat to his authority, and he made them the prime targets of his efforts to consolidate power. Initially he was successful. The Mkhedrioni was destroyed (paradoxically, with the help of the Russian military), its leaders put in jail, and other militias merged into the National Guard. In May 1991, Gamsakhurdia swept presidential elections with 87 percent of the vote. Strong nationalist credentials allowed him to make compromises that would not have been accepted from more moderate politicians. He established reasonably good relations with the Russian military in Georgia, incorporated many former Communists in his government, and struck a power-sharing deal with the Abkhaz nationalists (though he failed to stop the conflict in South Ossetia). It seemed that Gamsakhurdia was on his way to reconstructing state institutions—albeit in a nation-state format and in an autocratic style—just like other postcommunist or post-Soviet states. His success was short-lived, however. The defection of his closest lieutenants in August 1991 eventually led to his ouster in a January 1992 coup.

Why did the state collapse again, and this time in a more dramatic way? The breakdown of legitimacy should not have played a similar role, as Gamsakhurdia was democratically elected and still enjoyed considerable support at the time of the coup. His autocratic style, intolerance of opposition, persecution of independent media, and crude ethnic nationalism gained him mostly deserved, though often exaggerated, criticism by liberal intellectuals and opposition politicians. Those politicians later helped to legitimize the coup as a "democratic revolution" against the regime of personal dictatorship and "parochial fascism" and argued that Gamsakhurdia had abused his democratically acquired power to a degree that justified insurrection. But it is quite clear that liberal opponents were not able to topple the regime on their own, as their ideas hardly had roots beyond a thin layer of urban, modernized elites. Gamsakhurdia himself and his supporters blamed it all on a Russian conspiracy. A certain level of Russian support for the insurgents cannot be ruled out, as both sides depended on the local Russian military for arms supplies, and preferential Russian treatment of one of the parties would have been of decisive importance. But even if one believes this to be true, it still would not explain fully why Russian efforts were successful in Georgia as opposed to other parts of Russia's "near abroad." Economic crisis had already begun, but it cannot provide a sufficient explanation either. This was a period when some (hopefully temporary) reduction in living standards was considered acceptable by most of the population as a sacrifice for independence and democracy, and later Shevardnadze's government was excused for a much more drastic economic decline.

There were probably two immediate grounds for the collapse of Gamsakhurdia's regime. One was his erratic personality, which bordered on mental instability;[9] the other, a resurgence of anarchic political culture in the behavior of his opposition. He failed to translate his popularity into a successful effort to build state institutions. Once he alienated most of his key supporters, there were no institutions on which to fall back. Their defection re-created a situation of "divided rule," or practical ungovernability. In fighting him, they took the same attitudes as they had against the Communist regime; the fact that he was elected by the people made no difference.

The new winners had a much worse starting position than Gamsakhurdia had had in the fall of 1990. The enthusiasm of the national independence movement—and with it, any kind of public spirit—was over; the ousting of the first democratically elected and popular president caused a birth trauma to democracy and resulted in public apathy. The anarchic spirit of the victorious militias left small space for the functioning of remaining state institutions, whose credibility had significantly eroded under the attacks from first the anticommunist, then the anti-Gamsakhurdia oppositions. The nation was deeply divided between supporters of Gamsakhurdia and his opponents. Shevardnadze was invited in as a last hope.

Factors of Reconstructing Statehood

In the first two years of Shevardnadze's rule the disintegration of statehood went even further, and only after some time did the country hit bottom and start to recover. Shevardnadze's relative success in rebuilding the Georgian state can be attributed to two sets of factors. One was his shrewd application of the traditional technology of power. Being in this regard almost the exact opposite of Gamsakhurdia, he was very good at entering coalitions when he needed them, using contradictions between his rivals, and only striking against his enemies when the time was ripe. He was brought to power by the warlords Tengiz Kitovani and Ioseliani, fought together with them against the Zviadists, and removed Kitovani with the help of Ioseliani. But he swiftly appealed to public support when he had a disagreement with the latter. He used Russian help against the Zviadists but relied on Western help in resisting Russian insistence on dominating

---

9. This was the impression of many people who had personal contact with him. Tengiz Sigua, his defected prime minister and one of the leaders of the coup, repeatedly referred to his mental problems as a major justification of the coup (see, for instance, Broladze 1992).

the Caucasus. When he was not in a strong position to win, he accepted reality as it was and prevented the conflict from becoming too intense (his relations with Abashidze are an illustration of this). He even managed to use his greatest failures, such as the military defeat in Abkhazia, to his advantage (it helped him to destroy the warlords). This technique, however, required time and explains the slow pace of his success.

Another set of explanatory variables should be sought in the field of political legitimacy. However skillful a political gambler Shevardnadze was, he would not have been able to engage in the political game, much less win it, without sufficient political capital. Although he did not control guns[10] or effective institutions, he had to rely on some kind of legitimacy—that is, he had to be able to claim representation of important political values and to build support around them. There were two such major values which he came to represent: state order and international recognition. These bases are quite different from those on which Gamsakhurdia's legitimacy rested: nationalism (in both senses—national independence and ethnic antiminority nationalism) and personal charisma.

Although it took Shevardnadze some time to restore a modicum of order, he was quite fast in delivering international recognition and assistance. This depended on the unique circumstance that, in his previous political incarnation, he had been foreign minister of another, much more powerful state and became globally famous by playing a central role in such world-historical events as the unification of Germany. Nobody in Georgia could conceivably compete with him in this realm. His international approval also put him in conspicuous contrast to Gamsakhurdia: one of the reasons the latter was abandoned by many of his close supporters was that he led Georgia in the direction of becoming a pariah state.

That this unique degree of international fame constituted the major part of his starting political capital correlates with the central point about "failed" or "quasi-" states made in the literature on Africa. When rulers of such a state cannot "gain political authority primarily from internal legitimacy, bureaucratic efficiency, nurturing of local revenue resources, or attractiveness of foreign investors," they use international recognition of their sovereignty as the major resource, since it gives them access to resources from foreign states and international organizations (Reno 1998, 18; Jackson 1990, 13–31). Apart from accessibility of resources such as for-

---

10. Shevardnadze is reported to have said during the meeting of leaders of Caucasian states with President Yeltsin of Russia, "If I had 200 men who were loyal to me I wouldn't be here" (Fairbanks 1997, 103).

eign assistance, which had been crucial for economic stabilization,[11] recognition had special moral value for a country that had recently emerged from political nonexistence: such occasions as Georgia's joining the United Nations (UN) or the Organization for Security and Cooperation in Europe (and, more recently, the European Council and the World Trade Organization) were extensively used by state propaganda and portrayed as the personal achievements of Shevardnadze. It was on the image of this indispensability that he started building his internal legitimacy—and was later able to translate this into real power.

Without this "translation," however, Georgia would have been forever stuck in the reality of the "failed state." Thus arose the idea of basic law and order as the basis for Shevardnadze's internal legitimacy. Here his record as Georgia's Communist Party first secretary from 1972 to 1985, while disconcerting for the nationalist portion of the new coalition, resonated with the wishes of the broad population to see order restored, and their notion of orderly life corresponded with the Communist past.

This does not mean that Shevardnadze did not try to appeal to nationalist feelings as well. Once the war in Abkhazia broke out in August 1992, the new regime tried to define it as a "patriotic war" and hoped to mend the divide caused by the Christmas coup. This attempt failed. The opposition of Gamsakhurdia's supporters was a considerable impediment for government troops, as the Zviadist-controlled regions lay on the route that Georgian troops had to take to Abkhazia. At some points Gamsakhurdia even conspired with the separatists. This delegitimized Gamsakhurdia among some parts of the population but did not breach the gap with the Zviadists. The Zviadists presented the war as a Russian conspiracy, implemented through Shevardnadze, to deprive Georgia of Abkhazia. (The result of the war only strengthened this belief.) The nationalist card appeared not to work as a major state-building tool after Gamsakhurdia, the symbol of Georgian nationalism, was ousted and, for many, discredited. Arguably, the radical version of nationalism as represented by the national independence movement had to exhaust itself. Georgia probably had to be defeated in all its wars before it could start to rebuild. Military defeats were also helpful in discrediting the militias and warlords who actually waged those wars.

Shevardnadze's reliance on the value of basic order correlated with the choice of institution from which he started rebuilding his power base: the

---

11. In its 1995 budget—the first annual budget the Georgian parliament managed to pass—international loans, grants, and aid constituted 53.55 percent of all revenues *(Georgian Chronicle,* January 1995).

police. In this sense, the start of the process may be dated to September 14, 1993, when the first open disagreement occurred between Shevardnadze and Ioseliani, the major Georgian warlord. The disagreement was caused by Shevardnadze's decision to dismiss one of Ioseliani's lieutenants from the position of minister of the interior and to assume those responsibilities himself. Ioseliani threatened to withdraw his support, which, in the face of a new Zviadist insurrection, would have challenged the new regime in a fundamental way, so Shevardnadze resigned. Several thousand panicked people rallied in his support, at some point even going down on their knees asking Shevardnadze to reverse his decision—which he did. Ioseliani had to accept the change and even continue to stand by Shevardnadze for another year and a half. He had no other choice, since the power abuses by the Mkhedrioni had made him and his group extremely unpopular.

This episode demonstrated in a dramatic, almost theatrical fashion both the centrality of order as a basic political value and the centrality of control over law enforcement bodies in the power struggle. Not that the police were efficient, but they were the only institutionalized armed force accepting control by political authority. Military defeat in Abkhazia had weakened the militias that had been the Georgian army, thus enabling the police to confront their remnants; fresh recollections of abuses by the Mkhedrioni and other groups provided an additional motivation for the police to recapture the authority previously lost by the state, and their attempt to do so gained public support.

As for the army, from March 1994 it was put under the control of a general from the Soviet school who made it no longer a threat to power, as no new militia would be created under its umbrella. Since rebuilding the army was not Shevardnadze's priority, it was not a problem that the allegiance of the minister to Russia rather than to his own country was suspect: the Russian-speaking and politically unambitious general was isolated in Georgia. The growing strength of Shevardnadze inevitably led to an open conflict with the Mkhedrioni, which, at least since spring 1995, had developed an obvious alliance with the head of the Security Service, Igor Giorgadze. Shevardnadze used a failed attempt on his own life in August of the same year that was allegedly masterminded and carried out by Giorgadze and his allies in the Mkhedrioni to destroy both and to establish control over the Security Service. This move completed the building of a minimalist Weberian state in Georgia (or, more precisely, in that part of Georgia actually controlled by the government). For carrying out this task, Shevardnadze was rewarded with a victory in the November 1995 elections. During his previous three and a half years in power, the country had lost about 15 percent of its territory, its GDP had shrank several times, and up to one-fifth of the population had fled poverty and lawlessness to other countries, but he managed to restore basic order and ran as the symbol of "stability" (Gachechiladze 1997, 24–29).

Further Challenges and Developments

If the failed state of 1992–93 is taken as a reference point, Shevardnadze's success may be considered spectacular. He made Georgia a state, albeit a weak one. But if one assumes that "weak" statehood is an intermediary condition between efficacy and failure, the question faced by Georgia at the moment should be whether the chronic inefficiency of the state bureaucracy and the failure to ensure an even and orderly territorial distribution of power—both characteristics of contemporary Georgian politics— are so serious that a new collapse of statehood is possible. Is the state gradually moving in the direction of overcoming these problems and becoming effective, or is it stuck in current contradictions and doomed to "muddle through" indefinitely? I do not think confident answers can be given to these questions at this point. But we can review the arguments in favor of both positive and negative expectations.

A pessimist would argue that the same methods that Shevardnadze used in his effort to ensure basic stability hamper further development of the state. For instance, corruption may be the buzzword in Georgia now, and it is recognized as the most urgent problem by government, opposition, and independent analysts. President Shevardnadze symbolically defined two consecutive years—1997 and 1998—as years of accelerated struggle with corruption. But no significant results were achieved. Why such a total failure? Shevardnadze's success in stabilizing the country was based on a very skillful balancing act: he did not upset actual or potential opponents by any attempt at sweeping change in the existing constellation of political forces, but took that arrangement as given and tried instead to play one actor against the other, making himself indispensable for preserving the balance. Corruption was an important stabilizing factor in this regard because it made different major players interested in the preservation of the status quo. Real measures against institutionalized structural corruption, then, would imply serious changes in the balance of power and possibly push some powerful actors to challenge political authority. Hence, arguably, Shevardnadze only talks the anticorruption talk, but has not yet—and probably never will—even try to walk the walk.

The problem of the police is most frequently mentioned in this respect. The police were Shevardnadze's major ally in his fight against the warlords. But the police are also widely recognized as probably the most corrupt institution, or at least the most conspicuously corrupt, and this issue is very widely discussed in the media. However, even the most reform-minded politicians hesitate to take on the police for their abuses of power, as an open conflict with this power institution would call into question the politicians' future. In private or semi-private situations politicians try to spread the message that at this moment of development a corrupt police is a guarantee of the country's stability, since this is the only way the police may be kept happy and supportive of the reformist government. Reform efforts, according to this theory, should first be concentrated on other areas (such as the economy or the judiciary); only after those areas are stabilized can the government afford to take decisive measures against police corruption. The failure of the government to attack corruption in this central area, however, inevitably leads to a loss of credibility and a discrediting of the very ideas of reform. This failure breeds political cynicism, which erodes the foundation of legitimacy of state power altogether and reduces its capacity to meet serious challenges as they arise.

Whereas 1996 and 1997 were relatively calm and stable, 1998 brought new troubles (or strong reminders of the old ones), putting Georgia's stability into question again (see my analysis in Nodia 2000). In February, the president narrowly survived another attempt on his life, and in a week's time some of the alleged perpetrators of the terrorist attack (from the Zviadist camp) took four UN military observers hostage. Although these episodes could be interpreted as an occasional outburst of terrorism, May brought a big disaster when a six-day-long war broke out in the district of Gali between Georgian guerrillas and Abkhaz forces. The war brought a new humiliating defeat to Georgia, with at least 239 casualties and about 40,000 Georgians who had spontaneously returned to their homes in Gali becoming refugees for the second time in several years (U.S. Department of State 1998). The government, which was believed to have supported the guerrillas covertly, was blamed for the whole affair; it again appeared impotent, incompetent, not in charge. Understandably, the second wave of refugees were furious. They were driven to the region of Mingrelia, the former Zviadist stronghold, where Shevardnadze was especially unpopular. There were justified fears that the region could become a problem again. In October, a military mutiny occurred in the town of Senaki (in Mingrelia) under the leadership of an erstwhile Zviadist rebel who had ostensibly reconciled with the government. The mutineers demanded Shevardnadze's resignation and restoration of the "legitimate" (that is, Zviadist) government. (The mutiny was defeated on the same day.) Parallel to these developments, hitherto hidden tensions between Tbilisi and Ajaria became open and acute, as parliamentarians supporting Abashidze started to boycott the Georgian parliament. Economics played a role as well: all this, together with the impact of the Russian financial crisis and against the backdrop of the Georgian government's general inability to raise taxes, caused a fiscal crisis and created pressures on the national currency, the lari, which the National Bank could no longer protect. Once the lari was allowed to float on December 7, it lost about 50 percent of its value and continued to gradually fall thereafter. The IMF, disappointed with Georgia's failure to improve tax collection, ceased its financial support, dealing another blow to the country's international credibility.

These events invited a new sense of pessimism and disenchantment, and indeed they demonstrated the fragility of the Georgian political balance and the limited resources of the state in meeting its basic obligations. However, if the record of the year is scrutinized not against the backdrop of bright expectations but against the more modest reference point of the "failed state" of several years earlier, hopeful signs may be found even in these negative events. The government took credit for not allowing the Gali conflict in May to develop into a full-scale war. This acknowledgment caused many derogatory remarks, but if we compare this situation with August 1992, when Shevardnadze could not stop his warlords from initiating a war, it does demonstrate important improvements. More important, the mutiny in Senaki did not find any popular support—contrary to its organizers' expectations—even in the most disgruntled and economically devastated region of Mingrelia. Thus, however good the reasons are for people to be angry, they still are not inclined to try to change the situation through fighting. Currency devaluation was painful for many people, but it did not cause a major economic crisis, and economic growth continued, although at a more modest rate. Though there was no success in fighting corruption, society (as represented both by nongovernmental organizations and by the media) became visibly more outspoken in opposing the abuse of power by government bodies. One element may be singled out as the most hopeful aspect of recent Georgian developments: despite strong pressures to the contrary, near-anarchy was overcome and the present level of political order is maintained without attempts to establish an authoritarian regime. In saying this, I appeal not just to the unconditional value of liberty, but to the stabilizing role of democracy. With the exception of a few fringe groups, all political actors seem to accept the democratic rules of the game.

Another issue to be discussed here is the role and impact of international assistance. It is probably too early to make any far-reaching assessments on this subject. A persuasive case can be made that international assistance was a crucial positive factor in reconstructing a basic level of political order in Georgia (what I called a transition from a "failed state" to a "weak state"). Shevardnadze used his image as an indispensable procurer of international assistance (both material and political) as initial capital, which he later expanded into defeating major warlord adversaries and reconstructing a minimalist Weberian state on at least most of his country's territory. It is another question, however, what real role international donors such as the IMF, the World Bank, or the European Union will play in solving Georgia's future problems.

Here, a comparison with African "failed" or "weak" states may be of significant value. As William Reno has argued, in the cold war period international aid may have had a negative effect on weak states, as their rulers learned to manipulate external actors and thus maintained their positions by attracting foreign resources rather than enhancing the efficiency of their bureaucracies or creating an investment-friendly environment. Although in the post–cold war era international donors such as the IMF or the World Bank started to attach strict conditions to their grants and credits in order to force rulers to develop "real" statehood, local rulers still manage to find a way around those requirements (Reno 1998, 18–26). So even though IMF and World Bank efforts in Georgia are met with some level of resistance and criticism (as they are everywhere), most experts agree that the major conditions attached to international credits imply basic measures of fiscal discipline and economic reform and are only to be welcomed. Before its cooperation with the IMF started in 1994, the Georgian state did not have any economic policy at all and was not even capable of passing a budget. The first positive results from cooperation with the IMF were quick to arrive. On the other hand, many politicians and experts argue that many World Bank programs are inefficient: most of the money goes to Western consultants who are not necessarily good, while state debt accumulates. The state bureaucracy also transfers its own responsibility to foreign organizations and has a financial interest in specific programs without any incentive to care about its own efficiency. Thus these programs, it is argued, only help maintain existing bureaucratic inefficiencies without pushing for reform.

I am not in a position to evaluate the pros and cons of this debate, but a specific example may be helpful. In 1998, the IMF ceased its stabilization credits to Georgia, as the latter had failed to meet its obligations. Most notably, the IMF referred to a failure of the Georgian government to in-crease tax collection (*Black Sea Press* 1998a, 1998b). This requirement is undeniably crucial for the development of Georgian statehood: if the Geor-gian government succeeds in a sizeable and lasting improvement in this area, and if there is a demonstrable link between the IMF pressure and this change, one could make a strong argument that the overall impact of in-ternational financial organizations on Georgian stateness is positive.

The Fragility of the Georgian State: An Interpretation

I have tried to analyze the factors and processes that first caused the failure of the state and later its partial reconstruction in Georgia. But a more gen-eral question arises: Why did the Georgian state prove so fragile in com-parison with most other post-Soviet states, even neighboring ones? Was it just bad luck that an erratic character like Gamsakhurdia became its first president and wasted the resource of wide popular mobilization for inde-pendent statehood, or is it just good luck that Georgia happened to have such a resource as Shevardnadze, who managed to make a difference with his international connections and shrewd scheming (so that, after his exit, Georgia may still return to chaos)? This kind of reasoning—and one hears it all the time both inside and outside Georgia—is simplistic. There is no theoretical necessity to exclude the decisive role of the personal factor when it comes to explaining a brief episode of history within an individual coun-try. The comparison between the cases of Georgia and Uganda in Chapter 17 may be useful for demonstrating that when it comes to oscillations be-tween state collapse and the regeneration of relatively stable but still weak statehood, the quality of political leadership leads us a long way: Gam-sakhurdia and Idi Amin contributed a great deal to state collapse, whereas Shevardnadze and Yoweri Museveni may take considerable credit for state rehabilitation.

But the general fragility of the state requires another set of explanatory variables. One of the major features of state "normalcy" undoubtedly is that its institutions are foolproof in the sense that they insulate a given so-ciety from the idiosyncrasies of individual leaders. In the context of com-parison between the vulnerabilities of postcommunist and African states, two distinct dimensions make these comparison more than superficial. The first is the postcolonial context, which results in the "foreign-ness" of state institutions and hence explains their deficient legitimacy. The other is the context of multiethnicity and ethnic conflict. I would argue that in the case of Georgia, the former has greater explanatory value than the latter.

Georgia definitely suffers greatly from the same malaise of antipolitics that is typical for postcommunist countries and has been analyzed by such authors as Václav Havel (1985), Gaspar Tamasz (1994, 30–34), and Charles H. Fairbanks, Jr. (1997). The Communist regime parodied and discredited things political, such as political parties, ideologies, institutions, and the notion of a "public good" as such. The label of "falsity" firmly stuck to the public sphere, and politics was a priori considered a "dirty business," with the values of goodness and truth sought only in the private domain. This attitude already contained the seeds of the disintegration of the state—or at least it weakened the immunity of the political system from anarchic antipolitical forces as they emerged.

The fact that it led to a destruction of the state only in some cases (Bosnia, Georgia, and Tajikistan) is often ascribed to the fact that in most East European states the antipolitical malaise was balanced by "the tradition of national cohesion and a strong state" (Fairbanks 1997, 109). This appears to be true in general, but I would like to be more specific about how exactly "the tradition of a strong state" could have an impact after decades of communism. In countries such as Poland or Czechoslovakia, dissident antipolitics took the shape of developing a "civil society," a world of truth that had to serve as an alternative to the false public world tainted by communist ideology. Fairbanks interprets this as a flight "from the public world, from the political" (Fairbanks 1997, 96). I do not agree, however, that civil society, even in the interpretation of the East European dissidents, represented a flight from the public world. In the Hegelian understanding of the term, which I accept, civil society is an intermediary between the family and the state—that is, it is already the public (rather than the private) world, but not yet necessarily political in the sense of a direct positive relation to the state. This understanding applies to East European dissidents' interpretation of civil society as well: it was a conscious attempt to construct an alternative public world and as such contained the seeds of both the political and the antipolitical. It was antipolitical insofar as politics was identified with communist rule, and it was the difference between state and civil society that was stressed. But it would be no less legitimate, especially in the Georgian context, to put a stress on the contrast between civil society as something existing in the public sphere and familistic networks. In whatever way East European intellectuals conceptualized "civil society," the actual presence of independent associations and networks and the level of development of public discourse that was made possible as a result of the quest for "civil society" proved crucial for a fairly rapid and successful political transformation. In both the Polish and Czech cases, there is some demonstrable continuity between "civil society" constructed under communism and the new political elites who took charge of political transformation.

The comparison with Georgia makes the importance of this point evident. Although some groups and individuals represented dissent in Georgia and went to prison for their beliefs, there was no concept of "civil society" in dissident discourse. Instead, that discourse was dominated by motives of national independence and rejection of communism in the name of the abstract idea of democracy. There was no conscious effort to build an alternative public domain under the name of "civil society" (or any other name). As a result, the only social institutions that were available in Georgia in the period when the public sphere as constructed by the communist state was delegitimized and collapsed was the domain of familistic relations. These relations were in part reminiscent of the "amoral familism" as described by Edward Banfield with respect to southern Italian society (Banfield 1958). Indeed, ethnic nationalist ideology, implying a notion of the nation as an extended family, was the only ideology that had a chance of public appeal. Arguably, however, the major difference between civil society and familistic networks is that the former (even when contrasted with the state) upholds the notion of the "public good" (which makes it able to underpin a "normal" state), whereas the latter know only of the "family good" (thus tending to correlate with a "failed" state). Current attempts to construct a "civil society" in Georgia are aimed at creating something to which the state can relate, so that it does not depend solely on the rulers' ability to maneuver between different "strongmen" or procure grants and credits from international donors. The possibility of success in this attempt in Georgia should not be underestimated, but development of this area must be considered critical by the elite and other important political actors.

Although the above argument may apply to an array of postcommunist countries, only some (Bosnia, Georgia, and Tajikistan) became examples of failed states. Of these three, only Georgia has partially recovered; the other two remain in the "failed state" category. Can an explanation be found for this specificity? Do these three countries have anything in common that would explain why each should have failed at some point?

Bosnia suffers from a lack of national cohesion in an environment where ethnic identity matters most: out of its three major ethnic groups, two identify with neighboring states, Serbia and Croatia, that have irredentist claims to Bosnian territory (though in the Croatian case these claims were less openly expressed), while the only group that identifies itself with Bosnia per se, the Bosnian Muslims, finds itself in a minority. After a war that brought about ethnic homogenization of territories controlled by these respective ethnic groups, Bosnia is only artificially and ostensibly kept together, against the wishes of the majority of people living on its territory, by the international community in a face-saving effort by the West not to (formally) surrender to ethnic separatists or admit that "ethnic cleansing" actually works. In that sense, Bosnia has a very slim chance of becoming a "real" state—not because multiethnic states are not viable in principle, but because in the specific Bosnian case there is no core around which the state can be reconstructed and because indigenous centripetal forces that might keep it together do not exist. This does not exclude, however, eventual development of "normal" statehood in each of its constituent parts.

Georgia is a different story. Though it is indeed multi ethnic, it still has a clear ethnic majority—a core group that identifies itself with the state of Georgia (this core constituted 70 percent of the population in 1989, and its share undoubtedly has increased since then due to emigration by minorities). Furthermore, Georgia's most numerous ethnic minorities (Armenians, Azeris, and Russians) have never challenged its integrity. One can imagine that Armenians and Azeris, who live in distinct communities abutting the borders with their eponymous states, may at some point fall for irredentist slogans. It is also possible that subethnic groups among the Georgians (for instance, Ajarians, who are Muslim, and Mingrelians, who use a vernacular linked to Georgian that is incomprehensible to other Georgians) might also develop separatist aspirations. But even in this worst-case scenario, Georgia will still be viable, as the majority of its population will consider Georgia "its" state. The secessionist movements in Abkhazia and South Ossetia constituted a very serious challenge to Georgian statehood. It is uncertain how these problems will be settled eventually, and conceivably Georgia may never actually restore control over these territories. But whatever has happened and will happen in the future, if the Georgian state fails, it will not be caused by a lack of ethnic homogeneity.[12] On the contrary, as I have argued elsewhere, it was a breakdown of the Georgian state

---

12. Here also a comparison with weak African states may be made. The chronic inefficiency of government in many African countries is often blamed in part on a lack of cultural homogeneity—that is, on an ethnic diversity in the absence of a clear "core" ethnic group. This would not apply to Georgia, though. See, for instance, Widner (1995).

in the center that caused the war in Abkhazia and its eventual de facto secession (Nodia 1998b, 31–33).

Tajikistan is a less clear case. It is not in a region where ideological ethnic nationalism calls the shots, but it also suffers from very weak national cohesion and a very weak sense of statehood. These appear to be losing in competition with regional loyalties, on the one hand (although the latter did not develop into distinct political claims), and religious movements, on the other. A strong and distinct core political community around which the country could unite is yet to be molded. Once the political regime collapsed, it was difficult to restore a unified order (as was similarly the case in neighboring Afghanistan). In the long run, religiously motivated groups will have greater chances to succeed if outside forces (namely, Russia and Uzbekistan) allow them.

Georgia is different in this respect as well. The idea of Georgian nationhood as the basis for an independent state was distinctly formulated and came to dominate political discourse as soon as Gorbachev's political liberalization allowed free expression. It was never seriously contested afterward. It is another matter how much this national idea translated into actual national cohesion—that is, an ability to mobilize for specific political goals defined on the basis of some common good for the political community.

I believe that at least a partial explanation for the peculiar difficulties of Georgia's state-building should be sought in its civilizational-political marginality. Broadly speaking, modern statehood may be constructed in two ways. One is autocratic, when modern statehood retains a certain continuity with traditional structures of power and patriarchal traditions and is built on them through a series of modifications (a top-to-bottom model). Another is democratic (though not necessarily liberal), when traditional patriarchal power structures are explicitly rejected through some kind of revolutionary action and a new political regime is built whose legitimacy rests on popular will (a bottom-up model). This latter project requires certain capacities (broadly called "social capital") within a society that claims to constitute a new political community. In particular, it requires some critical amount of trust, social cohesion, and solidarity that make possible a certain level of political mobilization around slogans and values. In emergent democracies, these slogans and values are more often nationalist (though they may have a socialist component as well). Social capital also implies a capacity to translate this mass mobilization into fairly coherent, protracted, and targeted political action that culminates in the creation of stable and effective political institutions. In short, this requires an active society with a high capacity for social and political self-organization. This capacity is also sometimes called "political culture" in a normative sense, "political traditions," or "civil society" (if the latter term is not reduced to meaning only nongovernmental organizations and the media).

Since a democratic model of modern statehood mostly succeeded in the West, a strong perception has been created that this kind of society and, respectively, this model of state-building are essentially "Western." I will try neither to question nor to confirm this, since for my objectives it suffices to say that this perception was universally shared in post-Soviet countries, including Georgia. A choice in favor of the Western model of building statehood usually correlated with a "pro-Western orientation"—that is, the self-perception that a given nation intrinsically "belongs" to Western civilization or feels compelled to follow the Western path.

In the post-Soviet countries, the best example of such an orientation and model of building statehood has been the Baltic states. Lithuanians, Latvians, and Estonians had full consensus that they really belonged to Europe and were separated from it only because of foreign occupation—so, when independent, they should base their political organization on the popular will and implement it through broad popular mobilization. Cohesion of the polity would be glued by the national idea. Theirs are also quite obviously the most effective states in the post-Soviet area. On the other pole are the Central Asian states, whose populations (at least their "core" or "titular" ones) did not consider themselves part of Western civilization and did not feel compelled to create a new type of political power based on popular mobilization. Hence, their post-Soviet political regimes mainly continue the Soviet model with some modifications. Tajikistan is the only exception: its total chaos, resulting from an attempt to change the political regime from below, only strengthened other Central Asian leaders (and, it appears, the majority of Central Asian populations as well) in their belief that the "Western way" was not for them. So far, Central Asian regimes have also been fairly stable, and statehood has not been challenged there. (Their experience, however, is not usually included among the "success stories" of the region, since they did not make much of an attempt at transitions to democracy.)

The states of the Caucasus, and in particular Georgia, represent an ambiguous case. Georgian elites expressly opted for a "pro-Western orientation" and a Western type of political conduct (or what they perceived as such). Baltic national-democratic movements served as a reference point for the Georgians: they agreed or disagreed on tactical points, but assumed that the general direction and targets were the same. But Georgian society lacked those social-political capacities associated with "Western" ways: "national cohesion," "political culture," and "social capital."[13] Georgian political ambitions did not correlate with Georgian social capacities. Georgian society, at least in the initial stages of independent statehood, did not display capacities necessary for building democratically based state institutions, but the pro-Western orientation of its elite also did not allow it to tolerate autocratic, openly repressive regimes associated in the popular mind with "Eastern" or "Asian" ways. Once President Gamsakhurdia displayed clear autocratic leanings, he was ousted. But stability could not be achieved this way either. As a result, rejection of both Soviet totalitarianism and nationalist autocracy resulted in near anarchy, where only personal and familialistic loyalties worked.

However, this pro-Western choice, though dominating political discourse for the most part, was more ambiguous in Georgia than in the Baltic. There has always been an alternative trend that is based not so much on anti-Western sentiment, but more often on the perception that "we are not good enough to follow Western ways" (meaning: "not organized enough," or "not disciplined enough") and that therefore Georgia has to turn to greater autocracy (and, therefore, to orient itself toward Russia in foreign politics).

While supporters of this trend never came to power on the national level, this option of building statehood developed in the autonomous region of Ajaria, which, as I said earlier, represents an openly autocratic model of building statehood on Georgian soil. Whereas most of Georgia's political elite tries to imitate the West, Ajaria's elite looks for its inspiration elsewhere. As its ideologist Alexander Chachia put it, "[T]he most important feature [Georgians] always had was the patriarchal mentality characteristic of oriental civilization" (Kalandadze 1999). "Orthodox Christianity and Islam correspond with patriarchal ways and the mentality of our nation. That's why a Georgian Orthodox Christian will always have more in common with an Iraqi Muslim than with a Protestant" (Todua 1999). Abashidze became the leader of Georgia's Revival, the major opposition coalition for the parliamentary elections of 1999 (which includes several other parties not based in Ajaria), and he was the coalition's candidate for president in April 2000. The formation of this coalition might be considered a bid to export the Ajarian model to the rest of Georgia. Apart from attracting a protest vote, the main appeal of the Ajarian model has been its

---

13. Barbara Cristophe (1999) tries to conceptualize this lack of social capital based on the concept of "neo-patrimonialism."

claim to represent state efficacy in contrast to the deficiencies of stateness as demonstrated by the Tbilisi model. Ajaria has been stable while Georgia has been going through different stages of turmoil. Hence, it may be used as a confirmation of the frequently voiced opinion that "we are not ready for democracy yet" or "Western democracy is not for us."

Ajarianization of the whole of Georgia is unlikely, as was demonstrated by the spectacular defeat of Abashidze's coalition in the October 1999 elections and Shevardnadze's overwhelming victory in the 2000 elections. Moreover, few of the pragmatic allies of Abashidze would share Chachia's ideas, which sound exotic for most Georgian elites.[14] But the very presence of such an option shows that, although Georgian political elites mainly try to follow Western ways and have achieved some success (Georgia's admission to the Council of Europe and the World Trade Organization in 1999 are most important recognitions of this), this choice is not based on a firm and unambiguous consensus in society. Although turning toward a "non-Western," openly autocratic model is highly unlikely, this lack of unambiguous consensus in favor of Western liberal-democratic values (with skepticism toward it fed by actual deficiencies in the capacities of Georgian society for democratic self-organization) may be a serious impediment to future steps toward the "normalization" of statehood in Georgia.

This conclusion does not imply an overall pessimism with regard to Georgian statehood, however. Full normalization of Georgian statehood will be an uphill battle for its political elites, and it is highly unlikely that the state will overcome its multiple deficiencies in the foreseeable future. The prospect of a return to a chaotic condition will also be looming on the horizon for some time to come. But "social capital" or "political culture" are not constants. They may evolve, and as the experience of other countries has shown, they are not insurmountable obstacles to an elite-led effort to build "normal" statehood. The burning ambition of most Georgian elites to join the club of advanced "Western" nations may be an important driving factor in this.

References

Adgilobrivi tsarmomadgenlobiti organoebis—sakrebuloebis—1998 tslis 15 noembris archevnebi (Statistikuri masalebi).1999. [15 November 1998 elections to local representative bodies—sakrebulos (Statistical data)]. Tbilisi.

---

14. Chachia himself came to Ajaria after spending years in Russia, and his thinking bears the strong influence of Russian "Eurasianist" theories that have never been popular in Georgia.

Banfield, Edward C. 1958. *The Moral Basis of a Backward Society.* Glencoe: Free Press.

Black Sea Press. 1993. "Georgian President Warns about Strict Measures in Response to 'Fiscal Terrorism.'" 23 November.

———. 1998a. "Reasons for Fiscal Crisis in Georgia Are Not Only Economic." 16 October.

———. 1998b. "IMF Mission Will Come to Georgia on December 11." 7 December.

———. 1999a. "Georgia Will Receive the Next Tranche from the IMF Only after It Shows Specific Results in Tax-Collection." 10 February.

———. 1999b. "Aslan Abashidze Charged Tbilisi with an Attempt to Institute an Economic Blockade against Ajaria." 26 July.

Broladze, Nodar. 1992. "Nam ieshche rano imet' prezidenta." *Nezavisimaya gazeta.* 10 January: 1.

Coppieters, Bruno, Alexei Zverev, and Dmitri Trenin, eds. 1995. *Commonwealth and Independence in Post-Soviet Eurasia.* London: Portland.

Cristophe, Barbara. 1999 "The Legacy of the Neo-Patrimonial State: A Forgotten Dimension in Explaining Ethnic Conflict in Post-Socialist Transcaucasia " European University Viadrina Frankfurt (Oder). Photocopy.

Fairbanks, Charles H., Jr. 1997. "The Public Void: Antipolitics in the Former Soviet Union." Pp. 91–114 in *The End of Politics? Exploration into Modern Antipolitics,* ed. Andreas Schedler. New York: St. Martin's.

Gachechiladze, Revaz. 1997. *Population Migration in Georgia and Its Socio-Political Consequences.* Tbilisi: United Nations Development Programme—Georgia.

Havel, Václav. 1985. *The Power of the Powerless: Citizens against the State in Central-Eastern Europe.* London: Hutchinson.

Jackson, Robert H. 1990. *Quasi-States: Sovereignty, International Relations, and the Third World.* Cambridge: Cambridge University Press.

Kalandadze, Jonny. 1999. "Interviu politolog Alexandre Chachiastan." *Alia.* 30 January: 3.

Mark, David E. 1996. "Eurasia Letter: Russia and the New Transcaucasus." *Foreign Policy* 105 (winter): 141–59.

Migdal, Joel. 1988. *Strong Societies and Weak States: State-Society Relations and State Capabilities in the Third World.* Princeton: Princeton University Press.

Nodia, Ghia. 1995. "Georgia's Identity Crisis." *Journal of Democracy* 1: 104–16.

———1998a. "The Conflict in Abkhazia: National Projects and Political Circumstances." Pp. 14–48 in *Georgians and Abkhazians: The Search for a Peace Settlement,* ed. Bruno Coppieters, Ghia Nodia, and Yury Anchabadze. Cologne: BIOst.

———. 1998b. *Causes and Visions of Conflict in Abkhazia.* Working paper (winter), Berkeley Program in Soviet and Post-Soviet Studies, University of California, Berkeley.

———. 2000. "A New Cycle of Instability in Georgia: New Troubles and Old Problems." Pp. 188–203 in *Crossroads of Conflict: Security and Foreign Policy in the Southern Tier,* ed. Gary K. Bertsch et al. New York: Routledge.

Ramishvili, Davit, Alexi Alexishvili, Vazha Petriashvili, and Davit Amaghlodeli. 1999. "Taxes and Taxation Policy." *Bulletin of the Georgian Center for Strategic Studies and Development* 29: 3.

Reno, William. 1998. *Warlord Politics and African States.* Boulder: Lynne Rienner.

Tamasz, Gaspar. 1994. "The Legacy of Dissent." *Uncaptive Minds* 7, no. 2: 18–34.

Todua, Irakli. 1999. "Alexandre Chachia: chven gavimarjvebt." *Asaval-Dasavali.* 8 February: 9.

United Nations Development Programme (UNDP). 1996. *Human Development Report: Georgia 1996.* Tbilisi: UNDP.

U.S. Department of State. 1998. "Georgia Country Report on Human Rights Practices for 1998." Obtained at www.state.gov/www/global/human_rights/1998_hrp_report/georgiavhtml.

Widner, Jennifer A. 1995. "State and Statelessness in Late-Twentieth-Century Africa." *Daedalus* 124, no. 3 (summer): 142–50.

Zartman, I. William, ed. 1995. *Collapsed States: The Disintegration and Restoration of Legitimate Authority.* Boulder: Lynne Rienner.

Zverev, Alexei. 1996. "Ethnic Conflicts in the Caucasus." Pp. 13–71 in *Contested Borders in the Caucasus,* ed. Bruno Coppieters. Brussels: VUB University Press.

17

After the Fall:
State Rehabilitation in Uganda

CRAWFORD YOUNG

Uganda offers a useful African comparison for Georgia. Its itinerary bears some resemblance to that of its Caucasus counterpart. From relative strength at the time of independence, it followed a dramatic downward spiral into the land of the failed state in the Idi Amin years. A slight recovery occurred during the second A. Milton Obote regime, then came a far more robust rehabilitation of the state under Yoweri Museveni, Uganda's president since 1986. The important lesson emerging from these paired cases is that an episode of state failure, even if extending over several years, is not necessarily fatal.

States, one discovers, are not so easy to destroy. Fragments of their institutional organs may persist even when the central nervous system is no longer fully operative. A legal system, even if for a period it becomes merely phantasmal, can spring back to life, fully clothed by the codification of state commands embodied in shelves of legal texts. Imprinted on societal memory is a set of recollections of a "normal state": security it is expected to provide, services it is assumed to assure, rituals of statehood it is presumed to perform. These expectations serve as a legitimating reservoir for renewed assertions of state authority.

Yet the pathway to rehabilitation is far from easy. A number of state failures littered the 1990s African landscape: Congo-Kinshasa, Somalia, Liberia, and Sierra Leone are only the clearest examples. Yet cases of clear restoration of once-failed states are harder to find. Ghana, from a low point of state weakness, though not outright failure, achieved impressive recovery beginning in the mid-1980s. Mozambique, a reasonable candidate for the state-failure roster by the mid-1980s, when it could neither feed nor protect much of its population, has since restored peace, achieved a degree of reconciliation, and displayed robust macroeconomic statistics in the second half of the 1990s. But the state remains enfeebled, unusually reliant on a large international nongovernmental organization sector. In Africa, only Uganda constitutes a reasonably clear case of substantial state rehabilitation after several years of consignment to the failed-state contingent. On the Eurasian side, Tajikistan rivals Georgia in outright failure in the wake of the disintegration of the Soviet Union. But Georgia alone shows clear evidence of state recovery, as Chapter 16 shows.

In the classificatory language employed in this chapter, I follow the same definitions as in Chapter 16. A "strong" (or perhaps better, "normal") state is one that has the basic capacity to perform the functions and to implement the policies that civil society and state agents believe to fall within the domain of state responsibility. A "weak" state meets minimum Weberian definitions of institutions of rule and is able to carry out some basic functions but is far from performing according to domestic and international expectations of a "normal" state. A "failed" state continues to enjoy formal recognition by the international system, but its institutions fail to meet even minimum definitions of governmental authority and operation. In this inquiry, I will track the analysis used by Ghia Nodia in Chapter 16, establishing first Uganda's baseline of relative state strength in the terminal colonial period and the first independence years, examining the decline and then fall into outright failure in the last Obote years and under the Amin regime, and then analyzing the trajectory of rehabilitation, at first slender and precarious in the second Obote period, but then rapid and extensive in the Museveni era.[1]

In its final form in the 1950s, the British colonial administration operated a well-organized state, exercising extensive and effective control over its African subjects. Whether one places stress on the hegemonic force of the central colonial institutions (Young 1994), or on the potency of "decentralized despotism" operating through the chiefly intermediaries (Mam-

---

1. I will follow normal Ugandan conventions in referring to the first regime under Obote, who was prime minister and then president from 1962 to 1971, as "Obote I," and his second coming as head of state from 1980 to 1984 as "Obote II." Idi Amin held power from 1971 to 1979. The years 1979–1980 and 1985–1986 were interregnum periods with several short-lived heads of state; these interregnums are not treated here.

dani 1996), terminal colonial Uganda was a well-ordered polity. Emergent nationalism was channeled into the emergent district and national representative institutions, whose powers were gradually enlarged. The rapid economic expansion of the postwar years, although partly attributable to an unusually favorable international trade environment, also reflected effective state management. In the period from 1946 to the independence year of 1962, Uganda's gross domestic product (GDP) increased five-fold. Government expenditures, a mere £4.5 million in 1947, had multiplied to £32.3 million in 1962 (Ghai 1966). An export-oriented economy, built largely on cotton and coffee, assured a modest but expanding level of well-being in the countryside. Cotton production, although introduced with a large dose of compulsion, expanded naturally by the postwar period. Coffee cultivation, very profitable in the 1950s in spite of high taxation levels, spread rapidly in ecologically suitable areas.

State action expanded significantly during this period. A large proportion of the country's agricultural buying and processing was by state action taken from private Asian operators and placed in the hands of the Ugandan cooperative movement (for example, through the compulsory acquisition of cotton ginneries, with large credit infusions to African cooperative unions; Young, Sherman, and Rose 1981). The administrative hierarchies in regional government were doubled by rapidly expanding technical services. The physical infrastructure—transportation, communication, education, and health facilities—experienced comparable growth. By the time of independence, all parts of the country were within a day's journey of the capital.

The country was demarcated into thirteen major subdivisions, four of which had the status of kingdoms. Below this tier, whose command personnel were European, a hierarchy of chiefs extended state authority down to the individual subject, from counties, through subcounties, to villages. By the postwar period, intermediary chiefs above the village level, whose authority depended on state appointment, met some educational and performance (as well as ancestral) criteria for selection and drew stipends (Richards 1959). A "graduated tax" (essentially, a head tax) was effectively collected from the great majority of households. Although the military means of coercion at the hands of state were modest—a single 700-troop battalion of the pan-territorial King's African Rifles (Omara-Otunnu 1987, 51)—an uncontested monopoly of force lay with the colonial administration.

Thus, at the hour of independence in 1962, the Ugandan successors to British colonial managers inherited an effective state. Its major institutions, at first, functioned smoothly. The technical services performed efficiently

in their respective domains. Politically, a power-sharing arrangement enjoyed reasonably broad support. No party won a clear majority in the independence elections, but the coalition formed between the Uganda People's Congress (UPC) and the Buganda Kabaka Yekka ("The king alone,"
or KY) held 55 of 77 parliamentary seats.

Some analysts argue that the newly independent Uganda was in reality
a "weak state" (Migdal 1988, Khadiagala 1995). But research conducted
in the mid-1960s on the operation of the independent state through its rural policies and local government institutions suggests otherwise (Leys
1967; Vincent 1971; Burke 1964; *Uganda District Government and Politics* 1977). State "strength" is necessarily relative to its overall environment
and resources; Uganda at its peak did not match the Georgia of high Stalinism. But the institutions of governance extended downward to the village capillaries of the system, the basic fabric of public order was assured,
and the state was capable of implementing the policies it chose to pursue.
Research carried out with several Ugandan collaborators in seven districts
regarding farmers' attitudes toward cooperative societies and government
agricultural services in 1966–67 revealed a generally positive orientation
toward the key rural policy instruments of the state (Young, Sherman, and
Rose 1981, 102–19). Among both elites and ordinary citizens relative optimism prevailed; both expected continued improvement in their level of
well-being, hopes that were generally fulfilled until the later 1960s as the
terminal colonial momentum of economic growth and state revenue expansion persisted.

The transition to African rule posed a set of challenges to governance
that had been suppressed under alien colonial hegemony. The racial division of labor during colonial times, wherein Europeans ruled, Asians
owned and operated much of the private economy, and Africans were farmers and workers, would be inverted: Africans ruled, Asians operated at their
sufferance, and Europeans withdrew, few having intended permanent settlement.

On the periphery, some local disputes flared around issues of ethnic ascendancy in district governments; one, in the Ruwenzori Mountains in the
western frontier, expanded into a low-intensity insurgency that simmered
until 1983 (Rubongoya 1995; Doornbos 1970). In the semiarid zones of
the far northeast, a pastoral region deemed economically unproductive by
the colonial state, a limited and purely preemptive administration existed;
the independent government found itself unable to impose more extensive
control in the area, in spite of garrisoning a newly formed battalion in the
zone shortly after independence (Ocan 1994; Wozei 1977). Religious fac-

tionalism deeply embedded itself into the national party system and the district governments (Mudoola 1996; Welbourn 1965).

Most serious of all was the uneasy relationship between the central government and the kingdom of Buganda. Situated at the center of Uganda, with a quarter of the country's total population and an even larger share of its economic production and wealth, Buganda had long regarded itself as distinct from the rest of the territory. In the eyes of the Ganda (the ethnic population), the kingdom enjoyed a treaty relationship with the United Kingdom between nearly equal partners; other parts of Uganda came under British rule by forcible subjugation, with important assistance from Buganda. Throughout the decolonization negotiations during the final colonial decade, Buganda opposed often truculent resistance to power-transfer schemes that appeared through the law of numbers in national parliamentary elections to subordinate Buganda to Ugandans from other regions (Apter 1961; Wrigley 1996; Young 1977; Low 1971). In 1961, the kingdom announced its intention to secede, a threat that was never carried out.

A precarious compromise took form on the eve of independence. Obote, who was at the time the leader of the largest national party (the UPC), became prime minister with the support of the Ganda royalist party (KY), which swept virtually all the seats in Buganda. In return, the king (*kabaka*) of Buganda, Sir Edward Mutesa, became president, thus preserving a formal ritual ascendancy of the kingdom. However, from the outset Obote chafed under the constraints on central authority posed by the semifederal status of Buganda and, to a lesser extent, the other kingdom districts, granted in the final independence negotiations in order to win the reluctant agreement of Buganda to the new constitution.

The state that Obote directed in the first years of independence, these limits on its cohesion and unity of purpose notwithstanding, was clearly "normal" in the eyes of its domestic citizenry as well as those of the international community. In the future envisioned by Obote and many of his contemporaries in the first generation of African rulers, the merely normal far from sufficed (Ingham 1994). Merely managing the state legacy of the colonial heritage fell short of the transformative ambitions then current. A unified, centralized state, employing comprehensive economic planning and acquiring substantial control over the economy, held the secrets to besting the beasts of underdevelopment—poverty, ignorance, and disease. Strengthening the state, for Obote, was an imperative. The ultimate paradox of Obote I was that the series of steps taken to enlarge state hegemony set in motion a corrosive process of state-weakening.

The liberal democratic constitution, with its semifederal elements and parliamentary system, constrained for a time the state-building project. Tensions with Buganda gradually increased. Opposition fermented within the ranks of the UPC itself (Mutibwa 1992, 32–41). A shadowy coalition of Buganda and other southern Ugandan forces took shape in reaction to perceived "northern" domination under Obote, aspiring to oust him through parliamentary means. In February 1966, a motion passed parliament, with a single dissenting voice, calling for an inquiry into allegations of embezzlement of Congolese gold by Obote and his key henchmen.

Obote seized the occasion to force a confrontation, arresting five southern ministers during a cabinet meeting, suspending the constitution, declaring himself head of state in place of the Bugandan monarch, and imposing a state of emergency. Buganda fell into the Obote trap by providing the pretext for a military showdown, which the kingdom was certain to lose; in May 1966, the Bugandan government ordered central government institutions to evacuate its territory. The Ugandan army, now under the command of Idi Amin, became a central player by assaulting the royal palace, driving the *kabaka* into exile, and imposing a harsh military occupation of the Bugandan countryside (Kabaka of Buganda 1967).

By 1967, Obote had in place a centralizing constitution tailored to his ambitions for full personal ascendancy. The kingdoms were dissolved, local government councils were shorn of their autonomy, and district commissioners as central agents were invested with undivided powers of regional administration. The "revolutionary-centralization" ethos of the new basic law aimed at "permanently strengthening the centre at the expense of the periphery . . . conferred wide-ranging powers on the central government in diverse spheres, and greatly enhanced the executive and legislative powers of the President at the expense of the cabinet, judiciary and legislature" (Mutibwa 1992, 59). Representative institutions were never renewed, since no new national elections were held; parliamentary legitimacy decayed. Most opposition members were induced to cross the carpet; those that remained were put out of business in December 1969, when opposition parties were banned as "dangerous to peace and order." Uganda thus became a one-party state. Civil society was placed under state tutelage as well, as independent unions were driven to cover and associational life shriveled.

The realm of ideology also became a centralizing weapon for Obote (Mittelman 1975). Although a central state role in the economy, building on tendencies already pronounced in the terminal colonial era, was a core aspiration from the outset, in the first Obote years no specific doctrinal form appeared in state discourse. A "Move to the Left" was announced in 1969, elaborated in a "Common Man's Charter" duly approved by a party congress of the UPC, now fully under presidential control. Socialist tropes began to pervade state discourse. Although Obote critics on the left passed caustic judgment on his lack of doctrinal rigor (Gershenberg 1972), and his apologists argued the essential pragmatism of his socialist orientation (Ingham 1994), these measures did strike further at the Asian mercantile class, as did the government's proclaimed intent to assume a 60 percent state equity in the eighty-four leading foreign enterprises in Uganda, with compensation to be provided from profits over a fifteen-year period (Mittelman 1975, 124). Actual implementation fell well short of the initial proclamation, but the scope of the state's self-aggrandizing ambitions fundamentally altered the perspectives of private economic interests, whether from overseas or resident Asians and Europeans.

The generalized failure of socialist orientation in Africa was far from clear until well into the 1980s (Young 1982). At the time, the state-enhancing aspirations fit conventional African patterns of the pursuit of legitimation, accumulation, and hegemony. However, negative consequences swiftly appeared, which more than offset any immediate advantages. Capital flight, particularly by the Asian community, swelled to significant proportions. Inflation, until then a minor irritant, began to accelerate. Shortages of basic consumer commodities appeared for the first time since World War II. Key external donors, in particular the United States and the United Kingdom, grew uneasy about (U.S.) or downright hostile to (U.K.) the drift of the Obote socialist project.

The downward spiral of state-weakening was well underway by 1970. The most important region, Buganda, was physically subdued but sullen and brooding, deeply antagonistic to the regime. The apparent potency of Obote's personal rule concealed its own growing isolation and declining legitimacy. The president became increasingly reliant on his security forces, whose commander was of uncertain loyalty. The economy was visibly fraying at the edges.

The seizure of power by Amin in January 1971 set the stage for the spectacle of state failure. Although the trigger for his coup was the knowledge that Obote was about to remove him from army command (Decalo 1976), Amin had little difficulty in assembling an eighteen-point indictment of the preceding regime. The sharply deflated legitimation of the Obote order found expression in the popular euphoria that greeted the coup. Although enthusiasm was greatest in Buganda, where animosity toward Obote was most intense, few publicly mourned his eclipse. Asian business saw brighter days ahead with the end of rhetorical socialism. The United States, the United Kingdom, and Israel especially welcomed the coup, and the last two, many believe, were accessories to the conspiracy (Turyahikayo-Rugyema 1998, 17–18).

More than in the Georgian case, the rapid decline into state failure in Uganda is partly attributable to the singular personal deficiencies of Amin, a soldier of limited literacy and negligible sense of statecraft catapulted into state leadership by the accidents of military history (Gwyn 1977; Mazrui 1975). Although his commanding physique, his earthy and populist political style, and his audacity cast a brief spell of enchantment, the flaws in the exercise of power by an individual so poorly suited by background, education, training, and experience to managing the affairs of a sovereign state soon became evident. By 1972, Amin was confronted by a badly executed but threatening incursion from Tanzania by armed supporters of the former regime and by the first of a number of internal conspiracies. Suspicion of those who might become inimical descended into paranoiac unleashing of the multiple security agencies he created against real or imagined enemies. Disappearances and assassinations, including such spectacular victims as the chief justice of Uganda and the archbishop of the Church of Uganda, began to multiply. Initial admiration became tinged with fear, then downright terror as the Amin regime degenerated into a capricious tyranny. The number of victims remains unknown; there were certainly tens of thousands, perhaps more.

Among the other core vectors of state failure were the bitter conflict within the security forces themselves, successive ethnic purges, and the proliferation of security services with unclear mandates and little to curb their violent impulses. In the final Obote years, competitive ethnic recruiting flourished, as Obote sought to expand and solidify Lango and Acholi contingents, who by ethno-regional affinity fulfilled the requirements of his ethnic security map (Enloe 1980), while Amin was filling the military ranks with new recruits from his far northwest homeland. Many of the Lango and Acholi soldiers were slaughtered in the immediate aftermath of the Amin coup, which they tried to resist. Killings within the armed forces continued throughout the Amin period, as successive northern sources of recruitment (Lugbara, Madi) became perceived as unreliable. In the final phases, the elusive search for a personally loyal and reliable army led to substantial recruitment of southern Sudanese and Congolese. Meanwhile, the task of intimidation of the citizenry was simultaneously pursued by the sinister State Research Bureau and diverse other agencies. Particularly targeted were members of the professional and educated classes, many thousands of whom fled into exile in other parts of Africa, Europe, and North America, stripping the state of an important fraction of its skilled human resources.

Economically, the road from state weakness to failure began with the 1972 expulsion of the vast majority of the Asian community, which then numbered 83,000, of whom 43,000 held Ugandan citizenship. Amin, invoking the divine inspiration of a dream instructing him that "the Asian problem was becoming extremely explosive and that God was directing me to act immediately to save the situation" (Mittelman 1975, 229), gave Asians ninety days to liquidate their affairs and depart. Although some Asian citizens were subsequently exempted, only 10,000 remained by 1975; an estimated $1 billion in property was confiscated. These "racial cleansing" measures, like the coup itself, were initially very popular. Asian domination of much of the economy, perhaps above all the virtual control of wholesale and retail trade, inevitably generated deep resentments. A 1966–67 survey showed that 93.2 percent of the farmers interviewed believed that Asian traders rarely or never conducted business honestly (Young, Sherman, and Rose 1981, 106).[2]

The damaging consequences of these sweeping confiscations were intensified by the ways in which seized properties were redistributed. Asian enterprises were parceled out to regime cronies, military personnel, and other acolytes without regard to the recipients' capacity to manage the booty. For the shops in particular, a common outcome was liquidation of the inventory, then abandonment of the enterprise. Inflation was further energized, and shortages became endemic. The formal economy shrank rapidly, partly replaced by a *magendo,* or underground market. The nearly complete disjuncture between state and market at the end of the Amin era is one clear marker of state failure.

Trade in both cotton and coffee, which accounted for about three-quarters of Uganda's export earnings at the time of independence, suffered from deepening dislocations of the formal economy. The cotton trade was particularly savaged: by the later Amin years, cotton exports virtually vanished. Consumer goods were no longer available as an inducement; infrastructural services in seed, fertilizer, and insecticide distribution ceased; and even hoes could not be found in the cotton-producing areas. Payment for cotton deliveries was made in chits of doubtful negotiability. Coffee, as a

---

2. Enthusiasm for African traders was not much greater. Some 30 percent of respondents believed that African traders carried out their business honestly only some of the time, and 53.5 percent felt they were never honest.

perennial crop, was not so quick to shrink when the state abandoned its supportive role. Furthermore, whereas cotton was too bulky to smuggle, clandestine coffee trade with neighboring Kenya, Rwanda, and Congo-Kinshasa sustained some output. In the final months of the Amin regime, when the state had lost almost all of its sources of revenue, the remaining coffee output was seized by the military and exported by air to the United Kingdom for barter acquisition of basic supplies for the regime's inner military core—the infamous "whiskey run." Production of secondary commodities such as tea, copper, and sugar virtually stopped.

In the last year of the Obote regime, GDP had increased 11 percent, and there was a record output of cotton and coffee. Export revenues had doubled over the decade of Obote I. Even though policy choices of the late 1960s were beginning to undermine the economy, the far more systematically destructive actions that were to follow in the Amin years produced a pattern of sustained decline that lay outside the remembered experience of the citizenry. During 1973–80, Uganda suffered an annual average decline in per capita GNP of 6.2 percent, the worst performance in Africa save only for war-torn Angola (World Bank 1989, 221).

Despite its vanishing legitimacy and evaporating resource base, the Amin regime could not be overturned from within. Its fall came only following a final desperate gambit by Amin to occupy his restless army and distract the public: an invasion of Tanzania, to annex a corridor to the sea to which Amin had occasionally laid claim. Tanzania, finally provoked beyond endurance, responded by invading Uganda, seizing the capital and sending Amin into flight (Turyahikayo-Rugyema 1998, 108–15).

Uganda during its failed-state years did not entirely vanish institutionally. Bits and pieces of its institutions continued to function by inertial force. The educational system operated, discovering that it could function largely through the support of the local community and religious networks. Makerere University never missed an academic year; those serving as external examiners reported that graduate quality remained high. The judicial system continued, with local magistrates behaving as though the rule of law existed.[3] As long as the litigation did not implicate the regime and its security obsessions, no interference was likely.

To some extent, an illusion of Uganda was externally sustained by its continued international recognition, as "quasi-state" theory prescribes (Jackson 1990). The Organization of African Unity supplied a prestigious plat-

---

3. This observation was confirmed in field research by Lynn Khadiagala in 1996 and 1997 on women and the legal system at the local level (Khadiagala 1999).

form for Amin as the embodiment of Uganda by holding its 1975 summit conference in Kampala, by virtue of which Amin became chief spokesperson for Africa during the ensuing year. His discovery of his Islamic identity in 1972 and his abandonment of his one-time Israeli sponsors in favor of Arab solidarity earned funds and favor from some quarters in the Arab world, especially Libya. His embrace of anti-imperialist discourse by the mid-1970s attracted Soviet diplomatic interest and arms supplies.

At the same time, the excesses of Amin isolated Uganda. The nascent human rights community targeted Uganda as a prime offender. The now-large Ugandan exile community supplied a flood of documented data on abuses. The irrepressible buffoonery of Amin attracted ridicule: his threats to invade South Africa with his "Suicide Battalion," to extinguish Israel, to collect food for starving English citizens (Turyahikayo-Rugyema 1998, 68–79). In 1973, the United States closed its embassy in Kampala; in 1977, the U.S. Congress enacted a trade embargo against Uganda, citing massive human rights abuses. When Tanzania invaded Uganda in 1979 to oust Amin at the same moment that the Soviet invasion of Afghanistan was provoking a global crisis, there was some discomfort in African capitals, but most of the world quietly applauded.

As compared with Georgia, state failure came to Uganda through different avenues. In the latter, much more blame was attributable to the singular persona of the ruler himself. Uganda did not yet have warlords challenging public order. Disorder was perhaps more total in Georgia, but it was briefer in duration. The institutional infrastructure of the old order in Georgia was undoubtedly denser and more authoritative; state hegemony bore more directly and thoroughly on the subject of a Leninist state. There was no Ugandan counterpart to the Communist Party and its *nomenklatura*. The collapse of the former system was more abrupt and complete in Georgia.

Some similarities, however, may be detected, above all in the nature of transitional dynamics beyond state failure. In both countries, the pattern of centralized state direction of the economy had virtually collapsed. The conditions of generalized disorder and the dominance of the parallel economy created huge challenges in the building of a stable public market economy. Such a project was inescapably tributary to support from the international financial institutions and the available donor community, now only Western. (By 1986, when Uganda's state recovery began in earnest, the Soviet Union was withdrawing from its African aid commitments.) Thus discourse and practice in economic macromanagement had to conform to the canon of the "Washington consensus."

A security apparatus capable of meeting the Weberian definition of stateness itself had to be constructed from scratch in both cases. The Russian army, although it continued to play a role of fluctuating value to Georgian state consolidation, was not organized in a fashion permitting national units to revert to the newly independent republics (in contrast to the colonial-era East African King's African Rifles, which had an exclusively Ugandan battalion). In Uganda, the Amin army simply dissolved, as did its other murderous security agencies, with some fragments subsequently reappearing as insurgent militias. This process was repeated when the Obote II era ended. A wholly new army had to be built—a process that sowed the seeds of destruction of the successor regime. Politically, a new regime whose legitimacy both domestically and internationally could rest on something other than force was critical. A major factor in both cases was gifted leadership: Eduard Shevardnadze in Georgia, Yoweri Museveni in Uganda.

Neither of these two leaders emerged right away. In Uganda, in the interim during 1979–80 until elections could be held, Tanzania played an important tutelary role in mediating the regional, ideological, and personal disputes that divided the fractious exiled opposition who returned with the Tanzanian army. In the elections organized in 1980, two of the three main parties from 1962 reemerged: the UPC and the Democratic Party (DP). The conditions were hardly propitious for orderly elections. But the evidence is powerful that, although the DP really won, the UPC managed to distort the results with Tanzanian support to return Obote to power; the observer group from the British Commonwealth chose to close its eyes to the evident fraud and to give the results its blessing (Mutibwa 1992, 139–52).

During the abbreviated Obote II period from 1980 to 1985, some normalcy was restored in state management of the economy. Obote entirely abandoned earlier socialist visions and sought the support of the international financial institutions and the Western donor community. The latter were more than receptive; state failure in Africa was still a novelty, and the opportunity to demonstrate the possibilities of restorative therapy enticed the international community. Widely held views on the diabolic nature of the Amin regime, whose final life-support system relied on demonic sources such as Libya and the Soviet Union, reinforced the inclination to assist a martyred country and citizenry. With substantial external assistance, a degree of economic stabilization was achieved by 1982, and some rehabilitation of infrastructure was begun. But these modest accomplishments were soon swallowed up in the deepening insecurity and precarious legitimacy of the Obote restoration.

The Amin army broke into fragments, some retreating into Congo-Kinshasa and Sudan, reforming into insurgent militias. Some of its armories, especially in the northeastern district of Karamoja, were abandoned and looted by local would-be warriors. Obote sought to create a new army around the core of Ugandan exile elements who accompanied the Tanzanian army in its 1979 invasion. Although some effort was made to make the force nationally representative (except for Buganda), the new army soon became, in popular perceptions and actual numbers, a largely Lango and Acholi force (Omara-Otunnu 1987, 158). By 1981, no fewer than five armed groups were in existence, offering still modest but ominous insurgent challenges to Obote II. The most determined and resourceful of these adversaries proved to be the National Resistance Army (NRA) led by Yoweri Museveni.[4]

From small beginnings, Museveni built a rebel army of 15,000, mostly of Ankole, Ganda, and other southern Ugandans, but including 4,000 Rwandan Tutsi who had long been exiled in Uganda. Its main theater of operations was the Luwero triangle, a Buganda zone of several hundred square kilometers northwest of Kampala. The Obote army assigned the task of rooting out the NRA mostly to Acholi troops; their mission not only failed in its objective but was conducted with exceptional brutality, leaving an estimated 300,000 fatalities from 1982 to 1985 (Ofcansky 1996, 52). The consequences proved fatal for Obote: as word of the savagery of the campaign crept out, the donor community backed away from its initial engagement. Animosity toward the regime intensified, especially in southern Uganda and, above all, in Buganda. The fragile economic recovery fell apart, as soaring defense expenditures unhinged the budget and resulted in suspension of support from the international financial institutions. Most ominous of all, tensions built within the army, with Acholi soldiers convinced that they alone were sent to the front, while the Lango co-ethnics of Obote were withheld from combat (Omara-Otunnu 1987, 162–63). The senior Acholi general Tito Okello overthrew Obote in July 1985.

The military regime that followed enjoyed little support and demonstrated less capacity to consolidate its rule. Unsuccessful efforts to negotiate a settlement with the NRA consumed the final months of 1985. In January 1986, Museveni and his army marched into Kampala and seized power, the second occasion in Africa in which a post-independence insur-

---

4. He provides a detailed account of his insurgent campaign in his autobiography (Museveni 1997).

gent movement had conquered the state from the periphery (the first was Chad in 1982), foreshadowing a wave of such takeovers in the 1990s.

Though its military triumph was complete, the political prospects for the new regime of the National Resistance Movement (NRM) were problematic. The guerrilla campaign was conducted with skill and the NRM exhibited unusual discipline, but Museveni's force had a narrow ethnic base. Power seizure by an insurgent force has little intrinsic legitimacy; the extant political forces in Uganda had played little part in the campaign. The discourse of insurgency was freighted with the phraseology of the radical left, and Libyan hands were detected in the supply and arming of the NRM (Omara-Otunnu 1987, 161). These associations led to initial suspicion as to the orientation of the new regime among the Western donor community, by now the only possible source of financial support. Last but by no means least, for the second time within a decade an entire army dissolved, mostly into its home areas, with some troops quickly reforming into local militias. Acholiland was traumatized by the fear that vengeance would be exacted for the role of its soldiers in the Luwero triangle. Large quantities of arms vanished into hidden caches, black markets, or private hands.

The NRM rose to the initial challenge of its legitimation imperative with considerable skill. One of its first measures was to create a new system of local government, instituting five tiers of councils, beginning with elected village assemblies vested with authority for self-rule. The higher tiers were constituted by indirect election at first. However, with the adoption of a carefully constructed Local Government Act in 1997, the direct-election principle was extended to all levels. The launching of the local assemblies, initially labelled National Resistance Councils, generated extensive participation and high enthusiasm, and the NRM's decentralizing ethos of empowering "civil society" attracted laudatory international notice.

A second prong of the legitimation campaign was initiation in 1988 of what was to be a protracted constitution-drafting process (Furley and Katalikawe 1997). A broadly representative commission was appointed and charged with undertaking broad popular consultation. This process extended over several years, leading to a 1993 draft and election of a constituent assembly to finalize and adopt the constitution, finally promulgated in 1995. An extraordinary volume of constitutional seminars and public discussion sessions took place at all levels. Although those critical of the Museveni order viewed the consultative exertions as populist mythology, the degree of participation, if not real influence, was exceptional. In its affirmation of liberal-democratic constitutional precepts and in some of

its innovative features, such as the guarantees of female political representation, the 1995 constitution is a worthy document.

A third and more controversial element in the legitimation project was
transforming an essentially military guerrilla organization into an inclusive
national political movement. Museveni blamed the old political parties for
erecting electoral processes on religious and ethnic divisions and believed
that multiparty systems inevitably politicize difference and embed identity
politics in electoral politics. Hence by metamorphosis the guerrilla van-
guard became the NRM, which vociferously denied that it was a "party"
but claimed to represent all Ugandans. Article 70 of the 1995 constitution
stipulates that a "movement political system" is "broad-based, inclusive
and non-partisan" and embodies such virtues as participatory democracy,
accountability, transparency, equal access to leadership roles for all citizens,
and individual merit as the basis for electoral choice. The movement system asserts its distinctiveness from the discredited single-party systems
once prevalent in Africa by its omission of an official binding doctrine and
its tolerance of the existence of political parties, but not their electoral participation nor public campaigning. The constitution leaves open a future
return to a multiparty system by referendum. Such a consultation occurred
in 2000; Museveni placed all his weight behind defeat of the multiparty
option, an outcome assured by a boycott of the referendum by multiparty
supporters.

A fourth and important dimension assuring a degree of legitimation for
the Museveni regime is the degree of political latitude for public debate
and open criticism—substantially more than existed in Obote I or II. A vigorous and critical opposition press operates, as do private radios with popular "talk shows" of political commentary. Parliament, some of whose
members have known associations with political parties, has been surprisingly vigilant, particularly in uncovering corruption. Army commander
Salim Saleh (his nom de guerre), a half-brother of Museveni, was driven
from office in 1999 by parliamentary revelations of his sordid business
transactions. These gains notwithstanding, criticism grows of the Museveni regime's human rights record, the subject of a blistering attack in the
U.S. Department of State's 2000 annual review of global human rights.

The NRM regime, especially in its early years, proved adept at enlarging
its political base. According to Amii Omara-Otunnu, the initial composition of the ruling council was more than 90 percent southerners, half of
whom were from Museveni's own Ankole ethnic group (Omara-Otunnu
1987, 177). This disproportion quickly changed in an inclusive direction,

however. One by one, most of the initial insurgent militias were negotiated into the movement framework, with some of their leaders taking government posts and some followers incorporated into the army. Thus, by 1988, the NRM enjoyed basic control of most of the country's territory, although acceptance of its rule was tenuous and reluctant in a number of areas in the north.

After Uganda's initial flirtation with radical populism in the economic sphere, the hard constraints of its circumstances reordered the regime's perspectives. By 1987, the NRM had mastered the policy language of the "Washington consensus" and had established rapidly warming relationships with international financial institutions. Successful implementation of successive stabilization programs soon transformed Uganda into a model pupil of structural adjustment pedagogy. In reward, large volumes of aid began to flow, totaling $2 billion by 1995 and continuing at a level of several hundred million dollars annually in subsequent years (Ofcansky 1996, 119). The Ugandan shilling was stabilized in value and made freely convertible by 1993; whereas $1 purchased 7 shillings in 1962, it exchanged for 100,000 by the time of the stabilization. After years of hyperinflation, monetary stability was a major accomplishment.

Liberalization of the economy proceeded systematically in the 1990s. All price controls were eliminated by 1994. The poorly performing state agricultural monopolies were ended, with immediate benefits to producers. In the case of coffee, producers of which received only 15 percent of the export price under the regime of the Coffee Marketing Board monopoly, the abolition of that board and the intense competition among buyers that followed raised the farmers' share of the export price to roughly 75 percent (Brett 1993). In terms of macroeconomic measures, the Ugandan performance under NRM auspices was exceptional: a 3.3 percent increase in per capita GNP from 1987 to 1997 (World Bank 1998, 6). Only two countries in Africa performed better: the Seychelles and Botswana. In 1998, large billboards featuring the impressive economic growth statistics greeted the Kampala citizenry in a number of locations.

Although one may debate whether Uganda today merits the label of "strong state," it certainly approaches the standard of normalcy within the universe of African states. Reasonably effective institutions of rule operate at the central level, and a creative if under-resourced infrastructure of regional and local governance is in place. Much of public infrastructure has been restored, and basic services in the key domains of education and health are operating. In contrast to their counterparts in Georgia, Ugandan public servants are regularly paid and come closer to receiving a living wage. The quality of governance and effectiveness of rule in Uganda is probably better than at any other time since the first moments of independence.

But large uncertainties remain, and there is an underlying fragility to the Ugandan resurrection. Some observers are pessimistic about future prospects; Thomas Ofcansky, for example, assessed the outlook as "bleak" (Ofcansky 1996, 155). Many Ugandans are very critical of what is perceived as an autocratic drift, with Museveni seemingly determined to cling to power indefinitely. Insurgencies in the north (by the Lord's Resistance Army) and the west (by the Allied Democratic Force) simmer on, operating from bases in neighboring countries (Sudan and Congo-Kinshasa, respectively); the Ugandan counterpart to the Georgian warlord comes into view. The open commitment of the Ugandan army in support of the 1998 Congo-Kinshasa rebellion against the Laurent Kabila regime has proved costly. Outside of its core areas of support in the southwest, the NRM popular backing appears to have eroded, and relations with the key region of Buganda have cooled.

How to balance the indisputable successes of the Museveni regime against its undeniable liabilities is a judgment that will vary with each observer. The assessment with which Ghia Nodia concluded Chapter 16 is relevant here as well: transitions are inherently risky, and a full collapse of statehood is always a possibility. But in both Uganda and Georgia the question is open: equally possible is a consolidation of state restoration and achievement of a genuinely democratic polity consonant with the cultural heritage of the respective societies.

References

Apter, David. 1961. *The Political Kingdom in Uganda*. Princeton: Princeton University Press.

Brett, E. A. 1993. *Providing for the Rural Poor: Institutional Decay and Transformation in Uganda*. Kampala: Fountain.

Burke, Fred G. 1964. *Local Government and Politics in Uganda*. Syracuse: Syracuse University Press.

Decalo, Samuel. 1976. *Coups and Army Rule in Africa: Studies in Military Style*. New Haven: Yale University Press.

Doornbos, Martin. 1970. "Kumunyana and Rwenzururu: Two Responses to Ethnic Inequality." Pp. 1072–87 in *Protest and Power in Black Africa,* ed. Robert I. Rotberg and Ali A. Mazrui. New York: Oxford University Press.

Enloe, Cynthia H. 1980. *Ethnic Soldiers: State Security in Divided Societies*. Athens: University of Georgia Press.

Furley, Oliver, and James Katalikawe. 1997. "Constitutional Reform in Uganda: The New Approach." *African Affairs* 96, no. 383 (April): 243–60.

Gershenberg, Irvin. 1972. "Slouching toward Socialism: Obote's Uganda." *African Studies Review* 15, no. 1 (April): 79–85.

Ghai, Dharam P. 1966. *Taxation for Development: A Case Study of Uganda.* Nairobi: East African Publishing House.

Gwyn, David. 1977. *Idi Amin: Deathlight of Africa.* Boston: Little, Brown.

Ingham, Kenneth. 1994. *Obote: A Political Biography.* London: Routledge.

Jackson, Robert H. 1990. *Quasi-States: Sovereignty, International Relations, and the Third World.* Cambridge: Cambridge University Press.

Kabaka of Buganda. 1967. *The Desecration of My Kingdom.* London: Constable.

Khadiagala, Gilbert M. 1995. "State Collapse and Reconstruction in Uganda." Pp. 33–48 in *Collapsed States: The Disintegration and Restoration of Legitimate Authority,* ed. I. William Zartman. Boulder: Lynne Rienner.

Khadiagala, Lynn. 1999. "Law, Power, and Justice: The Administration of Women's Property Rights in Uganda." Ph.D. diss., University of Wisconsin-Madison.

Leys, Colin. 1967. *Politicians and Policies: An Essay on Politics in Acholi, Uganda, 1962–65.* Nairobi: East African Publishing House.

Low, D. Anthony. 1971. *Buganda in Modern History.* Berkeley: University of California Press.

Mamdani, Mahmood. 1996. *Citizen and Subject: Contemporary Africa and the Legacy of Colonialism.* Princeton: Princeton University Press.

Mazrui, Ali A. 1975. *Soldiers and Kinsmen in Uganda: The Making of a Military Ethnocracy.* Beverly Hills: Sage.

Migdal, Joel. 1988. *Strong Societies and Weak States: State-Society Relations and State Capabilities in the Third World.* Princeton: Princeton University Press.

Mittelman, James H. 1975. *Ideology and Politics in Uganda: From Obote to Amin.* Ithaca: Cornell University Press.

Mudoola, Dan M. 1996. *Religion, Ethnicity and Politics in Uganda.* Kampala: Fountain.

Museveni, Yoweri. 1997. *Sowing the Mustard Seed.* London: Macmillan.

Mutibwa, Phares. 1992. *Uganda since Independence: A Study of Unfulfilled Hopes.* Kampala: Fountain.

Ocan, Charles. 1994. "Pastoral Crisis and Social Change in Karamoja." Pp. 97–142 in *Uganda: Studies in Living Conditions, Popular Movements and Constitutionalism,* ed. Mahmood Mamdani and Joe Oloka-Onyango. Kampala: JEP Books.

Ofcansky, Thomas. 1996. *Uganda: The Tarnished Pearl of Africa.* Boulder: Westview.

Omara-Otunnu, Amii. 1987. *Politics and the Military in Uganda 1890–1985.* New York: St. Martin's.

Richards, Audrey, ed. 1959. *East African Chiefs: A Study of Political Development Uganda and Tanganyika Tribes.* New York: Praeger.

Rubongoya, Joshua B. 1995. "The Bakonjo-Baamba and Uganda: Colonial and Postcolonial Integration and Ethnocide." *Studies in Conflict and Terrorism* 18: 75–92.

Turyahikayo-Rugyema, Benoni. 1998. *Idi Amin Speaks: An Annotated Selection of His Speeches.* Madison: African Studies Program, University of Wisconsin.

Uganda District Government and Politics 1947–1967. 1977. Madison: African Studies Program, University of Wisconsin.

Vincent, Joan. 1971. *African Elite: Big Men of a Small Town.* New York: Columbia University Press.

Welbourn, F. M. 1965. *Religion and Politics in Uganda.* Nairobi: East African Publishing House.

World Bank. 1989. *Sub-Saharan Africa from Crisis to Sustainable Growth: A Long-Term Perspective Study.* Washington: World Bank.

———. 1998. *African Development Indicators 1998–99.* Washington: World Bank.

Wozei, M. M. 1977. "Karamoja." Pp. 201–22 in *Uganda District Government and Politics 1947–1967.* Madison: African Studies Program, University of Wisconsin.

Wrigley, Christopher. 1996. *Kingship and State: The Buganda Dynasty.* Cambridge: Cambridge University Press.

Young, Crawford. 1977. "Buganda." Pp. 193–234 in *African Kingships in Perspective,* ed. René Lemarchand. London: Frank Cass.

———. 1982. *Ideology and Development in Africa.* New Haven: Yale University Press.

———. 1994. *The African Colonial State in Comparative Perspective.* New Haven: Yale University Press.

Young, Crawford, Neal Sherman, and Tim H. Rose. 1981. *Cooperatives and Development: Agricultural Politics in Ghana and Uganda.* Madison: University of Wisconsin Press.

18

The Effective State in Postcolonial Africa and Post-Soviet Eurasia: Hopeless Chimera or Possible Dream?

MARK R. BEISSINGER
AND CRAWFORD YOUNG

The reader who has persisted to these final pages will harbor no doubts as to the magnitude of the crises challenging states in Africa and Eurasia. Although states in other regions of the world exhibit similar symptoms of dysfunctional authority (Cambodia, Afghanistan, Yugoslavia, and Haiti immediately come to mind), no other regions contain such a large percentage of debilitated states afflicted by such substantial long-term contractions in their capacities. In their very essence, the crises of the state in postcolonial Africa and post-Soviet Eurasia are a crisis of stateness itself. They revolve around the capacity of public institutions to rule effectively, to create security within their orbit of territorial sovereignty, to generate legitimacy for their operation, to assure a revenue base adequate for their functioning, and to supply the conditions for a prospering economy and welfare of citizenry.

In both regions, the symptoms of ill health were first detected within the economic realm. In Africa, the Organization of African Unity's 1979 summit took official note of mediocre economic performance on the continent and mandated the study that led to the 1980 Lagos Plan of Action. Simultaneously, African directors of the World Bank invited an inquiry that in 1981 provided the intellectual rationale for the wave of "structural adjustment" programs that stretched across the region. In the former Soviet Union, the sense of malaise and dissatisfaction with economic performance characteristic of the "era of stagnation" began about the same time, ultimately leading to the emergence of Mikhail Gorbachev's program of *perestroika*. Initially, economic reform alone was contemplated, without fundamental adjustment of the political framework. Reform architects presumed that restructuring could be accomplished within a few years and that its beneficial effects would follow in short order.

Thus, through somewhat different though intriguingly interactive itineraries, by the end of the 1980s the political foundations of African and Eurasian states and economics came into question. In an astonishing moment of enthusiasm, Soviet state socialism and African single-party and military neopatrimonial autocracies were stripped of their mystique of invulnerability and swept aside. The "third wave" of democratization (Huntington 1991)—a seemingly irresistible historical tide—rolled over both regions. Attending this tsunami initially was the euphoric expectation that shedding the discredited, venality-ridden, and often predatory state structures of the former political monopolies in favor of multiparty electoral democracies would swiftly create legitimate and effective governance and in turn provide a facilitative environment for economic liberalization. The redemptive archangel of civil society would spur the institutions of rule to accountable, transparent, and responsive behavior.

Such hopes faded during the 1990s. Along with them disappeared the illusion that early exits from state crises were likely in either Africa or the former Soviet Union. Perhaps the most salient overall conclusion to emerge from the chapters in this book, as well as from other papers contributed to our 1999 conference that we were unable to include in this volume, is the protracted nature of the process of political and economic adaptation in course in both regions. The initial inclination of these changes invoked the notion of "transition," around which a large literature emerged. In this perspective, the essence of historical process was the movement from one dominant political order to another: from Soviet state socialism and African patrimonial autocracy to a liberal democracy and market economy, within a finite time frame. Our contributors suggest a different formulation. Rather than convergence of these disparate continents toward liberal democracy, we have witnessed instead a convergence toward a crisis of the state in its most fundamental sense. To be sure, there has been an indisputable departure from the old order, which in its entirety remains discredited. Whatever the disillusions of the present, no mere restoration of the ancien régime in either region is conceivable. Such outcomes are precluded both by the impossibility of securing domestic acceptance and by the incompatibility of these prior regimes with the evolving international normative order.

However, there no longer appears to be a clearly defined end point to the processes of adaptation in course. Although the tug of liberal democracy and market economy is strong as a referential emblem of "normality" and as a global cachet of respectability, given the enormous problems of stateness that afflict these regions there is no longer a certainty that these represent the eventual destinations. Rather, the interaction between the pressures of globalization, the contradictory processes of state-rebuilding, and activated social forces may well be producing some new equilibrium— one that is influenced by norms of constitutionalism and capitalism but falls far short of the theorized end point.

In this initial conclusion of a protracted period of flux and adaptation in African and post-Soviet states, we may suggest vindication of the synergy of our crossregional comparison. Each region has sufficient analytical wholeness to permit the comparative venture: the commonalities imposed by long enclosure within the Russian and Soviet imperial domains for Eurasia and the shared experience of colonial subjugation for Africa. Both superimposed structures of hegemony that proved difficult to erase and that in their transcendence unleashed an unfolding dialectic of decline. In our introduction we acknowledged in some detail the important historical and cultural differences. However, we return here to underline the framework of comparability. The key point is that, in both regions, the dissolution of the former political order produced a challenge of adaptation of immense proportions. At issue was not a transition from authoritarian capitalism to liberal democracy, as in a Spain, a Brazil, or a Taiwan. The challenge in both areas was a virtual reinvention of the state and a comprehensive reordering of the economy. The magnitude and intrinsic difficulties of such a challenge were widely underestimated, within and without. Its common scope provides additional comparative ligaments for this work.

Politically, though it made pretensions to perfected citizenship, the Soviet totalitarian state until its death throes held its citizens in thrall to subjecthood. The theory and practice of "civil society" existed only in the *samizdat* interstices eluding the reach of state power. In Africa, after a brief moment of flourishing in the final colonial years, civil society organizations were mostly driven into the sterile embrace of the party-state as subordinated ancillary bodies, if not proscribed altogether. Political liberalization had little tradition of embedded practice or social capital on which to build. As space for contestation opened in the former Soviet Union, the transcripts of solidarity available for rapid mobilization were primarily around ethno-national ideologies, ironically in part a product of the ethno-federal forms of state organization chosen by Vladimir Lenin and Joseph Stalin. Although no comparable predominance of ethnic mobilization existed in Africa, the political vacuum left behind by decades of autocracy and exclusionary politics gave rise to a democratic ferment dominated by animosity to former regimes and rulers. Similar was a rejection of the past as "failure."

Economically, a sense of comprehensive failure was, if anything, more complete. State socialism was beyond the palliatives of *perestroika*. The centrally planned command economy assured a minimal level of security and consumption to its populace but was transparently incapable of competing with advanced capitalist economies. The mythology of officially declared double-digit growth rates lost its credibility as Soviet elites realized they not only were falling behind Western Europe and Japan but were being overtaken by South Korea and Taiwan. In much of Africa, the 1980s were a decade of absolute decline in per capita incomes. Economies were comprehensively parastatalized, with or without benefit of socialist ideology. Capitalist Nigeria in 1999 still had more than a thousand state-owned enterprises ("Nigeria in Civvy Street" 1999, 18). Although the practice of command economics was much less far-reaching, the degree of state intervention in the economy—a product of both paternalistic colonial state practice and the vision of state-led development that was conventional wisdom in the 1960s—was extensive. So also was the total fraction of wage employment, which was state-dependent in many countries.

To appreciate the magnitude of economic adjustment imposed on the two regions, one needs to reckon with the historic depth of state-centered economies and the contemporary predominance of the "Washington consensus" in defining the reform options (discussed in Chapters 11 and 12). In Eurasia, agricultural collectivization was six decades old by the time its reform was first contemplated. Even in the Baltic states and Moldova, where private cultivation had lasted two decades longer than in the rest of the former Soviet Union, no active agriculturalists had ever experienced private farming. Aversion to the risk of leaving the collective womb was inevitable. For the urban economy, the financial, legal, and judicial institutions indispensable to a private economy required huge adaptations or innovations beyond the reach of "shock therapy" (Hendley 1999). In Africa, agricultural policy since the 1950s had tended to treat the peasant sector as a fiscal resource; in addition, basic food-crop pricing policies privileged the more politically dangerous urban populations (Bates 1981). Both aspects of policy negatively affected marketed agricultural production. Although socialist orientation did not define ideological discourse for all states, its policy impact was important (Young 1982). Success in "building socialism" was minimal, but socialism's artisans were quite effective in blocking capitalism. Thus, in both regions, ventures in economic liberalization encountered the weakness or absence of supportive institutional infrastructure and the relative absence of the economic operatives necessary for a market economy.

Although each region contains broad similarities supportive of our comparative project, one finds within each region a large range of variation: states that are coalescing and making progress toward coherent authority; states that are chronically weak; and states that have, for all practical purposes, collapsed. In the post-Soviet region the Baltic states stand out as far more closely approximating the image of a "normal" European state than the other successor states. As we pointed out in the introduction to this volume, although some aspects of our analysis of state crises apply to all the states in the region (particularly, the issue of corruption), many do not. In Uzbekistan, Turkmenistan, and Belarus the breakdown of state institutions has been more circumscribed than in Russia, Ukraine, Moldova, Kazakhstan, Kyrgyzstan, Tajikistan, Armenia, Georgia, and Azerbaijan for different reasons—in large part because political and economic reform have also been quite limited. In general, in the post-Soviet region state weakness has been significantly more of a problem than has been state collapse, though examples of the latter (Tajikistan, Georgia from 1991 to 1993, and, on a substate basis, contemporary Chechnya) exist as well. In Africa, South Africa and the Arab tier of states on the Mediterranean shores of the continent stand somewhat apart; in those areas, the attributes of crisis discussed in these chapters would apply only to Algeria. A number of states in Africa have enjoyed reasonable stability over time—with no extralegal regime changes—and at least modest economic success (for example, Tunisia and Botswana). During the 1990s, the emergence of actual state collapse as an outcome (as occurred in Somalia, Liberia, and Sierra Leone) sharply extended the range of possible variation in outcome (Zartman 1994). The notion of "state crisis" that undergirds this volume pulls our attention to those cases and conditions where the concept applies. In both regions, this is a substantial majority of states, but in reflecting on the previous chapters one needs remember that the analysis is not of universal application, and explaining the variations is precisely where possibilities for pathways beyond crisis potentially emerge.

The impossibility across much of these regions to achieve political and economic reform as a genuine transition has had important consequences. Abandonment of state socialism and patrimonial autocracy necessarily involved a massive scaling back of the state's role. But in many countries this process went well beyond any planned reduction in the scope of state action to encompass a broad weakening of the very fabric of stateness. The legacy of previous policies was, for many, a heavy external debt and empty treasuries. Austerity measures—however necessary—frequently brought a sharp reduction in the real value of civil service wages, irregularities in their payment, and the inevitable bureaucratic demoralization and loss of effectiveness that followed. Adjustment policies also required purging the state payroll of numerous redundant employees, who had poor prospects for alternative employment. According to the official texts of economic reform, the slimmed state would emerge strengthened in effectiveness (World Bank 1997): "*moins d'état, mieux d'état*" (a smaller state, a better state), in the epigram of former Senegalese president Abdou Diouf. The reality in both regions, our authors have shown, was a widespread deflation in state capacities. The frequent result, as Achille Mbembe argues, was the emergence of patterns of private indirect government supplanting the state (Mbembe 1999).

Another possible outcome, identified by William Reno in Chapter 5, is the ruler's reliance on a "shadow state"—a framework of rule outside of formal institutions based on private uses of state prerogatives and assets. Mobutu Sese Seko of Congo-Kinshasa, for example, essentially abandoned any notion of "governance" by 1979 and directed his political skills to siphoning state resources into a network of prebendal clienteles and personal wealth that prolonged his survival. The formal functions of the state became all but irrelevant (Joseph 1987; Chabal and Daloz 1998). Certainly, prebendalist patterns have become prominent in post-Soviet Eurasia as well, though the degree to which the "shadow state" model applies, as Reno recognizes, is more limited in comparison with the pattern of partial transfer of state functions to private actors identified by Mbembe (1999). Here, the weight of state penetration and pre-independence legacies would seem to be critical in explaining some of the divergence in the ways in which state breakdown has occurred in the two regions.

A further consequence of state weakening in some cases has been the loss of control of significant swaths of territory and consolidation of various insurgent militias. This pattern emerges only in the 1990s on any scale in both world regions. In post-Soviet Eurasia, it is found in Tajikistan, Moldova, and parts of the Caucasus; in Africa, in two major theaters—an arc extending from the Horn south and west to Angola and the two Congos, and a smaller zone from Liberia through Guinea-Bissau. The availability of vast amounts of military equipment both within the former Soviet Union and for sale abroad either by cash-starved states, their security forces (either officially or unofficially), or private intermediaries has fed internal wars in both Eurasia and Africa. Significantly, mercenary soldiers from the former Soviet Union now appear with some regularity in the internal wars in Africa—an example of the ways in which disorder in these two regions is multiplicative on a global scale rather than additive. In Africa, warlords have acquired skill and experience in the mercantile operations needed to convert high-value resources such as gold and diamonds into weapons and supplies for their militia (Reno 1998). In Eurasia, as Charles Fairbanks, Jr., detailed in Chapter 6, warlords have emerged from criminal elements (as in Georgia and Dagestan), newly formed business elites (such as Surat Huseinov in Azerbaijan), or former *nomenklatura* (as in Moldova) with many of these same skills, though more frequently in Eurasia warlordism has evolved out of ethnic or civil warfare rather than the other way around.

In both world regions the inability of the state to provide the adequate infrastructure and regulatory framework necessary for a market economy has produced significant parallel economies and the penetration of criminal elements into major sectors of state and economic activity. Chapter 4 unraveled the mafia operations in the Russian case; Jean-François Bayart, Stephen Ellis, and Béatrice Hibou (1999) document the criminalization of the state in parts of Africa. These phenomena have their roots in patterns of behavior prior to the initiation of market reforms. Informalization of the economy spread in the former Soviet Union to overcome the rigidities of central planning, and the array of fixers and intermediaries who honed their skills in late Soviet times became natural practitioners of post-1991 illicit commerce. These patterns of behavior had become common within the governing apparatus of the Soviet state, but became dominant motifs only as marketization proceeded and law enforcement institutions crumbled. In Africa, apart from the growing volume of narcotics traffic (with Nigeria as its largest entrepôt), illicit economic activity is less diversified and sophisticated but, as in Eurasia, involves widespread scavenging of high-value and readily transportable goods (such as diamonds, gold, timber, and coffee) and their export through black market channels.

The deepening awareness of state weakness that runs through the chapters of this book subtly alters the problematic of reform. Liberalization, political or economic, is emptied of content if its object, the state, lacks minimal capacity. Stateness, or a restoration of the basic capacity of the state to exercise rule, must inevitably enter the calculus of democratization and market reform. The designation of the "state" as the chosen theme of the World Bank's 1997 development report reflects a growing recognition of this fact. So also do the more subdued tones in which the international donor community asserts democratization as a core condition for external assistance. Chapters 16 and 17, comparing state restoration in Georgia and Uganda, respectively, reflected this concern, which also ran through Chapters 3, 9, 10, and 11. Without effective political authority, neither a liberal-democratic order nor a market economy can prosper.

Economic reform, many believe, has shown some beneficial effect in Africa and parts of Eurasia. Macroeconomic performance measures in much of Africa appeared to improve in the mid-1990s. However, the record, Peter Lewis concluded in Chapter 12, remains mixed, although it is better than in the "lost decade" of the 1980s. But the overall data communicate ambiguous messages. Above all, for many countries, "structural adjustment" resonates poorly with publics, and economic reform lacks a strong domestic constituency. In Africa, its visible beneficiaries are often immigrant mercantile groups (Asians or Levantines). In Eurasia, the explosion of inequality often associated with the rise of the "new Russians" (or in Kazakhstan, the "Kazanovas") carries no legitimacy among populations who have grown impoverished and have long been intolerant toward economic disparity. Moreover, the dead weight of the bloated state-enterprise sector has proven difficult to divest in ways that protect against "crony capitalism." This phenomenon is observed on a far more blatant scale in Russia, where "shock therapy" reform resulted in a large transfer of state assets to the erstwhile *nomenklatura* or to buccaneering insiders. As Lilia Shevtsova pointed out in Chapter 9, the Russian public is skeptical about the post-Soviet economy and polity, which it characterizes harshly as a "criminal oligarchic regime," "phony capitalism," or "crony capitalism." African publics as well find continuing evidence confirming their now deep-seated suspicions of predatory behavior by states and their leading agents.[1]

---

1. To cite one illustration, evidence recently surfaced that the late, unlamented Nigerian dictator Sani Abacha had formed through family intermediaries in league with two former ministers a shell company to purchase for 20 cents on the dollar $2.5 billion of Nigerian debt to Russia incurred for the catastrophic and still all-but-inoperative Ajaokuta steel project. The Nigerian treasury was then ordered to provide full payment of the debt to this combine ("Nigeria Investigates" 1998), which has swallowed some $8 billion without producing any steel. The public also learned that the acute oil-product shortage in the late Abacha period, which paralyzed domestic transport and caused acute suffering, was artificially sustained by deliberate delays in repairing Nigerian refineries serving the domestic market, for which funds were appropriated more than once, so that Abacha and his cronies could continue collecting

Still, no alternative has come into view to the slow, arduous effort to institutionalize some closer approximation to a market economy. The dysfunctionality of past state economic macromanagement, whether under state socialism or neopatrimonial statism, is indisputable. Acerbic criticism of market reforms is widespread, yet no intellectual formulation of a different broad policy choice has emerged. This absence of an alternative in the wake of the collapse of socialism has been crucial to sustaining marketization projects in both regions.

Moreover, in both regions most states are dependent on the international financial institutions and the Western donor community. The "Washington consensus" has perhaps softened around the edges, but its core doctrines remain intact. Eurasian or African states have, in practice, some latitude in the energy with which they implement International Monetary Fund or World Bank agreements but cannot escape the basic strictures that govern the periodic bargaining on debt rescheduling and aid injections.

On the political side, "transitology" thinking at first prevailed: post-Soviet Eurasian and postcolonial African states were embarked on an epic voyage from authoritarianism to democracy, with the founding elections as defining moments of historical change. In Africa, these founding elections often involved substantial external funding and international observer teams, emblematic of the increasing role of international judgments concerning respectability. By the mid-1990s many of the same teams of international observers were shuttling between the African continent and Eurasia to oversee implementation of democratic norms. In Africa, a significant number of changes in rulers did occur—between twelve and eighteen, depending on one's mode of calculation, and some long-standing incumbents experienced spectacular defeat (for example, in Zambia, Malawi, Benin, and Madagascar). But in a larger number of cases, ruling parties survived the multiparty challenge by virtue of the inherent resource advantage obtained by those who control the state apparatus or by varying degrees of manipulation and fraud. In Eurasia, the collapse of the Soviet Union by definition brought new leaders to the fore or at a minimum empowered local elites once subject to the tutelage of the center. But only in the Baltic states did electoral parliamentary regimes take root and was the *apparatchik* class superseded. In the Russian Federation, Shevtsova showed, although party competition existed at the parliamentary level, the core of the system was a "superpresidency," which, through its manipulation and con-

---

lucrative commissions on gasoline imports. For the ordinary Nigerian, military rule was a "lootocracy."

trol of state resources, dominated the political process—a phenomenon that has only been reinforced with the accession to power of President Vladimir Putin. Similar patterns prevailed in Ukraine, Moldova, Georgia, and Armenia, while in Azerbaijan, Belarus, and the states of Central Asia autocracies or semiautocratic regimes prevailed.

The powerful momentum for political liberalization has unmistakably ebbed in both regions. The euphoria of the early 1990s has given way to a more subdued, even somber, mood. Vadim Volkov (in Chapter 4) and Shevtsova wondered whether pressures have been building in Russia for some more overtly authoritarian form of rule, driven by a sense of state weakness, economic dislocation, and general insecurity. In Russia, Putin's efforts to rebuild the state by challenging the power of oligarchs and regional bosses have raised questions about the degree to which such an effort is compatible with political pluralism. In Ukraine and Moldova, an incipient and delicate pluralism muddles through only by careful regional and ethnic balancing. Pressures for further liberalization are weak in Central Asia, Belarus, and much of the Caucasus. Nowhere outside the Baltic states have signs arisen of the institutionalization of effective party competition that would indicate movement toward democratic consolidation, and in a number of instances (Russia, Azerbaijan, Kazakhstan, Kyrgyzstan, and Belarus) we have witnessed an unmistakable erosion of progress, as empowered elites have sought to load electoral processes in their favor or avoid them entirely. In Africa, the most painstaking analysis of democratic experiments concludes that in many instances *"big-man democracy* is emerging, in which the formal trappings of democracy coexist with neopatrimonial political practice" (Bratton and van de Walle 1997, 233). The second round of competitive elections in the late 1990s were in general less openly and effectively competitive than were the founding elections. In contrast to the significant number of alternations produced by the initial wave of elections, incumbents lost the second round only in Benin and Madagascar; ironically, in both these instances, previous incumbents returned to power. Richard Joseph, an active participant in the movement to support African democratization in its early phases, suggested in Chapter 10 that an important part of democratization's actual enactment must be understood as performance and display—virtual democracy, a notion widely invoked in contemporary Russia as well. Elections in Africa, Joseph argued, are "instances of significant contestation and participation but not exercises in which the citizenry could effect an alternation in executive power among the leaders and parties."

Whatever the degree of virtuality or even "illiberalism" (Zakaria 1997), the importance of the electoral process itself is undeniable. In Africa, the enormous psychological and political consequence of the generally fairly conducted 1999 elections in South Africa and Nigeria in providing a reservoir of legitimacy to two regimes critical to the entire continent serves to underline this point. Also worth recollecting is that the sole unambiguously successful, internationally brokered and nurtured resolution of a protracted postcolonial civil war in Africa in the 1990s occurred in Mozambique, where incorporation of the insurgents through the electoral mechanism was crucial to the peace making process. In Eurasia as well, notwithstanding the limits of electoralism and the predominance of "big men," one cannot imagine an alternative source of ultimate legitimation. Even Saparmurad Niiazov, who introduced a neototalitarian rule to Turkmenistan, including a Stalin-like cult of personality, and saw fit in 1994 to extend his term in office to 2003 through a referendum (albeit Soviet-style, with 99.9 percent approval), spurned suggestions that he assume the title "President for Life," and made soundings about increasing the role played by parliament—all in an attempt to attract foreign investment.

Other aspects of political liberalization have produced changes in the routines and practices of politics that seem permanent. The observation of basic human rights is greatly improved if still highly imperfect. Even the pattern of violation has altered. In Russia, for instance, the abuse of human rights has devolved to the local and regional level in accordance with the larger breakdown of state authority. In both regions, active domestic human rights organizations have emerged and draw sustenance from the greatly strengthened international network of such bodies, as well as the enhanced salience of such issues in the international normative order. The range of freedom of expression is vastly enlarged, and in most areas independent media provide a vehicle for its articulation. A ramifying sector of nongovernmental organizations has taken root. However elusive the definition of "civil society" may be, something loosely corresponding to most of its meanings clearly now exists in most parts of Africa and Eurasia. By any standard, these are important changes.

A particularly striking contrast between the two regions lies in the impact of the military on political liberalization. In post-Soviet Eurasia, in spite of serious dislocation, economic distress, episodic crises, and periods of state failure, the military has never seized power. Civil wars have brought militia-backed groupings to power in Georgia, Tajikistan, and Azerbaijan; coup attempts have been reported to have occurred in Azerbaijan, Georgia, and Chechnya; and rumors of coups have been rife within Russia and Armenia at various times. But the type of direct military intervention in politics that has been characteristic of African politics has so far been absent. In Africa, although coups are far less frequent since the democratization movement took hold, since 1990 army power seizures have occurred in Algeria, Burundi, Comoros, the Gambia, the Ivory Coast, Niger (twice), and Guinea-Bissau. In addition, armed insurgents have swept from the periphery into the capitals in Chad, both Congos, Ethiopia, Rwanda, Somalia, and Uganda.

Chapter 6 provided illumination on this point. The Russian army and its successors were long the core of imperial power, and the military has a long tradition of professionalism and service to civilian authority. Although the Soviet armed forces on the eve of the Soviet collapse were perhaps not as formidable as cold war demonology suggested, in numbers and equipment Gorbachev commanded a massive military machine. Its voracious budgetary appetites played no small part in the downward spiral of the Soviet state. As Fairbanks details, an unforeseen outcome of the demise of the Soviet Union was the rapid decomposition of its military instrument, put on dramatic display in the initial Chechen disgrace of the Russian army. The consequences of the breakdown of the military as an institution were the de facto privatization of various military functions and the multiplication of irregular militia of diverse sorts. In the non-Russian republics, new armies were created, in some instances drawing on fragments of the Soviet army, in other instances on local police or paramilitary forces. None of these became effective fighting forces. In some instances (Kazakhstan and Kyrgyzstan), the rates of desertion are high; in other instances, morale remains low and infrastructure has deteriorated. All are starved of resources, and many require nonbudget sources of revenue to survive, such as sale of their equipment or performing private security services. The result is what Fairbanks termed a feudalization of the security function of the state and the multiplication of local warlords. However, the logic of survival has not driven public or private militaries to seek control of the state itself—in part because such rule would not be viewed as legitimate within populations, in part because of internalized norms of behavior within the military itself.

In Africa, the historic trajectory of the military role in politics differs substantially, explaining some of the contrasting outcomes at present. At the time of political independence, African militaries were small, lightly armed infantry constabularies still under European command; security forces were the last spheres in which Africanization began. Uganda, for example, had a single 700-man battalion in 1962 (Omara-Otunnu 1987, 51); giant Nigeria had a mere 7,600 troops on the eve of independence (Peters 1997, 77). The rapid creation of more substantial armed forces enjoyed priority everywhere, both as an emblem of statehood itself and in response to the belief that the newly sovereign state acquired by this fact an enlarged security imperative. Although the military coup in Africa was pioneered by the Egyptian Free Officers in 1952, the phenomenon became general practice beginning in 1965, when a wave of coups occurred within a few months (in Nigeria, Algeria, Ghana, the Central African Republic, Benin, Burkina Faso, and Congo-Kinshasa). As single-party monopolies eliminated any other means of incumbent removal, the military coup became a central feature of the African political environment; more than eighty successful army takeovers occurred in the period prior to the democratization era. There were two crucial consequences. First, as the armies periodically assumed direct political roles, they tended to become internally politicized. Second, all rulers became sensitized to the constant possibility of military intervention; to forestall coups, ethnic security maps shaped the choice of key commanders and military demographics (Enloe 1980). A further phase in the dynamics of military politics in Africa opened in 1979 in Uganda, when for the first time an insurgent militia (backed in this case by the Tanzanian army) marched into the capital to seize power, dispersing and dissolving the existing security forces. Their weapons entered the black market, and their soldiers often reformed into diverse militia, fueling warlord politics. Similar power seizures from the periphery occurred in Uganda again in 1986; in Chad (1982 and 1990); in Ethiopia, Eritrea, and Somalia (1991); and in both Congos (1997). A consequence has been, in roughly a third of African polities, a loss by the state of one of its defining attributes—a monopoly of the means of coercion—through the proliferation of insurgent militias. Although not usually constituted on an ethnic principle, these militias normally have a marked ethno-regional profile. National armies by and large lack capacity and cannot acquire sufficient external reinforcement from more powerful states or the swiftly expanding private security market to defeat militias. Resolution of such conflicts generally requires absorption of segments of the militia into national armies. In Eurasia, similar patterns of absorption of paramilitary units have occurred at times in Georgia, Chechnya, and Tajikistan, but the extent to which these armies subsequently took a role in politics was minimal. The military factor looms large in the African search for political and economic reform. The possibility of direct military intervention remains significant. The pronounced ethnic imbalances, a product of prolonged incumbencies by patrimonial autocrats, threaten the communal equilibrium of a liberalized state. The proliferation of militias creates zones of insecurity damaging to economic recovery. Younger officers remember with envy that a number of their superiors used periods of military rule to acquire fortunes; most have retained their illicitly acquired assets, and few have faced punishment. Indeed, amnesty for former military rulers is usually the necessary ransom for their retreat.

In both regions, complex cultural pluralism is a defining feature of politics, but the fashion in which societal identities intersect stateness (with its inevitable discourse of nationhood) contrasts sharply. Eurasia lies securely within the zone of "titular nationalities," with political units formed around ethnicities on the basis of Soviet ethno-federalism. The problems generated by the legacies of this type of ethnically hierarchical, territorialized system have to do with the treatment of minorities within nationalizing political units, arbitrary assignment of a group to hierarchical subordination of another group's unit, groups locked out of privileges enjoyed by others, and (in a context of state weakness) a decline of state capacity due to the outbidding generated by asymmetry. The African state system, by contrast, succeeds a colonial partition in which cultural realities on the ground were rarely relevant. Here, as Francis Deng argued in Chapter 14, the state as artificial container creates a different discourse about nationhood, incites intergroup competition for control over the state, and internationalizes group conflict due to the ways in which groups straddle state boundaries.

In the vast territory between Dublin and Tokyo, virtually all states (the United Kingdom, Belgium, and Switzerland are the main exceptions) take the name of their dominant nationality. When the Russian empire was recast as the Soviet Union, this logic was imported from western Europe and applied as a mechanism by which the non-Russian periphery could be kept within the Leninist realm. These then became, by the curious logic of *uti possidetis,* the necessary successor states when the Soviet Union itself imploded (Buchanan 1999).[2] Populations who do not belong to the "titular nationalities" are constituted as "national minorities." Once enjoying extraterritorial privileges outside the ethno-federal hierarchy, the ethnic Russians in many of the new post-Soviet states became a significant national minority with the demise of the Soviet Union. Aside from Russians, almost

---

2. *Uti possidetis* originated as a concept in Roman private law, stipulating that immovable private property remains in the possession of its holder until some legal finding alters its status. By migration into international public law, the concept came to translate into the principle of intangibility of boundaries in state succession, a bedrock principle in Africa above all. In application to instances of state breakdown, such as in the former Yugoslavia and the Soviet Union, this means that the successor states inherit the boundaries of the principal administrative subdivisions of the fragmenting state.

all of the successor states have other significant national minorities with their own challenges of cultural survival within the context of nationalizing states. The nationalizing policies of most of the successor states (and even of ethno-federal subunits within successor states) are a direct continuation of ethno-federal assumptions as well. These in turn have generated conflict between nationalizing states and national minorities (Brubaker 1996). There also remain the abiding legacies of Stalin's decisions concerning the status of groups within the ethno-federal hierarchy and the assignment of units with status lower than that of a union republic to one of the existing union republics. The Abkhaz and South Ossetian conflicts within Georgia and the Nagorno-Karabakh conflict in Azerbaijan belong to the latter category, while the Volga Tatar and Chechen conflicts belong to the former. Finally, some groups (Crimean Tatars, Poles, and Gagauz, for instance) were locked out of the ethno-federal hierarchy entirely; the conflicts surrounding them in the post-Soviet context tend to revolve around issues of establishing a nonexistent territoriality or provision of rights in the absence of territoriality. The bloodiest conflicts in Eurasia (Chechnya, Nagorno-Karabakh, Abkhazia, Pridnestr) have fundamentally concerned ethno-national control over territorial units (i.e., sovereignty versus self-determination) rather than conflict over control of the state from within by culturally distinguished segments (the regional conflict in Tajikistan being an exception) or the attempt to impose a genocidal scheme on society.

By contrast, in Africa, with a handful of exceptions (Lesotho, Swaziland, Botswana), the territorial state is not coincident with a self-conscious cultural entity.[3] The legitimating discourse of "nation" thus refers to a shared history of colonial subjugation and a purely territorial unit of consciousness. Whatever its artificiality, the territorial state has acquired not only the protective armor of *uti possidetis* as the foundational principle of the African state system, but also the inertial acceptance of long familiarity. As well, independent states made vigorous use of their control of educational systems and media to act as pedagogues of "nationhood," practices that had more effect than many appreciate. Particularly striking in the large zones of disorder in contemporary Africa is the relative absence of ethnic self-determination movements. "Congo" clearly persists in a popular social consciousness in the absence of a state institutional structure able to provide basic services or assert its residual authority in large parts of Congo-Kinshasa:

---

3. Somalia is an apparent exception as well, but as its collapsed condition indicates, identities operate at multiple levels, with warlord politics now situated at clan and subclan levels.

witness the strong popular reaction to Rwandan and Ugandan "invasions" in support of Congolese rebels, encountered even in regions under loose insurgent control.

Gail Lapidus and Deng both argued that, even in an environment of state weakness, communal conflict need not overwhelm public order. Lapidus in Chapter 13 recalled that many feared that the collapse of the Soviet Union "would precipitate an uncontrollable escalation of ethno-political conflict and violence within and among the states of the region." Although rapid ethno-national mobilization and widespread violence did occur in the final months of the Soviet Union, and some national minorities in the successor states did unleash secession struggles in the immediate aftermath of the collapse, the latter have subsided into low-intensity stalemates, and no new violent ethnic conflicts emerged in the late 1990s. The imperative of stabilization as well as the impossibility of purely military "solutions" when military institutions themselves have come undone (as the first Chechen war well illustrated) have motivated new rulers to pursue accommodative policies. The Russian Federation acknowledges variable degrees of "sovereignty" and effective autonomy for its twenty-one ethno-federal republics, and has retained the "titular nationality" policy for these subdivisions. Indeed, the negotiation of privileges with the center led under President Boris Yeltsin to the proliferation of an astounding variety of arrangements, weakening central control over local governors and generating resentment among Russians against the privileges of minorities. But asymmetric ethno-federalism has so far contained secessionist impulses (except among the Chechens, with whom serious negotiations concerning autonomy never occurred). Elsewhere in the post-Soviet states, Russian minorities have for the most part been given full citizenship and some cultural rights, though the extent to which they are discriminated against in practice remains an open question. As Lapidus argued, the close scrutiny by European monitoring organizations, applying the congealing international norms applicable to "national minorities," has acted to constrain state behavior. The price of the coveted respectability is conformity to these standards.

Deng comes to a similar conclusion. Sovereignty, he suggested, ceases to be a doctrine insulating states against external scrutiny, becoming instead "postulated as a normative concept of responsibility, which requires a system of governance that is based on democratic popular citizen participation, constructive management of diversities, respect for fundamental rights, and equitable distribution of national wealth and opportunities for development." Dominant understandings of ethnicity in Africa have altered as well over the post-independence period. In the 1950s, the very lexicon of identity connoted backwardness. The ethnic group was a mere "tribe," an artifact of traditionality that obstructed the highway of modernity. A primary justification for the centralized, unitary state under single-party rule was the imperative of "nation-building," which required banishing ethnic consciousness to the far periphery of the private sphere. Today there is a far greater disposition to acknowledge ethnicity as a natural form of consciousness and the medium through which cultural heritage is reproduced—a development Deng regards as essential to the effective accommodation of diversity. The deadliest disasters to have disfigured contemporary Africa arose when a multicultural society fell in thrall to the use of the state apparatus to impose a project of communal hegemony. The genocidal tragedies in Rwanda (1994) and Burundi (especially 1972 and 1993) illustrate the terrible dangers of such practices. So also does the grim fate of Sudan, torn by civil war from its 1956 independence until today save for a decade's remission from 1972 to 1983, when the southern regions, which cannot accept Arabism and Islam as exclusive definitions of the national personality, were accorded autonomy (Deng 1995).

The texture of cultural pluralism in Africa differs substantially from that in Eurasia. The ideological texts asserting the supreme value of ethno-national identity and the self-determination and sovereignty claims that accompany it are far more elaborated and salient in Eurasia. African identities, apart from Arabhood in the north, are more fluid, multilayered, and circumstantial than their Eurasian counterparts. Secessionist movements in Eurasia are invariably ethno-national; in Africa, important separatist movements, such as those in southern Sudan, Eritrea, Biafra, Katanga, or Casamance, are based on territorial subdivisions. The social energies underlying them may well be ethnic (e.g., for the Igbo in Biafra), but the self-determination claim is made on behalf of an extant provincial entity.[4] This in turn, we suggest, reflects the contrasting concepts of state as nation: the ethno-national versus the territorial.

In the domain of gender as well, we observe contrasting outcomes, as Aili Mari Tripp's Chapter 15 demonstrated. In Eurasia, the post-Soviet

---

4. The Casamance separatist movement in southern Senegal is an intriguing case in point. Though many perceive this movement as a Diola insurgency, its independence claims are based on a territory, and its arguments are partly rooted in demands made by French residents in colonial times for recognition as a distinct colonial territory. The discourse of insurgency never advances Diola grievances per se, nor does it call for collective mobilization of the group under the banner of ethnic consciousness. Indeed, many Diola oppose the movement, and large numbers of the Senegalese army combating it are Diola. See Lambert (1998).

states and their derelictions have resulted in a measurable decline in gender equities. In Africa, in contrast, liberalization has produced significant gains for women. A number of African states include a reserved proportion of parliamentary seats for women. In addition, the new space opened in civil society has, in a number of countries, created opportunities for diverse women's organizations to flourish, perhaps less important for their political significance than for their capacity to improve female well-being.

Finally, international system factors bear importantly on the quest for effective state authority. In the economic realm, both regions are heavily dependent on the international financial and external donor communities. This dependence subjects them to the intrusive scrutiny and monitoring of international financial institutions and global capital markets. Although the pressures for political conditionalities in international assistance bargaining have faded, respectability remains an important commodity. Its preservation requires, at the least, formal observation of the external signs of liberal democracy: regular conduct of competitive elections with multiple parties. Monitoring, however, has not prevented a tendency in both regions for incumbents to entrench and prolong their rule by loading the process. Nor, in reality, is external supervision sufficient to bring about a genuine market economy.

Within each world region the phenomenon of state weakness has important interstate consequences. As Donald Rothchild argued in Chapter 8, when weakness decants into failure, and when zones of disorder appear, the neighboring states are directly affected. Armed conflict has a strong tendency to spill over: flows of refugees, trade dislocations, use of neighboring territory by insurgents as a sanctuary. This in turn creates the temptation to intervene, either in support of the regime or to back its insurgents. State weakness thus sets in motion further weakening of the inhibitions inherent in the notion of sovereignty.

The character of the imperial legacy imparts a different dynamic to international intervention in Eurasia than in Africa. In Eurasia, Russia lays claim to a special right of intervention in pursuit of its interests in what it labels its "near abroad." Substantial Russian military operations have occurred in Tajikistan, Georgia, Armenia, and Moldova. Particularly in the Caucasus, there is a singular interlocking of security logics. For different reasons, violent crises, even those associated with humanitarian disasters, are unlikely to induce interventions by the outside world in Africa. The residual possessive vision that Russia harbors toward the "near abroad" precludes international responses by other states, as the international silence with respect to Chechnya well illustrates. In Africa, memories of the

Somalia fiasco remain fresh. Even the shame of the inaction in response to the ghastly Rwanda genocide is unlikely to produce extra-African intervention in response to an African crisis. The African state system itself is groping toward a formula for peacekeeping, even peace making, within the continent. Liberia and Sierra Leone were initial testing grounds for a regional African intervention force, mainly composed of Nigerian troops. The ambiguous results bear witness to the intrinsic difficulties of the task. By contrast, in Eurasia, such multilateral schemes would be viewed by Russia as an attack on its claims to remaining a "great power" in the region.

As the contributions to this volume attest, the quest for the effective state is a long-term project and remains in many ways the defining attribute of politics in both Eurasia and Africa. Partly liberalized economies, semi-democracies, and weak states are the likely modal outcomes for an extended period, with substantial variation around a mean of troubled performance. For some in both regions, gilded memories of the seeming certainties of the state socialism or patrimonial autocracy of yesteryear awaken nostalgic longings. But the past is unredeemable and irretrievable. A protracted struggle can only continue, without illusions as to its difficulty. Certainly, despite the disruptions involved, state weakness and semireformed economies and polities are preferable outcomes to state collapse or failure to initiate any political or market reform at all. Notwithstanding its enormous problems, Eduard Shevardnadze's Georgia must be judged an improvement over Imomali Rakhmonov's Tajikistan or Aleksandr Lukashenka's Belarus by most measures of human rights and economic development, as is Yoweri Museveni's Uganda over Omar Bashir's Sudan or Laurent Kabila's Congo. As Chapters 16 and 17 detail, with effective leadership and support from the international community, collapsed states can be moved to varying conditions of weakness. Many of the unmitigated catastrophes of state collapse that emerged in both regions could have been avoided in the presence of effectual leadership. But this in itself speaks to the fragility of the arrangements that leaders such as Shevardnadze and Museveni leave behind.

In the long term, the question that will haunt most of Africa and Eurasia is not whether unreformed autocracies will be forced to initiate change or even whether collapsed states can be pieced back together into weak but intact varieties through skillful statecraft. Rather, it is whether the transitions from state weakness to state effectiveness, from semidemocracy to genuine democracy, and from protracted economic decline to sustained economic growth can be made. Given what we have detailed in this volume as the centrality of the obstacle that problems of stateness pose to further headway in democratic and market transitions, we expect that significant progress in democratization and market transition will first require tackling the seemingly more intractable issues of corruption, the criminalization of the state, its incapacity for enforcing rules, and its institutional and territorial incoherence. This is not to argue that progress will not be made; the variability in outcomes in both regions speaks to its possibility. But the factors that impede progress on these issues in particular are deeply ingrained in the historical development of these states and are not easily removed. The quest for transcending the crises of the state in Africa and Eurasia can therefore be expected to dominate political processes in both regions for many years to come.

References

Bates, Robert. 1981. *Markets and States in Tropical Africa*. Berkeley: University of California Press.

Bayart, Jean-François, Stephen Ellis, and Béatrice Hibou. 1998. *The Criminalization of the State in Africa*. London: James Currey.

Bratton, Michael, and Nicolas van de Walle. 1997. *Democratic Experiments in Africa: Regime Transitions in Comparative Perspective*. Cambridge: Cambridge University Press.

Brubaker, Rogers. 1996. *Nationalism Reframed: Nationhood and the National Question in the New Europe*. Cambridge: Cambridge University Press.

Buchanan, Allen. 1999. "Secession and State Breakdown." Paper presented at conference on "Beyond State Crisis? The Quest for the Efficacious State in Africa and Eurasia." Madison, Wisc., March.

Chabal, Patrick, and Jean-Pascal Daloz. 1998. *Africa Works: Disorder as Political Instrument*. London: James Currey.

Deng, Francis M. 1995. *War of Visions: Conflict of Identities in the Sudan*. Washington: Brookings Institution Press.

Enloe, Cynthia H. 1980. *Ethnic Soldiers: State Security in Divided Societies*. Athens: University of Georgia Press.

Hendley, Kathryn. 1999. "State Institutions and the Limits of Externally Induced Economic Transition." Paper presented at conference on "Beyond State Crisis? The Quest for the Efficacious State in Africa and Eurasia." Madison, Wisc., March.

Huntington, Samuel P. 1991. *The Third Wave: Democratization in the Late Twentieth Century*. Norman: University of Oklahoma Press.

Joseph, Richard. 1987. *Democracy and Prebendal Politics in Nigeria: The Rise and Fall of the Second Republic*. Cambridge: Cambridge University Press.

Lambert, Michael. 1998. "Casamance: Ethnicity or Nationalism?" *Africa* 68, no. 4: 585–602.

Mbembe, Achille. 1999. *Du gouvernement privé indirect*. Dakar: CODESRIA.

"Nigeria Investigates Ex-Ministers in a Fraud It Puts at $2.5 Billion." 1998. *New York Times*. 3 December: A6.

"Nigeria in Civvy Street." 1999. *Economist* 351 (19–25 June): 17–18.

Omara-Otunnu, Amii. 1987. *Politics and the Military in Uganda, 1890–1985*. New York: St. Martin's.

Peters, Jimi. 1997. *The Nigerian Military and the State*. London: I. B. Tauris.

Reno, William. 1998. *Warlord Politics and African States*. Boulder: Lynne Rienner.

World Bank 1997. *The State in a Changing World: World Development Report 1997*. New York: Oxford University Press.

Young, Crawford. 1982. *Ideology and Development in Africa*. New Haven: Yale University Press.

Zakaria, Fareed. 1997. "The Rise of Illiberal Democracy." *Foreign Affairs* 76, no. 6 (November–December): 22–43.

Zartman, I. William, ed . 1994. *Collapsed States: The Disintegration and Restoration of Legitimate Authority*. Boulder: Lynne Rienner.

Contributors

Mark R. Beissinger is Professor of Political Science at the University of Wisconsin–Madison. He is the author and editor of a number of books, including *Scientific Management, Socialist Discipline, and Soviet Power* (Harvard University Press, 1988), *The Nationalities Factor in Soviet Politics and Society* (Westview, 1990), and *Nationalist Mobilization and the Collapse of the Soviet State: A Tidal Approach to the Study of Nationalism* (Cambridge University Press, 2002).

Francis M. Deng, author or editor of more than twenty books, is Distinguished Professor of Political Science at the City University of New York Graduate Center, and Special Representative of the United Nations Secretary-General on Internally Displaced Persons. Formerly a Senior Fellow at the Brookings Institution, he helped establish the African Studies branch of the Brookings Foreign Policy Studies program. His background includes academic appointments both in his home country of Sudan and in several U.S. universities, as well as public service as Human Rights Officer in the United Nations Secretariat, as Sudanese Ambassador to Canada, the Scandinavian countries and the United States, and as Minister of State for Foreign Affairs.

Charles H. Fairbanks, Jr. is a research professor of international relations at the School of Advanced International Studies (SAIS) of Johns Hopkins University, and Director of its Central Asian Institute. Prior to joining the faculty of SAIS, Fairbanks served in the U.S. Department of State as a member of the Policy Planning Staff and as a Deputy Assistant Secretary. He is author of numerous articles and editor of a forthcoming book on the lessons from the unexpected collapse of communism.

487

David Holloway is Raymond A. Spruance Professor of International History in the Departments of Political Science and History, and Director of the Institute for International Studies at Stanford University. He is the author of *The Soviet Union and the Arms Race* (1983) and *Stalin and the Bomb* (1984), both published by Yale University Press.

Richard Joseph is Asa G. Candler Professor of Political Science at Emory University. He is the author of *Radical Nationalism in the Cameroon* (Clarendon Press, 1977) and *Democracy and Prebendal Politics in Nigeria* (Cambridge University Press, 1987), as well as editor of *Gaullist Africa: Cameroon under Ahmadu Ahidjo* (Fourth Dimension Publishers, 1978) and *State, Conflict, and Democracy in Africa* (Lynne Rienner, 1999). He directed the African Governance Program of the Carter Center from 1988 to 1994, and is currently serving as Director of the Institute of Caribbean and International Studies at St. George's University, Grenada.

Gail W. Lapidus is Senior Fellow at the Institute for International Studies at Stanford University and directs a project on ethnic conflict and regional security at its Center for International Security and Cooperation. A Professor of Political Science at the University of California at Berkeley from 1976 to 1994, she is the author of numerous books and articles on Soviet and post-Soviet politics, society, and foreign policy. Her recent work has focused on ethnopolitical developments in the Russian Federation and the war in Chechnya.

Peter M. Lewis is Associate Professor of Political Science at American University. He has published extensively on the political economy of structural adjustment and democratization in Africa. Among his publications are a number of articles on the dilemmas of economic and political reform in Nigeria.

Achille Mbembe is the author of many books, including *On the Postcolony* (University of California Press, 2001). He served for several years, ending in 2000, as Executive Secretary of the Council for the Development of Social Sciences in Africa (CODESRIA) in Dakar, Senegal, and earlier held a faculty post in the Department of History at the University of Pennsylvania. He is currently Senior Researcher at the Institute of Social and Economic Research, University of the Witwatersrand, Johannesburg, South Africa.

Ghia Nodia is Chair of the Caucasian Institute for Peace, Democracy, and Development, an independent research institute in Tbilisi, Georgia, and is also a sociology professor at Tbilisi State University. He holds degrees in philosophy from the Tbilisi State University and the Academy of Sciences of Georgia. During the last ten years his major research interests have been concentrated in regional security, state-building and democratization in the Caucasus, and theories of nationalism and its fate in the post-cold war context.

William Reno is Associate Professor of Political Science at Northwestern University. He is the author of *Warlord Politics and African States* (Lynne Rienner, 1998) and other work on the politics of state collapse in Africa. His current research involves field work in Central Asia, and Eastern and Central Africa to compare business and protection strategies in the context of very weak or absent state structures.

Donald Rothchild is Professor of Political Science at the University of California at Davis. His recent books include *Managing Ethnic Conflict in Africa: Pressures and Incentives for Cooperation* (Brookings, 1997), and (as co-author) *Sovereignty as Responsibility: Conflict Management in Africa* (Brookings, 1996); as well, he is co-editor of *The International Spread of Ethnic Conflict: Fear, Diffusion, and Escalation* (Princeton University Press, 1998). His current project, with Philip Roeder, involves a global study on power sharing and peacemaking.

Lilia Shevtsova is a Senior Associate of the Carnegie Endowment for International Peace and heads its Project on Post-Communist Institutions; she holds a doctorate from the Institute of International Relations and the Academy of Sciences in Moscow. She served as Deputy Director of the Institute of International Economic and Political Studies of the Russian Academy of Sciences and as a Director of the Center of Political Studies. She is the author of four books, the most recent, published in 1999 by the Carnegie Endowment, *Yeltsin's Russia: Myths and Realities.*

Peter J. Stavrakis is Associate Professor of Political Science at the University of Vermont and former Deputy Director of the Kennan Institute for Advanced Russian Studies of the Woodrow Wilson International Center for Scholars. His scholarly work includes contemporary Russian and Ukrainian politics, Russian regionalism, U.S. foreign assistance, and bureaucratic reform in the Soviet successor states. He is editor of *Beyond the Monolith: The Emergence of Regionalism in Post-Soviet Russia* (Woodrow Wilson Center Press/Johns Hopkins University Press, 1997), and author of *Moscow and Greek Communism, 1944–1949* (Cornell University Press, 1989).

Stephen John Stedman is a senior research scholar at the Center for International Security and Cooperation, Stanford University. His numerous publications deal with international security and conflict resolution in Africa. He is author of *Peacemaking in Civil War: International Mediation in Zimbabwe* (Lynne Rienner, 1991), and editor of *South Africa: The Political Economy of Transformation* (Lynne Rienner, 1994), as well as two other books. He received his doctorate from Stanford University in 1988.

Aili Mari Tripp is Associate Professor of Political Science and Women's Studies at the University of Wisconsin–Madison, where she serves as Director of the Women's Studies Research Center. Her publications include *Women and Politics in Uganda* (University of Wisconsin Press, 2000) and *Changing the Rules: The Politics of Liberalization and the Urban Informal Economy in Tanzania* (University of California Press, 1997). She has also published on women and politics in Africa, societal responses to economic reform, and the political impact of transformations of associational life in Africa.

Vadim Volkov teaches political science and sociology at the European University in Saint Petersburg, and is the author of fifteen articles and book chapters, a number of which have appeared in English. He received his doctorate in sociology from Cambridge University in 1995. His current research focuses on organized violence, the formation of markets, and the dynamics of contemporary Russian statehood.

Crawford Young is H. Edwin Young and Rupert Emerson Professor of Political Science at the University of Wisconsin–Madison, where he has taught since 1963. His major books include *Politics in the Congo* (Princeton University Press, 1965), *The Politics of Cultural Pluralism* (University of Wisconsin Press, 1976), *Ideology and Development in Africa* (Yale University Press, 1982), *The Rise and Decline of the Zairian State* (co-authored with Thomas Turner, University of Wisconsin Press, 1985), and *The African Colonial State in Comparative Perspective* (Yale University Press, 1994). He has also taught in Congo-Kinshasa, Uganda, and Senegal.

Index

491